W9-BQE-807

No Longer the Property of NOLS

NORTH OLYMPIC
LIBRARY SYSTEM
PORT ANGELES, WA 98362

A PATTERN LANGUAGE

TOWNS · BUILDINGS · CONSTRUCTION

A Pattern Language is the second in a series of books which describe an entirely new attitude to architecture and planning. The books are intended to provide a complete working alternative to our present ideas about architecture, building, and planning—an alternative which will, we hope, gradually replace current ideas and practices.

volume 1 THE TIMELESS WAY OF BUILDING

volume 2 A PATTERN LANGUAGE

volume 3 THE OREGON EXPERIMENT

Center for Environmental Structure

BERKELEY, CALIFORNIA

A
PATTERN
LANGUAGE

TOWNS · BUILDINGS · CONSTRUCTION

Christopher Alexander

Sara Ishikawa   Murray Silverstein

with

Max Jacobson   Ingrid Fiksdahl-King   Shlomo Angel

NEW YORK

OXFORD UNIVERSITY PRESS

1977

Copyright © 1977 by Christopher Alexander
Library of Congress Catalogue Card Number: 74-22874
ISBN 0-19-501919-9

printing, last digit: 30 29 28 27 26 25 24 23 22 21
Printed in the United States of America
on acid-free paper

USING THIS BOOK

CONTENTS

A PATTERN LANGUAGE

Volume 1, *The Timeless Way of Building*, and Volume 2, *A Pattern Language*, are two halves of a single work. This book provides a language, for building and planning; the other book provides the theory and instructions for the use of the language. This book describes the detailed patterns for towns and neighborhoods, houses, gardens, and rooms. The other book explains the discipline which makes it possible to use these patterns to create a building or a town. This book is the sourcebook of the timeless way; the other is its practice and its origin.

The two books have evolved very much in parallel. They have been growing over the last eight years, as we have worked on the one hand to understand the nature of the building process, and on the other hand to construct an actual, possible pattern language. We have been forced by practical considerations, to publish these two books under separate covers; but in fact, they form an indivisible whole. It is possible to read them separately. But to gain the insight which we have tried to communicate in them, it is essential that you read them both.

The Timeless Way of Building describes the fundamental nature of the task of making towns and buildings.

It is shown there, that towns and buildings will not be able to become alive, unless they are made by all the people in society, and unless these people share a common pattern language, within which to make these buildings, and unless this common pattern language is alive itself.

In this book, we present one possible pattern language, of the kind called for in *The Timeless Way*. This language is extremely practical. It is a language that we have distilled from our own building and planning efforts over the last eight years. You can use it to work with your neighbors, to improve your town and neighborhood. You can use it to design a house for yourself, with your family; or to work with other people to design an office or a workshop or a public building like a school. And you can use it to guide you in the actual process of construction.

The elements of this language are entities called patterns. Each pattern describes a problem which occurs over and over again in our environment, and then describes the core of the solution to that problem, in such a way that you can use this solution a million times over, without ever doing it the same way twice.

For convenience and clarity, each pattern has the same format. First, there is a picture, which shows an archetypal example of that pattern. Second, after the picture, each pattern has an introductory paragraph, which sets the context for the pattern, by explaining how it helps to complete certain larger patterns. Then there are three diamonds to mark the beginning of the problem. After the diamonds there is a headline, in bold type. This

headline gives the essence of the problem in one or two sentences. After the headline comes the body of the problem. This is the longest section. It describes the empirical background of the pattern, the evidence for its validity, the range of different ways the pattern can be manifested in a building, and so on. Then, again in bold type, like the headline, is the solution—the heart of the pattern—which describes the field of physical and social relationships which are required to solve the stated problem, in the stated context. This solution is always stated in the form of an instruction—so that you know exactly what you need to do, to build the pattern. Then, after the solution, there is a diagram, which shows the solution in the form of a diagram, with labels to indicate its main components.

After the diagram, another three diamonds, to show that the main body of the pattern is finished. And finally, after the diamonds there is a paragraph which ties the pattern to all those smaller patterns in the language, which are needed to complete this pattern, to embellish it, to fill it out.

There are two essential purposes behind this format. First, to present each pattern connected to other patterns, so that you grasp the collection of all 253 patterns as a whole, as a language, within which you can create an infinite variety of combinations. Second, to present the problem and solution of each pattern in such a way that you can judge it for yourself, and modify it, without losing the essence that is central to it.

Let us next understand the nature of the connection between patterns.

The patterns are ordered, beginning with the very largest, for regions and towns, then working down through neighborhoods, clusters of buildings, buildings, rooms and alcoves, ending finally with details of construction.

This order, which is presented as a straight linear sequence, is essential to the way the language works. It is presented, and explained more fully, in the next section. What is most important about this sequence, is that it is based on the connections between the patterns. Each pattern is connected to certain "larger" patterns which come above it in the language; and to certain "smaller" patterns which come below it in the language. The pattern helps to complete those larger patterns which are "above" it, and is itself completed by those smaller patterns which are "below" it.

Thus, for example, you will find that the pattern ACCESSIBLE GREEN (60), is connected first to certain larger patterns: SUBCULTURE BOUNDARY (13), IDENTIFIABLE NEIGHBORHOOD (14), WORK COMMUNITY (41), and QUIET BACKS (59). These appear on its first page. And it is also connected to certain smaller patterns: POSITIVE OUTDOOR SPACE (107), TREE PLACES (171), and GARDEN WALL (173). These appear on its last page.

What this means, is that IDENTIFIABLE NEIGHBORHOOD, SUBCULTURE BOUNDARY, WORK COMMUNITY, and QUIET BACKS are incomplete, unless they contain an ACCESSIBLE GREEN; and that an ACCESSIBLE GREEN is itself incomplete, unless it contains POSITIVE OUTDOOR SPACE, TREE PLACES, and a GARDEN WALL.

And what it means in practical terms is that, if you

want to lay out a green according to this pattern, you must not only follow the instructions which describe the pattern itself, but must also try to embed the green within an IDENTIFIABLE NEIGHBORHOOD or in some SUB-CULTURE BOUNDARY, and in a way that helps to form QUIET BACKS; and then you must work to complete the green by building in some POSITIVE OUTDOOR SPACE, TREE PLACES, and a GARDEN WALL.

In short, no pattern is an isolated entity. Each pattern can exist in the world, only to the extent that is supported by other patterns: the larger patterns in which it is embedded, the patterns of the same size that surround it, and the smaller patterns which are embedded in it.

This is a fundamental view of the world. It says that when you build a thing you cannot merely build that thing in isolation, but must also repair the world around it, and within it, so that the larger world at that one place becomes more coherent, and more whole; and the thing which you make takes its place in the web of nature, as you make it.

Now we explain the nature of the relation between problems and solutions, within the individual patterns.

Each solution is stated in such a way that it gives the essential field of relationships needed to solve the problem, but in a very general and abstract way—so that you can solve the problem for yourself, in your own way, by adapting it to your preferences, and the local conditions at the place where you are making it.

For this reason, we have tried to write each solution in a way which imposes nothing on you. It contains only those essentials which cannot be avoided if you really

want to solve the problem. In this sense, we have tried, in each solution, to capture the invariant property common to all places which succeed in solving the problem.

But of course, we have not always succeeded. The solutions we have given to these problems vary in significance. Some are more true, more profound, more certain, than others. To show this clearly we have marked every pattern, in the text itself, with two asterisks, or one asterisk, or no asterisks.

In the patterns marked with two asterisks, we believe that we have succeeded in stating a true invariant: in short, that the solution we have stated summarizes a *property* common to *all possible ways* of solving the stated problem. In these two-asterisk cases we believe, in short, that it is not possible to solve the stated problem properly, without shaping the environment in one way or another according to the pattern that we have given—and that, in these cases, the pattern describes a deep and inescapable property of a well-formed environment.

In the patterns marked with one asterisk, we believe that we have made some progress towards identifying such an invariant: but that with careful work it will certainly be possible to improve on the solution. In these cases, we believe it would be wise for you to treat the pattern with a certain amount of disrespect—and that you seek out variants of the solution which we have given, since there are almost certainly possible ranges of solutions which are not covered by what we have written.

Finally, in the patterns without an asterisk, we are certain that we have *not* succeeded in defining a true

invariant—that, on the contrary, there are certainly ways of solving the problem different from the one which we have given. In these cases we have still stated a solution, in order to be concrete—to provide the reader with at least one way of solving the problem—but the task of finding the true invariant, the true property which lies at the heart of all possible solutions to this problem, remains undone.

We hope, of course, that many of the people who read, and use this language, will try to improve these patterns—will put their energy to work, in this task of finding more true, more profound invariants—and we hope that gradually these more true patterns, which are slowly discovered, as time goes on, will enter a common language, which all of us can share.

You see then that the patterns are very much alive and evolving. In fact, if you like, each pattern may be looked upon as a hypothesis like one of the hypotheses of science. In this sense, each pattern represents our current best guess as to what arrangement of the physical environment will work to solve the problem presented. The empirical questions center on the problem—does it occur and is it felt in the way we have described it?—and the solution—does the arrangement we propose in fact resolve the problem? And the asterisks represent our degree of faith in these hypotheses. But of course, no matter what the asterisks say, the patterns are still hypotheses, all 253 of them—and are therefore all tentative, all free to evolve under the impact of new experience and observation.

Let us finally explain the status of this language, why

we have called it "A Pattern Language" with the emphasis on the word "A," and how we imagine this pattern language might be related to the countless thousands of other languages we hope that people will make for themselves, in the future.

The Timeless Way of Building says that every society which is alive and whole, will have its own unique and distinct pattern language; and further, that every individual in such a society will have a unique language, shared in part, but which as a totality is unique to the mind of the person who has it. In this sense, in a healthy society there will be as many pattern languages as there are people—even though these languages are shared and similar.

The question then arises: What exactly is the status of this published language? In what frame of mind, and with what intention, are we publishing this language here? The fact that it is published as a book means that many thousands of people can use it. Is it not true that there is a danger that people might come to rely on this one printed language, instead of developing their own languages, in their own minds?

The fact is, that we have written this book as a first step in the society-wide process by which people will gradually become conscious of their own pattern languages, and work to improve them. We believe, and have explained in *The Timeless Way of Building*, that the languages which people have today are so brutal, and so fragmented, that most people no longer have any language to speak of at all—and what they do have is not based on human, or natural considerations.

We have spent years trying to formulate this language, in the hope that when a person uses it, he will be so impressed by its power, and so joyful in its use, that he will understand again, what it means to have a living language of this kind. If we only succeed in that, it is possible that each person may once again embark on the construction and development of his own language—perhaps taking the language printed in this book, as a point of departure.

And yet, we do believe, of course, that this language which is printed here is something more than a manual, or a teacher, or a version of a possible pattern language. Many of the patterns here are archetypal—so deep, so deeply rooted in the nature of things, that it seems likely that they will be a part of human nature, and human action, as much in five hundred years, as they are today. We doubt very much whether anyone could construct a valid pattern language, in his own mind, which did not include the pattern ARCADES (119) for example, or the pattern ALCOVES (179).

In this sense, we have also tried to penetrate, as deep as we are able, into the nature of things in the environment: and hope that a great part of this language, which we print here, will be a core of any sensible human pattern language, which any person constructs for himself, in his own mind. In this sense, at least a part of the language we have presented here, is the archetypal core of all possible pattern languages, which can make people feel alive and human.

SUMMARY OF THE LANGUAGE

A pattern language has the structure of a network. This is explained fully in *The Timeless Way of Building*. However, when we use the network of a language, we always use it as a *sequence*, going through the patterns, moving always from the larger patterns to the smaller, always from the ones which create structures, to the ones which then embellish those structures, and then to those which embellish the embellishments. . . .

Since the language is in truth a network, there is no one sequence which perfectly captures it. But the sequence which follows, captures the broad sweep of the full network; in doing so, it follows a line, dips down, dips up again, and follows an irregular course, a little like a needle following a tapestry.

The sequence of patterns is both a summary of the language, and at the same time, an index to the patterns. If you read through the sentences which connect the groups of patterns to one another, you will get an overview of the whole language. And once you get this overview, you will then be able to find the patterns which are relevant to your own project.

And finally, as we shall explain in the next section, this sequence of patterns is also the "base map," from

which you can make a language for your own project, by choosing the patterns which are most useful to you, and leaving them more or less in the order that you find them printed here.

❖ ❖ ❖

We begin with that part of the language which defines a town or community. These patterns can never be "designed" or "built" in one fell swoop—but patient piecemeal growth, designed in such a way that every individual act is always helping to create or generate these larger global patterns, will, slowly and surely, over the years, make a community that has these global patterns in it.

1. INDEPENDENT REGIONS

within each region work toward those regional policies which will protect the land and mark the limits of the cities;

2. THE DISTRIBUTION OF TOWNS

3. CITY COUNTRY FINGERS

4. AGRICULTURAL VALLEYS

5. LACE OF COUNTRY STREETS

6. COUNTRY TOWNS

7. THE COUNTRYSIDE

through city policies, encourage the piecemeal formation of those major structures which define the city;

    8. MOSAIC OF SUBCULTURES

    9. SCATTERED WORK

    10. MAGIC OF THE CITY

    11. LOCAL TRANSPORT AREAS

build up these larger city patterns from the grass roots, through action essentially controlled by two levels of self-governing communities, which exist as physically identifiable places;

    12. COMMUNITY OF 7000

    13. SUBCULTURE BOUNDARY

    14. IDENTIFIABLE NEIGHBORHOOD

    15. NEIGHBORHOOD BOUNDARY

connect communities to one another by encouraging the growth of the following networks;

    16. WEB OF PUBLIC TRANSPORTATION

    17. RING ROADS

    18. NETWORK OF LEARNING

    19. WEB OF SHOPPING

    20. MINI-BUSES

establish community and neighborhood policy to control the character of the local environment according to the following fundamental principles;

    21. FOUR-STORY LIMIT

both in the neighborhoods and the communities, and in between them, in the boundaries, encourage the formation of local centers;

around these centers, provide for the growth of housing in the form of clusters, based on face-to-face human groups;

between the house clusters, around the centers, and especially in the boundaries between neighborhoods, encourage the formation of work communities;

between the house clusters and work communities, allow the local road and path network to grow informally, piecemeal;

in the communities and neighborhoods, provide public open land where people can relax, rub shoulders and renew themselves;

58. CARNIVAL

59. QUIET BACKS

60. ACCESSIBLE GREEN

61. SMALL PUBLIC SQUARES

62. HIGH PLACES

63. DANCING IN THE STREET

64. POOLS AND STREAMS

65. BIRTH PLACES

66. HOLY GROUND

in each house cluster and work community, provide the smaller bits of common land, to provide for local versions of the same needs;

67. COMMON LAND

68. CONNECTED PLAY

69. PUBLIC OUTDOOR ROOM

70. GRAVE SITES

71. STILL WATER

72. LOCAL SPORTS

73. ADVENTURE PLAYGROUND

74. ANIMALS

within the framework of the common land, the clusters, and the work communities encourage transformation of

the smallest independent social institutions: the families, workgroups, and gathering places. The family, in all its forms;

the workgroups, including all kinds of workshops and offices and even children's learning groups;

the local shops and gathering places.

This completes the global patterns which define a town or a community. We now start that part of the language which gives shape to groups of buildings, and individual buildings, on the land, in three dimensions. These are the patterns which can be "designed" or "built"—the patterns which define the individual buildings and the space between buildings; where we are dealing for the first time with patterns that are under the control of individuals or small groups of individuals, who are able to build the patterns all at once.

The first group of patterns helps to lay out the overall arrangement of a group of buildings: the height and number of these buildings, the entrances to the site, main parking areas, and lines of movement through the complex;

fix the position of individual buildings on the site, within the complex, one by one, according to the nature of the site, the trees, the sun: this is one of the most important moments in the language;

within the buildings' wings, lay out the entrances, the gardens, courtyards, roofs, and terraces: shape both the volume of the buildings and the volume of the space between the buildings at the same time—remembering that indoor space and outdoor space, yin and yang, must always get their shape together;

when the major parts of buildings and the outdoor areas have been given their rough shape, it is the right time to give more detailed attention to the paths and squares between the buildings;

now, with the paths fixed, we come back to the buildings: within the various wings of any one building, work out the fundamental gradients of space, and decide how the movement will connect the spaces in the gradients;

within the framework of the wings and their internal gradients of space and movement, define the most important areas and rooms. First, for a house;

then the same for offices, workshops, and public buildings;

add those small outbuildings which must be slightly independent from the main structure, and put in the access from the upper stories to the street and gardens;

prepare to knit the inside of the building to the outside, by treating the edge between the two as a place in its own right, and making human details there;

decide on the arrangement of the gardens, and the places in the gardens;

go back to the inside of the building and attach the necessary minor rooms and alcoves to complete the main rooms;

fine tune the shape and size of rooms and alcoves to make them precise and buildable;

give all the walls some depth, wherever there are to be
alcoves, windows, shelves, closets, or seats;

*At this stage, you have a complete design for an in-
dividual building. If you have followed the patterns
then, you have a scheme of spaces, either marked on
the ground, with stakes, or on a piece of paper, accurate
to the nearest foot or so. You know the height of rooms,
the rough size and position of windows and doors, and
you know roughly how the roofs of the building, and
the gardens are laid out.*

The next, and last part of the language, tells how to

make a buildable building directly from this rough scheme of spaces, and tells you how to build it, in detail.

Before you lay out structural details, establish a philosophy of structure which will let the structure grow directly from your plans and your conception of the buildings;

205. STRUCTURE FOLLOWS SOCIAL SPACES

206. EFFICIENT STRUCTURE

207. GOOD MATERIALS

208. GRADUAL STIFFENING

within this philosophy of structure, on the basis of the plans which you have made, work out the complete structural layout; this is the last thing you do on paper, before you actually start to build;

209. ROOF LAYOUT

210. FLOOR AND CEILING LAYOUT

211. THICKENING THE OUTER WALLS

212. COLUMNS AT THE CORNERS

213. FINAL COLUMN DISTRIBUTION

put stakes in the ground to mark the columns on the site, and start erecting the main frame of the building according to the layout of these stakes;

214. ROOT FOUNDATIONS

215. GROUND FLOOR SLAB

216. BOX COLUMNS

within the main frame of the building, fix the exact positions for openings—the doors and windows—and frame these openings;

as you build the main frame and its openings, put in the following subsidiary patterns where they are appropriate;

build outdoor details to finish the outdoors as fully as the indoor spaces;

complete the building with ornament and li͙ and your own things;

CHOOSING A LANGUAGE
FOR YOUR PROJECT

All 253 patterns together form a language. They create a coherent picture of an entire region, with the power to generate such regions in a million forms, with infinite variety in all the details.

It is also true that any small sequence of patterns from this language is itself a language for a smaller part of the environment; and this small list of patterns is then capable of generating a million parks, paths, houses, workshops, or gardens.

For example, consider the following ten patterns:

PRIVATE TERRACE ON THE STREET (140)
SUNNY PLACE (161)
OUTDOOR ROOM (163)
SIX-FOOT BALCONY (167)
PATHS AND GOALS (120)
CEILING HEIGHT VARIETY (190)
COLUMNS AT THE CORNERS (212)
FRONT DOOR BENCH (242)
RAISED FLOWERS (245)
DIFFERENT CHAIRS (251)

This short list of patterns is itself a language: it is one of a thousand possible languages for a porch, at the front of a house. One of us chose this small language, to build

a porch onto the front of his house. This is the way the language, and its patterns, helped to generate this porch.

I started with PRIVATE TERRACE ON THE STREET (140). That pattern calls for a terrace, slightly raised, connected to the house, and on the street side. SUNNY PLACE (161) suggests that a special place on the sunny side of the yard should be intensified and made into a place by the use of a patio, balcony, outdoor room, etc. I used these two patterns to locate a raised platform on the south side of the house.

To make this platform into an OUTDOOR ROOM (163), I put it half under the existing roof overhang, and kept a mature pyracanthus tree right smack in the middle of the platform. The overhead foliage of the tree added to the roof-like enclosure of the space. I put a wind screen of fixed glass on the west side of the platform too, to give it even more enclosure.

I used SIX-FOOT BALCONY (167) to determine the size of the platform. But this pattern had to be used judiciously and not blindly—the reasoning for the pattern has to do with the minimum space required for people to sit comfortably and carry on a discussion around a small side-table. Since I wanted space for at least two of these conversation areas—one under the roof for very hot or rainy days, and one out under the sky for days when you wanted to be full in the sun, the balcony had to be made 12 x 12 feet square.

Now PATHS AND GOALS (120): Usually, this pattern deals with large paths in a neighborhood, and comes much earlier in a language. But I used it in a special way. It says that the paths which naturally get formed by people's walking, on the land, should be preserved and intensified. Since the path to our front door cut right across the corner of the place where I had planned to put the platform, I cut the corner of the platform off.

The height of the platform above the ground was determined by CEILING HEIGHT VARIETY (190). By building the platform approximately one foot above the ground line, the ceiling height of the covered portion came out at between 6 and 7 feet—just right for a space as small as this. Since this height above the ground level is just about right for sitting, the pattern FRONT DOOR BENCH (242) was automatically satisfied.

There were three columns standing, supporting the roof over

the old porch. They had to stay where they are, because they hold the roof up. But, following COLUMNS AT THE CORNERS (212), the platform was very carefully tailored to their positions—so that the columns help define the social spaces on either side of them.

Finally, we put a couple of flower boxes next to the "front door bench"—it's nice to smell them when you sit there—according to RAISED FLOWERS (245). And the old chairs you can see in the porch are DIFFERENT CHAIRS (251).

You can see, from this short example, how powerful and simple a pattern language is. And you are now, perhaps ready to appreciate how careful you must be, when you construct a language for yourself and your own project.

The finished porch

The character of the porch is given by the ten patterns in this short language. In just this way, each part of the environment is given its character by the collection of patterns which we choose to build into it. The character of what you build, will be given to it by the language of patterns you use, to generate it.

For this reason, of course, the task of choosing a language for your project is fundamental. The pattern language we have given here contains 253 patterns. You can therefore use it to generate an almost unimaginably large number of possible different smaller languages, for all the different projects you may choose to do, simply by picking patterns from it.

We shall now describe a rough procedure by which you can choose a language for your own project, first by taking patterns from this language we have printed here, and then by adding patterns of your own.

1. First of all, make a copy of the master sequence (pages xix–xxxiv) on which you can tick off the patterns which will form the language for your project. If you don't have access to a copying machine, you can tick off patterns in the list printed in the book, use paper clips to mark pages, write your own list, use paper markers—whatever you like. But just for now, to explain it clearly, we shall assume that you have a copy of the list in front of you.

2. Scan down the list, and find the pattern which best describes the overall scope of the project you have in mind. This is the starting pattern for your project. Tick it. (If there are two or three possible candidates, don't worry: just pick the one which seems best: the others will fall in place as you move forward.)

3. Turn to the starting pattern itself, in the book, and read it through. Notice that the other patterns mentioned by name at the beginning and at the end, of the pattern you are reading, are also possible candidates for your language. The ones at the beginning will tend to be "larger" than your project. Don't include them, unless

you have the power to help create these patterns, at least in a small way, in the world around your project. The ones at the end are "smaller." Almost all of them will be important. Tick all of them, on your list, unless you have some special reason for not wanting to include them.

4. Now your list has some more ticks on it. Turn to the next highest pattern on the list which is ticked, and open the book to that pattern. Once again, it will lead you to other patterns. Once again, tick those which are relevant—especially the ones which are "smaller" that come at the end. As a general rule, do not tick the ones which are "larger" unless you can do something about them, concretely, in your own project.

5. When in doubt about a pattern, don't include it. Your list can easily get too long: and if it does, it will become confusing. The list will be quite long enough, even if you only include the patterns you especially like.

6. Keep going like this, until you have ticked all the patterns you want for your project.

7. Now, adjust the sequence by adding your own material. If there are things you want to include in your project, but you have not been able to find patterns which correspond to them, then write them in, at an appropriate point in the sequence, near other patterns which are of about the same size and importance. For example, there is no pattern for a sauna. If you want to include one, write it in somewhere near BATHING ROOM (144) in your sequence.

8. And of course, if you want to change any patterns, change them. There are often cases where you may have a personal version of a pattern, which is more true, or

more relevant for you. In this case, you will get the most "power" over the language, and make it your own most effectively, if you write the changes in, at the appropriate places in the book. And, it will be most concrete of all, if you change the name of the pattern too—so that it captures your own changes clearly.

Suppose now that you have a language for your project. The way to use the language depends very much on its scale. Patterns dealing with towns can only be implemented gradually, by grass roots action; patterns for a building can be built up in your mind, and marked out on the ground; patterns for construction must be built physically, on the site. For this reason we have given three separate instructions, for these three different scales. For towns, see page 3; for buildings, see page 463; for construction, see page 935.

The procedures for each of these three scales are described in much more detail with extensive examples, in the appropriate chapters of *The Timeless Way of Building*. For the town—see chapters 24 and 25; for an individual building—see chapters 20, 21, and 22; and for the process of construction which describes the way a building is actually built see chapter 23.

Finally, a note of caution. This language, like English, can be a medium for prose, or a medium for poetry. The difference between prose and poetry is not that different languages are used, but that the same language is used, differently. In an ordinary English sentence, each word has one meaning, and the sentence too, has one simple meaning. In a poem, the meaning is far more dense. Each word carries several meanings; and the sentence as a whole carries an enormous density of interlocking meanings, which together illuminate the whole.

The same is true for pattern languages. It is possible to make buildings by stringing together patterns, in a rather loose way. A building made like this, is an assembly of patterns. It is not dense. It is not profound. But it is also possible to put patterns together in such a way that many many patterns overlap in the same physical space: the building is very dense; it has many meanings captured in a small space; and through this density, it becomes profound.

In a poem, this kind of density, creates illumination, by making identities between words, and meanings, whose identity we have not understood before. In "O Rose thou art sick," the rose is identified with many

greater, and more personal things than any rose—and the poem illuminates the person, and the rose, because of this connection. The connection not only illuminates the words, but also illuminates our actual lives.

> O Rose thou art sick.
> The invisible worm,
> That flies in the night
> In the howling storm:
>
> Has found out thy bed
> Of crimson joy:
> And his dark secret love
> Does thy life destroy.

WILLIAM BLAKE

The same exactly, happens in a building. Consider, for example, the two patterns BATHING ROOM (144) and STILL WATER (71). One defines a part of a house where you can bathe yourself slowly, with pleasure, perhaps in company; a place to rest your limbs, and to relax. The other is a place in a neighborhood, where this is water to gaze into, perhaps to swim in, where children can sail boats, and splash about, which nourishes those parts of ourselves which rely on water as one of the great elements of the unconscious.

Suppose now, that we make a complex of buildings where individual bathing rooms are somehow connected to a common pond, or lake, or pool—where the bathing room merges with this common place; where there is no sharp distinction between the individual and family processes of the bathing room, and the common pleasure of the common pool. In this place, these two patterns

exist in the same space; they are identified; there is a compression of the two, which requires less space, and which is more profound than in a place where they are merely side by side. The compression illuminates each of the patterns, sheds light on its meaning; and also illuminates our lives, as we understand a little more about the connections of our inner needs.

But this kind of compression is not only poetic and profound. It is not only the stuff of poems and exotic statements, but to some degree, the stuff of every English sentence. To some degree, there is compression in every single word we utter, just because each word carries the whisper of the meanings of the words it is connected to. Even "Please pass the butter, Fred" has some compression in it, because it carries overtones that lie in the connections of these words to all the words which came before it.

Each of us, talking to our friends, or to our families, makes use of these compressions, which are drawn out from the connections between words which are given by the language. The more we can feel all the connections in the language, the more rich and subtle are the things we say at the most ordinary times.

And once again, the same is true in building. The compression of patterns into a single space, is not a poetic and exotic thing, kept for special buildings which are works of art. It is the most ordinary economy of space. It is quite possible that all the patterns for a house might, in some form be present, and overlapping, in a simple one-room cabin. The patterns do not need to be strung out, and kept separate. Every building, every room,

every garden is better, when all the patterns which it needs are compressed as far as it is possible for them to be. The building will be cheaper; and the meanings in it will be denser.

It is essential then, once you have learned to use the language, that you pay attention to the possibility of compressing the many patterns which you put together, in the smallest possible space. You may think of this process of compressing patterns, as a way to make the cheapest possible building which has the necessary patterns in it. It is, also, the only way of using a pattern language to make buildings which are poems.

TOWNS

We begin with that part of the language which defines a town or a community. These patterns can never be "designed" or "built" in one fell swoop—but patient piecemeal growth, designed in such a way that every individual act is always helping to create or generate these larger global patterns, will, slowly and surely, over the years, make a community that has these global patterns in it.

❖ ❖ ❖

The first 94 patterns deal with the large-scale structure of the environment: the growth of town and country, the layout of roads and paths, the relationship between work and family, the formation of suitable public institutions for a neighborhood, the kinds of public space required to support these institutions.

We believe that the patterns presented in this section can be implemented best by piecemeal processes, where each project built or each planning decision made is sanctioned by the community according as it does or does not help to form certain large-scale patterns. *We do not believe that these large patterns, which give so much structure to a town or of a neighborhood, can be created by centralized authority, or by laws, or by master plans.* We believe instead that they can emerge gradually and organically, almost of their own accord, if every act of building, large or small, takes on the responsibility for gradually shaping its small corner of the world to make these larger patterns appear there.

In the next few pages we shall describe a planning

3

process which we believe is compatible with this piece-meal approach.

1. The core of the planning process we propose is this: The region is made up of a hierarchy of social and political groups, from the smallest and most local groups —families, neighborhoods, and work groups—to the largest groups—city councils, regional assemblies.

Imagine for example a metropolitan region composed very roughly of the following groups, each group a coherent political entity:

A. The region: 8,000,000 people.
B. The major city: 500,000 people.
C. Communities and small towns: 5–10,000 people each.
D. Neighborhoods: 500–1000 people each.
E. House clusters and work communities: 30–50 people each.
F. Families and work groups: 1–15 people each.

2. *Each group makes its own decisions about the environment it uses in common.* Ideally, each group actually owns the common land at its "level." And higher groups do not own or control the land belonging to lower groups—they only own and control the common land that lies *between* them, and which serves the higher group. For instance, a community of 7000 might own the public land lying between its component neighborhoods, but not the neighborhoods themselves. A cooperative house cluster would own the common land between the houses, but not the houses themselves.

3. Each of these groups takes responsibility for those patterns relevant to its own internal structure.

Thus, we imagine, for example, that the various

groups we have named might choose to adopt the following patterns:

A. Region: INDEPENDENT REGIONS

DISTRIBUTION OF TOWNS

CITY COUNTRY FINGERS . . .

B. City: MOSAIC OF SUBCULTURES

SCATTERED WORK

THE MAGIC OF THE CITY . . .

C. Community: COMMUNITY OF 7000

SUBCULTURE BOUNDARY . . .

4. Each neighborhood, community, or city is then
free to find various ways of persuading its constituent
groups and individuals to implement these patterns
gradually.

In every case this will hinge on some kind of incentive. However, the actual incentives chosen might vary
greatly, in their power, and degree of enforcement.
Some patterns, like CITY COUNTRY FINGERS, might be
made a matter of regional law—since nothing less can
deter money-hungry developers from building everywhere. Other patterns, like MAIN GATEWAY, BIRTH
PLACES, STILL WATER, might be purely voluntary. And
other patterns might have various kinds of incentives,
intermediate between these extremes.

For example, NETWORK OF PATHS AND CARS, ACCES-
SIBLE GREENS, and others might be formulated so that
tax breaks will be given to those development projects
which help to bring them into existence.

5. As far as possible, implementation should be loose
and voluntary, based on social responsibility, and not on
legislation or coercion.

Suppose, for example, that there is a citywide decision

5

to increase industrial uses in certain areas. Within the process here defined, the city could not implement this policy over the heads of the neighborhoods, by zoning or the power of eminent domain or any other actions. They can suggest that it is important, and can increase the flow of money to any neighborhoods willing to help implement this larger pattern. They can implement it, in short, if they can find local neighborhoods willing to see their own future in these terms, and willing to modify their own environment to help make it happen locally. As they find such neighborhoods, then it will happen gradually, over a period of years, as the local neighborhoods respond to the incentives.

6. Once such a process is rolling, a community, having adopted the pattern HEALTH CENTER, for example, might invite a group of doctors to come and build such a place. The team of users, designing the clinic would work from the HEALTH CENTER pattern, and all the other relevant patterns that are part of the community's language. They would try to build into their project any higher patterns that the community has adopted—NINE PER CENT PARKING, LOCAL SPORTS, NETWORK OF PATHS AND CARS, ACCESSIBLE GREEN, etc.

7. It is of course possible for individual acts of building to begin working their way toward these larger communal patterns, even before the neighborhood, community, and regional groups are formed.

Thus, for example, a group of people seeking to get rid of noisy and dangerous traffic in front of their houses might decide to tear up the asphalt, and build a GREEN STREET there instead. They would present their case to

6

the traffic department based on the arguments presented in the pattern, and on an analysis of the existing street pattern.

Another group wanting to build a small communal workshop, in a neighborhood currently zoned for residential use only, can argue their case based on SCATTERED WORK, SETTLED WORK, etc., and possibly get the city or zoning department to change the zoning regulation on this matter, and thereby slowly work toward introducing patterns, one at a time within the current framework of codes and zoning.

We have worked out a partial version of this process at the Eugene campus of the University of Oregon. That work is described in Volume 3, *The Oregon Experiment*. But a university is quite different from a town, because it has a single centralized owner, and a single source of funds. It is inevitable, therefore, that the process by which individual acts can work together to form larger wholes without restrictive planning from above, can only partly be put into practice there.

The theory which explains how large patterns can be built piecemeal from smaller ones, is given in Chapters 24 and 25 of The Timeless Way of Building.

At some time in the future, we hope to write another volume, which explains the political and economic processes needed to implement this process fully, in a town.

Do what you can to establish a world government, with a thousand independent regions, instead of countries;

I. INDEPENDENT REGIONS

Metropolitan regions will not come to balance until each one is small and autonomous enough to be an independent sphere of culture.

There are four separate arguments which have led us to this conclusion: 1. The nature and limits of human government. 2. Equity among regions in a world community. 3. Regional planning considerations. 4. Support for the intensity and diversity of human cultures.

1. There are natural limits to the size of groups that can govern themselves in a human way. The biologist J. B. S. Haldane has remarked on this in his paper, "On Being the Right Size":

. . . just as there is a best size for every animal, so the same is true for every human institution. In the Greek type of democracy all the citizens could listen to a series of orators and vote directly on questions of legislation. Hence their philosophers held that a small city was the largest possible democratic state. . . . (J. B. S Haldane, "On Being the Right Size," *The World of Mathematics, Vol. II*, J. R. Newman, ed. New York: Simon and Schuster, 1956, pp. 962–67).

It is not hard to see why the government of a region becomes less and less manageable with size. In a population of N persons, there are of the order of N^2 person-to-person links needed to keep channels of communication open. Naturally, when N goes beyond a certain limit, the channels of communication needed for democracy and justice and information are simply too clogged, and too complex; bureaucracy overwhelms human processes.

And, of course, as N grows the number of levels in the hierarchy of government increases too. In small countries like Denmark there are so few levels, that any private citizen can have access to the Minister of Education. But this kind of direct access is quite impossible in larger countries like England or the United States.

We believe the limits are reached when the population of a region reaches some 2 to 10 million. Beyond this size, people become remote from the large-scale processes of government. Our estimate may seem extraordinary in the light of modern history: the nation-states have grown mightily and their governments hold power over tens of millions, sometimes hundreds of millions, of people. But these huge powers cannot claim to have a natural size.

They cannot claim to have struck the balance between the needs of towns and communities, and the needs of the world community as a whole. Indeed, their tendency has been to override local needs and repress local culture, and at the same time aggrandize themselves to the point where they are out of reach, their power barely conceivable to the average citizen.

2. Unless a region has at least several million people in it, it will not be large enough to have a seat in a world government, and will therefore not be able to supplant the power and authority of present nation-states.

We found this point expressed by Lord Weymouth of Warminster, England, in a letter to the *New York Times*, March 15, 1973:

WORLD FEDERATION: A THOUSAND STATES

. . . the essential foundation stone for world federation on a democratic basis consists of regionalization within centralized government. . . . This argument rests on the idea that world government is lacking in moral authority unless each delegate represents an approximately equal portion of the world's population. Working backward from an estimate of the global population in the year 2000, which is anticipated to rise to the 10,000 million mark, I suggest that we should be thinking in terms of an ideal regional state at something around ten million, or between five and fifteen million, to give greater flexibility. This would furnish the U.N. with an assembly of equals of 1000 regional representatives: a body that would be justified in claiming to be truly representative of the world's population.

Weymouth believes that Western Europe could take some of the initiative for triggering this conception of world government. He looks for the movement for regional autonomy to take hold in the European Parliament at Strasbourg; and hopes that power can gradually be transferred from Westminister, Paris, Bonn, etc., to regional councils, federated in Strasbourg.

I am suggesting that in the Europe of the future we shall see England split down into Kent, Wessex, Mercia, Anglia and Northumbria, with an independent Scotland, Wales and Ireland, of course. Other European examples will include Brittany, Bavaria and Calabria. The national identities of our contemporary Europe will have lost their political significance.

3. Unless the regions have the power to be self-governing, they

will not be able to solve their own environmental problems. The arbitrary lines of states and countries, which often cut across natural regional boundaries, make it all but impossible for people to solve regional problems in a direct and humanly efficient way.

An extensive and detailed analysis of this idea has been given by the French economist Gravier, who has proposed, in a series of books and papers, the concept of a Europe of the Regions, a Europe decentralized and reorganized around regions which cross present national and subnational boundaries. (For example, the Basel-Strasbourg Region includes parts of France, Germany, and Switzerland; the Liverpool Region includes parts of England and parts of Wales). See Jean-François Gravier, "L'Europe des regions," in 1965 Internationale Regio Planertagung, Schriften der Regio 3, Regio, Basel, 1965, pp. 211–22; and in the same volume see also Emrys Jones, "The Conflict of City Regions and Administrative Units in Britain," pp. 223–35.

4. Finally, unless the present-day great nations have their power greatly decentralized, the beautiful and differentiated languages, cultures, customs, and ways of life of the earth's people, vital to the health of the planet, will vanish. In short, we believe that independent regions are the natural receptacles for language, culture, customs, economy, and laws and that each region should be separate and independent enough to maintain the strength and vigor of its culture.

The fact that human cultures within a city can only flourish when they are at least partly separated from neighboring cultures is discussed in great detail in MOSAIC OF SUBCULTURES (8). We are suggesting here that the same argument also applies to regions —that the regions of the earth must also keep their distance and their dignity in order to survive as cultures.

In the best of medieval times, the cities performed this function. They provided permanent and intense spheres of cultural influence, variety, and economic exchange; they were great communes, whose citizens were co-members, each with some say in the city's destiny. We believe that the independent region can become the modern polis—the new commune—that human entity which provides the sphere of culture, language, laws, services, economic exchange, variety, which the old walled city or the polis provided for its members.

Therefore:

Wherever possible, work toward the evolution of independent regions in the world; each with a population between 2 and 10 million; each with its own natural and geographic boundaries; each with its own economy; each one autonomous and self-governing; each with a seat in a world government, without the intervening power of larger states or countries.

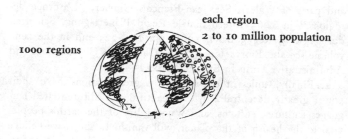

1000 regions

each region
2 to 10 million population

❖ ❖ ❖

Within each region encourage the population to distribute itself as widely as possible across the region—THE DISTRIBUTION OF TOWNS (2). . . .

within each region work toward those regional policies which will protect the land and mark the limits of the cities:

2 THE DISTRIBUTION OF TOWNS

. . . consider now the character of settlements within the region: what balance of villages, towns, and cities is in keeping with the independence of the region—INDEPENDENT REGIONS (1)?

If the population of a region is weighted too far toward small villages, modern civilization can never emerge; but if the population is weighted too far toward big cities, the earth will go to ruin because the population isn't where it needs to be, to take care of it.

Two different necessities govern the distribution of population in a region. On the one hand, people are drawn to cities: they are drawn by the growth of civilization, jobs, education, economic growth, information. On the other hand, the region as a social and ecological whole will not be properly maintained unless the people of the region are fairly well spread out across it, living in many different kinds of settlements—farms, villages, towns, and cities—with each settlement taking care of the land around it. Industrial society has so far been following only the first of these necessities. People leave the farms and towns and villages and pack into the cities, leaving vast parts of the region depopulated and undermaintained.

In order to establish a reasonable distribution of population within a region, we must fix two separate features of the distribution: its statistical character and its spatial character. First, we must be sure that the statistical distribution of towns, by size, is appropriate: we must be sure that there are many small towns and few large ones. Second, we must then be sure that the spatial distribution of towns within the region is appropriate: we must be sure that the towns in any given size category are evenly spread out across the region, not highly concentrated.

In practice, the statistical distribution will take care of itself. A large number of studies has shown that the natural demographic and political and economic processes at work in city growth and population movement will create a distribution of

towns with many small towns and few large ones; and indeed, the nature of this distribution does correspond, roughly, to the logarithmic distribution that we propose in this pattern. Various explanations have been given by Christaller, Zipf, Herbert Simon, and others; they are summarized in Brian Berry and William Garrison, "Alternate Explanations of Urban Rank-Size Relationships," *Annals of the Association of American Geographers*, Vol. 48, March 1958, No. 1, pp. 83–91.

Let us assume, then, that towns will have the right distribution of sizes. But are they adjacent to one another, or are they spread out? If all the towns in a region, large, medium, and small, were crammed together in one continuous urban area, the fact that some are large and some are small, though interesting politically, would have no ecological meaning whatsoever. As far as the ecology of the region is concerned, it is the *spatial* distribution of the towns which matters, not the statistics of political boundaries within the urban sprawl.

Two arguments have led us to propose that the towns in any one size category should be uniformly distributed across the region: an economic argument and an ecological argument.

Economic. All over the world, underdeveloped areas are facing economic ruin because the jobs, and then the people, move toward the largest cities, under the influence of their economic gravity. Sweden, Scotland, Israel, and Mexico are all examples. The population moves toward Stockholm, Glasgow, Tel Aviv, Mexico City —as it does so, new jobs get created in the city, and then even more people have to come to the city in search of jobs. Gradually the imbalance between city and country becomes severe. The city becomes richer, the outlying areas continuously poorer. In the end the region may have the highest standard of living in the world at its center, yet only a few miles away, at its periphery, people may be starving.

This can only be halted by policies which guarantee an equal sharing of resources, and economic development, across the entire region. In Israel, for example, there has been some attempt to pour the limited resources with which the government can subsidize economic growth into those areas which are most backward economically. (See "Urban Growth Policies in Six

European Countries," Urban Growth Policy Study Group, Office of International Affairs, HUD, Washington, D.C., 1972.)

Ecological. An overconcentrated population, in space, puts a huge burden on the region's overall ecosystem. As the big cities grow, the population movement overburdens these areas with air pollution, strangled transportation, water shortages, housing shortages, and living densities which go beyond the realm of human reasonableness. In some metropolitan centers, the ecology is perilously close to cracking. By contrast, a population that is spread more evenly over its region minimizes its impact on the ecology of the environment, and finds that it can take care of itself and the land more prudently, with less waste and more humanity:

This is because the actual urban superstructure required per inhabitant goes up radically as the size of the town increases beyond a certain point. For example, the *per capita* cost of high rise flats is much greater than that of ordinary houses; and the cost of roads and other transportation routes increases with the number of commuters carried. Similarly, the *per capita* expenditure on other facilities such as those for distributing food and removing wastes is much higher in cities than in small towns and villages. Thus, if everybody lived in villages the need for sewage treatment plants would be somewhat reduced, while in an entirely urban society they are essential, and the cost of treatment is high. Broadly speaking, it is only by decentralization that we can increase self-sufficiency—and self-sufficiency is vital if we are to minimize the burden of social systems on the ecosystems that support them. The Ecologist, *Blueprint for Survival*, England: Penguin, 1972, pp. 52–53.)

Therefore:

Encourage a birth and death process for towns within the region, which gradually has these effects:

1. **The population is evenly distributed in terms of different sizes—for example, one town with 1,000,000 people, 10 towns with 100,000 people each, 100 towns with 10,000 people each, and 1000 towns with 100 people each.**

2. **These towns are distributed in space in such a way that within each size category the towns are homogeneously distributed all across the region.**

This process can be implemented by regional zoning policies, land grants, and incentives which encourage industries to locate according to the dictates of the distribution.

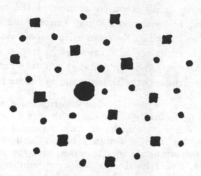

towns of 1,000,000 – 250 miles apart
towns of 100,000 – 80 miles apart
towns of 10,000 – 25 miles apart
towns of 1,000 – 8 miles apart

❖ ❖ ❖

As the distribution evolves, protect the prime agricultural land for farming—AGRICULTURAL VALLEYS (4); protect the smaller outlying towns, by establishing belts of countryside around them and by decentralizing industry, so that the towns are economically stable—COUNTRY TOWNS (6). In the larger more central urban areas work toward land policies which maintain open belts of countryside between the belts of city—CITY COUNTRY FINGERS (3). . .

3 CITY COUNTRY FINGERS**

. . . the distribution of towns required to make a balanced region—DISTRIBUTION OF TOWNS (2)—can be further helped by controlling the balance of urban land and open countryside within the towns and cities themselves.

❖ ❖ ❖

Continuous sprawling urbanization destroys life, and makes cities unbearable. But the sheer size of cities is also valuable and potent.

People feel comfortable when they have access to the countryside, experience of open fields, and agriculture; access to wild plants and birds and animals. For this access, cities must have boundaries with the countryside near every point. At the same time, a city becomes good for life only when it contains a great density of interactions among people and work, and different ways of life. For the sake of this interaction, the city must be continuous—not broken up. In this pattern we shall try to bring these two facts to balance.

Let us begin with the fact that people living in cities need contact with true rural land to maintain their roots with the land that supports them. A 1972 Gallup poll gives very strong evidence for this fact. The poll asked the question: "If you could live anywhere, would you prefer a city, suburban area, small town, or farm?" and received the following answers from 1465 Americans:

City	13%
Suburb	13
Small town	32
Farm	23

And this dissatisfaction with cities is getting worse. In 1966, 22 percent said they preferred the city—in 1972, only six years later, this figure dropped to 13 percent. ("Most don't want to live in a city," George Gallup, *San Francisco Chronicle*, Monday, December 18, 1972, p. 12.)

It is easy to understand why city people long for contact with

22

the countryside. Only 100 years ago 85 percent of the Americans lived on rural land; today 70 percent live in cities. Apparently we cannot live entirely within cities—at least the kinds of cities we have built so far—our need for contact with the countryside runs too deep, it is a biological necessity:

> Unique as we may think we are, we are nevertheless as likely to be genetically programmed to a natural habitat of clean air and a varied green landscape as any other mammal. To be relaxed and feel healthy usually means simply allowing our bodies to react in the way for which one hundred millions of years of evolution has equipped us. Physically and genetically, we appear best adapted to a tropical savanna, but as a cultural animal we utilize learned adaptations to cities and towns. For thousands of years we have tried in our houses to imitate not only the climate, but the setting of our evolutionary past: warm, humid air, green plants, and even animal companions. Today, if we can afford it, we may even build a greenhouse or swimming pool next to our living room, buy a place in the country, or at least take our children vacationing on the seashore. The specific physiological reactions to natural beauty and diversity, to the shapes and colors of nature (especially to green), to the motions and sounds of other animals, such as birds, we as yet do not comprehend. But it is evident that nature in our daily life should be thought of as a part of the biological need. It cannot be neglected in the discussions of resource policy for man. (H. H. Iltis, P. Andres, and O. L. Loucks, in *Population Resources Environment: Issues in Human Ecology*, P. R. Ehrlich and A. H. Ehrlich, San Francisco: Freeman and Co., 1970, p. 204.)

But it is becoming increasingly difficult for city dwellers to come into contact with rural life. In the San Francisco Bay Region 21 square miles of open space is lost each year (Gerald D. Adams, "The Open Space Explosion," *Cry California*, Fall 1970, pp. 27–32.) As cities get bigger the rural land is farther and farther away.

With the breakdown of contact between city dwellers and the countryside, the cities become prisons. Farm vacations, a year on the farm for city children, and retirement to the country for old people are replaced by expensive resorts, summer camps, and retirement villages. And for most, the only contact remaining is the weekend exodus from the city, choking the highways and the few organized recreation centers. Many weekenders return to the city on Sunday night with their nerves more shattered than when they left.

*When the countryside is far away
the city becomes a prison.*

If we wish to re-establish and maintain the proper connection between city and country, and yet maintain the density of urban interactions, it will be necessary to stretch out the urbanized area into long sinuous fingers which extend into the farmland, shown in the diagram below. Not only will the city be in the form of narrow fingers, but so will the farmlands adjacent to it.

The maximum width of the city fingers is determined by the maximum acceptable distance from the heart of the city to the countryside. We reckon that everyone should be within 10 minutes' walk of the countryside. This would set a maximum width of 1 mile for the city fingers.

The minimum for any farmland finger is determined by the minimum acceptable dimensions for typical working farms. Since 90 percent of all farms are still 500 acres or less and there is no respectable evidence that the giant farm is more efficient (Leon H. Keyserling, *Agriculture and the Public Interest,* Conference on Economic Progress, Washington, D. C., February 1965), these fingers of farmland need be no more than 1 mile wide.

The implementation of this pattern requires new policies of three different kinds. With respect to the farmland, there must be policies encouraging the reconstruction of small farms, farms that fit the one-mile bands of country land. Second, there must be policies which contain the cities' tendency to scatter in every direction. And third, the countryside must be truly public, so that people can establish contact with even those parts of the land that are under private cultivation.

Imagine how this one pattern would transform life in cities.

3   CITY COUNTRY FINGERS

Every city dweller would have access to the countryside; the open country would be a half-hour bicycle ride from downtown. Therefore:

Keep interlocking fingers of farmland and urban land, even at the center of the metropolis. The urban fingers should never be more than 1 mile wide, while the farmland fingers should never be less than 1 mile wide.

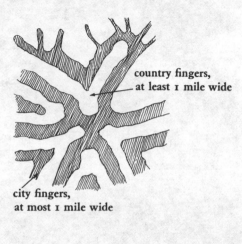

country fingers, at least 1 mile wide

city fingers, at most 1 mile wide

❖ ❖ ❖

Whenever land is hilly, keep the country fingers in the valleys and the city fingers on the upper slopes of hillsides—AGRICULTURAL VALLEYS (4). Break the city fingers into hundreds of distinct self-governing subcultures—MOSAIC OF SUBCULTURES (8), and run the major roads and railways down the middle of these city fingers—WEB OF PUBLIC TRANSPORTATION (16), RING ROADS (17). . . .

4 AGRICULTURAL VALLEYS*

. . . this pattern helps maintain the INDEPENDENT REGIONS (1)
by making regions more self-sufficient agriculturally; and it will
create CITY COUNTRY FINGERS (3) almost automatically by preserving agricultural land in urban areas. But just exactly which
land ought to be preserved, and which land built upon?

✧ ✧ ✧

**The land which is best for agriculture happens to be best
for building too. But it is limited—and once destroyed, it
cannot be regained for centuries.**

In the last few years, suburban growth has been spreading
over all land, agricultural or not. It eats up this limited resource
and, worse still, destroys the possibility of farming close to cities
once and for all. But we know, from the arguments of CITY
COUNTRY FINGERS (3), that it is important to have open farmland near the places where people live. Since the arable land
which can be used for farming lies mainly in the valleys, it is
essential that the valley floors within our urban regions be left untouched and kept for farming.

The most complete study of this problem that we know, comes
from Ian McHarg (*Design With Nature*, New York: Natural
History Press, 1969). In his "Plan for the Valleys" (Wallace-
McHarg Associates, Philadelphia, 1963), he shows how town
development can be diverted to the hillsides and plateaus, leaving
the valleys clear. The pattern is supported, also, by the fact that
there are several possible practical approaches to the task of
implementation (McHarg, pp. 79–93).

Therefore:

**Preserve all agricultural valleys as farmland and protect
this land from any development which would destroy or
lock up the unique fertility of the soil. Even when valleys**

27

are not cultivated now, protect them: keep them for farms and parks and wilds.

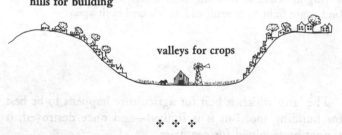

hills for building

valleys for crops

❖ ❖ ❖

Keep town and city development along the hilltops and hillsides—CITY COUNTRY FINGERS (3). And in the valleys, treat the ownership of the land as a form of stewardship, embracing basic ecological responsibilities—THE COUNTRYSIDE (7). . . . .

28

5 LACE OF COUNTRY
STREETS

. . . according to the pattern CITY COUNTRY FINGERS (3), there is a rather sharp division between city land and rural land. But at the ends of city fingers, where the country fingers open out, there is a need for an additional kind of structure. This structure has traditionally been the suburbs. But. . .

❖ ❖ ❖

The suburb is an obsolete and contradictory form of human settlement.

Many people want to live in the country; and they also want to be close to a large city. But it is geometrically impossible to have thousands of small farms, within a few minutes of a major city center.

To live well in the country, you must have a reasonable piece of land of your own—large enough for horses, cows, chickens, an orchard—and you must have immediate access to continuous open countryside, as far as the eye can see. To have quick access to the city, you must live on a road, within a few minutes' drive from city centers, and with a bus line outside your door.

It is possible to have both, by arranging country roads around large open squares of countryside or farmland, with houses closely packed along the road, but only one house deep. Lionel March lends support to this pattern in his paper, "Homes, and the Fringe" (Land Use and Built Form Studies, Cambridge, England, 1968). March shows that such a pattern, fully developed, could work for millions of people even in a country as small and densely populated as England.

A "lace of country streets" contains square miles of open countryside, fast roads from the city at the edge of these square miles, houses clustered along the roads, and footpaths stretching out from the city, crisscrossing the countryside.

1. Square miles of open countryside. We believe that one square mile is the smallest piece of open land which still maintains the integrity of the countryside. This figure is derived from the requirements of small farms, presented in the argument for CITY COUNTRY FINGERS (3).

6 COUNTRY TOWNS*

. . . this pattern forms the backbone of the DISTRIBUTION OF TOWNS (2), which requires that scores of smaller country towns support the larger towns and cities of the region.

❖ ❖ ❖

The big city is a magnet. It is terribly hard for small towns to stay alive and healthy in the face of central urban growth.

During the last 30 years, 30 million rural Americans have been forced to leave their farms and small towns and migrate to crowded cities. This forced migration continues at the rate of 800,000 people a year. The families that are left behind are not able to count on a future living in the country: about half of them live on less than $3000 a year.

And it is not purely the search for jobs that has led people away from small towns to the cities. It is also a search for information, for connection to the popular culture. In Ireland and India, for example, lively people leave the villages where there is some work, and some little food, and they go to the city, looking for action, for better work, for a better life.

Unless steps are taken to recharge the life of country towns, the cities will swamp those towns which lie the nearest to them; and will rob those which lie furthest out of their most vigorous inhabitants. What are the possibilities?

1. Economic reconstruction. Incentives to business and industry to decentralize and locate in small towns. Incentives to the inhabitants of small towns to begin grassroots business and production ventures. (See, for example, the bill introduced by Joe Evins in the House of Representatives, *Congressional Record* —House, October 3, 1967, 27687.)

2. Zoning. Zoning policy to protect small towns and the countryside around them. Greenbelt zoning was defined by Ebenezer Howard at the turn of the century and has yet to be taken seriously by American governments.

3. Social services. There are connections between small towns

34

and cities that take the form of social services, that are irreplaceable: small town visits, farm weekends and vacations for city dwellers, schools and camps in the countryside for city children, small town retirement for old people who do not like the pace of city life. Let the city invite small towns to provide these services, as grassroots ventures, and the city, or private groups, will pay for the cost of the service.

Therefore:

Preserve country towns where they exist; and encourage the growth of new self-contained towns, with populations between 500 and 10,000, entirely surrounded by open countryside and at least 10 miles from neighboring towns. Make it the region's collective concern to give each town the wherewithal it needs to build a base of local industry, so that these towns are not dormitories for people who work in other places, but real towns—able to sustain the whole of life.

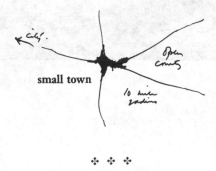

small town

❖ ❖ ❖

Treat each of these small towns as a political community, with full provision for all the stages of human life—COMMUNITY OF 7000 (12), LIFE CYCLE (26). Treat the belt of open country which surrounds the town as farm land which belongs to the people and can be freely used by them—THE COUNTRYSIDE (7). . . .

7 THE COUNTRYSIDE*

. . . within each region, in between the towns, there are vast areas of countryside—farmland, parkland, forests, deserts, grazing meadows, lakes, and rivers. The legal and ecological character of this countryside is crucial to the balance of the region. When properly done, this pattern will help to complete THE DISTRIBUTION OF TOWNS (2), CITY COUNTRY FINGERS (3), AGRICULTURAL VALLEYS (4), LACE OF COUNTRY STREETS (5) and COUNTRY TOWNS (6).

❖ ❖ ❖

I conceive that land belongs for use to a vast family of which many are dead, few are living, and countless members are still unborn.

—a Nigerian tribesman

Parks are dead and artificial. Farms, when treated as private property, rob the people of their natural biological heritage—the countryside from which they came.

Property is theft

In Norway, England, Austria, it is commonly understood people have a right to picnic in farmland, and walk and provided they respect the animals and crops. And the r also true—there is no wilderness which is abandoned ! processes—even the mountainsides are terraced, r grazed and cared for.

We may summarize these ideas by saying that th kind of nonurban land—*the countryside.* Ther

37

no farms; no uncharted wilderness. Every piece of countryside
has keepers who have the right to farm it, if it is arable; or the
obligation to look after it, if it is wild; and every piece of land
is open to the people at large, provided they respect the organic
processes which are going on there.

The central conception behind this view of the land is
given by Aldo Leopold in his essay, "The Land Ethic" (*A Sand
County Almanac*, New York: Oxford University Press, 1949);
Leopold believes that our relationship to the land will provide the
framework for the next great ethical transformation in the human
community:

This extension of ethics, so far studied only by philosophers, is
actually a process in ecological evolution. Its sequences may be
described in ecological as well as in philosophical terms. An ethic,
ecologically, is a limitation on freedom of action in the struggle for
existence. An ethic, philosophically, is a differentiation of social from
anti-social conduct. These are two definitions of one thing. The thing
has its origin in the tendency of interdependent individuals or groups
to evolve modes of co-operation. The ecologist calls these symbioses.
Politics and economics are advanced symbioses in which the original
free-for-all competition has been replaced, in part, by co-operative
mechanisms with an ethical content. . . .

All ethics so far evolved rest upon a single premise: that the individual is a member of a community of interdependent parts. His
instincts prompt him to compete for his place in that community, but
his ethics prompt him also to co-operate. . . .
The land ethic simply enlarges the boundaries of the community
to include soils, waters, plants, and animals, or collectively: the
land. . . .

Within the framework of this ethic, parks and campgrounds
conceived as "pieces of nature" for people's recreation, without
regard for the intrinsic value of the land itself, are dead things
and immoral. So also are farms conceived as areas "owned" by
the farmers for their own exclusive profit. If we continue to
treat the land as an instrument for our enjoyment, and as a
source of economic profit, our parks and camps will become more
artificial, more plastic, more like Disneyland. And our farms will
become more and more like factories. The land ethic replaces the
idea of public parks and public campgrounds with the concept
of a single countryside.

7 THE COUNTRYSIDE

One example of support for this idea lies in the *Blueprint for Survival*, and the proposal there to give traditional communities stewardship over certain estuaries and marshes. These wetlands are the spawning grounds for the fish and shellfish which form the base of the food chain for 60 per cent of the entire ocean harvest, and they can only be properly managed by a group who respects them as a cooperating part in the chain of life. (The Ecologist, England: Penguin, 1972, p. 41.)

The residential forests of Japan provide another example. A village grows up along the edge of a forest; the villagers tend the forest. Thinning it properly is one of their responsibilities. The forest is available to anyone who wants to come there and partake in the process:

> The farmhouses of Kurume-machi stand in a row along the main road for about a mile. Each house is surrounded by a belt of trees of similar species, giving the aspect of a single large forest. The main trees are located so as to produce a shelter-belt. In addition, these small forests are homes for birds, a device for conserving water, a source of firewood and timber, which is selectively cut, and a means of climate control, since the temperature inside the residential forest is cooler in summer and warmer in winter.
>
> It should be noted that these residential forests, established more than 300 years ago, are still intact as a result of the careful selective cutting and replacement program followed by the residents. (John L. Creech, "Japan—Like a National Park," *Yearbook of Agriculture* 1963, U. S. Department of Agriculture, pp. 525–28.)

Therefore:

Define all farms as parks, where the public has a right to be; and make all regional parks into working farms.

Create stewardships among groups of people, families and cooperatives, with each stewardship responsible for one part of the countryside. The stewards are given a lease for the land, and they are free to tend the land and set ground rules for its use—as a small farm, a forest, marshland, desert, and so forth. The public is free to visit the land, hike there, picnic, explore, boat, so long as they conform to the ground rules. With such a setup, a farm near a city might have picnickers in its fields every day during the summer.

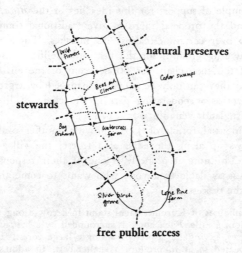

natural preserves

stewards

free public access

❖ ❖ ❖

Within each natural preserve, we imagine a limited number of houses—HOUSE CLUSTER (37)—with access on unpaved country lanes—GREEN STREETS (51). . . .

through city policies, encourage the piecemeal formation of those major structures which define the city:

8. MOSAIC OF SUBCULTURES

9. SCATTERED WORK

10. MAGIC OF THE CITY

11. LOCAL TRANSPORT AREAS

8 MOSAIC OF SUBCULTURES**

. . . the most basic structure of a city is given by the relation of urban land to open country—CITY COUNTRY FINGERS (3). Within the swaths of urban land the most important structure must come from the great variety of human groups and subcultures which can co-exist there.

❖ ❖ ❖

The homogeneous and undifferentiated character of modern cities kills all variety of life styles and arrests the growth of individual character.

Compare three possible alternative ways in which people may be distributed throughout the city:

1. In the heterogeneous city, people are mixed together, irrespective of their life style or culture. This seems rich. Actually it dampens all significant variety, arrests most of the possibilities for differentiation, and encourages conformity. It tends to reduce all life styles to a common denominator. What appears heterogeneous turns out to be homogeneous and dull.

The heterogeneous city.

2. In a city made up of ghettos, people have the support of the most basic and banal forms of differentiation—race or economic status. The ghettos are still homogeneous internally, and

City of ghettos.

43

do not allow a significant variety of life styles to emerge. People in the ghetto are usually forced to live there, isolated from the rest of society, unable to evolve their way of life, and often intolerant of ways of life different from their own.

3. In a city made of a large number of subcultures relatively small in size, each occupying an identifiable place and separated from other subcultures by a boundary of nonresidential land, new ways of life can develop. People can choose the kind of subculture they wish to live in, and can still experience many ways of life different from their own. Since each environment fosters mutual support and a strong sense of shared values, individuals can grow.

Mosaic of subcultures.

This pattern for a mosaic of subcultures was originally proposed by Frank Hendricks. His latest paper dealing with it is "Concepts of environmental quality standards based on life styles," with Malcolm MacNair (Pittsburg, Pennsylvania: University of Pittsburgh, February 1969). The psychological needs which underlie this pattern and which make it necessary for subcultures to be spatially separated in order to thrive have been described by Christopher Alexander, "Mosaic of Subcultures," Center for Environmental Structure, Berkeley, 1968. The following statement is an excerpt from that paper.

I.

We are the hollow men,
We are the stuffed men.
Leaning together
Headpiece filled with straw. Alas.
. . . .
Shape without form, shade without color,
Paralyzed force, gesture without motion;
. . .

—T. S. Eliot

Many of the people who live in metropolitan areas have a weak character. In fact, metropolitan areas seem almost marked by the fact that the people in them have markedly weak character, compared with the character which develops in simpler and more rugged situations. This weakness of character is the counterpart of another, far more visible feature of metropolitan areas: the homogeneity and lack of variety among the people who live there. Of course, weakness of character and lack of variety, are simply two sides of the same coin: a condition in which people have relatively undifferentiated selves. Character can only occur in a self which is strongly differentiated and whole: by definition, a society where people are relatively homogeneous, is one where individual selves are not strongly differentiated.

Let us begin with the problem of variety. The idea of men as millions of faceless nameless cogs pervades 20th century literature. The nature of modern housing reflects this image and sustains it. The vast majority of housing built today has the touch of mass-production. Adjacent apartments are identical. Adjacent houses are identical. The most devastating image of all was a photograph published in *Life* magazine several years ago as an advertisement for a timber company: The photograph showed a huge roomful of people; all of them had exactly the same face. The caption underneath explained: In honor of the chairman's birthday, the shareholders of the corporation are wearing masks made from his face.

These are no more than images and indications. . . . But where do all the frightening images of sameness, human digits, and human cogs, come from? Why have Kafka and Camus and Sartre spoken to our hearts?

Many writers have answered this question in detail—[David Riesman in *The Lonely Crowd*; Kurt Goldstein in *The Organism*; Max Wertheimer in *The Story of Three Days*; Abraham Maslow in *Motivation and Personality*; Rollo May in *Man's Search for Himself*, etc.]. Their answers all converge on the following essential point: Although a person may have a different mixture of attributes from his neighbour, he is not truly different, until he has a strong center, until his uniqueness is integrated and forceful. At present, in metropolitan areas, this seems not to be the case. Different though they are in detail, people are forever leaning on one another, trying to be whatever will not displease the others, afraid of being themselves.

People do things a certain way "because that's the way to get them done" instead of "because we believe them right." Compromise, going along with the others, the spirit of committees and all that it implies—in metropolitan areas, these characteristics have been made to appear adult, mature, well-adjusted. But euphemisms do little to disguise the fact that people who do things because that's the way to get along with others, instead of doing what they believe in, do it because it avoids coming to terms with their own self, and standing

on it, and confronting others with it. It is easy to defend this weakness of character on the grounds of expediency. But however many excuses are made for it, in the end weakness of character destroys a person; no one weak in character can love himself. The self-hate that it creates is not a condition in which a person can become whole.

By contrast, the person who becomes whole, states his own nature, visibly, and outwardly, loud and clear, for everyone to see. He is not afraid of his own self; he stands up for what he is; he is himself, proud of himself, recognising his shortcomings, trying to change them, but still proud of himself and glad to be himself.

But it is hard to allow that you which lurks beneath the surface to come out and show itself. It is so much easier to live according to the ideas of life which have been laid down by others, to bend your true self to the wheel of custom, to hide yourself in demands which are not yours, and which do not leave you full.

It seems clear, then, that variety, character, and finding your own self, are closely interwoven. In a society where a man can find his own self, there will be ample variety of character, and character will be strong. In a society where people have trouble finding their own selves, people will seem homogeneous, there will be less variety, and character will be weak.

If it is true that character is weak in metropolitan areas today, and we want to do something about it, the first thing we must do, is to understand *how* the metropolis has this effect.

II.

How does a metropolis create conditions in which people find it hard to find themselves?

We know that the individual forms his own self out of the values, habits and beliefs, and attitudes which his society presents him with. [George Herbert Mead, *Mind, Self and Society*.] In a metropolis the individual is confronted by a vast tableau of different values, habits and beliefs and attitudes. Whereas, in a primitive society, he had merely to integrate the traditional beliefs (in a sense, there was a self already there for the asking), in modern society each person has literally to fabricate a self, for himself, out of the chaos of values which surrounds him.

If, every day you do something, you meet someone with a slightly different background, and each of these peoples' response to what you do is different even when your actions are the same, the situation becomes more and more confusing. The possibility that you can become secure and strong in yourself, certain of what you are, and certain of what you are doing, goes down radically. Faced constantly with an unpredictable changing social world, people no longer generate the strength to draw on themselves; they draw more and more on the approval of others; they look to see whether people are smiling when they say something, and if they are, they go on saying

it, and if not, they shut up. In a world like that, it is very hard for anyone to establish any sort of inner strength.

Once we accept the idea that the formation of the self is a social process, it becomes clear that the formation of a strong social self depends on the strength of the surrounding social order. When attitudes, values, beliefs and habits are highly diffuse and mixed up as they are in a metropolis, it is almost inevitable that the person who grows up in these conditions will be diffuse and mixed up too. Weak character is a direct product of the present metropolitan society.

This argument has been summarized in devastating terms by Margaret Mead [*Culture, Change and Character Structure*]. A number of writers have supported this view empirically: Hartshorne, H. and May, M. A., *Studies in the Nature of Character*, New York, Macmillan, 1929; and "A Summary of the Work of the Character Education Inquiry," *Religious Education*, 1930, Vol. 25, 607–619 and 754–762. "Contradictory demands made upon the child in the varied situations in which he is responsible to adults, not only prevent the organisation of a consistent character, but actually compel inconsistency as the price of peace and self-respect." . . .

But this is not the end of the story. So far we have seen how the diffusion of a metropolis creates weak character. But diffusion, when it becomes pronounced, creates a special kind of superficial uniformity. When many colors are mixed, in many tiny scrambled bits and pieces, the overall effect is grey. This greyness helps to create weak character in its own way.

In a society where there are many voices, and many values, people cling to those few things which they all have in common. Thus Margaret Mead (*op. cit.*): "There is a tendency to reduce all values to simple scales of dollars, school grades, or some other simple quantitative measure, whereby the extreme incommensurables of many different sets of cultural values can be easily, though superficially, reconciled." And Joseph T. Klapper [*The Effects of Mass Communication*, Free Press, 1960]:

"Mass society not only creates a confusing situation in which people find it hard to find themselves—it also . . . creates chaos, in which people are confronted by impossible variety—the variety becomes a slush, which then concentrates merely on the most obvious."

. . . It seems then, that the metropolis creates weak character in two almost opposite ways; first, because people are exposed to a chaos of values; second, because they cling to the superficial uniformity common to all these values. *A nondescript mixture of values will tend to produce nondescript people.*

III.

There are obviously many ways of solving the problem. Some of these solutions will be private. Others will involve a variety of social processes including, certainly, education, work, play, and

family. I shall now describe one particular solution, which involves the large scale social organisation of the metropolis.

The solution is this. *The metropolis must contain a large number of different subcultures, each one strongly articulated, with its own values sharply delineated, and sharply distinguished from the others. But though these subcultures must be sharp and distinct and separate, they must not be closed; they must be readily accessible to one another, so that a person can move easily from one to another, and can settle in the one which suits him best.*

This solution is based on two assumptions:

1. A person will only be able to find his own self, and therefore to develop a strong character, if he is in a situation where he receives support for his idiosyncrasies from the people and values which surround him.

2. In order to find his own self, he also needs to live in a milieu where the possibility of many different value systems is explicitly recognized and honored. More specifically, he needs a great variety of choices, so that he is not misled about the nature of his own person, can see that there are many kinds of people, and can find those whose values and beliefs correspond most closely to his own.

. . . one mechanism which might underly people's need for an ambient culture like their own: Maslow has pointed out that the process of self actualisation can only start after other needs, like the need for food and love, and *security*, have already been satisfied. [*Motivation and Personality*, pp. 84–89.] Now the greater the mixture of kinds of persons in a local urban area, and the more unpredictable the strangers near your house, the more afraid and insecure you will become. In Los Angeles and New York this has reached the stage where people are constantly locking doors and windows, and where a mother does not feel safe sending her fifteen year old daughter to the corner mailbox. People are afraid when they are surrounded by the unfamiliar; the unfamiliar is dangerous. But so long as this fear is an unsolved problem, it will override the rest of their lives. Self-actualisation will only be able to happen when this fear is overcome; and that in turn, can only happen, when people are in familiar territory, among people of their own kind, whose habits and ways they know, and whom they trust.

. . . However, if we encourage the appearance of distinct subcultures, in order to satisfy the demands of the first assumption, *then we certainly do not want to encourage these subcultures to be tribal or closed*. That would fly in the face of the very quality which makes the metropolis so attractive. It must be possible, therefore, for people to move easily from one subculture to another, and for them to choose whichever one is most to their taste; and they must be able

to do all of this at any moment in their lives. Indeed, if it ever becomes necessary, the law must guarantee each person freedom of access to every subculture. . . .

IV.

It seems clear, then, that the metropolis should contain a large number of mutually accessible subcultures. But why should those subcultures be separated in space. Someone with an aspatial bias could easily argue that these subcultures could, and should, coexist in the same space, since the essential links which create cultures are links between people.

I believe this view, if put forward, would be entirely wrong. I shall now present arguments to show that the articulation of subcultures is an ecological matter; that distinct subcultures will only survive, as distinct subcultures, if they are physically separated in space.

First, there is no doubt that people from different subcultures actually require different things of their environment. Hendricks has made this point clearly. People of different age groups, different interests, different emphasis on the family, different national background, need different kinds of houses, they need different sorts of outdoor environment round about their houses, and above all, they need different kinds of community services. These services can only become highly specialised, in the direction of a particular subculture, if they are sure of customers. They can only be sure of customers if customers of the same subculture live in strong concentrations. People who want to ride horses all need open riding; Germans who want to be able to buy German food may congregate together, as they do around German town, New York; old people may need parks to sit in, less traffic to contend with, nearby nursing services; bachelors may need quick snack food places; Armenians who want to go to the orthodox mass every morning will cluster around an Armenian church; street people collect around their stores and meeting places; people with many small children will be able to collect around local nurseries and open play space.

This makes it clear that different subcultures need their own activities, their own environments. But subcultures not only need to be concentrated in space to allow for the concentration of the necessary activities. They also need to be concentrated so that one subculture does not dilute the next: indeed, from this point of view they not only need to be internally concentrated—but also physically separated from one another. . . .

We cut the quote short here. The rest of the original paper presents empirical evidence for the need to separate subcultures spatially, and—in this book—we consider that as part of another pattern. The argument is given, with empirical details, in SUBCULTURE BOUNDARY (13).

Therefore:

Do everything possible to enrich the cultures and subcultures of the city, by breaking the city, as far as possible, into a vast mosaic of small and different subcultures, each with its own spatial territory, and each with the power to create its own distinct life style. Make sure that the subcultures are small enough, so that each person has access to the full variety of life styles in the subcultures near his own.

hundreds of different subcultures

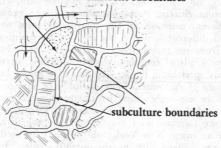

subculture boundaries

❖ ❖ ❖

We imagine that the smallest subcultures will be no bigger than 150 feet across; the largest perhaps as much as a quarter of a mile —COMMUNITY OF 7000 (12), IDENTIFIABLE NEIGHBORHOOD (14), HOUSE CLUSTER (37). To ensure that the life styles of each subculture can develop freely, uninhibited by those which are adjacent, it is essential to create substantial boundaries of nonresidential land between adjacent subcultures—SUBCULTURE BOUNDARY (13). . . .

9 SCATTERED WORK**

. . . this pattern helps the gradual evolution of MOSAIC OF SUB-CULTURES (8), by placing families and work together, and so intensifying the emergence of highly differentiated subcultures, each with its individual character.

❖ ❖ ❖

The artificial separation of houses and work creates intolerable rifts in people's inner lives.

In modern times almost all cities create zones for "work" and other zones for "living" and in most cases enforce the separation by law. Two reasons are given for the separation. First, the work-

Concentration and segregation of work . . . leads to dead neighborhoods.

places need to be near each other, for commercial reasons. Second, workplaces destroy the quiet and safety of residential neighborhoods.

But this separation creates enormous rifts in people's emotional lives. Children grow up in areas where there are no men, except on weekends; women are trapped in an atmosphere where they are expected to be pretty, unintelligent housekeepers; men are forced to accept a schism in which they spend the greater part of their waking lives "at work, and away from their families" and then the other part of their lives "with their families, away from work."

Throughout, this separation reinforces the idea that work is a toil, while only family life is "living"—a schizophrenic view which creates tremendous problems for all the members of a family.

In order to overcome this schism and re-establish the connection between love and work, central to a sane society, there needs to be a redistribution of all workplaces throughout the areas where people live, in such a way that children are near both men and women during the day, women are able to see themselves both as loving mothers and wives and still capable of creative work, and men too are able to experience the hourly connection of their lives as workmen and their lives as loving husbands and fathers.

What are the requirements for a distribution of work that can overcome these problems?

1. Every home is within 20–30 minutes of many hundreds of workplaces.
2. Many workplaces are within walking distance of children and families.
3. Workers can go home casually for lunch, run errands, work half-time, and spend half the day at home.
4. Some workplaces are in homes; there are many opportunities for people to work from their homes or to take work home.
5. Neighborhoods are protected from the traffic and noise generated by "noxious" workplaces.

The only pattern of work which does justice to these requirements is a pattern of scattered work: a pattern in which work is strongly decentralized. To protect the neighborhoods from the noise and traffic that workplaces often generate, some noisy work

places can be in the boundaries of neighborhoods, communities and subcultures—see SUBCULTURE BOUNDARY (13); others, not noisy or noxious, can be built right into homes and neighborhoods. In both cases, the crucial fact is this: *every home is within a few minutes of dozens of workplaces.* Then each household would have the chance to create for itself an intimate ecology of home and work: all its members have the option of arranging a workplace for themselves close to each other and their friends. People can meet for lunch, children can drop in, workers can run home. And under the prompting of such connections the workplaces themselves will inevitably become nicer places, more like homes, where life is carried on, not banished for eight hours.

This pattern is natural in traditional societies, where workplaces are relatively small and households comparatively self-sufficient. But is it compatible with the facts of high technology and the concentration of workers in factories? How strong is the need for workplaces to be near each other?

The main argument behind the centralization of plants, and their gradual increase in size, is an economic one. It has been demonstrated over and again that there are economies of scale in production, advantages which accrue from producing a huge number of goods or services in one place.

However, large centralized organizations are not intrinsic to mass production. There are many excellent examples which demonstrate the fact that where work is substantially scattered, people can still produce goods and services of enormous complexity. One of the best historical examples is the Jura Federation of watchmakers, formed in the mountain villages of Switzerland in the early 1870's. These workers produced watches in their home workshops, each preserving his independence while coordinating his efforts with other craftsmen from the surrounding villages. (For an account of this federation, see, for example, George Woodcock, *Anarchism: A History of Libertarian Ideas and Movements,* Cleveland: Meridian Books, 1962, pp. 168–69.)

In our own time, Raymond Vernon has shown that small, scattered workplaces in the New York metropolitan economy, respond much faster to changing demands and supplies, and that the degree of creativity in agglomerations of small businesses is vastly greater than that of the more cumbersome and centralized

industrial giants. (See Raymond Vernon, *Metropolis* 1985, Chapter 7: External Economics.)

To understand these facts, we must first realize that the city itself is a vast centralized workspace and that all the benefits of this centralization are potentially available to every work group that is a part of the city's vast work community. In effect, the urban region as a whole acts to produce economies of scale by bringing thousands of work groups within range of each other. If this kind of "centralization" is properly developed, it can support an endless number of combinations between small, scattered workgroups; and it can lend great flexibility to the modes of production. "Once we understand that modern industry does not necessarily bring with it financial and physical concentration, the growth of smaller centers and a more widespread distribution of genuine benefits of technology will, I think, take place" (Lewis Mumford, *Sticks and Stones*, New York, 1924, p. 216).

Remember that even such projects as complicated and seemingly centralized as the building of a bridge or a moon rocket, can be organized this way. Contracting and subcontracting procedures make it possible to produce complicated industrial goods and services by combining the efforts of hundreds of small firms. The Apollo project drew together more than 30,000 independent firms to produce the complicated spaceships to the moon.

Furthermore, there is evidence that the agencies which set up such multiple contracts look for small, semi-autonomous firms. They know instinctively that the smaller, more self-governing the group, the better the product and the service (*Small Sellers and Large Buyers in American Industry*, Business Research Center, College of Business Administration, Syracuse University, New York, 1961).

Let us emphasize: we are not suggesting that the decentralization of work should take precedence over a sophisticated technology. We believe that the two are compatible: it is possible to fuse the human requirements for interesting and creative work with the exquisite technology of modern times. It is possible to make television sets, xerox machines and IBM typewriters, automobiles, stereo sets and washing machines under human working conditions. We mention in particular the xerox and IBM typewriters because they have played a vital role for us, the authors of

this book. We could not have made this book together, in the communal way we have done, without these machines: and we consider them a vital part of the new decentralized society we seek.

A small factory in Zemun, Yugoslavia; the work group is building a corn picking machine, an item they themselves decided to produce and sell in the marketplace.

Therefore:

Use zoning laws, neighborhood planning, tax incentives, and any other means available to scatter workplaces throughout the city. Prohibit large concentrations of work, without family life around them. Prohibit large concentrations of family life, without workplaces around them.

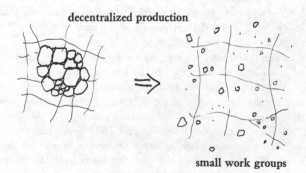

decentralized production

small work groups

9 SCATTERED WORK

✧ ✧ ✧

The scattered work itself can take a great variety of forms. It can occur in belts of industry, where it is essential for an industry to occupy an acre or more between subcultures—SUBCULTURE BOUNDARY (13), INDUSTRIAL RIBBON (42); it can occur in work communities, which are scattered among the neighborhoods— NEIGHBORHOOD BOUNDARY (15), WORK COMMUNITY (41); and it can occur in individual workshops, right among the houses— HOME WORKSHOP (157). The size of each workplace is limited only by the nature of human groups and the process of self-governance. It is discussed in detail in SELF-GOVERNING WORK-SHOPS AND OFFICES (80). . . .

. . . next to the MOSAIC OF SUBCULTURES (8), perhaps the most important structural feature of a city is the pattern of those centers where the city life is most intense. These centers can help to form the mosaic of subcultures by their variety; and they can also help to form CITY COUNTRY FINGERS (3), if each of the centers is at a natural meeting point of several fingers. This pattern was first written by Luis Racionero, under the name "Downtowns of 300,000."

There are few people who do not enjoy the magic of a great city. But urban sprawl takes it away from everyone except the few who are lucky enough, or rich enough, to live close to the largest centers.

This is bound to happen in any urban region with a single high density core. Land near the core is expensive; few people can live near enough to it to give them genuine access to the city's life; most people live far out from the core. To all intents and purposes, they are in the suburbs and have no more than occasional access to the city's life. This problem can only be solved by decentralizing the core to form a multitude of smaller cores, each devoted to some special way of life, so that, even though decentralized, each one is still intense and still a center for the region as a whole.

The mechanism which creates a single isolated core is simple. Urban services tend to agglomerate. Restaurants, theaters, shops, carnivals, cafes, hotels, night clubs, entertainment, special services, tend to cluster. They do so because each one wants to locate in that position where the most people are. As soon as one nucleus has formed in a city, each of the interesting services—especially those which are most interesting and therefore require the largest catch basin—locate themselves in this one nucleus. The one nucleus keeps growing. The downtown becomes enormous. It becomes rich, various, fascinating. But gradually, as the metropolitan area grows, the average distance from an individual house

to this one center increases; and land values around the center rise so high that houses are driven out from there by shops and offices—until soon no one, or almost no one, is any longer genuinely in touch with the magic which is created day and night within this solitary center.

The problem is clear. On the one hand people will only expend so much effort to get goods and services and attend cultural events, even the very best ones. On the other hand, real variety and choice can only occur where there is concentrated, centralized activity; and when the concentration and centralization become too great, then people are no longer willing to take the time to go to it.

If we are to resolve the problem by decentralizing centers, we must ask what the minimum population is that can support a central business district with the magic of the city. Otis D. Duncan in "The Optimum Size of Cities" (*Cities and Society*, P. K. Hatt and A. J. Reiss, eds., New York: The Free Press, 1967, pp. 759–72), shows that cities with more than 50,000 people have a big enough market to sustain 61 different kinds of retail shops and that cities with over 100,000 people can support sophisticated jewelry, fur, and fashion stores. He shows that cities of 100,000 can support a university, a museum, a library, a zoo, a symphony orchestra, a daily newspaper, AM and FM radio, but that it takes a population of 250,000 to 500,000 to support a specialized professional school like a medical school, an opera, or all of the TV networks.

In a study of regional shopping centers in metropolitan Chicago, Brian K. Berry found that centers with 70 kinds of retail shops serve a population base of about 350,000 people (*Geography of Market Centers and Retail Distribution*, New Jersey: Prentice-Hall, 1967, p. 47). T. R. Lakshmanan and Walter G. Hansen, in "A Retail Potential Model" (*American Institute of Planners Journal*, May 1965, pp. 134–43), showed that full-scale centers with a variety of retail and professional services, as well as recreational and cultural activities, are feasible for groups of 100,000 to 200,000 population.

It seems quite possible, then, to get very complex and rich urban functions at the heart of a catch basin which serves no more than 300,000 people. Since, for the reasons given earlier, it is

desirable to have as many centers as possible, we propose that the city region should have one center for each 300,000 people, with the centers spaced out widely among the population, so that every person in the region is reasonably close to at least one of these major centers.

To make this more concrete, it is interesting to get some idea of the range of distances between these centers in a typical urban region. At a density of 5000 persons per square mile (the density of the less populated parts of Los Angeles) the area occupied by 300,000 will have a diameter of about nine miles; at a higher density of 80,000 persons per square mile (the density of central Paris) the area occupied by 300,000 people has a diameter of about two miles. Other patterns in this language suggest a city much more dense than Los Angeles, yet somewhat less dense than central Paris—FOUR-STORY LIMIT (21), DENSITY RINGS (29). We therefore take these crude estimates as upper and lower bounds. If each center serves 300,000 people, they will be at least two miles apart and probably no more than nine miles apart.

One final point must be discussed. The magic of a great city comes from the enormous specialization of human effort there. Only a city such as New York can support a restaurant where you can eat chocolate-covered ants, or buy three-hundred-year-old books of poems, or find a Caribbean steel band playing with American folk singers. By comparison, a city of 300,000 with a second-rate opera, a couple of large department stores, and half a dozen good restaurants is a hick town. It would be absurd if the new downtowns, each serving 300,000 people, in an effort to capture the magic of the city, ended up as a multitude of second-class hick towns.

This problem can only be solved if each of the cores not only serves a catch basin of 300,000 people but also offers some kind of special quality which none of the other centers have, so that each core, though small, serves several million people and can therefore generate all the excitement and uniqueness which become possible in such a vast city.

Thus, as it is in Tokyo or London, the pattern must be implemented in such a way that one core has the best hotels, another the best antique shops, another the music, still another has the fish and sailing boats. Then we can be sure that every person is

within reach of at least one downtown and also that all the downtowns are worth reaching for and really have the magic of a great metropolis.

Therefore:

Put the magic of the city within reach of everyone in a metropolitan area. Do this by means of collective regional policies which restrict the growth of downtown areas so strongly that no one downtown can grow to serve more than 300,000 people. With this population base, the downtowns will be between two and nine miles apart.

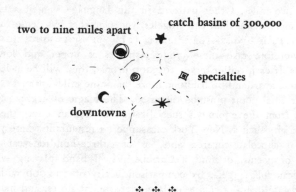

❖ ❖ ❖

Treat each downtown as a pedestrian and local transport area—LOCAL TRANSPORT AREAS (11), PROMENADE (31), with good transit connections from the outlying areas—WEB OF PUBLIC TRANSPORTATION (16); encourage a rich concentration of night life within each downtown—NIGHT LIFE (33), and set aside at least some part of it for the wildest kind of street life—CARNIVAL (58), DANCING IN THE STREET (63). . . .

II LOCAL TRANSPORT AREAS**

. . . superimposed over the MOSAIC OF SUBCULTURES (8), there is a need for a still larger cellular structure: the local transport areas. These areas, 1–2 miles across, not only help to form sub-cultures, by creating natural boundaries in the city, but they can also help to generate the individual city fingers in the CITY COUNTRY FINGERS (3), and they can help to circumscribe each downtown area too, as a special self-contained area of local trans-portation—MAGIC OF THE CITY (10).

❖ ❖ ❖

Cars give people wonderful freedom and increase their opportunities. But they also destroy the environment, to an extent so drastic that they kill all social life.

The value and power of the car have proved so great that it seems impossible to imagine a future without some form of private, high-speed vehicle. Who will willingly give up the degree of freedom provided by cars? At the same time, it is undeniably true that cars turn towns to mincemeat. Somehow local areas must be saved from the pressure of cars or their future equivalents.

It is possible to solve the problem as soon as we make a distinc-tion between short trips and long trips. Cars are not very good for short trips inside a town, and it is on these trips that they do their greatest damage. But they are good for fairly long trips, where they cause less damage. The problem will be solved if towns are divided up into areas about one mile across, with the idea that cars may be used for trips which leave these areas, but that other, slower forms of transportation will be used for all trips inside these areas—foot, bike, horse, taxi. All it needs, physically, is a street pattern that discourages people from using private cars for trips within these areas, and encourages the use of walking, bikes, horses, and taxis instead—but allows the use of cars for trips which leave the area.

Let us start with a list of the obvious social problems created by the car:

Air pollution

Noise
Danger
Ill health
Congestion
Parking problem
Eyesore

The first two are very serious, but are not inherent in the car; they could both be solved, for instance, by an electric car. They are, in that sense, temporary problems. Danger will be a persistent feature of the car so long as we go on using high-speed vehicles for local trips. The widespread lack of exercise and consequent ill health created by the use of motor-driven vehicles will persist unless offset by an amount of daily exercise at least equal to a 20 minute walk per day. And finally, the problems of congestion and loss of speed, difficulty and cost of parking, and eyesore are all direct results of the fact that the car is a very large vehicle which consumes a great deal of space.

The fact that cars are large is, in the end, the most serious aspect of a transportation system based on the use of cars, since it is inherent in the very nature of cars. Let us state this problem in its most pungent form. A man occupies about 5 square feet of space when he is standing still, and perhaps 10 square feet when he is walking. A car occupies about 350 square feet when it is standing still (if we include access), and at 30 miles an hour, when cars are 3 car lengths apart, it occupies about 1000 square feet. As we know, most of the time cars have a single occupant. This means that when people use cars, each person occupies almost 100 times as much space as he does when he is a pedestrian.

If each person driving occupies an area 100 times as large as he does when he is on his feet, this means that people are 10 times as far apart. *In other words, the use of cars has the overall effect of spreading people out, and keeping them apart.*

The effect of this particular feature of cars on the social fabric is clear. People are drawn away from each other; densities and corresponding frequencies of interaction decrease substantially. Contacts become fragmented and specialized, since they are localized by the nature of the interaction into well-defined indoor places—the home, the workplace, and maybe the homes of a few isolated friends.

It is quite possible that the collective cohesion people need to form a viable society just cannot develop when the vehicles which people use force them to be 10 times farther apart, on the average, than they have to be. This states the possible social cost of cars in its strongest form. *It may be that cars cause the break-down of society, simply because of their geometry.*

At the same time that cars cause all these difficulties, they also have certain unprecedented virtues, which have in fact led to their enormous success. These virtues are:

> Flexibility
> Privacy
> Door-to-door trips, without transfer
> Immediacy

These virtues are particularly important in a metropolitan region which is essentially two-dimensional. Public transportation can provide very fast, frequent, door-to-door service, along certain arteries. But in the widely spread out, two-dimensional character of a modern urban region, public transportation by itself cannot compete successfully with cars. Even in cities like London and Paris, with the finest urban public transportation in the world, the trains and buses have fewer riders every year because people are switching to cars. They are willing to put up with all the delays, congestion, and parking costs, because apparently the convenience and privacy of the car are more valuable.

Under *theoretical* analysis of this situation, the only kind of transportation system which meets all the needs is a system of individual vehicles, which can use certain high-speed lines for long cross-city trips and which can use their own power when they leave the public lines in local areas. The systems which come closest to this theoretical model are the various Private Rapid Transit proposals; one example is the Westinghouse Starr-car—a system in which tiny two-man vehicles drive on streets locally and onto high-speed public rails for long trips.

However, the Starrcar-type systems have a number of disadvantages. They make relatively little contribution to the problem of space. The small cars, though smaller than a conventional car, still take up vastly more space than a person. Since the private cars will not be capable of long cross-country trips, they must be

treated as a "second vehicle"—and are rather expensive. They make no contribution to the health problem, since people are still sitting motionless while they travel. The system is relatively antisocial, since people are still encapsulated in "bubbles" while they travel. It is highly idealistic, since it works if everyone has a Starrcar, but makes no allowance for the great variety of movement which people actually desire, i.e., bikes, horses, jalopies, old classic cars, family buses.

We propose a system which has the advantages of the Starrcar system but which is more realistic, easier to implement, and, we believe, better adapted to people's needs. The essence of the system lies in the following two propositions:

1. For local trips, people use a variety of low-speed, low-cost vehicles (bicycles, tricycles, scooters, golf carts, bicycle buggies, horses, etc.), which take up less room than cars and which all leave their passengers in closer touch with their environment and with one another.

Many ways of getting around on local trips.

2. People still own, and use, cars and trucks—but mainly for long trips. We assume that these cars can be made to be quiet, nonpolluting, and simple to repair, and that people simply consider them best suited for long distance travel. It will still be possible for people to use a car or a truck for a local trip, either in a case of emergency, or for some special convenience. However, the town is constructed in such a way that it is actually expensive and inconvenient to use cars for local trips—so that people only do it when they are willing to pay for the very great social costs of doing so.

Therefore:

Break the urban area down into local transport areas,
each one between 1 and 2 miles across, surrounded by a
ring road. Within the local transport area, build minor
local roads and paths for internal movements on foot, by
bike, on horseback, and in local vehicles; build major roads
which make it easy for cars and trucks to get to and from
the ring roads, but place them to make internal local trips
slow and inconvenient.

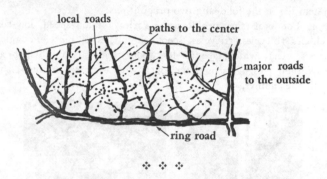

❖ ❖ ❖

To keep main roads for long distance traffic, but not for internal local traffic, lay them out as parallel one way roads, and keep
these parallel roads away from the center of the area, so that they
are very good for getting to the ring roads, but inconvenient for
short local trips—PARALLEL ROADS (23). Lay out abundant footpaths and bike paths and green streets, at right angles to the main
roads, and make these paths for local traffic go directly through
the center—GREEN STREETS (51), NETWORK OF PATHS AND CARS
(52), BIKE PATHS AND RACKS (56); sink the ring roads around
the outside of each area, or shield the noise they make some other
way—RING ROADS (17); keep parking to a minimum within the
area, and keep all major parking garages near the ring roads—
NINE PER CENT PARKING (22), SHIELDED PARKING (97); and
build a major interchange within the center of the area—INTER-
CHANGE (34). . . .

68

build up these larger city patterns from the grass roots, through action essentially controlled by two levels of self-governing communities, which exist as physically identifiable places;

12. COMMUNITY OF 7000

13. SUBCULTURE BOUNDARY

14. IDENTIFIABLE NEIGHBORHOOD

15. NEIGHBORHOOD BOUNDARY

12 COMMUNITY OF 7000*

. . . the MOSAIC OF SUBCULTURES (8) is made up of a great number of large and small self-governing communities and neighborhoods. Community of 7000 helps define the structure of the large communities.

Individuals have no effective voice in any community of more than 5000–10,000 persons.

People can only have a genuine effect on local government when the units of local government are autonomous, self-governing, self-budgeting communities, which are small enough to create the possibility of an immediate link between the man in the street and his local officials and elected representatives.

This is an old idea. It was the model for Athenian democracy in the third and fourth centuries B.C.; it was Jefferson's plan for American democracy; it was the tack Confucius took in his book on government, *The Great Digest.*

For these people, the practice of exercising power over local matters was itself an experience of intrinsic satisfaction. Sophocles wrote that life would be unbearable were it not for the freedom to initiate action in a small community. And it was considered that this experience was not only good in itself, but was the only way of governing that would not lead to corruption. Jefferson wanted to spread out the power not because "the people" were so bright and clever, but precisely because they were prone to error, and it was therefore dangerous to vest power in the hands of a few who would inevitably make big mistakes. "Break the country into wards" was his campaign slogan, so that the mistakes will be manageable and people will get practice and improve.

Today the distance between people and the centers of power that govern them is vast—both psychologically and geographically. Milton Kotler, a Jeffersonian, has described the experience:

The process of city administration is invisible to the citizen who sees little evidence of its human components but feels the sharp pain of taxation. With increasingly poor public service, his desires and needs are more insistently expressed. Yet his expressions of need seem

71

to issue into thin air, for government does not appear attentive to his demands. This disjunction between citizen and government is the major political problem of city government, because it embodies the dynamics of civil disorder. . . . (Milton Kotler, Neighborhood Foundations, Memorandum #24; "Neighborhood corporations and the reorganization of city government," unpub. ms., August 1967.)

There are two ways in which the physical environment, as it is now ordered, promotes and sustains the separation between citizens and their government. First, the size of the political community is so large that its members are separated from its leaders simply by their number. Second, government is invisible, physically located out of the realm of most citizens' daily lives. Unless these two conditions are altered, political alienation is not likely to be overcome.

1. *The size of the political community.* It is obvious that the larger the community the greater the distance between the average citizen and the heads of government. Paul Goodman has proposed a rule of thumb, based on cities like Athens in their prime, that no citizen be more than two friends away from the highest member of the local unit. Assume that everyone knows about 12 people in his local community. Using this notion and Goodman's rule we can see that an optimum size for a political community would be about 12^3 or 1728 households or 5500 persons. This figure corresponds to an old Chicago school estimate of 5000. And it is the same order of magnitude as the size of ECCO, the neighborhood corporation in Columbus, Ohio, of 6000 to 7000, described by Kotler (*Committee on Government Operations*, U.S. Senate, 89th Congress, Second Session, Part 9, December 1966).

The editors of *The Ecologist* have a similar intuition about the proper size for units of local government. (See their *Blueprint for Survival*, Penguin Books, 1972, pp. 50–55.) And Terence Lee, in his study, "Urban neighborhood as a socio-spatial schema," *Ekistics 177*, August 1970, gives evidence for the importance of the spatial community. Lee gives 75 acres as a natural size for a community. At 25 persons per acre, such a community would accommodate some 2000 persons; at 60 persons per acre, some 4500.

2. *The visible location of local government.* Even when local

branches of government are decentralized in function, they are often still centralized in space, hidden in vast municipal city-county buildings out of the realm of everyday life. These places are intimidating and alienating. What is needed is for every person to feel at home in the place of his local government with his ideas and complaints. A person must feel that it is a forum, that it is his directly, that he can call and talk to the person in charge of such and such, and see him personally within a day or two.

For this purpose, local forums must be situated in highly visible and accessible places. They could, for instance, be located in the most active marketplace of each community of 5000 to 7000. We discuss this possibility more fully under LOCAL TOWN HALL (44), but we emphasize it here, since the provision of a political "heart," a political center of gravity, is an essential part of a political community.

Community meeting of several thousand.

Therefore:

Decentralize city governments in a way that gives local control to communities of 5,000 to 10,000 persons. As nearly as possible, use natural geographic and historical boundaries to mark these communities. Give each community the power to initiate, decide, and execute the affairs that con-

73

cern it closely: land use, housing, maintenance, streets, parks, police, schooling, welfare, neighborhood services.

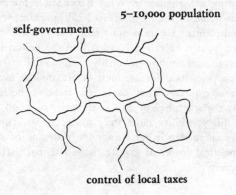

5–10,000 population

self-government

control of local taxes

❖ ❖ ❖

Separate the communities from one another by means of substantial areas—SUBCULTURE BOUNDARY (13); subdivide each community into 10 or 20 independent neighborhoods, each with a representative on the community council—IDENTIFIABLE NEIGHBORHOOD (14); provide a central place where people have a chance to come together—ECCENTRIC NUCLEUS (28), PROMENADE (31); and in this central place provide a local town hall, as a focal point for the community's political activity—LOCAL TOWN HALL (44). . . .

I3 SUBCULTURE BOUNDARY*

. . . the MOSAIC OF SUBCULTURES (8) and its individual subcultures, whether they are COMMUNITIES OF 7000 (12) or IDENTIFIABLE NEIGHBORHOODS (14), need to be completed by boundaries. In fact, the mere creation of the boundary areas, according to this pattern, will begin to give life to the subcultures between the boundaries, by giving them a chance to be themselves.

❖ ❖ ❖

The mosaic of subcultures requires that hundreds of different cultures live, in their own way, at full intensity, next door to one another. But subcultures have their own ecology. They can only live at full intensity, unhampered by their neighbors, if they are physically separated by physical boundaries.

In MOSAIC OF SUBCULTURES (8) we have argued that a great variety of subcultures in a city is not a racist pattern which forms ghettos, but a pattern of opportunity which allows a city to contain a multitude of different ways of life with the greatest possible intensity.

But this mosaic will only come into being if the various subcultures are insulated from one another, at least enough so that no one of them can oppress, or subdue, the life style of its neighbors, nor, in return, feel oppressed or subdued. As we shall see, this requires that adjacent subcultures are separated by swaths of open land, workplaces, public buildings, water, parks, or other natural boundaries.

The argument hinges on the following fact. Wherever there is an area of homogeneous housing in a city, its inhabitants will exert strong pressure on the areas adjacent to it to make them conform to their values and style. For example, the "straight" people who lived near the "hippie" Haight Ashbury district in San Francisco in 1967 were afraid that the Haight would send their land values down, so they put pressure on City Hall to get the Haight "cleaned up"—that is, to make the Haight more like their own area. This seems to happen whenever one subculture is

76

very different in style from another one next to it. People will be afraid that the neighboring area is going to "encroach" on their own area, upset their land values, undermine their children, send the "nice" people away, and so forth, and they will do everything they can to make the next door area like their own.

Carl Werthman, Jerry Mandel, and Ted Dienstfrey (*Planning and the Purchase Decision: Why People Buy in Planned Communities*, University of California, Berkeley, July 1965) have noticed the same phenomenon even among very similar subcultures. In a study of people living in tract developments, they found that the tension created by adjacencies between dissimilar social groups disappeared when there was enough open land, unused land, freeway, or water between them. In short, a physical barrier between the adjacent subcultures, if big enough, took the heat off.

Obviously, a rich mix of subcultures will not be possible if each subculture is being inhibited by pressure from its neighbors. *The subcultures must therefore be separated by land, which is not residential land, and by as much of it as possible.*

There is another kind of empirical observation which supports this last statement. If we look around a metropolitan area, and pinpoint the strongly differentiated subcultures, those with character, we shall always find that they are near boundaries and hardly ever close to other communities. For example, in San Francisco the two most distinctive areas are Telegraph Hill and Chinatown. Telegraph Hill is surrounded on two sides by the docks. Chinatown is bounded on two sides by the city's banking area. The same is true in the larger Bay Area. Point Richmond and Sausalito,

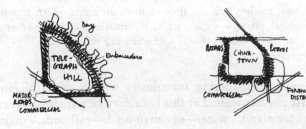

Subculture boundaries.

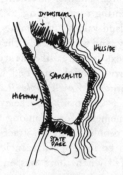

two of the most distinctive communities in the greater Bay Area, are both almost completely isolated. Sausalito is surrounded by hills and water; Point Richmond by water and industrial land. Communities which are cut off to some extent are free to develop their own character.

Further support for our argument comes from ecology. In nature, the differentiation of a species into subspecies is largely due to the process of geographic speciation, the genetic changes which take place during a period of spatial isolation (see, for example, Ernst Mayr, *Animal Species and Evolution*, Cambridge, 1963, Chapter 18: "The Ecology of Speciation," pp. 556–85). It has been observed in a multitude of ecological studies that members of the same species develop distinguishable traits when separated from other members of the species by physical boundaries like a mountain ridge, a valley, a river, a dry strip of land, a cliff, or a significant change in climate or vegetation. In just the same way, differentiation between subcultures in a city will be able to take place most easily when the flow of those elements which account for cultural variety—values, style, information, and so on—is at least partially restricted between neighboring subcultures.

Therefore:

Separate neighboring subcultures with a swath of land at least 200 feet wide. Let this boundary be natural—wilderness, farmland, water—or man-made—railroads, major roads, parks, schools, some housing. Along the seam be-

78

tween two subcultures, build meeting places, shared functions, touching each community.

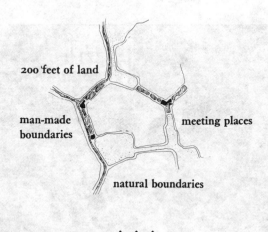

200 feet of land

man-made
boundaries

meeting places

natural boundaries

❖ ❖ ❖

Natural boundaries can be things like THE COUNTRYSIDE (7), SACRED SITES (24), ACCESS TO WATER (25), QUIET BACKS (59), ACCESSIBLE GREEN (60), POOLS AND STREAMS (64), STILL WATER (71). Artificial boundaries can include RING ROADS (17), PARALLEL ROADS (23), WORK COMMUNITIES (41), INDUSTRIAL RIBBONS (42), TEENAGE SOCIETY (84), SHIELDED PARKING (97). The interior organization of the subculture boundary should follow two broad principles. It should concentrate the various land uses to form functional clusters around activity—ACTIVITY NODES (30), WORK COMMUNITY (41). And the boundary should be accessible to both the neighboring communities, so that it is a meeting ground for them—ECCENTRIC NUCLEUS (28) . . .

I4 IDENTIFIABLE
NEIGHBORHOOD**

. . . the MOSAIC OF SUBCULTURES (8) and the COMMUNITY OF 7000 (12) are made up of neighborhoods. This pattern defines the neighborhoods. It defines those small human groups which create the energy and character which can bring the larger COMMUNITY OF 7000 (12) and the MOSAIC OF SUBCULTURES (8) to life.

People need an identifiable spatial unit to belong to.

Today's pattern of development destroys neighborhoods.

They want to be able to identify the part of the city where they live as distinct from all others. Available evidence suggests, first, that the neighborhoods which people identify with have extremely small populations; second, that they are small in area; and third, that a major road through a neighborhood destroys it.

1. What is the right population for a neighborhood?

The neighborhood inhabitants should be able to look after their own interests by organizing themselves to bring pressure on city hall or local governments. This means the families in a neighborhood must be able to reach agreement on basic decisions about public services, community land, and so forth. Anthropological evidence suggests that a human group cannot coordinate itself to reach such decisions if its population is above 1500, and many people set the figure as low as 500. (See, for example, Anthony Wallace, *Housing and Social Structure*, Philadelphia Housing Au-

81

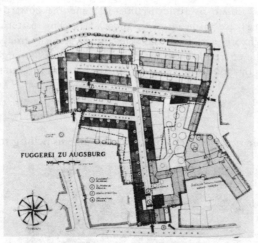

A famous neighborhood: the Fuggerei in Augsburg.

thority, 1952, available from University Microfilms, Inc., Ann
Arbor, Michigan, pp. 21–24.) The experience of organizing community meetings at the local level suggests that 500 is the more
realistic figure.

2. As far as the physical diameter is concerned, in Philadelphia,
people who were asked which area they really knew usually limited themselves to a small area, seldom exceeding the two to three
blocks around their own house. (Mary W. Herman, "Comparative
Studies of Identification Areas in Philadelphia," City of Philadelphia Community Renewal Program, Technical Report No. 9,
April 1964.) One-quarter of the inhabitants of an area in Mil-
waukee considered a neighborhood to be an area no larger than
a block (300 feet). One-half considered it to be no more than
seven blocks. (Svend Riemer, "Villagers in Metropolis," *British
Journal of Sociology*, 2, No. 1, March 1951, pp. 31–43.)

3. The first two features, by themselves, are not enough. A
neighborhood can only have a strong identity if it is protected
from heavy traffic. Donald Appleyard and Mark Lintell have
found that the heavier the traffic in an area, the less people think
of it as home territory. Not only do residents view the streets
with heavy traffic as less personal, but they feel the same about

the houses along the street. ("Environmental Quality of City Streets," by Donald Appleyard and Mark Lintell, Center for Planning and Development Research, University of California, Berkeley, 1971.)

neighborhood with light traffic   2000 vehicles/day
200 vehicles/peak hour   15–20 mph   Two-way

Residents speaking on "neighboring and visiting"
> *I feel it's home. There are warm people on this street. I don't feel alone.*
> *Everbody knows each other.*
> *Definitely a friendly street.*

Residents speaking on "home territory"
> *The street life doesn't intrude into the home . . . only happiness comes in from the street.*
> *I feel my home extends to the whole block.*

neighborhood with moderate traffic   6000 vehicles/day
550 vehicles/peak hour   25 mph   Two-way

Residents speaking on "neighboring and visiting"
> *You see the neighbors but they aren't close friends.*
> *Don't feel there is any community any more, but people say hello.*

Residents speaking on "home territory"
> *It's a medium place—doesn't require any thought.*

neighborhood with heavy traffic   16,000 vehicles/day
1900 vehicles/peak hour   35–40 mph   One-way

Residents speaking on "neighboring and visiting"
> *It's not a friendly street—no one offers help.*
> *People are afraid to go into the street because of the traffic.*

Residents speaking on "home territory"
> *It is impersonal and public.*
> *Noise from the street intrudes into my home.*

How shall we define a major road? The Appleyard-Lintell study found that with more than 200 cars per hour, the quality of the neighborhood begins to deteriorate. On the streets with 550 cars per hour people visit their neighbors less and never gather in the street to meet and talk. Research by Colin Buchanan indicates that major roads become a barrier to free pedestrian movement when "most people (more than 50%) . . . have to adapt their movement to give way to vehicles." This is based on "an average delay to all crossing pedestrians of 2 seconds . . . as a very rough guide to the borderline between acceptable and unacceptable conditions," which happens when the traffic reaches some 150 to 250 cars per hour. (Colin D. Buchanan, *Traffic in Towns*, London: Her Majesty's Stationery Office, 1963, p. 204.) Thus any street with greater than 200 cars per hour, at any time, will probably seem "major," and start to destroy the neighborhood identity.

A final note on implementation. Several months ago the City of Berkeley began a transportation survey with the idea of deciding the location of all future major arteries within the city. Citizens were asked to make statements about areas which they wanted to protect from heavy traffic. This simple request has caused widespread grass roots political organizing to take place: at the time of this writing more than 30 small neighborhoods have identified themselves, simply in order to make sure that they succeed in keeping heavy traffic out. In short, the issue of traffic is so fundamental to the fact of neighborhoods, that neighborhoods emerge, and crystallize, as soon as people are asked to decide where they want nearby traffic to be. Perhaps this is a universal way of implementing this pattern in existing cities.

Therefore:

Help people to define the neighborhoods they live in, not more than 300 yards across, with no more than 400 or 500 inhabitants. In existing cities, encourage local groups to organize themselves to form such neighborhoods. Give the neighborhoods some degree of autonomy as far as taxes and land controls are concerned. Keep major roads outside these neighborhoods.

max. population of 500

max diameter of 300 yards

❖ ❖ ❖

Mark the neighborhood, above all, by gateways wherever main paths enter it—MAIN GATEWAYS (53)—and by modest boundaries of non-residential land between the neighborhoods—NEIGHBOR-HOOD BOUNDARY (15). Keep major roads within these boundaries —PARALLEL ROADS (23); give the neighborhood a visible center, perhaps a common or a green—ACCESSIBLE GREEN (60)—or a SMALL PUBLIC SQUARE (61); and arrange houses and workshops within the neighborhood in clusters of about a dozen at a time— HOUSE CLUSTER (37), WORK COMMUNITY (41). . . .

15 NEIGHBORHOOD BOUNDARY*

. . . the physical boundary needed to protect subcultures from one another, and to allow their ways of life to be unique and idiosyncratic, is guaranteed, for a COMMUNITY OF 7000 (12), by the pattern SUBCULTURE BOUNDARY (13). But a second, smaller kind of boundary is needed to create the smaller IDENTIFIABLE NEIGHBORHOOD (14).

❖ ❖ ❖

The strength of the boundary is essential to a neighborhood. If the boundary is too weak the neighborhood will not be able to maintain its own identifiable character.

The cell wall of an organic cell is, in most cases, as large as, or larger, than the cell interior. It is not a surface which divides inside from outside, but a coherent entity in its own right, which preserves the functional integrity of the cell and also provides for a multitude of transactions between the cell interior and the ambient fluids.

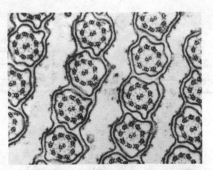

Cell with cell wall: The cell wall is a place in its own right.

We have already argued, in SUBCULTURE BOUNDARY (13), that a human group, with a specific life style, needs a boundary around it to protect its idiosyncrasies from encroachment and dilution by surrounding ways of life. This subculture boundary,

then, functions just like a cell wall—it protects the subculture and creates space for its transactions with surrounding functions.

The argument applies as strongly to an individual neighborhood, which is a subculture in microcosm.

However, where the subculture boundaries require wide swaths of land and commercial and industrial activity, the neighborhood boundaries can be much more modest. Indeed it is not possible for a neighborhood of 500 or more to bound itself with shops and streets and community facilities; there simply aren't enough to go around. Of course, the few neighborhood shops there are— the STREET CAFE (88), the CORNER GROCERY (89)—will help to form the edge of the neighborhood, but by and large the boundary of neighborhoods will have to come from a completely different morphological principle.

From observations of neighborhoods that succeed in being well-defined, both physically and in the minds of the townspeople, we have learned that the single most important feature of a neighborhood's boundary is *restricted access into the neighborhood:* neighborhoods that are successfully defined have definite and relatively few paths and roads leading into them.

For example, here is a map of the Etna Street neighborhood in Berkeley.

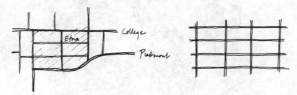

*Our neighborhood, compared with
a typical part of a grid system.*

There are only seven roads into this neighborhood, compared with the fourteen which there would be in a typical part of the street grid. The other roads all dead end in T junctions immediately at the edge of the neighborhood. Thus, while the Etna Street neighborhood is not literally walled off from the community, access into it is subtly restricted. The result is that people do not come into the neighborhood by car unless they have

business there; and when people are in the neighborhood, they recognize that they are *in* a distinct part of town. Of course, the neighborhood was not "created" deliberately. It was an area of Berkeley which has become an identifiable neighborhood because of this accident in the street system.

An extreme example of this principle is the Fuggerei in Augsburg, illustrated in IDENTIFIABLE NEIGHBORHOOD (14). The Fuggerei is entirely bounded by the backs of buildings and walls, and the paths into it are narrow, marked by gateways.

Indeed, if access is restricted, this means, *by definition*, that those few points where access is possible, will come to have special importance. In one way or another, subtly, or more obviously, they will be gateways, which mark the passage into the neighborhood. We discuss this more fully in MAIN GATEWAYS (53). But the fact is that every successful neighborhood is identifiable because it has some kind of gateways which mark its boundaries: the boundary comes alive in peoples' minds because they recognize the gateways.

In case the idea of gateways seems too closed, we remark at once that the boundary zone—and especially those parts of it around the gateways—must also form a kind of public meeting ground, where neighborhoods come together. If each neighborhood is a self-contained entity, then the community of 7000 which the neighborhoods belong to will not control any of the land internal to the neighborhoods. But it will control *all* of the land *between* the neighborhoods—the boundary land—because this boundary land is just where functions common to all 7000 people must find space. In this sense the boundaries not only serve to protect individual neighborhoods, but simultaneously function to unite them in their larger processes.

Therefore:

Encourage the formation of a boundary around each neighborhood, to separate it from the next door neighborhoods. Form this boundary by closing down streets and limiting access to the neighborhood—cut the normal number of streets at least in half. Place gateways at those points where the restricted access paths cross the boundary; and

make the boundary zone wide enough to contain meeting places for the common functions shared by several neighborhoods.

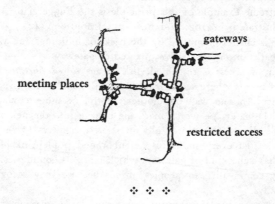

❖ ❖ ❖

The easiest way of all to form a boundary around a neighborhood is by turning buildings inward, and by cutting off the paths which cross the boundary, except for one or two at special points which become gateways—MAIN GATEWAYS (53); the public land of the boundary may include a park, collector roads, small parking lots, and work communities—anything which forms a natural edge—PARALLEL ROADS (23), WORK COMMUNITY (41), QUIET BACKS (59), ACCESSIBLE GREEN (60), SHIELDED PARKING (97), SMALL PARKING LOTS (103). As for the meeting places in the boundary, they can be any of those neighborhood functions which invite gathering: a park, a shared garage, an outdoor room, a shopping street, a playground—SHOPPING STREET (32), POOLS AND STREAMS (64), PUBLIC OUTDOOR ROOM (69), GRAVE SITES (70), LOCAL SPORTS (72), ADVENTURE PLAYGROUND (73). . . .

connect communities to one another by encouraging
the growth of the following networks:

16. WEB OF PUBLIC TRANSPORTATION

17. RING ROADS

18. NETWORK OF LEARNING

19. WEB OF SHOPPING

20. MINI-BUSES

16 WEB OF PUBLIC TRANSPORTATION*

. . . the city, as defined by CITY COUNTRY FINGERS (3), spreads out in ribbon fashion, throughout the countryside, and is broken into LOCAL TRANSPORT AREAS (11). To connect the transport areas, and to maintain the flow of people and goods along the fingers of the cities, it is now necessary to create a web of public tranportation.

The system of public transportation—the entire web of airplanes, helicopters, hovercraft, trains, boats, ferries, buses, taxis, mini-trains, carts, ski-lifts, moving sidewalks —can only work if all the parts are well connected. But they usually aren't, because the different agencies in charge of various forms of public transportation have no incentives to connect to one another.

Here, in brief, is the general public transportation problem. A city contains a great number of places, distributed rather evenly across a two-dimensional sheet. The trips people want to make are typically between two points at random in this sheet. No one linear system (like a train system), can give direct connections between the vast possible number of point pairs in the city.

It is therefore only possible for systems of public transportation to work, if there are rich connections between a great variety of *different* systems. But these connections are not workable, unless they are genuine fast, short, connections. The waiting time for a connection must be short. And the walking distance between the two connecting systems must be very short.

This much is obvious; and everyone who has thought about public transportation recognizes its importance. However, obvious though it is, it is extremely hard to implement.

There are two practical difficulties, both of which stem from the fact that different kinds of public transportation are usually in the hands of different agencies who are reluctant to cooperate. They are reluctant to cooperate, partly because they are actually in competition, and partly just because cooperation makes life harder for them.

This is particularly true along commuting corridors. Trains, buses, mini-buses, rapid transit, ferries, and maybe even planes and helicopters compete for the same passenger market along these corridors. When each mode is operated by an independent agency there is no particular incentive to provide feeder services to the more inflexible modes. Many services are even reluctant to provide good feeder connections to rapid transit, trains, and ferries, because their commuter lines are their most lucrative lines. Similarly, in many cities of the developing world, mini-buses and *collectivos* provide public transportation along the main commuting corridors, pulling passengers away from buses. This leaves the mainlines served by small vehicles, while almost empty buses reach the peripheral lines, usually because the public bus company is required to serve these areas, even at a loss.

The solution to the web of public transportation, then, hinges on the possibility of solving the coordination problem of the different systems. This is the nut of the matter. We shall now propose a way of solving it. The traditional way of looking at public transportation assumes that lines are primary and that the interchanges needed to connect the lines to one another are secondary. We propose the opposite: namely, that interchanges are primary and that the transport lines are secondary elements which connect the interchanges.

Imagine the following organization: each interchange is run by the community that uses it. The community appoints an interchange chief for every interchange, and gives him a budget, and a directive on service. The interchange chief coordinates the service at his interchange; he charters service from any number of transport companies—the companies, themselves, are in free competition with one another to create service.

In this scheme, responsibility for public transportation shifts from lines to interchanges. The interchanges are responsible for connecting themselves to each other, and the community which

uses the interchange decides what kinds of service they want to have passing through it. It is then up to the interchange chief to persuade these transport modes to pass through it.

Slowly, a service connecting interchanges will build up. One example which closely follows our model, and shows that this model is capable of producing a higher level of service than any centralized agency can produce, is the famous Swiss Railway System.

The Swiss railway system . . . is the densest network in the world. At great cost and with great trouble, it has been made to serve the needs of the smallest localities and most remote valleys, not as a paying proposition but because such was the will of the people. It is the outcome of fierce political struggles. In the 19th century, the "democratic railway movement" brought the small Swiss communities into conflict with the big towns, which had plans for centralisation. . . . And if we compare the Swiss system with the French which, with admirable geometrical regularity, is entirely centered on Paris so that the prosperities or the decline, the life or death of whole regions has depended on the quality of the link with the capital, we see the difference between a centralised state and a federal alliance. The railway map is the easiest to read at a glance, but let us now superimpose on it another showing economic activity and the movement of population. The distribution of industrial activity all over Switzerland, even in the outlying areas, accounts for the strength and stability of the social structure of the country and prevented those horrible 19th century concentrations of industry, with their slums and rootless proletariat. (Colin Ward, "The Organization of Anarchy," in *Patterns of Anarchy*, by Leonard I. Krimerman and Lewis Perry, New York, 1966.)

Therefore:

Treat interchanges as primary and transportation lines as secondary. Create incentives so that all the different modes of public transportation—airplanes, helicopters, ferries, boats, trains, rapid transit, buses, mini-buses, ski-lifts, escalators, travelators, elevators—plan their lines to connect the interchanges, with the hope that gradually many different lines, of many different types, will meet at every interchange.

Give the local communities control over their interchanges so that they can implement the pattern by giving

contracts only to those transportation companies which are willing to serve these interchanges.

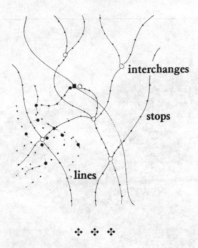

❖ ❖ ❖

Keep all the various lines that converge on a single interchange, and their parking, within 600 feet, so that people can transfer on foot—INTERCHANGE (34). It is essential that the major stations be served by a good feeder system, so people are not forced to use private cars at all—MINI-BUSES (20). . . .

17 RING ROADS

. . . the ring roads which this pattern specifies, help to define and generate the LOCAL TRANSPORT AREAS (11); if they are placed to make connections between INTERCHANGES (34), they also help to form the WEB OF PUBLIC TRANSPORTATION (16).

It is not possible to avoid the need for high speed roads in modern society; but it is essential to place them and build them in such a way that they do not destroy communities or countryside.

Even though the rush of freeways and superhighways built in the 1950's and 1960's is slowing down, because of widespread local protest, we cannot avoid high speed roads altogether. There is, at present, no prospect for a viable alternative which can provide for the vast volume of movement of cars and trucks and buses which a modern city lives on economically and socially.

At the same time, however, high speed roads do enormous damage when they are badly placed. They slice communities in half; they cut off waterfronts; they cut off access to the countryside; and, above all, they create enormous noise. For hundreds of yards, even a mile or two, the noise of every superhighway roars in the background.

To resolve these obvious dilemmas that come with the location and construction of high speed roads, we must find ways of building and locating these roads, so that they do not destroy communities and shatter life with their noise. We can give three requirements that, we believe, go to the heart of this policy:

1. Every community that has coherence as an area of local transportation—LOCAL TRANSPORT AREAS (11)—is never split by a high speed road, but rather has at least one high speed road adjacent to it. This allows rapid auto travel from one such community out to other communities and to the region at large.

2. It must be possible for residents of each local transport area to reach the open countryside without crossing a high speed road—see CITY COUNTRY FINGERS (3). This means, very roughly,

that high speed roads must always be placed in such positions that at least one side of every local transport area has direct access to open country.

3. Most important of all, high speed roads must be shielded acoustically to protect the life around them. This means that they must either be sunken, or shielded by earth berms, parking structures, or warehouses, which will not be damaged by the noise.

Therefore:

Place high speed roads (freeways and other major arteries) so that:

1. **At least one high speed road lies tangent to each local transport area.**
2. **Each local transport area has at least one side not bounded by a high speed road, but directly open to the countryside.**
3. **The road is always sunken, or shielded along its length by berms, or earth, or industrial buildings, to protect the nearby neighborhoods from noise.**

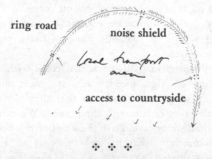

❖ ❖ ❖

Always place the high speed roads on boundaries between subcultures—SUBCULTURE BOUNDARY (13) and never along waterfronts—ACCESS TO WATER (25). Place industry and big parking garages next to the roads, and use them, whenever possible, as extra noise shields—INDUSTRIAL RIBBONS (42), SHIELDED PARKING (c). . . .

98

18 NETWORK OF LEARNING*

. . . another network, not physical like transportation, but conceptual, and equal in importance, is the network of learning: the thousands of interconnected situations that occur all over the city, and which in fact comprise the city's "curriculum": the way of life it teaches to its young.

❖ ❖ ❖

In a society which emphasizes teaching, children and students—and adults—become passive and unable to think or act for themselves. Creative, active individuals can only grow up in a society which emphasizes learning instead of teaching.

There is no need to add to the criticism of our public schools. The critique is extensive and can hardly be improved on. The processes of learning and teaching, too, have been exhaustively studied. . . . The question now is what to do. (George Dennison, *Lives of Children*, New York: Vintage Books, 1969, p. 3.)

To date, the most penetrating analysis and proposal for an alternative framework for education comes from Ivan Illich in his book, *De-Schooling Society*, and his article, "Education without Schools: How It Can Be Done," in the *New York Review of Books*, New York, 15 (12): 25–31, special supplement, July 1971.

Illich describes a style of learning that is quite the opposite from schools. It is geared especially to the rich opportunities for learning that are natural to every metropolitan area:

The alternative to social control through the schools is the voluntary participation in society through *networks* which provide access to all its resources for learning. In fact these networks now exist, but they are rarely used for educational purposes. The crisis of schooling, if it is to have any positive consequence, will inevitably lead to their incorporation into the educational process. . . .

Schools are designed on the assumption that there is a secret to everything in life; that the quality of life depends on knowing that secret; that secrets can be known only in orderly successions; and that only teachers can properly reveal these secrets. An individual with a schooled mind conceives of the world as a pyramid of classified packages accessible only to those who carry the proper tags.

New educational institutions would break apart this pyramid. Their purpose must be to facilitate access for the learner: to allow him to look into the windows of the control room or the parliament, if he cannot get in the door. Moreover, such new institutions should be channels to which the learner would have access without credentials or pedigree—public spaces in which peers and elders outside his immediate horizon now become available. . . .

While network administrators would concentrate primarily on the building and maintenance of roads providing access to resources, the pedagogue would help the student to find the path which for him could lead fastest to his goal. If a student wants to learn spoken Cantonese from a Chinese neighbor, the pedagogue would be available to judge their proficiency, and to help them select the textbook and methods most suitable to their talents, character, and the time available for study. He can counsel the would-be airplane mechanic on finding the best places for apprenticeship. He can recommend books to somebody who wants to find challenging peers to discuss African history. Like the network administrator, the pedagogical counselor conceives of himself as a professional educator. Access to either could be gained by individuals through the use of educational vouchers. . . .

In addition to the tentative conclusions of the Carnegie Commission reports, the last year has brought forth a series of important documents which show that responsible people are becoming aware of the fact that schooling for certification cannot continue to be counted upon as the central educational device of a modern society. Julius Nyere of Tanzania has announced plans to integrate education with the life of the village. In Canada, the Wright Commission on post-secondary education has reported that no known system of formal education could provide equal opportunities for the citizens of Ontario. The president of Peru has accepted the recommendation of his commission on education, which proposes to abolish free schools in favor of free educational opportunities provided throughout life. In fact he is reported to have insisted that this program proceed slowly at first in order to keep teachers in school and out of the way of true educators. (Abridged from pp. 76 and 99 in *Deschooling Society* by Ivan Illich. Vol. 44 in World Perspectives Series, edited by Ruth Nanda Anshen, New York: Harper & Row, 1971.)

In short, the educational system so radically decentralized becomes congruent with the urban structure itself. People of all walks of life come forth, and offer a class in the things they know and love: professionals and workgroups offer apprenticeships in their offices and workshops, old people offer to teach whatever their life work and interest has been, specialists offer tutoring in their special subjects. Living and learning are the

same. It is not hard to imagine that eventually every third or fourth household will have at least one person in it who is offering a class or training of some kind.

Therefore:

Instead of the lock-step of compulsory schooling in a fixed place, work in piecemeal ways to decentralize the process of learning and enrich it through contact with many places and people all over the city: workshops, teachers at home or walking through the city, professionals willing to take on the young as helpers, older children teaching younger children, museums, youth groups traveling, scholarly seminars, industrial workshops, old people, and so on. Conceive of all these situations as forming the backbone of the learning process; survey all these situations, describe them, and publish them as the city's "curriculum"; then let students, children, their families and neighborhoods weave together for themselves the situations that comprise their "school" paying as they go with standard vouchers, raised by community tax. Build new educational facilities in a way which extends and enriches this network.

network directory

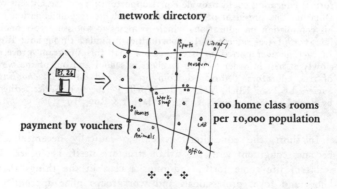

payment by vouchers

100 home class rooms per 10,000 population

❖ ❖ ❖

Above all, encourage the formation of seminars and workshops in people's homes—HOME WORKSHOP (157); make sure that

each city has a "path" where young children can safely wander on their own—CHILDREN IN THE CITY (57); build extra public "homes" for children, one to every neighborhood at least—CHILDREN'S HOME (86); create a large number of work-oriented small schools in those parts of town dominated by work and commercial activity—SHOPFRONT SCHOOLS (85); encourage teenagers to work out a self-organized learning society of their own —TEENAGE SOCIETY (84); treat the university as scattered adult learning for all the adults in the region—UNIVERSITY AS A MARKETPLACE (43); and use the real work of professionals and tradesmen as the basic nodes in the network—MASTER AND APPRENTICES (83). . . .

19 WEB OF SHOPPING*

. . . this pattern defines a piecemeal process which can help to locate shops and services where they are needed, in such a way that they will strengthen the MOSAIC OF SUBCULTURES (8), SUBCULTURE BOUNDARIES (13), and the decentralized economy needed for SCATTERED WORK (9) and LOCAL TRANSPORT AREAS (11).

Shops rarely place themselves in those positions which best serve the people's needs, and also guarantee their own stability.

Large parts of towns have insufficient services. New shops which could provide these services often locate near the other shops and major centers, instead of locating themselves where they are needed. In an ideal town, where the shops are seen as part of the society's necessities and not merely as a way of making profit for the shopping chains, the shops would be much more widely and more homogeneously distributed than they are today.

It is also true that many small shops are unstable. Two-thirds of the small shops that people open go out of business within a year. Obviously, the community is not well served by unstable businesses, and once again, their economic instability is largely linked to mistakes of location.

To guarantee that shops are stable, as well as distributed to meet community needs, each new shop must be placed where it will fill a gap among the other shops offering a roughly similar service and also be assured that it will get the threshold of customers which it needs in order to survive. We shall now try to express this principle in precise terms.

The characteristics of a stable system of shops is rather well known. It relies, essentially, on the idea that each unit of shopping has a certain catch basin—the population which it needs in order

to survive—and that units of any given type and size will therefore be stable if they are evenly distributed, each one at the
center of a catch basin large enough to support it.

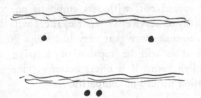

Catch basins.

The reason that shops and shopping centers do not always,
automatically, distribute themselves according to their appropriate
catch basins is easily explained by the situation known as Hotel-
ling's problem. Imagine a beach in summer time—and, somewhere along the beach, an ice-cream seller. Suppose now, that
you are also an ice-cream seller. You arrive on the beach. Where
should you place yourself in relation to the first ice-cream seller?
There are two possible solutions.

Two approaches to the ice-cream problem.

In the first case, you essentially decide to split the beach with
the other ice-cream seller. You take half the beach, and leave him
half the beach. In this case, you place yourself as far away from
him as you can, in a position where half the people on the beach
are nearer to you than to him.

In the second case, you place yourself right next to him. You
decide, in short, to try and compete with him—and place yourself in such a way as to command the whole beach, not half of it.

Every time a shop, or shopping center opens, it faces a similar choice. It can either locate in a new area where there are no other competing businesses, or it can place itself exactly where all the other businesses are already in the hope of attracting their customers away from them.

The trouble is, very simply, that people tend to choose the second of these two alternatives, because it seems, on the surface, to be safer. In fact, however, the first of the two choices is both better and safer. It is better for the customers, who then have stores to serve them closer to their homes and work places than they do now; and it is safer for the shopkeepers themselves since—in spite of appearances—their stores are much more likely to survive when they stand, without competition, in the middle of a catch basin which needs their services.

Let us now consider the global nature of a web which has this character. In present cities, shops of similar types tend to be clustered in shopping centers. They are forced to cluster, in part because of zoning ordinances, which forbid them to locate in so-called residential areas; and they are encouraged to cluster by their mistaken notion that competition with other shops will serve them better than roughly equal sharing of the available customers. In the "peoples" web we are proposing, shops are far more evenly spread out, with less emphasis on competition and greater emphasis on service. Of course, there will still be competition, enough to make sure that very bad shops go out of business, because each shop will be capable of drawing customers from the nearby catch basins if it offers better service—but the accent is on cooperation instead of competition.

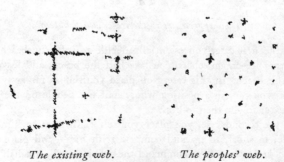

The existing web.   *The peoples' web.*

To generate this kind of homogeneous people's web, it is only necessary that each new shop follow the following three-step procedure when it chooses a location:

1. Identify all other shops which offer the service you are interested in; locate them on the map.

2. Identify and map the location of potential consumers. Wherever possible, indicate the density or total number of potential consumers in any given area.

3. Look for the biggest gap in the existing web of shops in those areas where there are potential consumers.

The gap in services.

Two colleagues of ours have tested the efficiency and potential stability of the webs created by this procedure. ("Computer Simulation of Market Location in an Urban Area," S. Angel and F. Loetterle, CES files, June 1967.) They chose to study markets. They began with a fixed area, a known population density and purchasing power, and a random distribution of markets of different sizes. They then created new markets and killed off old markets according to the following rules. (1) Among all of the existing markets, erase any that do not capture sufficient business to support their given size; (2) among all of the possible locations for a new market, find the one which would most strongly support a new market; (3) find that size for the new market that would be most economically feasible; (4) find that market among all those now existing that is the least economically feasible, and erase it from the web; (5) repeat steps (2) through (4) until no further improvement in the web can be made.

Under the impact of these rules, the random distribution of

markets at the beginning leads gradually to a fluctuating, pulsating distribution of markets which remains economically stable throughout its changes.

Now of course, even if shops of the *same* kind are kept apart by this procedure, shops of *different* kinds will tend to cluster. This follows, simply, from the convenience of the shopper. If we follow the rules of location given above—always locating a new shop in the biggest gap in the web of similar shops—then, within that gap there are still quite a large number of different possible places to locate: and naturally, we shall try to locate near the largest cluster of other shops within that gap, to increase the number of people coming past the shop, in short, to make it more convenient for shoppers.

The clusters which emerge have been thoroughly studied by Berry. It turns out that the *levels* of clustering are remarkably similar, even though their spacing varies greatly according to population density. (See *Geography of Market Centers and Retail Distribution*, B. Berry, Englewood Cliffs, New Jersey: Prentice-Hall, Inc., 1967, pp. 32–33.) The elements in this web of clustering correspond closely to patterns defined in this language.

Therefore:

When you locate any individual shop, follow a three-step procedure:

1. Identify all other shops which offer the service you are interested in; locate them on the map.
2. Identify and map the location of potential consumers. Wherever possible, indicate the density or total number of potential consumers in any given area.
3. Look for the biggest gap in the existing web of shops in those areas where there are potential consumers.
4. Within the gap in the web of similar shops, locate your shop next to the largest cluster of other kinds of shops.

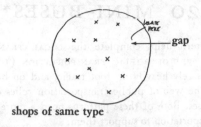

shops of same type

We estimate, that under the impact of this rule, a web of shopping with the following overall characteristics will emerge:

	Population	Distance Apart (Miles)
MAGIC OF THE CITY (10)	300,000	10*
PROMENADES (31)	50,000	4*
SHOPPING STREETS (32)	10,000	1.8*
MARKETS OF MANY SHOPS (46)	4,000	1.1*
CORNER GROCERIES (89)	1,000	0.5*

* These distances are calculated for an overall population density of 5000 per square mile. For a population density of D persons/ square mile, divide the distances by $\sqrt{D/5000}$. . . .

20 MINI-BUSES*

. . . this pattern helps complete the LOCAL TRANSPORT AREAS
(11) and the WEB OF PUBLIC TRANSPORTATION (16). The local
transport areas rely heavily on foot traffic, and on bikes and carts
and horses. The web of public transportation relies on trains and
planes and buses. Both of these patterns need a more flexible kind
of public transportation to support them.

**Public transportation must be able to take people from
any point to any other point within the metropolitan area.**

Buses and trains, which run along lines, are too far from most
origins and destinations to be useful. Taxis, which can go from
point to point, are too expensive.

To solve the problem, it is necessary to have a kind of vehicle
which is half way between the two—half like a bus, half like a
taxi—a small bus which can pick up people at any point and take
them to any other point, but which may also pick up other passengers on the way, to make the trip less costly than a taxi fare.

Recent research, and full-scale experiments, have shown that a
system of mini-buses, on call by telephone, can function in this
fashion, taking people from door to door in 15 minutes, for no
more than 50 cents a ride (1974): and that the system is efficient
enough to support itself. It works just like a taxi, except that it
picks up and drops off other passengers while you are riding; it
goes to the nearest corner to save time—not to your own front
door; and it costs a quarter of an average taxi fare.

The system hinges, to a certain extent, on the development of
sophisticated new computer programs. As calls come in, the computer examines the present movements of all the various mini-
buses, each with its particular load of passengers, and decides
which bus can best afford to pick up the new passenger, with the
least detour. Two-way radio contact keeps the mini-buses in communication with the dispatcher at the computer switchboard. All
this, and other details, are discussed fully in a review of current

Canadian mini-bus.

dial-a-bus research: *Summary Report—The Dial-a-Ride Transportation System,* M.I.T. Urban Systems Laboratory, Report # USL-TR-70-10, March 1971.

Dial systems for buses are actually coming into existence now because they are economically feasible. While conventional fixed-route public transport systems are experiencing a dangerous spiral of lower levels of service, fewer passengers, and increased public subsidies, over 30 working dial-a-bus systems are presently in successful operation throughout the world. For example, a dial-a-bus system in Regina, Saskatchewan, is the *only* part of the Regina Transit System which supports itself (*Regina Telebus Study: Operations Report, and Financial Report,* W. G. Atkinson et al., June 1972). In Batavia, New York, dial-a-bus is the sole means of public transport, serving a population of 16,000 at fares of 40 to 60 cents per ride.

We finish this pattern by reminding the reader of two vital problems of public transportation, which underline the importance of the mini-bus approach.

First, there are very large numbers of people in cities who cannot drive; we believe the mini-bus system is the only realistic way of meeting the needs of all these people.

Their numbers are much larger than one would think. They are, in effect, a silent minority comprising the uncomplaining old and physically handicapped, the young and the poor. In 1970, over 20 percent of U.S. households did not own a car. Fifty-seven and five-tenths percent of all households with incomes under $3000 did not own a car. For households headed by persons 65 years of age or older, 44.9 percent did not own a car. Of the youths between 10 and 18 years of age, 80 percent are dependent on others, including public

transit, for their mobility. Among the physically disabled about 5.7 million are potential riders of public transportation if the system could take them door-to-door. (Sumner Myers, "Turning Transit Subsidies into 'Compensatory Transportation,'" *City*, Vol. 6, No. 3, Summer 1972, p. 20.)

Second, quite apart from these special needs, the fact is that a web of public transportation, with large buses, boats, and trains, will not work anyway, without a mini-bus system. The large systems need feeders: some way of getting to the stations. If people have to get in their cars to go to the train, then, once in the car, they stay in it and do not use the train at all. The mini-bus system is essential for the purpose of providing feeder service in the larger web of public transportation.

Therefore:

Establish a system of small taxi-like buses, carrying up to six people each, radio-controlled, on call by telephone, able to provide point-to-point service according to the passengers' needs, and supplemented by a computer system which guarantees minimum detours, and minimum waiting times. Make bus stops for the mini-buses every 600 feet in each direction, and equip these bus stops with a phone for dialing a bus.

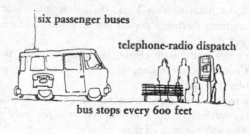

six passenger buses

telephone-radio dispatch

bus stops every 600 feet

❖ ❖ ❖

Place the bus stops mainly along major roads, as far as this can be consistent with the fact that no one ever has to walk more than 600 feet to the nearest one—PARALLEL ROADS (23); put one in every INTERCHANGE (34); and make each one a place where a few minutes' wait is pleasant—BUS STOP (92). . . .

establish community and neighborhood policy to control the character of the local environment according to the following fundamental principles:

21. FOUR-STORY LIMIT

22. NINE PER CENT PARKING

23. PARALLEL ROADS

24. SACRED SITES

25. ACCESS TO WATER

26. LIFE CYCLE

27. MEN AND WOMEN

21 FOUR-STORY LIMIT**

. . . within an urban area, the density of building fluctuates. It will, in general, be rather higher toward the center and lower toward the edges—CITY COUNTRY FINGERS (3), LACE OF COUNTRY STREETS (5), MAGIC OF THE CITY (10). However, throughout the city, even at its densest points, there are strong human reasons to subject all buildings to height restrictions.

There is abundant evidence to show that high buildings make people crazy.

High buildings have no genuine advantages, except in speculative gains for banks and land owners. They are not cheaper, they do not help create open space, they destroy the townscape, they destroy social life, they promote crime, they make life difficult for children, they are expensive to maintain, they wreck the open spaces near them, and they damage light and air and view. But quite apart from all of this, which shows that they aren't very sensible, empirical evidence shows that they can actually damage people's minds and feelings.

"The Ministry of Truth—Minitrue, in Newspeak—was startlingly different from any other object in sight. It was an enormous pyramidal structure of glittering white concrete, soaring up terrace after terrace 300 metres in the air." (George Orwell, 1984)

There are two separate bodies of evidence for this. One shows the effect of high-rise housing on the mental and social well being of families. The other shows the effect of large buildings, and high buildings, on the human relations in offices and workplaces. We present the first of these two bodies of evidence in the text which follows. The second, concerning offices and workplaces, we have placed in BUILDING COMPLEX (95), since it has implications not just for the height of buildings but also for their total volume.

We wish to stress, however, that the seemingly one-sided concern with housing in the paragraphs which follow, is only apparent. The underlying phenomenon—namely, mental disorder and social alienation created by the height of buildings—occurs equally in housing and in workplaces.

The strongest evidence comes from D. M. Fanning ("Families in Flats," *British Medical Journal*, November 18, 1967, pp. 382–86). Fanning shows a direct correlation between incidence of mental disorder and the height of people's apartments. The higher people live off the ground, the more likely are they to suffer mental illness. And it is not simply a case of people prone to mental illness choosing high-rise apartments. Fanning shows that the correlation is strongest for the people who spend the most time in their apartments. Among the families he studied, the correlation was strongest for women, who spend the most time in their apartments; it was less strong for children, who spend less time in the apartments; and it was weakest for men, who spend the least amount of time in their apartments. This strongly suggests that sheer time spent in the high-rise is itself what causes the effect.

A simple mechanism may explain this: high-rise living takes people away from the ground, and away from the casual, everyday society that occurs on the sidewalks and streets and on the gardens and porches. It leaves them alone in their apartments. The decision to go out for some public life becomes formal and awkward; and unless there is some specific task which brings people out in the world, the tendency is to stay home, alone. The forced isolation then causes individual breakdowns.

Fanning's findings are reinforced by Dr. D. Cappon's clinical experiences reported in "Mental Health and the High Rise," Canadian Public Health Association, April 1971:

There is every reason to believe that high-rise apartment dwelling has adverse effects on mental and social health. And there is sufficient clinical, anecdotal and intuitive observations to back this up. Herewith, in no particular order ranking, a host of factors:

In my experience as Mental Health Director in a child guidance clinic in York Township, Toronto, for 5 years, I saw numerous children who had been kinetically deprived . . . and kinetic deprivation is the worst of the perceptual, exploratory kinds, for a young child, leaving legacies of lethargy, or restlessness, antisocial acting out or withdrawal, depersonalization or psychopathy.

Young children in a high-rise are much more socially deprived of neighborhood peers and activities than their S.F.D. (Single Family Dwelling) counterparts, hence they are poorly socialized and at too close quarters to adults, who are tense and irritable as a consequence.

Adolescents in a high-rise suffer more from the "nothing-to-do" ennui than those of a S.F.D., with enhanced social needs for "drop in centres" and a greater tendency to escapism. . . .

Mothers are more anxious about their very young ones, when they can't see them in the street below, from a convenient kitchen window.

There is higher passivity in the high-rise because of the barriers to active outlets on the ground; such barriers as elevators, corridors; and generally there is a time lapse and an effort in negotiating the vertical journey. TV watching is extended in the high-rise. This affects probably most adversely the old who need kinesia and activity, in proportion, as much as the very young do. Though immobility saves them from accidents, it also shortens their life in a high-rise. . . .

A Danish study by Jeanne Morville adds more evidence (*Borns Brug af Friarsaler*, Disponering Af Friarsaler, Etageboligomrader Med Saerlig Henblik Pa Borns Legsmuligheder, S.B.I., Denmark, 1969):

Children from the high blocks start playing out of doors on their own at a later age than children from the low blocks: Only 2% of the children aged two to three years in the high point blocks play on their own out of doors, while 27% of the children in the low blocks do this.

Among the children aged five years in the high point blocks 29% do not as yet play on their own out of doors, while in the low blocks all the children aged five do so. . . . The percentage of young children playing out of doors on their own decreases with the height of their homes; 90% of all the children from the three lower floors in the high point blocks play on their own out of doors, while only 59% of the children from the three upper floors do so. . . .

Young children in the high blocks have fewer contacts with playmates than those in the low blocks· Among children aged one, two and three years, 86% from the low blocks have daily contact with playmates; this applies to only 29% from the high blocks.

More recently, there is the evidence brought forward by Oscar Newman in *Defensible Space*. Newman compared two adjacent housing projects in New York—one high-rise, the other a collection of relatively small three-story walk-up buildings. The two projects have the same overall density, and their inhabitants have roughly the same income. *But Newman found that the crime rate in the high-rise was roughly twice that in the walk-ups.*

At what height do the effects described by Fanning, Cappon, Morville, and Newman begin to take hold? It is our experience that in both housing and office buildings, the problems begin when buildings are more than four stories high.

At three or four stories, one can still walk comfortably down to the street, and from a window you can still feel part of the street scene: you can see details in the street—the people, their faces, foliage, shops. From three stories you can yell out, and catch the attention of someone below. Above four stories these connections break down. The visual detail is lost; people speak of the scene below as if it were a game, from which they are completely detached. The connection to the ground and to the fabric of the town becomes tenuous; the building becomes a world of its own: with its own elevators and cafeterias.

We believe, therefore, that the "four-story limit" is an appropriate way to express the proper connection between building height and the health of a people. Of course, it is the spirit of the pattern which is most essential. Certainly, a building five stories high, perhaps even six, might work if it were carefully handled. But it is difficult. On the whole, we advocate a four-story limit, with only occasional departures, throughout the town.

Finally, we give the children of Glasgow the last word.

To fling a "piece," a slice of bread and jam, from a window down to a child in the street below has been a recognised custom in Glasgow's tenement housing. . . .

THE JEELY PIECE SONG
by Adam McNaughton

I'm a skyscraper wean, I live on the nineteenth flair,
On' I'm no' gaun oot tae play ony mair,
For since we moved tae oor new hoose I'm wastin' away,
'Cos I'm gettin' wan less meal ev'ry day,

Refrain

Oh, ye canny fling pieces oot a twenty-storey flat,
Seven hundred hungry weans will testify tae that,
If it's butter, cheese or jeely, if the breid is plain or pan,
The odds against it reachin' us is ninety-nine tae wan.

. . . .

We've wrote away tae Oxfam tae try an' get some aid,
We've a' joined thegither an' formed a "piece" brigade,
We're gonny march tae London tae demand oor Civil Rights,
Like "Nae mair hooses ower piece flingin' heights."

Therefore:

In any urban area, no matter how dense, keep the majority of buildings four stories high or less. It is possible that certain buildings should exceed this limit, but they should never be buildings for human habitation.

four storys

❖ ❖ ❖

Within the framework of the four-story limit the exact height of individual buildings, according to the area of floor they need, the area of the site, and the height of surrounding buildings, is given by the pattern NUMBER OF STORIES (96). More global variations of density are given by DENSITY RINGS (29). The horizontal subdivision of large buildings into smaller units, and separate smaller buildings, is given by BUILDING COMPLEX (95). HOUSING HILL (39) and OFFICE CONNECTIONS (82) help to shape multi-storied apartments and offices within the constraints of a four-story limit. And finally, don't take the four-story limit too literally. Occasional exceptions from the general rule are very important—HIGH PLACES (62). . . .

22 NINE PER CENT
PARKING**

. . . the integrity of local transport areas and the tranquility of local communities and neighborhoods depend very much on the amount of parking they provide. The more parking they provide, the less possible it will be to maintain these patterns, because the parking spaces will attract cars, which in turn violate the local transport areas and neighborhoods—LOCAL TRANSPORT AREAS (11), COMMUNITY OF 7000 (12), IDENTIFIABLE NEIGHBORHOOD (14). This pattern proposes radical limits on the distribution of parking spaces, to protect communities.

Very simply—when the area devoted to parking is too great, it destroys the land.

*In downtown Los Angeles over 60 per cent
of the land is given over to the automobile.*

Very rough empirical observations lead us to believe that it is not possible to make an environment fit for human use when more than 9 per cent of it is given to parking.

Our observations are very tentative. We have yet to perform systematic studies—our observations rely on our own subjective estimates of cases where "there are too many cars" and cases where "the cars are all right." However, we have found in our preliminary observations, that different people agree to a remarkable extent about these estimates. This suggests that we are dealing with a phenomenon which, though obscure, is nonetheless substantial.

An example of an environment which has the threshold density of 9 per cent parking, is shown in our key photograph: a quadrant

of the University of Oregon. Many people we have talked to feel intuitively that this area is beautiful now, but that if more cars were parked there it would be ruined.

What possible functional basis is there for this intuition? We conjecture as follows: people realize, subconsciously, that the physical environment is the medium for their social intercourse. It is the environment which, when it is working properly, creates the potential for all social communion, including even communion with the self.

We suspect that when the density of cars passes a certain limit, and people experience the feeling that there are too many cars, what is really happening is that subconsciously they feel that the cars are overwhelming the environment, that the environment is no longer "theirs," that they have no right to be there, that it is not a place for people, and so on. After all, the effect of the cars reaches far beyond the mere presence of the cars themselves. They create a maze of driveways, garage doors, asphalt and concrete surfaces, and building elements which people cannot use. When the density goes beyond the limit, we suspect that people feel the social potential of the environment has disappeared. Instead of inviting them out, the environment starts giving them the message that the outdoors is not meant for them, that they should stay indoors, that they should stay in their own buildings, that social communion is no longer permitted or encouraged.

We have not yet tested this suspicion. However, if it turns out to be true, it may be that this pattern, which seems to be based on such slender evidence, is in fact one of the most crucial patterns there is, and that it plays a key role in determining the difference between environments which are socially and psychologically healthy and those which are unhealthy.

We conjecture, then, that environments which are human, and not destroyed socially or ecologically by the presence of parked cars, have less than 9 per cent of the ground area devoted to parking space; and that parking lots and garages must therefore never be allowed to cover more than 9 per cent of the land.

It is essential to interpret this pattern in the strictest possible way. The pattern becomes meaningless if we allow ourselves to place the parking generated by a piece of land A, on another adjacent piece of land B, thus keeping parking on A below 9 per

cent, but raising the parking on B to more than 9 per cent. In other words, each piece of land must take care of itself; we must not allow ourselves to solve this problem on one piece of land at the expense of some other piece of land. A town or a community can only implement the pattern according to this strict interpretation by defining a grid of independent "parking zones"—each zone 1 to 10 acres in area—which cover the whole community, and then insisting that the rule be applied, independently, and strictly, inside every parking zone.

The 9 per cent rule has a clear and immediate implication for the balance between surface parking and parking in garages, at different parking densities. This follows from simple arithmetic. Suppose, for example, that an area requires 20 parking spaces per acre. Twenty parking spaces will consume about 7000 square feet, which would be 17 per cent of the land if it were all in surface parking. To keep 20 cars per acre in line with the 9 per cent rule, at least half of them will have to be parked in garages. The table below gives similar figures for different densities:

Cars per acre	Per cent on surface	Per cent in two story garages	Per cent in three story garages
12	100	—	—
17	50	50	—
23	50	—	50
30	—	—	100

What about underground parking? May we consider it as an exception to this rule? Only if it does not violate or restrict the use of the land above. If, for example, a parking garage is under a piece of land which was previously used as open space, with great trees growing on it, then the garage will almost certainly change the nature of the space above, because it will no longer be possible to grow large trees there. Such a parking garage is a violation of the land. Similarly, if the structural grid of the garage— 60 foot bays—constrains the structural grid of the building above, so that this building is not free to express its needs, this is a violation too. Underground parking may be allowed only in those rare cases where it does not constrain the land above at all: under a major road, perhaps, or under a tennis court.

We see then, that the 9 per cent rule has colossal implications.

Since underground parking will only rarely satisfy the conditions we have stated, the pattern really says that almost no part of the urban area may have more than 30 parking spaces per acre. *This will create large changes in the central business district.* Consider a part of a typical downtown area. There may be several hundred commuters per acre working there; and, under today's conditions, many of them park their cars in garages. But if it is true that there cannot be more than 30 parking spaces per acre, then either the work will be forced to decentralize, or the workers will have to rely on public transportation. It seems, in short, that this simple pattern, based on the social psychology of the environment, leads us to the same far reaching social conclusions as the patterns WEB OF PUBLIC TRANSPORTATION (16) and SCATTERED WORK (9).

Therefore:

Do not allow more than 9 per cent of the land in any given area to be used for parking. In order to prevent the "bunching" of parking in huge neglected areas, it is necessary for a town or a community to subdivide its land into "parking zones" no larger than 10 acres each and to apply the same rule in each zone.

parking zones

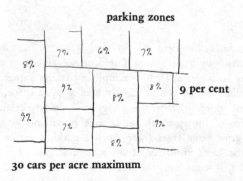

30 cars per acre maximum

❖ ❖ ❖

Two later patterns say that parking must take one of two forms: tiny, surface parking lots, or shielded parking structures—

SHIELDED PARKING (97), SMALL PARKING LOTS (103). If you accept these patterns the 9 per cent rule will put an effective upper limit of 30 parking spaces per acre, on every part of the environment. Present-day on-street parking, with driveways, which provides spaces for about 35 cars per acre on the ground is ruled out. And those present-day high density business developments which depend on the car are also ruled out. . . .

23 PARALLEL ROADS

. . . in earlier patterns, we have proposed that cities should be subdivided into local transport areas, whose roads allow cars to move in and out from the ring roads, but strongly discourage internal movement across the area—LOCAL TRANSPORT AREAS (11), RING ROADS (17)—and that these transport areas themselves be further subdivided into communities and neighborhoods, with the provision that all major roads are in the boundaries between communities and neighborhoods—SUBCULTURE BOUNDARY (13), NEIGHBORHOOD BOUNDARY (15). Now, what should the arrangement of these roads be like, to help the flow required by LOCAL TRANSPORT AREAS (11), and to maintain the boundaries?

The net-like pattern of streets is obsolete. Congestion is choking cities. Cars can average 60 miles per hour on freeways, but trips across town have an average speed of only 10 to 15 miles per hour.

Certainly, in many cases, we want to get rid of cars, not help them to go faster. This is fully discussed in LOCAL TRANSPORT AREAS (11). But away from the areas where children play and people walk or use their bikes, there still need to be certain streets which carry cars. The question is: How can these streets be designed to carry the cars faster and without congestion?

It turns out that the loss of speed on present city streets is caused mainly by crossing movements: left-hand turns across traffic and four-way intersections. (G. F. Newell, "The Effect of Left Turns on the Capacity of Traffic Intersection," *Quarterly of Applied Mathematics*, XVII, April 1959, pp. 67–76.)

To speed up traffic it is therefore necessary to create a network of major roads in which there are no four-way intersections, and no left-hand turns across traffic. This can easily be done if the major roads are alternating, one-way parallel roads, a few hundred feet apart, with smaller local roads opening off them, and the only connections between the parallel roads given by larger freeways crossing them at two- or three-mile intervals.

Parallel roads.

This pattern has been discussed at considerable length in three papers ("The Pattern of Streets," C. Alexander, *AIP Journal*, September 1966; Criticisms by D. Carson and P. Roosen-Runge, and Alexander's reply, in *AIP Journal*, September 1967.) We refer the reader to these original papers for the full derivation of all the geometric details. Our present statement is a radically condensed version. Here we concentrate mainly on one puzzling question—that of detours—because this is for many people the most surprising aspect of the full analysis.

The pattern of parallel roads—since it contains no major cross streets—creates many detours not present in today's net-like pattern. At first sight it seems likely that these detours will be impossibly large. However, in the papers mentioned above it is shown in detail that they are in fact perfectly reasonable. We summarize the argument below.

It is possible to calculate the probable detour for any trip of a given length through this proposed parallel road system as a function of the distance between the cross roads. Next, the probability of any given trip length may be obtained from actual studies of metropolitan auto trips. These two types of probabilities can finally be combined to yield an overall mean trip length and overall mean detours as shown below.

Trip Length, miles	1	2	3	4	5	7	10	4.12 (Overall Mean Trip Length)
Proportion of Trip Lengths %*	28	11	11	9	9	24	8	
miles between cross roads			Mean Detour, miles					Overall Mean Detour
1	.12	.05	.04	.03	.02	.01	.01	.05
2	.45	.24	.15	.11	.09	.07	.04	.21
3	.79	.58	.36	.25	.20	.15	.11	.41

* Data for distribution of trip lengths was obtained from Edward M. Hall, "Travel Characteristics of Two San Diego Suburban Developments," *Highway Research Board Bulletin 2039*, Washington, D. C., 1958, pp. 1–19, Figure 11. These data are typical for metropolitan areas all over the Western world.

We see, therefore, that even with cross roads two miles apart, the lack of cross streets only increases trip lengths by 5 per cent. *At the same time, the average speed of trips will increase from 15 miles per hour to about 45 miles per hour, a threefold increase.* The huge savings in time and fuel costs will more than offset the slight increase in distance.

Referring back for a moment to the table of detours, it will be noticed that the highest detours occur for the shortest trips. We have argued elsewhere—LOCAL TRANSPORT AREAS (11)—that to preserve the quality of the city's environment it is necessary to discourage the use of the automobile for very short trips, and to encourage walking, bikes, buses, and horses instead. The pattern of parallel roads has precisely the feature which local transport areas need. It makes longer trips vastly more efficient, while discouraging the very short auto trips, and so provides the local transport area with just the internal structure which it needs to support its function.

Although this pattern seems strange at first sight, it is in fact already happening in many parts of the world and has already proved its worth. For example, Berne, Switzerland, is one of the few cities in Europe that does not suffer from acute traffic congestion. When one looks at a map of Berne, one can see that its old center is formed by five long parallel roads with almost no cross streets. We believe that it has little congestion in the old center precisely because it contains the pattern. In many large cities today, the same insight is being implemented piecemeal—in the form of more and more one-way streets: in New York the alternating one-way Avenues, in downtown San Francisco the one-way major streets.

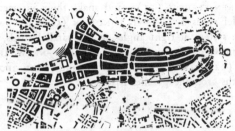

Berne's five main parallel streets.

Therefore:

Within a local transport area build no intersecting major roads at all; instead, build a system of parallel and alternating one-way roads to carry traffic to the RING ROADS (17). In existing towns, create this structure piecemeal, by gradually making major streets one-way and closing cross streets. Keep parallel roads at least 100 yards apart (to make room for neighborhoods between them) and no more than 300 or 400 yards apart.

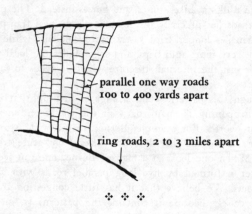

parallel one way roads
100 to 400 yards apart

ring roads, 2 to 3 miles apart

❖ ❖ ❖

The parallel roads are the only *through* roads in a LOCAL TRANSPORT AREA (11). For access from the parallel roads to public buildings, house clusters, and individual houses use safe, slow, narrow roads which are not through roads—LOOPED LOCAL ROADS (49), GREEN STREETS (51)—and make their intersections with the parallel roads a "T"—T JUNCTION (50). Keep the pedestrian path system at right angles to the parallel roads, and raised above them where the two must run parallel—NETWORK OF PATHS AND CARS (52), RAISED WALK (55). Provide a ROAD CROSSING (54) where paths cross the parallel roads.

24 SACRED SITES*

. . . in every region and every town, indeed in every neighborhood, there are special places which have come to symbolize the area, and the people's roots there. These places may be natural beauties or historic landmarks left by ages past. But in some form they are essential.

❖ ❖ ❖

People cannot maintain their spiritual roots and their connections to the past if the physical world they live in does not also sustain these roots.

Informal experiments in our communities have led us to believe that people agree, to an astonishing extent, about the sites which do embody people's relation to the land and to the past. It seems, in other words, as though "the" sacred sites for an area exist as objective communal realities.

If this is so, it is then of course essential that these specific sites be preserved and made important. Destruction of sites which have become part of the communal consciousness, in an agreed and widespread sense, must inevitably create gaping wounds in the communal body.

Traditional societies have always recognized the importance of these sites. Mountains are marked as places of special pilgrimage; rivers and bridges become holy; a building or a tree, or rock or stone, takes on the power through which people can connect themselves to their own past.

But modern society often ignores the psychological importance of these sites. They are bulldozed, developed, changed, for political and economic reasons, without regard for these simple but fundamental emotional matters; or they are simply ignored.

We suggest the following two steps.

1. In any geographic area—large or small—ask a large number of people which sites and which places make them feel the most contact with the area; which sites stand most for the important values of the past, and which ones embody their connection to the land. Then insist that these sites be actively preserved.

2. Once the sites are chosen and preserved, embellish them in

a way which intensifies their public meaning. We believe that the best way to intensify a site is through a progression of areas which people pass through as they approach the site. This is the principle of "nested precincts," discussed in detail under the pattern HOLY GROUND (66).

A garden which can be reached only by passing through a series of outer gardens keeps its secrecy. A temple which can be reached only by passing through a sequence of approach courts is able to be a special thing in a man's heart. The magnificence of a mountain peak is increased by the difficulty of reaching the upper valleys from which it can be seen; the beauty of a woman is intensified by the slowness of her unveiling; the great beauty of a river bank—its rushes, water rats, small fish, wild flowers—are violated by a too direct approach; even the ecology cannot stand up to the too direct approach—the thing will simply be devoured.

We must therefore build around a sacred site a series of spaces which gradually intensify and converge on the site. The site itself becomes a kind of inner sanctum, at the core. And if the site is very large—a mountain—the same approach can be taken with special places from which it can be seen—an inner sanctum, reached past many levels, which is not the mountain, but a garden, say, from which the mountain can be seen in special beauty.

Therefore:

Whether the sacred sites are large or small, whether they are at the center of the towns, in neighborhoods, or in the deepest countryside, establish ordinances which will protect them absolutely—so that our roots in the visible surroundings cannot be violated.

sacred sites

acts of preservation

133

Give every sacred site a place, or a sequence of places, where people can relax, enjoy themselves, and feel the presence of the place—QUIET BACKS (59), ZEN VIEW (134), TREE PLACES (171), GARDEN SEAT (176). And above all, shield the approach to the site, so that it can only be approached on foot, and through a series of gateways and thresholds which reveal it gradually—HOLY GROUND (66). . . . .

25 ACCESS TO WATER*

. . . water is always precious. Among the special natural places covered by SACRED SITES (24), we single out the ocean beaches, lakes, and river banks, because they are irreplaceable. Their maintenance and proper use require a special pattern.

People have a fundamental yearning for great bodies of water. But the very movement of the people toward the water can also destroy the water.

Either roads, freeways, and industries destroy the water's edge and make it so dirty or so treacherous that it is virtually inaccessible; or when the water's edge is preserved, it falls into private hands.

Access to water is blocked.

But the need that people have for water is vital and profound. (See, for example, C. G. Jung, *Symbols of Transformation*, where Jung takes bodies of water which appear in dreams as a consistent representation of the dreamer's unconscious.)

The problem can be solved only if it is understood that people will build places *near* the water because it is entirely natural; but that the land immediately along the water's edge must be preserved for common use. To this end the roads which can destroy the water's edge must be kept back from it and only allowed near it when they lie at right angles to it.

Life forms around the water's edge.

The width of the belt of land along the water may vary with the type of water, the density of development along it, and the ecological conditions. Along high density development, it may be no more than a simple stone promenade. Along low density development, it may be a common parkland extending hundreds of yards beyond a beach.

Therefore:

When natural bodies of water occur near human settlements, treat them with great respect. Always preserve a belt of common land, immediately beside the water. And allow dense settlements to come right down to the water only at infrequent intervals along the water's edge.

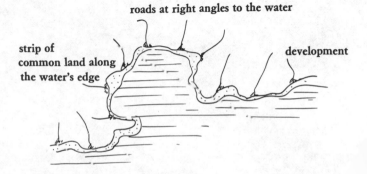

roads at right angles to the water

strip of
common land along
the water's edge

development

The width of the common land will vary with the type of water and the ecological conditions. In one case, it may be no more than a simple stone promenade along a river bank a few feet wide—PROMENADE (31). In another case, it may be a swath of dunes extending hundreds of yards beyond a beach—THE COUNTRYSIDE (7). In any case, do not build roads along the water within one mile of the water; instead, make all the approach roads at right angles to the edge, and very far apart—PARALLEL ROADS (23). If parking is provided, keep the lots small—SMALL PARKING LOTS (103). . . .

. . . a real community provides, in full, for the balance of human experience and human life—COMMUNITY OF 7000 (12). To a lesser extent, a good neighborhood will do the same—IDENTIFIABLE NEIGHBORHOOD (14). To fulfill this promise, communities and neighborhoods must have the range of things which life can need, so that a person can experience the full breadth and depth of life in his community.

❖ ❖ ❖

**All the world's a stage,
And all the men and women merely players:
They have their exits and their entrances;
And one man in his time plays many parts,
His acts being seven ages.**

As, first the infant,
Mewling and puking in the nurse's arms.
And then the whining schoolboy, with his satchel
And shining morning face, creeping like snail
Unwillingly to school. And then the lover,
Sighing like furnace, with a woeful ballad
Made to his mistress' eyebrow. Then the soldier,
Full of strange oaths, and bearded like the pard,
Jealous in honour, sudden and quick in quarrel,
Seeking the bubble reputation
Even in the cannon's mouth. And then the justice,
In fair round belly with good capon lined,
With eyes severe and beard of formal cut,
Full of wise saws and modern instances;
And so he plays his part. The sixth age shifts
Into the lean and slipper'd pantaloon,
With spectacles on nose and pouch on side;
His youthful hose, well saved, a world too wide
For his shrunk shank; and his big manly voice,
Turning again toward childish treble, pipes
And whistles in his sound. Last scene of all,
That ends this strange eventful history,
Is second childishness and mere oblivion,
Sans teeth, sans eyes, sans taste, sans every thing.
(Shakespeare, *As You Like It*, II.viii.)

To live life to the fullest, in each of the seven ages, each age must be clearly marked, by the community, as a distinct well-marked time. And the ages will only seem clearly marked if the

ceremonies which mark the passage from one age to the next are firmly marked by celebrations and distinctions.

By contrast, in a flat suburban culture the seven ages are not at all clearly marked; they are not celebrated; the passages from one age to the next have almost been forgotten. Under these conditions, people distort themselves. They can neither fulfill themselves in any one age nor pass successfully on to the next. Like the sixty-year-old woman wearing bright red lipstick on her wrinkles, they cling ferociously to what they never fully had.

This proposition hinges on two arguments.

A. The cycle of life is a definite psychological reality. It consists of discrete stages, each one fraught with its own difficulties, each one with its own special advantages.

B. Growth from one stage to another is not inevitable, and, in fact, it will not happen unless the community contains a balanced life cycle.

A. The Reality of the Life Cycle.

Everyone can recognize the fact that a person's life traverses several stages—infancy to old age. What is perhaps not so well understood is the idea that each stage is a discrete reality, with its own special compensations and difficulties; that each stage has certain characteristic experiences that go with it.

The most inspired work along these lines has come from Erik Erikson: "Identity and the Life Cycle," in *Psychological Issues*, Vol. 1, No. 1, New York: International Universities Press, 1959; and *Childhood and Society*, New York: W. W. Norton, 1950.

Erikson describes the sequence of phases a person must pass through as he matures and suggests that each phase is characterized by a specific developmental task—a successful resolution of some life conflict—and that this task must be solved by a person before he can move wholeheartedly forward to the next phase. Here is a summary of the stages in Erikson's scheme, adapted from his charts:

1. *Trust vs. mistrust:* the infant; relationship between the infant and mother; the struggle for confidence that the environment will nourish.

2. *Autonomy vs. shame and doubt:* the very young child; relationship between the child and parents; the struggle to stand on

one's own two feet, to find autonomy in the face of experiences of shame and doubt as to one's capacity for self-control.

3. *Initiative vs. guilt:* the child; relationship to the family, the ring of friends; the search for action, and the integrity of one's acts; to make and eagerly learn, checked by the fear and guilt of one's own aggressions.

4. *Industry vs. inferiority:* the youngster; relationship to the neighborhood, the school; adaptation to the society's tools; the sense that one can make things well, alone, and with others, against the experience of failure, inadequacy.

5. *Identity vs. identity diffusion:* youth, adolescence; relationship to peers and "outgroups" and the search for models of adult life; the search for continuity in one's own character against confusion and doubt; a moratorium; a time to find and ally oneself with creeds and programs of the world.

6. *Intimacy vs. isolation:* young adults; partners in friendship, sex, work; the struggle to commit oneself concretely in relations with others; to lose and find oneself in another, against isolation and the avoidance of others.

7. *Generativity vs. stagnation:* adults; the relationship between a person and the division of labor, and the creation of a shared household; the struggle to establish and guide, to create, against the failure to do so, and the feelings of stagnation.

8. *Integrity vs. despair:* old age; the relationship between a person and his world, his kind, mankind; the achievement of wisdom; love for oneself and one's kind; to face death openly, with the forces of one's life integrated; vs. the despair that life has been useless.

B. But growth through the life cycle is not inevitable.

It depends on the presence of a balanced community, a community that can sustain the give and take of growth. Persons at each stage of life have something irreplaceable to give and to take from the community, and it is just these transactions which help a person to solve the problems that beset each stage. Consider the case of a young couple and their new child. The connection between them is entirely mutual. Of course, the child "depends" on the parents to give the care and love that is required to resolve the conflict of trust that goes with infancy. But simultaneously,

the child gives the parents the experience of raising and bearing, which helps them to meet their conflict of generativity, unique to adulthood.

We distort the situation if we abstract it in such a way that we consider the parent as "having" such and such a personality when the child is born and then, remaining static, impinging upon a poor little thing. For this weak and changing little being moves the whole family along. Babies control and bring up their families as much as they are controlled by them; in fact, we may say that the family brings up a baby by being brought up by him. Whatever reaction patterns are given biologically and whatever schedule is predetermined developmentally must be considered to be a series of potentialities for changing patterns of mutual regulation. [Erikson, ibid. p. 69.]

Similar patterns of mutual regulation occur between the very old and the very young; between adolescents and young adults, children and infants, teenagers and younger teenagers, young men and old women, young women and old men, and so on. And these patterns must be made viable by prevailing social institutions and those parts of the environment which help to maintain them —the schools, nurseries, homes, cafes, bedrooms, sports fields, workshops, studios, gardens, graveyards. . . .

We believe, however, that the balance of settings which allow normal growth through the life cycle has been breaking down. Contact with the entire cycle of life is less and less available to each person, at each moment in time. In place of natural communities with a balanced life cycle we have retirement villages, bedrooms suburbs, teenage culture, ghettos of unemployed, college towns, mass cemeteries, industrial parks. Under such conditions, one's chances for solving the conflict that comes with each stage in the life cycle are slim indeed.

To re-create a community of balanced life cycles requires, first of all, that the idea take its place as a principal guide in the development of communities. *Each building project, whether the addition to a house, a new road, a clinic, can be viewed as either helping or hindering the right balance for local communities.* We suspect that the community repair maps, discussed in *The Oregon Experiment,* Chapter V (Volume 3 in this series), can play an especially useful role in helping to encourage the growth of a balanced life cycle.

But this pattern can be no more than an indication of work

that needs to be done. Each community must find ways of taking stock of its own relative "balance" in this respect, and then define a growth process which will move it in the right direction. This is a tremendously interesting and vital problem; it needs a great deal of development, experiment, and theory. If Erikson is right, and if this kind of work does not come, it seems possible that the development of trust, autonomy, initiative, industry, identity, intimacy, generativity, integrity may disappear entirely.

STAGE	IMPORTANT SETTINGS	RITES OF PASSAGE
1. INFANT *Trust*	Home, crib, nursery, garden	Birth place, setting up the home . . . . out of the crib, making a place
2. YOUNG CHILD *Autonomy*	Own place, couple's realm, children's realm, commons, connected play	Walking, making a place, special birthday
3. CHILD *Initiative*	Play space, own place, common land, neighborhood, animals	First ventures in town . . . . joining
4. YOUNGSTER *Industry*	Children's home, school, own place, adventure play, club, community	Puberty rites, private entrance paying your way
5. YOUTH *Identity*	Cottage, teenage society, hostels, apprentice, town and region	Commencement, marriage, work, building
6. YOUNG ADULT *Intimacy*	Household, couple's realm, small work group, the family, network of learning	Birth of a child, creating social wealth . . building
7. ADULT *Generativity*	Work community, the family town hall, a room of one's own	Special birthday, gathering, change in work
8. OLD PERSON *Integrity*	Settled work, cottage, the family, independent regions	Death, funeral, grave sites

Therefore:

Make certain that the full cycle of life is represented and balanced in each community. Set the ideal of a balanced life cycle as a principal guide for the evolution of communities. This means:

1. That each community include a balance of people at every stage of the life cycle, from infants to the very old; and include the full slate of settings needed for all these stages of life;

2. That the community contain the full slate of settings which best mark the ritual crossing of life from one stage to the next.

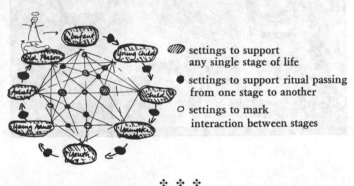

settings to support
any single stage of life

● settings to support ritual passing
from one stage to another

○ settings to mark
interaction between stages

❖ ❖ ❖

The rites of passage are provided for, most concretely, by HOLY GROUND (66). Other specific patterns which especially support the seven ages of man and the ceremonies of transition are HOUSEHOLD MIX (35), OLD PEOPLE EVERYWHERE (40), WORK COMMUNITY (41), LOCAL TOWN HALL (44), CHILDREN IN THE CITY (57), BIRTH PLACES (65), GRAVE SITES (70), THE FAMILY (75), YOUR OWN HOME (79), MASTER AND APPRENTICES (83), TEENAGE SOCIETY (84), SHOPFRONT SCHOOLS (85), CHILDREN'S HOME (86), ROOMS TO RENT (153), TEENAGER'S COTTAGE (154), OLD AGE COTTAGE (155), SETTLED WORK (156), MARRIAGE BED (187).

27 MEN AND WOMEN

. . . and just as a community or neighborhood must have a proper balance of activities for people of all the different ages— COMMUNITY OF 7000 (12), IDENTIFIABLE NEIGHBORHOOD (14), LIFE CYCLE (26)—so it must also adjust itself and its activities to the balance of the sexes, and provide, in equal part, the things which reflect the masculine and feminine sides of life.

The world of a town in the 1970's is split along sexual lines. Suburbs are for women, workplaces for men; kindergartens are for women, professional schools for men; supermarkets are for women, hardware stores for men.

Since no aspect of life is purely masculine or purely feminine, a world in which the separation of the sexes is extreme, distorts reality, and perpetuates and solidifies the distortions. Science is dominated by a masculine, and often mechanical mentality; foreign diplomacy is governed by war, again the product of the masculine ego. Schools for young children are swayed by the world of women, as are homes. The house has become the domain of woman to such a ridiculous extreme that home builders and developers portray an image of homes which are delicate and perfectly "nice," like powder rooms. The idea that such a home could be a place where things are made or vegetables grown, with sawdust around the front door, is almost inconceivable.

The pattern or patterns which could resolve these problems are, for the moment, unknown. We can hint at the kinds of buildings and land use and institutions which would bring the problem into balance. But the geometry cannot be understood until certain social facts are realized, and given their full power to influence the environment. *In short, until both men and women are able to mutually influence each part of a town's life, we shall not know what kinds of physical patterns will best co-exist with this social order.*

Therefore:

Make certain that each piece of the environment—each building, open space, neighborhood, and work community —is made with a blend of both men's and women's instincts. Keep this balance of masculine and feminine in mind for every project at every scale, from the kitchen to the steel mill.

man's spirit   woman's spirit

❖ ❖ ❖

No large housing areas without workshops for men; no work communities which do not provide for women with part-time jobs and child care—SCATTERED WORK (9). Within each place which has a balance of the masculine and feminine, make sure that individual men and women also have room to flourish, in their own right, distinct and separate from their opposites—A ROOM OF ONE'S OWN (141). . . .

*both in the neighborhoods and the communities, and
in between them, in the boundaries, encourage the
formation of local centers:*

28 ECCENTRIC NUCLEUS*

. . . so far, we have established an overall height restriction on the city, with its attendant limitation on average density—FOUR-STORY LIMIT (21). If we assume, also, that the city contains major centers for every 300,000 people, spaced according to the rules in MAGIC OF THE CITY (10), it will then follow that the overall density of the city slopes off from these centers: the highest density near to them, the lowest far away. This means that any individual COMMUNITY OF 7000 (12) will have an overall density, given by its distance from the nearest downtown. The question then arises: How should density vary locally, within this community; what geometric pattern should the density have? The question is complicated greatly by the principle of SUBCULTURE BOUNDARY (13), which requires that communities are surrounded by their services, instead of having their services at their geometric centers. This pattern, and the next, defines a local distribution of density which is compatible with this context.

The random character of local densities confuses the identity of our communities, and also creates a chaos in the pattern of land use.

Let us begin by considering the typical configuration of the residential densities in a town. There is an overall slope to the densities: they are high toward the center and lower toward the outskirts. But there is no recognizable structure within this overall slope: no clearly visible repeating pattern we can see again and again within the city. Compare this with the contours of a mountain range. In a mountain range, there is a great deal of recognizable structure; we see systematic ridges and valleys, foothills, bowls, and peaks which have arisen naturally from geological processes; and all this structure is repeated again and again, from place to place, within the whole.

Of course, this is only an analogy. But it does raise the question: Is it natural, and all right, if density configurations in a town are so random; or would a town be better off if there was some more visible coherent structure, some kind of systematic variation in the pattern of the densities?

What happens when the local densities in a town vary in their present rambling, incoherent fashion? The high density areas, potentially capable of supporting intense activity cannot actually do so because they are too widely spread. And the low density areas, potentially capable of supporting silence and tranquility when they are concentrated, are also too diffusely scattered. The result: the town has neither very intense activity, nor very intense quiet. Since we have many arguments which show how vital it is for a town to give people both intense activity, and also deep and satisfying quiet—SACRED SITES (24), ACTIVITY NODES (30), PROMENADE (31), QUIET BACKS (59), STILL WATER (71)—it seems quite likely, then, that this randomness of density does harm to urban life.

We believe, indeed, that a town would be far better off if it did contain a coherent pattern of densities. We present a systematic account of the factors which might naturally influence the pattern of density—in the hope of showing what kind of coherent pattern might be sensible and useful. The argument has five steps.

1. We may assume, reasonably, that some kind of center, formed by local services, will occur at least once in every community of 7000. This center will typically be the kind we have called a SHOPPING STREET (32). In WEB OF SHOPPING (19) we have shown that shopping streets occur about once for every 10,000 persons.

2. From the arguments presented in SUBCULTURE BOUNDARY (13), we know that this center of activity, since it is a service, should occur in the boundary between subcultures, should help to form the boundary between subcultures, and should therefore be located in the area of the boundary—not *inside* the community, but *between* communities.

3. We know, also, that this center must be in just that part of the boundary which is closest to the center of the larger town or city. This follows from a dramatic and little known series of results which show that catch basins of shopping centers are not

circles, as one might naïvely suppose, but half-circles, with the half-circle on that side of the center away from the central city, because people always go to that shopping center which lies toward the center of their city, never to the one which lies toward the city's periphery.

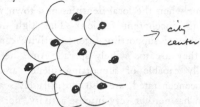

Brennan's catch basins.

This phenomenon was originally discovered by Brennan in his post-war studies of Wolverhampton (T. Brennan, *Midland City*, London: Dobson, 1948). It has, since then, been confirmed and studied by several writers, most notably Terence Lee, "Perceived Distance as a Function of Direction in the City," *Environment and Behavior*, June 1970, 40–51. Lee has shown that the phenomenon is not only caused by the fact that people are simply more familiar with the roads and paths that lie toward the center, and use them more often, but that their very perception of distance varies with direction, and that distances along lines toward the center are seen as much shorter than distances along lines away from the center.

Since we certainly want the community to correspond with the catch basin of its "center" it is essential, then, that the center be placed off-center—in fact, at that point in the community which lies toward the center of the larger city. This is, of course, compatible with the notion discussed already, that the center should lie in the boundary of the community.

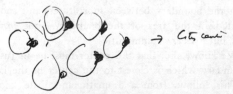

Eccentric centers.

4. Even though the center lies on one side of the community, forming a boundary of the community, we may also assume that the center does need to bulge into the community just a little. This follows from the fact that, even though services do need to be in the boundary of the community, not in its middle, still, people do have some need for the psychological center of their community to be at least somewhere toward the geometric center of gravity. If we make the boundary bulge toward the geometric center, then this axis will naturally form a center—and, further, its catch basin, according to the data given above, will correspond almost perfectly with the community.

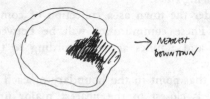

The inward bulge.

5. Finally, although we know that the center needs to be mainly in the boundary, we do not know exactly just how large it needs to be. At the edge of the city, where the overall density is low—the center will be small. At the center of the city, where the overall density is higher, it will be larger, because the greater density of population supports more services. In both cases, it will be in the boundary. If it is too large to be contained at one point, it will naturally extend itself along the boundary, but still within the boundary, thus forming a lune, a partial horseshoe, long or short, according to its position in the greater city.

A partial horseshoe.

These rules are rather simple. If we follow them, we shall find a beautiful gradient of overlapping imbricated horseshoes, not unlike the scales of a fish. If the city gradually gets this highly coherent structure, then we can be sure that the articulation of dense areas, and areas of little density, will be so clear that both activity and quiet can exist, each intense, unmixed, and each available to everyone.

Therefore:

Encourage growth and the accumulation of density to form a clear configuration of peaks and valleys according to the following rules:

1. **Consider the town as a collection of communities of 7000. These communities will be between ¼ mile across and 2 miles across, according to their overall density.**

2. **Mark that point in the boundary of each community which is closest to the nearest major urban center. This point will be the peak of the density, and the core of the "eccentric" nucleus.**

3. **Allow the high density to bulge in from the boundary, toward the center of gravity of the community, thus enlarging the eccentric nucleus toward the center.**

4. **Continue this high density to form a ridge around the boundary in horseshoe fashion—with the length of the horseshoe dependent on the overall mean gross density, at that part of the city, and the bulge of the horseshoe toward the center of the region, so that the horseshoes form a gradient, according to their position in the region. Those close to a major downtown are almost complete; those further away are only half complete; and those furthest from centers are shrunken to a point.**

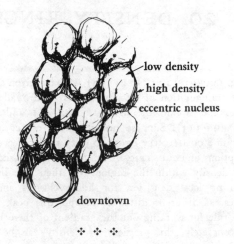

low density
high density
eccentric nucleus

downtown

❖ ❖ ❖

Given this overall configuration, now calculate the average densities at different distances from this ridge of high density, according to the computations given in the next pattern—DENSITY RINGS (29); keep major shopping streets and promenades toward the dense part of the horseshoe—ACTIVITY NODES (30), PROMENADE (31), SHOPPING STREET (32); and keep quiet areas toward the open part of the horseshoe—SACRED SITES (24), QUIET BACKS (59), STILL WATER (71). . . .

29   DENSITY RINGS*

. . . in ECCENTRIC NUCLEUS (28) we have given a general form
for the configuration of density "peaks" and "valleys," with respect to the MOSAIC OF SUBCULTURES (8) and SUBCULTURE
BOUNDARIES (13). Suppose now that the center of commercial
activity in a COMMUNITY OF 7000 (12) is placed according to the
prescriptions of ECCENTRIC NUCLEUS (28), and according to the
overall density within the region. We then face the problem of
establishing local densities, for house clusters and work communities, at different distances around this peak. This pattern
gives a rule for working out the gradient of these local densities.
Most concretely, this gradient of density can be specified, by
drawing rings at different distances from the main center of
activity and then assigning different densities to each ring, so
that the densities in the succeeding rings create the gradient of
density. The gradient will vary from community to community—
both according to a community's position in the region, and according to the cultural background of the people.

**People want to be close to shops and services, for excite-
ment and convenience. And they want to be away from
services, for quiet and green. The exact balance of these
two desires varies from person to person, but in the aggregate it is the balance of these two desires which determines the gradient of housing densities in a neighborhood.**

In order to be precise about the gradient of housing densities,
let us agree at once, to analyze the densities by means of three
concentric semi-circular rings, of equal radial thickness, around
the main center of activity.
[We make them semi-circles, rather than full circles, since it has
been shown, empirically, that the catch basin of a given local

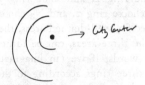

Rings of equal thickness.

center is a half-circle, on the side away from the city—see discussion in ECCENTRIC NUCLEUS (28) and the references to Brennan and Lee given in that pattern. However, even if you do not accept this finding, and wish to assume that the circles are full circles, the following analysis remains essentially unchanged.] We now define a density gradient, as a set of three densities, one for each of the three rings.

A density gradient.

Imagine that the three rings of some actual neighborhood have densities D_1, D_2, D_3. And assume, now, that a new person moves into this neighborhood. As we have said, within the given density gradient, he will choose to live in that ring, where his liking for green and quiet just balances his liking for access to shops and public services. This means that each person is essentially faced with a choice among three alternative density-distance combinations:

Ring 1. The density D_1, with a distance of about R_1 to shops.
Ring 2. The density D_2, with a distance of about R_2 to shops.
Ring 3. The density D_3, with a distance of about R_3 to shops.

Now, of course, each person will make a different choice—according to his own personal preference for the balance of density and distance. Let us imagine, just for the sake of argument, that all the people in the neighborhood are asked to make this choice (forgetting, for a moment, which houses are available). Some will

choose ring 1, some ring 2, and some ring 3. Suppose that N_1 choose ring 1, N_2 choose ring 2, and N_3 choose ring 3. Since the three rings have specific, well-defined areas, the numbers of people who have chosen the three areas, can be turned into hypothetical densities. In other words, if we (in imagination) distribute the people among the three rings according to their choices, we can work out the hypothetical densities which would occur in the three rings as a result.

Now we are suddenly faced with two fascinating possibilities:
I. These new densities are different from the actual densities.
II. These new densities are the same as the actual densities.

Case I is much more likely to occur. But this is unstable—since people's choices will tend to change the densities. Case II, which is less likely to occur, is stable—since it means that people, choosing freely, will together re-create the very same pattern of density within which they have made these choices. This distinction is fundamental.

If we assume that a given neighborhood, with a given total area, must accommodate a certain number of people (given by the average density of people at that point in the region), then there is just *one* configuration of densities which is stable in this sense. We now describe a computational procedure which can be used to obtain this stable density configuration.

Before we explain the computational procedure, we must explain how very fundamental and important this kind of stable density configuration is.

In today's world, where density gradients are usually not stable, in our sense, most people are forced to live under conditions where the balance of quiet and activity does not correspond to their wishes or their needs, because the total number of available houses and apartments at different distances is inappropriate. What happens, then, is that the rich, who can afford to pay for what they want, are able to find houses and apartments with the balance that they want; the not so rich and poor are forced to take the leavings. All this is made legitimate by the middle-class economics of "ground rent"—the idea that land at different distances from centers of activity, commands different prices, because more or less people want to be at those distances. But actually the fact of differential ground rent is an economic

mechanism which springs up, within an unstable density configuration, to compensate for its instability.

We want to point out that in a neighborhood with a stable density configuration (stable in our sense of the word), the land would not need to cost different prices at different distances, because the total available number of houses in each ring would exactly correspond to the number of people who wanted to live at those distances. With demand equal to supply in every ring, the ground rents, or the price of land, could be the same in every ring, and everyone, rich and poor, could be certain of having the balance they require.

We now come to the problem of computing the stable densities for a given neighborhood. The stability depends on very subtle psychological forces; so far as we know these forces cannot be represented in any psychologically accurate way by mathematical equations, and it is therefore, at least for the moment, impossible to give a mathematical model for the stable density. Instead, we have chosen to use the fact that each person can make choices about his required balance of activity and quiet, and to use people's choices, within a simple game, as the source of the computation. In short, we have constructed a game, which allows one to obtain the stable density configuration within a few minutes. This game essentially simulates the behavior of the real system, and is, we believe, far more reliable than any mathematical computation.

DENSITY GRADIENTS GAME

1. First draw a map of the three concentric half rings. Make it a half-circle—if you accept the arguments of ECCENTRIC NUCLEUS (28)—otherwise a full circle Smooth this half-circle to fit the horseshoe of the highest density—mark its center as the center of that horseshoe.

2. If the overall radius of the half-circle is R, then the mean radii of the three rings are R_1, R_2, R_3 given by:

$$R_1 = R/6$$
$$R_2 = 3R/6$$
$$R_3 = 5R/6$$

3. Make up a board for the game, which has the three concentric circles shown on it, with the radii marked in blocks, so people can understand them easily, i.e., 1000 feet = 3 blocks.

4. Decide on the total population of this neighborhood. This is

the same as settling on an *overall* average net density for the area. It will have to be roughly compatible with the overall pattern of density in the region. Let us say that the total population of the community is N families.

5. Find ten people who are roughly similar to the people in the community—vis-à-vis cultural habits, background, and so on. If possible, they should be ten of the people in the actual community itself.

6. Show the players a set of photographs of areas that show typical best examples of different population densities (in families per gross acre), and leave these photographs on display throughout the game so that people can use them when they make their choices.

7. Give each player a disk, which he can place on the board in one of the three rings.

8. Now, to start the game, decide what percentage of the total population is to be in each of the three rings. It doesn't matter what percentages you choose to start with—they will soon right themselves as the game gets under way—but, for the sake of simplicity, choose multiples of 10 per cent for each ring, i.e., 10 per cent in ring 1, 30 per cent in ring 2, 60 per cent in ring 3.

9. Now translate these percentages into actual densities of families per net acre. Since you will have to do this many times during the course of the game, it is advisable to construct a table which translates percentages directly into densities. You can make up such a table by inserting the values for N and R which you have chosen for your community into the formulae below. The formulae are based on the simple arithmetic of area, and population. R is expressed in hundreds of yards—roughly in blocks. The densities are expressed in *families per gross acre*. Multiply each ring density by a number between 1 and 10, according to the per cent in that ring. Thus, if there are 30 per cent in ring 3, the density there is 3 times the entry in the formulae, or $24N/5\pi R^2$.

$$10\%$$

Ring 1 $8N/\pi R^2$
Ring 2 $8N/3\pi R^2$
Ring 3 $8N/5\pi R^2$

10. Once you have found the proper densities, from the formulae, write them on three slips of paper, and place these slips into their appropriate rings, on the game board.

11. The slips define a tentative density configuration for the community. Each ring has a certain typical distance from the center. And each ring has a density. Ask people to look carefully at the pictures which represent these densities, and then to decide which of the three rings gives them the best balance of quiet and green, as against access to shops. Ask each person to place his disk in the ring he chooses.

12. When all ten disks are on the board, this defines a new distribution of population. Probably, it is different from the one you started with. Now make up a new set of percentages, half-way between the one you originally defined, and the one which people's disks define, and, again, round off the percentages to the nearest 10 per cent. Here is an example of the way you can get new percentages.

Old percentages	People's disks		New percentages
10%	3 = 30%	$\longrightarrow$	20%
30%	4 = 40%	$\longrightarrow$	30%
60%	3 = 30%	$\longrightarrow$	50%

As you see, the new ones are not perfectly half-way between the other two—but as near as you can get, and still have multiples of ten.

13. Now go back to step 9, and go through 9, 10, 11, 12 again and again, until the percentages defined by people's disks are the same as the ones you defined for that round. If you turn these last stable percentages into densities, you have found the stable density configuration for this community. Stop, and have a drink all round.

In our experiments, we have found that this game reaches a stable state very quickly indeed. Ten people, in a few minutes, can define a stable density distribution. We have presented the results of one set of games in the table which follows below.

STABLE DENSITY DISTRIBUTIONS FOR
DIFFERENT SIZED COMMUNITIES

These figures are for semi-circular communities.

Radius in blocks	Population in families	Density in families per gross acre		
		Ring 1	Ring 2	Ring 3
2	150	15	9	5
3	150	7	5	2
3	300	21	7	5
4	300	7	3	2
4	600	29	7	4
6	600	15	4	2
6	1200	36	9	3
9	1200	18	5	1

It is essential to recognize that the densities given in this table cannot wisely be used just as they stand. The figures will vary with the exact geometry of the neighborhood and with different cultural attitudes in different subcultures. For this reason, we consider it essential that the people of a given community, who want to apply this pattern, play the game themselves, in order to find a stable gradient of densities for their own situation. The numbers we have given above are more for the sake of illustration than anything else.

Therefore:

Once the nucleus of a community is clearly placed— define rings of decreasing local housing density around this nucleus. If you cannot avoid it, choose the densities from the foregoing table. But, much better, if you can possibly manage it, play the density rings game, to obtain these densities, from the intuitions of the very people who are going to live in the community.

❖ ❖ ❖

Within the rings of density, encourage housing to take the form of housing clusters—self-governing cooperatives of 8 to 15 households, their physical size varying according to the density— HOUSE CLUSTER (37). According to the densities in the different rings, build these houses as free-standing houses—HOUSE CLUSTER (37), ROW HOUSES (38), or higher density clusters of housing— HOUSING HILL (39). Keep public spaces—PROMENADE (31), SMALL PUBLIC SQUARES (61)—to those areas which have a high enough density around them to keep them alive—PEDESTRIAN DENSITY (123). . . .

30 ACTIVITY NODES**

. . . this pattern forms those essential nodes of life which help to generate IDENTIFIABLE NEIGHBORHOOD (14), PROMENADE (31), NETWORK OF PATHS AND CARS (52), and PEDESTRIAN STREET (100). To understand its action, imagine that a community and its boundary are growing under the influence of COMMUNITY OF 7000 (12), SUBCULTURE BOUNDARY (13), IDENTIFIABLE NEIGHBORHOOD (14), NEIGHBORHOOD BOUNDARY (15), ECCENTRIC NUCLEUS (28), and DENSITY RINGS (29). As they grow, certain "stars" begin to form, where the most important paths meet. These stars are potentially the vital spots of a community. The growth of these stars and of the paths which form them need to be guided to form genuine community crossroads.

Community facilities scattered individually through the city do nothing for the life of the city.

One of the greatest problems in existing communities is the fact that the available public life in them is spread so thin that it has no impact on the community. It is not in any real sense available to the members of the community. Studies of pedestrian behavior make it clear that people seek out concentrations of other people, whenever they are available (for instance, Jan Gehl, "Mennesker til Fods (Pedestrians)," *Arkitekten*, No. 20, 1968).

To create these concentrations of people in a community, facilities must be grouped densely round very small public squares which can function as nodes—with all pedestrian movement in the community organized to pass through these nodes. Such nodes require four properties.

First, each node must draw together the main paths in the surrounding community. The major pedestrian paths should converge on the square, with minor paths funneling into the major ones, to create the basic star-shape of the pattern. This is much harder to do than one might imagine. To give an example of the difficulty which arises when we try to build this relationship into a town, we show the following plan—a scheme of

ours for housing in Peru—in which the paths are all convergent on a very small number of squares.

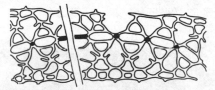

Public paths converge on centers of action.

This is not a very good plan—it is too stiff and formal. But it is possible to achieve the same relationship in a far more relaxed manner. In any case the relationship between paths, community facilities, and squares is vital and hard to achieve. It must be taken seriously, from the very outset, as a major feature of the city.

Second, to keep the activity concentrated, it is essential to make the squares rather small, smaller than one might imagine. A square of about 45 × 60 feet can keep the normal pace of public life well concentrated. This figure is discussed in detail under SMALL PUBLIC SQUARE (61).

Third, the facilities grouped around any one node must be chosen for their symbiotic relationships. It is not enough merely to group communal functions in so-called community centers. For example, church, cinema, kindergarten, and police station are all community facilities, but they do not support one another mutually. Different people go to them, at different times, with different things in mind. There is no point in grouping them together. To create intensity of action, the facilities which are placed together round any one node must function in a cooperative manner, and must attract the same kinds of people, at the same times of day. For example, when evening entertainments are grouped together, the people who are having a night out can use any one of them, and the total concentration of action increases—see NIGHT LIFE (33). When kindergartens and small parks and gardens are grouped together, young families with children may use either, so their total attraction is increased.

Fourth, these activity nodes should be distributed rather evenly

across the community, so that no house or workplace is more than a few hundred yards from one. In this way a contrast of "busy and quiet" can be achieved at a small scale—and large dead areas can be avoided.

Nodes of different size.

Therefore:

Create nodes of activity throughout the community, spread about 300 yards apart. First identify those existing spots in the community where action seems to concentrate itself. Then modify the layout of the paths in the community to bring as many of them through these spots as possible. This makes each spot function as a "node" in the

path network. Then, at the center of each node, make a small public square, and surround it with a combination of community facilities and shops which are mutually supportive.

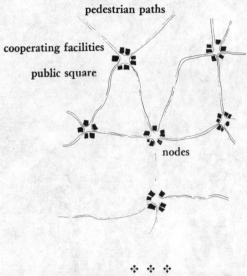

pedestrian paths

cooperating facilities

public square

nodes

❖ ❖ ❖

Connect those centers which are most dense, with a wider, more important path for strolling—PROMENADE (31); make special centers for night activities—NIGHT LIFE (33); whenever new paths are built, make certain that they pass through the centers, so that they intensify the life still further—PATHS AND GOALS (120); and differentiate the paths so they are wide near the centers and smaller away from them—DEGREES OF PUBLICNESS (36). At the heart of every center, build a small public square—SMALL PUBLIC SQUARES (61), and surround each square with an appropriate mix of mutually self-reinforcing facilities—WORK COMMUNITY (41), UNIVERSITY AS A MARKETPLACE (43), LOCAL TOWN HALL (44), HEALTH CENTER (47), BIRTH PLACES (65), TEENAGE SOCIETY (84), SHOPFRONT SCHOOL (85), INDIVIDUALLY OWNED SHOPS (87), STREET CAFE (88), BEER HALL (90), FOOD STANDS (93). . . .

31 PROMENADE**

. . . assume now that there is an urban area, subdivided into subcultures and communities each with its boundaries. Each subculture in the MOSAIC OF SUBCULTURES (8), and each COMMUNITY OF 7000 (12) has a promenade as its backbone. And each promenade helps to form ACTIVITY NODES (30) along its length, by generating the flow of people which the activity nodes need in order to survive.

❖ ❖ ❖

Each subculture needs a center for its public life: a place where you can go to see people, and to be seen.

The promenade, "paseo," "passegiata," evening stroll, is common in the small towns of Italy, Spain, Mexico, Greece, Yugoslavia, Sicily, and South America. People go there to walk up and down, to meet their friends, to stare at strangers, and to let strangers stare at them.

Throughout history there have been places in the city where people who shared a set of values could go to get in touch with each other. These places have always been like street theaters: they invite people to watch others, to stroll and browse, and to loiter:

In Mexico, in any small town plaza every Thursday and Sunday night with the band playing and the weather mild, the boys walk this way, the girls walk that, around and around, and the mothers and fathers sit on iron-scrolled benches and watch. (Ray Bradbury, "The girls walk this way; the boys walk that way . . ." *West*, Los Angeles Times Sunday Magazine, April 5, 1970.)

In all these places the beauty of the promenade is simply this: people with a shared way of life gather together to rub shoulders and confirm their community.

Is the promenade in fact a purely Latin institution? Our experiments suggest that it is not. The fact is that the kinds of promenades where this strolling happens are not common in a city, and they are especially uncommon in a sprawling urban region. But experiments by Luis Racionero at the Department of

Architecture at the University of California, Berkeley, have shown that wherever the possibility of this public contact *does* exist, people will seek it, as long as it is close enough. Racionero interviewed 37 people in several parts of San Francisco, living various distances from a promenade, and found that people who lived within 20 minutes used it, while people who lived more than 20 minutes away did not.

	Use the promenade	Do not use the promenade
People who live less than 20 minutes away	13	1
People who live more than 20 minutes away	5	18

It seems that people, of all cultures, may have a general need for the kind of human mixing which the promenade makes possible; but that if it is too far, the effort to get there simply outweighs the importance of the need. In short, to make sure that all the people in a city can satisfy this need, there must be promenades at frequent intervals.

Exactly how frequent should they be? Racionero establishes 20 minutes as the upper limit, but his survey does not investigate frequency of use. We know that the closer the promenade is, the more often people will use it. We guess that if the promenade is within 10 minutes or less, people will use it often—perhaps even once or twice a week.

The relation between the catch basin of the promenade, and the actual physical paved area of the promenade itself, is extremely critical. We show in PEDESTRIAN DENSITY (123), that places with less than one person for every 150 to 300 square feet of paved surface, will seem dead and uninviting. It is therefore essential to be certain that the number of people who might, typically, be out strolling on the promenade, is large enough to maintain this pedestrian density along its length. To check this relation, we calculate as follows:

A 10-minute walk amounts to roughly 1500 feet (150 feet per minute), which is probably also about the right length for the promenade itself. This means that the catch basin for a promenade has a shape roughly like this:

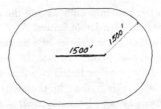

A promenade and its catch basin.

This area contains 320 acres. If we assume an average density of 50 people per gross acre, then there are 16,000 people in the area. If one-fifth of this population uses the promenade once a week, for an hour between 6 and 10 p.m., then at any given moment between those hours, there are some 100 people on the promenade. If it is 1500 feet long, at 300 square feet per person, it can therefore be 20 feet wide, at the most, and would be better if it were closer to 10 feet wide. It is feasible, but only just.

We see then, that a promenade 1500 feet long, with the catch basin we have defined and the population density stated, should be able to maintain a lively density of activity, provided that it is not more than about 20 feet wide. *We want to emphasize that a promenade will not work unless the pedestrian density is high enough, and that a calculation of this kind must always be made to check its feasibility.*

The preceding figures are meant to be illustrative. They establish a rough order of magnitude for promenades and their catch basin populations. But we have also seen successful promenades for populations of 2000 (a fishing village in Peru); and we have seen a promenade for 2,000,000 (Las Ramblas in Barcelona). They both work, although they are very different in character. The small one with its catch basin of 2000 works, because the cultural habit of the paseo is so strong there, a higher percentage of the people use it more often, and the density of people on the promenade is less than we would imagine—it is so beautiful that people enjoy it even if it is not so crowded. The large one works as a citywide event. People are willing to drive a long distance to it—they may not come as often, but when they do, it is worth the ride—it is exciting—packed—teeming with people.

We imagine the pattern of promenades in a city to be just as varied—a continuum ranging from small local promenades serv-

ing 2000 people to large intense ones serving the entire city—each different in character and density of action.

Finally, what are the characteristics of a successful promenade? Since people come to see people and to be seen, a promenade must have a high density of pedestrians using it. It must therefore be associated with places that in themselves attract people, for example, clusters of eating places and small shops.

A promenade in Paris.

Further, even though the real reasons for coming might have to do with seeing people and being seen, people find it easier to take a walk if they have a "destination." This destination may be real, like a coke shop or cafe, or it may be partly imaginary, "let's walk round the block." But the promenade must provide people with a strong goal.

It is also important that people do not have to walk too far between the most important points along the promenade. Informal observation suggests that any point which is more than 150 feet from activity becomes unsavory and unused. In short, good promenades are part of a path through the most active parts of the community; they are suitable as destinations for an evening walk; the walk is not too long, and nowhere on it desolate: no point of the stroll is more than 150 feet from a hub of activity.

A variety of facilities will function as destinations along the promenade: ice cream parlors, coke shops, churches, public gardens, movie houses, bars, volleyball courts. Their potential will depend on the extent to which it is possible to make provisions for people to stay: widening of pedestrian paths, planting of trees, walls to lean against, stairs and benches and niches for sitting,

opening of street fronts to provide sidewalk cafes, or displays of activities or goods where people might like to linger.

Therefore:

Encourage the gradual formation of a promenade at the heart of every community, linking the main activity nodes, and placed centrally, so that each point in the community is within 10 minutes' walk of it. Put main points of attraction at the two ends, to keep a constant movement up and down.

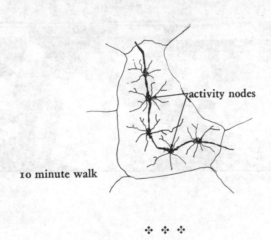

❖ ❖ ❖

No matter how large the promenade is, there must be enough people coming to it to make it dense with action, and this can be precisely calculated by the formula of PEDESTRIAN DENSITY (123). The promenade is mainly marked by concentrations of activity along its length—ACTIVITY NODES (30); naturally, some of these will be open at night—NIGHT LIFE (33); and somewhere on the promenade there will be a concentration of shops—SHOPPING STREET (32). It might also be appropriate to include CARNIVAL (58) and DANCING IN THE STREET (63) in very large promenades. The detailed physical character of the promenade is given by PEDESTRIAN STREET (100) and PATH SHAPE (121). . . . .

173

32 SHOPPING STREET*

. . . this pattern helps to complete the MAGIC OF THE CITY (10) and PROMENADE (31). And, each time a shopping street gets built, it will also help to generate the WEB OF SHOPPING (19).

❖ ❖ ❖

Shopping centers depend on access: they need locations near major traffic arteries. However, the shoppers themselves don't benefit from traffic: they need quiet, comfort, and convenience, and access from the pedestrian paths in the surrounding area.

This simple and obvious conflict has almost never been effectively resolved. On the one hand, we have shopping strips. Here the shops are arranged along the major traffic arteries. This is convenient for cars, but it is not convenient for pedestrians. A strip does not have the characteristics which pedestrian areas need.

Shopping strip—for cars.

On the other hand, we have those "pre-automobile" shopping streets in the center of old towns. Here the pedestrians' needs are taken into account, at least partially. But, as the town spreads out and the streets become congested, they are inconvenient to reach; and again the cars dominate the narrow streets.

The modern solution is the shopping center. They are usually located along, or near to, major traffic arteries, so they

Old shopping street—inconvenient for cars and people.

are convenient for cars; and they often have pedestrian precincts in them—so that, in theory at least, they are comfortable
and convenient for pedestrians. But they are usually isolated, in
the middle of a vast parking lot, and thereby disconnected from
the pedestrian fabric of the surrounding areas. In short, you cannot walk to them.

New shopping center—only for cars.

To be convenient for traffic, and convenient for people walking, and connected to the fabric of the surrounding town, the
shops must be arranged along a street, itself pedestrian, but
opening off a major traffic artery, perhaps two, with parking behind, or underneath, to keep the cars from isolating the shops
from surrounding areas.

We observed this pattern growing spontaneously in certain
neighborhoods of Lima, Peru: a wide road is set down for automobile traffic, and the shops begin to form themselves, in
pedestrian streets that are perpendicular off-shoots off this road.

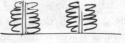

Shopping streets growing spontaneously in Lima, Peru.

This pattern is also the form of the famous Stroget in Copenhagen. The Stroget is the central shopping spine for the city; it is extremely long—almost a mile—and is entirely pedestrian, only cut periodically by roads which run at right angles to it.

Therefore:

Encourage local shopping centers to grow in the form of short pedestrian streets, at right angles to major roads and opening off these roads—with parking behind the shops, so that the cars can pull directly off the road, and yet not harm the shopping street.

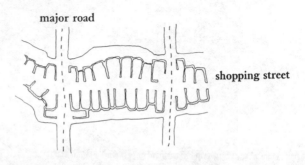

177

Treat the physical character of the street like any other PEDES-
TRIAN STREET (100) on the NETWORK OF PATHS AND CARS (52),
at right angles to major PARALLEL ROADS (23); have as many
shops as small as possible —INDIVIDUALLY OWNED SHOPS (87);
where the shopping street crosses the road, make the crossing wide,
giving priority to the pedestrians— ROAD CROSSING (54); parking
can easily be provided by a single row of parking spaces in an
alley lying behind the shops—all along the backs of the shops, off
the alley, with the parking spaces walled, and perhaps even given
canvas roofs, so that they don't destroy the area—SHIELDED PARK-
ING (97), CANVAS ROOFS (244). Make sure that every shopping
street includes a MARKET OF MANY SHOPS (46), and some HOUSING
IN BETWEEN (48). . . .

33 NIGHT LIFE*

. . . every community has some kind of public night life—MAGIC OF THE CITY (10), COMMUNITY OF 7000 (12). If there is a promenade in the community, the night life is probably along the promenade, at least in part—PROMENADE (31). This pattern describes the details of the concentration of night time activities.

❖ ❖ ❖

Most of the city's activities close down at night; those which stay open won't do much for the night life of the city unless they are together.

This pattern is drawn from the following seven points:

1. People enjoy going out at night; a night on the town is something special.

2. If evening activities such as movies, cafes, ice cream parlors, gas stations, and bars are scattered throughout the community, each one by itself cannot generate enough attraction.

One bar by itself is a lonely place at night.

3. Many people do *not* go out at night because they feel they have no place to go. They do not feel like going out to a specific establishment, *but they do feel like going out.* An evening center, particularly when it is full of light, functions as a focus for such people.

4. Fear of the dark, especially in those places far away from one's own back yard, is a common experience, and quite simple to understand. Throughout our evolution night has been a time to stay quiet and protected, not a time to move about freely.

A cluster of night spots creates life in the street.

5. Nowadays this instinct is anchored in the fact that at night street crimes are most prevalent in places where there are too few pedestrians to provide natural surveillance, but enough pedestrians to make it worth a thief's while, in other words, dark, isolated night spots invite crime. A paper by Shlomo Angel, "The Ecology of Night Life" (Center for Environmental Structure, Berkeley, 1968), shows the highest number of street crimes occurring in those areas where night spots are scattered. Areas of very low or very high night pedestrian density are subject to much less crime.

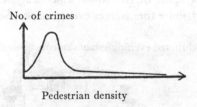

Isolated night spots invite crime.

6. It is difficult to estimate the exact number of night spots that need to be grouped to create a sense of night life. From observation, we guess that it takes about six, minimum.

7. On the other hand, massive evening centers, combining evening services which a person could not possibly use on the same night, are alienating. For example, in New York the Lincoln Center for the Performing Arts makes a big splash at night, but it makes no sense. No one is going to the ballet and the theater and a concert during one night on the town. And centralizing these places robs the city as a whole of several centers of night life.

All these arguments together suggest small, scattered centers of mutually enlivening night spots, the services grouped to form cheery squares, with lights and places to loiter, where people can spend several hours in an interesting way. Here are some examples of small groups of mutually sustaining night activities.

A movie theater, a restaurant and a bar, and a bookstore open till midnight; a smoke shop.

A laundromat, liquor store and cafe; and a meeting hall and beer hall.

Lodge hall, bowling alley, bar, playhouse.

A terminal, a diner, hotels, nightclubs, casinos.

Therefore:

Knit together shops, amusements, and services which are open at night, along with hotels, bars, and all-night diners to form centers of night life: well-lit, safe, and lively places that increase the intensity of pedestrian activity at night by drawing all the people who are out at night to the same few spots in the town. Encourage these evening centers to distribute themselves evenly across the town.

clustered evening establishments

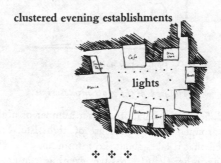

❖ ❖ ❖

Treat the physical layout of the night life area exactly like any other ACTIVITY NODE (30), except that *all* of its establishments are open at night. The evening establishments might include LOCAL TOWN HALL (44), CARNIVAL (58), DANCING IN THE STREET (63), STREET CAFE (88), BEER HALL (90), TRAVELER'S INN (91). . . .

. . . this pattern defines the points which generate the WEB OF
PUBLIC TRANSPORTATION (16). It also helps to complete LOCAL
TRANSPORT AREAS (11) by guaranteeing the possibility of interchanges at the center of each transport area, where people can
change from their bikes, or local mini-buses, to the long distance
transit lines that connect different transport areas to one another.

❖ ❖ ❖

**Interchanges play a central role in public transportation.
Unless the interchanges are working properly, the public
transportation system will not be able to sustain itself.**

Everyone needs public transportation sometimes. But it is the
steady users who keep it going. If the steady users do not keep it
going, then there is no system for the occasional user. To maintain
a steady flow of users, interchanges must be extremely convenient
and easy to use: 1. Workplaces and the housing for people who
especially need public transportation must be distributed rather
evenly around interchanges. 2. The interchanges must connect up
with the surrounding flow of pedestrian street life. 3. It must be
easy to change from one mode of travel to another.

In more detail:

1. Workers are the bread and butter of the transportation
system. If the system is to be healthy, all the workplaces in town
must be within walking distance of the interchanges. Furthermore, the distribution of workplaces around interchanges should
be more or less even—see SCATTERED WORK (9). When they are
concentrated around one or two, the rush hour flow crowds the
trains, and creates inefficiencies in the system as a whole.

Furthermore, some of the area around interchanges should be
given over to houses for those people who rely entirely on public
transportation—especially old people. Old people depend on
public transportation; they make up a large proportion of the
system's regular users. To meet their needs, the area around interchanges must be zoned so that the kind of housing that suits
them will develop there—OLD PEOPLE EVERYWHERE (40).

2. The interchange must be convenient for people walking from their homes and jobs, and it must be safe. People will not use an interchange if it is dingy, derelict, and deserted. This means that the interchange must be continuous with local pedestrian life. Parking lots must be kept to one side, so that people do not have to walk across them to get to the station. And there must be enough shops and kiosks in the interchange, to keep a steady flow of people moving in and out of it and through it.

3. If the system is going to be successful, there must be no more than a few minutes' walk—600 feet at the most—between points of transfer. And the distance should decrease as the trips become more local: from bus to bus, 100 feet maximum; from rapid transit to bus, 200 feet maximum; from train to rapid transit, 300 feet maximum. In rainy climates the connecting paths should be almost entirely covered—ARCADES (119). What's more, the most important transfer connections should not involve crossing streets: if necessary sink the roads or build bridges to make the transfer smooth.

For details on the organization of interchanges, see "390 Requirements for Rapid Transit Stations," Center for Environmental Structure, 1964, partly published in "Relational Complexes in Architecture" (Christopher Alexander, Van Maren King, Sara Ishikawa, Michael Baker, *Architectural Record*, September 1966, pp. 185–90).

Therefore:

At every interchange in the web of transportation follow these principles:

1. **Surround the interchange with workplaces and housing types which specially need public transportation.**

2. **Keep the interior of the interchange continuous with the exterior pedestrian network, and maintain this continuity by building in small shops and kiosks and by keeping parking to one side.**

3. **Keep the transfer distance between different modes of transport down to 300 feet wherever possible, with an absolute maximum of 600 feet.**

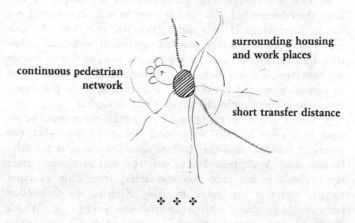

continuous pedestrian network

surrounding housing and work places

short transfer distance

❖ ❖ ❖

Recognize that the creation of workplaces around every interchange contributes to the development of SCATTERED WORK (9). Place HOUSING HILLS (39), OLD PEOPLE EVERYWHERE (40), and WORK COMMUNITIES (41) round the interchange; treat the outside of the interchange as an ACTIVITY NODE (30) to assure its continuity with the pedestrian network; treat the transfers as ARCADES (119) where necessary to keep them under cover; give every interchange a BUS STOP (92) on the MINI-BUS (20) network. . . .

around these centers, provide for the growth of housing in the form of clusters, based on face to face human groups:

35. HOUSEHOLD MIX

36. DEGREES OF PUBLICNESS

37. HOUSE CLUSTER

38. ROW HOUSES

39. HOUSING HILL

40. OLD PEOPLE EVERYWHERE

35 HOUSEHOLD MIX*

. . . the mix of households in an area does almost more than anything else to generate, or destroy, the character of an IDENTIFIABLE NEIGHBORHOOD (14), of a HOUSE CLUSTER (37), of a WORK COMMUNITY (41), or, most generally of all, of a LIFE CYCLE (26). The question is, what kind of mix should a well-balanced neighborhood contain?

❖ ❖ ❖

No one stage in the life cycle is self-sufficient.

People need support and confirmation from people who have reached a different stage in the life cycle, at the same time that they also need support from people who are at the same stage as they are themselves.

However, the needs which generate separation tend to overwhelm the need for mixture. Present housing patterns tend to keep different types of households segregated from each other. There are vast areas of two-bedroom houses, other areas of studio and one-bedroom apartments, other areas of three- and four-bedroom houses. This means that we have corresponding areas of single people, couples, and small families with children, segregated by type.

The effects of household segregation are profound. In the pattern LIFE CYCLE (26), we have suggested that normal growth through the stages of life requires contact, at each stage, with people and institutions from *all* the other ages of man. Such contact is completely foiled if the housing mix in one's neighborhood is skewed toward one or two stages only. On the other hand, when the balance of life cycles is well related to the kinds of housing that are available in a neighborhood, the possibilities for contact become concrete. Each person can find in the face-to-face life of his neighborhood at least passing contact with people from every stage of life. Teenagers see young couples, old people watch the very young, people living alone draw sustenance from large families, youngsters look to the middle-aged for models, and so on: it is all a medium through which people feel their way through life.

This need for a mix of housing must be offset against the need to be near people similar in age and way of life to oneself. Taking these two needs together, what is the right balance for the housing mix?

The right balance can be derived straightforwardly from the statistics of the region. First, determine the percentage of each household type for the region as a whole; second, use the same percentages to guide the gradual growth of the housing mix within the neighborhood. For example, if 40 per cent of a metropolitan region's households are families, 25 per cent are couples, 20 per cent are individuals, and 10 per cent group households, then we would expect the houses in each neighborhood to have roughly the same balance.

Let us ask, finally, how large a group should the mix be applied to? We might try to create a mix in every house (obviously absurd), or in every cluster of a dozen houses, or in every neighborhood, or merely in every town (this last has almost no significant effect). We believe that the mix will only work if it exists in a human group small enough to have some internal political and human intercourse—this could be a cluster of a dozen families, or a neighborhood of 500 people.

Therefore:

Encourage growth toward a mix of household types in every neighborhood, and every cluster, so that one-person households, couples, families with children, and group households are side by side.

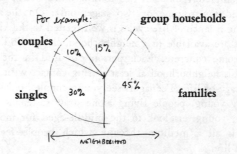

❖ ❖ ❖

Make especially sure there are provisions for old people in every neighborhood—OLD PEOPLE EVERYWHERE (40), and that even with this mix, young children will have enough playmates—CONNECTED PLAY (68); and build the details of the different kinds of households, according to the appropriate more detailed patterns to reinforce the mix—THE FAMILY (75), HOUSE FOR A SMALL FAMILY (76), HOUSE FOR A COUPLE (77), HOUSE FOR ONE PERSON (78). . . .

36 DEGREES OF PUBLICNESS**

. . . within the neighborhoods—IDENTIFIABLE NEIGHBORHOOD (14)—there are naturally some areas where life is rather concentrated ACTIVITY NODES (30), others where it is slower, and others in between—DENSITY RINGS (29). It is essential to differentiate groups of houses and the paths which lead to them according to this gradient.

❖ ❖ ❖

People are different, and the way they want to place their houses in a neighborhood is one of the most basic kinds of difference.

Some people want to live where the action is. Others want more isolation. This corresponds to a basic human personality dimension, which could be called the "extrovert-introvert" dimension, or the "community loving–privacy loving" dimension. Those who want the action like being near services, near shops, they like a lively atmosphere outside their houses, and they are happy to have strangers going past their houses all the time. Those who want more isolation like being away from services and shops, enjoy a very small scale in the areas outside their houses, and don't want strangers going past their houses. (See for example, Nancy Marshall, "Orientations Toward Privacy: Environmental and Personality Components," James Madison College, Michigan State University, East Lansing, Michigan.)

The variation of different people along the extrovert-introvert dimension is very well described by Frank Hendricks and Malcolm MacNair in "Concepts of Environmental Quality Standards Based on Life Styles," report to the American Public Health Association, February 12, 1969, pp. 11–15. The authors identify several kinds of persons and characterize each by the relative amount of time spent in extroverted activities and in introverted activities. Francis Loetterle has shed further light on the problem in "Environment Attitudes and Social Life in Santa Clara County," Santa Clara County Planning Department, San Jose,

California, 1967. He asked 3300 households how far they wanted to be from various community services. The results were: 20 per cent of the households interviewed wanted to be located less than three blocks from commercial centers; 60 per cent wanted to be located between four and six blocks away; 20 per cent wanted to be located more than six blocks away (mean block size in Santa Clara County is 150 yards). The exact distances apply only to Santa Clara. But the overall result overwhelmingly supports our contention that people vary in this way and shows that they have quite different needs as far as the location and character of houses is concerned.

To make sure that the different kinds of people can find houses which satisfy their own particular desires, we suggest that each cluster of houses, and each neighborhood should have three kinds of houses, in about equal numbers: those which are nearest to the action, those which are half-way between, and those which are almost completely isolated. And, to support this pattern we need, also, three distinct kinds of paths:

1. Paths along services, wide and open for activities and crowds, paths that connect activities and encourage busy through traffic.

2. Paths remote from services, narrow and twisting, to discourage through traffic, with many at right angles and dead ends.

3. Intermediate types of paths linking the most remote and quiet paths to the most central and busy ones.

This pattern is as important in the design of a cluster of a few houses as it is in the design of a neighborhood. When we were helping a group of people to design their own cluster of houses, we first asked each person to consider his preference for location on the basis of extrovert-introvert. Three groups emerged: four "extroverts" who wished to be as near the pedestrian and community action as possible, four "introverts" who desired as much remoteness and privacy as possible, and the remaining four who wanted a bit of both. The site plan they made, using this pattern, is shown below, with the positions which the three kinds of people chose.

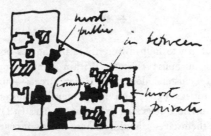

*In one house cluster: private homes,
public homes, and in-between.*

Therefore:

**Make a clear distinction between three kinds of homes
—those on quiet backwaters, those on busy streets, and
those that are more or less in between. Make sure that those
on quiet backwaters are on twisting paths, and that these
houses are themselves physically secluded; make sure that
the more public houses are on busy streets with many
people passing by all day long and that the houses themselves are relatively exposed to the passers-by. The in-
between houses may then be located on the paths half-way
between the other two. Give every neighborhood about
equal numbers of these three kinds of homes.**

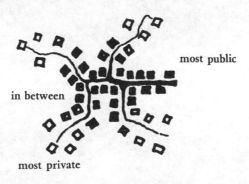

most public

in between

most private

❖ ❖ ❖

Use this pattern to help differentiate the houses both in neighborhoods and in house clusters. Within a neighborhood, place higher density clusters along the busier streets—HOUSING HILL (39), ROW HOUSES (38), and lower density clusters along the backwaters—HOUSE CLUSTER (37), ROW HOUSES (38). The actual busy streets themselves should either be PEDESTRIAN STREETS (100) or RAISED WALKS (55) on major roads; the backwaters GREEN STREETS (51), or narrow paths with a distinct PATH SHAPE (121). Where lively streets are wanted, make sure the density of housing is high enough to generate the liveliness—PEDESTRIAN DENSITY (123). . . .

. . . the fundamental unit of organization within the neighborhood—IDENTIFIABLE NEIGHBORHOOD (14)—is the cluster of a dozen houses. By varying the density and composition of different clusters, this pattern may also help to generate DENSITY RINGS (29), HOUSEHOLD MIX (35), and DEGREES OF PUBLICNESS (36).

❖ ❖ ❖

People will not feel comfortable in their houses unless a group of houses forms a cluster, with the public land between them jointly owned by all the householders.

When houses are arranged on streets, and the streets owned by the town, there is no way in which the land immediately outside the houses can reflect the needs of families and individuals living in those houses. The land will only gradually get shaped to meet their needs if they have direct control over the land and its repair.

This pattern is based on the idea that the cluster of land and homes immediately around one's own home is of special importance. It is the source for gradual differentiation of neighborhood land use, and it is the natural focus of neighborly interaction.

Herbert Gans, in *The Levittowners* (New York: Pantheon, 1967), has collected some powerful evidence for this tendency. Gans surveyed visiting habits on a typical block tract development. Of the 149 people he surveyed, *all of them were engaged in some pattern of regular visiting with their neighbors.* The interesting finding is the morphology of this visiting pattern.

Consider the following diagram—one like it can be made for almost every house in a tract. There is a house on either side, one or two across the street, and one directly behind, across a garden fence.

Ninety-three per cent of all the neighborhood visiting engaged in by the subjects is confined to this spatial cluster.

*On a typical block each home is
at the center of its own cluster.*

And when asked "Whom do you visit most?" 91 per cent
said the people they visit most are immediately across the street
or next door.

The beauty of this finding is its indication of the strength of
the *spatial* cluster to draw people together into neighborly contact. *The most obvious and tribal-like cluster—the homes on
either side and across the street—forms roughly a circle, and it
is there that most contact occurs.* And if we add to this shape
the home immediately behind, although it is separated by private
gardens and a fence, we can account for nearly all the visiting
that goes on in the Levittown neighborhood.

*We conclude that people continue to act according to the
laws of a spatial cluster, even when the block layout and the
neighborhood plan do their best to destroy this unit and make it
anonymous.*

Gans' data underscore our intuitions: people want to be part
of a neighborly spatial cluster; contact between people sharing
such a cluster is a vital function. And this need stands, even
when people are able to drive and see friends all over the city.

What about the size of the cluster? What is the appropriate
size? In Gans' investigations each home stands at the center of
a cluster of five or six other homes. But this is certainly not a
natural limit for a housing cluster since the Levittown block layouts are so confining. In our experience, when the siting of the
homes is attuned to the cluster pattern, the natural limit arises
entirely from the balance between the informality and coherence
of the group.

The clusters seem to work best if they have between 8 and 12 houses each. With one representative from each family, this is the number of people that can sit round a common meeting table, can talk to each other directly, face to face, and can therefore make wise decisions about the land they hold in common. With 8 or 10 households, people can meet over a kitchen table, exchange news on the street and in the gardens, and generally, without much special attention, keep in touch with the whole of the group. When there are more than 10 or 12 homes forming a cluster, this balance is strained. We therefore set an upper limit of around 12 on the number of households that can be naturally drawn into a cluster. Of course, the average size for clusters might be less, perhaps around 6 or 8; and clusters of 3, 4, or 5 homes can work perfectly well.

Now, assuming that a group of neighbors, or a neighborhood association, or a planner, wants to give some expression to this pattern, what are the critical issues?

First, the geometry. In a new neighborhood, with houses built on the ground, we imagine quite dramatic clusters, with the houses built around or to the side of common land; and with a core to the cluster that gradually tapers off at the edges.

A cluster of 12 houses.

In existing neighborhoods of free-standing houses, the pattern must be brought into play gradually by relaxing zoning ordinances, and allowing people to gradually knit together clusters out of the existing grid—see COMMON LAND (67) and THE FAMILY (75). It is even possible to implement the pattern with

ROW HOUSES (38) and HOUSING HILLS (39). In this case the configuration of the rows, and the wings of the apartment building, form the cluster.

In all cases common land which is shared by the cluster is an essential ingredient. It acts as a focus and physically knits the group together. This common land can be as small as a path or as large as a green.

On the other hand, care must be taken not to make the clusters too tight or self-contained, so that they exclude the larger community or seem too constricting and claustrophobic. There needs to be some open endedness and overlapping among clusters.

Overlapping clusters in a Turkish village.

Along with the shape of the cluster, the way in which it is owned is critical. *If the pattern of ownership is not in accord with the physical properties of the cluster, the pattern will not take hold.* Very simply, the cluster must be owned and maintained by its constituent households. The households must be able to organize themselves as a corporation, capable of owning all the common land they share. There are many examples of tiny, user-owned housing corporations such as this. We know several places in our region where such experiments are under way, and places where they have been established for many years. And we have heard, from visitors to the Center, of similar developments in various parts of the world.

We advocate a system of ownership where the deed to one home carries with it part ownership in the cluster to which the home belongs; and ideally, this in turn carries with it part owner-

ship in the neighborhood made up of several clusters. In this way, every owner is automatically a shareholder in several levels of public land. And each level, beginning with the homes in their clusters, is a political unit with the power to control the processes of its own growth and repair.

Under such a system, the housing, whether in low or high density neighborhoods, can gradually find its way toward an abiding expression of the cluster. And the clusters themselves will come to support a quality of neighborhood life that, from our broken down neighborhoods now, we can only dimly perceive.

The unavowed secret of man is that he wants to be confirmed in his being and his existence by his fellow men and that he wishes them to make it possible for him to confirm them, and . . . not merely in the family, in the party assembly or in the public house, but also in the course of neighborly encounters, perhaps when he or the other steps out of the door of his house or to the window of his house and the greeting with which they greet each other will be accompanied by a glance of well-wishing, a glance in which curiosity, mistrust, and routine will have been overcome by a mutual sympathy: the one gives the other to understand that he affirms his presence. This is the indispensable minimum of humanity. (Martin Buber, *Gleanings*, New York: Simon and Schuster, 1969, p. 94.)

Therefore:

Arrange houses to form very rough, but identifiable clusters of 8 to 12 households around some common land and paths. Arrange the clusters so that anyone can walk through them, without feeling like a trespasser.

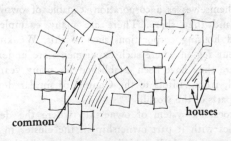

common   houses

Use this pattern as it is for low densities, up to about 15 houses per acre; at higher densities, modify the cluster with the additional structure given by ROW HOUSES (38) or HOUSING HILL (39). Always provide common land between the houses—COMMON LAND (67) and a shared common workshop—HOME WORKSHOP (157). Arrange paths clearly—CIRCULATION REALMS (98)—and lay these paths out in such a way that they create busier paths and backwaters, even within the cluster—DEGREES OF PUBLICNESS (36); keep parking in SMALL PARKING LOTS (103), and make the houses in the cluster suit the households which will live there—THE FAMILY (75), HOUSE FOR A SMALL FAMILY (76), HOUSE FOR A COUPLE (77), HOUSE FOR ONE PERSON (78), YOUR OWN HOME (79). . . .

38 ROW HOUSES*

. . . in certain parts of a community, the detached homes and gardens of a HOUSE CLUSTER (37) will not work, because they are not dense enough to generate the denser parts of DENSITY RINGS (29) and DEGREES OF PUBLICNESS (36). To help create these larger patterns, it is necessary to build row houses instead.

At densities of 15 to 30 houses per acre, row houses are essential. But typical row houses are dark inside, and stamped from an identical mould.

Above 15 houses per acre, it is almost impossible to make houses freestanding without destroying the open space around them; the open space which is left gets reduced to nothing more than shallow rings around the houses. And apartments do not solve the problem of higher densities; they keep people off the ground and they have no private gardens.

Row houses solve these problems. But row houses, in their conventional form, have problems of their own. Conventional row houses all conform, approximately, to the following diagram. The houses have a short frontage and a long depth, and share the party wall along their long side.

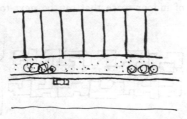

Typical row house pattern.

Because of the long party walls, many of the rooms are poorly lit. The houses lack privacy—there is nowhere in the houses or their yards that is very far from a party wall. The small yards are made even worse by the fact that they are at the short ends of the house, so that only a small part of the indoor space can be

adjacent to the garden. And there is almost no scope for individual variation in the houses, with the result that terraces of row houses are often rather sterile.

These four problems of row houses can easily be solved by making the houses long and thin, along the paths, like cottages. In this case, there is plenty of room for subtle variations from house to house—each plan can be quite different; and it is easy to arrange the plan to let the light in.

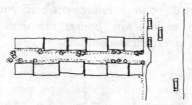

Houses long and thin along the path.

This kind of house has 30 per cent of its perimeter fixed and 70 per cent free for individual variations. A house in a conventional terrace of row houses has 70 per cent of its perimeter fixed and only 30 per cent open to individual variations. So the house can take on a variety of shapes, with a guarantee of a reasonable amount of privacy for its garden and for most of the house, an increase in the amount of light into the house, and an increase in the amount of indoor space that can be next to outdoor areas.

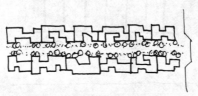

Crinkling and variation.

These advantages of the long thin row house are so obvious, it is natural to wonder why they aren't used more often. The reason is, of course, that roads do not permit it. So long as houses front directly onto roads, it is imperative that they have

the shortest frontage possible, so as to save the cost of roads and services—the cost of roads is a large part of any housing budget. But in the pattern we propose, we have been able to avoid this difficulty altogether, by making the houses front only onto paths —which don't cost much—and it is then these paths which connect to the roads, at right angles, in the way prescribed by NETWORK OF PATHS AND CARS (52).

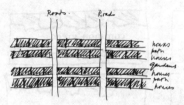

Roads away from houses.

Finally, a word on density. As we see from the sketch below, it is possible to build a two-story house of 1200 square feet on an area 30 x 20, using a total area (path, house, garden) of about 1300 square feet, and it is even possible to manage with an *absolute* minimum of 1000 square feet.

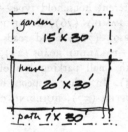

1300 square feet of land per house.

It is therefore possible to build row houses at a density of 30 per net acre. Without parking, or with less parking, this figure could conceivably be even higher.

Therefore.

For row houses, place houses along pedestrian paths that run at right angles to local roads and parking lots, and give each house a long frontage and a shallow depth.

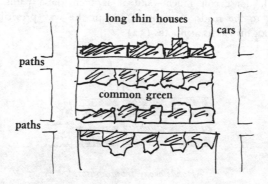

❖ ❖ ❖

Make the individual houses and cottages as long and thin along the paths as possible—LONG THIN HOUSE (109); vary the houses according to the different household types—THE FAMILY (75), HOUSE FOR A SMALL FAMILY (76), HOUSE FOR A COUPLE (77), HOUSE FOR ONE PERSON (78); build roads across the paths, at right angles to them—PARALLEL ROADS (23), NETWORK OF PATHS AND CARS (52), with small parking lots off the roads—SMALL PARKING LOTS (103). In other respects build row houses in clusters—HOUSE CLUSTER (37), BUILDING COMPLEX (95). . . .

. . . at the still higher densities required in the inner ring of the community's DENSITY RINGS (29), and wherever densities rise above 30 houses per acre or are four stories high—FOUR-STORY LIMIT (21), the house clusters become like hills.

❖ ❖ ❖

Every town has places in it which are so central and desirable that at least 30–50 households per acre will be living there. But the apartment houses which reach this density are almost all impersonal.

In the pattern YOUR OWN HOME (79), we discuss the fact that every family needs its own home with land to build on, land where they can grow things, and a house which is unique and clearly marked as theirs. A typical apartment house, with flat walls and identical windows, cannot provide these qualities.

The form of the HOUSING HILL comes essentially from three requirements. First, people need to maintain contact with the ground and with their neighbors, far more contact than high-rise living permits. Second, people want an outdoor garden or yard. This is among the most common reasons for their rejecting apartment living. And third, people crave for variation and uniqueness in their homes, and this desire is almost always constrained by high-rise construction, with its regular façades and identical units.

1. Connection to the ground and to neighbors. The strongest evidence comes from D. M. Fanning ("Families in Flats," *British Medical Journal,* November 1967, pp. 382–86). Fanning shows a direct correlation between incidence of mental disorder and high-rise living. These findings are presented in detail in FOUR-STORY LIMIT (21). High-rise living, it appears, has a terrible tendency to leave people alone, stranded, in their apartments. Home life is split away from casual street life by elevators, hallways, and long stairs. The decision to go out for some public life becomes formal and awkward; and unless there is some specific task which brings people out in the world, the tendency is to stay home, alone.

Fanning also found a striking lack of communication between families in the high-rise flats he studied. Women and children were especially isolated. The women felt they had little reason to take the trip from their apartment to the ground, except to go shopping. They and their children were effectively imprisoned in their apartments, cut off from the ground and from their neighbors.

Contact is impossible.

It seems as if the ground, the common ground between houses, is the medium through which people are able to make contact with one another and with themselves. Living on the ground, the yards around houses join those of the neighbors, and, in the best arrangements, they also adjoin neighborhood byways. Under these conditions it is easy and natural to meet with people. Children playing in the yard, the flowers in the garden, or just the weather outside provide endless topics for conversations. This kind of contact is impossible to maintain in high-rise apartments.

2. Private gardens. In the Park Hill survey (J. F. Demors, "Park Hill Survey," *O.A.P.*, February 1966, p. 235), about one-third of the high-rise residents interviewed said they missed the chance to putter around in their garden.

The need for a small garden, or some kind of private outdoor space, is fundamental. It is equivalent, at the family scale, to the biological need that a society has to be integrated with its country-

side—CITY COUNTRY FINGERS (3). In all traditional architec
tures, wherever building is essentially in the hands of the people,
there is some expression of this need. The miniature gardens of
Japan, outdoor workshops, roof gardens, courtyards, backyard
rose gardens, communal cooking pits, herb gardens—there are
thousands of examples. But in modern apartment structures this
kind of space is simply not available.

3. Identity of each unit. During the course of a seminar held
at the Center for Environmental Structure, Kenneth Radding
made the following experiment. He asked people to draw their
dream apartment, from the outside, and stuck the drawing on a
small piece of cardboard. He then asked them to place the cardboard on a grid representing the façade of a huge apartment
house, and asked them to move their "homes" around, until they
liked the position they were in. Without fail, people wanted
their apartments to be on the *edge* of the building, or set off
from other units by blank walls. No one wanted his own apartment to be lost in a grid of apartments.

In another survey we visited a nineteen-story apartment
building in San Francisco. The building contained 190 apartments each with a balcony. The management had set very rigid
restrictions on the use of these balconies—no political posters,
no painting, no clothes drying, no mobiles, no barbecues, no
tapestries. But even when confined by such restrictions, over half
of the residents were still able, in some way, to personalize their
balconies with plants in pots, carpets, and furniture. In short, in
the face of the most extreme regimentation people try to give
their apartments a unique face.

What building form is compatible with these three basic
requirements? First of all, to maintain a strong and direct connection to the ground, the building must be no higher than
four stories—FOUR-STORY LIMIT (21). Also, and perhaps more
important, we believe that each "house" must be within a few
steps of a rather wide and gradual stair that rises directly from
the ground. If the stair is open, somewhat rambling, and very
gradual, it will be continuous with the street and the life of the
street. Furthermore, if we take this need seriously, the stair must
be connected at the ground to a piece of land, owned in common

by the residents—this land organized to form a semi-private green.

Concerning the private gardens. They need sunlight and privacy—two requirements hard to satisfy in ordinary balcony arrangements. The terraces must be south-facing, large, and intimately connected to the houses, and solid enough for earth, and bushes, and small trees. This suggests a kind of housing hill; with a gradual slope toward the south and a garage for parking below the "hill."

And for identity—the only genuine solution to the problem of identity is to let each family gradually build and rebuild its own home on a terraced superstructure. If the floors of this structure are capable of supporting a house and some earth, each unit is free to take its own character and develop its own tiny garden.

Although these requirements bring to mind a form similar to Safdie's Habitat, it is important to realize that Habitat fails to solve two of the three problem discussed here. It has private gardens; but it fails to solve the problem of connection to the ground—the units are strongly separated from the casual life of the street;—and the mass-produced dwellings are anonymous, far from unique.

The following sketch for an apartment building—originally made for the Swedish community of Märsta, near Stockholm—includes all the essential features of a housing hill.

Apartment building for Märsta, near Stockholm.

Therefore:

To build more than 30 dwellings per net acre, or to

build housing three or four stories high, build a hill of houses. Build them to form stepped terraces, sloping toward the south, served by a great central open stair which also faces south and leads toward a common garden . . .

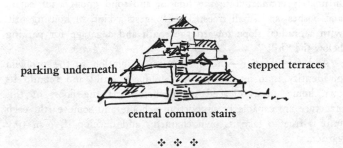

parking underneath   stepped terraces

central common stairs

❖ ❖ ❖

Let people lay out their own houses individually, upon the terraces, just as if they were land—YOUR OWN HOME (79). Since each terrace overlaps the one below it, each house has its garden on the house below—ROOF GARDENS (118). Leave the central stair open to the air, but give it a roof, in wet or snowy climates—perhaps a glass roof—OPEN STAIRS (158); and place the common land right at the bottom of the stair with playgrounds, flowers, and vegetables for everyone—COMMON LAND (67), CONNECTED PLAY (68), VEGETABLE GARDEN (177). . . .

40 OLD PEOPLE EVERYWHERE**

. . . when neighborhoods are properly formed they give the people there a cross section of ages and stages of development—IDENTIFIABLE NEIGHBORHOOD (14), LIFE CYCLE (26), HOUSEHOLD MIX (35); however, the old people are so often forgotten and left alone in modern society, that it is necessary to formulate a special pattern which underlines their needs.

Old people need old people, but they also need the young, and young people need contact with the old.

There is a natural tendency for old people to gather together in clusters or communities. But when these elderly communities are too isolated or too large, they damage young and old alike. The young in other parts of town, have no chance of the benefit of older company, and the old people themselves are far too isolated.

Treated like outsiders, the aged have increasingly clustered together for mutual support or simply to enjoy themselves. A now familiar but still amazing phenomenon has sprung up in the past decade: dozens of good-sized new towns that exclude people under 65. Built on cheap, outlying land, such communities offer two-bedroom houses starting at $18,000 plus a refuge from urban violence . . . and generational pressures. (*Time*, August 3, 1970.)

But the choice the old people have made by moving to these communities and the remarks above are a serious and painful reflection of a very sad state of affairs in our culture. The fact is that contemporary society shunts away old people; and the more shunted away they are, the deeper the rift between the old and young. The old people have no choice but to segregate themselves —they, like anyone else, have pride; they would rather not be with younger people who do not appreciate them, and they feign satisfaction to justify their position.

And the segregation of the old causes the same rift inside each individual life: as old people pass into old age communities their ties with their own past become unacknowledged, lost, and there-

fore broken. Their youth is no longer alive in their old age—the two become dissociated; their lives are cut in two.

In contrast to the situation today, consider how the aged were respected and needed in traditional cultures:

> Some degree of prestige for the aged seems to have been practically universal in all known societies. This is so general, in fact, that it cuts across many cultural factors that have appeared to determine trends in other topics related to age. (*The Role of Aged in Primitive Society*, Leo W. Simmons, New Haven: Yale University Press, 1945, p. 69.)

More specifically:

> . . . Another family relationship of great significance for the aged has been the commonly observed intimate association between the very young and the very old. Frequently they have been left together at home while the able-bodied have gone forth to earn the family living. These oldsters, in their wisdom and experience, have protected and instructed the little ones, while the children, in turn, have acted as the "eyes, ears, hands, and feet" of their feeble old friends. Care of the young has thus very generally provided the aged with a useful occupation and a vivid interest in life during the long dull days of senescence. (Ibid. p. 199.)

Clearly, old people cannot be integrated socially as in traditional cultures unless they are first integrated physically—unless they share the same streets, shops, services, and common land with everyone else. But, at the same time, they obviously need other old people around them; and some old people who are infirm need special services.

And of course old people vary in their need or desire to be among their own age group. The more able-bodied and independent they are, the less they need to be among other old people, and the farther they can be from special medical services. The variation in the amount of care they need ranges from complete nursing care; to semi-nursing care involving house calls once a day or twice a week; to an old person getting some help with shopping, cooking, and cleaning; to an old person being completely independent. Right now, there is no such fine differentia-

tion made in the care of old people—very often people who simply need a little help cooking and cleaning are put into rest homes which provide total nursing care, at huge expense to them, their families, and the community. It is a psychologically debilitating situation, and they turn frail and helpless because that is the way they are treated.

We therefore need a way of taking care of old people which provides for the full range of their needs:

1. It must allow them to stay in the neighborhood they know best—hence some old people in every neighborhood.

2. It must allow old people to be together, yet in groups small enough not to isolate them from the younger people in the neighborhood.

3. It must allow those old people who are independent to live independently, without losing the benefits of communality.

4. It must allow those who need nursing care or prepared meals, to get it, without having to go to nursing homes far from the neighborhood.

All these requirements can be solved together, very simply, if every neighborhood contains a small pocket of old people, not concentrated all in one place, but fuzzy at the edges like a swarm of bees. This will both preserve the symbiosis between young and old, *and* give the old people the mutual support they need within the pockets. Perhaps 20 might live in a central group house, another 10 or 15 in cottages close to this house, but interlaced with other houses, and another 10 to 15 also in cottages, still further from the core, in among the neighborhood, yet always within 100 or 200 yards of the core, so they can easily walk there to play chess, have a meal, or get help from the nurse.

The number 50 comes from Mumford's argument:

> The first thing to be determined is the number of aged people to be accommodated in a neighborhood unit; and the answer to this, I submit, is that the normal age distribution in the community as a whole should be maintained. This means that there should be from five to eight people over sixty-five in every hundred people; so that in a neighborhood unit of, say, six hundred people, there would be between thirty and fifty old people. (Lewis Mumford, *The Human Prospect*, New York, 1968, p. 49.)

As for the character of the group house, it might vary from

case to case. In some cases it might be no more than a commune, where people cook together and have part-time help from young girls and boys, or professional nurses. However, about 5 per cent of the nation's elderly need full-time care. This means that two or three people in every 50 will need complete nursing care. Since a nurse can typically work with six to eight people, this suggests that every second or third neighborhood group house might be equipped with complete nursing care.

Therefore:

Create dwellings for some 50 old people in every neighborhood. Place these dwellings in three rings . . .
1. **A central core with cooking and nursing provided.**
2. **Cottages near the core.**
3. **Cottages further out from the core, mixed among the other houses of the neighborhood, but never more than 200 yards from the core.**

. . . in such a way that the 50 houses together form a single coherent swarm, with its own clear center, but interlocked at its periphery with other ordinary houses of the neighborhood.

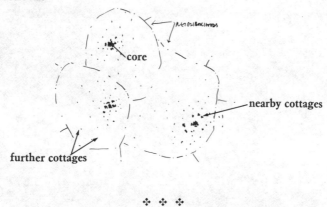

* * *

Treat the core like any group house; make all the cottages, both those close to and those further away, small—OLD AGE

COTTAGE (155), some of them perhaps connected to the larger family houses in the neighborhood—THE FAMILY (75); provide every second or third core with proper nursing facilities; somewhere in the orbit of the old age pocket, provide the kind of work which old people can manage best—especially teaching and looking after tiny children—NETWORK OF LEARNING (18), CHILDREN'S HOME (86), SETTLED WORK (156), VEGETABLE GARDEN (177). . . .

*between the house clusters, around the centers, and
especially in the boundaries between neighborhoods,
encourage the formation of work communities;*

41 WORK COMMUNITY**

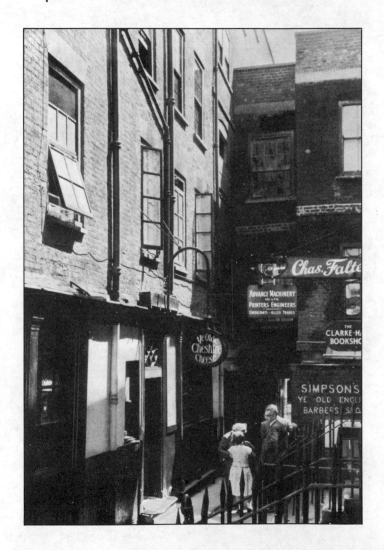

. . . according to the pattern SCATTERED WORK (9), work is entirely decentralized and woven in and out of housing areas. The effect of SCATTERED WORK—can be increased piecemeal, by building individual work communities, one by one, in the boundaries between the neighborhoods; these work communities will then help to form the boundaries—SUBCULTURE BOUNDARY (13), NEIGHBORHOOD BOUNDARY (15)—and above all in the boundaries, they will help to form ACTIVITY NODES (30).

❖ ❖ ❖

If you spend eight hours of your day at work, and eight hours at home, there is no reason why your workplace should be any less of a community than your home.

When someone tells you where he "lives," he is always talking about his house or the neighborhood his house is in. It sounds harmless enough. But think what it really means. Why should the people of our culture choose to use the word "live," which, on the face of it applies to every moment of our waking lives, and apply it only to a special portion of our lives—that part associated with our families and houses. The implication is straightforward. The people of our culture believe that they are less alive when they are working than when they are at home; and we make this distinction subtly clear, by choosing to keep the word "live" only for those places in our lives where we are not working. Anyone who uses the phrase "where do you live" in its everyday sense, accepts as his own the widespread cultural awareness of the fact that no one really "lives" at his place of work—there is no song or music there, no love, no food—that he is not alive while working, not living, only toiling away, and being dead.

As soon as we understand this situation it leads at once to outrage. Why should we accept a world in which eight hours of the day are "dead"; why shall we not create a world in which our work is as much part of life, as much alive, as anything we do at home with our family and with our friends?

This problem is discussed in other patterns—SCATTERED WORK (9), SELF-GOVERNING WORKSHOPS AND OFFICES (80). Here we

focus on the implications which this problem has for the physical and social nature of the *area* in which a workplace sits. If a person spends eight hours a day working in a certain area, and the nature of his work, its social character, and its location, are all chosen to make sure that he is living, not merely earning money, then it is certainly essential that the area immediately around his place of work be a *community*, just like a neighborhood but oriented to the pace and rhythms of work, instead of the rhythms of the family.

For workplaces to function as communities, five relationships are critical:

1. *Workplaces must not be too scattered, nor too agglomerated, but clustered in groups of about 15.*

We know from SCATTERED WORK (9) that workplaces should be decentralized, but they should not be so scattered that a single workplace is isolated from others. On the other hand, they should not be so agglomerated that a single workplace is lost in a sea of others. The workplaces should therefore be grouped to form strongly identifiable communities. The communities need to be small enough so that one can know most of the people working in them, at least by sight—and big enough to support as many amenities for the workers as possible—lunch counters, local sports, shops, and so on. We guess the right size may be between 8 and 20 establishments.

2. *The workplace community contains a mix of manual jobs, desk jobs, craft jobs, selling, and so forth.*

Most people today work in areas which are specialized: medical buildings, car repair, advertising, warehousing, financial, etc. This kind of segregation leads to isolation from other types of work and other types of people, leading in turn to less concern, respect, and understanding of them. We believe that a world where people are socially responsible can only come about where there is a value intrinsic to every job, where there is dignity associated with all work. This can hardly come about when we are so segregated from people who do different kinds of work from us.

3. *There is a common piece of land within the work community, which ties the individual workshops and offices together.*

A shared street does a little to tie individual houses and places together; but a shared piece of common land does a great deal

more. If the workplaces are grouped around a common courtyard where people can sit, play volleyball, eat lunches, it will help the contact and community among the workers.

4. *The work community is interlaced with the larger community in which it is located.*

A work community, though forming a core community by itself, cannot work well in complete isolation from the surrounding community. This is already discussed to some extent in SCATTERED WORK (9) and MEN AND WOMEN (27). In addition, both work community and residential community can gain by sharing facilities and services—restaurants, cafes, libraries. Thus it makes sense for the work community to be open to the larger community with shops and cafes at the seam between them.

5. *Finally, it is necessary that the common land, or courtyards, exist at two distinct and separate levels.* On the one hand, the courtyards for common table tennis, volleyball, need half-a-dozen workgroups around them at the most—more would swamp them. On the other hand, the lunch counters and laundries and barbershops need more like 20 or 30 workgroups to survive. For this reason the work community needs two levels of clustering.

Therefore:

Build or encourage the formation of work communities —each one a collection of smaller clusters of workplaces which have their own courtyards, gathered round a larger common square or common courtyard which contains shops and lunch counters. The total work community should have no more than 10 or 20 workplaces in it.

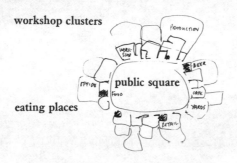

workshop clusters

public square

eating places

Make the square at the heart of the community a public square with public paths coming through it—SMALL PUBLIC SQUARES (61); either in this square, or in some attached space, place opportunities for sports—LOCAL SPORTS (72); make sure that the entire community is always within three minutes' walk of an ACCESSIBLE GREEN (60); lay out the individual smaller courtyards in such a way that people naturally gather there—COURTYARDS WHICH LIVE (115); keep the workshops small—SELF-GOVERNING WORKSHOPS AND OFFICES (80); encourage communal cooking and eating over and beyond the lunch counters—STREET CAFE (88), FOOD STANDS (93), COMMUNAL EATING (147). . . . .

42 INDUSTRIAL RIBBON*

. . . in a city where work is decentralized by SCATTERED WORK (9), the placing of industry is of particular importance since it usually needs a certain amount of concentration. Like WORK COMMUNITIES (41), the industry can easily be placed to help in the formation of the larger boundaries between subcultures—SUBCULTURE BOUNDARY (13).

❖ ❖ ❖

Exaggerated zoning laws separate industry from the rest of urban life completely, and contribute to the plastic unreality of sheltered residential neighborhoods.

It is true, obviously, that industry creates smoke, smells, noise, and heavy truck traffic; and it is therefore necessary to prevent the heaviest industry, especially, from interfering with the calm and safety of the places where people live.

But it is also true that in the modern city industry gets treated like a disease. The areas where it exists are assumed to be dirty and derelict. They are kept to the "other side of the tracks," swept under the rug. And people forget altogether that the things which surround them in their daily lives—bread, chemicals, cars, oil, gaskets, radios, chairs—are all made in these forbidden industrial zones. Under these conditions it is not surprising that people treat life as an unreal charade, and forget the simplest realities and facts of their existence.

Since the 1930's various efforts have been made, on behalf of the workers, to make factories green and pleasant. This social welfare approach to the nature of industries is once again unreal, in the opposite direction. A workshop, where things are being made, is not a garden or a hospital. The gardens which surround the new industrial "parks" are more for show than for the workers anyway since a few small inner courts or gardens would be far more useful to the workers themselves. And the contribution of an industrial park to the social and emotional life of the surrounding city is almost nil.

What is needed is a form of industry which is small enough so that it does not need to be so sharply segregated; genuine, so that it seems like a workshop, because it is a workshop; placed

The social welfare "green" industrial park.

in such a way that the truck traffic which it generates does not endanger nearby neighborhoods; and formed along the edge of neighborhoods so that it is not a dangerous, forgotten zone, but so that it is a real part of life, accessible to children from the surrounding houses, woven into the fabric of city life, in a way that properly reflects its huge importance in the scheme of things.

But many industries are not small. They need large areas to function properly. A survey of planned industrial districts shows that 71.2 per cent of the industries require 0 to 5.0 acres, 13.6 per cent require 5 to 10 acres, and 9.9 per cent require 10 to 25 acres. (Robert E. Boley, *Industrial Districts Restudied: An Analysis of Characteristics*, Urban Land Institute, Technical Bulletin No. 41, 1961.) These industries can only fit into a NEIGHBORHOOD BOUNDARY (15) or SUBCULTURE BOUNDARY (13) if the boundary is wide enough. Ribbons whose width varies between 200 and 500 feet, with sites varying in length between 200 and 2000 feet, will be able to provide the necessary range of one to 25-acre sites in compact blocks, and are still narrow enough to keep communities on opposite sides of the ribbon reasonably connected.

The industrial ribbons require truck access and some rail transport. Truck roads and rail spurs should always be located in the center of the ribbon, so that the edges of the ribbon remain open

Truck traffic from an industrial area
to a nearby freeway destroys a neighborhood.

to the community. Even more important, the ribbons must be placed so that they do not generate a heavy concentration of dangerous and noisy truck traffic *through* neighborhoods. Since most truck traffic comes to and from the freeways, this means that the industrial ribbons must be placed fairly near to RING ROADS (17).

Therefore:

Place industry in ribbons, between 200 and 500 feet wide, which form the boundaries between communities. Break these ribbons into long blocks, varying in area between 1 and 25 acres; and treat the edge of every ribbon as a place where people from nearby communities can benefit from the offshoots of the industrial activity.

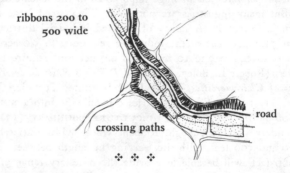

ribbons 200 to 500 wide

crossing paths

road

❖ ❖ ❖

Place the ribbons near enough to RING ROADS (17) so that trucks can pass directly from the ribbons to the ring road, without having to pass through any other intermediate areas. Develop the internal layout of the industrial ribbon like any other work community, though slightly more spread out—WORK COMMUNITY (41). Place the important buildings of each industry, the "heart" of the plant, toward the edge of the ribbon to form usable streets and outdoor spaces—POSITIVE OUTDOOR SPACE (106), BUILDING FRONTS (122).

43 UNIVERSITY AS A MARKETPLACE

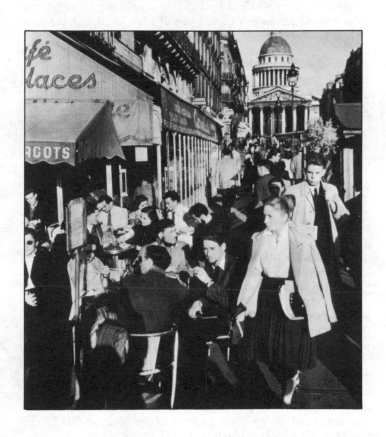

. . . the NETWORK OF LEARNING (18) has established the importance of a whole society devoted to the learning process with decentralized opportunities for learning. The network of learning can be greatly helped by building a university, which treats the learning process as a normal part of adult life, for all the people in society.

❖ ❖ ❖

Concentrated, cloistered universities, with closed admission policies and rigid procedures which dictate who may teach a course, kill opportunities for learning.

The original universities in the middle ages were simply collections of teachers who attracted students because they had something to offer. They were marketplaces of ideas, located all over the town, where people could shop around for the kinds of ideas and learning which made sense to them. By contrast, the isolated and over-administered university of today kills the variety and intensity of the different ideas at the university and also limits the student's opportunity to shop for ideas.

To re-create this kind of academic freedom and the opportunity for exchange and growth of ideas two things are needed.

First, the social and physical environment must provide a setting which encourages rather than discourages individuality and freedom of thought. Second, the environment must provide a setting which encourages the student to see for himself which ideas make sense—a setting which gives him the maximum opportunity and exposure to a great variety of ideas, so that he can make up his mind for himself.

The image which most clearly describes this kind of setting is the image of the traditional marketplace, where hundreds of tiny stalls, each one developing some specialty and unique flavor which can attract people by its genuine quality, are so arranged that a potential buyer can circulate freely, and examine the wares before he buys.

What would it mean to fashion the university after this model?

1. *Anyone can take a course.* To begin with, in a university marketplace there are no admission procedures. Anyone, at any age, may come forward and seek to take a class. In effect, the "course catalog" of the university is published and circulated at large, in the newspapers and on radio, and posted in public places throughout the region.

2. *Anyone can give a course.* Similarly, in a university marketplace, anyone can come forward and offer a course. There is no hard and fast distinction between teachers and the rest of the citizenry. If people come forward to take the course, then it is established. There will certainly be groups of teachers banding together and offering interrelated classes; and teachers may set prerequisities and regulate enrollment however they see fit. But, like a true marketplace, the students create the demand. If over a period of time no one comes forward to take a professor's course, then he must change his offering or find another way to make a living.

Many courses, once they are organized, can meet in homes and meeting rooms all across the town. But some will need more space or special equipment, and all the classes will need access to libraries and various other communal facilities. The university marketplace, then, needs a physical structure to support its social structure.

Certainly, a marketplace could never have the form of an isolated campus. Rather it would tend to be open and public, woven through the city, perhaps with one or two streets where university facilities are concentrated.

In an early version of this pattern, written expressly for the University of Oregon in Eugene, we described in detail the physical setting which we believe complements the marketplace of ideas. We advised:

Make the university a collection of small buildings, situated along pedestrian paths, each containing one or two educational projects. Make all the horizontal circulation among these projects, in the public domain, at ground floor. This means that all projects open directly to a pedestrian path, and that the upper floors of buildings are connected directly to the ground, by stairs and entrances. Connect all the pedestrian paths, so that, like a marketplace, they form one major pedestrian system, with many entrances and openings off it. The over-

all result of this pattern, is that the environment becomes a collection of relatively low buildings, opening off a major system of pedestrian paths, each building containing a series of entrances and staircases, at about 50 foot intervals.

We still believe that this image of the university, as a marketplace scattered through the town, is correct. Most of these details are given by other patterns, in this book: BUILDING COMPLEX (95), PEDESTRIAN STREET (100), ARCADES (119), and OPEN STAIRS (158).

Finally, how should a university marketplace be administered? We don't know. Certainly a voucher system where everyone has equal access to payment vouchers seems sensible. And some technique for balancing payment to class size is required, so teachers are not simply paid according to how many students they enroll. Furthermore, some kind of evaluation technique is needed, so that reliable information on courses and teachers filters out to the towns people.

There are several experiments going forward in higher education today which may help to solve these administrative questions. The Open University of England, the various "free" universities, such as Heliotrope in San Francisco, the 20 branches of the University Without Walls all over the United States, the university extension programs, which gear their courses entirely to working people—they are all examples of institutions experimenting with different aspects of the marketplace idea.

Therefore:

Establish the university as a marketplace of higher education. As a social conception this means that the university is open to people of all ages, on a full-time, part-time, or course by course basis. Anyone can offer a class. Anyone can take a class. Physically, the university marketplace has a central crossroads where its main buildings and offices are, and the meeting rooms and labs ripple out from this crossroads—at first concentrated in small buildings along pedestrian streets and then gradually becoming more dispersed and mixed with the town.

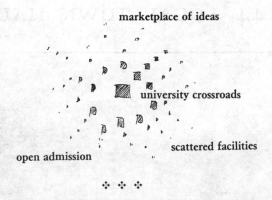

marketplace of ideas

university crossroads

open admission

scattered facilities

❖ ❖ ❖

Give the university a PROMENADE (31) at its central cross-roads; and around the crossroads cluster the buildings along streets—BUILDING COMPLEX (95), PEDESTRIAN STREET (100). Give this central area access to quiet greens—QUIET BACKS (59); and a normal distribution of housing—HOUSING IN BETWEEN (48); as for the classes, wherever possible let them follow the model of MASTER AND APPRENTICES (83). . . .

44 LOCAL TOWN HALL*

. . . according to COMMUNITY OF 7000 (12), the political and economic life of the city breaks down into small, self-governing communities. In this case, the process of local government needs a physical place of work; and the design and placing of this physical place of work can help to create and to sustain the COMMUNITY OF 7000 by acting as its physical and social focus.

❖ ❖ ❖

Local government of communities and local control by the inhabitants, will only happen if each community has its own physical town hall which forms the nucleus of its political activity.

We have argued, in MOSAIC OF SUBCULTURES (8), COMMUNITY OF 7000 (12), and IDENTIFIABLE NEIGHBORHOOD (14), that every city needs to be made of self-governing groups, which exist at two different levels, the communities with populations of 5000 to 10,000 and the neighborhoods with populations of 200 to 1000.

These groups will only have the political force to carry out their own, locally determined plans, if they have a share of the taxes which their inhabitants generate, and if the people in the groups have a genuine, daily possibility of access to the local government which represents them. Both require that each group has its own seat of government, no matter how modest, where the people of the neighborhood feel comfortable, and where they know that they can get results.

This calls up a physical image of city government which is quite the opposite of the huge city halls that have been built in the last 75 years. A *local* town hall would contain two basic features:

1. It is community territory for the group it serves; it is made in a way which invites people in for service, spontaneously, to debate policy, and the open space around the building is shaped to sustain people gathering and lingering.

2. It is located at the heart of the local community and is within walking distance of everyone it serves.

1. The town hall as community territory.

The weakness of community government is due in part to the kinds of policies created and maintained by the city hall bureaucracy. And we believe this situation is largely supported and bolstered by the physical nature of city hall. In other words, the physical existence of a city hall undermines local community government, even where the city hall staff is sympathetic to "neighborhood participation."

The key to the problem lies in the experience of powerlessness at the community level. When a man goes to city hall to take action on a neighborhood or community issue, he is at once on the defensive: the building and the staff of city hall serve the entire city; his problem is very small beside the problems of the city as a whole. And besides, everyone is busy-busy and unfamiliar. He is asked to fill out paper forms and make appointments, though perhaps the connection between these forms and appointments and his problem are not very clear. Soon the people in the neighborhoods feel more and more remote from city hall, from the center of decision-making and from the decisions themselves which influence their lives. Quickly the syndrome of powerlessness grows.

In an earlier publication, we presented a body of evidence to substantiate the growth of this syndrome (*A Pattern Language Which Generates Multi-Service Centers*, Center for Environmental Structure, Berkeley, 1968, pp. 80–87). There we discovered that centralized service programs reached very few of the people in their target areas; the staff of these centers quickly took on the red tape mentality, even where they were chosen specifically to support neighborhood programs; and, most damaging of all, the centers themselves were seen as alien places, and the experience of using them was, on the whole, debilitating to the people.

Like all syndromes, this one can only be broken if it is attacked on its several fronts simultaneously. This means, for example, organizing neighborhoods and communities to take control of the functions that concern them; revising city charters to grant

power to local groups; *and making places, in communities and neighborhoods, that act as home bases for the consolidation of this power—the local town halls.*

What might these local town halls be like if they are to be effective in breaking down the syndrome of powerlessness?

The evidence shows that people can and will articulate their needs if given the proper setting and means. Creating this setting goes hand in hand with community organization. If the local town hall is gradually to become a source of real neighborhood power, it must help the process of community organization. This means, essentially, that the building be built around the *process* of community organization, and that the place be clearly recognizable *as community territory.*

When we translate the idea of community organization and community territory into physical terms, they yield two components: an arena and a zone of community projects.

The community needs a public forum, equipped with sound system, benches, walls to put up notices, where people are free to gather; a place which belongs to the community where people would naturally come whenever they think something should be done about something. *We call this public forum the arena.*

And the community needs a place where people can have access to storefronts, work space, meeting rooms, office equipment. Once a group is ready to move, it takes typewriters, duplicating machines, telephones, etc., to carry through with a project and develop broad based community support—and this in turn needs cheap and readily accessible office space. We call this space the community projects zone—see NECKLACE OF COMMUNITY PROJECTS (45) for details.

2. *The location of local town halls.*

If these local town halls are to be successful in drawing people in, the question of their location must be taken seriously. From earlier work on the location of multi-service centers, we are convinced that town halls can die if they are badly located: *twenty times as many people drop into community centers when they are located near major intersections* as when they are buried in the middle of residential blocks.

Here, for example, is a table which shows the number of

people who dropped in at a service center while it was located on a residential street, versus the number of people who dropped in after it was relocated on a major commercial street, close to a main pedestrian intersection.

	Number of people dropping in, per day	Number of people with appointments, per day
Before the move	1–2	15–20
Two months after the move	15–20	about 50
Six months after the move	about 40	about 50

The details of this investigation are given in *A Pattern Language Which Generates Multi-Service Centers* (pp. 70–73). The conclusion reached there, is that community centers can afford to be within a block of the major pedestrian intersections, but if they are farther away, they are virtually dead as centers of local service.

This information must be interpreted to suit the different scales of neighborhood and community. We imagine, in a neighborhood of 500, the neighborhood town hall would be quite small and informal; perhaps not even a separate building at all, but a room with an adjoining outdoor room, on an important corner of the neighborhood. In a community of 7000, something more is required: a building the size of a large house, with an outdoor area developed as a forum and meeting place, located on the community's main promenade.

Therefore:

To make the political control of local functions real, establish a small town hall for each community of 7000, and even for each neighborhood; locate it near the busiest intersection in the community. Give the building three parts: an arena for public discussion, public services around the arena, and space to rent out to ad hoc community projects.

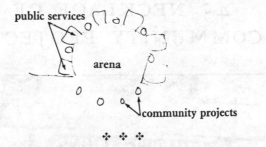

❖ ❖ ❖

Arrange the arena so that it forms the heart of a community crossroads; and make it small, so that a crowd can easily gather there—ACTIVITY NODES (30), SMALL PUBLIC SQUARES (61), PEDESTRIAN DENSITY (123). Keep all the public services around this square as small as possible—SMALL SERVICES WITHOUT RED TAPE (81); and provide ample space for the community projects, in a ring around the building, so that they form the outer face of the town hall—NECKLACE OF COMMUNITY PROJECTS (45). . . . .

45 NECKLACE OF
COMMUNITY PROJECTS

. . . LOCAL TOWN HALL (44) calls for small centers of local government at the heart of every community. This pattern embellishes the local town hall and other public institutions like it—UNIVERSITY AS A MARKETPLACE (43) and HEALTH CENTER (47)—with a ground for community action.

❖ ❖ ❖

The local town hall will not be an honest part of the community which lives around it, unless it is itself surrounded by all kinds of small community activities and projects, generated by the people for themselves.

A lively process of community self-government depends on an endless series of ad hoc political and service groups, functioning freely, each with a proper chance to test its ideas before the townspeople. The spatial component of this idea is crucial: this process will be stymied if people cannot get started in an office on a shoestring.

We derive the geometry of this pattern from five requirements:

1. Small, grass roots movements, unpopular at their inception, play a vital role in society. They provide a critical opposition to established ideas; their presence is a direct correlate of the right to free speech; a basic part of the self-regulation of a successful society, which will generate counter movements whenever things get off the track. Such movements need a place to manifest themselves, in a way which puts their ideas directly into the public domain. At this writing, a quick survey of the East Bay shows about 30 or 40 bootstrap groups that are suffering for lack of such a place: for example, Alcatraz Indians, Bangla Desh Relief, Solidarity Films, Tenant Action Project, November 7th Movement, Gay Legal Defense, No on M, People's Translation Service. . . .

2. But as a rule these groups are small and have very little money. To nourish this kind of activity, the community must provide minimal space to any group of this sort, rent free, with some limit on the duration of the lease. The space must be like a

small storefront and have typewriters, duplicating machines, and telephones; and access to a meeting room.

3. To encourage the atmosphere of honest debate, these storefront spaces must be near the town hall, the main crossroads of public life. If they are scattered across the town, away from the main town hall, they cannot seriously contend with the powers that be.

4. The space must be highly visible. It must be built in a way which lets the group get their ideas across, to people on the street. And it must be physically organized to undermine the natural tendency town governments have to wall themselves in and isolate themselves from the community once they are in power.

5. Finally, to bring these groups into natural contact with the community, the fabric of storefronts should be built to include some of the stable shops and services that the community needs—barbershop, cafe, laundromat.

These five requirements suggest a necklace of rather open storefront spaces around the local town hall. This necklace of spaces is a physical embodiment of the political process in an open society: everyone has access to equipment, space to mount a campaign, and the chance to get their ideas into the public arena.

Therefore:

Allow the growth of shop-size spaces around the local town hall, and any other appropriate community building. Front these shops on a busy path, and lease them for a minimum rent to ad hoc community groups for political work, trial services, research, and advocate groups. No ideological restrictions.

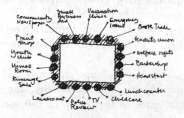

❖ ❖ ❖

Make each shop small, compact, and easily accessible like INDIVIDUALLY OWNED SHOPS (87); build small public spaces for loitering amongst them—PUBLIC OUTDOOR ROOM (69). Use them to form the building edge—BUILDING FRONTS (122), BUILDING EDGE (160), and keep them open to the street—OPENING TO THE STREET (165). . . .

46 MARKET OF
MANY SHOPS**

. . . we have proposed that shops be widely decentralized and placed in such a way that they are most accessible to the communities which use them—WEB OF SHOPPING (19). The largest groups of shops are arranged to form pedestrian streets or SHOPPING STREETS (32) which will almost always need a market to survive. This pattern describes the form and economic character of markets.

❖ ❖ ❖

It is natural and convenient to want a market where all the different foods and household goods you need can be bought under a single roof. But when the market has a single management, like a supermarket, the foods are bland, and there is no joy in going there.

It is true that the large supermarkets do have a great variety of foods. But this "variety" is still centrally purchased, centrally warehoused, and still has the staleness of mass merchandise. In addition, there is no human contact left, only rows of shelves and then a harried encounter with the check-out man who takes your money.

The only way to get the human contact back, and the variety of food, and all the love and care and wisdom about individual foods which shopkeepers who know what they are selling can bring to it, is to create those markets once again in which individual owners sell different goods, from tiny stalls, under a common roof.

As it stands, supermarkets are likely to get bigger and bigger, to conglomerate with other industries, and to go to all lengths to dehumanize the experience of the marketplace. Horn and Hardart, for example, have been contemplating this scheme:

. . . the customer either drives her car or walks onto a moving ramp, is conveyed decorously through the whole store, selects her groceries by viewing samples displayed in lighted wall panels (or unlocking the cases with a special key or her credit card), and chooses her meat and produce via closed circuit TV. She then drives around to a separate warehouse area to collect her order, paid for by a uni-

247

versal credit card system. . . . Most of the people would be invisible.
. . . (Jennifer Cross, *The Supermarket Trap*, New York: Berkeley
Medallion, 1971).

Now contrast this with the following description of an old-
fashioned market place in San Francisco:

If you visit the Market regularly you come to have favorite stalls,
like the one with the pippin and Hauer apples from Watsonville.
The farmer looks at each apple as he chooses it and places it in the
bag, reminding you to keep them in a cool place so they will remain
crisp and sweet. If you display interest, he tells you with pride about
the orchard they come from and how they were grown and cared
for, his blue eyes meeting yours. His English is spoken with a slight
Italian accent so you wonder about the clear blue eyes, light brown
hair and long-boned body until he tells you about the part of northern Italy where he was born.
There is a handsome black man offering small mountains of melons
where the stalls end. Tell him you are not enough of an expert to
choose one you would like to have perfect for the day after tomor-
row, and he will not only pick one out that he assures you will be
just right (as it turns out to be), but gives you a lesson in choosing
your next melon, whether cranshaw, honeydew or watermelon,
wherever you may happen to buy it. He cares that you will always
get a good one and enjoy it. ("The Farmers Go to Market," *California Living*, San Francisco Chronicle Sunday Magazine, February
6, 1972.)

There is no doubt that this is far more human and enlivening
than the supermarket conveyor belt. The critical question lies
with the economics of the operation. Is there a reasonable
economic basis for a marketplace of many shops? Or are markets
ruled out by the efficiencies of the supermarket?

There do not seem to be any economic obstacles more serious
than those which accompany the start of any business. The major
problem is one of coordination—coordination of individual shops
to form one coherent market and coordination of many similar
shops, from several markets, to make bulk purchase arrangements.

If individual shops are well located, they can operate competi-
tively, at profit margins of up to 5 per cent of sales ("Expenses in
Retail Business," National Cash Register, Dayton, Ohio, p. 15).
According to National Cash Register figures, this profit margin
stays the same, regardless of size, for all convenience food stores.
The small stores are often undercut by supermarkets because they
are located by themselves, and therefore cannot offer shoppers

the same variety at one stop, as the supermarket. However, if many of these small shops are clustered and centrally located, and together they offer a variety comparable to the supermarket, then they can compete effectively with the chain supermarkets.

The one efficiency that chain stores do maintain is the efficiency of bulk purchase. But even this can be offset if groups of similar shops, all over the town, coordinate their needs and set up bulk purchase arrangements. For example, in the Bay Area there are a number of flower vendors running their business from small carts on the street. Although each vendor manages his own affairs independently, all the vendors go in together to buy their flowers. They gain enormously by purchasing their flowers in bulk and undersell the established florists three to one.

Of course, it is difficult for a market of many shops to get started—it is hard to find a place and hard to finance it. We propose a very rough and simple structure in the beginning, that can be filled in and improved over time. The market in the photo, in Lima, Peru, began with nothing more than free-standing columns and aisles. The shops—most of them no more than six feet by nine—were built up gradually between the columns.

A market in Peru . . .

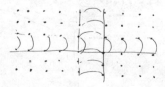

. . . began with nothing more than columns.

A spectacular example of a simple wood structure that has been modified and enlarged over the years is the Pike Place Market in Seattle, Washington.

The Pike Place Market—a market of many shops in Seattle.

Therefore:

Instead of modern supermarkets, establish frequent marketplaces, each one made up of many smaller shops which are autonomous and specialized (cheese, meat, grain, fruit, and so on). Build the structure of the market as a minimum, which provides no more than a roof, columns which define aisles, and basic services. Within this structure allow the different shops to create their own environment, according to their individual taste and needs.

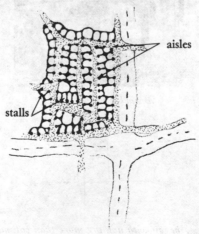

❖ ❖ ❖

Make the aisles wide enough for small delivery carts and for a dense throng of pedestrians—perhaps 6 to 12 feet wide—BUILD-ING THOROUGHFARE (101); keep the stalls extremely small so that the rent is low—perhaps no more than six feet by nine feet—shops which need more space can occupy two—INDIVIDUALLY OWNED SHOPS (87); define the stalls with columns at the corners only—COLUMNS AT THE CORNERS (212); perhaps even let the owners make roofs for themselves—CANVAS ROOFS (244); connect the aisles with the outside so that the market is a direct continuation of the pedestrian paths in the city just around it—PEDESTRIAN STREET (100). . . .

47 HEALTH CENTER*

. . . the explicit recognition of the life cycle as the basis for every individual life will do a great deal to help people's health in the community—LIFE CYCLE (26); this pattern describes the more specific institutions which help people to care for themselves and their health.

More than 90 per cent of the people walking about in an ordinary neighborhood are unhealthy, judged by simple biological criteria. This ill health cannot be cured by hospitals or medicine.

Hospitals put the emphasis on sickness. They are enormously expensive; they are inconvenient because they are too centralized; and they tend to create sickness, rather than cure it, because doctors get paid when people are sick.

By contrast, in traditional Chinese medicine, people pay the doctor only when they are healthy; when they are sick, he is obliged to treat them, without payment. The doctors have incentives to keep people well.

A system of health care which is actually capable of keeping people healthy, in both mind and body, must put its emphasis on health, not sickness. It must therefore be physically decentralized so that it is as close as possible to people's everyday activities. And it must be able to encourage people in daily practices that lead to health. The core of the solution, as far as we can see, must be a system of small, widely distributed, health centers, which encourage physical activities—swimming, dancing, sports, and fresh air—and provide medical treatment only as an incidental side of these activities.

There is converging evidence and speculation in the health

care literature that health centers with these characteristics, organized according to the philosophy of health maintenance, are critical. (See, for example: William H. Glazier, "The Task of Medicine," *Scientific American*, Vol. 228, No. 4, April 1973, pp. 13–17; and Milton Roemer, "Nationalized Medicine for America," *Transaction*, September 1971, p. 31.)

We know of several attempts to develop health care programs which are in line with this proposal. In most of the cases, though, the programs fall short in their hopes because, despite their good intentions, they still tend to cater to the sick, they do not work to maintain health. Take, for example, the so-called "community mental health centers" encouraged by the United States National Institute of Mental Health during the late 1960's. On paper, these centers are intended to encourage health, not cure sickness.

In practice it is a very different story. We visited one of the most advanced, in San Anselmo, California. The patients sit around all day long; their eyes are glazed; they are half-enthusiastically doing "clay therapy" or "paint therapy." One patient came up to us and said, "Doctor," his eyes shining with happiness, "this is a wonderful mental health center; it is the very best one I have ever been in." In short, the patients are kept as patients; they understand themselves to be patients; in certain cases they even revel in their role as patients. They have no useful occupation, no work, nothing useful they can show at the end of a day, nothing to be proud of. The center, for all its intentions to be human, in fact reinforces the patients' idea of their own sickness and encourages the behavior of sickness, even while it is preaching and advocating health.

The same is true for the Kaiser-Permanente program in California. The Kaiser hospitals have been hailed in a recent article as "ones which shift the emphasis away from treatment of illness and toward the maintenance of health (William H. Glazier, "The Task of Medicine"). Members of Kaiser are entitled to a multi-phasic examination yearly, intended to give every member a complete picture of the state of his health. But the conception of health which is created by this multi-phasic program is still "freedom from sickness." It is essentially negative. There is no effort made toward the positive creation and maintenance of actual, blooming, health. And besides, the Kaiser Center

is still nothing but a giant hospital. People are treated as numbers; the center is so large and concentrated that the doctors cannot possibly see their patients as people in their natural communities. They see them as patients.

The only health center we know which actually devoted itself to health instead of sickness was the famous Peckham Health Center in England. The Peckham Center was a club, run by two doctors, focused on a swimming pool, a dance floor, and a cafe. In addition, there were doctors' offices, and it was understood that families—never individuals—would receive periodic check-ups as part of their activities around the swimming and dancing. Under these conditions, people used the center regularly, during the day and at night. The question of their health became fused with the ordinary life of the community, and this set the stage for a most extraordinary kind of health care.

For example, it seems that many of the mothers in working-class pre-war England, were ashamed of their own bodies. This shame reached such proportions that they were ashamed of suckling and holding their own babies, and in many cases they actually did not want their babies as a result. The Peckham Center was able to dismantle this syndrome entirely by its emphasis on health. The program of swimming and dancing, coupled with the family checkups, allowed women to become proud of their own bodies; they no longer felt afraid of their own newborn babies, no longer felt shame about their bodies; the babies felt wanted; and the incidence of emotional disturbance and childhood psychosis among the children in later years was drastically reduced within the Peckham population, starting exactly from the year when the health center began its operation.

This kind of profound biological connection between physical health, family life, and emotional welfare was truly the beginning of a new era in human biology. It is described, beautifully, and at length, by two doctors from Peckham Center (Innes Pearse and Lucy Crocker, *The Peckham Experiment, A Study in the Living Structure of Society*, New Haven: Yale University Press, 1946). Only when biological ideas of this depth and power are taken seriously will it be possible to have real health centers, instead of sickness centers.

Therefore:

Gradually develop a network of small health centers, perhaps one per community of 7000, across the city; each equipped to treat everyday disease—both mental and physical, in children and adults—but organized essentially around a functional emphasis on those recreational and educational activities which help keep people in good health, like swimming and dancing.

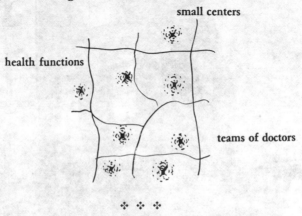

small centers

health functions

teams of doctors

❖ ❖ ❖

Keep the medical teams small and independent—SMALL SERVICES WITHOUT RED TAPE (81), but coordinated with each other and other clinics, like BIRTH PLACES (65)—throughout the town. Give each center some functions that fuse with the ordinary course of local work and recreation: swimming pool, workshops, sauna, gym, vegetable garden, greenhouse. But don't force these facilities to form a continuous "health park"—knit them together loosely with other parts of the town—HOUSING IN BETWEEN (48), LOCAL SPORTS (72), ADVENTURE PLAYGROUND (73), HOME WORKSHOP (157), VEGETABLE GARDEN (177). Perhaps the most important subsidiary pattern for helping people to keep healthy is the opportunity for swimming; ideally, try and put a swimming pool on every block—STILL WATER (71). . . .

. . . most housing is in residential neighborhoods, and in the clusters within neighborhoods—IDENTIFIABLE NEIGHBORHOOD (14), HOUSE CLUSTER (37); and according to our patterns these housing areas need to be separated by boundaries which contain public land and work communities—SUBCULTURE BOUNDARY (13), NEIGHBORHOOD BOUNDARY (15), WORK COMMUNITY (41). But even these work communities, and boundaries, and shopping streets, must contain houses which have people living in them.

❖ ❖ ❖

Wherever there is a sharp separation between residential and nonresidential parts of town, the nonresidential areas will quickly turn to slums.

The personal rhythms of maintenance and repair are central to the well being of any part of a community, because it is only these rhythms which keep up a steady sequence of adaptations and corrections in the organization of the whole. Slums happen when these rhythms break down.

Now in a town, the processes of maintenance and repair hinge on the fact of user ownership. In other words, the places where people are user-owners are kept up nicely; the places where they are not, tend to run down. When people have their own homes among shops, workplaces, schools, services, the university, these places are enhanced by the vitality that is natural to their homes. They extend themselves to make it personal and comfortable. A person will put more of himself into his home than into any of the other places where he spends his time. And it is unlikely that a person can put this kind of feeling into two places, two parts of his life. We conclude that many parts of the environment have the arid quality of not being cared for personally, for the simple reason that indeed nobody lives there.

It is only where houses are mixed in between the other functions, in twos and threes, in rows and tiny clusters, that the personal quality of the households and house-building activities gives energy to the workshops and offices and services.

Therefore:

Build houses into the fabric of shops, small industry, schools, public services, universities—all those parts of cities which draw people in during the day, but which tend to be "nonresidential." The houses may be in rows or "hills" with shops beneath, or they may be free-standing, so long as they mix with the other functions, and make the entire area "lived-in."

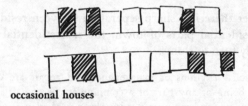

occasional houses

❖ ❖ ❖

Make sure that, in spite of its position in a public area, each house still has enough private territory for people to feel at home in it—YOUR OWN HOME (79). If there are several houses in one area, treat them as a cluster or as a row—HOUSE CLUSTER (37), ROW HOUSES (38). . . .

*between the house clusters and work communities,
allow the local road and path network to grow
informally, piecemeal:*

49 LOOPED LOCAL ROADS**

. . . assume that neighborhoods, house clusters, work communities, and major roads are more or less defined—LOCAL TRANSPORT
AREAS (11), IDENTIFIABLE NEIGHBORHOOD (14), PARALLEL ROADS
(23), HOUSE CLUSTER (37), WORK COMMUNITY (41). Now, for
the layout of the local roads.

Nobody wants fast through traffic going by their homes.

Through traffic is fast, noisy, and dangerous. At the same time
cars are important, and cannot be excluded altogether from the
areas where people live. Local roads must provide access to houses
but prevent traffic from coming through.

This problem can only be solved if all roads which have houses
on them are laid out to be "loops." We define a looped road as
any road in a road network so placed that no path along other
roads in the road network can be shortened by travel along the
"loop."

The loops themselves must be designed to discourage high
volumes or high speeds: this depends on the total number of
houses served by the loop, the road surface, the road width, and
the number of curves and corners. Our observations suggest that a
loop can be made safe so long as it serves less than 50 cars. At
one and one-half cars per house, such a loop serves 30 houses; at
one car per house, 50 houses; at one-half car per house, 100
houses.

Here is an example of an entire system of looped local roads
designed for a community of 1500 houses in Peru.

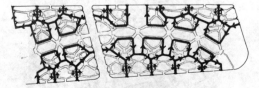

Looped local roads in Lima.

Even a simple grid can be changed to have looped local roads.

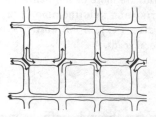

A way of closing streets to form looped local roads.

Dead-end streets are also loops, according to the definition. However, cul-de-sacs are very bad from a social standpoint—they force interaction and they feel claustrophobic, because there is only one entrance. When auto traffic forms a dead end, make sure that the pedestrian path is a through path, leading into the cul-de-sac from one direction, and out of it in another direction.

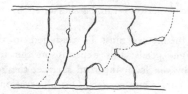

Pedestrian paths which go beyond a dead end.

Recognize also that many roads which appear looped are actually not. This map looks as though it has looped roads. Actually, only one or two of these roads are looped in the functional sense defined.

These are not looped local roads.

Therefore:

Lay out local roads so that they form loops. A loop is defined as any stretch of road which makes it impossible for cars that don't have destinations on it to use it as a shortcut. Do not allow any one loop to serve more than 50 cars, and keep the road really narrow—17 to 20 feet is quite enough.

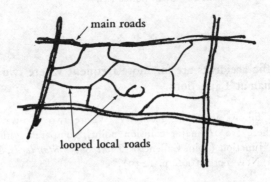

main roads

looped local roads

❖ ❖ ❖

Make all the junctions between local roads three-way T junctions, never four-way intersections—T JUNCTIONS (50); wherever there is any possibility of life from buildings being oriented toward the road, give the road a very rough surface of grass and gravel, with paving stones for wheels of cars—GREEN STREETS (51); keep parking off the road in driveways—SMALL PARKING LOTS (103) and CAR CONNECTION (113); except where the roads are very quiet, run pedestrian paths at right angles to them, not along them, and make buildings open off these paths, not off the roads—NETWORK OF PATHS AND CARS (52). . . .

50 T JUNCTIONS*

. . . if major roads are in position—PARALLEL ROADS (23), and
you are in the process of defining the local roads, this pattern
gives the nature of the intersections. It will also greatly influence
the layout of the local roads, and will help to generate their loop-
like character—LOOPED LOCAL ROADS (49).

**Traffic accidents are far more frequent where two roads
cross than at T junctions.**

This follows from the geometry. Where two two-way roads
cross, there are 16 major collision points, compared with three
for a T junction (John Callendar, *Time Saver Standards*, Fourth
Edition, New York, 1966, p. 1230).

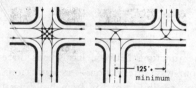

Sixteen collision points. . . . Three collision points.

Maps from an empirical study which compares the number of
accidents over a period of five years for different street patterns
are shown below. They show clearly that T junctions have many
fewer accidents than four-way intersections (from *Planning for
Man and Motor*, by Paul Ritter, p. 307).

Further evidence shows that the T junction is safest if it is a
right-angled junction. When the angle deviates from the right
angle, it is hard for drivers to see round the corner, and accidents
increase (Swedish National Board of Urban Planning, "Principles
for Urban Planning with Respect to Road Safety," *The Scaft
Guidelines 1968, Publication* No. 5, Stockholm, Sweden, p. 11).

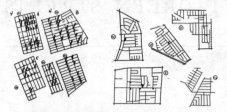

Accidents at different intersections.

Therefore:

Lay out the road system so that any two roads which meet at grade, meet in three-way T junctions as near 90 degrees as possible. Avoid four-way intersections and crossing movements.

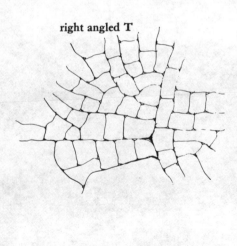

right angled T

✣ ✣ ✣

At busy junctions, where pedestrian paths converge, make a special raised crossing for pedestrians, something more than the usual crosswalk—ROAD CROSSING (54). . . .

51 GREEN STREETS**

. . . this pattern helps to give the character of local roads. Even though it only defines the surface of the road, and the position of parking, the gradual emergence of this pattern in an area, can be used, piecemeal, to create LOOPED LOCAL ROADS (49), T JUNCTIONS (50), and COMMON LAND (67). This pattern was inspired by a beautiful road in the north of Denmark, built by Anne-Marie Rubin, and illustrated here.

❖ ❖ ❖

There is too much hot hard asphalt in the world. A local road, which only gives access to buildings, needs a few stones for the wheels of the cars; nothing more. Most of it can still be green.

In a typical low density American suburb, more than 50 per cent of the land is covered with concrete or asphalt paving. In some areas, like downtown Los Angeles, it is more than 65 per cent.

This concrete and asphalt have a terrible effect on the local environment. They destroy the microclimate; they do nothing useful with the solar energy that falls on them; they are unpleasant to walk on; there is nowhere to sit; nowhere for children to play; the natural drainage of the ground is devastated; animals and plants can hardly survive.

The fact is that asphalt and concrete are only suitable for use on high speed roads. They are unsuitable, and quite unnecessary, on local roads, where a few cars are moving in and out. When local roads are paved, wide and smooth, like major roads, drivers are encouraged to travel past our houses at 35 or 40 miles per hour. What is needed, instead, on local roads is a grassy surface that is adapted to the primary uses of the common land between the buildings, with just enough hard paving to cope with the few cars that do go on it.

The best solution is a field of grass, with paving stones set into it. This arrangement provides for animals and children and makes the street a focal point for the neighborhood. On hot summer

days the air over the grass surface is 10 to 14 degrees cooler than the air over an asphalt road. And the cars are woven into this scheme, but they do not dominate it.

Paving stones.

Of course, such a scheme raises immediately the question of parking. How shall it be organized? It is possible to arrange for parking on green streets, so long as it is parking for residents and their guests, only. When overflow parking from shopping streets and work communities sprawls onto streets that were intended to be quiet neighborhoods, the character of the neighborhood is drastically altered. The residents generally resent this situation. Often it means they cannot park in front of their own homes. The neighborhood becomes a parking lot for strangers who care nothing about it, who simply store their cars there.

The green street will only work if it is based on the principle that the street need not, and should not, provide for more parking than its people need. Parking for visitors can be in small parking lots at the ends of the street; parking for people in the individual houses and workshops can either be in the same parking lots or in the driveways of the buildings.

This does not imply that commercial activities, shops, and businesses should be excluded from residential areas. In fact, as we have said in SCATTERED WORK (9), it is extremely important to build such functions into neighborhoods. The point is, however, that businesses cannot assume when they move into a neighborhood that they have the right to a huge amount of free parking. They must pay for their parking; and they must pay for it in a way which is consistent with the environmental needs of the neighborhood.

Therefore:

On local roads, closed to through traffic, plant grass all over the road and set occasional paving stones into the grass to form a surface for the wheels of those cars that need access to the street. Make no distinction between street and sidewalk. Where houses open off the street, put in more paving stones or gravel to let cars turn onto their own land.

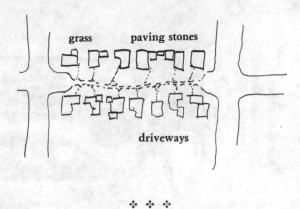

❖ ❖ ❖

When a road is a green street, it is so pleasant that it naturally tends to attract activity to it. In this case, the paths and the green street are one—COMMON LAND (67). However, even when the street is green, it may be pleasant to put in occasional very small lanes, a few feet wide, at right angles to the green streets, according to NETWORK OF PATHS AND CARS (52). In order to preserve the greenness of the street, it will be essential, too, to keep parked cars in driveways on the individual lots, or in tiny parking lots, at the ends of the street, reserved for the house owners and their visitors—SMALL PARKING LOTS (103). Fruit trees and flowers will make the street more beautiful—FRUIT TREES (170), RAISED FLOWERS (245)—and the paving stones which form the beds for cars to drive on, can themselves be laid with cracks between them and with grass and moss and flowers in the cracks between the stones—PAVING WITH CRACKS BETWEEN THE STONES (247). . . .

52 NETWORK OF PATHS
AND CARS**

. . . roads may be governed by PARALLEL ROADS (23), LOOPED LOCAL ROADS (49), GREEN STREETS (51); major paths by ACTIVITY NODES (30), PROMENADE (31), and PATHS AND GOALS (120). This pattern governs the interaction between the two.

Cars are dangerous to pedestrians; yet activities occur just where cars and pedestrians meet.

It is common planning practice to separate pedestrians and cars. This makes pedestrian areas more human and safer. However, this practice fails to take account of the fact that cars and pedestrians also need each other: and that, in fact, a great deal of urban life occurs at just the point where these two systems meet. Many of the greatest places in cities, Piccadilly Circus, Times Square, the Champs Elysées, are alive because they are at places where pedestrians and vehicles meet. New towns like Cumbernauld, in Scotland, where there is total separation between the two, seldom have the same sort of liveliness.

The same thing is true at the local residental scale. A great deal of everyday social life occurs where cars and pedestrians meet. In Lima, for example, the car is used as an extension of the house: men, especially, often sit in parked cars, near their houses, drinking beer and talking. And in one way or another, something like this happens everywhere. Conversation and discussion grow naturally around the lots where people wash their cars. Vendors set themselves up where cars and pedestrians meet; they need all the traffic they can get. Children play in parking

Children like cars.

lots—perhaps because they sense that this is the main point of arrival and departure; and of course because they like the cars. Yet, at the same time, it is essential to keep pedestrians separate from vehicles: to protect children and old people; to preserve the tranquility of pedestrian life.

To resolve the conflict, it is necessary to find an arrangement of pedestrian paths and roads, so that the two are separate, but meet frequently, with the points where they meet recognized as focal points. In general, this requires two orthogonal networks, one for roads, one for paths, each connected and continuous, crossing at frequent intervals (our observations suggest that most points on the path network should be within 150 feet of the nearest road), meeting, when they meet, at right angles.

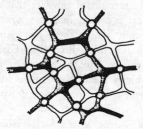

Two orthogonal networks.

In practice, there are several possible ways of forming this relationship between the roads and paths.

It can be done within the system of fast one-way roads about 300 feet apart described in PARALLEL ROADS (23). Between the roads there are pedestrian paths running at right angles to the roads, with buildings opening off the pedestrian paths. Where the

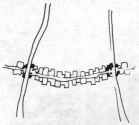

Path between parallel roads.

paths intersect the roads there are small parking lots with space for kiosks and shops.

It can be applied to an existing neighborhood—as it is in the following sequence of plans drawn by the People's Architects, Berkeley, California. This shows a beautiful and simple way of creating a path network in an existing grid of streets, by closing off alternate streets, in each direction. As the drawings show, it can be done gradually.

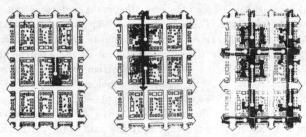

The growth of a path network in a street grid.

Different again, is our project for housing in Lima. Here the two orthogonal systems are laid out as follows:

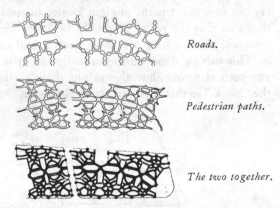

Roads.

Pedestrian paths.

The two together.

In all these cases, we see a global pattern, in which roads and paths are created more or less at the same time—and therefore brought into the proper relationship. However, it is essential to recognize that in most practical applications of this pattern, it is

not necessary to locate the roads and paths together. Most typically of all, there is an existing road system: and the paths can be put in one by one, piecemeal, at right angles to the existing roads. Slowly, very slowly, a coherent path network will be created by the accumulation of these piecemeal acts.

Finally, note that this kind of separation of cars from pedestrians is only appropriate where traffic densities are medium or medium high. At low densities (for instance, a cul-de-sac gravel road serving half-a-dozen houses), the paths and roads can obviously be combined. There is no reason even to have sidewalks—GREEN STREETS (51). At very high densities, like the Champs Elysées, or Piccadilly Circus, a great deal of the excitement is actually created by the fact that pedestrian paths are running *along* the roads. In these cases the problem is best solved by extra wide sidewalks—RAISED WALKS (55)—which actually contain the resolution of the conflict in their width. The edge away from the road is safe—the edge near the road is the place where the activities happen.

Therefore:

Except where traffic densities are very high or very low, lay out pedestrian paths at right angles to roads, not along them, so that the paths gradually begin to form a second network, distinct from the road system, and orthogonal to it. This can be done quite gradually—even if you put in one path at a time, but always put them in the middle of the "block," so that they run across the roads.

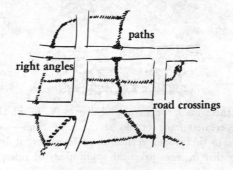

❖ ❖ ❖

Where paths have to run along major roads—as they do occasionally—build them 18 inches higher than the road, on one side of the road only, and twice the usual width—RAISED WALK (55); on GREEN STREETS (51) the paths can be in the road since there is nothing but grass and paving stones there; but even then, occasional narrow paths at right angles to the green streets are very beautiful. Place the paths in detail according to PATHS AND GOALS (120); shape them according to PATH SHAPE (121). Finally, treat the important street crossings as crosswalks, raised to the level of the pedestrian path—so cars have to slow down as they go over them—ROAD CROSSING (54). . . .

53 MAIN GATEWAYS**

. . . at various levels in the structure of the town, there are identifiable units. There are neighborhoods—IDENTIFIABLE NEIGHBORHOOD (14), clusters—HOUSE CLUSTER (37), communities of work—WORK COMMUNITY (41); and there are many smaller building complexes ringed around some realms of circulation—BUILDING COMPLEX (95), CIRCULATION REALMS (98). All of them get their identity most clearly from the fact that you pass through a definite gateway to enter them—it is this gateway acting as a threshold which creates the unit.

Any part of a town—large or small—which is to be identified by its inhabitants as a precinct of some kind, will be reinforced, helped in its distinctness, marked, and made more vivid, if the paths which enter it are marked by gateways where they cross the boundary.

Many parts of a town have boundaries drawn around them. These boundaries are usually in people's minds. They mark the end of one kind of activity, one kind of place, and the beginning of another. In many cases, the activities themselves are made more sharp, more vivid, more alive, if the boundary which exists in people's minds is also present physically in the world.

A boundary around an important precinct, whether a neighborhood, a building complex, or some other area, is most critical at those points where paths cross the boundary. If the point where the path crosses the boundary is invisible, then to all intents and purposes the boundary is not there. It will be there, it will be felt, only if the crossing is marked. And essentially, the crossing of a boundary by a path can only be marked by a gateway. That is why all forms of gateway play such an important role in the environment.

A gateway can have many forms: a literal gate, a bridge, a passage between narrowly separated buildings, an avenue of trees, a gateway through a building. All of these have the same function: they mark the point where a path crosses a boundary and help

maintain the boundary. All of them are "things"—not merely holes or gaps, but solid entities.

Gateways mark the point of transition.

In every case, the crucial feeling which this solid thing must create is the feeling of transition.

Therefore:

Mark every boundary in the city which has important human meaning—the boundary of a building cluster, a neighborhood, a precinct—by great gateways where the major entering paths cross the boundary.

Make the gateways solid elements, visible from every line of approach, enclosing the paths, punching a hole through a building, creating a bridge or a sharp change of level—but above all make them "things," in just the same way specified for MAIN ENTRANCE (110), but make them larger. Whenever possible, emphasize the feeling of transition for the person passing through the gateway, by allowing change of light, or surface, view, crossing water, a change of level—ENTRANCE TRANSITION (112). In every case, treat the main gateway as the starting point of the pedestrian circulation inside the precinct—CIRCULATION REALMS (98). . . .

. . . under the impetus of PARALLEL ROADS (23) and NETWORK OF PATHS AND CARS (52), paths will gradually grow at right angles to major roads—not along them as they do now. This is an entirely new kind of situation, and requires an entirely new physical treatment to make it work.

❖ ❖ ❖

Where paths cross roads, the cars have power to frighten and subdue the people walking, even when the people walking have the legal right-of-way.

This will happen whenever the path and the road are at the same level. No amount of painted white lines, crosswalks, traffic lights, button operated signals, ever quite manage to change the fact that a car weighs a ton or more, and will run over any pedestrian, unless the driver brakes. Most often the driver does brake. But everyone knows of enough occasions when brakes have failed, or drivers gone to sleep, to be perpetually wary and afraid.

The people who cross a road will only feel comfortable and safe if the road crossing is a physical obstruction, which physically guarantees that the cars must slow down and give way to pedestrians. In many places it is recognized by law that pedestrians have the right-of-way over automobiles. Yet at the crucial points where paths cross roads, the *physical* arrangement gives priority to *cars*. The road is continuous, smooth, and fast, interrupting the pedestrian walkway at the junctions. This continuous road surface actually implies that the car has the right-of-way.

What should crossings be like to accommodate the needs of the pedestrians?

The fact that pedestrians feel less vulnerable to cars when they are about 18 inches above them, is discussed in the next pattern RAISED WALK (55). The same principle applies, even more powerfully, where pedestrians have to cross a road. The pedestrians who cross must be extremely visible from the road. Cars should also be forced to slow down when they approach the crossing. If the pedestrian way crosses 6 to 12 inches above the road-

way, and the roadway slopes up to it, this satisfies both requirements. A slope of 1 in 6, or less, is safe for cars and solid enough
to slow them down. To make the crossing even easier to see from
a distance and to give weight to the pedestrian's right to be there,
the pedestrian path could be marked by a canopy at the edge of
the road—CANVAS ROOFS (244).

Almost a road crossing . . . but no bump.

We know that this pattern is rather extraordinary. For this
reason, we consider it quite essential that readers do not try to
use it on every road, for formalistic reasons, but only on those
roads where it is badly needed. We therefore complete the problem statement by defining a simple experiment which you can do
to decide whether or not a given crossing needs this treatment.

Go to the road in question several times, at different times of
day. Each time you go, count the number of seconds you have to
wait before you can cross the road. If the average of these waiting times is more than two seconds, then we recommend you use
the pattern. (On the basis of Buchanan's statement that roads become threatening to pedestrians when the volume of traffic on
them creates an average delay of two seconds or more, for people
trying to cross on foot. See the extensive discussion, Colin
Buchanan et al., *Traffic in Towns*, HMSO, London, 1963, pp.
203–13.) If you cannot do this experiment, or the road is not
yet built, you may be able to guess, by using the chart below. It
shows which combinations of volume and width will typically
create more than a two-second average delay.

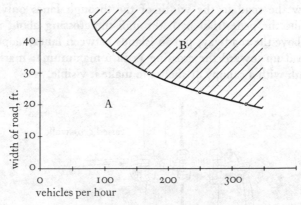

Roads that fall in the shaded region require special crossings.

One final note. This pattern may be impossible to implement, in places where traffic engineers are still in control. Nevertheless the functional issue is vital, and must not be ignored. A big wide road, with several lanes of heavy traffic can form an almost impenetrable barrier. In this case, you can solve the problem, at least partially, by creating islands—certainly one in the middle, and perhaps extra islands, between adjacent lanes. This has a huge effect on a person's capacity to cross the road, for a very simple reason. If you are trying to cross a wide road, you have to wait for a gap to occur simultaneously in each of the lanes. It is the waiting for this coincidence of gaps that creates the problem. But if you can hop, from island to island, each time a gap occurs in any one lane, one lane at a time, you can get across in no time at all—because the gaps which occur in individual lanes are many many times more frequent, than the big gaps in all lanes at the same time. So, if you can't raise the crossing, at least use islands, like stepping stones.

Therefore:

At any point where a pedestrian path crosses a road that has enough traffic to create more than a two second delay to people crossing, make a "knuckle" at the crossing:

narrow the road to the width of the through lanes only; continue the pedestrian path through the crossing about a foot above the roadway; put in islands between lanes; slope the road up toward the crossing (1 in 6 maximum); mark the path with a canopy or shelter to make it visible.

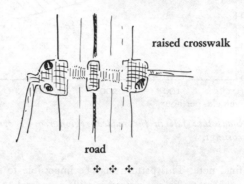

raised crosswalk

road

❖ ❖ ❖

On one side or the other of the road make the pedestrian path swell out to form a tiny square, where food stands cluster round a bus stop—SMALL PUBLIC SQUARES (61), BUS STOP (92), FOOD STANDS (93); provide one or two bays for standing space for buses and cars—SMALL PARKING LOTS (103), and when a path must run from the road crossing along the side of the road, keep it to one side only, make it as wide as possible, and raised above the roadway—RAISED WALK (55). Perhaps build the canopy as a trellis or canvas roof—TRELLISED WALK (174), CANVAS ROOFS (244). . . .

55 RAISED WALK*

. . . this pattern helps complete the NETWORK OF PATHS AND CARS (52) and ROAD CROSSINGS (54). It is true that in most cases, pedestrian paths which follow the path network will be running across roads, not next to them. But still, from time to time, especially along major PARALLEL ROADS (23), between one road crossing and the next, there is a need for paths along the road. This pattern gives these special paths their character.

Where fast moving cars and pedestrians meet in cities, the cars overwhelm the pedestrians. The car is king, and people are made to feel small.

This cannot be solved by keeping pedestrians separate from cars; it is in their nature that they have to meet, at least occasionally—NETWORK OF PATHS AND CARS (52). What can be done at those points where cars and pedestrians do meet?

On an ordinary street, cars make pedestrians feel small and vulnerable because the sidewalks are too narrow and too low. When the sidewalk is too narrow, you feel you are going to fall off, or get pushed off—and there is always a chance that you will step off just in front of a passing car. When the sidewalk is too low, you feel that cars can easily mount the sidewalk, if they go out of control, and crush you. It is clear, then, that pedestrians will feel comfortable, powerful, safe, and free in their movements when the walks they walk on are both wide enough to keep the

Traditional raised walk in Pichucalis, Mexico.

people well away from the cars, and high enough to make it quite impossible for any car to drive up on them by accident.

We first consider the width. What is the appropriate width for a raised walk? The famous example, of course, is the Champs Elysées, where the sidewalk is more than 30 feet wide, and very comfortable. In our own experience, a walk of half this width, along a typical shopping street with traffic, is still comfortable; but 12 feet or less, and a pedestrian begins to feel cramped and threatened by cars. A conventional sidewalk is often no more than 6 feet wide; and people really feel the presence of the cars. How can we afford the extra width which people need in order to be comfortable? One way: instead of putting sidewalks along both sides of a road, we can put a double width raised walk along one side of the road only, with road crossings at intervals of 200 to 300 feet. This means, of course, that there can only be shops along one side of the road.

What is the right height for a raised walk? Our experiments suggest that pedestrians begin to feel secure when they are about 18 inches above the cars. There are a number of possible reasons for this finding.

One possible reason. When the car is down low and the pedestrian world physically higher, pedestrians feel, symbolically, that they are more important than the cars and therefore feel secure.

Another possible reason. It may be that the car overwhelms the pedestrian because of a constant, unspoken possibility that a runaway car might at any moment mount the curb and run him down. A car can climb an ordinary six inch curb easily. For the pedestrian to feel certain that a car could not climb the curb, the curb height would have to be greater than the radius of a car tire (10 to 15 inches).

Another possible reason. Most people's eye level is between 51 and 63 inches. A typical car has an overall height of 55 inches. Although tall people can see over cars, even for them, the cars fill the landscape since a standing person's normal line of sight is 10 degrees below the horizontal (Henry Dreyfus, *The Measure of Man*, New York, 1958, sheet F). To put a car 12 feet away completely below a pedestrian's line of sight, it would have to be on a road some 18 to 30 inches below the pedestrian.

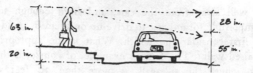

Keep the cars below a person's line of sight.

Therefore:

We conclude that any pedestrian path along a road carrying fast-moving cars should be about 18 inches above the road, with a low wall or railing, or balustrade along the edge, to mark the edge. Put the raised walk on only one side of the road—make it as wide as possible.

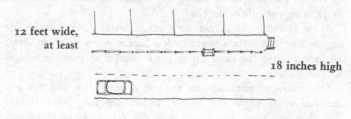

12 feet wide, at least

18 inches high

❖ ❖ ❖

Protect the raised walk from the road, by means of a low wall —SITTING WALL (243). An arcade built over the walk, will, with its columns, give an even greater sense of comfort and protection —ARCADES (119). At the end of blocks and at special points where a car might pull in to pick up or drop passengers, build steps into the raised walk, large enough so people can sit there and wait in comfort—STAIR SEATS (125). . . .

56 BIKE PATHS AND RACKS*

. . . within a LOCAL TRANSPORT AREA (11) there is a heavy concentration of small vehicles like bikes, electric carts, perhaps even horses, which need a system of bike paths. The bike paths will play a very large role in helping to create the local transport areas, and may also help to modify LOOPED LOCAL ROADS (49) and NETWORK OF PATHS AND CARS (52).

Bikes are cheap, healthy, and good for the environment; but the environment is not designed for them. Bikes on roads are threatened by cars; bikes on paths threaten pedestrians.

In making the environment safe for bikes, the following problems must be solved:

1. Bikes are threatened where they meet or cross heavy automobile traffic.

2. They are also threatened by parked cars. Parked cars make it difficult for the bike rider to see other people, and they make it difficult for other people to see him. In addition, since the bike rider usually has to ride close to parked cars, he is always in danger of someone opening a car door in front of him.

3. Bikes endanger pedestrians along pedestrian paths; yet people often tend to ride bikes along pedestrian paths, not roads, because they are the shortest routes.

4. Where bikes are in heavy use, for instance around schools and universities, they can lay a pedestrian precinct to waste in their own way, just as cars can.

An obvious solution to these problems is to create a completely independent system of bike paths. However, it is doubtful that this is a viable or desirable solution. The study "Students on Wheels" (Jany, Putney, and Ritter, Department of Landscape Architecture, University of Oregon, Eugene, Oregon, 1972) shows that bike riders and nonbike riders want a mixed system, so long as it is reasonably safe.

We also think that it is essential for bike paths to run in streets

and along pedestrian paths: if bikes are forced onto a separate system, it will almost certainly be violated by people taking short-cuts across the other networks. And laws which would keep bikes completely off the road and path systems would be discouraging to the already hasseled bike riders. Wherever possible, then, bike paths should coincide with roads and major pedestrian paths.

Where bike paths coincide with major roads, they must be separated from the roadway. It helps put the bike rider in a safer position with respect to the cars if the bike path is raised a few inches from the road; or separated by a row of trees.

Where bike paths run alongside local roads, parking should be removed from that side of the road; the bike surface may simply be part of the road and level with it. An article by Bascome in the *Oregon Daily Emerald* (October 1971) suggested that bike lanes along streets should always be on the sunny side of the street.

Where bike paths coincide with major pedestrian paths, they should be separate from the paths, perhaps a few inches below them. Here, the change in level gives the pedestrian a sense of safety from the bikes.

Quiet paths and certain pedestrian precincts should be com-pletely protected from bikes for the same reasons that they need to be protected from cars. This can be handled by making the bike path system bypass these places, or by enclosing these places with steps or low walls which force bike riders to dismount and walk their bikes.

Therefore:

Build a system of paths designated as bike paths, with the following properties: the bike paths are marked clearly with a special, easily recognizable surface (for example, a red asphalt surface). As far as possible they run along local roads, or major pedestrian paths. Where a bike path runs along a local road, its surface may be level with the road —if possible, on the sunny side; where a bike path runs along a pedestrian path, keep it separate from that path and a few inches below it. Bring the system of bike paths to

within 100 feet of every building, and give every building a
bike rack near its main entrance.

bike path system

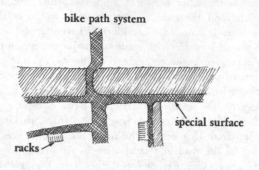

special surface

racks

❖ ❖ ❖

Build the racks for bikes to one side of the main entrance, so
that the bikes don't interfere with people's natural movement in
and out—MAIN ENTRANCE (110), and give it some shelter, with
the path from the racks to the entrance also under shelter—
ARCADES (119); keep the bikes out of quiet walks and quiet
gardens—QUIET BACKS (59), GARDEN WALL (173). . . .

57 CHILDREN IN
THE CITY

. . . roads, bike paths, and main pedestrian paths are given their position by PARALLEL ROADS (23), PROMENADE (31), LOOPED LOCAL ROADS (49), GREEN STREETS (51), NETWORK OF PATHS AND CARS (52), BIKE PATHS AND RACKS (56). Some of them are safe for children, others are less safe. Now, finally, to complete the paths and roads, it is essential to define at least one place, right in the very heart of cities, where children can be completely free and safe. If handled properly, this pattern can play a great role in helping to create the NETWORK OF LEARNING (18).

❖ ❖ ❖

If children are not able to explore the whole of the adult world round about them, they cannot become adults. But modern cities are so dangerous that children cannot be allowed to explore them freely.

The need for children to have access to the world of adults is so obvious that it goes without saying. The adults transmit their ethos and their way of life to children through their actions, not through statements. Children learn by doing and by copying. If the child's education is limited to school and home, and all the vast undertakings of a modern city are mysterious and inaccessible, it is impossible for the child to find out what it really means to be an adult and impossible, certainly, for him to copy it by doing.

This separation between the child's world and the adult world is unknown among animals and unknown in traditional societies. In simple villages, children spend their days side by side with farmers in the fields, side by side with people who are building houses, side by side, in fact, with all the daily actions of the men and women round about them: making pottery, counting money, curing the sick, praying to God, grinding corn, arguing about the future of the village.

But in the city, life is so enormous and so dangerous, that children can't be left alone to roam around. There is constant danger from fast-moving cars and trucks, and dangerous machinery. There is a small but ominous danger of kidnap, or rape,

or assault. And, for the smallest children, there is the simple danger of getting lost. A small child just doesn't know enough to find his way around a city.

The problem seems nearly insoluble. But we believe it can be at least partly solved by enlarging those parts of cities where small children can be left to roam, alone, and by trying to make sure that these protected children's belts are so widespread and so far-reaching that they touch the full variety of adult activities and ways of life.

We imagine a carefully developed childrens' bicycle path, within the larger network of bike paths. The path goes past and through interesting parts of the city; and it is relatively safe. It is part of the overall system and therefore used by everyone. It is not a special children's "ride"—which would immediately be shunned by the adventurous young—but it does have a special name, and perhaps it is specially colored.

The path is always a bike path; it never runs beside cars. Where it crosses traffic there are lights or bridges. There are many homes and shops along the path—adults are nearby, especially the old enjoy spending an hour a day sitting along this path, themselves riding along the loop, watching the kids out of the corner of one eye.

And most important, the great beauty of this path is that it passes along and even through those functions and parts of a town which are normally out of reach: the place where newspapers are printed, the place where milk arrives from the countryside and is bottled, the pier, the garage where people make doors and windows, the alley behind restaurant row, the cemetery.

Therefore:

As part of the network of bike paths, develop one system of paths that is extra safe—entirely separate from automo-

biles, with lights and bridges at the crossings, with homes and shops along it, so that there are always many eyes on the path. Let this path go through every neighborhood, so that children can get onto it without crossing a main road. And run the path all through the city, down pedestrian streets, through workshops, assembly plants, warehouses, interchanges, print houses, bakeries, all the interesting "invisible" life of a town—so that the children can roam freely on their bikes and trikes.

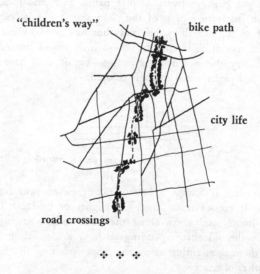

❖ ❖ ❖

Line the children's path with windows, especially from rooms that are in frequent use, so that the eyes upon the street make it safe for the children—STREET WINDOWS (164); make it touch the children's places all along the path—CONNECTED PLAY (68), ADVENTURE PLAYGROUND (73), SHOPFRONT SCHOOLS (85), CHILDREN'S HOME (86), but also make it touch other phases of the life cycle—OLD PEOPLE EVERYWHERE (40), WORK COMMUNITY (41), UNIVERSITY AS A MARKETPLACE (43), GRAVE SITES (70), LOCAL SPORTS (72), ANIMALS (74), TEENAGE SOCIETY (84). . . .

*in the communities and neighborhoods provide pub-
lic open land where people can relax, rub shoulders
and renew themselves;*

58 CARNIVAL

. . . once in a while, in a subculture which is particularly open to it, a promenade may break into a wilder rhythm—PROMENADE (31), NIGHT LIFE (33)—and perhaps every promenade may have a touch of this.

❖ ❖ ❖

Just as an individual person dreams fantastic happenings to release the inner forces which cannot be encompassed by ordinary events, so too a city needs its dreams.

Under normal circumstances, in today's world the entertainments which are available are either healthy and harmless—going to the movies, watching TV, cycling, playing tennis, taking helicopter rides, going for walks, watching football—or downright sick and socially destructive—shooting heroin, driving recklessly, group violence.

But man has a great need for mad, subconscious processes to come into play, without unleashing them to such an extent that they become socially destructive. There is, in short, a need for socially sanctioned activities which are the social, outward equivalents of dreaming.

In primitive societies this kind of process was provided by the rites, witch doctors, shamans. In Western civilization during the last three or four hundred years, the closest available source of this outward acknowledgment of underground life has been the circus, fairs, and carnivals. In the middle ages, the market place itself had a good deal of this kind of atmosphere.

Today, on the whole, this kind of experience is gone. The circuses and the carnivals are drying up. But the need persists. In the Bay Area, the annual Renaissance Fair goes a little way to meet the need—but it is much too bland. We imagine something more along the following lines: street theater, clowns, mad games in the streets and squares and houses; during certain weeks, people may live in the carnival; simple food and shelter are free; day and night people mixing; actors who mingle with the crowd and involve you, willy nilly, in processes whose end cannot be

299

foreseen; fighting—two men with bags on a slippery log, in front of hundreds; Fellini—clowns, death, crazy people, brought into mesh.

Remember the hunchbacked dwarf in *Ship of Fools*, the only reasonable person on the ship, who says "Everyone has a problem; but I have the good fortune to wear mine on my back, where everyone can see it."

Therefore:

Set aside some part of the town as a carnival—mad sideshows, tournaments, acts, displays, competitions, dancing, music, street theater, clowns, transvestites, freak events, which allow people to reveal their madness; weave a wide pedestrian street through this area; run booths along the street, narrow alleys; at one end an outdoor theater; perhaps connect the theater stage directly to the carnival street, so the two spill into and feed one another.

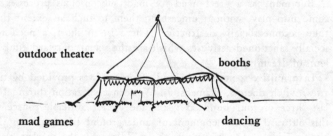

outdoor theater   booths

mad games   dancing

❖ ❖ ❖

Dancing in the street, food stands, an outdoor room or two, a square where the theater is, and tents and canvas will all help to make it even livelier—SMALL PUBLIC SQUARES (61), DANCING IN THE STREET (63), PUBLIC OUTDOOR ROOM (69), FOOD STANDS (93), PEDESTRIAN STREET (100), CANVAS ROOFS (244). . . .

59 QUIET BACKS*

. . . the work places are given their general position by SCAT-TERED WORK (9) and their detailed organization and distribution by WORK COMMUNITIES (41). It is essential though, that they be supported by some kind of quiet, which is complementary to the work. This pattern, and the next few patterns, gives the structure of that quiet.

❖ ❖ ❖

Any one who has to work in noise, in offices with people all around, needs to be able to pause and refresh himself with quiet in a more natural situation.

The walk along the Seine, through the middle of Paris, is a classic "quiet back" in the middle of a fast city. People drop down from the streets and the traffic and the commerce to stroll along the river, where the mood is slow and reflective.

The need for such places has often been recognized in universities, where there are quiet walks where people go to think, or pause, or have a private talk. A beautiful case is the University of Cambridge: each college has its "backs"—quiet courts stretching down to the River Cam. But the need for quiet backs goes far beyond the university. It exists everywhere where people work in densely populated, noisy areas.

To meet this need, we may conceive all buildings as having a front and a back. If the front is given over to the street life—cars, shopping paths, delivery—then the back can be reserved for quiet.

If the back is to be quiet, a place where you can hear only natural sounds—winds, birds, water—it is critical that it be protected. At the same time, it must be some way from the buildings which it serves. This suggests a walk, some distance behind the buildings, perhaps separated from them by their private small gardens, completely protected by substantial walls and dense planting along its length.

An example we know is the walk through the cathedral close in Chichester. There is a high brick wall on each side of this walk and flowers planted all along it. It leads away from the cathedral,

parallel but set back from the town's major road. On this path, less than a block from the major crossroads of the town, you can hear the bees buzzing.

If a number of these walks are connected, one to another, then slowly, there emerges a ribbon-like system of tiny backs, pleasant alleyways behind the commotion of the street. Since the sound of water plays such a powerful role in establishing the kind of quiet that is required, these paths should always connect up with the local POOLS AND STREAMS (64). And the longer it can be, the better.

Therefore:

Give the buildings in the busy parts of town a quiet "back" behind them and away from the noise. Build a walk along this quiet back, far enough from the building so that it gets full sunlight, but protected from noise by walls and distance and buildings. Make certain that the path is not a natural shortcut for busy foot traffic, and connect it up with other walks, to form a long ribbon of quiet alleyways which converge on the local pools and streams and the local greens.

shield of buildings

natural quiet

✥ ✥ ✥

If possible, place the backs where there is water—POOLS AND STREAMS (64), STILL WATER (71), and where there are still great trees unharmed by traffic—TREE PLACES (171); connect them to ACCESSIBLE GREENS (60); and protect them from noise with walls or buildings—GARDEN WALL (173). . . .

. . . at the heart of neighborhoods, and near all work communities, there need to be small greens—IDENTIFIABLE NEIGHBORHOOD (14), WORK COMMUNITY (41). Of course it makes the most sense to locate these greens in such a way that they help form the boundaries and neighborhoods and backs—SUBCULTURE BOUNDARY (13), NEIGHBORHOOD BOUNDARY (15), QUIET BACKS (59).

❖ ❖ ❖

People need green open places to go to; when they are close they use them. But if the greens are more than three minutes away, the distance overwhelms the need.

Parks are meant to satisfy this need. But parks, as they are usually understood, are rather large and widely spread through the city. Very few people live within three minutes of a park.

Our research suggests that even though the need for parks is very important, and even though it is vital for people to be able to nourish themselves by going to walk, and run, and play on open greens, this need is very delicate. The only people who make full, daily use of parks are those who live less than three minutes from them. The other people in a city who live more than 3 minutes away, don't need parks any less; but distance discourages use and so they are unable to nourish themselves, as they need to do.

This problem can only be solved if hundreds of small parks— or greens—are scattered so widely, and so profusely, that every house and every workplace in the city is within three minutes walk of the nearest one.

In more detail: The need for parks within a city is well recognized. A typical example of this awareness is given by the results of a 1971 citizen survey on open space conducted by the Berkeley City Planning Department. The survey showed that the great majority of people living in apartments want two kinds of outdoor spaces above all others: (a) a pleasant, usable private balcony and (b) a quiet public park within walking distance.

But the critical effect of distance on the usefulness of such

parks is less well known and understood. In order to study this problem, we visited a small park in Berkeley, and asked 22 people who were in the park how often they came there, and how far they had walked to the park. Specifically, we asked each person three questions:

a. Did you walk or drive?
b. How many blocks have you come?
c. How many days ago did you last visit the park?

On the basis of the first question we rejected five subjects who had come by car or bike. The third question gave for each person a measure of the number of times per week that person comes to the park. For example, if he last came three days ago, we may estimate that he typically comes once per week. This is more reliable than asking the frequency directly, since it relies on a fact which the person is sure of, not on his judgment of a rather intangible frequency.

We now construct a table showing the results. In the first column, we write the number of blocks people walked to get to the park. In the second column we write a measure of the area of the ring-shaped zone which lies at that distance. The area of this ring-shaped zone is proportional to the difference of two squares. For example, the measure of area of the ring at three blocks, is $3^2 - 2^2 = 5$.

Radius R Blocks	Measure of area of the ring at Radius R	Trips/ week	P. (Relative probability of trips, for any one person)	Log P.
1	1	19.5	19.5	1.29
2	3	26	8.7	.94
3	5	11	2.2	.34
4	7	6	0.9	T.95
5	9	0	—	—
6	11	0	—	—
7	13	0	—	—
8	15	6	0.4	T.60
9	17	0	—	—
10	19	3	0.2	T.30
11	21	0	—	—
12	23	2.5	0.1	T.0

Analysis of visiting pattern to a local green

In the third column, we write the number of people who have come from that distance, each person multiplied by the number of trips per week he makes to the park. This gives us a measure of the total number of trips per week, which originate in that ring.

In the fourth column we write the number of trips per week divided by the area of the ring. If we assume that people are distributed throughout the entire area at approximately even density, this gives us a measure of the probability that any one person, in a given ring, will make a trip to the park in a given week.

In the fifth column we write the logarithm (base 10) of this probability measure P.

Simple inspection of these data shows that while the probability measure, P, drops in half between one and two blocks, it drops by a factor of four between two and three blocks. Its rate of decrease diminishes from then on. This indicates that an individual's use of a park changes character radically if he lives more than three blocks away.

For more precision let us examine the relationship between distance and the logarithm of P. Under normal circumstances, the frequency of access to a given center will vary according to some distance decay function, such as $P = Ae^{-Br}$, where A and B are constants, and r is the radius. This means that if behavior and motivation are constant with respect to distance, and we plot the log of P against the radius, we should get a straight line. Any aberration from the straight line will show us the threshold where one kind of behavior and motivation changes to another. This plot is shown below:

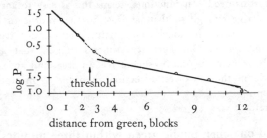

Beyond two or three blocks use of the green drops off drastically.

We see that the resulting curve is S-shaped. It starts going down at a certain angle, then gets much steeper, and then flattens out again. Apparently there is a threshold somewhere between 2 and 3 blocks, where people's behavior and motivation change drastically.

Those people who live in close proximity to a green follow a high intensity use function—it has a steep gradient and it is very sensitive to increasing distance. But those people who live far from a green appear to adopt a low intensity use function (indicated by a shallower gradient), and their behavior is not as sensitive to distance. It is as if those people with ready access to a green display a full, free responsiveness to it; while people far away have lost their awareness of it and have suffered a reduced sensitivity to the pleasures of the green—for thees people, the green has ceased to be a vital element in their neighborhood life.

Apparently, within a two to three block radius (a three-minute walking distance) people are able to satisfy their need for access to a green, but a greater distance seriously interferes with their ability to meet this need.

This inference is rather unexpected. We know that people who are close to a green go to it fairly often, presumably because they need the relaxation. The people who live more than three minutes walk from the green also need the relaxation, presumably. But in their case the distance prevents them from meeting their need. It seems then, that to meet this need, everyone—and that means every house and every workplace—must be within three minutes of such a park.

One question remains. How large must a green be in order to satisfy this need? In functional terms this is easy to answer. It must be large enough so that, at least in the middle of it, you feel that you are in touch with nature, and away from the hustle and bustle. Our current estimates suggest that a green should be as much as 60,000 square feet in area, and at least 150 feet wide in the narrowest direction in order to meet this requirement.

Therefore:

Build one open public green within three minutes' walk —about 750 feet—of every house and workplace. This

means that the greens need to be uniformly scattered at
1500-foot intervals, throughout the city. Make the greens
at least 150 feet across, and at least 60,000 square feet in
area.

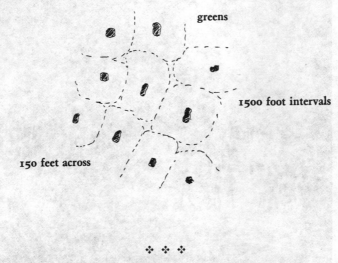

❖ ❖ ❖

Pay special attention to old trees, look after them—TREE
PLACES (171); shape the green so that it forms one or more
positive room-like spaces and surround it with trees, or walls, or
buildings, but not roads or cars—POSITIVE OUTDOOR SPACE
(106), GARDEN WALL (173); and perhaps set aside some part
of the green for special community functions—HOLY GROUND
(66), GRAVE SITES (70), LOCAL SPORTS (72), ANIMALS (74),
SLEEPING IN PUBLIC (94). . . .

61 SMALL PUBLIC SQUARES**

. . . this pattern forms the core which makes an ACTIVITY NODE (30): it can also help to generate a node, by its mere existence, provided that it is correctly placed along the intersection of the paths which people use most often. And it can also help to generate a PROMENADE (31), a WORK COMMUNITY (41), an IDENTIFIABLE NEIGHBORHOOD (14), through the action of the people who gather there. But it is essential, in every case, that it is not too large.

❖ ❖ ❖

A town needs public squares; they are the largest, most public rooms, that the town has. But when they are too large, they look and feel deserted.

It is natural that every public street will swell out at those important nodes where there is the most activity. And it is only these widened, swollen, public squares which can accommodate the public gatherings, small crowds, festivities, bonfires, carnivals, speeches, dancing, shouting, mourning, which must have their place in the life of the town.

But for some reason there is a temptation to make these public squares too large. Time and again in modern cities, architects and planners build plazas that are too large. They look good on drawings; but in real life they end up desolate and dead.

Our observations suggest strongly that open places intended as public squares should be very small. As a general rule, we have found that they work best when they have a diameter of about 60 feet—at this diameter people often go to them, they become favorite places, and people feel comfortable there. When the diameter gets above 70 feet, the squares begin to seem deserted and unpleasant. The only exceptions we know are places like the Piazza San Marco and Trafalgar Square, which are great town centers, teeming with people.

What possible functional basis is there for these observations? First, we know from the pattern, PEDESTRIAN DENSITY (123),

*The squares in Lima: one small and alive,
the other huge and deserted.*

that a place begins to seem deserted when it has more than about
300 square feet per person.

On this basis a square with a diameter of 100 feet will begin
to seem deserted if there are less than 33 people in it. There are
few places in a city where you can be sure there will always be 33
people. On the other hand, it only takes 4 people to give life to
a square with a diameter of 35 feet, and only 12 to give life to
a square with a diameter of 60 feet. Since there are far far better
chances of 4 or 12 people being in a certain place than 33, the
smaller squares will feel comfortable for a far greater percentage
of the time.

The second possible basis for our observations depends on the
diameter. A person's face is just recognizable at about 70 feet;
and under typical urban noise conditions, a loud voice can just
barely be heard across 70 feet. This may mean that people feel
half-consciously tied together in plazas that have diameters of

70 feet or less—where they can make out the faces and half-hear the talk of the people around them; and this feeling of being at one with a loosely knit square is lost in the larger spaces. Roughly similar things have been said by Philip Thiel ("An Architectural and Urban Space Sequence Notation." unpublished ms., University of California, Department of Architecture, August 1960, p. 5) and by Hans Blumenfeld ("Scale in Civic Design," *Town Planning Review*, April 1953, pp. 35-46). For example, Blumenfeld gives the following figures: a person's face can be recognized at up to 70 or 80 feet; a person's face can be recognized as "a portrait," in rich detail, at up to about 48 feet.

Our own informal experiments show the following results. Two people with normal vision can communicate comfortably up to 75 feet. They can talk with raised voice, and they can see the general outlines of the expression on one another's faces. This 75 foot maximum is extremely reliable. Repeated experiments gave the same distance again and again, ±10 per cent. At 100 feet it is uncomfortable to talk, and facial expression is no longer clear. Anything above 100 feet is hopeless.

Therefore:

Make a public square much smaller than you would at first imagine; usually no more than 45 to 60 feet across, never more than 70 feet across. This applies only to its width in the short direction. In the long direction it can certainly be longer.

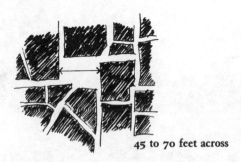

45 to 70 feet across

An even better estimate for the size of the square: make a guess about the number of people who will typically be there (say, P), and make the area of the square no greater than 150 to 300P square feet—PEDESTRIAN DENSITY (123); ring the square around with pockets of activity where people congregate—ACTIVITY POCKETS (124); build buildings round the square in such a way that they give it a definite shape, with views out into other larger places—POSITIVE OUTDOOR SPACE (106), HIERARCHY OF OPEN SPACE (114), BUILDING FRONTS (122), STAIR SEATS (125); and to make the center of the square as useful as the edges, build SOMETHING ROUGHLY IN THE MIDDLE (126). . . .

62 HIGH PLACES*

. . . according to FOUR-STORY LIMIT (21), most roofs in the community are no higher than four stories, about 40 or 50 feet. However, it is very important that this height limit be punctuated, just occasionally, by higher buildings which have special functions. They can help the character of the SMALL PUBLIC SQUARES (61) and HOLY GROUND (66); they can give particular identity to their communities, provided that they do not occur more frequently than one in each COMMUNITY OF 7000 (12).

❖ ❖ ❖

The instinct to climb up to some high place, from which you can look down and survey your world, seems to be a fundamental human instinct.

The tiniest hamlets have a dominating landmark—usually the church tower. Great cities have hundreds of them. The instinct to build these towers is certainly not merely Christian; the same thing happens in different cultures and religions, all over the world. Persian villages have pigeon towers; Turkey, its minarets; San Gimignano, its houses in the form of towers; castles, their lookouts; Athens, its Acropolis; Rio, its rock.

These high places have two separate and complementary functions. They give people a place to climb up to, from which they can look down upon their world. And they give people a place which they can see from far away and orient themselves toward, when they are on the ground.

Listen to Proust:

Combray at a distance, from a twenty-mile radius, as we used to see it from the railway when we arrived there every year in Holy Week, was no more than a church epitomising the town, representing it, speaking of it and for it to the horizon, and as one drew near, gathering close about its long, dark cloak, sheltering from the wind, on the open plain, as a shepherd gathers his sheep, the woolly grey backs of its blocking houses. . . .

From a long way off one could distinguish and identify the steeple of Sainte-Hilaire inscribing its unforgetable form upon a horizon beneath which Combray had not yet appeared; when from the train

which brought us down from Paris at Eastertime my father caught sight of it, as it slipped into every fold of the sky in turn, its little iron cock veering continually in all directions, he could say: "Come, get your wraps together, we are there." (Marcel Proust, *Swann's Way*.)

Oxford: the city of dreaming spires.

High places are equally important, too, as places from which to look down: places that give a spectacular, comprehensive view of the town. Visitors can go to them to get a sense of the entire area they have come to; and the people who live there can do so too—to reassess the shape and scope of their surroundings. But these visits to the high places will have no freshness or exhilaration if there is a ride to the top in a car or elevator. To get a full sense of the magnificence of the view, it seems necessary to work for it, to leave the car or elevator, and to climb. The act of climbing, even if only for a few steps, clears the mind and prepares the body.

As for distribution, we suggest about one of these high places for each community of 7000, high enough to be seen throughout the community. If high places are less frequent, they tend to be too special, and they have less power as landmarks.

Therefore:

Build occasional high places as landmarks throughout the city. They can be a natural part of the topography, or towers, or part of the roofs of the highest local building— but, in any case, they should include a physical climb.

317

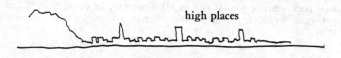

high places

✣ ✣ ✣

Elaborate the area around the base of the high place—it is a
natural position for a SMALL PUBLIC SQUARE (61); give the stair
which leads up to the top, openings with views out, so that
people can stop on the stair, sit down, look out, and be seen while
they are climbing—STAIR SEATS (125), ZEN VIEW (134), OPEN
STAIRS (158). . . .

63 DANCING IN THE STREET*

. . . several patterns have laid the groundwork for evening activity in public—MAGIC OF THE CITY (10), PROMENADE (31), NIGHT LIFE (33), CARNIVAL (58), SMALL PUBLIC SQUARES (61). To make these places alive at night, there is nothing like music and dancing; this pattern simply states the physical conditions which will encourage dancing and music to fill the streets.

❖ ❖ ❖

Why is it that people don't dance in the streets today?

All over the earth, people once danced in the streets; in theater, song, and natural speech, "dancing in the street" is an image of supreme joy. Many cultures still have some version of this activity. There are the Balinese dancers who fall into a trance whirling around in the street; the mariachi bands in Mexico—every town has several squares where the bands play and the neighborhood comes out to dance; there is the European and American tradition of bandstands and jubilees in the park; there is the *bon odori* festival in Japan, when everybody claps and dances in the streets.

But in those parts of the world that have become "modern" and technically sophisticated, this experience has died. Communities are fragmented; people are uncomfortable in the streets, afraid with one another; not many people play the right kind of music; people are embarrassed.

Certainly there is no way in which a change in the environment, as simple as the one which we propose, can remedy these circumstances. But we detect a change in mood. The embarrassment and the alienation are recent developments, blocking a more basic need. And as we get in touch with these needs, things start to happen. People remember how to dance; everyone takes up an instrument; many hundreds form little bands. At this writing, in San Francisco, Berkeley, and Oakland there is a controversy over "street musicians"—bands that have spontaneously begun playing in streets and plazas whenever the weather is good— where should they be allowed to play, do they obstruct traffic, shall people dance?

It is in this atmosphere that we propose the pattern. Where there is feeling for the importance of the activity re-emerging, then the right setting can actualize it and give it roots. The essentials are straightforward: a platform for the musicians, perhaps with a cover; hard surface for dancing, all around the bandstand; places to sit and lean for people who want to watch and rest; provision for some drink and refreshment (some Mexican bandstands have a beautiful way of building tiny stalls into the base of the bandstand, so that people are drawn though the dancers and up to the music, for a fruit drink or a beer); the whole thing set somewhere where people congregate.

Therefore:

Along promenades, in squares and evening centers, make a slightly raised platform to form a bandstand, where street musicians and local bands can play. Cover it, and perhaps build in at ground level tiny stalls for refreshment. Surround the bandstand with paved surface for dancing—no admission charge.

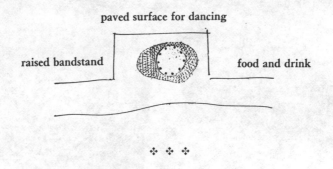

paved surface for dancing

raised bandstand   food and drink

❖ ❖ ❖

Place the bandstand in a pocket of activity, toward the edge of a square or a promenade—ACTIVITY POCKETS (124); make it a room, defined by trellises and columns—PUBLIC OUTDOOR ROOM (69); build FOOD STANDS (93) around the bandstand; and for dancing, maybe colored canvas canopies, which reach out over portions of the street, and make the street, or parts of it, into a great, half-open tent—CANVAS ROOFS (244). . . .

64 POOLS AND STREAMS*

. . . the land, in its natural state, is hardly ever flat, and was, in its most primitive condition, overrun with rills and streams which carried off the rainwater. There is no reason to destroy this natural feature of the land in a town—SACRED SITES (24), ACCESS TO WATER (25)—in fact, it is essential that it be preserved, or recreated. And in doing so it will be possible to deepen several larger patterns—boundaries between neighborhoods can easily be formed by streams—NEIGHBORHOOD BOUNDARY (15), quiet backs can be made more tranquil—QUIET BACKS (59), pedestrian streets can be made more human and more natural—PEDESTRIAN STREET (100).

We came from the water; our bodies are largely water; and water plays a fundamental role in our psychology. We need constant access to water, all around us; and we cannot have it without reverence for water in all its forms. But everywhere in cities water is out of reach.

Even in the temperate climates that are water rich, the natural sources of water are dried up, hidden, covered, lost. Rainwater runs underground in sewers; water reservoirs are covered and fenced off; swimming pools are saturated with chlorine and fenced off; ponds are so polluted that no one wants to go near them any more.

And especially in heavily populated areas water is scarce. We cannot possibly have the daily access to it which we and our children need, unless all water, in all its forms, is exposed, preserved, and nourished in an endless local texture of small pools, ponds, reservoirs, and streams in every neighborhood.

There are various ways of expressing the connection between people and water. The biologist, L. J. Henderson, observed that the saline content of human blood is essentially the same as that of the sea, because we came from the sea. Elaine Morgan, an anthropologist, speculates that during the drought of the Pliocene era, we went back to the sea and lived 10 million years as sea mam-

mals in the shallow waters along the edge of the ocean. Apparently, this hypothesis explains a great deal about the human body, the way in which it is adapted to water, which is otherwise obscure (*The Descent of Woman*, New York: Bantam Books, 1973).

Furthermore, among psychoanalysts it is common to consider the bodies of water that appear in people's dreams as loaded with meaning. Jung and the Jungian analysts take great bodies of water as representing the dreamer's unconscious. We even speculate, in light of the psychoanalytic evidence, that going into the water may bring a person closer to the unconscious processes in his life. We guess that people who swim and dive often, in lakes and pools and in the ocean, may be closer to their dreams, more in contact with their unconscious, than people who swim rarely. Several studies have in fact demonstrated that water has a positive therapeutic effect; that it sets up growth experience. (For references, see Ruth Hartley et al., *Understanding Children's Play*, Columbia University Press, New York: 1964, Chapter V).

All of this suggests that our lives are diminished if we cannot establish rich and abiding contact with water. But of course, in most cities we cannot. Swimming pools, lakes, and beaches are few in number and far away. And consider also the water supply. Our only contact with this water is to turn on the tap. We take the water for granted. But as marvelous as the high technology of water treatment and distribution has become, it does not satisfy the emotional need to make contact with the local reservoirs, and to understand the cycle of water: its limits and its mystery.

But it is possible to imagine a town where there are many hundreds of places near every home and workplace where there is water. Water to swim in, water to sit beside, water where you can dangle your feet. Consider, for example, the running water: the brooks and streams. Today they are paved over and forced underground. Instead of building with them, and alongside them, planners simply get them out of the way, as if to say: "the vagaries of nature have no place in a rational street grid." But we can build in ways which maintain contact with water, in ponds and pools, in reservoirs, and in brooks and streams. We can

even build details that connect people with the collection and run-off of rain water.

Think of the shallow ponds and pools that children need. It is possible for these pools and ponds to be available throughout the city, close enough for children to walk to. Some can be part of the larger pools. Others can be bulges of streams that run through the city, where a balanced ecology is allowed to develop along their edges—ponds with ducks and carp, with edges safe enough for children to come close.

And consider the system of local and distribution reservoirs. We can locate local reservoirs and distribution reservoirs so that people can get at them; we might build them as kinds of shrines, where people can come to get in touch with the source of their water supply; the place immediately around the water an atmosphere inviting contemplation. These shrines could be set into the public space: perhaps as one end of a promenade, or as a boundary of common land between two communities.

Indian stepped well.

And think of running water, in all its possible forms. People who have been deprived of it in their daily surroundings go to great lengths to get out of their towns into the countryside, where they can watch a river flow, or sit by a stream and gaze at the water. Children are fascinated by running water. They use it endlessly, to play in, to throw sticks and see them disappear, to run little paper boats along, to stir up mud and watch it clear gradually.

Natural streams in their original streambeds, together with their surrounding vegetation, can be preserved and maintained. Rainwater can be allowed to assemble from rooftops into small pools and to run through channels along garden paths and public pedestrian paths, where it can be seen and enjoyed. Fountains can be built in public places. And in those cities where streams have been buried, it may even be possible to unravel them again.

The buried streams.

In summary, we propose that every building project, at every scale, take stock of the distribution of water and the access to water in its neighborhood. Where there is a gap, where nourishing contact with water is missing, then each project should make some attempt, on its own and in combination with other projects, to bring some water into the environment. There is no other way to build up an adequate texture of water in cities: we need pools for swimming, ornamental and natural pools, streams of rain water, fountains, falls, natural brooks and streams running through towns, tiny garden pools, and reservoirs we can get to and appreciate.

Therefore:

Preserve natural pools and streams and allow them to run through the city; make paths for people to walk along them and footbridges to cross them. Let the streams form natural barriers in the city, with traffic crossing them only infrequently on bridges.

Whenever possible, collect rainwater in open gutters and allow it to flow above ground, along pedestrian paths and in front of houses. In places without natural running water, create fountains in the streets.

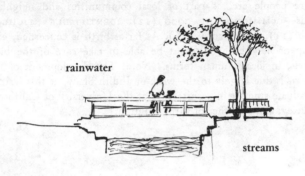

rainwater

streams

❖ ❖ ❖

If at all possible, make all the pools and swimming holes part of the running water—not separate—since this is the only way that pools are able to keep alive and clean without the paraphernalia of pumps and chlorine—STILL WATER (71). Sometimes, here and there, give the place immediately around the water the atmosphere of contemplation; perhaps with arcades, perhaps some special common land, perhaps one end of a promenade—PROMENADE (31), HOLY GROUND (66), ARCADES (119). . . .

65 BIRTH PLACES

. . . both birth and death need recognition throughout society, where people are, as part of local communities and neighborhoods—COMMUNITY OF 7000 (12), IDENTIFIABLE NEIGHBORHOOD (14), LIFE CYCLE (26). As far as birth is concerned, each group of neighborhoods must be able to take care of the birth process, in local, human terms. (Note: The development of this pattern is due largely to the work of Judith Shaw, at this writing a graduate student in architecture at the University of California, Berkeley, and a mother of three children.)

It seems unlikely that any process which treats childbirth as a sickness could possibly be a healthy part of a healthy society.

"Pregnancy is no state of emergency from which the mother may hopefully be returned to 'normality' after the birth of the child. . . . It is a highly active, potent, developmental process of the family going forward to its natural culmination in delivery." (I. H. Pearse and L. H. Crocker, *The Peckham Experiment*, New Haven: Yale University Press, 1946, p. 153.)

The existing obstetrics service in most hospitals follows a well outlined procedure. Having a baby is thought of as an illness and the stay in the hospital as recuperation. Women who are about to deliver are treated as "patients" about to undergo surgery. They are sterilized. Their genitals are scrubbed and shaved. They are gowned in white, and put on a table to be moved back and forth between the various parts of the hospital. Women in labor are put in cubicles to pass the time with virtually no social contact. This time can last for many hours. It is a time when father and children could be present to provide encouragement. But this is not permitted. Delivery usually takes place in a "delivery room" which has the proper "table" for childbirth.

Except for the particular workings of the delivery table the room has the same properties as an operating theater. The birth becomes a time for separation rather than togetherness. It may be as long as 12 hours before the mother is even allowed to touch her baby, and if she was sedated for the delivery, even longer before she may see her husband.

For about fifteen years there has been a subtle movement to try and recapture the essence of childbirth as a natural phenomenon. There has been no loud protest against obstetricians and hospital rules, but a rather quiet one: several good books, word of mouth, concerned professionals and nonprofessionals, the La Leche League, a few groups around the country whose prime concern is with birth, and the re-emergence of the nurse-midwife. The original effort of these people was aimed at "natural" childbirth, the name being applied in an attempt to bring the concept of childbirth back to a normal physiological occurrence. Lately the focus of the effort has been expanded to include an altered environment for childbirth and to include the family in a positive way. (For an architectural slant, see Lewis Mumford, *The Urban Prospect*, New York: Harcourt Brace and World, 1968, p. 25.)

We quote now from Judith Shaw's description of a good birth place. She is describing a place comparable to a small nursing home, perhaps associated with a local health center, and with emergency connections to the local hospital:

A small basket for the baby would be provided. . . . The nurse-midwife would be there always to provide post-partum care. . . . The nurse-midwife, who lives in, would have a small suite containing a bedroom, sitting room-kitchen and bath. . . .
The eating place would be communal. Each baby would have a place too (his movable basket) so that the mother can bring her child with her to feed or to watch. . . . The pattern FARMHOUSE KITCHEN (139) could play an important role in this building. . . . families can come not only to have babies but have their pre-natal care, learn methods of natural childbirth, possibly child care, maybe just to talk and in general to become familiar with the place they will come to for the delivery.
The birthing place should have accommodations for the entire family. They can occupy a suite in which they live and in which the mother gives birth to the baby. . . . Since the delivery would take place in the family suite, the baby, mother, and the family can be

together immediately. Each suite would have to be equipped with running water and a simple table on which to lay the baby, wash it and give it its initial examination.

Therefore:

Build local birth places where women go to have their children: places that are specially tailored to childbirth as a natural, eventful moment—where the entire family comes for prenatal care and education; where fathers and midwives help during the hours of labor and birth.

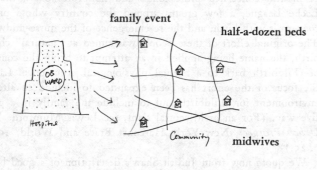

❖ ❖ ❖

Include rooms where after the birth the mother and her baby can stay together with the other members of the family—sleep together, eat together, cook together—COMMON AREAS AT THE HEART (129), COUPLE'S REALM (136), FARMHOUSE KITCHEN (139); provide a partly private garden to walk in—HALF-HIDDEN GARDEN (111), GARDEN WALL (173); for the shape of the building, gardens, parking, and surroundings, begin with BUILDING COMPLEX (95). . . .

66 HOLY GROUND*

. . . we have defined the need for a full life cycle, with rites of passage between stages of the cycle—LIFE CYCLE (26); and we have recommended that certain pieces of land be set aside because of their importance and meaning—SACRED SITES (24). This pattern gives the detailed organization of the space around these places. The organization is so powerful, that to some extent it can itself create the sacredness of sites, perhaps even encourage the slow emergence of coherent rites of passage.

❖ ❖ ❖

What is a church or temple? It is a place of worship, spirit, contemplation, of course. But above all, from a human point of view, it is a gateway. A person comes into the world through the church. He leaves it through the church. And, at each of the important thresholds of his life, he once again steps through the church.

The rites that accompany birth, puberty, marriage, and death are fundamental to human growth. Unless these rites are given the emotional weight they need, it is impossible for a man or woman to pass thoroughly from one stage of life to another.

In all traditional societies, where these rites are treated with enormous power and respect, the rites, in one form or another, are supported by parts of the physical environment which have the character of gates. Of course, a gate, or gateway, by itself cannot create a rite. But it is also true that the rites cannot evolve in an environment which specifically ignores them or makes them trivial. A hospital is no place for a baptism; a funeral home makes it impossible to feel the meaning of a funeral.

In functional terms, it is essential that each person have the opportunity to enter into some kind of social communion with his fellows at the times when he himself or his friends pass through these critical points in their lives. And this social communion at this moment needs to be rooted in some place which is recognized as a kind of spiritual gateway for these events.

What physical shape or organization must this "gateway" have

in order to support the rites of passage, and in order to create the sanctity and holiness and feeling of connection to the earth which makes the rites significant.

Of course, it will vary in detail, from culture to culture. Whatever it is exactly that is held to be sacred—whether it is nature, god, a special place, a spirit, holy relics, the earth itself, or an idea—it takes different forms, in different cultures, and requires different physical environments to support it.

However, we do believe that one fundamental characteristic is invariant from culture to culture. In all cultures it seems that whatever it is that is holy will only be felt as holy, if it is hard to reach, if it requires layers of access, waiting, levels of approach, a gradual unpeeling, gradual revelation, passage through a series of gates. There are many examples: the Inner City of Peking; the fact that anyone who has audience with the Pope must wait in each of seven waiting rooms; the Aztec sacrifices took place on stepped pyramids, each step closer to the sacrifice; the Ise shrine, the most famous shrine in Japan, is a nest of precincts, each one inside the other.

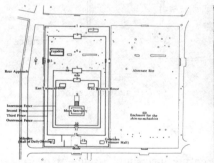

Layers of access.

Even in an ordinary Christian church, you pass first through the churchyard, then through the nave; then, on special occasions, beyond the altar rail into the chancel and only the priest himself is able to go into the tabernacle. The holy bread is sheltered by five layers of ever more difficult approach.

This layering, or nesting of precincts, seems to correspond to

a fundamental aspect of human psychology. We believe that every community, regardless of its particular faith, regardless of whether it even has a faith in any organized sense, needs some place where this feeling of slow, progressive access through gates to a holy center may be experienced. When such a place exists in a community, even if it is not associated with any particular religion, we believe that the feeling of holiness, in some form or other, will gradually come to life there among the people who share in the experience.

Therefore:

In each community and neighborhood, identify some sacred site as consecrated ground, and form a series of nested precincts, each marked by a gateway, each one progressively more private, and more sacred than the last, the innermost a final sanctum that can only be reached by passing through all of the outer ones.

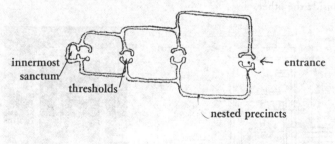

innermost sanctum — thresholds — nested precincts — entrance

❖ ❖ ❖

At each threshold between precincts build a gate—MAIN GATE-WAYS (53); at each gate, a place to pause with a new view toward the next most inner place—ZEN VIEW (134); and at the inner-most sanctum, something very quiet and able to inspire—perhaps a view, or no more than a simple tree, or pool—POOLS AND STREAMS (64), TREE PLACES (171). . . .

*in each house cluster and work community, provide
the smaller bits of common land, to provide for local
versions of the same needs:*

67 COMMON LAND**

. . . just as there is a need for public land at the neighborhood level—ACCESSIBLE GREEN (60), so also, within the clusters and work communities from which the neighborhoods are made, there is a need for smaller and more private kinds of common land shared by a few work groups or a few families. This common land, in fact, forms the very heart and soul of any cluster. Once it is defined, the individual buildings of the cluster form around it—HOUSE CLUSTER (37), ROW HOUSES (38), HOUSING HILL (39), WORK COMMUNITY (41).

Without common land no social system can survive.

In pre-industrial societies, common land between houses and between workshops existed automatically—so it was never necessary to make a point of it. The paths and streets which gave access to buildings were safe, social spaces, and therefore functioned automatically as common land.

But in a society with cars and trucks, the common land which can play an effective social role in knitting people together no longer happens automatically. Those streets which carry cars and trucks at more than crawling speeds, definitely do not function as common land; and many buildings find themselves entirely isolated from the social fabric because they are not joined to one another by land they hold in common. In such a situation common land must be provided, separately, and with deliberation, as a social necessity, as vital as the streets.

The common land has two specific social functions. First, the land makes it possible for people to feel comfortable outside their buildings and their private territory, and therefore allows them to feel connected to the larger social system—though not necessarily to any specific neighbor. And second, common land acts as a meeting place for people.

The first function is subtle. Certainly one's immediate neighbors are less important in modern society than in traditional

337

society. This is because people meet friends at work, at school, at meetings of interest groups and therefore no longer rely exclusively on neighbors for friendship. (See for instance, Melvin Webber, "Order in Diversity: Community Without Propinquity," *Cities and Space,* ed. Lowdon Wingo, Baltimore: Resources for the Future, 1963; and Webber, "The Urban Place and the Nonplace Urban Realm," in Webber et al., *Explorations into Urban Structure,* Philadelphia, 1964, pp. 79–153.)

To the extent that this is true, the common land between houses might be less important than it used to be as a meeting ground for friendship. But the common land between buildings may have a deeper psychological function, which remains important, even when people have no relation to their neighbors. In order to portray this function, imagine that your house is separated from the city by a gaping chasm, and that you have to pass across this chasm every time you leave your house, or enter it. The house would be disturbingly isolated; and you, in the house, would be isolated from society, merely by this physical fact. In psychological terms, we believe that a building without common land in front of it is as isolated from society as if it had just such a chasm there.

There is a new emotional disorder—a type of agoraphobia—making its appearance in today's cities. Victims of this disorder are afraid to go out of their houses for any reason—even to mail a letter or to go to the corner grocery store—literally, they are afraid of the marketplace—the agora. We speculate—entirely without evidence—that this disorder may be reinforced by the absence of common land, by an environment in which people feel they have no "right" to be outside their own front doors. If this is so, agoraphobia would be the most concrete manifestation of the breakdown of common land.

The second social function of common land is straightforward. Common land provides a *meeting ground* for the fluid, common activities that a house cluster shares. The larger pieces of public land which serve neighborhoods—the parks, the community facilities—do not fill the bill. They are fine for the neighborhood as a whole. But they do not provide a base for the functions that are common to a cluster of households.

Lewis Mumford:

Even in housing estates that are laid out at twelve families to the acre—perhaps one should say especially there—there is often a lack of common meeting places for the mothers, where, on a good day, they might come together under a big tree, or a pergola, to sew or gossip, while their infants slept in a pram or their runabout children grubbed around in a play pit. Perhaps the best part of Sir Charles Reilly's plans for village greens was that they provided for such common activities: as the planners of Sunnyside, Long Island, Messrs. Stein and Wright, had done as early as 1924. (*The Urban Prospect*, New York: Harcourt, Brace and World, 1968, p. 26.)

How much common land must there be? There must be enough to be useful, to contain children's games and small gatherings. And enough land must be common so that private land doesn't dominate it psychologically. We guess that the amount of common land needed in a neighborhood is on the order of 25 per cent of the land held privately. This is the figure that the greenbelt planners typically devoted to their commons and greens. (See Clarence Stein, *Toward New Towns in America*, Cambridge: M.I.T. Press, 1966.)

With cooperation among the people, it is possible to build this pattern piecemeal, into our existing neighborhoods by closing streets.

Berkeley street transformed to neighborhood commons.

Therefore:

Give over 25 per cent of the land in house clusters to common land which touches, or is very very near, the

homes which share it. Basic: be wary of the automobile; on no account let it dominate this land.

common meeting ground   25 per cent common

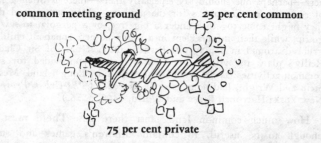

75 per cent private

Shape the common land so it has some enclosure and good sunlight—SOUTH FACING OUTDOORS (105), POSITIVE OUTDOOR SPACE (106); and so that smaller and more private pieces of land and pockets always open onto it—HIERARCHY OF OPEN SPACE (114); provide communal functions within the land—PUBLIC OUTDOOR ROOM (69), LOCAL SPORTS (72), VEGETABLE GARDEN (177); and connect the different and adjacent pieces of common land to one another to form swaths of connected play space—CONNECTED PLAY (68). Roads can be part of common land if they are treated as GREEN STREETS (51). . . .

68 CONNECTED PLAY*

. . . suppose the common land that connects clusters to one another is being provided—COMMON LAND (67). Within this common land, it is necessary to identify play space for children and, above all, to make sure that the relationship between adjacent pieces of common land allows this play space to form.

❖ ❖ ❖

If children don't play enough with other children during the first five years of life, there is a great chance that they will have some kind of mental illness later in their lives.

Children need other children. Some findings suggest that they need other children even more than they need their own mothers. And empirical evidence shows that if they are forced to spend their early years with too little contact with other children, they will be likely to suffer from psychosis and neurosis in their later years.

Alone . . .

Since the layout of the land between the houses in a neighborhood virtually controls the formation of play groups, it therefore has a critical effect on people's mental health. A typical suburban subdivision with private lots opening off streets almost confines

342

children to their houses. Parents, afraid of traffic or of their neighbors, keep their small children indoors or in their own gardens: so the children never have enough chance meetings with other children of their own age to form the groups which are essential to a healthy emotional development.

We shall show that children will only be able to have the access to other children which they need, if each household opens onto some kind of safe, connected common land, which touches at least 64 other households.

First, let us review the evidence for the problem. The most dramatic evidence comes from the Harlows' work on monkeys. The Harlows have shown that monkeys isolated from other infant monkeys during the first six months of life are incapable of normal social, sexual, or play relations with other monkeys in their later lives:

> They exhibit abnormalities of behavior rarely seen in animals born in the wild. They sit in their cages and stare fixedly into space, circle their cages in a repetitively stereotyped manner, and clasp their heads in their hands or arms and rock for long periods of time . . . the animal may chew and tear at its body until it bleeds . . . similar symptoms of emotional pathology are observed in deprived children in orphanages and in withdrawn adolescents and adults in mental hospitals. (Henry F. Harlow and Margaret K. Harlow, "The Effect of Rearing Conditions on Behavior," *Bull. Menniger Clinic*, 26, 1962, pp. 213–14.)

It is well known that infant monkeys—like infant human beings—have these defects if brought up without a mother or a mother surrogate. It is not well known that the effects of separation from other infant monkeys are even stronger than the effects of maternal deprivation. Indeed, the Harlows showed that although monkeys can be raised successfully without a mother, provided that they have other infant monkeys to play with, they cannot be raised successfully by a mother alone, without other infant monkeys, even if the mother is entirely normal. They conclude: "It seems possible that the infant-mother affectional system is dispensable, whereas the infant-infant system is a sine-qua-non for later adjustment in all spheres of monkey life." (Harry F. Harlow and Margaret K. Harlow, "Social Deprivation in Monkeys," *Scientific American*, 207, No. 5, 1962, pp. 136–46.)

The first six months of a rhesus monkey's life correspond to the first three years of a child's life. Although there is no formal evidence to show that lack of contact during these first three years damages human children—and as far as we know, it has never been studied—there is very strong evidence for the effect of isolation between the ages of four to ten.

Herman Lantz questioned a random sample of 1,000 men in the United States Army, who had been referred to a mental hygiene clinic because of emotional difficulties. (Herman K. Lantz, "Number of Childhood Friends as Reported in the Life Histories of a Psychiatrically Diagnosed Group of 1,000," *Marriage and Family Life*, May 1956, pp. 107–108.) Army psychiatrists classified each of the men as normal, suffering from mild psychoneurosis, severe psychoneurosis, or psychosis. Lantz then put each man into one of three categories: those who reported having five friends or more at any typical moment when they were between four and ten years old, those who reported an average of about two friends, and those who reported having no friends at that time. The following table shows the relative percentages in each of the three friendship categories separately. The results are astounding:

	5 or More Friends	About 2 Friends	No Friends
Normal	39.5	7.2	0.0
Mild psychoneurosis	22.0	16.4	5.0
Severe psychoneurosis	27.0	54.6	47.5
Psychosis	0.8	3.1	37.5
Other	10.7	18.7	10.0
	100.0	100.0	100.0

Among people who have five friends or more as children, 61.5 per cent have mild cases, while 27.8 per cent have severe cases. Among people who had no friends, only 5 per cent have mild cases, and 85 per cent have severe cases.

On the positive side, an informal account by Anna Freud shows how powerful the effect of contact among tiny children can be on the emotional development of the children. She describes five young German children who lost their parents during infancy

in a concentration camp, and then looked after one another inside the camp until the war ended, at which point they were brought to England. (Anna Freud and Sophie Dann, "An Experiment in Group Upbringing," *Reading in Child Behavior and Development*, ed. Celia Stendler, New York, 1964, pp. 122–40.) She describes the beautiful social and emotional maturity of these tiny children. Reading the account, one feels that these children, at the age of three, were more aware of each other and more sensitive to each other's needs than many people ever are.

It is almost certain, then, that contact is essential, and that lack of contact, when it is extreme, has extreme effects. A considerable body of literature beyond that which we have quoted, is given in Christopher Alexander, "The City as a Mechanism for Sustaining Human Contact," *Environment for Man*, ed. W. R. Ewald, Indiana University Press, Bloomington, 1967, pp. 60–109.

If we assume that informal, neighborhood contact between children is a vital experience, we may then ask what kinds of neighborhoods support the formation of spontaneous play groups. The answer, we believe, is some form of safe common land, connected to a child's home, and from which he can make contact with several other children. The critical question is: How many households need to share this connected play space?

The exact number of households that are required depends on the child population within the households. Let us assume that children represent about one-fourth of a given population (slightly less than the modal figure for suburban households), and that these children are evenly distributed in age from 0 to 18. Roughly speaking, a given pre-school child who is x years old will play with children who are $x - 1$ or x or $x + 1$ years old. In order to have a reasonable amount of contact, and in order for playgroups to form, each child must be able to reach at least five children in his age range. Statistical analysis shows that for each child to have a 95 per cent chance of reaching five such potential playmates, each child must be in reach of 64 households.

The problem may be stated as follows: In an infinite population of children, one-sixth are the right age and five-sixths are the wrong age for any given child. A group of r children is

chosen at random. The probability that this group of r children contains 5 or more right-age children in it is $1 - \sum\limits_{k=0}^{4} P_{r, k}$, where $P_{r, k}$ is the hypergeometric distribution. If we now ask what is the least r which makes $1 - \sum\limits_{k=0}^{4} P_{r, k} > 0.95$, r turns out to be 54.

If we need 54 children, we need a total population of $4(54) = 216$, which at 3.4 persons per household, needs 64 households.

Sixty-four is a rather large number of households to share connected common land. In fact, in the face of this requirement, there is a strong temptation to try to solve the problem by grouping 10 or 12 homes in a cluster. But this will not work: while it is a useful configuration for other reasons—HOUSE CLUSTER (37) and COMMON LAND (67)—by itself it will not solve the problem of connected play space for children. There must also be safe paths to connect the bits of common land.

Connecting paths.

Therefore:

Lay out common land, paths, gardens, and bridges so that groups of at least 64 households are connected by a

swath of land that does not cross traffic. Establish this land as the connected play space for the children in these households.

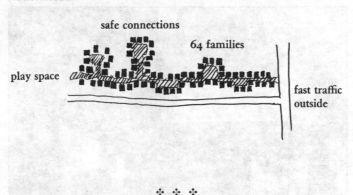

❖ ❖ ❖

Do this by connecting several HOUSE CLUSTERS (37) with GREEN STREETS (51) and safe paths. Place the local CHILDREN'S HOME (86) in this play space. Within the play space, make sure the children have access to mud, and plants, and animals, and water—STILL WATER (71), ANIMALS (74); set aside one area where there is all kinds of junk that they can use to make things —ADVENTURE PLAYGROUND (73). . . .

69 PUBLIC OUTDOOR ROOM**

. . . the common land in MAIN GATEWAYS (53), ACCESSIBLE GREEN (60), SMALL PUBLIC SQUARES (61), COMMON LAND (67), PEDESTRIAN STREET (100), PATHS AND GOALS (120) needs at least some place where hanging out and being "out" in public become possible. For this purpose it is necessary to distinguish one part of the common land and to define it with a little more elaboration. Also, if none of the larger patterns exist yet, this pattern can act as a nucleus, and help them to crystallize around it.

❖ ❖ ❖

There are very few spots along the streets of modern towns and neighborhoods where people can hang out, comfortably, for hours at a time.

Men seek corner beer shops, where they spend hours talking and drinking; teenagers, especially boys, choose special corners too, where they hang around, waiting for their friends. Old people like a special spot to go to, where they can expect to find others; small children need sand lots, mud, plants, and water to play with in the open; young mothers who go to watch their children often use the children's play as an opportunity to meet and talk with other mothers.

Because of the diverse and casual nature of these activities, they require a space which has a subtle balance of being defined and yet not too defined, so that any activity which is natural to the neighborhood at any given time can develop freely and yet has something to start from.

For example, it would be possible to leave an outdoor room unfinished, with the understanding it can be finished by people who live nearby, to fill whatever needs seem most pressing. It may need sand, or water faucets, or play equipment for small children—ADVENTURE PLAYGROUND (73); it may have steps and seats, where teenagers can meet—TEENAGE SOCIETY (84); someone may build a small bar or coffee shop in a house that opens into the area, with an arcade, making the arcade a place to eat and

drink—FOOD STANDS (93); there may be games like chess and checkers for old people.

Modern housing projects especially suffer from the lack of this kind of space. When indoor community rooms are provided, they are rarely used. People don't want to plunge into a situation which they don't know; and the degree of involvement created in such an enclosed space is too intimate to allow a casual passing interest to build up gradually. On the other hand, vacant land is not enclosed enough. It takes years for anything to happen on vacant land; it provides too little shelter, and too little "reason to be there."

What is needed is a framework which is just enough defined so that people naturally tend to stop there; and so that curiosity naturally takes people there, and invites them to stay. Then, once community groups begin to gravitate toward this framework, there is a good chance that they will themselves, if they are permitted, create an environment which is appropriate to their activities.

We conjecture that a small open space, roofed, with columns, but without walls at least in part, will just about provide the necessary balance of "openness" and "closedness."

A beautiful example of the pattern was built by Dave Chapin and George Gordon with architecture students from Case Western Reserve in Cleveland, Ohio. They built a sequence of public out-

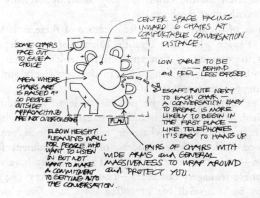

Public outdoor room built by Chapin and Gordon in Cleveland, Ohio.

door rooms on the grounds and on the public land surrounding a local mental health clinic. According to staff reports, these places changed the life of the clinic dramatically: many more people than had been usual were drawn into the outdoors, public talk was more animated, outdoor space that had always been dominated by automobiles suddenly became human and the cars had to inch along.

In all, Chapin and Gordon and their crew built seven public outdoor rooms in the neighborhood. Each one was slightly different, varying according to views, orientation, size.

We have also discovered a version of this pattern from medieval society. Apparently, in the twelfth and thirteenth centuries there were many such public structures dotted through the towns. They were the scene of auctions, open-air meetings, and market fairs. They are very much in the spirit of the places we are proposing for neighborhoods and work communities.

Outdoor rooms in England and Peru.

Therefore:

In every neighborhood and work community, make a

piece of the common land into an outdoor room—a partly enclosed place, with some roof, columns, without walls, perhaps with a trellis; place it beside an important path and within view of many homes and workshops.

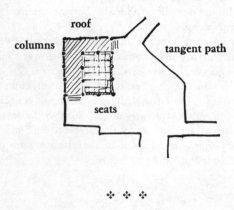

❦ ❦ ❦

Place the outdoor room where several paths are tangent to it, like any other common area—COMMON AREAS AT THE HEART (129); in the bulge of a path—PATH SHAPE (121); or around a square—ACTIVITY POCKETS (124); use surrounding BUILDING EDGES (160) to define part of it; build it like any smaller outdoor room, with columns, and half-trellised roofs—OUTDOOR ROOM (163); perhaps put an open courtyard next to it—COURTYARDS WHICH LIVE (115), an ARCADE (119) around the edge, or other simple cover—CANVAS ROOFS (244), and seats for casual sitting— STAIR SEATS (125), SEAT SPOTS (241). . . .

70 GRAVE SITES*

. . . according to LIFE CYCLE (26) the transitions of a person's life must be available and visible in every community. Death is no exception. This pattern helps to integrate the fact of death with the public spaces of each neighborhood, and, by its very existence, helps to form IDENTIFIABLE NEIGHBORHOODS (14), and HOLY GROUND (66) and COMMON LAND (67).

No people who turn their backs on death can be alive. The presence of the dead among the living will be a daily fact in any society which encourages its people to live.

Huge cemeteries on the outskirts of cities, or in places no one ever visits, impersonal funeral rites, taboos which hide the fact of death from children, all conspire to keep the fact of death away from us, the living. If you live in a modern suburb, ask yourself how comfortable you would be if your house were next to a graveyard. Very likely the thought frightens you. But this is only because we are no longer used to it. We shall be healthy, when graves of friends and family, and memorials to the people of the recent and the distant past, are intermingled with our houses, in small grave yards, as naturally as winter always comes before the spring.

In every culture there is some form of intense ceremony surrounding death, grieving for the dead, and disposal of the body. There are thousands of variations, but the point is always to give the community of friends left alive the chance to reconcile themselves to the facts of death: the emptiness, the loss; their own transience.

These ceremonies bring people into contact with the experience of mortality, and in this way, they bring us closer to the facts of life, as well as death. When these experiences are integrated with the environment and each person's life, we are able to live through them fully and go on. But when circumstances or custom prevent us from making contact with the experience of mortality, and living with it, we are left depressed, diminished,

less alive. There is a great deal of clinical evidence to support this notion.

In one documented case, a young boy lost his grandmother; the people around him told him that she had merely "gone away" to "protect his feelings." The boy was uneasily aware that something had happened, but in this atmosphere of secrecy, could not know it for what it was and could not therefore experience it fully. Instead of being protected, he became a victim of a massive neurosis, which was only cured, many years later, when he finally recognized, and lived through the fact of his grandmother's death.

This case, and others which make it abundantly clear that a person must live through the death of those he loves as fully as possible, in order to remain emotionally healthy, have been described by Eric Lindemann. We have lost the crucial reference for this work, but two other papers by Lindemann converge on the same point: "Symptomatology and Management of Acute Grief," *American Journal of Psychiatry*, 1944, *101*, 141–48; and "A Study of Grief: Emotional Responses to Suicide," *Pastoral Psychology*, 1953, 4(39), 9–13. We also recommend a recent paper by Robert Kastenbaum, on the ways in which children explore their mortality: "The Kingdom Where Nobody Dies," *Saturday Review*, January 1973, pp. 33–38.

A concrete honeycomb graveyard in Colma, California. The superintendant of the cemetery said, "Families will never see the sinking . . . which so distressed them in older parts of the cemetery. . . ."

In the big industrial cities, during the past 100 years, the ceremonies of death and their functional power for the living have

been completely undermined. What were once beautifully simple forms of mourning have been replaced by grotesque cemeteries, plastic flowers, everything but the reality of death. And above all, the small graveyards which once put people into daily contact with the fact of death, have vanished—replaced by massive cemeteries, far away from people's daily business.

What must be done to set things right? We can solve the problem by fusing some of the old ritual forms with the kinds of situations we face today.

1. Most important, it is essential to break down the scale of modern cemeteries, and to reinstate the connection between burial grounds and local communities. Intense decentralization: a person can choose a spot for himself, in parks, common lands, on his land.

2. The right setting requires some enclosure; paths beside the gravesites; the graves visible, and protected by low walls, edges, trees.

3. Property rights. There must be some legal basis for hallowing small pieces of ground—to give a guarantee that the ground a person chooses will not be sold and developed.

4. With increasing population, it is obviously impossible to go on and on covering the land with graves or memorials. We suggest a process similar to the one followed in traditional Greek villages. The graveyards occupy a fixed area, enough to cope with the dead of 200 years. After 200 years, remains are put out to sea—except for those whose memory is still alive.

5. The ritual itself has to evolve from a group with some shared values, at least a family, perhaps a group that shares a religious view. Three of the basics: friends carrying the casket through the streets in procession; simple pine coffins or urns; gathering round the grave.

Therefore:

Never build massive cemeteries. Instead, allocate pieces of land throughout the community as grave sites—corners of parks, sections of paths, gardens, beside gateways—where memorials to people who have died can be ritually placed with inscriptions and mementos which celebrate their life.

356

Give each grave site an edge, a path, and a quiet corner
where people can sit. By custom, this is hallowed ground.

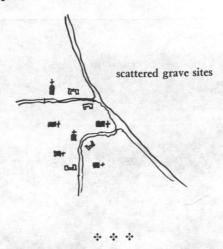

scattered grave sites

❖ ❖ ❖

If possible, keep them in places which are quiet—QUIET BACKS
(59); and provide a simple seat or a bench under a tree, where
people can be alone with their memories—TREE PLACES (171),
SEAT SPOTS (241). . . .

71 STILL WATER*

. . . the patterns ACCESS TO WATER (25) and POOLS AND STREAMS (64) provide a variety of kinds of water throughout the community. This pattern helps to embellish the still waters—the pools and ponds and swimming holes—and provide them with a safe edge for children. It also helps to differentiate the public space in HOUSE CLUSTER (37), WORK COMMUNITY (41), HEALTH CENTER (47), COMMON LAND (67), LOCAL SPORTS (72).

To be in touch with water, we must above all be able to swim; and to swim daily, the pools and ponds and holes for swimming must be so widely scattered through the city, that each person can reach one within minutes.

We have already explained, in POOLS AND STREAMS (64), how important it is to be in touch with water—and how the ordinary water of an area can, if left open, be a natural component of the everyday ecology of a community.

In this pattern we go a little further, and put the emphasis on swimming. On the one hand, adults cannot have any substantial contact with water unless they can swim in it, and for this purpose the body of water must be large enough and deep enough to swim in. On the other hand, the highly chlorinated, private, walled, and fenced off swimming pools, which have become common in rich people's suburbs, work directly against the very forces we have described in POOLS AND STREAMS (64), and make the touch of water almost meaningless, because it is so private and so antiseptic.

We believe that the swimming cannot come into its proper place, unless everyone who wants to can swim every day: and this means, that, to all intents and purposes, there needs to be a swimming pool on every block, almost in every cluster, and at least in every neighborhood, within no more than about 100 yards of every house.

In this pattern, we shall therefore try to establish a model for a kind of "swimming hole": public, so that it becomes a communal

function, not a wholly private one; and safe, so that this public water can be deep enough for swimming without being dangerous to tiny children playing at the edge.

For millions of years, children have grown up in perfect safety along the edge of oceans, rivers, and lakes. Why is a swimming pool so dangerous? The answer depends simply on the edge.

. . . the edge . . .

As a rule, the natural edges between water and shore are marked by a slow, rough transition. There is a certain well-marked sequence of changes in materials, texture, and ecology as one passes from land to water. The human consequences of this transition are important: it means that people can walk lazily along the edge, without concern for their safety; they can sit at the edge and have their feet in the water, or walk along with the water around their ankles.

Children can play in the water safely when the edge is gradual. A baby crawling into a lake comes to no abrupt surprises; he stops when the water gets too deep, and goes back out again. It has even been shown that children teach themselves to swim when they are free to play around a pool with an extremely gradual slope toward the deep. In such a pool, some children have even learned to swim before they can walk. Even the rocks at the steep edge of a rock-bound lake are not that surprising—because the sandy earth further from the edge gives way to rocks, which change their angle and their texture, as one comes to the sharp edge.

But a swimming pool, and any kind of water with a hard and artificial edge, has none of this gradualness. A child may be run-

ning along, at top speed, when splash, suddenly he finds himself in six feet of water.

The abrupt edge, most serious for children, has its effects in psychological terms for adults too. Although they are not literally endangered by the edge—since they can learn its dangers—the presence of an ecologically wrong kind of abruptness is disconcerting—and destroys the peace and calm which water often has.

It is therefore essential that every water's edge, whether on a pond, or lake, or swimming pool, or river, or canal, be made so that it has a natural gradient, which changes as a person comes up to the edge, and goes on changing as the water is first very shallow, and then gradually gets deeper.

Of course, some deep water is essential for swimming; but the edge of the deep water must not be directly accessible. Instead, the edge around the deep end needs to be protected by a wall or a fence; and islands can be built there, for people to swim to, and to dive from.

Therefore:

In every neighborhood, provide some still water—a pond, a pool—for swimming. Keep the pool open to the public at all times, but make the entrance to the pool only from the shallow side of the pool, and make the pool deepen gradually, starting from one or two inches deep.

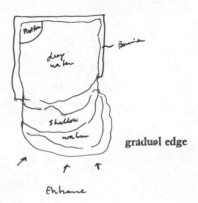

gradual edge

If possible, arrange the pool as part of a system of natural running water, so that it purifies itself, and does not have to be chlorinated—POOLS AND STREAMS (64). Make sure the pool has southern exposure—SOUTH FACING OUTDOORS (105). If possible, embellish the edge of the pool with a small outdoor room or trellis, where people can sit and watch—PUBLIC OUTDOOR ROOM (69), TRELLISED WALK (174), SITTING WALL (243). . . .

72 LOCAL SPORTS*

. . . all the areas where people live and work—especially the
WORK COMMUNITIES (41) and the areas looked after by the
preventive programs of the HEALTH CENTER (47)—need to be
completed by provisions for sports and exercise. This pattern
defines the nature and distribution of this exercise.

❖ ❖ ❖

**The human body does not wear out with use. On the
contrary, it wears down when it is not used.**

In agricultural society, people use their bodies every day in
many different ways. In urban society, most people use their
minds, but not their bodies; or they use their bodies only in a
routine way. This is devastating. There is ample empirical evidence that physical health depends on daily physical activity.

Perhaps the most striking evidence for the unbalance in our
way of life comes from a comparison of the death rates between
groups that have been able to live lives that include daily physical activity with those that have not. For example, in the age
group 60 to 64, 1 per cent of the men in the heavy exercise category died during the follow-up year, whereas 5 per cent of those
in the no-exercise group died. (See P. B. Johnson et al., *Physical
Education, A Problem Solving Approach to Health and Fitness*,
University of Toledo, Holt, Rinehart and Winston, 1966.)

There are very few modern societies where these facts are
taken seriously. China and Cuba come to mind. In these societies,
people work both with their hands and with their minds. Work-
days embrace both kinds of skills. Doctors are as apt to be
building houses as practicing medicine; and builders are often
sitting in administrative sessions.

In any society which has reached this stage, the gross physical
atrophy of human bodies will not occur. But in any society which
has not learned this wisdom, it is necessary, as a kind of interim
solution, to scatter opportunities for physical activity, so that
they are close at hand, indeed next door, to every house and
place of work. Small fields, swimming pools, gyms, game courts,
must be as frequent as corner groceries and restaurants. Ideally,

364

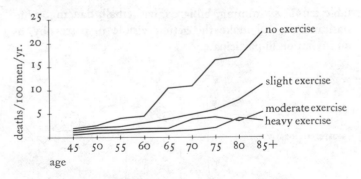

You will probably live longer if you exercise regularly. (Graph adapted from E. G. Hammond, "Some Preliminary Findings on Physical Complaints from a Prospective Study of 1,064,004 Men and Women," American Journal of Public Health, 54:11, 1964).

local sports would form a natural part of every neighborhood and work community. We imagine these facilities as nonprofit centers, supported by the people who use them, perhaps coordinated with a program of health prevention like the swimming and dancing at the Pioneer Health Center in Peckham—see HEALTH CENTER (47).

Sports also have a special life of their own, which cannot be duplicated. Throwing the ball around, shouting out, winning a crushing victory, losing a long drawn out match, getting a wild ball back on the net somehow, anyhow—these are moments that cannot be captured by a job of work. They are entirely different; perhaps they cater especially to what E. Hart calls the psycho-emotional component of muscular activity. ("The Need for Physical Activity," in S. Maltz, ed., *Health Readings*, Wm. Brown Book Company, Iowa, 1968, p. 240.) In any case, it is a kind of vitality that cannot be replaced.

Therefore:

Scatter places for team and individual sports through every work community and neighborhood: tennis, squash,

table tennis, swimming, billiards, basketball, dancing, gymnasium . . . and make the action visible to passers-by, as an invitation to participate.

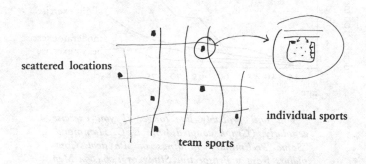

scattered locations

individual sports

team sports

❖ ❖ ❖

Treat the sports places as a special class of recognizable simple buildings, which are open, easy to get into, with changing rooms and showers—BUILDING COMPLEX (95), BATHING ROOM (144); combine them with community swimming pools, where they exist —STILL WATER (71); keep them open to people passing—BUILDING THOROUGHFARE (101), OPENING TO THE STREET (165), and provide places where people can stop and watch—SEAT SPOTS (241), SITTING WALL (243). . . .

73 ADVENTURE PLAYGROUND

. . . inside the local neighborhood, even if there is common land where children can meet and play—COMMON LAND (67), CONNECTED PLAY (68); it is essential that there be at least one smaller part, which is differentiated, where the play is wilder, and where the children have access to all kinds of junk.

❖ ❖ ❖

A castle, made of cartons, rocks, and old branches, by a group of children for themselves, is worth a thousand perfectly detailed, exactly finished castles, made for them in a factory.

Play has many functions: it gives children a chance to be together, a chance to use their bodies, to build muscles, and to test new skills. But above all, play is a function of the imagination. A child's play is his way of dealing with the issues of his growth, of relieving tensions and exploring the future. It reflects directly the problems and joys of his social reality. Children come to terms with the world, wrestle with their pictures of it, and reform these pictures constantly, through those adventures of imagination we call play.

Any kind of playground which disturbs, or reduces, the role of imagination and makes the child more passive, more the recipient of someone else's imagination, may look nice, may be clean, may be safe, may be healthy—but it just cannot satisfy the fundamental need which play is all about. And, to put it bluntly, it is a waste of time and money. Huge abstract sculptured playlands are just as bad as asphalt playgrounds and jungle gyms. They are not just sterile; they are useless. The functions they perform have nothing to do with the child's most basic needs.

This need for adventurous and imaginative play is taken care of handily in small towns and in the countryside, where children have access to raw materials, space, and a somewhat comprehensible environment. In cities, however, it has become a pressing concern. The world of private toys and asphalt playgrounds does not provide the proper settings for this kind of play.

The basic work on this problem has come from Lady Allen of

No playing.

Hurtwood. In a series of projects and publications over the past twenty years, Lady Allen has developed the concept of the adventure playground for cities, and we refer the reader, above all, to her work. (See, for example, her book, *Planning for Play*, Cambridge: MIT Press, 1968.) We believe that her work is so substantial, that, by itself, it establishes the essential pattern for neighborhood playgrounds.

Colin Ward has also written an excellent review, "Adventure Playgrounds: A Parable of Anarchy," *Anarchy* 7, September 1961. Here is a description of the Grimsby playground, from that review:

> At the end of each summer the children saw up their shacks and shanties into firewood which they deliver in fantastic quantities to old age pensioners. When they begin building in the spring, "it's just a hole in the ground—and they crawl into it." Gradually the holes give way to two-storey huts. Similarly with the notices above their dens. It begins with nailing up "Keep Out" signs. After this come more personal names like "Bughold Cave" and "Dead Man's Cave," but by the end of the summer they have communal names like "Hospital" or "Estate Agent." There is an everchanging range of activities due entirely to the imagination and enterprise of the children themselves. . . .

Therefore:

Set up a playground for the children in each neighborhood. Not a highly finished playground, with asphalt and

swings, but a place with raw materials of all kinds—nets, boxes, barrels, trees, ropes, simple tools, frames, grass, and water—where children can create and re-create playgrounds of their own.

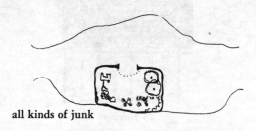

all kinds of junk

❖ ❖ ❖

Make sure that the adventure playground is in the sun—SUNNY PLACE (161); make hard surfaces for bikes and carts and toy trucks and trolleys, and soft surfaces for mud and building things—BIKE PATHS AND RACKS (56), GARDEN GROWING WILD (172), CHILD CAVES (203); and make the boundary substantial with a GARDEN WALL (173) or SITTING WALL (243). . . .

. . . even when there is public land and private land for individual buildings—COMMON LAND (67), YOUR OWN HOME (79), there is no guarantee that animals can flourish there. This pattern helps to form GREEN STREETS (51) and COMMON LAND (67) by giving them the qualities they need to sustain animal life.

❖ ❖ ❖

Animals are as important a part of nature as the trees and grass and flowers. There is some evidence, in addition, which suggests that contact with animals may play a vital role in a child's emotional development.

Yet while it is widely accepted that we need "parks"—at least access to some kind of open space where trees and grass and flowers grow—we do not yet have the same kind of wisdom where sheep, horses, cows, goats, birds, snakes, rabbits, deer, chickens, wildcats, gulls, otters, crabs, fish, frogs, beetles, butterflies, and ants are concerned.

Ann Dreyfus, a family therapist in California, has told us about the way that animals like goats and rabbits help children in their therapy. She finds that children who cannot make contact with people, are nevertheless able to establish contact with these animals. Once this has happened and feelings have started to flow again, the children's capacity for making contact starts to grow again, and eventually spreads out to family and friends.

But animals are almost missing from cities. In a city there are, broadly speaking, only three kinds of animal: pets, vermin, and animals in the zoo. None of these three provides the emotional sustenance nor the ecological connections that are needed. Pets are pleasant, but so humanized that they have no wild free life of their own. And they give human beings little opportunity to experience the animalness of animals. Vermin—rats, cockroaches—are animals which are peculiar to cities and which depend ecologically on miserable and disorganized conditions, so they are naturally considered as enemies. Animals in the zoo are more or less inaccessible to most of the human population—except as

372

occasional curiosities. Besides, it has been said that animals living under the conditions which a zoo provides are essentially psychotic —that is, entirely disturbed from their usual mode of existence— so that it is probably wrong to keep them there—and certainly they can in no way re-create the missing web of animal life which cities need.

Looking in or looking out—what's the difference?

It is perfectly possible to reintroduce animals into the natural ecology of cities in a useful and functioning sense, provided that arrangements are made which allow this and do not create a nuisance.

Examples of ecologically useful animals in a city: horses, ponies, donkeys—for local transportation and sport. Pigs—to recycle garbage and for meat. Ducks and chickens—as a source of eggs and meat. Cows—for milk. Goats—milk. Bees—honey and pollination of fruit trees. Birds—to maintain insect balance.

There are essentially two difficulties to overcome. (1) Many of these animals have been driven out of cities by law because they interrupt traffic, leave dung on the street, and carry disease. (2) Many of the animals cannot survive without protection under modern urban conditions. It is necessary to make specific provisions to overcome these difficulties.

Therefore:

Make legal provisions which allow people to keep any animals on their private lots or in private stables. Create a piece of fenced and protected common land, where animals

are free to graze, with grass, trees, and water in it. Make at least one system of movement in the neighborhood which is entirely asphalt-free—where dung can fall freely without needing to be cleaned up.

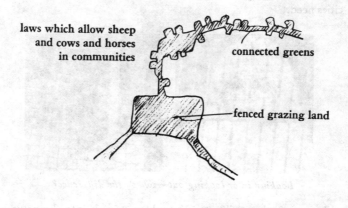

laws which allow sheep and cows and horses in communities

connected greens

fenced grazing land

❖ ❖ ❖

Make sure that the green areas—GREEN STREETS (51), ACCESSIBLE GREEN (60)—are all connected to one another to form a continuous swath throughout the city for domestic and wild animals. Place the animal commons near a children's home and near the local schools, so children can take care of the animals —CHILDREN'S HOME (86); if there is a lot of dung, make sure that it can be used as a fertilizer—COMPOST (178). . . .

within the framework of the common land, the clusters and the work communities, encourage transformation of the smallest independent social institutions: the families, workgroups, and gathering places. First, the family, in all its forms;

75 THE FAMILY*

. . . assume now, that you have decided to build a house for yourself. If you place it properly, this house can help to form a cluster, or a row of houses, or a hill of houses—HOUSE CLUSTER (37), ROW HOUSES (38), HOUSING HILL (39)—or it can help to keep a working community alive—HOUSING IN BETWEEN (48). This next pattern now gives you some vital information about the social character of the household itself. If you succeed in following this pattern, it will help repair LIFE CYCLE (26) and HOUSEHOLD MIX (35) in your community.

❖ ❖ ❖

The nuclear family is not by itself a viable social form.

Until a few years ago, human society was based on the extended family: a family of at least three generations, with parents, children, grandparents, uncles, aunts, and cousins, all living together in a single or loosely knit multiple household. But today people move hundreds of miles to marry, to find education, and to work. Under these circumstances the only family units which are left are those units called nuclear families: father, mother, and children. And many of these are broken down even further by divorce and separation.

Unfortunately, it seems very likely that the nuclear family is not a viable social form. It is too small. Each person in a nuclear family is too tightly linked to other members of the family; any one relationship which goes sour, even for a few hours, becomes critical; people cannot simply turn away toward uncles, aunts, grandchildren, cousins, brothers. Instead, each difficulty twists the family unit into ever tighter spirals of discomfort; the children become prey to all kinds of dependencies and oedipal neuroses; the parents are so dependent on each other that they are finally forced to separate.

Philip Slater describes this situation for American families and finds in the adults of the family, especially the women, a terrible, brooding sense of deprivation. There are simply not enough people around, not enough communal action, to give the ordinary

377

experience around the home any depth or richness. (Philip E. Slater, *The Pursuit of Loneliness*, Boston: Beacon Press, 1970, p. 67, and throughout.)

It seems essential that the people in a household have at least a dozen people round them, so that they can find the comfort and relationships they need to sustain them during their ups and downs. Since the old extended family, based on blood ties, seems to be gone—at least for the moment—this can only happen if small families, couples, and single people join together in voluntary "families" of ten or so.

In his final book, *Island*, Aldous Huxley portrayed a lovely vision of such a development:

"How many homes does a Palanese child have?"
"About twenty on the average."
"Twenty? My God!"
"We all belong," Susila explained, "to a MAC—a Mutual Adoption Club. Every MAC consists of anything from fifteen to twenty-five assorted couples. Newly elected brides and bridegrooms, old-timers with growing children, grandparents and great-grandparents—everybody in the club adopts everyone else. Besides our own blood relations, we all have our quota of deputy mothers, deputy fathers, deputy aunts and uncles, deputy brothers and sisters, deputy babies and toddlers and teen-agers."
Will shook his head. "Making twenty families grow where only one grew before."
"But what grew before was *your* kind of family. . . ." As though reading instructions from a cookery book, "Take one sexually inept wage slave," she went on, "one dissatisfied female, two or (if preferred) three small television addicts; marinate in a mixture of Freudism and dilute Christianity; then bottle up tightly in a four-room flat and stew for fifteen years in their own juice. *Our* recipe is rather different: Take twenty sexually satisfied couples and their offspring; add science, intuition and humor in equal quantities; steep in Tantrik Buddhism and simmer indefinitely in an open pan in the open air over a brisk flame of affection."
"And what comes out of your open pan?" he asked.
"An entirely different kind of family. Not exclusive, like your families, and not predestined, not compulsory. An inclusive, unpredestined and voluntary family. Twenty pairs of fathers and mothers, eight or nine ex-fathers and ex-mothers, and forty or fifty assorted children of all ages." (Aldous Huxley, *Island*, New York: Bantam, 1962, pp. 89–90.)

Physically, the setting for a large voluntary family must provide

for a balance of privacy and communality. Each small family, each person, each couple, needs a private realm, almost a private household of their own, according to their territorial need. In the movement to build communes, it is our experience that groups have not taken this need for privacy seriously enough. It has been shrugged off, as something to overcome. But it is a deep and basic need; and if the setting does not let each person and each small household regulate itself on this dimension, it is sure to cause trouble. We propose, therefore, that individuals, couples, people young and old—each subgroup—have its own legally independent household—in some cases, physically separate households and cottages, at least separate rooms, suites, and floors.

The private realms are then set off against the common space and the common functions. The most vital commons are the kitchen, the place to sit down and eat, and a garden. Common meals, at least several nights a week, seem to play the biggest role in binding the group. The meals, and taking time at the cooking, provide the kind of casual meeting time when everything else can be comfortably discussed: the child care arrangements, maintenance, projects—see COMMUNAL EATING (147).

This would suggest, then, a large family room-farmhouse kitchen, right at the heart of the site—at the main crossroads, where everyone would tend to meet toward the end of the day. Again, according to the style of the family, this might be a separate building, with workshop and gardens, or one wing of a house, or the entire first floor of a two or three story building.

There is some evidence that processes which generate large voluntary group households are already working in the society. (Cf. Pamela Hollie, "More families share houses with others to enhance 'life style,'" *Wall Street Journal*, July 7, 1972.)

One way to spur the growth of voluntary families: When someone turns over or sells their home or room or apartment, they first tell everyone living around them—their neighbors. These neighbors then have the right to find friends of theirs to take the place—and thus to extend their "family." If friends are able to move in, then they can arrange for themselves how to create a functioning family, with commons, and so on. They might build a connection between the homes, knock out a wall, add a

room. If the people immediately around the place cannot make the sale in a few months, then it reverts to the normal marketplace.

Therefore:

Set up processes which encourage groups of 8 to 12 people to come together and establish communal households. Morphologically, the important things are:

1. **Private realms for the groups and individuals that make up the extended family: couple's realms, private rooms, sub-households for small families.**
2. **Common space for shared functions: cooking, working, gardening, child care.**
3. **At the important crossroads of the site, a place where the entire group can meet and sit together.**

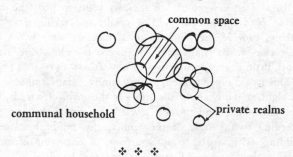

❖ ❖ ❖

Each individual household within the larger family must, at all costs, have a clearly defined territory of its own, which it controls—YOUR OWN HOME (79); treat the individual territories according to the nature of the individual households—HOUSE FOR A SMALL FAMILY (76), HOUSE FOR A COUPLE (77), HOUSE FOR ONE PERSON (78); and build common space between them, where the members of the different smaller households can meet and eat together—COMMON AREAS AT THE HEART (129), COMMUNAL EATING (147). For the shape of the building, gardens, parking, and surroundings, begin with BUILDING COMPLEX (95). . . .

76 HOUSE FOR A SMALL FAMILY*

. . . according to THE FAMILY (75), each nuclear family ought to be a member household of a larger group household. If this is not possible, do what you can, when building a house for a small family, to generate some larger, possible group household, by tying it together with the next door households; in any case, at the very least, form the beginning of a HOUSE CLUSTER (37).

❖ ❖ ❖

In a house for a small family, it is the relationship between children and adults which is most critical.

Many small households, not large enough to have a full fledged nursery, not rich enough to have a nanny, find themselves swamped by the children. The children naturally want to be where the adults are; their parents don't have the heart, or the energy, to keep them out of special areas; so finally the whole house has the character of a children's room—children's clothes, drawings, boots and shoes, tricycles, toy trucks, and disarray.

Yet, obviously few parents feel happy to give up the calm and cleanliness and quiet of the adult world in every square inch of their homes. To help achieve a balance, a house for a small family needs three distinct areas: a couple's realm, reserved for the adults; a children's realm, where children's needs hold sway; and a common area, between the two, connected to them both.

The couple's realm should be more than a room, although rooms are a part of it. It is territory which sustains them as two adults, a couple—not father and mother. Other parts of their lives are involved with children, friends, work; there must be a place which becomes naturally an expression of them as adults, alone. The children come in and out of this territory, but when they are there, they are clearly in the adults' world. See COUPLE'S REALM (136).

The children's world must also be looked upon as territory that they share, as children, CHILDREN'S REALM (137); here, it is important to establish that this is a part of the house, in balance with the others. Again, the critical feature is not that adults are

382

"excluded" but that, when they are in this world, they are in children's territory.

The common area contains those functions that the children and the adults share: eating together, sitting together, games, perhaps bathing, gardening—again, whatever captures their needs for shared territory. Quite likely, the common territory will be larger than the two other parts of the house.

Finally, realize that this pattern is different from the way most small family homes are made today. For example, a popular current conception, comparable to this, but quite different, is a suburban *two part house:* sleeping and commons.

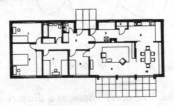

A typical suburban two part house.

Even though there is a "master bedroom" the sleeping part of the house is essentially one thing—the children are all around the master bedroom. This plan does not have the distinctions we are arguing for.

Here is a beautiful plan which does:

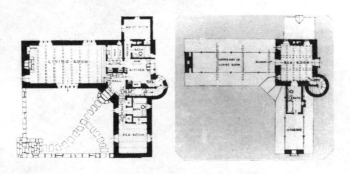

A three-part house—the couple's realm upstairs.

Therefore:

Give the house three distinct parts: a realm for parents, a realm for the children, and a common area. Conceive these three realms as roughly similar in size, with the commons the largest.

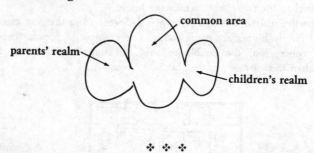

❖ ❖ ❖

Treat the house, like every house, as a distinct piece of territory —YOUR OWN HOME (79); build the three main parts according to the specific patterns for those parts—COMMON AREAS AT THE HEART (129), COUPLE'S REALM (136), BED CLUSTER (143) and connect the common areas, and the bed cluster according to the CHILDREN'S REALM (137). . . .

. . . again, ideally, every couple is a part of a larger group household—THE FAMILY (75). If this can not be so, try to build the house for the couple in such a way as to tie it together with some other households, to form the beginnings of a group household, or, if this fails, at least to form the beginnings of a HOUSE CLUSTER (37).

❖ ❖ ❖

In a small household shared by two, the most important problem which arises is the possibility that each may have too little opportunity for solitude or privacy.

Consider these forces:

1. Of course, the couple need a shared realm, where they can function together, invite friends, be alone together. This realm needs to be made up of functions which they share.

2. But it is also true that each partner is trying to maintain an individuality, and not be submerged in the identity of the other, or the identity of the "couple." Each partner needs *space* to nourish this need.

It is essential, therefore, that a small house be conceived as a place where the two people may be together but where, from time to time, either one of them may also be alone, in comfort, in dignity, and in such a way that the other does not feel left out or isolated. To this end, there must be two small places— perhaps rooms, perhaps large alcoves, perhaps a corner, screened off by a half-wall—places which are clearly understood as private territories, where each person can keep to himself, pursue his or her own activities.

Still, the problem of the balance of privacy in a couple's lives is delicate. Even with a small place of one's own, tenuously connected to the house, one partner may feel left out at various moments. While we believe that the solution proposed in this pattern helps, the problem will not be entirely settled until the couple itself is in some close, neighborly, and family-like rela-

tionship to other adults. Then, when one needs privacy, the other has other possibilities for companionship at hand. This idea and its physical implications are discussed in the pattern, THE FAMILY (75).

Once the opportunity for withdrawal is satisfied, there is also a genuine opportunity for the couple to be together; and then the house can be a place where genuine intimacy, genuine connection can happen.

There is one other problem, unique to a house for a couple, that must be mentioned. In the first years of a couple's life, as they learn more about each other, and find out if indeed they have a future together, the evolution of the house plays a vital role. Improving the house, fixing it up, enlarging it, provides a frame for learning about one another: it brings out conflict, and offers the chance, like almost no other activity, for concrete resolution and growth. This suggests that a couple find a place that they can change gradually over the years, and *not* build or buy for themselves a "dream" home from scratch. The experience of making simple changes in the house, and tuning it to their lives, provides some grist for their own growth. Therefore, it is best to start small, with plenty of room for growth and change.

Therefore:

Conceive a house for a couple as being made up of two kinds of places—a shared couple's realm and individual private worlds. Imagine the shared realm as half-public and half-intimate; and the private worlds as entirely individual and private.

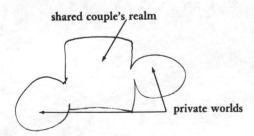

shared couple's realm

private worlds

❖ ❖ ❖

Again, treat the house as a distinct piece of territory, in some fashion owned by its users—YOUR OWN HOME (79). Lay out the common part, according to the pattern COUPLE'S REALM (136), and give both persons an individual world of their own where they can be alone—A ROOM OF ONE'S OWN (141). . . .

78 HOUSE FOR ONE PERSON*

. . . the households with one person in them, more than any other, need to be a part of some kind of larger household—THE FAMILY (75). Either build them to fit into some larger group household, or even attach them, as ancillary cottages to other, ordinary family households like HOUSE FOR A SMALL FAMILY (76) or HOUSE FOR A COUPLE (77).

❖ ❖ ❖

Once a household for one person is part of some larger group, the most critical problem which arises is the need for simplicity.

The housing market contains few houses or apartments specifically built for one person. Most often men and women who choose to live alone, live in larger houses and apartments, originally built for two people or families. And yet for one person these larger places are most often uncompact, unwieldy, hard to live in, hard to look after. Most important of all, they do not allow a person to develop a sense of self-sufficiency, simplicity, compactness, and economy in his or her own life.

The kind of place which is most closely suited to one person's needs, and most nearly overcomes this problem, is a place of the utmost simplicity, in which only the bare bones of necessity are there: a place, built like a ploughshare, where every corner, every table, every shelf, each flower pot, each chair, each log, is placed according to the simplest necessity, and supports the person's life directly, plainly, with the harmony of nothing that is not needed, and everything that is.

The plan of such a house will be characteristically different from other houses, primarily because it requires almost no differentiation of its spaces: it need only be one room. It can be a cottage or a studio, built on the ground or in a larger building, part of a group household or a detached structure. In essence, it is simply a central space, with nooks around it. The nooks replace the rooms in a larger house; they are for bed, bath, kitchen, workshop and entrance.

It is important to realize that very many of the patterns in this book can be built into a small house; small size does not pre-

clude richness of form. The trick is to intensify and to overlay; to compress the patterns; to reduce them to simple expressions; to make every inch count double. When it is well done, a small house feels wonderfully continuous—cooking a bowl of soup fills the house; there is no rattling around. This cannot happen if the place is divided into rooms.

We have found it necessary to call special attention to this pattern because it is nearly impossible to build a house this small in cities—there is no way to get hold of a very small lot. Zoning codes and banking practices prohibit such tiny lots; they prohibit "normal" lots from splitting down to the kind of scale that a house for one person requires. The correct development of this pattern will require a change in these ordinances.

Therefore:

Conceive a house for one person as a place of the utmost simplicity: essentially a one-room cottage or studio, with large and small alcoves around it. When it is most intense, the entire house may be no more than 300 to 400 square feet.

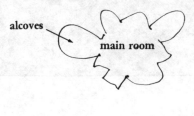

⬧ ⬧ ⬧

And again, make the house an individual piece of territory, with its own garden, no matter how small—YOUR OWN HOME (79); make the main room essentially a kind of farmhouse kitchen —FARMHOUSE KITCHEN (139), with alcoves opening off it for sitting, working, bathing, sleeping, dressing—BATHING ROOM (144), WINDOW PLACE (180), WORKSPACE ENCLOSURE (183), BED ALCOVE (188), DRESSING ROOM (189); if the house is meant for an old person, or for someone very young, shape it also according to the pattern for OLD AGE COTTAGE (155) or TEEN-AGER'S COTTAGE (154). . . .

79 YOUR OWN HOME**

. . . according to THE FAMILY (75), each individual household should be a part of a larger family group household. Whether this is so, or not, each individual household, must also have a territory of its own which it controls completely—HOUSE FOR A SMALL FAMILY (76), HOUSE FOR A COUPLE (77), HOUSE FOR ONE PERSON (78); this pattern, which simply sets down the need for such a territory, helps especially to form higher density house clusters like ROW HOUSES (38), HOUSING HILL (39), which often do not have well-defined individual territories for the separate households.

People cannot be genuinely comfortable and healthy in a house which is not theirs. All forms of rental—whether from private landlords or public housing agencies—work against the natural processes which allow people to form stable, self-healing communities.

Income property.

. . . in the imperishable primal language of the human heart house means my house, your house, a man's own house. The house is the winning throw of the dice which man has wrested from the uncanniness of universe; it is his defense against the chaos that threatens to invade him. Therefore his deeper wish is that it be his own house, that he not have to share with anyone other than his own family. (Martin Buber, *A Believing Humanism: Gleanings*, New York: Simon and Shuster, 1969, p. 93.)

This pattern is not intended as an argument in favor of "private

property," or the process of buying and selling land. Indeed, it
is very clear that all those processes which encourage speculation
in land, for the sake of profit, are unhealthy and destructive, because they invite people to treat houses as commodities, to build
things for "resale," and not in such a way as to fit their own
needs.

And just as speculation and the profit motive make it impossible for people to adapt their houses to their own needs, so
tenancy, rental, and landlords do the same. Rental areas are always
the first to turn to slums. The mechanism is clear and well known.
See, for example, George Sternlieb, *The Tenement Landlord*
(Rutgers University Press, 1966). The landlord tries to keep his
maintenance and repair costs as low as possible; the residents
have no incentive to maintain and repair the homes—in fact, the
opposite—since improvements add to the wealth of the landlord,
and even justify higher rent. And so the typical piece of rental
property degenerates over the years. Then landlords try to build
new rental properties which are immune to neglect—gardens are
replaced with concrete, carpets are replaced with lineoleum, and
wooden surfaces by formica: it is an attempt to make the new
units maintenance-free, and to stop the slums by force; but they
turn out cold and sterile and again turn into slums, because nobody loves them.

People will only be able to feel comfortable in their houses,
if they can change their houses to suit themselves, add on whatever they need, rearrange the garden as they like it; and, of
course, they can only do this in circumstances where they are
the legal owners of the house and land; and if, in high density
multi-story housing, each apartment, like a house, has a well-
defined volume, in which the owner can make changes as he likes.

This requires then, that every house is owned—in some fashion
—by the people that live in it; it requires that every house,
whether at ground level or in the air, has a well-defined volume
within which the family is free to make whatever changes they
want; and it requires a form of ownership which discourages
speculation.

Several approaches have been put forward in recent years to
solve the problem of providing each household with a "home."

At one extreme there are ideas like Habraken's high density "support" system, where families buy pads on publicly owned superstructures and gradually develop their own homes. And at the other extreme there are the rural communes, where people have forsaken the city to create their own homes in the country. Even modified forms of rental can help the situation if they allow people to change their houses according to their needs and give people some financial stake in the process of maintenance. This helps, because renting is often a step along the way to home ownership; but unless tenants can somehow recover their investments in money and labor, the hopeless cycle of degeneration of rental property and the degeneration of the tenants' financial capability will continue. (Cf. Rolf Goetze, "Urban Housing Rehabilitation," in Turner and Fichter, eds., *The Freedom to Build*, New York: Macmillan, 1972.)

A common element in all these cases is the understanding that the successful development of a household's "home" depends upon these features: Each household must possess a clearly defined site for both a house and an outdoor space, and the household must own this site in the sense that they are in full control of its development.

Therefore:

Do everything possible to make the traditional forms of rental impossible, indeed, illegal. Give every household its own home, with space enough for a garden. Keep the emphasis in the definition of ownership on control, not on financial ownership. Indeed, where it is possible to construct forms of ownership which give people control over their houses and gardens, but make financial speculation impossible, choose these forms above all others. In all cases give people the legal power, and the physical opportunity to modify and repair their own places. Pay attention to this rule especially, in the case of high density apartments: build the apartments in such a way that every individual apartment has a garden, or a terrace where vegetables will grow, and that even in this situation, each family

can build, and change, and add on to their house as they wish.

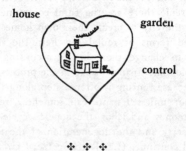

house   garden

control

❖ ❖ ❖

For the shape of the house, begin with BUILDING COMPLEX (95). For the shape of the lot, do not accept the common notion of a lot which has a narrow frontage and a great deal of depth. Instead, try to make every house lot roughly square, or even long along the street and shallow. All this is necessary to create the right relation between house and garden—HALF-HIDDEN GARDEN (111).

the workgroups, including all kinds of workshops and offices and even children's learning groups;

80 SELF-GOVERNING WORKSHOPS AND OFFICES**

. . . all kinds of work, office work and industrial work and agricultural work, are radically decentralized by SCATTERED WORK (9), and INDUSTRIAL RIBBONS (42) and grouped in small communities—WORK COMMUNITY (41). This pattern helps to generate these larger patterns by giving the fundamental nature of all work organizations, no matter what their type.

No one enjoys his work if he is a cog in a machine.

A man enjoys his work when he understands the whole and when he is responsible for the quality of the whole. He can only understand the whole and be responsible for the whole when the work which happens in society, all of it, is undertaken by small self-governing human groups; groups small enough to give people understanding through face-to-face contact, and autonomous enough to let the workers themselves govern their own affairs.

The evidence for this pattern is built upon a single, fundamental proposition: work is a form of living, with its own intrinsic rewards; any way of organizing work which is at odds with this idea, which treats work instrumentally, as a means only to other ends, is inhuman. Down through the ages people have described and proposed ways of working according to this proposition. Recently, E. F. Schumacher, the economist, has made a beautiful statement of this attitude (E. F. Schumacher, "Buddhist Economics," *Resurgence*, 275 Kings Road, Kingston, Surrey, Volume I, Number 11, January, 1968).

The Buddhist point of view takes the function of work to be at least threefold: to give a man a chance to utilize and develop his faculties; to enable him to overcome his ego-centeredness by joining with other people in a common task; and to bring forth the goods and services needed for a becoming existence. Again, the consequences that flow from this view are endless. To organize work in such a manner that it becomes meaningless, boring, stultifying, or nerve-racking for the worker would be little short of criminal; it would indicate a greater concern with goods than with people, an evil lack of compassion and a soul-destroying degree of attachment to the most

primitive side of this worldly existence. Equally, to strive for leisure as an alternative to work would be considered a complete misunderstanding of one of the basic truths of human existence, namely, that work and leisure are complementary parts of the same living process and cannot be separated without destroying the joy of work and the bliss of leisure.

From the Buddhist point of view, there are therefore two types of mechanization which must be clearly distinguished: one that enhances a man's skill and power and one that turns the work of man over to a mechanical slave, leaving man in a position of having to serve the slave. How to tell the one from the other? "The craftsman himself," says Ananda Coomaraswamy, a man equally competent to talk about the Modern West as the Ancient East, "the craftsman himself can always, if allowed to, draw the delicate distinction between the machine and the tool. The carpet loom is a tool, a contrivance for holding warp threads at a stretch for the pile to be woven round them by the craftsmen's fingers; but the power loom is a machine, and its significance as a destroyer of culture lies in the fact that it does the essentially human part of the work." It is clear, therefore, that Buddhist economics must be very different from the economics of modern materialism, since the Buddhist sees the essence of civilization not in a multiplication of wants but in the purification of human character. Character, at the same time, is formed primarily by a man's work. And work, properly conducted in conditions of human dignity and freedom, blesses those who do it and equally their products. The Indian philosopher and economist J. C. Kumarappa sums the matter up as follows:

"If the nature of the work is properly appreciated and applied, it will stand in the same relation to the higher faculties as food is to the physical body. It nourishes and enlivens the higher man and urges him to produce the best he is capable of. It directs his freewill along the proper course and disciplines the animal in him into progressive channels. It furnishes an excellent background for man to display his scale of values and develop his personality."

In contrast to this form of work stands the style of work that has been created by the technological progress of the past two hundred years. In this style workers are made to operate like parts of a machine; they create parts of no consequence, and have no responsibility for the whole. We may fairly say that the alienation of workers from the intrinsic pleasures of their work has been a primary product of the industrial revolution. The alienation is particularly acute in large organizations, where faceless workers repeat endlessly menial tasks to create products and services with which they cannot identify.

In these organizations, with all the power and benefits that the unions have been able to wrest from the hands of the owners, there is still evidence that workers are fundamentally unhappy with their work. In the auto industry, for example, the absentee rate on Mondays and Fridays is staggering—15 to 20 per cent; and there is evidence of "massive alcoholism, similar to what the Russians are experiencing with their factory workers" (Nicholas von Hoffman, *Washington Post*). The fact is that people cannot find satisfaction in work unless it is performed at a human scale and in a setting where the worker has a say.

Job dissatisfaction in modern industry has also led to industrial sabotage and a faster turnover of workers in recent years. A new super-automated General Motors assembly plant in Lordstown, Ohio, was sabotaged and shut down for several weeks. Absenteeism in the three largest automobile manufacturing companies has doubled in the past seven years. The turnover of workers has also doubled. Some industrial engineers believe that "American industry in some cases may have pushed technology too far by taking the last few bits of skill out of jobs, and that a point of human resistance has been reached" (Agis Salpukis, "Is the machine pushing man over the brink?" *San Francisco Sunday Examiner and Chronicle*, April 16, 1972).

Perhaps the most dramatic empirical evidence for the connection between work and life is that presented in the recent study, "Work in America," commissioned by Elliot Richardson, as Secretary of Health, Education and Welfare Department, 1972. This study finds that *the single best predictor of long life is not whether a person smokes or how often he sees a doctor, but the extent to which he is satisfied with his job.* The report identifies the two main elements of job dissatisfaction as the diminishing independence of workers, and the increasing simplification, fragmentation, and isolation of tasks—both of which are rampant in modern industrial and office work alike.

But for most of human history, the production of goods and services was for a far more personal, self-regulating affair; when each job of work was a matter of creative interest. And there is no reason why work can't be like that again, today.

For instance, Seymour Melman, in *Decision Making and Productivity*, compares the manufacture of tractors in Detroit and in

Coventry, England. He contrasts Detroit's managerial rule with Coventry's gang system and shows that the gang system produced high quality products and the highest wages in British industry. "The most characteristic feature of the decision-formulation process is that of mutuality in decision-making with final authority residing in the hands of the group workers themselves."

Other projects and experiments and evidence which indicate that modern work can be organized in this manner and still be compatible with sophisticated technology, have been collected by Hunnius, Garson, and Chase. See *Workers' Control*, New York: Vintage Books, 1973.

And another example comes from the reports by E. L. Trist, *Organizational Choice* and P. Herbst, *Autonomous Group Functioning*. These authors describe the organization of work in mining pits in Durham which was put into practice by groups of miners.

The composite work organization may be described as one in which the group takes over complete responsibility for the total cycle of operations involved in mining the coal-face. No member of the group has a fixed work-role. Instead, the men deploy themselves, depending on the requirements of the ongoing group task. Within the limits of technological and safety requirements they are free to evolve their way of organizing and carrying out their task.

[The experiment demonstrates] the ability of quite large primary work groups of 40–50 members to act as self-regulating, self-developing social organisms able to maintain ,themselves in a steady state of high productivity. (Quoted in Colin Ward, "The organization of anarchy," *Patterns of Anarchy*, Krimerman and Perry, eds., New York: Anchor Books, 1966, pp. 349–51.)

We believe that these small self-governing groups are not only most efficient, but also the only possible source of job satisfaction. They provide the only style of work that is nourishing and intrinsically satisfying.

Therefore:

Encourage the formation of self-governing workshops and offices of 5 to 20 workers. Make each group autonomous—with respect to organization, style, relation to other groups, hiring and firing, work schedule. Where the work

is complicated and requires larger organizations, several of these work groups can federate and cooperate to produce complex artifacts and services.

self-governing workshops

❖ ❖ ❖

House the workgroup in a building of its own—OFFICE CONNECTIONS (82), BUILDING COMPLEX (95); if the workgroup is large enough, and if it serves the public, break it down into autonomous departments, easily identifiable, with no more than a dozen people each—SMALL SERVICES WITHOUT RED TAPE (81); in any case, divide all work into small team work, either directly within the cooperative workgroup or under the departments, with the people of each team in common space—MASTER AND APPRENTICES (83) and SMALL WORK GROUPS (148). · · ·

81 SMALL SERVICES
WITHOUT RED TAPE*

. . . all offices which provide service to the public—WORK COM-MUNITY (41), UNIVERSITY AS A MARKETPLACE (43), LOCAL TOWN HALL (44), HEATH CENTER (47), TEENAGE SOCIETY (84) need subsidiary departments, where the members of the public go. And of course, piecemeal development of these small departments, one department at a time, can also help to generate these larger patterns gradually.

❖ ❖ ❖

Departments and public services don't work if they are too large. When they are large, their human qualities vanish; they become bureaucratic; red tape takes over.

There is a great deal of literature on the way red tape and bureaucracy work against human needs. See, for example, Gideon Sjoberg, Richard Brymer, and Buford Farris, "Bureaucracy and the Lower Class," Sociology and Social Research, 50, April, 1966, pp. 325–77; and Alvin W. Gouldner, "Red Tape as a Social Problem," in Robert Mertin, Reader in Bureaucracy, Free Press, 1952, pp. 410–18.

According to these authors, red tape can be overcome in two ways. First, it can be overcome by making each service program small and autonomous. A great deal of evidence shows that red tape occurs largely as a result of impersonal relationships in large institutions. When people can no longer communicate on a face-to-face basis, they need formal regulations, and in the lower echelons of the organization, these formal regulations are followed blindly and narrowly.

Second, red tape can be overcome by changing the passive nature of the clients' relation to service programs. There is considerable evidence to show that when clients have an active relationship with a social institution, the institution loses its power to intimidate them.

We have therefore concluded that no service should have more than 12 persons total (all staff, including clerks). We base this figure on the fact that 12 seems to be the largest number of

405

people that can sit down in a face-to-face discussion. It seems likely that a smaller staff size will work better still. Furthermore, each service should be relatively autonomous—subject only to a few simple, coordinative regulations from parent organizations—and that this should be emphasized by physical autonomy. In order to be physically autonomous, each service must have an area which is entirely under its own jurisdiction; with its own door on a public thoroughfare, and complete physical separation from other services.

This pattern applies equally to the departments of a city hall, a medical center, or to the local branches of a welfare agency. In most of these cases the pattern would require basic changes in administrative organization. However difficult they may be to implement, we believe these changes are required.

Therefore:

In any institution whose departments provide public service:

1. Make each service or department autonomous as far as possible.
2. Allow no one service more than 12 staff members total.
3. House each one in an identifiable piece of the building.
4. Give each one direct access to a public thoroughfare.

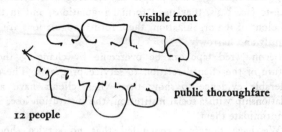

visible front

public thoroughfare

12 people

❖ ❖ ❖

Arrange these departments in space, according to the prescription of OFFICE CONNECTIONS (82) and BUILDING COMPLEX (95); if the public thoroughfare is indoors, make it a BUILDING THOROUGHFARE (101), and make the fronts of the services visible as a FAMILY OF ENTRANCES (102); wherever the services are in any way connected to the political life of the community, mix them with ad hoc groups created by the citizens or users— NECKLACE OF COMMUNITY PROJECTS (45); arrange the inside space of the department according to FLEXIBLE OFFICE SPACE (146); and provide rooms where people can team up in two's and three's—SMALL WORK GROUPS (148). . . . .

82 OFFICE CONNECTIONS*

... in any work community or any office, there are always various human groups—and it is always important to decide how these groups shall be placed, in space. Which should be near each other, which ones further apart? This pattern gives the answer to this question, and in doing so, helps greatly to construct the inner layout of a WORK COMMUNITY (41) or of SELF-GOVERN-ING WORKSHOPS AND OFFICES (80) or of SMALL SERVICES WITH-OUT RED TAPE (81).

If two parts of an office are too far apart, people will not move between them as often as they need to; and if they are more than one floor apart, there will be almost no communication between the two.

Current architectural methods often include a proximity matrix, which shows the amount of movement between different people and functions in an office or a hospital. These methods always make the tacit assumption that the functions which have the most movement between them should be closest together. *However, as usually stated, this concept is completely invalid.*

The concept has been created by a kind of Taylorian quest for efficiency, in which it is assumed that the less people walk about, the less of their salary is spent on "wasteful" walking. The logical conclusion of this kind of analysis is that, if it were only possible, people should not have to walk at all, and should spend the day vegetating in their armchairs.

The fact is that people work best only when they are healthy in mind and body. A person who is forced to sit all day long behind a desk, without ever stretching his legs, will become restless and unable to work, and inefficient in this way. Some walking is very good for you. It is not only good for the body, but also gives people an opportunity for a change of scene, a way

of thinking about something else, a chance to reflect on some detail of the morning's work or one of the everyday human problems in the office.

On the other hand, if a person has to make the same trip, many times, there is a point at which the length of the trip becomes time-consuming and annoying, and then inefficient, because it makes the person irritable, and finally critical when a person starts avoiding trips because they are too long and too frequent.

An office will function efficiently so long as the people who work there do not feel that the trips they have to take are a nuisance. Trips need to be short enough so they are not felt a nuisance—but they do not need to be any shorter.

The nuisance of a trip depends on the relationship between length and frequency. You can walk 10 feet to a file many times a day without being annoyed by it; you can walk 400 feet occasionally without being annoyed. In the graph below we plot the nuisance threshold for various combinations of length and frequency.

The graph is based on 127 observations in the Berkeley City Hall. People were asked to define all the trips they had to make regularly during the work week, to state their frequency, and then to state whether they considered the trip to be a nuisance.

The line on the graph shows the median of the distances said to be a nuisance for each different frequency. We define distances to the right of this line as nuisance distances. The nuisance distance for any trip frequency is the distance at which we predict that at least 50 per cent of all people will begin to consider this distance a nuisance.

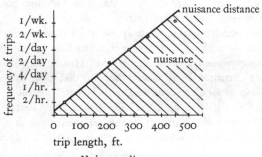

Nuisance distances.

So far, our discussion of proximity has been based on *horizontal* distances. How do stairs enter in? What part does vertical distance play in the experience of proximity? Or, to put it more precisely, what is the horizontal equivalent of one flight of stairs? Suppose two departments need to be within 100 feet of one another, according to the proximity graph—and suppose that they are for some reason on different stories, one floor apart. How much of the 100 feet does the stair eat up: with the stair between them, how far apart can they be horizontally?

We do not know the exact answer to this question. However, we do have some indirect evidence from an unpublished study by Marina Estabrook and Robert Sommer. As we shall see, this study shows that stairs play a much greater role, and eat up much more "distance" than you might imagine.

Estabrook and Sommer studied the formation of acquaintances in a three-story university building, where several different departments were housed. They asked people to name all the people they knew in departments other than their own. Their results were as follows:

Percent of people known:	When departments are:
12.2	on same floor
8.9	one floor apart
2.2	two floors apart

People knew 12.2 per cent of the people from other departments on the *same* floor as their own, 8.9 per cent of the people from other departments *one* floor apart from their own floor, and only 2.2 per cent of the people from other departments *two* floors apart from their own. In short, by the time departments are separated by two floors or more, there is virtually no informal contact between the departments.

Unfortunately, our own study of proximity was done before we knew about these findings by Estabrook and Sommer; so we have not yet been able to define the relation between the two kinds of distance. It is clear, though, that one stair must be equivalent to a rather considerable horizontal distance; and that two flights of stairs have almost three times the effect of a single stair. On the basis of this evidence, we conjecture that one stair is equal to about 100 horizontal feet in its effect on interaction

and feelings of distance; and that two flights of stairs are equal to about 300 horizontal feet.

Therefore:

To establish distances between departments, calculate the number of trips per day made between each two departments; get the "nuisance distance" from the graph above; then make sure that the physical distance between the two departments is less than the nuisance distance. Reckon one flight of stairs as about 100 feet, and two flights of stairs as about 300 feet.

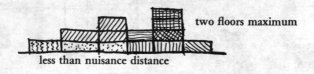

two floors maximum

less than nuisance distance

✧ ✧ ✧

Keep the buildings which house the departments in line with the FOUR-STORY LIMIT (21), and get their shape from BUILDING COMPLEX (95). Give every working group on upper storys its own stair to connect it directly to the public world—PEDESTRIAN STREET (100), OPEN STAIRS (158); if there are internal corridors between groups, make them large enough to function as streets—BUILDING THOROUGHFARE (101); and identify each workgroup clearly, and give it a well-marked entrance, so that people easily find their way from one to another—FAMILY OF ENTRANCES (102). . . .

8_3 MASTER AND APPRENTICES*

. . . the NETWORK OF LEARNING (18) in the community relies on the fact that learning is decentralized, and part and parcel of every activity—not just a classroom thing. In order to realize this pattern, it is essential that the individual workgroups, throughout industry, offices, workshops, and work communities, are all set up to make the learning process possible. This pattern, which shows the arrangement needed, therefore helps greatly to form SELF-GOVERNING WORKSHOPS AND OFFICES (80) as well as the NETWORK OF LEARNING (18).

The fundamental learning situation is one in which a person learns by helping someone who really knows what he is doing.

It is the simplest way of acquiring knowledge, and it is powerfully effective. By comparison, learning from lectures and books is dry as dust. But this situation has all but disappeared from modern society. The schools and universities have taken over and abstracted many ways of learning which in earlier times were always closely related to the real work of professionals, tradesmen, artisans, independent scholars. In the twelfth century, for instance, young people learned by working beside masters—helping them, making contact directly with every corner of society. When a young person found himself able to contribute to a field of knowledge, or a trade—he would prepare a master "piece"; and with the consent of the masters, become a fellow in the guild.

An experiment by Alexander and Goldberg has shown that a class in which one person teaches a small group of others is most likely to be successful in those cases where the "students" are actually helping the "teacher" to do something or solve some problem, which he is working on anyway—not when a subject of abstract or general interest is being taught. (Report to the Muscatine Committee, on experimental course ED. 10X, Department of Architecture, University of California, 1966.)

If this is generally true—in short, if students can learn best when they are acting as apprentices, and helping to do something

413

interesting—it follows that our schools and universities and offices and industries must provide physical settings which make this master-apprentice relation possible and natural: physical settings where communal work is centered on the master's efforts and where half a dozen apprentices—not more—have workspace closely connected to the communal work of the studio.

We know of an example of this pattern, in the Molecular Biology building of the University of Oregon. The floors of the building are made up of laboratories, each one under the direction of a professor of biology, each with two or three small rooms opening directly off the lab for graduate students working under the professor's direction.

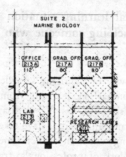

*Master-apprentice relationship
for a biology laboratory.*

We believe that variations of this pattern are possible in many different work organizations, as well as the schools. The practice of law, architecture, medicine, the building trades, social services, engineering—each discipline has the potential to set up its ways of learning, and therefore the environments in which its practitioners work, along these lines.

Therefore:

Arrange the work in every workgroup, industry, and office, in such a way that work and learning go forward hand in hand. Treat every piece of work as an opportunity for learning. To this end, organize work around a tradition of masters and apprentices: and support this form of

social organization with a division of the workspace into spatial clusters—one for each master and his apprentices—where they can work and meet together.

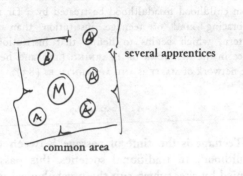

several apprentices

common area

❖ ❖ ❖

Arrange the workspaces as HALF-PRIVATE OFFICES (152) or WORKSPACE ENCLOSURES (183). Keep workgroups small, and give every group a common area, a common meeting space, and a place where they can eat together—COMMON AREAS AT THE HEART (129), COMMUNAL EATING (147), SMALL WORK GROUPS (148), SMALL MEETING ROOMS (151). . . .

84 TEEN-AGE SOCIETY

. . . the balanced LIFE CYCLE (26) requires that the transition from childhood to adulthood be treated by a far more subtle and embracing kind of teenage institution than a school; this pattern, which begins to define that institution, can take its place in the NETWORK OF LEARNING (18) and help contribute to the network of MASTERS AND APPRENTICES (83).

❖ ❖ ❖

Teenage is the time of passage between childhood and adulthood. In traditional societies, this passage is accompanied by rites which suit the psychological demands of the transition. But in modern society the "high school" fails entirely to provide this passage.

The most striking traditional example we know comes from an east African tribe. In order to become a man, a boy of this tribe embarks on a two year journey, which includes a series of more and more difficult tasks, and culminates in the hardest of all—to kill a lion. During his journey, families and villages all over the territory which he roams take him in, and care for him: they recognize their obligation to do so as part of his ritual. Finally, when the boy has passed through all these tasks, and killed his lion, he is accepted as a man.

In modern society, the transition cannot be so direct or simple. For reasons too complex to discuss here, the process of transition, and the time it takes have been extended and elaborated greatly. (See Edgar Friedenberg, *The Vanishing Adolescent*, Beacon Press, Boston, 1959 and *Coming of Age in America*, Random House Inc. N.Y., 1965). Teenage lasts, typically, from 12 to 18; six years instead of one or two. The simple sexual transformation, the change from childhood to maturity, has given way to a much vaster, slower change, in which the self of a person emerges

during a long struggle in which the person decides "what he or she is going to "be". Almost no one does what his father did before him; instead, in a world of infinite possibilities, it has to be worked out from nothing. This long process, new to the world since the industrial revolution is the process we call adolescence.

And this process of adolescence calls up an extraordinary hope. Since coming of age traditionally marks the birth of self, might not an extended coming of age bring with it a more profound and varied self-conception?

That is the hope; but so far it hasn't worked that way. Every culture that has an adolescent period has also a complicated adolescent problem. Throughout the technically developed world, puberty sets off a chain of forces that lead, in remarkably similar ways, to crisis and impasse. High rates of delinquency, school dropout, teenage suicide, drug addiction, and runaway are the dramatic forms this problem takes. And under these circumstances even "normal" adolescence is full of anxiety and, far from opening the doors to a more whole and complicated self, it tends to benumb us morally and intellectually.

The institution of the high school has particularly borne the brunt of the adolescent problem. Just at the time when teenagers need to band together freely in groups of their own making and explore, step back from, and explore again, the adult world: its work, love, science, laws, habits, travel, play, communications, and governance, they get treated as if they were large children. They have no more responsibility or authority in a high school than the children in a kindergarten do. They are responsible for putting away their things, and for playing in the school band, perhaps even for electing class leaders. But these things all happen in a kindergarten too. There is no new form of society, which is a microcosm of adult society, where they can test their growing adulthood in any serious way. And under these circumstances, the adult forces which are forming in them, lash out, and wreak terrible vengeance. Blind adults can easily, then, call this vengeance "delinquency."

This has finally been recognized by an official agency. In December 1973 the National Commission on the Reform of

Secondary Education, working with the Kittering Foundation, has come to the conclusion that the high schools in American cities are simply not working; that they are breaking down as institutions. They recommend that high school be non-compulsory after 14 years of age, and that teenagers be given many options for participation in society; that the size of high schools be reduced drastically, so that they are not so much a world apart from society; that each city provide opportunities for its young to work as apprentices in the local businesses and services,—and that such work be considered part of one's formal learning.

More specifically, we believe that the teenagers in a town, boys and girls from the ages of about 12 to 18, should be encouraged to form a miniature society, in which they are as differentiated, and as responsible mutually, as the adults in the full-scale adult society. It is necessary that they are responsible to one another, that they are able to play a useful role with respect to one another, that they have different degrees of power and authority according to their age and their maturity. It is necessary, in short, that their society is a microcosm of adult society, not an artificial society where people play at being adult, but the real thing, with real rewards, real tragedies, real work, real love, real friendship, real achievements, real responsibility. For this to happen it is necessary that each town have one or more actual teenage societies, partly enclosed, watched over, helped by adults, but run, essentially, by adults and the teenagers together.

Therefore:

Replace the "high school" with an institution which is actually a model of adult society, in which the students take on most of the responsibility for learning and social life, with clearly defined roles and forms of discipline. Provide adult guidance, both for the learning, and the social structure of the society; but keep them as far as feasible, in the hands of the students.

85 SHOPFRONT SCHOOLS

. . . the CHILDREN'S HOME (86) provides the beginning of learning and forms the foundation of the NETWORK OF LEARNING (18) in a community. As children grow older and more independent, these patterns must be supplemented by a mass of tiny institutions, schools and yet not schools, dotted among the living functions of the community.

❖ ❖ ❖

Around the age of 6 or 7, children develop a great need to learn by doing, to make their mark on a community outside the home. If the setting is right, these needs lead children directly to basic skills and habits of learning.

The right setting for a child is the community itself, just as the right setting for an infant learning to speak is his own home. For example:

On the first day of school we had lunch in one of the Los Angeles city parks. After lunch I gathered everyone, and I said, "Let's do some tree identification," and they all moaned. So I said, "Aw, come on, you live with these plants, you could at least know their names. What's the name of these trees we're sitting under?"
They all looked up, and in unison said "Sycamores." So I said, "What kind of sycamore?" and no one knew. I got out my *Trees of North America* book, and said, "Let's find out." There were only three kinds of sycamore in the book, only one on the West Coast, and it was called the California Sycamore. I thought it was all over, but I persisted, "We better make sure by checking these trees against the description in the book." So I started reading the text, "Leaves: six to eight inches." I fished a cloth measuring tape out of a box, handed it to Jeff, and said, "Go check out those leaves." He found that the leaves were indeed six to eight inches.
I went back to the book and read, " 'Height of mature trees, 30–50 feet.' How are we going to check that?" A big discussion followed, and we finally decided that I should stand up against one of the trees, they would back off as far as they could and estimate how many "Rusches" high the tree was. A little simple multiplication followed and we had an approximate tree height. Everyone was pretty involved by now, so I asked them "How else could you do it?" Eric was in the seventh grade and knew a little geometry, so he taught us how to measure the height by triangulation.

I was delighted just to have everyone's attention, so I went back to the book and kept reading. Near the bottom of the paragraph, came the clincher, "Diameter: one to three feet." So I handed over the measuring tape, and said, "Get me the diameter of that tree over there." They went over to the tree, and it wasn't until they were right on top of it that they realized that the only way to measure the diameter of a tree directly is to cut it down. But I insisted that we had to know the diameter of the tree, so two of them stretched out the tape next to the tree, and by eyeballing along one "edge" and then the other, they came up with eighteen inches.

I said, "Is that an accurate answer or just approximate?" They agreed it was only a guess, so I said, "How else could you do it?"

Right off, Daniel said, "Well you could measure all the way around it, lay that circle out in the dirt, and then measure across it." I was really impressed, and said, "Go to it." Meanwhile, I turned to the rest of the group, and said, "How else could you do it?"

Eric, who turned out to be a visualizer and was perhaps visualizing the tree as having two sides, said, "Well, you could measure all the way around it, and divide by two." Since I believe you learn at least as much from mistakes as from successes, I said, "Okay, try it." Meanwhile, Daniel was measuring across the circle on the ground, and by picking the right points on a somewhat lopsided circle came up with the same answer, "Eighteen inches." So I gave the tape to Eric, he measured around the tree, got sixty inches, divided by two, and got thirty for the diameter. He was naturally a little disappointed, so I said, "Well, I like your idea, maybe you just have the wrong number. Is there a better number to divide with than two?"

Right off, Michael said, "Well you could divide by three," and then thinking ahead quickly added, "and subtract two."

I said, "Great! Now you have a formula, check it out on that tree over there," pointing to one only about six inches in diameter. They went over, measured the circumference, divided by three, subtracted two, and checked it against a circle on the ground. The result was disappointing, so I told them try some more trees. They checked about three more trees and came back. "How did it work?"

"Well," Mark said, "Dividing by three works pretty well, but subtracting two isn't so good."

"How good is dividing by three?" I asked, and Michael replied, "It's not quite big enough."

"How big should it be?"

"About three and a half," said Daniel.

"No," said Michael, "It's more like three and an eighth."

At that point, these five kids, ranging in age from 9 to 12 were within two one hundredths of discovering π and I was having trouble containing myself. I suppose I could have extended the lesson by having them convert one-eighth to decimals, but I was too excited.

---

teenage society

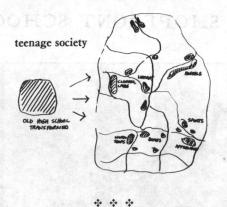

❖ ❖ ❖

Provide one central place which houses social functions, and a directory of classes in the community. Within the central place, provide communal eating for the students, opportunities for sports and games, a library and counseling for the network of learning which gives the students access to the classes, work communities, and home workshops that are scattered through the town—NETWORK OF LEARNING (18), LOCAL SPORTS (72), COMMUNAL EATING (147), HOME WORKSHOPS (157); for the shape of what buildings there are, begin with BUILDING COMPLEX (95). . . .

"Look," I said, "I want to tell you a secret. There's a magic number which is so special it has it own name. It's called π. And the magic is that once you know how big it is, you can take any circle, no matter how big or how small, and go from circumference to diameter, or diameter to circumference. Now here is how it works. . ."

After my explanation, we went around the park, estimating the circumferences of trees by guessing their diameter, or figuring the diameter by measuring the circumference and dividing by π. Later when I had taught them how to use a slide rule, I pointed out π to them and gave them a whole series of "tree" problems. Later still, I reviewed the whole thing with telephone poles and lighting standards, just to make sure that the concept of π didn't disappear into the obscurity of abstract mathematics. I know that I didn't really understand π until I got to college, despite an excellent math program in high school. But for those five kids at least, π is something real; it "lives" in trees and telephone poles. (Charles W. Rusch, "Moboc: The Mobile Open Classroom," School of Architecture and Urban Planning, University of California, Los Angeles, November 1973.)

A few children in a bus, visiting a city park with a teacher. That works because there are only a *few* children and one teacher. Any public school can provide the teacher and the bus. But they cannot provide the low student-teacher ratio, because the sheer size of the school eats up all the money in administrative costs and overheads—which end up making higher student ratios economically essential. So even though everyone knows that the secret of good teaching lies in low student-teacher ratios, the schools make this one central thing impossible to get, because they waste their money being large.

But as our example suggests, we can cut back on the overhead costs of large concentrated schools and lower the student-teacher ratio; simply by making our schools smaller. This approach to schooling—the mini-school or shopfront school—has been tried in a number of communities across the United States. See, for instance, Paul Goodman, "Mini-schools: a prescription for the reading problem," *New York Review of Books*, January 1968. To date, we know of no systematic empirical account of this experiment. But a good deal has been written about these schools. Perhaps the most interesting account is George Dennison's *The Lives of Children* (New York: Vintage Book, 1969):

I would like to make clear that in constrasting our own procedures with those of the public schools, I am not trying to criticize the teachers who find themselves embattled in the institutional setting and overburdened to the point of madness. . . . My point is precisely that the intimacy and small scale of our school should be imitated widely, since these things alone make possible the human contact capable of curing the diseases we have been naming with such frequency for the last ten years.

Now that "mini-schools" are being discussed (they have been proposed most cogently by Paul Goodman and Dr. Elliott Shapiro), it's worth saying that that's exactly what we were: the first of the mini-schools. . . .

By eliminating the expenses of the centralized school, Dennison found he was able to reduce the student-teacher ratio by a factor of three!

For the twenty-three children there were three full-time teachers, one part-time (myself), and several others who came at scheduled periods for singing, dancing, and music.

Public school teachers, with their 30 to 1 ratios, will be aware that we have entered the realm of sheer luxury. One of the things that will bear repeating, however, is that this luxury was purchased at a cost per child a good bit lower than that of the public system, for the similarity of operating costs does not reflect the huge capital investment of the public schools or the great difference in the quality of service. Not that our families paid tuition (hardly anyone did); I mean simply that our money was not drained away by vast administrative costs, bookkeeping, elaborate buildings, maintenance, enforcement personnel, and vandalism.

Charles Rusch, director of Moboc, Mobil Open Classroom, has made the same discovery:

. . . by eliminating the building and the salaries of all those persons who do not directly work with the children, the student/teacher ratio can be reduced from something like 35/1 to 10/1. In this one stroke many of the most pressing public school problems can be eliminated at no extra cost to the school or school district. Rusch, "Moboc: The Mobile Open Classroom," p. 7.

Therefore:

Instead of building large public schools for children 7 to 12, set up tiny independent schools, one school at a time. Keep the school small, so that its overheads are low and

a teacher-student ratio of 1:10 can be maintained. Locate it in the public part of the community, with a shopfront and three or four rooms.

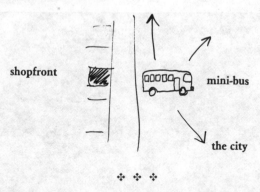

❖ ❖ ❖

Place the school on a pedestrian street—PEDESTRIAN STREET (100); near other functioning workshops—SELF-GOVERNING WORKSHOPS AND OFFICES (80) and within walking distance of a park—ACCESSIBLE GREEN (60). Make it an identifiable part of the building it is part of—BUILDING COMPLEX (95); and give it a good strong opening at the front, so that it is connected with the street—OPENING TO THE STREET (165). . . .

86 CHILDREN'S HOME*

. . . within each neighborhood there are hundreds of children. The children, especially the young ones, are helped in their relation to the world by the patterns CHILDREN IN THE CITY (57) and CONNECTED PLAY (68). However, these very general provisions in the form of public land need to be supported by some kind of communal place, where they can stay without their parents for a few hours, or a few days, according to necessity. This pattern is a part of the NETWORK OF LEARNING (18) for the youngest children.

❖ ❖ ❖

The task of looking after little children is a much deeper and more fundamental social issue than the phrases "baby-sitting" and "child care" suggest.

It is true, of course, that in a society where most children are in the care of single adults or couples, the mothers and fathers must be able to have their children looked after while they work or when they want to meet their friends. This is what child care and baby-sitting are for. It is, if you like, the adult's view of the situation.

But the fact is that the children themselves have unsatisfied needs which are equally pressing. They need access to other adults beyond their parents, and access to other children; and the situations in which they meet these other adults and other children need to be highly complex, subtle, full of the same complexities and intensities as family life—not merely "schools" and "kindergarten" and "playgrounds."

When we look at the children's needs, *and* at the needs of the adults, we realize that what is needed is a new institution in the neighborhood: *a children's home*—a place where children can be safe and well looked after, night and day, with the full range of opportunities and social activities that can introduce them, fully, to society.

To a certain extent, these needs were absorbed in the large, extended families of the past. In such a family, the variety of

adults and children of other ages had a positive value for the children. It brought them into contact with more human situations, allowed them to work out their needs with a variety of people, not just two.

However, as this kind of family has gradually disappeared, we have continued to hold fast to the idea that child-raising is the job of the family alone, especially the mother. But it is no longer viable. Here is Philip Slater discussing the difficulties that beset a small nuclear family focussing its attention on one or two children:

The new parents may not be as absorbed in material possessions and occupational self-aggrandizement as their own parents were. They may channel their parental vanity into different spheres, pushing their children to be brilliant artists, thinkers, and performers. But the hard narcissistic core on which the old culture was based will not be dissolved until the parent-child relationship itself is deintensified. . . .

Breaking the pattern means establishing communities in which (a) children are not socialized exclusively by their parents, (b) parents have lives of their own and do not live vicariously through their children (*The Pursuit of Loneliness*, Boston: Beacon Press, 1971, pp. 141–42).

The children's home we propose is a place which "de-intensifies the parent-child relationship" by bringing the child into authentic social relationships with several other adults and many other children.

1. Physically, it is a very large, rambling home, with a good-sized yard.

2. The house is within walking distance of the children's own homes. Terence Lee was found that young children who walk or bike to school learn more than those who go by bus or car. The mechanism is simple and startling. The children who walk or bike, remain in contact with the ground, and are therefore able to create a cognitive map which includes both home and school. The children who are taken by car, are whisked, as if by magic carpet, from one place to the other, and cannot maintain any cognitive map which includes both home and school. To all intents and purposes they feel lost when they are at school; they are perhaps even afraid that they have lost their mothers. (T. R. Lee, "On the relation between the school journey and social and emo-

tional adjustment in rural infant children," *British Journal of Educational Psychology*, 27:101, 1957.)

3. There is a core staff of two or three adults who manage the home; and at least one of them, preferably more, actually lives there. In effect, it is the real home of some people; it does not close down at night.

4. Parents and their children join a particular home. And then the children may come and stay there at any time, for an hour, an afternoon, sometimes for long overnight stays.

5. Payment might be made by the hour to begin with. If we assume $1 per hour as a base fee, and assume that a child might spend 20 hours a week there, the house needs about 30 member children to generate a monthly income of about $2500.

6. The home focuses on raising children in a big extended family setting. For example, the home might be the center of a local coffee klatch, where a few people meet every day and mix with the children.

7. In line with this atmosphere, the home itself should be relatively open, with a public path passing across the site. Silverstein has indicated that the child's sense of his first school being "separate" from society can be reduced if the play areas of the children's home are open to all passing adults and to all passing children. (Murray Silverstein, "The Child's Urban Environment," Proceedings of the Seventy-First National Convention of the Congress of Parents and Teachers, Chicago, Illinois, 1967, pp. 39–45.)

8. To keep the young children safe, and to make it possible to give them this great freedom without losing track of them altogether, the play areas may be sunk slightly, and surrounded by a low wall. If the wall is at seat height, it will encourage people to sit on it—giving them a place from which to watch the children playing, and the children a chance to talk to passers-by.

The children's home pattern has been tried, successfully, in a far more extreme form than we imagine here, in many kibbutzim where children are raised in collective nurseries, and merely visit their parents for a few hours per week. The fact that this very extreme version has been successful should remove any doubts about the workability of the much milder version which we are proposing.

Therefore:

In every neighborhood, build a children's home—a second home for children—a large rambling house or workplace—a place where children can stay for an hour or two, or for a week. At least one of the people who run it must live on the premises; it must be open 24 hours a day; open to children of all ages; and it must be clear, from the way that it is run, that it is a second family for the children —not just a place where baby-sitting is available.

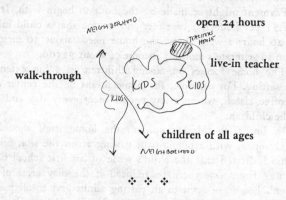

❖ ❖ ❖

Treat the building as a collection of small connected buildings —BUILDING COMPLEX (95); lay an important neighborhood path right through the building, so that children who are not a part of the school can see and get to know it by meeting the children who are—BUILDING THOROUGHFARE (101); attach it to the local ADVENTURE PLAYGROUND (73); make the teachers' house an integral part of the interior—YOUR OWN HOME (79); and treat the common space itself as the hearth of a larger family—THE FAMILY (75), COMMON AREAS AT THE HEART (129). . . .

the local shops and gathering places:

87 INDIVIDUALLY OWNED SHOPS**

. . . the STREET CAFE (88) and CORNER GROCERY (89) and all the individual shops and stalls in SHOPPING STREETS (32) and MARKETS OF MANY SHOPS (46) must be supported by an ordinance which guarantees that they will stay in local private hands, and not be owned by absentee landlords, or chain stores, or giant franchise operations.

When shops are too large, or controlled by absentee owners, they become plastic, bland, and abstract.

The profit motive creates a tendency for shops to become larger. But the larger they become, the less personal their service is, and the harder it is for other small shops to survive. Soon, the shops in the economy are almost entirely controlled by chain stores and franchises.

The franchises are doubly vicious. They create the image of individual ownership; they give a man who doesn't have enough capital to start his own store the chance to run a store that seems like his; and they spread like wildfire. But they create even more plastic, bland, and abstract services. The individual managers have almost no control over the goods they sell, the food they serve; policies are tightly controlled; the personal quality of individually owned shops is altogether broken down.

Shop run for money alone.   *Shop run as a way of life.*

Communities can only get this personal quality back if they prohibit all forms of franchise and chain stores, place limits on

433

the actual size of stores in a community, and prohibit absentee owners from owning shops. In short, they must do what they can to keep the wealth generated by the local community in the hands of that community.

Even then, it will not be possible to maintain this pattern unless the size of the shop spaces available for rent is small. One of the biggest reasons for the rise of large, nationally owned franchises is that the financial risks of starting a business are so enormous for the average individual. The failure of a single owner's business can be catastrophic for him personally; and it happens, in large part because he can't afford the rent. Many hundreds of tiny shops, with low rents, will keep the initial risk for a shop keeper who is starting, to a minimum.

Shops in Morocco, India, Peru, and the oldest parts of older towns, are often no more than 50 square feet in area. Just room for a person and some merchandise—but plenty big enough.

Fifty square feet.

Therefore:

Do what you can to encourage the development of individually owned shops. Approve applications for business licenses only if the business is owned by those people who actually work and manage the store. Approve new commercial building permits only if the proposed structure includes many very very small rental spaces.

owner occupied

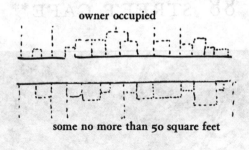

some no more than 50 square feet

❖ ❖ ❖

Treat each individual shop as an identifiable unit of a larger BUILDING COMPLEX (95); make at least some part of the shop part of the sidewalk, so that people walk through the shop as they are going down the street—OPENING TO THE STREET (165); and build the inside of the shop with all the goods as open and available as possible—THE SHAPE OF INDOOR SPACE (191), THICK WALLS (197), OPEN SHELVES (200). . . .

88 STREET CAFE**

. . . neighborhoods are defined by IDENTIFIABLE NEIGHBOR-HOOD (14); their natural points of focus are given by ACTIVITY NODES (30) and SMALL PUBLIC SQUARES (61). This pattern, and the ones which follow it, give the neighborhood and its points of focus, their identity.

❖ ❖ ❖

The street cafe provides a unique setting, special to cities: a place where people can sit lazily, legitimately, be on view, and watch the world go by.

The most humane cities are always full of street cafes. Let us try to understand the experience which makes these places so attractive.

We know that people enjoy mixing in public, in parks, squares, along promenades and avenues, in street cafes. The preconditions seem to be: the setting gives you the right to be there, by custom; there are a few things to do that are part of the scene, almost ritual: reading the newspaper, strolling, nursing a beer, playing catch; and people feel safe enough to relax, nod at each other, perhaps even meet. A good cafe terrace meets these conditions. But it has in addition, special qualities of its own: a person may sit there for hours—in public! Strolling, a person must keep up a pace; loitering is only for a few minutes. You can sit still in a park, but there is not the volume of people passing, it is more a private, peaceful experience. And sitting at home on one's porch is again different: it is far more protected; and there is not the mix of people passing by. But on the cafe terrace, you can sit still, relax, and be very public. As an experience it has special possibilities; "perhaps the next person . . ."; it is a risky place.

It is this experience that the street cafe supports. And it is one of the attractions of cities, for only in cities do we have the concentration of people required to bring it off. But this experience need not be confined to the special, extraordinary parts of town. In European cities and towns, there is a street cafe in every neighborhood—they are as ordinary as gas stations are in the United

States. And the existence of such places provides social glue for the community. They become like clubs—people tend to return to their favorite, the faces become familiar. When there is a successful cafe within walking distance of your home, in the neighborhood, so much the better. It helps enormously to increase the identity of a neighborhood. It is one of the few settings where a newcomer to the neighborhood can start learning the ropes and meeting the people who have been there many years.

The ingredients of a successful street cafe seem to be:

1. There is an established local clientele. That is, by name, location, and staff, the cafe is very much anchored in the neighborhood in which it is situated.

2. In addition to the terrace which is open to the street, the cafe contains several other spaces: with games, fire, soft chairs, newspapers. . . . This allows a variety of people to start using it, according to slightly different social styles.

3. The cafe serves simple food and drinks—some alcoholic drinks, but it is not a bar. It is a place where you are as likely to go in the morning, to start the day, as in the evening, for a nightcap.

When these conditions are present, and the cafe takes hold, it offers something unique to the lives of the people who use it: it offers a setting for discussions of great spirit—talks, two-bit lectures, half-public, half-private, learning, exchange of thought.

When we worked for the University of Oregon, we compared the importance of such discussion in cafes and cafe-like places, with the instruction students receive in the classroom. We interviewed 30 students to measure the extent that shops and cafes contributed to their intellectual and emotional growth at the University. We found that "talking with a small group of students in a coffee shop" and "discussion over a glass of beer" scored as high and higher than "examinations" and "laboratory study." Apparently the informal activities of shops and cafes contribute as much to the growth of students, as the more formal educational activities.

We believe this phenomenon is general. The quality that we tried to capture in these interviews, and which is present in a neighborhood cafe, is essential to all neighborhoods—not only student neighborhoods. It is part of their life-blood.

Therefore:

Encourage local cafes to spring up in each neighborhood. Make them intimate places, with several rooms, open to a busy path, where people can sit with coffee or a drink and watch the world go by. Build the front of the cafe so that a set of tables stretch out of the cafe, right into the street.

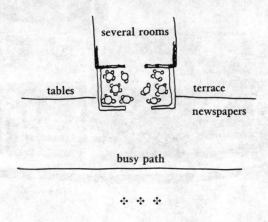

⁂

Build a wide, substantial opening between the terrace and the indoors—OPENING TO THE STREET (165); make the terrace double as A PLACE TO WAIT (150) for nearby bus stops and offices; both indoors and on the terrace use a great variety of different kinds of chairs and tables—DIFFERENT CHAIRS (251); and give the terrace some low definition at the street edge if it is in danger of being interrupted by street action—STAIR SEATS (125), SITTING WALL (243), perhaps a CANVAS ROOF (244). For the shape of the building, the terrace, and the surroundings, begin with BUILDING COMPLEX (95). . . .

89 CORNER GROCERY*

. . . the major shopping needs, in any community, are taken care of by the MARKET OF MANY SHOPS (46). However, the WEB OF SHOPPING (19) is not complete, unless there are also much smaller shops, more widely scattered, helping to supplement the markets, and helping to create the natural identity of IDENTIFIABLE NEIGHBORHOODS (14).

❖ ❖ ❖

It has lately been assumed that people no longer want to walk to local stores. This assumption is mistaken.

Indeed, we believe that people are not only *willing* to walk to their local corner groceries, but that the corner grocery plays an essential role in any healthy neighborhood: partly because it is just more convenient for individuals; partly because it helps to integrate the neighborhood as a whole.

Strong support for this notion comes from a study by Arthur D. Little, Inc., which found that neighborhood stores are one of the two most important elements in people's perception of an area *as a neighborhood* (*Community Renewal Program*, New York: Praeger Press, 1966). Apparently this is because local stores are an important destination for neighborhood walks. People go to them when they feel like a walk as well as when they need a carton of milk. In this way, as a generator of walks, they draw a residential area together and help to give it the quality of a neighborhood. Similar evidence comes from a report by the management of one of San Francisco's housing projects for the elderly. One of the main reasons why people resisted moving into some of the city's new housing projects, according to the rental manager, was that the projects were not located in "downtown locations, where . . . there is a store on every street corner." (*San Francisco Chronicle*, August 1971.)

To find out how far people will walk to a store we interviewed 20 people at a neighborhood store in Berkeley. We found that 80 per cent of the people interviewed walked, and that those who walked all came three blocks or less. Over half of

them had been to the store previously within two days. On the other hand, those who came by car usually came from more than four blocks away. We found the pattern to be similar at other public facilities in the neighborhoods that we surveyed. At distances around four blocks, or greater, people who rode outnumbered those who walked. It seems then, that corner groceries need to be within walking distance, three to four blocks or 1200 feet, of every home.

But can they survive? Are these stores doomed by the economics of scale? How many people does it take to support one corner grocery? We may estimate the critical population for grocery stores by consulting the yellow pages. For example, San Francisco, a city of 750,000, has 638 neighborhood grocery stores. This means that there is one grocery for every 1160 people, which corresponds to Berry's estimate—see WEB OF SHOPPING (19)—and corresponds also to the size of neighborhoods—see IDENTIFIABLE NEIGHBORHOOD (14).

It seems, then, that a corner grocery can survive under circumstances where there are 1000 people within three or four blocks—a net density of at least 20 persons per net acre, or six houses per net acre. Most neighborhoods do have this kind of density. One might even take this figure as a lower limit for a viable neighborhood, on the grounds that a neighborhood *ought* to be able to support a corner grocery, for the sake of its own social cohesion.

Finally, the success of a neighborhood store will depend on its location. It has been shown that the rents which owners of small retail businesses are willing to pay vary directly with the amount of pedestrian traffic passing by, and are therefore uniformly higher on street corners than in the middle of the block. (Brian J. L. Berry, *Geography of Market Centers and Retail Distribution*, Prentice Hall, 1967, p. 49.)

Therefore:

Give every neighborhood at least one corner grocery, somewhere near its heart. Place these corner groceries every 200 to 800 yards, according to the density, so that each one serves about 1000 people. Place them on corners, where

large numbers of people are going past. And combine them with houses, so that the people who run them can live over them or next to them.

small grocery

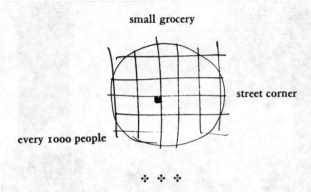

street corner

every 1000 people

❖ ❖ ❖

Prevent franchises and pass laws which prevent the emergence of those much larger groceries which swallow up the corner groceries—INDIVIDUALLY OWNED SHOPS (87). Treat the inside of the shop as a room, lined with goods—THE SHAPE OF INDOOR SPACE (191), THICK WALLS (197), OPEN SHELVES (200); give it a clear and wide entrance so that everyone can see it—MAIN ENTRANCE (110), OPENING TO THE STREET (165). And for the shape of the grocery, as a small building or as part of a larger building, begin with BUILDING COMPLEX (95). . . .

90 BEER HALL

. . . in an occasional neighborhood, which functions as the focus of a group of neighborhoods, or in a boundary between neighborhoods—NEIGHBORHOOD BOUNDARY (15)—or on the promenade which forms the focus of a large community—PROMENADE (31), NIGHT LIFE (33)—there is a special need for something larger and more raucous than a street cafe.

❖ ❖ ❖

Where can people sing, and drink, and shout and drink, and let go of their sorrows?

A public drinking house, where strangers and friends are drinking companions, is a natural part of any large community. But all too often, bars degenerate and become nothing more than anchors for the lonely. Robert Sommer has described this in "Design for Drinking," Chapter 8 of his book *Personal Space*, Englewood Cliffs, N.J.: Prentice-Hall, 1969.

. . . it is not difficult in any American city to find examples of the bar where meaningful contact is at a minimum. V. S. Pritchett describes the lonely men in New York City sitting speechlessly on a row of barstools, with their arms triangled on the bar before a bottle of beer, their drinking money before them. If anyone speaks to his neighbor under these circumstances, he is likely to receive a suspicious stare for his efforts. The barman is interested in the patrons as customers—he is there to sell, they are there to buy. . . .
   Another visiting Englishman makes the same point when he describes the American bar as a "hoked up saloon; the atmosphere is as chilly as the beer . . . when I asked a stranger to have a drink, he looked at me as if I were mad. In England if a guy's a guy, . . . each guy buys the other a drink. You enjoy each other's company, and everyone is happy. . . ." (Tony Kirby, "Who's Crazy?" *The Village Voice*, January 26, 1967, p. 39.)

Let us consider drinking more in the style of these English pubs. Drink helps people to relax and become open with one another, to sing and dance. But it only brings out these qualities when the setting is right. We think that there are two critical qualities for the setting:
   1. The place holds a crowd that is continuously mixing be-

tween functions—the bar, the dance floor, a fire, darts, the
bathrooms, the entrance, the seats; and these activities are concentrated and located round the edge so that they generate con-
tinual criss-crossing.

2. The seats should be largely in the form of tables for four
to eight set in open alcoves—that is, tables that are defined for
small groups, with walls, columns, and curtains—but open at
both ends.

The open alcove—supports the fluidity of the scene.

This form helps sustain the life of the group and lets people come
in and out freely. Also, when the tables are large, they invite
people to sit down with a stranger or another group.

Therefore:

**Somewhere in the community at least one big place
where a few hundred people can gather, with beer and
wine, music, and perhaps a half-dozen activities, so that
people are continuously criss-crossing from one to another.**

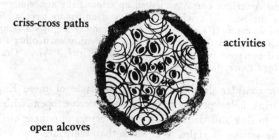

criss-cross paths

activities

open alcoves

446

❖ ❖ ❖

Put the tables in two-ended alcoves, roomy enough for people to pass through on their way between activities—ALCOVES (179); provide a fire, as the hub of one activity—THE FIRE (181); and a variety of ceiling heights to correspond to different social groupings—CEILING HEIGHT VARIETY (190). For the shape of the building, gardens, parking, and surroundings, begin with BUILDING COMPLEX (95). . . .

91 TRAVELER'S INN*

. . . any town or city has visitors and travelers passing through, and these visitors will naturally tend to congregate around the centers of activity—MAGIC OF THE CITY (10), ACTIVITY NODES (30), PROMENADE (31), NIGHT LIFE (33), WORK COMMUNITY (41). This pattern shows how the hotels which cater to these visitors can most effectively help to sustain the life of these centers.

❖ ❖ ❖

A man who stays the night in a strange place is still a member of the human community, and still needs company. There is no reason why he should creep into a hole, and watch TV alone, the way he does in a roadside motel.

At all times, except our own, the inn was a wonderful place, where strangers met for a night, to eat, and drink, play cards, tell stories, and experience extraordinary adventures. But in a modern motel every ounce of this adventure has been lost. The motel owner assumes that strangers are afraid of one another, so he caters to their fear by making each room utterly self-contained and self-sufficient.

But behind the fear, there is a deep need: the need for company—for stories, and adventures, and encounters. It is the business of an inn to create an atmosphere where people can experience and satisfy this need. The most extreme version is the Indian pilgrim's inn, or the Persian caravanserai. There people eat, and meet, and sleep, and talk, and smoke, and drink in one great space, protected from danger by their mutual company, and given entertainment by one another's escapades and stories.

The inspiration for this pattern came from Gita Shah's description of the Indian pilgrim's inn, in *The Timeless Way of Building:*

In India, there are many of these inns. There is a courtyard where the people meet, and a place to one side of the courtyard where they eat, and also on this side there is the person who looks after the Inn, and on the other three sides of the courtyard there are the rooms—in front of the rooms is an arcade, maybe one step up from

449

the courtyard, and about ten feet deep, with another step leading into the rooms. During the evening everyone meets in the courtyard, and they talk and eat together—it is very special—and then at night they all sleep in the arcade, so they are all sleeping together, round the courtyard.

And of course, the size is crucial. The atmosphere comes mainly from the fact that the people who run the place themselves live there and treat the entire inn as their household. A family can't handle more than 30 rooms.

Therefore:

Make the traveler's inn a place where travelers can take rooms for the night, but where—unlike most hotels and motels—the inn draws all its energy from the community of travelers that are there any given evening. The scale is small—30 or 40 guests to an inn; meals are offered communally; there is even a large space ringed round with beds in alcoves.

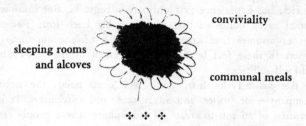

conviviality

sleeping rooms
and alcoves

communal meals

❖ ❖ ❖

The heart of the conviviality is the central area, where everyone can meet and talk and dance and drink—COMMON AREAS AT THE HEART (129), DANCING IN THE STREET (65), and BEER HALL (90). Provide the opportunity for communal eating, not a restaurant, but common food around a common table—COMMUNAL EATING (147); and, over and above the individual rooms there are at least some areas where people can lie down and sleep in public unafraid—SLEEPING IN PUBLIC (94), COMMUNAL SLEEPING (186). For the overall shape of the inn, its gardens, parking, and surroundings, begin with BUILDING COMPLEX (95). . . .

92 BUS STOP*

. . . within a town whose public transportation is based on MINI-BUSES (20), genuinely able to serve people, almost door to door, for a low price, and very fast, there need to be bus stops within a few hundred feet of every house and workplace. This pattern gives the form of the bus stops.

❖ ❖ ❖

Bus stops must be easy to recognize, and pleasant, with enough activity around them to make people comfortable and safe.

Bus stops are often dreary because they are set down independently, with very little thought given to the experience of waiting there, to the relationship between the bus stop and its surroundings. They are places to stand idly, perhaps anxiously, waiting for the bus, always watching for the bus. It is a shabby experience; nothing that would encourage people to use public transportation.

The secret lies in the web of relationships that are present in the tiny system around the bus stop. If they knit together, and reinforce each other, adding choice and shape to the experience, the system is a good one: but the relationships that make up such a system are extremely subtle. For example, a system as simple as a traffic light, a curb, and street corner can be enhanced by viewing it as a distinct node of public life: people wait for the light to change, their eyes wander, perhaps they are not in such a hurry. Place a newsstand and a flower wagon at the corner and the experience becomes more coherent.

The curb and the light, the paperstand and the flowers, the awning over the shop on the corner, the change in people's pockets—all this forms a web of mutually sustaining relationships.

The possibilities for each bus stop to become part of such a web are different—in some cases it will be right to make a system that will draw people into a private reverie—an old tree; another time one that will do the opposite—give shape to the social possibilities—a coffee stand, a canvas roof, a decent place to sit for people who are not waiting for the bus.

Two bus stops.

Therefore:

Build bus stops so that they form tiny centers of public life. Build them as part of the gateways into neighborhoods, work communities, parts of town. Locate them so that they work together with several other activities, at least a newsstand, maps, outdoor shelter, seats, and in various combinations, corner groceries, smoke shops, coffee bar, tree places, special road crossings, public bathrooms, squares. . . .

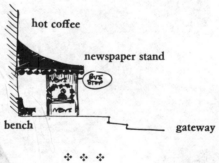

❖ ❖ ❖

Make a full gateway to the neighborhood next to the bus stop, or place the bus stop where the best gateway is already—MAIN GATEWAY (53); treat the physical arrangement according to the patterns for PUBLIC OUTDOOR ROOM (69), PATH SHAPE (121), and A PLACE TO WAIT (150); provide a FOOD STAND (93): place the seats according to sun, wind protection, and view—SEAT SPOTS (241). . . .

93 FOOD STANDS*

. . . throughout the neighborhood there are natural public gathering places—ACTIVITY NODES (30), ROAD CROSSINGS (54), RAISED WALKS (55), SMALL PUBLIC SQUARES (61), BUS STOPS (92). All draw their life, to some extent, from the food stands, the hawkers, and the vendors who fill the street with the smell of food.

❖ ❖ ❖

Many of our habits and institutions are bolstered by the fact that we can get simple, inexpensive food on the street, on the way to shopping, work, and friends.

The food stands which make the best food, and which contribute most to city life, are the smallest shacks and carts from which individual vendors sell their wares. Everyone has memories of them.

But in their place we now have shining hamburger kitchens, fried chicken shops, and pancake houses. They are chain operations, with no roots in the local community. They sell "plastic," mass-produced frozen food, and they generate a shabby quality of life around them. They are built to attract the eye of a person driving: the signs are huge; the light is bright neon. They are insensitive to the fabric of the community. Their parking lots around them kill the public open space.

If we want food in our streets contributing to the social life of the streets, not helping to destroy it, the food stands must be made and placed accordingly.

We propose four rules:

1. The food stands are concentrated at ROAD CROSSINGS (54) of the NETWORK OF PATHS AND CARS (52). It is possible to see them from cars and to expect them at certain kinds of intersections, but they do not have special parking lots around them—see NINE PER CENT PARKING (22).

2. The food stands are free to take on a character that is compatible with the neighborhood around them. They can be

455

freestanding carts, or built into the corners and crevices of existing buildings; they can be small huts, part of the fabric of the street.

3. The smell of the food is out in the street; the place can be surrounded with covered seats, sitting walls, places to lean and sip coffee, part of the larger scene, not sealed away in a plate glass structure, surrounded by cars. The more they smell, the better.

4. They are never franchises, but always operated by their owners. The best food always comes from family restaurants; and the best food in a foodstand always comes when people prepare the food and sell it themselves, according to their own ideas, their own recipes, their own choice.

Therefore:

Concentrate food stands where cars and paths meet— either portable stands or small huts, or built into the fronts of buildings, half-open to the street.

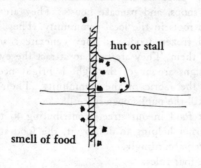

hut or stall

smell of food

❖ ❖ ❖

Treat these food stands as ACTIVITY POCKETS (124) when they are part of a square; Use canvas roofs to make a simple shelter over them—CANVAS ROOF (244); and keep them in line with the precepts of INDIVIDUALLY OWNED SHOPS (87): the best food always comes from people who are in business for themselves, who buy the raw food, and prepare it in their own style. . . .

94 SLEEPING IN PUBLIC

. . . this pattern helps to make places like the INTERCHANGE
(34), SMALL PUBLIC SQUARES (61), PUBLIC OUTDOOR ROOMS
(69), STREET CAFE (88), PEDESTRIAN STREET (100), BUILDING
THOROUGHFARE (101), A PLACE TO WAIT (150) completely
public.

It is a mark of success in a park, public lobby or a porch, when people can come there and fall asleep.

In a society which nurtures people and fosters trust, the fact
that people sometimes want to sleep in public is the most natural
thing in the world. If someone lies down on a pavement or a
bench and falls asleep, it is possible to treat it seriously as a need.
If he has no place to go—then, we, the people of the town, can
be happy that he can at least sleep on the public paths and
benches; and, of course, it may also be someone who does have
a place to go, but happens to like napping in the street.

But our society does not invite this kind of behavior. In our
society, sleeping in public, like loitering, is thought of as an
act for criminals and destitutes. In our world, when homeless
people start sleeping on public benches or in public buildings,
upright citizens get nervous, and the police soon restore "public
order."

Thus we cleared these difficult straits, my bicycle and I, together.
But a little further on I heard myself hailed. I raised my head and
saw a policeman. Elliptically speaking, for it was only later, by way
of induction, or deduction, I forget which, that I knew what it was.
What are you doing there? he said. I'm used to that question, I
understood it immediately. Resting, I said. Resting, he said. Resting, I
said. Will you answer my question? he cried. So it always is when
I'm reduced to confabulation. I honestly believe I have answered the
question I am asked and in reality I do nothing of the kind. I won't
reconstruct the conversation in all its meanderings. It ended in my understanding that my way of resting, my attitude when at rest, astride
my bicycle, my arms on the handlebars, my head on my arms, was a
violation of I don't know what, public order, public decency. . . .

What is certain is this, that I never rested in that way again, my

feet obscenely resting on the earth, my arms on the handlebars and on my arms my head, rocking and abandoned. It is indeed a deplorable sight, a deplorable example, for the people, who so need to be encouraged, in their bitter toil, and to have before their eyes manifestations of strength only, of courage and joy, without which they might collapse, at the end of the day, and roll on the ground. (Samuel Beckett, *Molloy*.)

It seems, at first, as though this is purely a social problem and that it can only be changed by changing people's attitudes. But the fact is, that these attitudes are largely shaped by the environment itself. In an environment where there are very few places to lie down and sleep people who sleep in public seem unnatural, because it is so rare.

Therefore:

Keep the environment filled with ample benches, comfortable places, corners to sit on the ground, or lie in comfort in the sand. Make these places relatively sheltered, protected from circulation, perhaps up a step, with seats and grass to slump down upon, read the paper and doze off.

soft benches   shelter   away from traffic

❖ ❖ ❖

Above all, put the places for sleeping along BUILDING EDGES (160); make seats there, and perhaps even a bed alcove or two in public might be a nice touch—BED ALCOVE (188), SEAT SPOTS (241); but above all, it will hinge on the attitudes which people have—do anything you can to create trust, so that people feel no fear in going to sleep in public and so that other people feel no fear of people sleeping in the street.

BUILDINGS

This completes the global patterns which define a town or a community. We now start that part of the language which gives shape to groups of buildings, and individual buildings, on the land, in three dimensions. These are the patterns which can be "designed" or "built"—the patterns which define the individual buildings and the space between buildings, where we are dealing for the first time with patterns that are under the control of individuals or small groups of individuals, who are able to build the patterns all at once.

We assume that, based on the instructions in "Summary of the Language," you have already constructed a sequence of patterns. We shall now go through a step-by-step procedure for building this sequence into a design.

1. The basic instruction is this: Take the patterns in the order of the sequence, one by one, and let the form grow from the fusion of these patterns, the site, and your own instincts.

2. It is essential to work on the site, where the project is to be built; inside the room that is to be remodeled; on the land where the building is to go up; and so forth. And as far as possible, work with the people that are actually going to use the place when it is finished: if you are the user, all the better. But, above all, work on the site, stay on the site, *let the site tell you its secrets.*

3. Remember too, that the form will grow gradually as you go through the sequence, beginning as something very loose and amorphous, gradually becoming more and more complicated, more refined and more differentiated, more finished. Don't rush this process. Don't

give the form more order than it needs to meet the patterns and the conditions of the site, each step of the way. In effect, as you build each pattern into the design, you will experience a single gestalt that is gradually becoming more and more coherent.

4. Take one pattern at a time. Open the page to the first one and read it again. The pattern statement describes the ways in which other patterns either influence this pattern, or are influenced by it. *For now,* this information is useful only in so far as it helps you to envision *the one pattern before you, as a whole.*

5. Now, try to imagine how, on your particular site, you can establish this pattern. Stand on the site with your eyes closed. Imagine how things might be, if the pattern, as you have understood it, had suddenly sprung up there overnight. Once you have an image of how it might be, walk about the site, pacing out approximate areas, marking the walls, using string and cardboard, and putting stakes in the ground, or loose stones, to mark the important corners.

6. Complete your thought about this pattern, before you go on to the next one. This means you must treat the pattern as an "entity"; and try to conceive of this entity, entire and whole, before you start creating any other patterns.

7. The sequence of the language will guarantee that you will not have to make enormous changes which cancel out your earlier decisions. Instead, the changes you make will get smaller and smaller, as you build in more and more patterns, like a series of progressive refinements, until you finally have a complete design.

8. Since you are building up your design, one pattern

at a time, it is essential to keep your design as fluid as possible, while you go from pattern to pattern. As you use the patterns, one after another, you will find that you keep needing to adjust your design to accommodate new patterns. It is important that you do this in a loose and relaxed way, without getting the design more fixed than necessary, and without being afraid to make changes. The design can change as it needs to, so long as you maintain the essential relationships and characteristics which earlier patterns have prescribed. You will see that it is possible to keep these essentials constant, and still make minor changes in the design. As you include each new pattern, you readjust the total gestalt of your design, to bring it into line with the pattern you are working on.

9. While you are imagining how to establish one pattern, consider the other patterns listed with it. Some are larger. Some are smaller. For the larger ones, try to see how they can one day be present in the areas you are working on, and ask yourself how the pattern you are now building can contribute to the repair or formation of these larger patterns.

10. For the smaller ones, make sure that your conception of the main pattern will allow you to make these smaller patterns within it later. It will probably be helpful if you try to decide roughly how you are going to build these smaller patterns in, when you come to them.

11. Keep track of the area from the very beginning so that you are always reasonably close to something you can actually afford. We have had many experiences in which people try to design their own houses, or other buildings, and then get discouraged because the final cost

is too high, and they have to go back and change it.

To do this, decide on a budget, and use a reasonable average square foot cost, to translate this budget into square feet of construction. Say for the sake of argument, that you have a budget of $30,000 for construction. With help from builders, find out what kind of square foot cost is reasonable for the kind of building you are making. For example, in 1976, in California, a reasonable house, compatible with the patterns in the last part of the language, can be built for some $28/ square foot. If you want expensive finishes, it will be more. With $36,000 for construction, this will give you some 1300 square feet.

12. Now, throughout the design process, keep this 1300-square-foot figure in mind. If you go to two stories, keep the ground area to 650 square feet. If you use only part of the upstairs volume, the ground floor can go as high as 800 or 900 square feet. If you decide to build rather elaborate outdoor rooms, walls, trellises, reduce the indoor area to make up for these outdoor costs— perhaps down to 1100 or 1200. And, each time you use a pattern to differentiate the layout of your building further, keep this total area in mind, so that you do not, ever, allow yourself to go beyond your budget.

13. Finally, make the essential points and lines which are needed to fix the pattern, on the site with bricks, or sticks or stakes. Try not to design on paper; even in the case of complicated buildings find a way to make your marks on the site.

More detailed instructions, and detailed examples of the design process in action, are given in chapters 20, 21, and 22 of *The Timeless Way of Building*.

The first group of patterns helps to lay out the overall arrangement of a group of buildings: the height and number of these buildings, the entrances to the site, main parking areas, and lines of movement through the complex;

95 BUILDING COMPLEX**

. . . this pattern, the first of the 130 patterns which deal specifically with buildings, is the bottleneck through which all languages pass from the social layouts of the earlier patterns to the smaller ones which define individual spaces.

Assume that you have decided to build a certain building. The social groups or institutions which the building is meant to house are given—partly by the facts peculiar to your own case, and partly, perhaps, by earlier patterns. Now this pattern and the next one—NUMBER OF STORIES (96), give you the basis of the building's layout on the site. This pattern shows you roughly how to break the building into parts. NUMBER OF STORIES helps you decide how high to make each part. Obviously, the two patterns must be used together.

A building cannot be a human building unless it is a complex of still smaller buildings or smaller parts which manifest its own internal social facts.

A building is a visible, concrete manifestation of a social group or social institution. And since every social institution has smaller groups and institutions within it, a human building will always reveal itself, not as a monolith, but as a complex of these smaller institutions, made manifest and concrete too.

A family has couples and groups within it; a factory has teams of workers; a town hall has divisions, departments within the large divisions, and working groups within these departments. A building which shows these subdivisions and articulations in its fabric is a human building—because it lets us live according to the way that people group themselves. By contrast, any monolithic building is denying the facts of its own social structure, and in denying these facts it is asserting other facts of a less human kind and forcing people to adapt their lives to them instead.

We have tried to make this feeling more precise by means of the following conjecture: the more monolithic a building is, and the less differentiated, the more it presents itself as an in-

human, mechanical factory. And when human organizations are housed in enormous, undifferentiated buildings, people stop identifying with the staff who work there as personalities and think only of the institution as an impersonal monolith, staffed by personnel. In short, the more monolithic the building is, the more it prevents people from being personal, and from making human contact with the other people in the building.

The strongest evidence for this conjecture that we have found to date comes from a survey of visitors to public service buildings in Vancouver, British Columbia. (*Preliminary Program for Massing Studies, Document 5: Visitor Survey*, Environmental Analysis Group, Vancouver, B.C., August 1970.) Two kinds of public service buildings were studied—old, three story buildings and huge modern office buildings. The reactions of visitors to the small building differed from the reactions of visitors to the large buildings in an extraordinary way. The people going to the small buildings most often mentioned friendly and competent staff as the important factor in their satisfaction with the service. In many cases the visitors were able to give names and describe the people with whom they had done business. Visitors to the huge office buildings, on the other hand, mentioned friendliness and staff competence rather infrequently. The great majority of these visitors found their satisfaction in "good physical appearance, and equipment."

In the monoliths, the visitors' experience is depersonalized. They stop thinking primarily of the people they are going to see and the quality of the relationship and focus instead on the building itself and its features. The staff becomes "personnel," interchangeable, and indifferent, and the visitors pay little attention to them as people—friendly or unfriendly, competent or incompetent.

We learn also from this study that in the large buildings visitors complained frequently about the "general atmosphere" of the building, without naming specific problems. There were no such complaints among the visitors to the smaller buildings. It is as if the monoliths induce a kind of free-floating anxiety in people: the environment "feels wrong," but it is hard to give a reason. It may be that the cause of the uneasiness is so simple— the place is too big, it is difficult to grasp, the people are like bees in a hive—that people are embarrassed to say it outright.

("If it is as simple as that, *I* must be wrong—after all, there are so many of these buildings.")

However it is, we take this evidence to indicate deep disaffection from the *human* environment in the huge, undifferentiated office buildings. The buildings impress themselves upon us as things: objects, commodities; they make us forget the people inside, as people; yet when we use these buildings we complain vaguely about the "general atmosphere."

It seems then that the degree to which a building is broken into visible parts *does* affect the human relations among people in the building. And if a building must, for psychological reasons, be broken into parts, it seems impossible to find any more natural way of breaking it down, than the one we have suggested. Namely, that the various institutions, groups, subgroups, activities, are visible in the concrete articulation of the physical building, on the grounds that people will only be fully able to identify with people in the building, when the building is a building *complex*.

A gothic cathedral—though an immense building—is an example of a building complex. Its various parts, the spire, the aisle, the nave, the chancel, the west gate, are a precise reflection of the social groups—the congregation, the choir, the special mass, and so forth.

And, of course, a group of huts in Africa, is human too, because it too is a complex of buildings, not one huge building by itself.

For a complex of buildings at high density, the easiest way of all, of making its human parts identifiable, is to build it up from narrow fronted buildings, each with its own internal stair. This is the basic structure of a Georgian terrace, or the brownstones of New York.

Therefore:

Never build large monolithic buildings. Whenever possible translate your building program into a building complex, whose parts manifest the actual social facts of the situation. At low densities, a building complex may take the form of a collection of small buildings connected by arcades, paths, bridges, shared gardens, and walls. At higher densities, a single building can be treated as a

building complex, if its important parts are picked out and made identifiable while still part of one three-dimensional fabric.

Even a small building, a house for example, can be conceived as a "building complex"—perhaps part of it is higher than the rest with wings and an adjoining cottage.

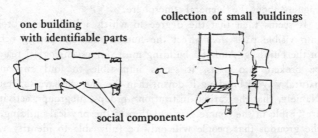

one building
with identifiable parts

collection of small buildings

social components

❖ ❖ ❖

At the highest densities, 3 or 4 stories, and along pedestrian streets, break the buildings into narrow, tall separate buildings, side by side, with common walls, each with its own internal or external stair. As far as possible insist that they be built piecemeal, one at a time, so that each one has time to be adapted to its neighbor. Keep the frontage as low as 25 or 30 feet. LONG THIN HOUSE (109), BUILDING FRONTS (122); MAIN ENTRANCE (110) and perhaps a part of an ARCADE (119) which connects to next door buildings.

Arrange the buildings in the complex to form realms of movement—CIRCULATION REALMS (98); build one building from the collection as a main building—the natural center of the site—MAIN BUILDING (99); place individual buildings where the land is least beautiful, least healthy—SITE REPAIR (104); and put them to the north of their respective open space to keep the gardens sunny—SOUTH-FACING OUTDOORS (105); subdivide them further, into narrow wings, no more than 25 or 30 feet across—WINGS OF LIGHT (107). For details of construction, start with STRUCTURE FOLLOWS SOCIAL SPACES (205). . . .

. . . assume now, that you know roughly how the parts of the building complex are to be articulated—BUILDING COMPLEX (95), and how large they are. Assume, also, that you have a site. In order to be sure that your building complex is workable within the limits of the site, you must decide how many stories its different parts will have. The height of each part must be constrained by the FOUR-STORY LIMIT (21). Beyond that, it depends on the area of your site, and the floor area which each part needs.

❖ ❖ ❖

Within the four-story height limit, just exactly how high should your buildings be?

To keep them small in scale, for human reasons, and to keep the costs down, they should be as low as possible. But to make the best use of land and to form a continuous fabric with surrounding buildings, they should perhaps be two or three or four stories instead of one. In this pattern we give rules for striking the balance.

Rule 1: Set a four-story height limit on the site. This rule comes directly from FOUR-STORY LIMIT (21) and the reasons for establishing this limit are described there.

Rule 2: For any given site, do not let the ground area covered by buildings exceed 50 per cent of the site. This rule requires that for any given site, where it belongs to a single household or a corporation, or whether it is a part of a larger site which contains several buildings, at least half of the site is left as open space. This is the limit of ground coverage within which reasonable site planning can take place. The rule therefore determines the maximum floor area that can be built with any given number of stories on a given site. The ratio of indoor area to site area (FAR—for floor area ratio) cannot thus exceed 0.5 in a single story building, 1.0 in a two story, 1.5 in a three story and 2.0 in a four story building.

If the total floor area you intend to build plus the built floor area that exists on the site is more than twice the area of the

site itself, then you are exceeding this limit. In this case, we advise that you cut back your program; build less space; perhaps build some of your project on another site.

Rule 3: Do not let the height of your building(s) vary too much from the predominant height of surrounding buildings. A rule of thumb: do not let your buildings deviate more than one story from surrounding buildings. On the whole, adjacent buildings should be *roughly* the same height.

Breaking the rule of thumb.

I live in a small one-story garden cottage at the back of a large house in Berkeley. All around the cottage there are two-story houses, some as close as thirty feet. I thought when I moved in, that a garden cottage would be secluded and I would have some private outdoor space. But instead I feel that I'm living in a goldfish bowl—every one of the second-story windows around me looks right down into my living room, or into my garden. The garden outside is useless, and I don't sit near the window.

Therefore:

First, decide how many square feet of built space you need, and divide by the area of the site to get the floor area ratio. Then choose the height of your buildings according to the floor area ratio and the height of the surrounding buildings from the following table. In no case build on more than 50 per cent of the land.

floor
area
ratio

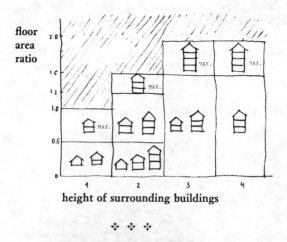

height of surrounding buildings

❖ ❖ ❖

Once you have the number of stories and the area of each part clear, decide which building or which part of the building will be the MAIN BUILDING (99). Vary the number of floors within the building—CASCADE OF ROOFS (116). Place the buildings on the site, with special reverence for the land, and trees, and sun—SITE REPAIR (104), SOUTH FACING OUTDOORS (105), TREE PLACES (171). In your calculations, remember that the effective area of the top story will be no more than three-quarters of the area of lower floors if it is in the roof, according to SHELTERING ROOF (117).

If the density is so high all around, that it is quite impossible to leave 50 per cent of the site open (as might be true in central London or New York), then cover the ground floor completely, but devote at least 50 per cent of the upper floors to open gardens—ROOF GARDEN (118).

Give each story a different ceiling height—bottom story biggest, top story smallest—and vary the column spacings accordingly—FINAL COLUMN DISTRIBUTION (213). The same building system applies, whether there are 1, 2, 3 or 4 stories—STRUCTURE FOLLOWS SOCIAL SPACES (205). . . .

97 SHIELDED PARKING*

. . . many patterns we have given discourage dependence on the use of cars; we hope that these patterns will gradually get rid, altogether, of the need for large parking lots and parking structures—LOCAL TRANSPORT AREAS (11), NINE PER CENT PARKING (22). However, in certain cases, unfortunately, large areas of parking are still necessary. Whenever this is so, this parking must be placed very early, to be sure that it does not destroy the BUILDING COMPLEX (95) altogether.

❖ ❖ ❖

Large parking structures full of cars are inhuman and dead buildings—no one wants to see them or walk by them. At the same time, if you are driving, the entrance to a parking structure is essentially the main entrance to the building—and it needs to be visible.

In NINE PER CENT PARKING (22), we have already defined an upper limit on the total amount of parking in a neighborhood. In SMALL PARKING LOTS (103) we give the best size and the distribution of the lots when they are on the ground. But in certain cases it is still necessary to build larger parking lots or parking structures. The environment can tolerate these larger lots and structures, provided that they are built so that they do not pollute the land around them.

This is a simple biological principle. In the human body, for example, there are waste products; the waste products are part of the way the body works, and obviously they must have a place. But the stomach and colon are built in such a way as to shield the other internal organs from the poisons carried by the wastes.

The same is true in a city. At this moment in history the city requires a certain limited amount of parking; and for the time being there is no getting away from that. But the parking must be built in such a way that it is shielded—by shops, houses, hills of

grassy earth, walls, or any other buildings of any kind—anything, so long as the interior of the parking structure and the cars are not visible from the surrounding land. On ground level, the shield is especially critical. Shops are useful since they generate their own pedestrian scale immediately. And since the need for parking often goes hand in hand with commercial development, shops are often very feasible economically.

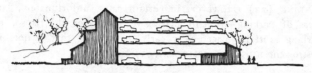

A shielded parking structure.

And of course, the houses themselves can serve the same function. In Paris, many of the most charming and beautiful apartment houses are arranged around courtyards, which permit parking inside, away from the street. There are few enough cars, so that they don't destroy the courtyard, for the houses; and the street is left free of parked cars entirely.

Along with the need to shield parking structures there is the equally pressing need on the part of a driver to be able to spot the parking structure quickly—and see how it is connected to the building he is headed for. One of the most frequent complaints about the parking near a building is not that it is too far away, but that you don't know where you can go to find a parking spot and still be sure of how to get back into the building.

This means that

1. Parking, which is specifically for the use of visitors, must be clearly marked from the directions of approach, even though the structure as a whole is shielded. The person who is coming by car will be looking for the building, not the parking lot. The entrance to parking must be marked as an important entrance—a gate —so that you can see it automatically, in the process of looking for the building. And it must be placed so that you find it about the same time that you see the building's main entrance.

2. While you are parking your car you must be able to see the exit from the parking area which will lead you into the building. This will let you search for the closest spots, and will mean that you don't have to walk around searching for the exit.

Therefore.

Put all large parking lots, or parking garages, behind some kind of natural wall, so that the cars and parking structures cannot be seen from outside. The wall which surrounds the cars may be a building, connected houses, or housing hills, earth berms, or shops.

Make the entrance to the parking lot a natural gateway to the buildings which it serves, and place it so that you can easily see the main entrance to the building from the entrance to the parking.

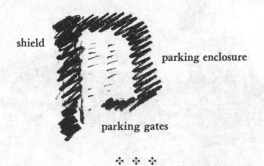

shield

parking enclosure

parking gates

❖ ❖ ❖

For shields see HOUSING HILL (39), HOUSING IN BETWEEN (48), INDIVIDUALLY OWNED SHOPS (87), OPEN STAIRS (158), GALLERY SURROUND (166). One of the cheapest ways of all to shield a parking lot is with canvas awnings—the canvas can be many colors: underneath, the light is beautiful—CANVAS ROOFS (244). Make certain that the major entrances of buildings are quite clearly visible from the place where you drive into parking lots, and from the places where you leave the parking lots on foot—CIRCULATION REALMS (98), FAMILY OF ENTRANCES (102), MAIN ENTRANCES (110). In covered parking structures, use a huge shaft of daylight as a natural direction which tells people where to walk to leave the parking—TAPESTRY OF LIGHT AND DARK (135); and finally, for the load-bearing structure, engineering, and construction, begin with STRUCTURE FOLLOWS SOCIAL SPACES (205). . . .

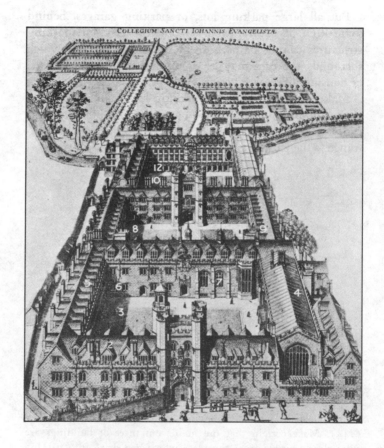

COLLEGIUM SANCTI IOHANNIS EVANGELISTÆ.

. . . once you have some rough idea how many buildings you are going to build—BUILDING COMPLEX (95), and how high they are to be—NUMBER OF STORIES (96), you can work out roughly what kind of layout they should have to make the access to them clear and comfortable. This pattern defines the overall philosophy of layout.

❖ ❖ ❖

In many modern building complexes the problem of disorientation is acute. People have no idea where they are, and they experience considerable mental stress as a result.

. . . the terror of being lost comes from the necessity that a mobile organism be oriented in its surroundings. Jaccard quotes an incident of native Africans who became disoriented. They were stricken with panic and plunged wildly into the bush. Witkin tells of an experienced pilot who lost his orientation to the vertical, and who described it as the most terrifying experience in his life. Many other writers in describing the phenomenon of temporary disorientation in the modern city, speak of the accompanying emotions of distress. (Kevin Lynch, *The Image of the City*, Cambridge, Mass.: MIT Press, 1960, p. 125.)

It is easiest to state the circulation problem for the case of a complete stranger who has to find his way around the complex of buildings. Imagine yourself as the stranger, looking for a particular address, within the building. From your point of view, the building is easy to grasp if someone can explain the position of this address to you, in a way you can remember easily, and carry in your head while you are looking for it. To put this in its most pungent form: *a person must be able to explain any given address within the building, to any other person, who does not know his way around, in one sentence.* For instance, "Come straight through the main gate, down the main path and turn into the second little gate, the small one with the blue grillwork—you can't miss my door."

At first sight, it might seem that the problem is only important for strangers—since a person who is familiar with a building can find his way around no matter how badly it is organized.

481

However, psychological theory suggests that the effect of badly laid out circulation has almost as bad an effect on a person who knows a building, as it does on a stranger. We may assume that every time a person goes toward some destination, he must carry some form of map or instruction in his mind. The question arises: How much of the time does he have to be consciously thinking about this map and his destination? If he spends a great deal of time looking out for landmarks, thinking about where to go next, then his time is entirely occupied, and leaves him little time for the process of reflection, tranquil contemplation, and thought.

We conclude that any environment which requires that a person pay attention to it constantly is as bad for a person who knows it, as for a stranger. A good environment is one which is easy to understand, without conscious attention.

What makes an environment easy to understand? What makes an environment confusing? Let us imagine that a person is going to a particular address within a building. Call this address A. The person who is looking for A does not go directly toward A—unless it happens to be visible from the point where he starts. Instead, he sets his journey up to form a series of steps, in which each step is a kind of temporary intermediate goal, and a taking off point for the next step. For example: First go through the gate, then to the second courtyard on the left, then to the right-hand arcade of the courtyard, and then through the third door. This sequence is a kind of map which the person has in his head. If it is always easy to construct such a map, it is easy to find your way around the building. If it is not easy, it is hard to find your way around.

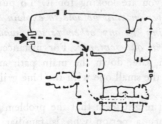

The way the map in your mind works.

A map works because it identifies a nested system of realms (in the case of our example the realms are first, the building itself, then the courtyard, then the arcade, then the room itself, the destination). The map guides you to the entrance of the largest realm, and from there to the entrance of the next largest realm, and so on. You make one decision at a time, and each decision you make narrows down the extent of the building which remains to be explored, until you finally narrow it down to the particular address you are looking for.

It seems reasonable to say that any useful map through a building complex must have this structure, and that any building complex in which you cannot create maps of this kind is confusing to be in. This is borne out by intuition. Consider these two examples; each has a system of realms which allows you to make such maps very easily.

An Oxford college. Here the college is made up of courts, each court has a collection of rooms called a "staircase" opening off it, and the individual suites of rooms open off these staircases. The realms are: College, Courts, Staircases, Rooms.

Manhattan. Here the city is made up of major areas, each major area has certain central streets and arteries. The realms are: Manhattan, Districts, Realms defined by the avenues, and Realms defined by cross streets and individual buildings. Manhattan is clear because the districts are so well defined, and the realms defined by the streets are subordinate to the realms defined by the avenues.

We conclude that in order to be clear, a building complex must follow three rules:

1. It is possible to identify a nested system of realms in the complex, the first and largest of these realms being the entire complex.

2. Each realm has a main circulation space, which opens directly from the entrances to that realm.

3. The entrances to any realm open directly off the circulation space of the next larger realm above it.

We emphasize finally, that these realms at every level must have *names*; and this requires, in turn, that they be well enough defined physically, so that they can in fact be named, and so that one knows where the realm of that name starts, and where it

stops. The realms do not have to be as precise as in the two examples we have given. But they must have enough psychological substance and existence so that they can honestly work as realms in somebody's mind.

Therefore:

Lay out very large buildings and collections of small buildings so that one reaches a given point inside by passing through a sequence of realms, each marked by a gateway and becoming smaller and smaller, as one passes from each one, through a gateway, to the next. Choose the realms so that each one can be easily named, so that you can tell a person where to go, simply by telling him which realms to go through.

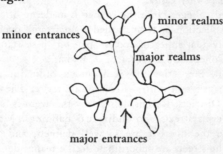

minor entrances

minor realms

major realms

major entrances

❖ ❖ ❖

Treat the first entrances to the whole system of circulation realms, the very largest ones, as gateways—MAIN GATEWAYS (53); make the major realms, which open off the gateways, pedestrian streets or common land—COMMON LAND (67), PEDESTRIAN STREET (100); then, make minor realms with individual buildings, and courtyards, and major indoor streets—MAIN BUILDING (99), BUILDING THOROUGHFARE (101), HIERARCHY OF OPEN SPACE (114), COURTYARDS WHICH LIVE (115); and mark the entrance to these minor realms with minor entrances that still stand out quite clearly—FAMILY OF ENTRANCES (102), MAIN ENTRANCE (110). Make the layout of paths consonant with PATHS AND GOALS (120). . . .

99 MAIN BUILDING*

. . . once you have decided more or less how people will move around within the BUILDING COMPLEX (95), and roughly how high the buildings will be—NUMBER OF STORIES (96)—it is time to try and find the natural heart or center of the building complex, to help complete its CIRCULATION REALMS (98).

A complex of buildings with no center is like a man without a head.

In circulation realms we have explained how people understand their surroundings and orient themselves in their surroundings by making mental maps. Such a map needs a point of reference: some point in the complex of buildings, which is very obvious, and so placed, that it is possible to refer all the other paths and buildings to it. A main building, which is also the functional soul of the complex, is the most likely candidate for this reference point. Without a main building, there is very little chance of any natural points of reference being strong enough to act as an organizer for one's mental map.

Furthermore, from the point of view of the group of users—the workers or the inhabitants—the sense of community and connection is heightened when one building or a part of one building is singled out and treated as a main building, common to all, the heart of the institution. Some examples: the meeting hall among a collection of government buildings; a guild hall in a work community; the kitchen and family room in a communal household; the merry-go-round in a park; a temple on sacred ground; the swimming pavilion in a health center; the workshop in an office.

Great care must be taken to pick that function which is actually the soul of the group, in human terms, for the main building. Otherwise, some irrelevant set of functions will dominate the building complex. The United Nations complex in New York fails for just this reason. The General Assembly, the heart and soul of the institution, is dwarfed by the bureaucratic Secretariat. And, indeed, this institution has suffered from the

red-tape mentality. (See the excellent series of articles by Lewis Mumford, discussing the U.N. buildings in *From the Ground Up*, Harvest Books, 1956, pp. 20–70.)
Therefore:

For any collection of buildings, decide which building in the group houses the most essential function—which building is the soul of the group, as a human institution. Then form this building as the main building, with a central position, higher roof.

Even if the building complex is so dense that it is a single building, build the main part of it higher and more prominent than the rest, so that the eye goes immediately to the part which is the most important.

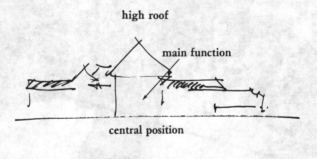

❖ ❖ ❖

Build all the main paths tangent to the main building, in arcades or glazed corridors, with a direct view into its main functions—COMMON AREAS AT THE HEART (129). Make the roof cascade down from the high roof over the main building to lower roofs over the smaller buildings—CASCADE OF ROOFS (116). And for the load bearing structure, engineering, and construction, begin with STRUCTURE FOLLOWS SOCIAL SPACES (205). . . .

100 PEDESTRIAN STREET**

. . . the earlier patterns—PROMENADE (31), SHOPPING STREET (32) and NETWORK OF PATHS AND CARS (52), all call for dense pedestrian streets; ROW HOUSES (38), HOUSING HILL (39), UNIVERSITY AS A MARKETPLACE (43), MARKET OF MANY SHOPS (46), all do the same; and within the BUILDING COMPLEX (95), CIRCULATION REALMS (98) calls for the same. As you build a pedestrian street, make sure you place it so that it helps to generate a NETWORK OF PATHS AND CARS (52), RAISED WALKS (55), and CIRCULATION REALMS (98) in the town around it.

❖ ❖ ❖

The simple social intercourse created when people rub shoulders in public is one of the most essential kinds of social "glue" in society.

In today's society this situation, and therefore this glue, is largely missing. It is missing in large part because so much of the actual process of movement is now taking place in indoor corridors and lobbies, instead of outdoors. This happens partly because the cars have taken over streets, and made them uninhabitable, and partly because the corridors, which have been built in response, encourage the same process. But it is doubly damaging in its effect.

It is damaging because it robs the streets of people. Most of the moving about which people do is indoors—hence lost to the street; the street becomes abandoned and dangerous.

And it is damaging because the indoor lobbies and corridors are most often dead. This happens partly because indoor space is not as public as outdoor space; and partly because, in a multi-story building each corridor carries a lower density of traffic than a public outdoor street. It is therefore unpleasant, even unnerving, to move through them; people in them are in no state to generate, or benefit from, social intercourse.

To recreate the social intercourse of public movement, as far as possible, the movement between rooms, offices, departments, buildings, must actually be outdoors, on sheltered walks, arcades, paths,

streets, which are truly public and separate from cars. Individual wings, small buildings, departments must as often as possible have their own entrances—so that the number of entrances onto the street increases and life comes back to the street.

In short, the solution to these two problems we have mentioned —the streets infected by cars and the bland corridors—is the pedestrian street. Pedestrian streets are both places to walk along (from car, bus, or train to one's destination) and places to pass through (between apartments, shops, offices, services, classes).

To function properly, pedestrian streets need two special properties. First, of course, no cars; but frequent crossings by streets with traffic, see NETWORK OF PATHS AND CARS (52): deliveries and other activities which make it essential to bring cars and trucks onto the pedestrian street must be arranged at the early hours of the morning, when the streets are deserted. Second, the buildings along pedestrian streets must be planned in a way which as nearly as possible eliminates indoor staircases, corridors, and lobbies, and leaves most circulation outdoors. This creates a street lined with stairs, which lead from all upstairs offices and rooms directly to the street, and many many entrances, which help to increase the life of the street.

Finally it should be noted that the pedestrian streets which seem most comfortable are the ones where the width of the street does not exceed the height of the surrounding buildings. (See "Vehicle free zones in city centers," *International Brief #16*, U.S. Department of Housing and Urban Development, Office of International Affairs, June 1972).

About square . . . or even narrower.

Therefore:

Arrange buildings so that they form pedestrian streets with many entrances and open stairs directly from the upper storys to the street, so that even movement between rooms is outdoors, not just movement between buildings.

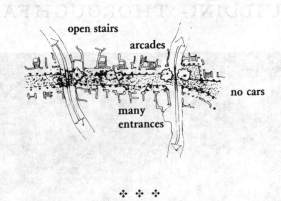

❖ ❖ ❖

The street absolutely will not work unless its total area is small enough to be well filled by the pedestrians in it—PEDESTRIAN DENSITY (123). Make frequent entrances and open stairs along the street, instead of building indoor corridors, to bring the people out; and give these entrances a family resemblance so one sees them as a system—FAMILY OF ENTRANCES (102), OPEN STAIRS (158); give people indoor and outdoor spaces which look on the street—PRIVATE TERRACE ON THE STREET (140), STREET WINDOWS (164), OPENING TO THE STREET (165), GALLERY SURROUND (166), SIX-FOOT BALCONY (167); and shape the street to make a space of it—ARCADE (119), PATH SHAPE (121). . . .

IOI BUILDING THOROUGHFARE

. . . if the building complex is built at high density, then at least part of the circulation cannot be made of outdoor PEDESTRIAN STREETS (100) because the buildings cover too much of the land; in this case, the main spines of the CIRCULATION REALMS (98) must take the form of building thoroughfares similar to pedestrian streets, but partly or wholly inside the buildings. Building thoroughfares replace the terrible corridors which destroy so much of modern building, and help to generate the indoor layout of a BUILDING COMPLEX (95).

❖ ❖ ❖

When a public building complex cannot be completely served by outdoor pedestrian streets, a new form of indoor street, quite different from the conventional corridor, is needed.

An indoor street.

The problem arises under two conditions.

1. *Cold weather.* In very cold climates to have all circulation outdoors inhibits social communication instead of helping it. Of course, a street can be roofed, particularly with a glass roof. But as soon as it becomes enclosed, it has a different social ecology and begins to function differently.

2. *High density.* When a building complex is so tightly packed

493

on the site that there is no reasonable space for outdoor streets because the entire building complex is a continuous two, three, or four story building, it becomes necessary to think of major thoroughfares in different terms.

To solve the problems posed by these conditions, streets must be replaced by indoor thoroughfares or corridors. But the moment we put them indoors and under cover, they begin to suffer from entirely new problems, which are caused by the fact that they get sterilized by their isolation. First, they become removed from the public realm, and are often deserted. People hardly ever feel free to linger in public corridors when they are off the street. And second, the corridors become so unfriendly that nothing ever happens there. They are designed for scuttling people through, but not for staying in.

In order to solve these new problems, created when we try to put a street indoors, the indoor streets—or building thoroughfares —need five specific characteristics.

1. Shortcut

Public places are meant to invite free loitering. The public places in community buildings (city halls, community centers, public libraries) especially need this quality, because when people feel free to hang around they will necessarily get acquainted with what goes on in the building and may begin to use it.

But people rarely feel free to stay in these places without an Official Reason. Goffman describes this situation as follows:

Being present in a public place without an orientation to apparent goals outside the situation is sometimes called lolling, when position is fixed, and loitering, when some movement is entailed. Either can be deemed sufficiently improper to merit legal action. On many of our city streets, especially at certain hours, the police will question anyone who appears to be doing nothing and ask him to "move along." (In London, a recent court ruling established that an individual has a right to walk on the street but no legal right merely to stand on it.) In Chicago, an individual in the uniform of a hobo can loll on "the stem," but once off this preserve he is required to look as if he were intent on getting to some business destination. Similarly, some mental patients owe their commitment to the fact that the police found them wandering on the streets at off hours without any apparent destination or purpose in mind. (Erving Goffman, *Behavior in Public Places*, New York: Free Press, 1963, p. 56.)

If a public space is to be really useful it must somehow help to counter the anti-loitering tendency in modern society. Specifically, we have observed these problems:

a. A person will not use a public place if he has to make a special motion toward it, a motion which indicates the intention to use the facility "officially."

b. If people are asked to state their reason for being in a place (for example, by a receptionist or clerk) they won't use it freely.

c. Entering a public space through doors, corridors, changes of level, and so on, tends to keep away people who are not entering with a specific goal in mind.

Places which overcome these problems, like the Galleria in Milan, all have a common characteristic: they all have public thoroughfares which slice through them, lined with places to stop and loiter and watch the scene.

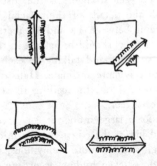

Shortcuts.

2. Width

An indoor street needs to be wide enough for people to feel comfortable walking or stopping along the way. Informal experiments help to determine how much space people need when they pass others. Since the likelihood of three people passing three people is not high, we consider as a maximum two people passing two people, or three people passing one person. Each person takes about two feet; there needs to be about one foot between two groups which pass, so that they do not feel crowded; and

495

people usually walk at least one foot away from the wall. The street width, therefore, should be *at least 11 feet*.

Our experiments also indicate that a person seated or standing at the edge of a street feels uncomfortable if anyone passes closer than five feet. Thus, in places in the street where seats, activities, entrances, and counters are placed, the street should widen to about 16 feet (one-sided) or 20 feet (two-sided).

3. Height

Ceiling heights should also feel comfortable for people walking or standing along an indoor street. According to CEILING HEIGHT VARIETY (190), the height of any space should be equal to the appropriate horizontal social distances between people for the given situation—the higher the ceiling, the more distant people seem from each other.

Edward Hall, in *The Hidden Dimension*, suggests that a comfortable distance between strangers is the distance at which you cannot distinguish the details of their facial features. He gives this distance as being between 12 and 16 feet. Thus, the ceiling height in an indoor street should be at least in that range.

Where people sit and stand talking to each other, the appropriate social distance is more intimate. Hall gives it a dimension of four to seven feet. Thus, the ceiling in activity and "edge" places should be seven feet.

This suggests, for a large indoor street, a ceiling that is high in the middle and low at the edges. In the middle, where people are passing through and are more anonymous, the ceiling may be 12 to 20 feet high, or even higher, according to the scale of the passage. Along the edges of the thoroughfare, where people are invited to stop and become slightly more engaged in the life of the building, the ceilings may be lower. Here are three sections through an indoor street which have this property.

Cross sections of an indoor street.

4. Wide entrance

As far as possible, the indoor street should be a continuation of the circulation outside the building. To this end, the path into the building should be as continuous as possible, and the entrance quite wide—more a gateway than a door. An entrance that is 15 feet wide begins to have this character.

5. Involvements along the edge

To invite the free loitering described above under *Short-cut*, the street needs a continuum of various "involvements" along its edge.

Rooms next to the street should have windows opening onto the street. We know it is unpleasant to walk down a corridor lined with blank walls. Not only do you lose the sense of where you are but you get the feeling that all the life in the building is on the other side of the walls, and you feel cut off from it. We guess that this contact with the public is not objectionable for the workers, so long as it is not too extreme, that is, as long as the workplace is protected either by distance or by a partial wall.

The corridor should be lined with seats and places to stop, such as newspaper, magazine, and candy stands, bulletin boards, exhibits, and displays.

Where there are entrances and counters of offices and services off the corridor, they should project into the corridor. Like activities, entrances and counters create places in the corridor, and should be combined with seats and other places to stop. In most public service buildings these counters and entrances are usually set back from corridors which makes them hard to see, and emphasizes the difference between the corridor as a place for passing through, and the office as a place where things happen. The problems can be solved if the entrances and counters project into the corridor and become part of it.

Therefore:

Wherever density or climate force the main lines of circulation indoors, build them as building thoroughfares. Place each thoroughfare in a position where it functions as a shortcut, as continuous as possible with the public street

outside, with wide open entrances. And line its edges with windows, places to sit, counters, and entrances which project out into the hall and expose the buildings' main functions to the public. Make it wider than a normal corridor—at least 11 feet wide and more usually, 15 to 20 feet wide; give it a high ceiling, at least 15 feet, with a glazed roof if possible and low places along the edge. If the street is several stories high, then the walkways along the edges, on the different stories, can be used to form the low places.

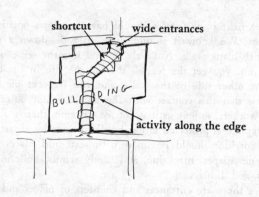

❖ ❖ ❖

Treat the thoroughfare as much like a PEDESTRIAN STREET (100) as possible, with OPEN STAIRS (158) coming into it from upper storys. Place entrances, reception points, and seats to form the pockets of activity under the lower ceilings at the edges— FAMILY OF ENTANCES (102), ACTIVITY POCKETS (124), RECEPTION WELCOMES YOU (149), WINDOW PLACE (180), CEILING HEIGHT VARIETY (190), and give these places strong natural light—TAPESTRY OF LIGHT AND DARK (135). Make a connection to adjacent rooms with INTERIOR WINDOWS (194) and SOLID DOORS WITH GLASS (237). To give the building thoroughfare the proper sense of liveliness, calculate its overall size according to PEDESTRIAN DENSITY (123). . . .

corner," but in every case the identification of "the one . . ."
can only make sense if the entire collection of possible entrances
can first be seen and understood *as a collection*. Then it is possible
to pick one particular entrance out, without conscious effort.

Therefore:

Lay out the entrances to form a family. This means:

**1. They form a group, are visible together, and each is
visible from all the others.**

**2. They are all broadly similar, for instance all porches,
or all gates in a wall, or all marked by a similar kind
of doorway.**

family of entrances

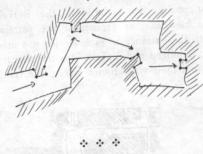

❖ ❖ ❖

In detail, make the entrances bold and easy to see—MAIN
ENTRANCE (110); when they lead into private domains, houses
and the like, make a transition in between the public street and
the inside—ENTRANCE TRANSITION (112); and shape the entrance itself as a room, which straddles the wall, and is thus
both inside and outside as a projecting volume, covered and
protected from the rain and sun—ENTRANCE ROOM (130). If it
is an entrance from an indoor street into a public office, make
reception part of the entrance room—RECEPTION WELCOMES
YOU (149). . . .

102 FAMILY OF ENTRANCES*

. . . this pattern is an embellishment of CIRCULATION REALMS (98). CIRCULATION REALMS portrayed a series of realms, in a large building or a building complex, with a major entrance or gateway into each realm and a collection of minor doorways, gates, and openings off each realm. This pattern applies to the relationship between these "minor" entrances.

❖ ❖ ❖

When a person arrives in a complex of offices or services or workshops, or in a group of related houses, there is a good chance he will experience confusion unless the whole collection is laid out before him, so that he can see the entrance of the place where he is going.

In our work at the Center we have encountered and defined several versions of this pattern. To make the general problem clear, we shall go through these cases and then draw out the general rule.

1. In our multi-service center project we called this pattern Overview of Services. We found that people could find their way around and see exactly what the building had to offer, if the various services were laid out in a horseshoe, directly visible from the threshold of the building. See *A Pattern Language Which Generates Multi-Service Centers*, pp. 123–26.

Overview of services.

2. Another version of the pattern, called Reception Nodes, was used for mental health clinics. In these cases we specified *one*

clearly defined main entrance, with main reception clearly visible inside this main entrance and each "next" point of reception then visible from the previous one, so that a patient who might be frightened or confused could find his way about by asking receptionists—and could always be directed to the next, *visible* receptionist down the line.

Reception nodes.

3. In our project for re-building the Berkeley City Hall complex, we used another version of the pattern. Within the indoor streets, the entrance to each service was made in a similar way—each one bulged out slightly into the street, so that people could easily find their way around among the resulting family of entrances.

Family of entrances.

4. We have also applied the pattern to houses which are laid out to form a cluster. In one example the pattern drew different house entrances together to make a mutually visible collection of them, and again gave each of them a similar shape.

In all these cases, the same central problem exists. A person who is looking for one of several entrances, and doesn't know his way around, needs to have some simple way of identifying the one entrance he wants. It can be identified as "the blue one," "the one with the mimosa bush outside," "the one with a big 18 on it," or "the last one on the right, after you get round the

103 SMALL PARKING LOTS*

. . . since a small parking lot is a kind of gateway—the place where you leave your car, and enter a pedestrian realm—this pattern helps to complete SHOPPING STREETS (32), HOUSE CLUSTER (37), WORK COMMUNITY (41), GREEN STREETS (51), MAIN GATEWAYS (53), CIRCULATION REALMS (98), and any other areas which need small and convenient amounts of parking. But above all, if it is used correctly, this pattern, together with SHIELDED PARKING (97), will help to generate NINE PER CENT PARKING (22) gradually, by increments.

Vast parking lots wreck the land for people.

In NINE PER CENT PARKING (22), we have suggested that the fabric of society is threatened by the mere existence of cars, if areas for parked cars take up more than 9 or 10 per cent of the land in a community.

We now face a second problem. Even when parked cars occupy less than 9 per cent of the land, they can still be distributed in two entirely different ways. They can be concentrated in a few huge parking lots; or they can be scattered in many tiny parking lots. The tiny parking lots are far better for the environment than the large ones, even when their total areas are the same.

Large parking lots have a way of taking over the landscape, creating unpleasant places, and having a depressing effect on the

The destruction of human scale.

504

open space around them. They make people feel dominated by cars; they separate people from the pleasure and convenience of being near their cars; and, if they are large enough to contain unpredictable traffic, they are dangerous for children, since children inevitably play in parking lots.

The problems stem essentially from the fact that a car is so much bigger than a person. Large parking lots, suited for the cars, have all the wrong properties for people. They are too wide; they contain too much pavement; they have no place to linger. In fact, we have noticed that people speed up when they are walking through large parking lots to get out of them as fast as possible.

It is hard to pin down the exact size at which parking lots become too big. Our observations suggest that parking lots for four cars are still essentially pedestrian and human in character; that lots for six cars are acceptable; but that any area near a parking lot which holds eight cars is already clearly identifiable as "car dominated territory."

This may be connected with the well-known perceptual facts about the number seven. A collection of less than five to seven objects can be grasped as one thing, and the objects in it can be grasped as individuals. A collection of more than five to seven things is perceived as "many things." (See G. Miller, "The Magical Number Seven, Plus or Minus Two: Some Limits on Our Capacity for Processing Information," in D. Beardslee and M. Wertheimer, eds., *Readings in Perception*, New York, 1958, esp. p. 103.) It may be true that the impression of a "sea of cars" first comes into being with about seven cars.

The small lots can be quite loosely placed.

Therefore:

Make parking lots small, serving no more than five to seven cars, each lot surrounded by garden walls, hedges, fences, slopes, and trees, so that from outside the cars are almost invisible. Space these small lots so that they are at least 100 feet apart.

five to seven cars

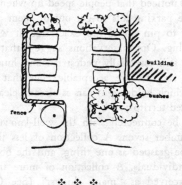

building

bushes

fence

❖ ❖ ❖

Place entrances and exits of the parking lots in such a way that they fit naturally into the pattern of pedestrian movement and lead directly, without confusion, to the major entrances to individual buildings—CIRCULATION REALMS (98). Shield even these quite modest parking lots with garden walls, and trees, and fences, so that they help to generate the space around them—POSITIVE OUTDOOR SPACE (106), TREE PLACES (171), GARDEN WALLS (173). . . .

*fix the position of individual buildings on the site,
within the complex, one by one, according to the
nature of the site, the trees, the sun: this is one of
the most important moments in the language;*

IO4 SITE REPAIR**

. . . the most general aspects of a building complex are established in BUILDING COMPLEX (95), NUMBER OF STORIES (96), and CIRCULATION REALMS (98). The patterns which follow, and all remaining patterns in the language, concern the design of one single building and its surroundings. This pattern explains the very first action you must take—the process of repairing the site. Since it tends to identify very particular small areas of any site as promising areas of development, it is greatly supported by BUILDING COMPLEX (95) which breaks buildings into smaller parts, and therefore makes it possible to tuck them into different corners of the site in the best places.

❖ ❖ ❖

Buildings must always be built on those parts of the land which are in the worst condition, not the best.

This idea is indeed very simple. But it is the exact opposite of what usually happens; and it takes enormous will power to follow it through.

What usually happens when someone thinks of building on a piece of land? He looks for the best site—where the grass is most beautiful, the trees most healthy, the slope of the land most even, the view most lovely, the soil most fertile—and that is just where he decides to put his house. The same thing happens whether the piece of land is large or small. On a small lot in a town the building goes in the sunniest corner, wherever it is most pleasant. On a hundred acres in the country, the buildings go on the most pleasant hillside.

It is only human nature; and, for a person who lacks a total view of the ecology of the land, it seems the most obvious and sensible thing to do. If you are going to build a building, ". . . build it in the best possible place."

But think now of the three-quarters of the available land which are not quite so nice. Since people always build on the one-quarter which is healthiest, the other three-quarters, already less healthy ecologically, become neglected. Gradually, they become

509

less and less healthy. Who is ever going to do anything on that corner of the lot which is dark and dank, where the garbage accumulates, or that part of the land which is a stagnant swamp, or the dry, stony hillside, where no plants are growing? Not only that. When we build on the best parts of the land, those beauties which are there already—the crocuses that break through the lawn each spring, the sunny pile of stones where lizards sun themselves, the favorite gravel path, which we love walking on—it is always these things which get lost in the shuffle. When the construction starts on the parts of the land which are already healthy, innumerable beauties are wiped out with every act of building.

People always say to themselves, well, of course, we can always start another garden, build another trellis, put in another gravel path, put new crocuses in the new lawn, and the lizards will find some other pile of stones. *But it just is not so.* These simple things take years to grow—it isn't all that easy to create them, just by wanting to. And every time we disturb one of these precious details, it may take twenty years, a lifetime even, before some comparable details grow again from our small daily acts.

If we always build on that part of the land which is most healthy, we can be virtually certain that a great deal of the land will always be less than healthy. If we want the land to be healthy all over—all of it—then we must do the opposite. We must treat every new act of building as an opportunity to mend some rent in the existing cloth; each act of building gives us the chance to make one of the ugliest and least healthy parts of the environment more healthy—as for those parts which are already healthy and beautiful—they of course need no attention. And in fact, we must discipline ourselves most strictly to *leave them alone,* so that our energy actually goes to the places which need it. This is the principle of site repair.

The fact is, that current development hardly ever does well by this pattern: everyone has a story about how some new building or road destroyed a place dear to them. The following news article from the San Francisco Chronicle (February 6, 1973) head-lined "Angry Boys Bulldoze House" struck us as the perfect case:

Two 13-year old boys—enraged over a swath of suburban homes being built in the midst of their rabbit-hunting turf—were arrested

after they admitted flattening one of the homes with a purloined bulldozer.

According to the Washoe County sheriff's office, the youths started up a bulldozer used at the construction site about four miles north of Reno, then plowed the sturdy vehicle through one of the homes four times late 'st Friday night.

The ranch-style house—which was nearly completed—was a shambles when workmen arrived yesterday morning. Damage was estimated at $7800 by the contractor. One of the boys told authorities the home along with several others nearby was ruining a "favorite rabbit-hunting preserve."

The two boys were booked on charges of felonious destruction.

The idea of site repair is just a beginning. It deals with the problem of how to minimize damage. But the most talented of traditional builders have always been able to use built form, not only to avoid damage, but also to improve the natural landscape. This attitude is so profoundly different from our current view of building, that concepts which will help us decide how to place buildings to *improve* the landscape don't even exist yet.

Therefore:

On no account place buildings in the places which are most beautiful. In fact, do the opposite. Consider the site and its buildings as a single living eco-system. Leave those areas that are the most precious, beautiful, comfortable, and healthy as they are, and build new structures in those parts of the site which are least pleasant now.

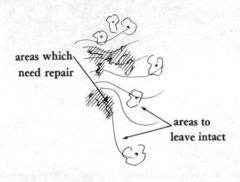

areas which need repair

areas to leave intact

Above all, leave trees intact and build around them with great care—TREE PLACES (171); keep open spaces open to the south of buildings, for the sun—SOUTH FACING OUTDOORS (105); try, generally, to shape space in such a way that each place becomes positive, in its own right—POSITIVE OUTDOOR SPACE (106). Repair slopes if they need it with TERRACED SLOPE (169), and leave the outdoors in its natural state as much as possible—GARDEN GROWING WILD (172). If necessary, push and shove the building into odd corners to preserve the beauty of an old vine, a bush you love, a patch of lovely grass—WINGS OF LIGHT (107), LONG THIN HOUSE (109). . . .

105 SOUTH FACING
OUTDOORS**

. . . within the general ideas of location which SITE REPAIR
(104) creates, this pattern governs the fundamental placing of
the building and the open space around it with respect to sun.

❖ ❖ ❖

**People use open space if it is sunny, and do not use it
if it isn't, in all but desert climates.**

This is perhaps the most important single fact about a building.
If the building is placed right, the building and its gardens will
be happy places full of activity and laughter. If it is done wrong,
then all the attention in the world, and the most beautiful details, will not prevent it from being a silent gloomy place.
Thousands of acres of open space in every city are wasted because
they are north of buildings and never get the sun. This is true
for public buildings, and it is true for private houses. The recently
built Bank of America building in San Francisco—a giant building built by a major firm of architects—has its plaza on the
north side. At lunchtime, the plaza is empty, and people eat
their sandwiches in the street, on the south side where the sun is.

North facing outdoors.

Just so for small private houses. The shape and orientation of
lots common in most developments force houses to be surrounded
by open space which no one will ever use because it isn't in the
sun.

A survey of a residential block in Berkeley, California, confirms this problem dramatically. Along Webster Street—an east-
west street—18 of 20 persons interviewed said they used only the
sunny part of their yards. Half of these were people living on

the north side of the street—*these people did not use their back-yards at all*, but would sit in the front yard, beside the sidewalk, to be in the south sun. The north-facing back yards were used primarily for storing junk. Not one of the persons interviewed indicated preference for a shady yard.

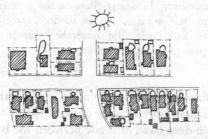

Favorite outdoor places to the south.

The survey also gave credence to the idea that sunny areas won't be used if there is a deep band of shade up against the house, through which you must pass to get to the sun. Four north facing backyards were large enough to be sunny toward the rear. In only one of these yards was the sunny area reported as being used—in just the one where it was possible to get to the sun without passing through a deep band of shade.

Although the idea of south-facing open space is simple, it has great consequences, and there will have to be major changes in land use to make it come right. For example, residential neighborhoods would have to be organized quite differently from the way they are laid out today. Private lots would have to be longer north to south, with the houses on the north side.

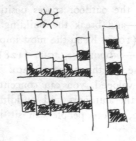

Blocks reorganized to catch the sun.

Note that this pattern was developed in the San Francisco Bay Area. Of course, its significance varies as latitude and climate change. In Eugene, Oregon, for example, with a rather rainy climate, at about 50° latitude, the pattern is even more essential: the south faces of the buildings are the most valuable outdoor spaces on sunny days. In desert climates, the pattern is less important; people will want to stay in outdoor spaces that have a balance of sun and shade. But remember that in one way or another, this pattern is absolutely fundamental.

Therefore:

Always place buildings to the north of the outdoor spaces that go with them, and keep the outdoor spaces to the south. Never leave a deep band of shade between the building and the sunny part of the outdoors.

building to the north

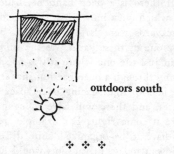

outdoors south

❖ ❖ ❖

Let HALF-HIDDEN GARDEN (111) influence the position of the outdoors too. Make the outdoor spaces positive—POSITIVE OUT-DOOR SPACE (106)—and break the building into narrow wings —WINGS OF LIGHT (107). Keep the most important rooms to the south of these wings—INDOOR SUNLIGHT (128); and keep storage, parking, etc, to the north—NORTH FACE (162). When the building is more developed, you can concentrate on the special sunny areas where the outdoors and building meet, and make definite places there, where people can sit in the sun—SUNNY PLACE (161). . . .

106 POSITIVE OUTDOOR
SPACE**

. . . in making SOUTH FACING OUTDOORS (105) you must both choose the place to build, and also choose the place for the outdoors. You cannot shape the one without the other. This pattern gives you the geometric character of the outdoors; the next one—WINGS OF LIGHT (107)—gives you the complementary shape of the indoors.

❖ ❖ ❖

Outdoor spaces which are merely "left over" between buildings will, in general, not be used.

There are two fundamentally different kinds of outdoor space: negative space and positive space. Outdoor space is negative when it is shapeless, the residue left behind when buildings—which are generally viewed as positive—are placed on the land. An outdoor space is positive when it has a distinct and definite shape, as definite as the shape of a room, and when its shape is as important as the shapes of the buildings which surround it. These two kinds of space have entirely different plan geometries, which may be most easily distinguished by their figure-ground reversal.

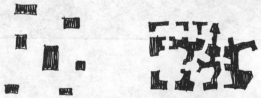

Buildings that create negative, leftover space . . .
buildings that create positive outdoor space.

If you look at the plan of an environment where outdoor spaces are negative, you see the buildings as figure, and the outdoor space as ground. There is no reversal. It is impossible to see the outdoor space as figure, and the buildings as ground. If you look at the plan of an environment where outdoor spaces are positive, you may see the buildings as figure, and outdoor spaces as ground—*and*, you may *also* see the outdoor spaces as

figure against the ground of the buildings. The plans have figure-ground reversal.

Another way of defining the difference between "positive" and "negative" outdoor spaces is by their degree of enclosure and their degree of convexity.

In mathematics, a space is convex when a line joining any two points inside the space itself lies totally inside the space. It is nonconvex, when some lines joining two points lie at least partly outside the space. According to this definition, the following irregular squarish space is convex and therefore positive; but the L-shaped space is not convex or positive, because the line joining its two end points cuts across the corner and therefore goes outside the space.

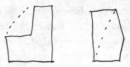

Convex and nonconvex.

Positive spaces are partly enclosed, at least to the extent that their areas seem bounded (even though they are not, in fact, because there are always paths leading out, even whole sides open), and the "virtual" area which seems to exist is *convex*. Negative spaces are so poorly defined that you cannot really tell where their boundaries are, and to the extent that you can tell, the shapes are *nonconvex*.

This space can be felt: it is distinct:—a place . . . and it is convex. This space is vague, amorphous, "nothing."

Now, what is the functional relevance of the distinction between "positive" and "negative" outdoor spaces. We put forward the following hypothesis. *People feel comfortable in spaces which are "positive" and use these spaces; people feel relatively uncomfortable in spaces which are "negative" and such spaces tend to remain unused.*

The case for this hypothesis has been most fully argued by Camillo Sitte, in *City Planning According to Artistic Principles* (republished by Random House in 1965). Sitte has analyzed a very large number of European city squares, distinguishing those which seem used and lively from those which don't, trying to account for the success of the lively squares. He shows, with example after example, that the successful ones—those which are greatly used and enjoyed—have two properties. On the one hand, they are partly enclosed; on the other hand, they are also open to one another, so that each one leads into the next.

The fact that people feel more comfortable in a space which is at least partly enclosed is hard to explain. To begin with, it is obviously not *always* true. For example, people feel very comfortable indeed on an open beach, or on a rolling plain, where there may be no enclosure at all. But in the smaller outdoor spaces —gardens, parks, walks, plazas—enclosure does, for some reason, seem to create a feeling of security.

It seems likely that the need for enclosure goes back to our most

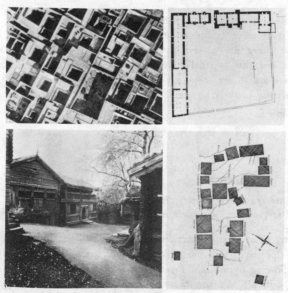

Four examples of positive outdoor space.

primitive instincts. For example, when a person looks for a place to sit down outdoors, he rarely chooses to sit exposed in the middle of an open space—he usually looks for a tree to put his back against; a hollow in the ground, a natural cleft which will partly enclose and shelter him. Our studies of people's space needs in workplaces show a similar phenomenon. To be comfortable, a person wants a certain amount of enclosure around him and his work—but not too much—see WORKSPACE ENCLOSURE (183). Clare Cooper has found the same thing in her study of parks: people seek areas which are partially enclosed and partly open—not too open, not too enclosed (Clare Cooper, Open Space Study, *San Francisco Urban Design Study*, San Francisco City Planning Dept., 1969).

Most often, positive outdoor space is created at the same time that other patterns are created. The following photograph shows one of the few places in the world where a considerable amount of building had no other purpose whatsoever except to create a positive outdoor space. It somehow underlines the pattern's urgency.

The square at Nancy.

When open space is negative, for example, L-shaped—it is always possible to place small buildings, or building projections, or walls in such a way as to break the space into positive pieces.

Transform this. . . . . .to this.

521

And when an existing open space is too enclosed, it may be possible to break a hole through the building to open the space up.

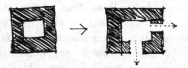

Transform this. . . . . .to this.

Therefore:

Make all the outdoor spaces which surround and lie between your buildings positive. Give each one some degree of enclosure; surround each space with wings of buildings, trees, hedges, fences, arcades, and trellised walks, until it becomes an entity with a positive quality and does not spill out indefinitely around corners.

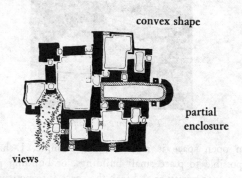

convex shape

partial
enclosure

views

❖ ❖ ❖

Place WINGS OF LIGHT (107) to form the spaces. Use open trellised walks, walls, and trees to close off spaces which are too exposed—TREE PLACES (171), GARDEN WALL (173), TRELLISED WALK (174); but make sure that every space is always open to

some larger space, so that it is not too enclosed—HIERARCHY OF OPEN SPACE (114). Use BUILDING FRONTS (122) to help create the shape of space. Complete the positive character of the outdoors by making places all around the edge of buildings, and so make the outdoors as much a focus of attention as the buildings—BUILDING EDGE (160). Apply this pattern to COURTYARDS WHICH LIVE (115), ROOF GARDENS (118), PATH SHAPE (121), OUTDOOR ROOM (163), GARDEN GROWING WILD (172).

107 WINGS OF LIGHT**

. . . at this stage, you have a rough position for the building or buildings on the site from SOUTH FACING OUTDOORS (105) and POSITIVE OUTDOOR SPACE (106). Before you lay out the interior of the building in detail, it is necessary to define the shapes of roofs and buildings in rather more detail. To do this, go back to the decisions you have already made about the basic social components of the building. In some cases, you will have made these decisions according to the individual case; in other cases you may have used the fundamental social patterns to define the basic entities— THE FAMILY (75), HOUSE FOR A SMALL FAMILY (76), HOUSE FOR A COUPLE (77), HOUSE FOR ONE PERSON (78), SELF-GOVERNING WORKSHOPS AND OFFICES (80), SMALL SERVICES WITHOUT RED TAPE (81), OFFICE CONNECTIONS (82), MASTER AND APPRENTICES (83), INDIVIDUALLY OWNED SHOPS (87). Now it is time to start giving the building a more definite shape based on these social groupings. Start by realizing that the building needn't be a massive hulk, but may be broken into wings.

Modern buildings are often shaped with no concern for natural light—they depend almost entirely on artificial light. But buildings which displace natural light as the major source of illumination are not fit places to spend the day.

A monster building—no concern for daylight inside.

This simple statement, if taken seriously, will make a revolution in the shape of buildings. At present, people take for granted that it is possible to use indoor space which is lit by artificial light; and buildings therefore take on all kinds of shapes and depths.

If we treat the presence of natural light as an *essential*—not optional—feature of indoor space, then no building could ever be more than 20–25 feet deep, since no point in a building which is more than about 12 or 15 feet from a window, can get good natural light.

Later on, in LIGHT ON TWO SIDES (159), we shall argue, even more sharply, that every room where people can feel comfortable must have not merely one window, but two, on different sides. This adds even further structure to the building shape: it requires not only that the building be no more than 25 feet deep, but also that its outer walls are continually broken up by corners and re-entrant corners to give every room two outside walls.

The present pattern, which requires that buildings be made up of long and narrow wings, lays the groundwork for the later pattern. Unless the building is first conceived as being made of long, thin wings, there is no possible way of introducing LIGHT ON TWO SIDES (159), in its complete form, later in the process. Therefore, we first build up the argument for this pattern, based on the human requirements for natural light, and later, in LIGHT ON TWO SIDES (159), we shall be concerned with the organization of windows within a particular room.

There are two reasons for believing that people must have buildings lit essentially by sun.

First, all over the world, people are rebelling against windowless buildings; people complain when they have to work in places without daylight. By analyzing words they use, Rapoport has shown that people are in a more positive frame of mind in rooms with windows than in rooms without windows. (Amos Rapoport, "Some Consumer Comments on a Designed Environment," *Arena*, January, 1967, pp. 176–78.) Edward Hall tells the story of a man who worked in a windowless office for some time, all the time saying that it was "just fine, just fine," and then abruptly quit. Hall says, "The issue was so deep, and so serious, that this man could not even bear to discuss it, since just discussing it would have opened the floodgates."

Second, there is a growing body of evidence which suggests that man actually *needs* daylight, since the cycle of daylight somehow plays a vital role in the maintenance of the body's circadian rhythms, and that the change of light during the day, though apparently variable, is in this sense a fundamental constant by which the human body maintains its relationship to the environment. (See, for instance, R. G. Hopkinson, *Architectural Physics: Lighting*, Department of Scientific & Industrial Research, Building Research Station, HMSO, London, 1963, pp. 116–17.) If this is true, then too much artificial light actually creates a rift between a person and his surroundings and upsets the human physiology.

Many people will agree with these arguments. Indeed, the arguments merely express precisely what all of us know already: that it is much more pleasant to be in a building lit by daylight than in one which is not. But the trouble is that many of the buildings which are built without daylight are built that way because of density. They are built compact, in the belief that it is necessary to sacrifice daylight in order to reach high densities.

Lionel March and Leslie Martin have made a major contribution to this discussion. (Leslie Martin and Lionel March, *Land Use and Built Form*, Cambridge Research, Cambridge University, April 1966.) Using the ratio of built floor area to total site area as a measure of density and the semi-depth of the building as a measure of daylight conditions, they have compared three different arrangements of building and open space, which they call S_0, S_1, and S_2.

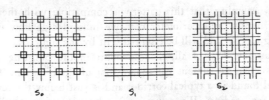

S_0 S_1 S_2

Three building types.

Of the three arrangements, S_2, in which buildings surround the outdoors with thin wings, gives the best daylight conditions

for a fixed density. It also gives the highest density for a fixed level of daylight.

There is another criticism that is often leveled against this pattern. Since it tends to create buildings which are narrow and rambling, it increases the perimeter of buildings and therefore raises building cost substantially. How big is the difference? The following figures are taken from a cost analysis of standard office buildings used by Skidmore Owings and Merrill, in the program BOP (Building Optimization). These figures illustrate costs for a typical floor of an office building and are based on costs of 21 dollars per square foot for the structure, floors, finishes, mechanical, and so on, not including exterior wall, and a cost of 110 dollars per running foot for the perimeter wall. (Costs are for 1969.)

Area (Sq. Ft.)	Shape	Perimeter Cost (S)	Perimeter Cost Per Sq. Ft. (S)	Total Cost Per Sq. Ft. (S)
15,000	120 X 125	$54,000	3.6	24.6
15,000	100 X 150	55,000	3.7	24.7
15,000	75 X 200	60,500	4.0	25.0
15,000	60 X 250	68,000	4.5	25.5
15,000	50 X 300	77,000	5.1	26.1

The extra perimeter adds little to building costs.

We see then, that at least in this one case, the cost of the extra perimeter adds very little to the cost of the building. The narrowest building costs only 6 per cent more than the squarest. We believe this case is fairly typical and that the cost savings to be achieved by square and compact building forms have been greatly exaggerated.

Now, assuming that this pattern is compatible with the problems of density and perimeter cost, we must decide how wide a building can be, and still be essentially lit by the sun.

We assume, first of all, that no point in the building should have less than 20 lumens per square foot of illumination. This is the level found in a typical corridor and is just below the level required for reading. We assume, second, that a place will only seem "naturally" lit, if more than 50 per cent of its light comes from the sky: that is, even the points furthest from the windows must be getting at least 10 lumens per square foot of their illumination from the sky.

Let us now look at a room analyzed in detail by Hopkinson and Kay. The room, a classroom, is 18 feet deep, 24 feet wide, with a window all along one side starting three feet above the floor. Walls have a reflectance of 40 per cent—a fairly typical value. With a standard sky, the desks 15 feet from the window are just getting 10 lumens per square foot from the sky—our minimum. Yet this is a rather well lit room. R. G. Hopkinson and J. G. Kay, *The Lighting of Buildings*, New York: Praeger, 1969, p. 108).

It is hard to imagine then, that many rooms more than 15 feet deep will meet our standards. Indeed, many patterns in this book will tend to reduce the window area—WINDOWS OVERLOOKING LIFE (192), NATURAL DOORS AND WINDOWS (221), DEEP REVEALS (223), SMALL PANES (239), so that in many cases rooms should be no more than 12 feet deep—more only if the walls are very light or the ceilings very high. We conclude, therefore, that a building wing that is truly a "wing of light" must be about 25 feet wide—never wider than 30 feet—with the interior rooms "one deep" along the wing. When buildings are wider than this, artificial light, of necessity, takes over.

A building which simply has to be wide—a large hall for example—can have the proper level of natural light if there are extra clerestory windows in the roof.

Therefore:

Arrange each building so that it breaks down into wings which correspond, approximately, to the most important natural social groups within the building. Make each wing long and as narrow as you can—never more than 25 feet wide.

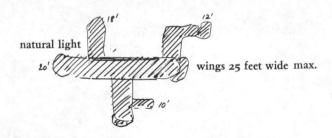

natural light   wings 25 feet wide max.

BUILDINGS

Use the wings to form outdoor areas which have a definite shape, like courts and rooms—POSITIVE OUTDOOR SPACE (106); connect the wings, whenever possible, to the existing buildings round about so that the building takes its place within a long and rambling continuous fabric—CONNECTED BUILDINGS (108). When you get further down and start defining individual rooms, make use of the daylight which the wings provide by giving each room LIGHT ON TWO SIDES (159).

Give each wing its own roof in such a way that all the wings together form a great cascade of roofs—CASCADE OF ROOFS (116); if the wing contains various houses, or workgroups, or a sequence of major rooms, build access to these rooms and groups of rooms from one side, from an arcade, or gallery, not from a central corridor—ARCADES (119), SHORT PASSAGES (132). For the load bearing structure of the wings, begin with STRUCTURE FOLLOWS SOCIAL SPACES (205). . . .

. . . this pattern helps to complete BUILDING COMPLEX (95), WINGS OF LIGHT (107), and POSITIVE OUTDOOR SPACE (106). It helps to create positive outdoor space, especially, by eliminating all the wasted areas between buildings. As you connect each building to the next you will find that you make the outdoor space positive, almost instinctively.

Isolated buildings are symptoms of a disconnected sick society.

Even in medium and high density areas where buildings are very close to each other and where there are strong reasons to connect them in a single fabric, people still insist on building isolated structures, with little bits of useless space around them.

These buildings pretend to be independent of one another— and this pretense leads to useless space around them.

Indeed, in our time, isolated, free-standing buildings are so common, that we have learned to take them for granted, without realizing that all the psycho-social disintegration of society is embodied in the fact of their existence.

It is easiest to understand this at the emotional level. The house, in dreams, most often means the self or person of the dreamer. A town of disconnected buildings, in a dream, would be a picture of society, made up of disconnected, isolated, selves. And the real towns which have this form, like dreams, embody just this meaning: they perpetuate the arrogant assumption that people stand alone and exist independently of one another.

When buildings are isolated and free standing, it is of course not necessary for the people who own them, use them, and repair them to interact with one another at all. By contrast, in a town where buildings lean against each other physically, the sheer fact of their adjacency forces people to confront their neighbors, forces them to solve the myriad of little problems which occur between them, forces them to learn how to adapt to other people's foibles, forces them to learn how to adapt to the realities outside them, which are greater, and more impenetrable than they are.

Not only is it true that connected buildings have these healthy consequences and that isolated buildings have unhealthy ones. It seems very likely—though we have no evidence to prove it—that, in fact, isolated buildings have become so popular, so automatic, so taken for granted in our time, because people seek refuge from the need to confront their neighbors, refuge from the need to work out common problems. In this sense, the isolated buildings are not only symptoms of withdrawal, but they also perpetuate and nurture the sickness.

If this is so, it is literally not too much to say that *in those parts of town where densities are relatively high,* isolated buildings, and the laws which create and enforce them, are undermining the fabric of society as forcibly and as persistently as any other social evil of our time.

By contrast, Sitte gives a beautiful discussion, with many examples, of the normal way that buildings were connected in ancient times:

The result is indeed astonishing, since from amongst 255 churches:
     41 have one side attached to other buildings
     96 have two sides attached to other buildings
    110 have three sides attached to other buildings
      2 have four sides obstructed by other buildings
     ·6 are free standing

255 churches in all; only 6 free-standing.

Regarding Rome then, it can be taken as a rule that churches were never erected as free-standing structures. Almost the same is true, in fact, for the whole of Italy. As is becoming clear, our modern attitude runs precisely contrary to this well-integrated and obviously thought-out procedure. We do not seem to think it possible that a new church can be located anywhere except in the middle of its building lot, so that there is space all around it. But this placement offers only disadvantages and not a single advantage. It is the least

favorable for building, since its effect is not concentrated anywhere but is scattered all about it. Such an exposed building will always appear like a cake on a serving-platter. To start with, any life-like organic integration with the site is ruled out. . . .

It is really a foolish fad, this craze for isolating buildings. . . . (Camillo Sitte, *City Planning According to Artistic Principles*, New York: Random House, 1965, pp. 25–31.)

A fabric of connected buildings.

Therefore:

Connect your building up, wherever possible, to the existing buildings round about. Do not keep set backs between buildings; instead, try to form new buildings as continuations of the older buildings.

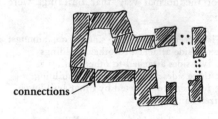

connections

❖ ❖ ❖

Connect buildings with arcades, and outdoor rooms, and court-yards where they cannot be connected physically, wall to wall— COURTYARDS WHICH LIVE (115), ARCADES (119), OUTDOOR ROOMS (163). . . .

109 LONG THIN HOUSE*

. . . for a very small house or office the pattern of WINGS OF
LIGHT (106) is almost automatically solved—no one would imagine that the house should be more than 25 feet wide. But in
such a house or office there are strong reasons to make the building even longer and thinner still. This pattern was originally
formulated by Christie Coffin.

**The shape of a building has a great effect on the relative
degrees of privacy and overcrowding in it, and this in turn
has a critical effect on people's comfort and well being.**

There is widespread evidence to show that overcrowding in
small dwellings causes psychological and social damage. (For
example, Wiliam C. Loring, "Housing Characteristics and Social Disorganization," *Social Problems*, January 1956; Chombart
de Lauwe, *Famille et Habitation*, Editions du Centre National
de la Recherche Scientifique, Paris, 1959; Bernard Lander,
Towards an Understanding of Juvenile Delinquency, New York:
Columbia University Press, 1954.) Everyone seems to be on top
of everyone else. Everything seems to be too near everything else.
Privacy for individuals or couples is almost impossible.

It would be simple to solve these problems by providing more
space—but space is expensive, and it is usually impossible to buy
more than a certain very limited amount of it. So the question is:
*For a given fixed area, which shape will create the greatest
feeling of spaciousness?*

There is a mathematical answer to this question.

The feeling of overcrowding is largely created by the mean
point-to-point distances inside a building. In a small house these
distances are small—as a result it is not possible to walk far inside
the house nor to get away from annoying disturbances; and it is
hard to get away from noise sources, even when they are in other
rooms.

To reduce this effect the building should have a shape for which the mean point-to-point distance is high. (For any given shape, we may compute the mean or average distance between two randomly chosen points within the shape). The mean point-to-point distance is low in compact shapes like circles and squares, and high in those distended shapes like long thin rectangles, and branched shapes, and tall narrow towers. These shapes increase the separation between places inside the building and therefore increase the relative privacy which people are able to get within a given area.

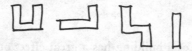

Buildings which increase the distance between points. . .

Of course, in practice there are limits on the long-thinness of a building. If it is too long and thin, the cost of walls becomes prohibitive, the cost of heating is too high, and the plan is not useful. But this is still no reason to settle only for box-like forms.

A small building can actually be much narrower than people imagine. It can certainly be much narrower than the 25 foot width proposed in WINGS OF LIGHT (107). We have seen successful buildings as narrow as 12 feet wide—indeed, Richard Neutra's own house in Los Angeles is even less.

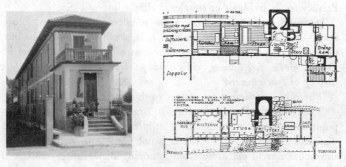

Long thin houses.

And a long thin house can also be a tower, or a pair of towers, connected at ground level. Towers, like floors can be much narrower than people realize. A building which is 12 feet square, and three stories high, with an exterior stair, makes a wonderful house. The rooms are so far apart, psychologically, that you feel as if you are in a mansion.

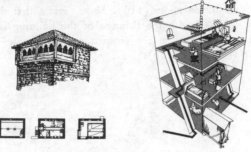

A Russian tower.

Therefore:

In small buildings, don't cluster all the rooms together around each other; instead string out the rooms one after another, so that distance between each room is as great as it can be. You can do this horizontally—so that the plan becomes a thin, long rectangle; or you can do it vertically —so that the building becomes a tall narrow tower. In either case, the building can be surprisingly narrow and still work—8, 10, and 12 feet are all quite possible.

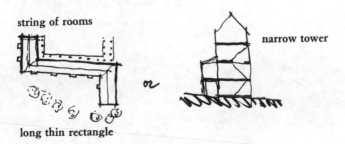

string of rooms

narrow tower

long thin rectangle

Use the long thin plan to help shape outdoor space on the site—POSITIVE OUTDOOR SPACE (106); the long perimeter of the building sets the stage for INTIMACY GRADIENT (127) and for the CASCADE OF ROOFS (116). Make certain that the privacy which is achieved with the thinness of the building is balanced with the communality at the crossroads of the house—COMMON AREAS AT THE HEART (129). . . .

*within the buildings' wings, lay out the entrances,
the gardens, courtyards, roofs and terraces: shape
both the volume of the buildings and the volume of
the space between the buildings at the same time—
remembering that indoor space and outdoor space, like
yin and yang, must always get their shape together.*

110 MAIN ENTRANCE**

. . . you have a rough position for your building on the site—SITE REPAIR (104), SOUTH FACING OUTDOORS (105), WINGS OF LIGHT (107). You also have an idea of the major circulation in the building complex and the lines of approach which lead toward the building—CIRCULATION REALMS (98), FAMILY OF ENTRANCES (102). Now it is time to fix the entrance of the building.

❖ ❖ ❖

Placing the main entrance (or main entrances) is perhaps the single most important step you take during the evolution of a building plan.

The position of main entrances controls the layout of the building. It controls movement to and from the building, and all the other decisions about layout flow from this decision. When the entrances are placed correctly, the layout of the building unfolds naturally and simply; when the entrances are badly placed, the rest of the building never seems quite right. It is therefore vital that the position of the main entrance (or entrances) be made early and correctly.

The functional problem which guides the placing of main entrances is simple. *The entrance must be placed in such a way that people who approach the bulding see the entrance or some hint of where the entrance is, as soon as they see the building itself.* This makes it possible for them to orient their movements toward the entrance as soon as they start moving toward the building, without having to change direction or change their plan of how they will approach the building.

The functional problem is rather obvious, but it is hard to overestimate the contribution it makes to a good building. We have had the experience over and again, that until this question is settled and an appropriate position chosen, a project is at a stalemate. And conversely, once the main entrances have been located and they can be felt to be in the right position, then other decisions begin to come naturally. This is true for single

Entrance shape.

543

houses, house clusters, small public buildings, large complexes of public buildings. Apparently, the pattern is basic, no matter the scale of the building.

Let us look into the functional question in more detail. Everyone finds it annoying to search around a building, or a precinct of buildings, looking for the proper entrance. When you know just where the entrance is, you don't have to bother thinking about it. It's automatic—you walk in, thinking about whatever's on your mind, looking at whatever catches your eye—you are not forced to pay attention to the environment simply to get around. Yet the entrances to many buildings are hard to find; they are not "automatic" in this sense.

There are two steps to solving the problem. First, the main entrances must be placed correctly. Second, they must be shaped so they are clearly visible.

1. Position

Consciously or unconsciously, a person walking works out his path some distance ahead, so as to take the shortest path. (See Tyrus Porter, *A Study of Path Choosing Behavior*, thesis, University of California, Berkeley, 1964). If the entrance is not visible when the building itself becomes visible, he cannot work out his path. To be able to work out his path, he must be able to see the entrance early, as soon as he sees the building.

And for other reasons too, the entrance needs to be the thing that you come to. If you have to walk a long distance along the building before you can enter, the chances are high that you will have to turn back after entering, and walk back in the direction you came from. This is not only annoying, but you may even begin to wonder whether you are going the right way and whether you haven't perhaps even missed the proper entrance. It is hard to pin this down numerically, but we suggest a threshold of some 50 feet. No one is bothered by a detour of 50 feet; if it gets much longer, it begins to be annoying.

Therefore, the first step in placing the entrances is to consider the main lines of approach to the site. Locate entrances so that, once the building(s) come into view, the entrance, too, comes into view; and the path toward the entrance is not more than 50 feet along the building.

Entrance position.

2. Shape

A person approaching a building needs to see the entrance clearly. Yet many of the people approaching the building are walking along the front of the building and parallel to it. Their angle of approach is acute. From this angle, many entrances are hardly visible. An entrance will be visible from an acute angled approach if:

　　a. The entrance sticks out beyond the building line.

　　b. The building is higher around the entrance, and this height is visible along the approach.

Entrance shape.

543

And of course, the relative color of the entrance, the light and shade immediately around it, the presence of mouldings and ornaments, may all play a part too. But above all, it is important that the entrance be strongly differentiated from its immediate surroundings.

Therefore:

Place the main entrance of the building at a point where it can be seen immediately from the main avenues of approach and give it a bold, visible shape which stands out in front of the building.

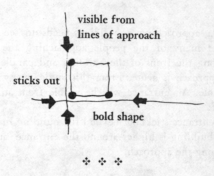

visible from
lines of approach

sticks out

bold shape

❖ ❖ ❖

If possible, make the entrance one of a family of similar entrances, so that they all stand out as visibly as possible within the street or building complex—FAMILY OF ENTRANCES (102); build that part of the entrance which sticks out, as a room, large enough to be a pleasant, light, and beautiful place—ENTRANCE ROOM (130) and bring the path between the street and this entrance room through a series of transitions of light and level and view—ENTRANCE TRANSITION (112). Make sure that the entrance has the proper relationship to parking—SHIELDED PARKING (97), CAR CONNECTION (113) . . .

I I I HALF-HIDDEN GARDEN*

. . . this pattern helps to form the fundamental layout of HOUSE CLUSTERS (37), ROW HOUSES (38), WORK COMMUNITY (41), YOUR OWN HOME (79), and BUILDING COMPLEX (95), because it influences the relative position of the buildings and their gardens. Since it affects the position of the buildings, and the shape and position of the gardens, it can also be used to help create SOUTH FACING OUTDOORS (105) and to help the general process of SITE REPAIR (104).

If a garden is too close to the street, people won't use it because it isn't private enough. But if it is too far from the street, then it won't be used either, because it is too isolated.

Start by thinking about the front gardens which you know. They are often decorative, lawns, flowers. But how often are people sitting there? Except at those special moments, when people want specifically to be watching the street, the front garden is nothing but a decoration. The half-private family groups, drinks with friends, playing ball with the children, lying in the grass—these need more protection than the typical front garden can create.

And the back gardens do not really solve the problem either. Those back gardens which are entirely isolated, entirely "in back" —are so remote from the street, that people often don't feel comfortable there either. Often the back garden is so remote from the street, that you can't hear people coming to the house; you have no sense of any larger, more open space, no sense of other people—only the enclosed, isolated, fenced-in world of one family. Children, so much more spontaneous and intuitive, give us a view in microcosm. How rarely they play in the full back garden; how much more often they prefer these side yards and gardens which have some privacy, yet also some exposure to the street.

It seems then, that the proper place for a garden is neither in front, nor fully behind. The garden needs a certain degree of privacy, yet also wants some kind of tenuous connection to the street and entrance. This balance can only be created in a situation where the garden is half in front, half in back—in a word, at the side, protected by a wall from too great an exposure to the street; and yet open enough, through paths, gates, arcades, trellises, so that people in the garden still have a glimpse of the street, a view of the front door or the path to the front door.

All this requires a revolution in the normal conception of a "lot." Lots are usually narrow along the street and deep. But to create half-hidden gardens, the lots must be long along the street, and shallow, so that each house can have a garden at its side. This gives the following archetype for house and half-hidden.

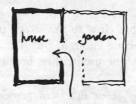

Archetype of a half-hidden garden.

There are many ways of developing this idea. One version we experienced in an old house where we once had our offices was particularly interesting.

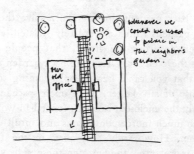

Another example.

The garden that *we* used was to the back, but behind the *next-door* house. It worked perfectly as a half-hidden garden for our house. We were able to sit there privately and have our lunch, and work on warm days, and still be in touch with the main entrance and even a glimpse of the street. But our own back garden was entirely hidden—and we never used it.

Therefore:

Do not place the garden fully in front of the house, nor fully to the back. Instead, place it in some kind of half-way position, side-by-side with the house, in a position which is half-hidden from the street, and half-exposed.

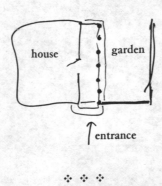

❖ ❖ ❖

If possible, use this pattern to influence the shape of house lots too, and make them as near double squares along the street as possible; build a partial wall around the garden, and locate the entrance to the house between the house and the garden, so that people in the garden can be private, yet still aware of the street, and aware of anybody coming up to the house—MAIN ENTRANCE (110), GARDEN WALL (173); allow the garden to grow wild— GARDEN GROWING WILD (172), and make the passage through, or alongside it, a major part of the transition between street and house—ENTRANCE TRANSITION (112). Half-hidden gardens may be COURTYARDS WHICH LIVE (115), ROOF GARDENS (118), or a PRIVATE TERRACE ON THE STREET (140). . . .

112 ENTRANCE TRANSITION**

. . . whatever kind of building or building complex you are making, you have a rough position for its major entrances—the gateways to the site from MAIN GATEWAYS (53); the entrances to individual buildings from FAMILY OF ENTRANCES (102), MAIN ENTRANCE (110). In every case, the entrances create a transition between the "outside"—the public world—and some less public inner world. If you have HALF-HIDDEN GARDENS (111) the gardens help to intensify the beauty of the transition. This pattern now elaborates and reinforces the transition which entrances and gardens generate.

Buildings, and especially houses, with a graceful transition between the street and the inside, are more tranquil than those which open directly off the street.

The experience of entering a building influences the way you feel inside the building. If the transition is too abrupt there is no feeling of arrival, and the inside of the building fails to be an inner sanctum.

An abrupt entrance—no transition.

The following argument may help to explain it. While people are on the street, they adopt a style of "street behavior." When they come into a house they naturally want to get rid of this street behavior and settle down completely into the more intimate spirit appropriate to a house. But it seems likely that they cannot do this unless there is a transition from one to the other which

helps them to lose the street behavior. The transition must, in effect, destroy the momentum of the closedness, tension and "distance" which are appropriate to street behavior, before people can relax completely.

Evidence comes from the report by Robert Weiss and Serge Bouterline, *Fairs, Exhibits, Pavilions, and their Audiences*, Cambridge, Mass., 1962. The authors noticed that many exhibits failed to "hold" people; people drifted in and then drifted out again within a very short time. However, in one exhibit people had to cross a huge, deep-pile, bright orange carpet on the way in. In this case, though the exhibit was no better than other exhibits, people stayed. The authors concluded that people were, in general, under the influence of their own "street and crowd behavior," and that while under this influence could not relax enough to make contact with the exhibits. But the bright carpet presented them with such a strong contrast as they walked in, that it broke the effect of their outside behavior, in effect "wiped them clean," with the result that they could then get absorbed in the exhibit.

Michael Christiano, while a student at the University of California, made the following experiment. He showed people photographs and drawings of house entrances with varying degrees of transition and then asked them which of these had the most "houseness." He found that the more changes and transitions a house entrance has, the more it seems to be "houselike." And the entrance which was judged most houselike of all is one which is approached by a long open sheltered gallery from which there is a view into the distance.

There is another argument which helps to explain the importance of the transition: people want their house, and especially the entrance, to be a private domain. If the front door is set back, and there is a transition space between it and the street, this domain is well established. This would explain why people are often unwilling to go without a front lawn, even though they do not "use it." Cyril Bird found that 90 per cent of the inhabitants of a housing project said their front gardens, which were some 20 feet deep, were just right or even too small—yet only 15 per cent of them ever used the gardens as a place to sit. ("Reactions to Radburn: A Study of Radburn Type Housing, in Hemel Hempstead," RIBA final thesis, 1960.)

So far we have spoken mainly about houses. But we believe this pattern applies to a wide variety of entrances. It certainly applies to all dwellings including apartments—even though it is usually missing from apartments today. It also applies to those public buildings which thrive on a sense of seclusion from the world: a clinic, a jewelry store, a church, a public library. It does not apply to public buildings or any buildings which thrive on the fact of being continuous with the public world.

Here are four examples of successful entrance transitions.

Each creates the transition with a different
combination of elements.

As you see from these examples, it is possible to make the transition itself in many different physical ways. In some cases, for example, it may be just inside the front door—a kind of entry court, leading to another door or opening that is more definitely inside. In another case, the transition may be formed by a bend in the path that takes you through a gate and brushes past the fuchsia on the way to the door. Or again, you might create a tran-

sition by changing the texture of the path, so that you step off the sidewalk onto a gravel path and then up a step or two and under a trellis.

In all these cases, what matters most is that the transition exists, as an actual physical place, between the outside and the inside, and that the view, and sounds, and light, and surface which you walk on change as you pass through this place. It is the physical changes—and above all the change of view—which creates the psychological transition in your mind.

Therefore:

Make a transition space between the street and the front door. Bring the path which connects street and entrance through this transition space, and mark it with a change of light, a change of sound, a change of direction, a change of surface, a change of level, perhaps by gateways which make a change of enclosure, and above all with a change of view.

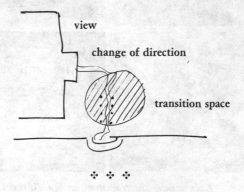

❖ ❖ ❖

Emphasize the momentary view which marks the transition by a glimpse of a distant place—ZEN VIEW (134); perhaps make a gateway or a simple garden gate to mark the entrance—GARDEN WALL (173); and emphasize the change of light—TAPESTRY OF LIGHT AND DARK (135), TRELLISED WALK (174). The transition runs right up to the front door, up to the ENTRANCE ROOM (130), and marks the beginning of the INTIMACY GRADIENT (127). . . .

113 CAR CONNECTION

. . . once you have the entrance of the building fixed and its transition clear—MAIN ENTRANCE (110), ENTRANCE TRANSITION (112)—it is necessary to work out how a person can approach the building by car. Of course, in a pedestrian precinct this will not apply; but generally the car itself must have a housing somewhere near the building; and when this is so, its place and character are critical.

❖ ❖ ❖

The process of arriving in a house, and leaving it, is fundamental to our daily lives; and very often it involves a car. But the place where cars connect to houses, far from being important and beautiful, is often off to one side and neglected.

This neglect can wreck havoc with the circulation in the house, especially in those houses with the traditional "front door and back door" relationship. Both family and visitors tend, more and more, to come and go by car. Since people always try to use the door nearest the car (see Vere Hole, et al., "Studies of 800 Houses in Conventional and Radburn Layouts," Building Research Station, Garston, Herts, England, 1966), the entrance nearest the parking spot always becomes the "main" entrance, even if it was not planned that way.

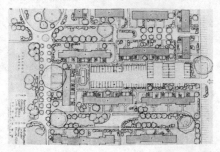

The car entrance becomes the main entrance —regardless of the plan.

If this entrance is a "back" door, then the back of the house becomes less a sanctuary for the family and perhaps the housewife feels uncomfortable about guests traipsing through. On the other hand, if this entrance is a formal "front" door, it is not really appropriate for family and good friends. In Radburn, the back doors face the parking lot, and the front doors face a pedestrian green. For families with cars, the back door, being on the car side, dominates exit and entry, yet visitors are "supposed" to come to the front door.

In order to ensure that both the kitchen and formal living room are conveniently located with respect to cars and that each space maintains its integrity in terms of use and privacy, there must be one and only one primary entrance into the house, and the kitchen and living room must be both directly accessible from this entrance. We do not mean that a house needs to have only one entrance. There is no reason why a house cannot have several entrances—indeed there are good reasons why it probably should have more than one. Secondary entrances, like patio and garden doors and teenager's private entrances, are very important. But they should never be placed so that they are in between the main entrance and the natural place to arrive by car—otherwise, they will compete with the main entrance and, again, confuse the way the house plan works.

Finally, it is essential to make something of the space which connects the house and the car, to make it a positive space—a space which supports the experience of coming and going. Essentially this means making a room out of the place for the car, the path from the car door to the house, and the front door. It may be achieved with columns, low walls, the edge of the house, plants, a trellised walk, a place to sit. This is the place we call the CAR CONNECTION (II3). A proper car connection is a place where people can walk together, lean, say goodbye; perhaps it is integrated with the structure and form of the house.

An ancient inn, built in the days of coach and horses, has a layout which treats the coach as a fundamental part of the environment and makes the connection between the two a significant part of the inn—so much so that it gives the inn its character. Airports, boathouses, stables, railway stations, all do the same. But for some reason, even though the car is so important to the

way of life in a modern house, the place where car and house meet is almost never treated seriously as a beautiful and significant place in its own right.

Therefore:

Place the parking place for the car and the main entrance, in such a relation to each other, that the shortest route from the parked car into the house, both to the kitchen and to the living rooms, is always through the main entrance. Make the parking place for the car into an actual room which makes a positive and graceful place where the car stands, not just a gap in the terrain.

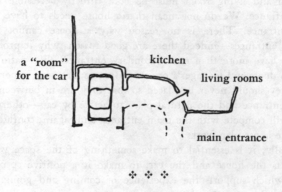

❖ ❖ ❖

Place both kitchen and main common living room just inside the main entrance—INTIMACY GRADIENT (127), COMMON AREAS AT THE HEART (129); treat the place for the car as if it were an actual outdoor room—OUTDOOR ROOM (163). If it is enclosed, build the enclosure according to STRUCTURE FOLLOWS SOCIAL SPACES (205); and make the path between this room and the front door a beautiful path, preferably the same as the one used by people who come on foot—ENTRANCE TRANSITION (112), ARCADES (119), PATHS AND GOALS (120), RAISED FLOWERS (245). If you can, put the car connection on the north face of the building—NORTH FACE (162). . . .

114 HIERARCHY OF
OPEN SPACE*

. . . the main outdoor spaces are given their character by SITE REPAIR (104), SOUTH FACING OUTDOORS (105) and POSITIVE OUTDOOR SPACE (106). But you can refine them, and complete their character by making certain that every space always has a view out into some other larger one, and that all the spaces work together to form hierarchies.

Outdoors, people always try to find a spot where they can have their backs protected, looking out toward some larger opening, beyond the space immediately in front of them.

In short, people do not sit facing brick walls—they place themselves toward the view or toward whatever there is in the distance that comes nearest to a view.

Simple as this observation is, there is almost no more basic statement to make about the way people place themselves in space. And this observation has enormous implications for the spaces in which people can feel comfortable. Essentially, it means that any place where people can feel comfortable has

1. A back.
2. A view into a larger space.

In order to understand the implications of this pattern, let us look at the three major cases where it applies.

In the very smallest of outdoor spaces, in private gardens, this pattern tells you to make a corner of the space as a "back" with a seat, looking out on the garden. If it is rightly made, this corner will be snug, but not at all claustrophobic.

Seat and garden.

558

Slightly larger in scale, there is the connection between a terrace or an outdoor room of some kind and a larger open space, the street or a square. The most common form of the pattern at this scale is the front stoop, which forms a definite enclosure and a back, off the public street.

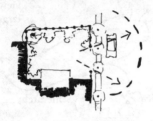

Terrace and street or square.

At the largest scale, this pattern tells you to open up public squares and greens, at one end, to great vistas. At this scale, the square itself acts as a kind of back which a person can occupy, and from which he can look out upon an even larger expanse.

Square and vista.

Therefore:

Whatever space you are shaping—whether it is a garden, terrace, street, park, public outdoor room, or courtyard, make sure of two things. First, make at least one smaller space, which looks into it and forms a natural back for it. Second, place it, and its openings, so that it looks into at least one larger space.

When you have done this, every outdoor space will have

a natural "back"; and every person who takes up the natural position, with his back to this "back," will be looking out toward some larger distant view.

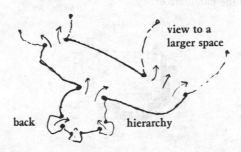

❖ ❖ ❖

For example: garden seats open to gardens—GARDEN SEAT (176), HALF-HIDDEN GARDEN (106); activity pockets open to public squares—ACTIVITY POCKETS (124), SMALL PUBLIC SQUARE (61); gardens open to local roads—PRIVATE TERRACE ON THE STREET (140), LOOPED LOCAL ROAD (49), roads open to fields—GREEN STREETS (51), ACCESSIBLE GREENS (60); fields open to the countryside, on a great vista—COMMON LAND (67), THE COUNTRYSIDE (7). Make certain that each piece of the hierarchy is arranged so that people can be comfortably settled within it, oriented out toward the next larger space. . . .

115 COURTYARDS
WHICH LIVE**

. . . within the general scheme of outdoor spaces, made positive according to the patterns POSITIVE OUTDOOR SPACE (106) and HIERARCHY OF OPEN SPACE (114), it is necessary to pay special attention to those smallest ones, less than 30 or 40 feet across—the courtyards—because it is especially easy to make them in such a way that they do not live.

The courtyards built in modern buildings are very often dead. They are intended to be private open spaces for people to use—but they end up unused, full of gravel and abstract sculptures.

Dead courtyard.

There seem to be three distinct ways in which these courtyards fail.

1. There is too little ambiguity between indoors and outdoors. If the walls, sliding doors, doors which lead from the indoors to the outdoors, are too abrupt, then there is no opportunity for a person to find himself half way between the two—and then, on the impulse of a second, to drift toward the outside. People need an ambiguous in-between realm—a porch, or a veranda, which they naturally pass onto often, as part of their ordinary life within the house, so that they can drift naturally to the outside.

2. There are not enough doors into the courtyard. If there is just one door, then the courtyard never lies between two activities inside the house; and so people are never passing through it, and enlivening it, while they go about their daily business. To overcome this, the courtyard should have doors on at least two op-

posite sides, so that it becomes a meeting point for different
activities, provides access to them, provides overflow from them,
and provides the cross-circulation between them.

3. They are too enclosed. Courtyards which are pleasant to
be in always seem to have "loopholes" which allow you to see
beyond them into some larger, further space. The courtyard
should never be perfectly enclosed by the rooms which surround
it, but should give at least a glimpse of some other space beyond.

Here are several examples of courtyards, large and small, from
various parts of the world, which are alive.

Courtyards which live.

Each one is partly open to the activity of the building that
surrounds it and yet still private. A person passing through the
courtyard and children running by can all be glimpsed and felt,
but they are not disruptive. Again, notice that all these courtyards have strong connections to other spaces. The photographs do
not tell the whole story; but still, you can see that the courtyards
look out, along paths, through the buildings, to larger spaces.
And most spectacular, notice the many different positions that
one can take up in each courtyard, depending on mood and
climate. There are covered places, places in the sun, places

spotted with filtered light, places to lie on the ground, places where a person can sleep. The edge and the corners of the courtyards are ambiguous and richly textured; in some places the walls of the buildings open, and connect the courtyard with the inside of the building, directly.

Therefore:

Place every courtyard in such a way that there is a view out of it to some larger open space; place it so that at least two or three doors open from the building into it and so that the natural paths which connect these doors pass across the courtyard. And, at one edge, beside a door, make a roofed veranda or a porch, which is continuous with both the inside and the courtyard.

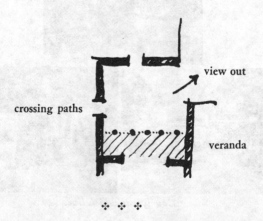

❖ ❖ ❖

Build the porch according to the patterns for ARCADE (119), GALLERY SURROUND (166), and SIX-FOOT BALCONY (167); make sure that it is in the sun—SUNNY PLACE (161); build the view out according to the HIERARCHY OF OPEN SPACE (114) and ZEN VIEW (134); make the courtyard like an OUTDOOR ROOM (163) and a GARDEN WALL (173) for more enclosure; make the height of the eaves around any courtyard of even height; if there are gable ends, hip them to make the roof edge level—ROOF LAYOUT (209); put SOMETHING ROUGHLY IN THE MIDDLE (126). . . .

116 CASCADE OF ROOFS*

. . . this pattern helps complete the BUILDING COMPLEX (95), NUMBER OF STORIES (96), MAIN BUILDING (99), and WINGS OF LIGHT (107), and it can also be used to help create these patterns. If you are designing a building from scratch, these larger patterns have already helped you to decide how high your buildings are; and they have given you a rough layout, in wings, with an idea of what spaces there are going to be in each floor of the wings. Now we come to the stage where it is necessary to visualize the building as a volume and, therefore, above all else, as a system of roofs.

Few buildings will be structurally and socially intact, unless the floors step down toward the ends of wings, and unless the roof, accordingly, forms a cascade.

This is a strange pattern. Several problems, from entirely different spheres, point in the same direction; but there is no obvious common bond which binds these different problems to one another—we have not succeeded in seizing the single kernel which forms the pivot of the pattern.

Let us observe, first, that many beautiful buildings have the form of a cascade: a tumbling arrangement of wings and lower wings and smaller rooms and sheds, often with a single highest center. Hagia Sophia, the Norwegian stave churches, and Palladio's villas are imposing and magnificent examples. Simple houses, small

Hagia Sophia

566

informal building complexes, and even clusters of mud huts are more modest ones.

What is it that makes the cascading character of these buildings so sound and so appropriate?

First of all, there is a social meaning in this form. The largest gathering places with the highest ceilings are in the middle because they are the social centers of activities; smaller groups of people, individual rooms, and alcoves fall naturally around the edges.

Second, there is a structural meaning in the form. Buildings tend to be of materials that are strong in compression; compressive strength is cheaper then tensile strength or strength in bending. Any building which stands in pure compression will tend toward the overall outline of an inverted catenary—ROOF LAYOUT (209). When a building does take this form, each outlying space acts to buttress the higher spaces. The building is stable in just the same way that a pile of earth, which has assumed the line of least resistance, is also stable.

And third, there is a practical consideration. We shall explain that ROOF GARDENS (118), wherever they occur, should not be over the top floor, but always on the same level as the rooms they serve. This means, naturally, that the building tends to get lower toward the edges since the roof gardens step down from the top toward the outer edge of the ground floor.

Why do these three apparently different problems lead to the same pattern? We don't know. But we suspect that there is some deeper essence behind the apparent coincidence. We leave the pattern intact in the hope that someone else will understand its meaning.

A sketch of Frank Lloyd Wright's.

Finally, a note on the application of the pattern. One must take care, in laying out large buildings, to make the cascade compatible with WINGS OF LIGHT (107). If you conceive of the cascade as pyramidal and the building is large, the middle section of the building will be cut off from daylight. Instead, the proper synthesis of cascades and wings of light will generate a building that tumbles down along relatively narrow wings, the wings turning corners and becoming lower where they will.

Therefore:

Visualize the whole building, or building complex, as a system of roofs.

Place the largest, highest, and widest roofs over those parts of the building which are most significant: when you come to lay the roofs out in detail, you will be able to make all lesser roofs cascade off these large roofs and form a stable self-buttressing system, which is congruent with the hierarchy of social spaces underneath the roofs.

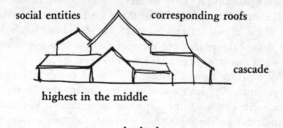

social entities   corresponding roofs

cascade

highest in the middle

❖ ❖ ❖

Make the roofs a combination of steeply pitched or domed, and flat shapes—SHELTERING ROOF (117), ROOF GARDEN (118). Prepare to place small rooms at the outside and ends of wings, and large rooms in the middle—CEILING HEIGHT VARIETY (190). Later, once the plan of the building is more exactly defined, you can lay out the roofs exactly to fit the cascade to individual rooms; and at that stage the cascade will begin to have a structural effect of great importance—STRUCTURE FOLLOWS SOCIAL SPACES (205), ROOF LAYOUT (209). . . .

117 SHELTERING ROOF**

. . . over the WINGS OF LIGHT (107), within the overall CASCADE OF ROOFS (116), some parts of the cascade are flat and some are steeply pitched or vaulted. This pattern gives the character of those parts which are steeply pitched or vaulted; the next one gives the character of those which must be flat.

The roof plays a primal role in our lives. The most primitive buildings are nothing but a roof. If the roof is hidden, if its presence cannot be felt around the building, or if it cannot be used, then people will lack a fundamental sense of shelter.

This sheltering function cannot be created by a pitched roof, or large roof, which is merely added to the top of an existing structure. The roof itself only shelters if it contains, embraces, covers, surrounds the process of living. This means very simply, that the roof must not only be large and visible, but it must also include living quarters *within* its volume, not only underneath it.

Compare the following examples. They show clearly how different roofs are, when they have living quarters within them and when they don't.

One roof lived in, the other stuck on.

The difference between these two houses comes largely from the fact that in one the roof is an integral part of the volume of the building, while in the other it is no more than a cap that has been set down on top of the building. In the first case, where the

building conveys an enormous sense of shelter, it is impossible to draw a horizontal line across the facade of the building and separate the roof from the inhabited parts of the building. But in the second case, the roof is so separate and distinct a thing, that such a line almost draws itself.

We believe that this connection between the geometry of roofs, and their capacity to provide psychological shelter, can be put on empirical grounds: first, there is a kind of evidence which shows that both children and adults naturally incline toward the sheltering roofs, almost as if they had archetypal properties. For example, here is Amos Rapoport on the subject:

. . . "roof" is a symbol of home, as in the phrase "a roof over one's head," and its importance has been stressed in a number of studies. In one study, the importance of images—i.e., symbols—for house form is stressed, and the pitched roof is said to be symbolic of shelter while the flat roof is not, and is therefore unacceptable on symbolic grounds. Another study of this subject shows the importance of these aspects in the choice of house form in England, and also shows that the pitched, tile roof is a symbol of security. It is considered, and even shown in a building-society advertisement, as an umbrella, and the houses directly reflect this view. (Amos Rapoport, *House Form and Culture*, Englewood Cliffs, N.J.: Prentice-Hall, 1969, p. 134.)

George Rand has drawn a similar point from his research. Rand finds that people are extremely conservative about their images of home and shelter. Despite 50 years of the flat roofs of the "modern movement," people still find the simple pitched roof the most powerful symbol of shelter. (George Rand, "Children's Images of Houses: A Prolegomena to the Study of Why People Still Want Pitched Roofs," *Environmental Design: Research and Practice*, Proceedings of the EDRA 3/AR 8 Conference, University of California at Los Angeles, William J. Mitchell, ed., January 1972, pp. 6–9–2 to 6–9–10.)

And the French psychiatrist, Menie Gregoire, makes the following observation about children:

At Nancy the children from the apartments were asked to draw a house. These children had been born in these apartment slabs which stand up like a house of cards upon an isolated hill. Without exception they each drew a small cottage with two windows and smoke curling up from a chimney on the roof. (M. Gregoire, "The Child in the High-Rise," *Ekistics*, May 1971, pp. 331–33.)

Such evidence as this can perhaps be dismissed on the grounds that it is culturally induced. But there is a second kind of evidence, more obvious, which lies in the simple fact of making the connection between the features of a roof and the feeling of shelter completely clear. In the passage which follows, we explain the geometric features which a roof must have in order to create an atmosphere of shelter.

1. The space under or on the roof must be useful space, space that people come into contact with daily. The whole feeling of shelter comes from the fact that the roof *surrounds* people at the same time that it covers them. You can imagine this taking either of the following forms. In both cases, the rooms under the roof are actually surrounded by the roof.

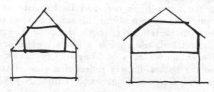

Two roof sections.

2. Seen from afar, the roof of the building must be made to form a massive part of the building. When you see the building, you see the roof. This is perhaps the most dramatic feature of a strong, sheltering roof.

What constitutes the charm to the eye of the old-fashioned country barn but its immense roof—a slope of gray shingle exposed to the weather like the side of a hill, and by its amplitude suggesting a bounty that warms the heart. Many of the old farmhouses, too, were modelled on the same generous scale, and at a distance little was visible but their great sloping roofs. They covered their inmates as a hen covereth her brood, and are touching pictures of the domestic spirit in its simpler forms. (John Burroughs, *Signs and Seasons*, New York: Houghton Mifflin, 1914, p. 252.)

3. And a sheltering roof must be placed so that one can touch it—touch it from outside. If it is pitched or vaulted, some

part of the roof must come down low to the ground, just in a place where there is a path, so that it becomes a natural thing to touch the roof edge as you pass it.

Roof edges you can touch.

Therefore:

Slope the roof or make a vault of it, make its entire surface visible, and bring the eaves of the roof down low, as low as 6′0″ or 6′6″ at places like the entrance, where people pause. Build the top story of each wing right into the roof, so that the roof does not only cover it, but actually surrounds it.

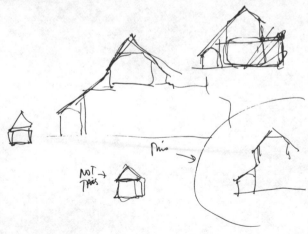

Get the exact shape of the cross section from ROOF VAULTS (220); use the space inside the top of the sloped roof for BULK STORAGE (145); where the roof comes down low, perhaps make it continuous with an ARCADE (119) or GALLERY SURROUND (166). Build the roof flat, not sloped, only where people can get out to it to use it as a garden—ROOF GARDENS (118); where rooms are built into the roof, make windows in the roof—DORMER WINDOWS (231). If the building plan is complex, get the exact way that different sloped roofs meet from ROOF LAYOUT (209). . . .

1 1 8 ROOF GARDEN*

. . . in between the sloping roofs created by SHELTERING ROOF (117), the roofs are flat where people can walk out on them. This pattern describes the best position for these roof gardens and specifies their character. If they are correctly placed, they will most often form the ends of WINGS OF LIGHT (107) at different stories and will, therefore, automatically help to complete the overall CASCADE OF ROOFS (116).

A vast part of the earth's surface, in a town, consists of roofs. Couple this with the fact that the total area of a town which can be exposed to the sun is finite, and you will realize that is is natural, and indeed essential, to make roofs which take advantage of the sun and air.

However, as we know from SHELTERING ROOF (117) and ROOF VAULTS (220), the flat shape is quite unnatural for roofs from psychological, structural, and climatic points of view. It is therefore sensible to use a flat roof only where the roof will actually become a garden or an outdoor room; to make as many of these "useful" roofs as possible; but to make all other roofs, which cannot be used, the sloping, vaulted, shell-like structures specified by SHELTERING ROOF (117) and ROOF VAULT (220).

Here is a rule of thumb: if possible, make at least one small roof garden in every building, more if you are sure people will actually use them. Make the remaining roofs steep roofs. Since, as we shall see, the roof gardens which work are almost always at the same level as some indoor rooms, this means that at least some part of the building's roofs will always be steep. We shall expect, then, that this pattern will generate a roof landscape in which roof gardens and steep roofs are mixed in almost every building.

We now consider the flat roof, briefly, on its own terms. Flat roof gardens have always been prevalent in dry, warm climates, where they can be made into livable environments. In the dense parts of towns in Mediterranean climates, nearly every roof is

576

habitable: they are full of green, private screens, with lovely views, places to cook out and eat and sleep. And even in temperate climates they are beautiful. They can be designed as rooms without ceilings, places that are protected from the wind, but open to the sky.

However, the flat roofs that have become architectural fads during the last 40 years are quite another matter. Gray gravel covered asphalt structures, these flat roofs are very rarely useful places; they are not gardens; and taken as a whole, they do not meet the psychological requirements that we have outlined in SHELTERING ROOF (117). To make the flat parts of roofs truly useful, and compatible with the need for sloping roofs, it seems necessary to build flat roof gardens off the indoor parts of the buildings. In other words, do not make them the highest part of the roof; let the highest parts of the roof slope; and make it possible to walk out to the roof garden from an interior room, without climbing special stairs. We have found that roof gardens that have this relationship are used far more intensely than those rooftops which must be reached by climbing stairs. The explanation is obvious: it is far more comfortable to walk straight out onto a roof and feel the comfort of part of the building behind and to one side of you, then it is to climb up to a place you cannot see.

Therefore:

Make parts of almost every roof system usable as roof gardens. Make these parts flat, perhaps terraced for planting, with places to sit and sleep, private places. Place the roof gardens at various stories, and always make it possible to walk directly out onto the roof garden from some lived-in part of the building.

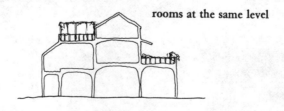

rooms at the same level

Remember to try and put the roof gardens at the open ends of
WINGS OF LIGHT (107) so as not to take the daylight away from
lower stories. Some roof gardens may be like balconys or galleries
or terraces—PRIVATE TERRACE ON THE STREET (140), GALLERY
SURROUND (166), SIX-FOOT BALCONY (167). In any case, place
the roof garden so that it is sheltered from the wind—SUNNY
PLACE (161), and give part of the roof some extra kind of shelter
—perhaps a canvas awning—so that people can stay on the roof
but keep out of the hot sun—CANVAS ROOFS (244). Treat each
individual garden much the way as any other garden, with
flowers, vegetables, outdoor rooms, canvas awnings, climbing
plants—OUTDOOR ROOMS (163), VEGETABLE GARDEN (177),
RAISED FLOWERS (245), CLIMBING PLANTS (246). . . .

when the major parts of buildings and the outdoor areas have been given their rough shape, it is the right time to give more detailed attention to the paths and squares between the buildings.

119 ARCADES**

. . . the CASCADE OF ROOFS (116) may be completed by arcades. Paths along the building, short paths between buildings, PEDESTRIAN STREET (100), paths between CONNECTED BUILDINGS (108), and parts of CIRCULATION REALMS (98) are all best as arcades. This is one of the most beautiful patterns in the language; it affects the total character of buildings as few other patterns do.

❖ ❖ ❖

Arcades—covered walkways at the edge of buildings, which are partly inside, partly outside—play a vital role in the way that people interact with buildings.

Buildings are often much more unfriendly than they need to be. They do not create the possibility of a connection with the public world outside. They do not genuinely invite the public in; they operate essentially as private territory for the people who are inside.

The problem lies in the fact that there are no strong connections between the territorial world within the building and the purely public world outside. There are no realms between the two kinds of spaces which are ambiguously a part of each—places that are both characteristic of the territory inside and, simultaneously, part of the public world.

The classic solution to this problem is the arcade: arcades create an ambiguous territory between the public world and the private world, and so make buildings friendly. But they need the following properties to be successful.

1. To make them public, the public path to the building must itself become a *place* that is partly inside the building; and this place must contain the character of the inside.

If the major paths through and beside the buildings are genuinely public, covered by an extension of the building, a low arcade, with openings into the building—many doors and windows and half-open walls—then people are drawn into the building; the action is on display, they feel tangentially a part of it. Perhaps they will watch, step inside, and ask a question.

2. To establish this place as a territory which is also *apart* from the public world, it must be felt as an extension of the building interior and therefore covered.

The arcade is the most simple and beautiful way of making such a territory. Arcades run along the building, where it meets the public world; they are open to the public, yet set partly into the building and at least seven feet deep.

3. Arcades don't work if the edges of the ceiling are too high. Keep the edges of the arcade ceilings low.

The edges of the ceiling are too high.

4. In certain cases, the effect of the arcade can be increased if the paths open to the public pass right through the building. This is especially effective in those places where the building wings are narrow—then the passage through the building need be no more than 25 feet long. It is very beautiful if these "tunnels" connect arcades on both sides of the wing. The importance of these arcades which pass right through a building, depends on the same functional effects as those described in BUILDING THOROUGHFARE (101).

Arcades which pass through buildings.

In those parts of the world where this pattern has taken hold, there are miles of linked and half-linked arcades and covered walks passing by and through the public parts of the town. This covered space then becomes the setting for much of the informal business of the city. Indeed, Rudofsky claims that such space "takes the place of the ancient forum." A good deal of his book,

Streets for People, is concerned with the arcade and the marvelous ambiguities of its space:

It simply never occurs to us to make streets into oases rather than deserts. In countries where their function has not yet deteriorated into highways and parking lots, a number of arrangements make streets fit for humans; pergole and awnings (that is, awnings spread across a street), tentlike structures, or permanent roofs. All are characteristic of the Orient, or countries with an oriental heritage, like Spain. The most refined street coverings, a tangible expression of civic solidarity—or, should one say, of philanthropy—are arcades. Unknown and unappreciated in our latitudes, the function of this singularly ingratiating feature goes far beyond providing shelter against the elements or protecting pedestrians from traffic hazards. Apart from lending unity to the streetscape, they often take the place of the ancient forums. Throughout Europe, North Africa, and Asia, arcades are a common sight because they also have been incorporated into "formal" architecture. Bologna's streets, to cite but one example, are accompanied by nearly twenty miles of portici. (Bernard Rudofsky, *Streets for People,* New York: Doubleday, 1969, p. 13.)

Simple and beautiful.

Therefore:

Wherever paths run along the edge of buildings, build arcades, and use the arcades, above all, to connect up the buildings to one another, so that a person can walk from place to place under the cover of the arcades.

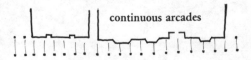

continuous arcades

Keep the arcade low—CEILING HEIGHT VARIETY (190); bring the roof of the arcade as low as possible—SHELTERING ROOF (117); make the columns thick enough to lean against—COLUMN PLACE (226); and make the openings between columns narrow and low—LOW DOORWAY (224), COLUMN CONNECTION (227)— either by arching them or by making deep beams or with lattice work—so that the inside feels enclosed—BUILDING EDGE (160), HALF-OPEN WALL (193). For construction see STRUCTURE FOLLOWS SOCIAL SPACES (205) and THICKENING THE OUTER WALLS (211). . . .

. . . once buildings and arcades and open spaces have been roughly fixed by BUILDING COMPLEX (95), WINGS OF LIGHT (107), POSITIVE OUTDOOR SPACE (106), ARCADES (119)—it is time to pay attention to the paths which run between the buildings. This pattern shapes these paths and also helps to give more detailed form to DEGREES OF PUBLICNESS (36), NETWORK OF PATHS AND CARS (52), and CIRCULATION REALMS (98).

❖ ❖ ❖

The layout of paths will seem right and comfortable only when it is compatible with the process of walking. And the process of walking is far more subtle than one might imagine.

Essentially there are three complementary processes:

1. As you walk along you scan the landscape for intermediate destinations—the furthest points along the path which you can see. You try, more or less, to walk in a straight line toward these points. This naturally has the effect that you will cut corners and take "diagonal" paths, since these are the ones which often form straight lines between your present position and the point which you are making for.

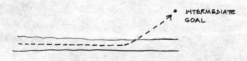

Path to a goal.

2. These intermediate destinations keep changing. The further you walk, the more you can see around the corner. If you always walk straight toward this furthest point and the furthest point keeps changing, you will actually move in a slow curve, like a missile tracking a moving target.

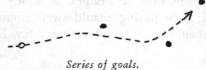

Series of goals.

3. Since you do not want to keep changing direction while you walk and do not want to spend your whole time re-calculating your best direction of travel, you arrange your walking process in such a way that you pick a temporary "goal"—some clearly visible landmark—which is more or less in the direction you want to take and then walk in a straight line toward it for a hundred yards, then, as you get close, pick another new goal, once more a hundred yards further on, and walk toward it. . . . You do this so that in between, you can talk, think, daydream, smell the spring, without having to think about your walking direction every minute.

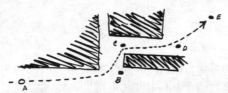

The actual path.

In the diagram above a person begins at A and heads for point E. Along the way, his intermediate goals are points B, C, and D. Since he is trying to walk in a roughly straight line toward E, his intermediate goal changes from B to C, as soon as C is visible; and from C to D, as soon as D is visible.

The proper arrangements of paths is one with enough intermediate goals, to make this process workable. If there aren't enough intermediate goals, the process of walking becomes more difficult, and consumes unnecessary emotional energy.

Therefore:

To lay out paths, first place goals at natural points of interest. Then connect the goals to one another to form the

paths. The paths may be straight, or gently curving between goals; their paving should swell around the goal. The goals should never be more than a few hundred feet apart.

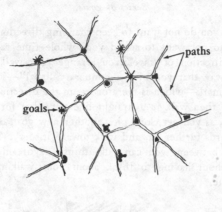

❖ ❖ ❖

All the ordinary things in the outdoors—trees, fountains, entrances, gateways, seats, statues, a swing, an outdoor room—can be the goals. See FAMILY OF ENTRANCES (102), MAIN ENTRANCE (110), TREE PLACES (171), SEAT SPOTS (241), RAISED FLOWERS (245); build the "goals" according to the rules of SOMETHING ROUGHLY IN THE MIDDLE (126); and shape the paths according to PATH SHAPE (121). To pave the paths use PAVING WITH CRACKS BETWEEN THE STONES (247). . . .

121 PATH SHAPE*

. . . paths of various kinds have been defined by larger patterns—PROMENADE (31), SHOPPING STREET (32), NETWORK OF PATHS AND CARS (52), RAISED WALK (55), PEDESTRIAN STREET (100), and PATHS AND GOALS (120). This pattern defines their shape: and it can also help to generate these larger patterns piecemeal, through the very process of shaping parts of the path.

❖ ❖ ❖

Streets should be for staying in, and not just for moving through, the way they are today.

For centuries, the street provided city dwellers with usable public space right outside their houses. Now, in a number of subtle ways, the modern city has made streets which are for "going through," not for "staying in." This is reinforced by regulations which make it a crime to loiter, by the greater attractions inside the side itself, and by streets which are so unattractive to stay in, that they almost force people into their houses.

From an environmental standpoint, the essence of the problem is this: streets are "centrifugal" not "centripetal": they drive people out instead of attracting them in. In order to combat this effect, the pedestrian world outside houses must be made into the kind of place where you stay, rather than the kind of place you move through. It must, in short, be made like a kind of outside public room, with a greater sense of enclosure than a street.

This can be accomplished if we make residential pedestrian streets subtly convex in plan with seats and galleries around the edges, and even sometimes roof the streets with beams or trelliswork.

Here are two examples of this pattern, at two different scales. First, we show a plan of ours for fourteen houses in Peru. The street shape is created by gradually stepping back the houses, in plan. The result is a street with a positive, somewhat elliptical shape. We hope it is a place that will encourage people to slow down and spend time there.

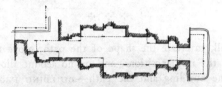

The path shape formed by fourteen houses.

The second example is a very small path, cutting through a neighborhood in the hills of Berkeley. Again, the shape swells out subtly, just in those places where it is good to pause and sit.

A spot along a path in the hills of Berkeley.

Therefore:

Make a bulge in the middle of a public path, and make the ends narrower, so that the path forms an enclosure which is a place to stay, not just a place to pass through.

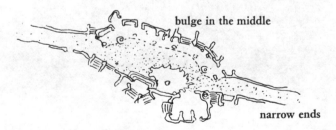

bulge in the middle

narrow ends

591

Above all, to create the shape of the path, move the building fronts into the right positions, and on no acount allow a set-back between the building and the path—BUILDING FRONTS (122); decide on the appropriate area for the "bulge" by using the arithmetic of PEDESTRIAN DENSITY (123); then form the details of the bulge with ARCADES (119), ACTIVITY POCKETS (124) and STAIR SEATS (125); perhaps even with a PUBLIC OUTDOOR ROOM (69); and give as much life as you can to the path all along its length with windows—STREET WINDOWS (164). . . .

122 BUILDING FRONTS*

. . . this pattern helps to shape the paths and buildings simultaneously; and so completes BUILDING COMPLEX (95), WINGS OF LIGHT (107), POSITIVE OUTDOOR SPACE (106), ARCADES (119), PATH SHAPE (121), and also ACTIVITY POCKETS (124).

❖ ❖ ❖

Building set-backs from the street, originally invented to protect the public welfare by giving every building light and air, have actually helped greatly to destroy the street as a social space.

In POSITIVE OUTDOOR SPACE (106) we have described the fact that buildings are not merely placed into the outdoors, but that they actually shape the outdoors. Since streets and squares have such enormous social importance, it is natural to pay close attention to the way that they are shaped by building fronts.

The early twentieth-century urge for "cleanliness" at all costs, and the social efforts to clean up slums, led social reformers to pass laws which make it necessary to place buildings several feet back from the street edge, to make sure that buildings cannot crowd the street and cut off sunshine, light, and air.

But, the set backs have destroyed the streets. Since it is possible to guarantee plenty of air and sun in buildings and streets in other ways—see, for example, FOUR-STORY LIMIT (21) and WINGS OF LIGHT (107)—it is essential to build the front of buildings on the street, so that the streets which they create are usable.

Finally, note that the positive shape of the street cannot be achieved by merely staggering building fronts. If the building fronts are adjusted to the shape of the outdoors, they will almost always take on a variety of slightly uneven angles.

Slight angles in the building fronts.

Therefore:

On no account allow set-backs between streets or paths or public open land and the buildings which front on them. The set-backs do nothing valuable and almost always destroy the value of the open areas between the buildings. Build right up to the paths; change the laws in all communities where obsolete by-laws make this impossible. And let the building fronts take on slightly uneven angles as they accommodate to the shape of the street.

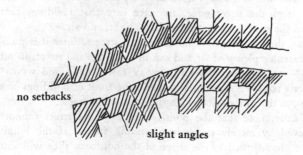

no setbacks

slight angles

❖ ❖ ❖

Detail the fronts of buildings, indeed the whole building perimeter, according to the pattern BUILDING EDGE (160). If some outdoor space is needed at the front of the building, make it part of the street life by making it a PRIVATE TERRACE ON THE STREET (140) or GALLERY SURROUND (166); and give the building many openings onto the street—STAIR SEATS (125), OPEN STAIRS (158), STREET WINDOWS (164), OPENING TO THE STREET (165), FRONT DOOR BENCH (242). . . .

123 PEDESTRIAN DENSITY*

. . . in various places there are pedestrian areas, paved so that people will congregate there or walk up and down—PROMENADE (31), SMALL PUBLIC SQUARES (61), PEDESTRIAN STREET (100), BUILDING THOROUGHFARE (101), PATH SHAPE (121). It is essential to limit the sizes of these places very strictly, especially the size of areas which are paved, so that they stay alive.

❖ ❖ ❖

Many of our modern public squares, though intended as lively plazas, are in fact deserted and dead.

In this pattern, we call attention to the relationship between the number of people in a pedestrian area, the size of the area, and a subjective estimate of the extent to which the area is alive.

We do not say categorically that the number of people per square foot *controls* the apparent liveliness of a pedestrian area. Other factors—the nature of the land around the edge, the grouping of people, what the people are doing—obviously contribute greatly. People who are running, especially if they are making noise, add to the liveliness. A small group attracted to a couple of folk singers in a plaza give much more life to the place than the same number sunning on the grass.

However, the number of square feet per person does give a reasonably crude estimate of the liveliness of a space. Christie Coffin's observations show the following figures for various public places in and around San Francisco. Her estimate of the liveliness of the places is given in the right-hand column.

	Sq. ft. per person	
Golden Gate Plaza, noon:	1000	Dead
Fresno Mall:	100	Alive
Sproul Plaza, daytime:	150	Alive
Sproul Plaza, evening:	2000	Dead
Union Square, central part:	600	Half-dead

Although these subjective estimates are clearly open to question, they suggest the following rule of thumb: At 150 square feet per person, an area is lively. If there are more than 500 square feet per person, the area begins to be dead.

Even if these figures are only correct to within an order of magnitude, we can use them to shape public pedestrian areas—squares, indoor streets, shopping streets, promenades.

To use the pattern it is essential to make a rough estimate of the number of people that are *typically* found in a given space at any moment of its use. In the front area of a market, for example, we might find that typically there are three people lingering and walking. Then we shall want the front of this market to form a little square, no larger than 450 square feet. If we estimate a pedestrian street will typically contain 35 people window shopping and walking, we shall want the street to form an enclosure of roughly 5000 square feet. (For an example of this calculation in a more complicated case—the case of a square in a public building that has yet to be built—see *A Pattern Language Which Generates Multi-Service Centers*, Alexander, Ishikawa, Silverstein, Center for Environmental Structure, 1968, p. 148.)

Therefore:

For public squares, courts, pedestrian streets, any place where crowds are drawn together, estimate the mean number of people in the place at any given moment (P), and make the area of the place between 150P and 300P square feet.

average number of people, P

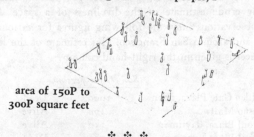

area of 150P to
300P square feet

❖ ❖ ❖

Embellish the density and feeling of life with areas at the edge which are especially crowded—STREET CAFE (88), ACTIVITY POCKETS (124), STAIR SEATS (125), PRIVATE TERRACE ON THE STREET (140), BUILDING EDGE (160), STREET WINDOWS (164), OPENING TO THE STREET (165), GALLERY SURROUND (166). . . .

124 ACTIVITY POCKETS**

. . . in many large scale patterns which define public space, the edge is critical: PROMENADE (31), SMALL PUBLIC SQUARES (61), PUBLIC OUTDOOR ROOM (69), PEDESTRIAN STREET (100), BUILDING THOROUGHFARE (101), PATH SHAPE (121). This pattern helps complete the edge of all these larger patterns.

The life of a public square forms naturally around its edge. If the edge fails, then the space never becomes lively.

In more detail: people gravitate naturally toward the edge of public spaces. They do not linger out in the open. If the edge does not provide them with places where it is natural to linger, the space becomes a place to walk through, not a place to stop. It is therefore clear that a public square should be surrounded by pockets of activity: shops, stands, benches, displays, rails, courts, gardens, news racks. In effect, the edge must be scalloped.

Further, the process of lingering is a gradual one; it happens; people do not make up their minds to stay; they stay or go, according to a process of gradual involvement. This means that the various pockets of activity around the edge should all be next to paths and entrances so that people pass right by them as they pass through. The goal-oriented activity of coming and going then has a chance to turn gradually into something more relaxed. And once many small groups form around the edge, it is likely that they will begin to overlap and spill in toward the center of the square. We therefore specify that pockets of activity must alternate with access points.

A conceptual diagram.

The scalloped edge must surround the space entirely. We may see this clearly as follows: draw a circle to represent the space, and darken some part of its perimeter to stand for the scalloped edge. Now draw chords which join different points along this darkened perimeter. As the length of the darkened edge gets smaller, the area of the space covered by these chords wanes drastically. This shows how quickly the life in the space will drop when the length of the scalloped edge gets shorter. To make the space lively, the scalloped edge must surround the space completely.

As the activities grow around the space,
it becomes more lively.

When we say that the edge must be scalloped with activity, we mean this conceptually—not literally. In fact, to build this pattern, you must build the activity pockets *forward* into the square: first rough out the major paths that cross the space and the spaces left over between these paths; then build the activity pockets into these "in-between" spaces, bringing them forward, into the square.

A pocket of activity which bulges into the square.

Therefore:

Surround public gathering places with pockets of activity —small, partly enclosed areas at the edges, which jut for-

ward into the open space between the paths, and contain activities which make it natural for people to pause and get involved.

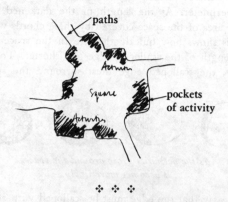

❖ ❖ ❖

Lead paths between the pockets of activity—PATHS AND GOALS (120)—and shape the pockets themselves with arcades and seats, and sitting walls, and columns and trellises—ARCADES (119), OUTDOOR ROOM (163), TRELLISED WALK (174), SEAT SPOTS (241), SITTING WALL (243); above all shape them with the fronts of buildings—BUILDING FRONTS (122); and include, within the pockets, newsstands—BUS STOPS (92), FOOD STANDS (93), gardens, games, small shops, STREET CAFES (88), and A PLACE TO WAIT (150). . . .

125 STAIR SEATS*

. . . we know that paths and larger public gathering places need a definite shape and a degree of enclosure, with people looking into them, not out of them—SMALL PUBLIC SQUARES (61), POSITIVE OUTDOOR SPACE (106), PATH SHAPE (121). Stairs around the edge do it just perfectly; and they also help embellish FAMILY OF ENTRANCES (102), MAIN ENTRANCES (110), and OPEN STAIRS (158).

Wherever there is action in a place, the spots which are the most inviting, are those high enough to give people a vantage point, and low enough to put them in action.

On the one hand, people seek a vantage point from which they can take in the action as a whole. On the other hand, they still want to be part of the action; they do not want to be mere onlookers. Unless a public space provides for both these tendencies, a lot of people simply will not stay there.

For a person looking at the horizon, the visual field is far larger below the horizon than above it. It is therefore clear that anybody who is "people-watching" will naturally try to take up a position a few feet above the action.

The trouble is that this position will usually have the effect of removing a person from the action. Yet most people want to be able to take the action in and to be part of it at the same time. This means that any places which are slightly elevated must also be within easy reach of passers-by, hence on circulation paths, and directly accessible from below.

The bottom few steps of stairs, and the balusters and rails along stairs, are precisely the kinds of places which resolve these tendencies. People sit on the edges of the lower steps, if they are wide enough and inviting, and they lean against the rails.

There is a simple kind of evidence, both for the reality of the forces described here and for the value of the pattern. When there are areas in public places which are both slightly raised and very accessible, people naturally gravitate toward them.

Stepped cafe terraces, steps surrounding public plazas, stepped porches, stepped statues and seats, are all examples.

Therefore:

In any public place where people loiter, add a few steps at the edge where stairs come down or where there is a change of level. Make these raised areas immediately accessible from below, so that people may congregate and sit to watch the goings-on.

public place

stair seats

❖ ❖ ❖

Give the stair seats the same orientation as SEAT SPOTS (241). Make the steps out of wood or tile or brick so that they wear with time, and show the marks of feet, and are soft to the touch for people sitting on them—SOFT TILE AND BRICK (248); and make the steps connect directly to surrounding buildings—CONNECTION TO THE EARTH (168). . . .

126 SOMETHING ROUGHLY
IN THE MIDDLE

. . . SMALL PUBLIC SQUARES (61), COMMON LAND (67), COURT-YARDS WHICH LIVE (115), PATH SHAPE (121) all draw their life from the activities around their edges—ACTIVITY POCKETS (124) and STAIR SEATS (125). But even then, the middle is still empty, and it needs embellishment.

❖ ❖ ❖

A public space without a middle is quite likely to stay empty.

We have discussed the fact that people tend to take up positions from which they are protected, partly, at their backs—HIERARCHY OF OPEN SPACE (114), and the way this fact tends to make the action grow around the edge of public squares—ACTIVITY POCKETS (124), STAIR SEATS (125). If the space is a tiny one, there is no need for anything beyond an edge. But if there is a reasonable area in the middle, intended for public use, it will be wasted unless there are trees, monuments, seats, fountains—a place where people can protect their backs, as easily as they can around the edge. This reason for setting something roughly in the middle of a square is obvious and practical. But perhaps there is an even more primitive instinct at work.

Imagine a bare table in your house. Think of the power of the instinct which tells you to put a candle or a bowl of flowers in the middle. And think of the power of the effect once you have done it. Obviously, it is an act of great significance; yet clearly it has nothing to do with activities at the edge or in the center.

Apparently the effect is purely geometrical. Perhaps it is the sheer fact that the space of the table is given a center, and the point at the center then organizes the space around it, and makes it clear, and puts it roughly at rest. The same thing happens in a courtyard or a public square. It is perhaps related to the man-

dala instinct, which finds in any centrally symmetric figure a powerful receptacle for dreams and images and for conjugations of the self. We believe that this instinct is at work in every courtyard and every square. Even in the Piazza San Marco, one of the few squares without an obvious center piece, the campanile juts out and creates an off beat center to the two plazas together.

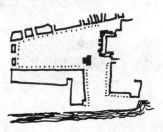

The campanile forms a rough center to the two piazzas.

Camillo Sitte, the great Italian planner, describes the evolution of such focal points and their functional significance in his book *City Planning According to Artistic Principles* (New York: Random House, 1965, pp. 20–31). But interestingly, he claims that the impulse to center something *perfectly* in a square is an "affliction" of modern times.

Imagine the open square of a small market town in the country, covered with deep snow and criss-crossed by several roads and paths that, shaped by the traffic, form the natural lines of communication. Between them are left irregularly distributed patches untouched by traffic. . . .
On exactly such spots, undisturbed by the flow of vehicles, rose the fountains and monuments of old communities. . . .

Therefore:

Between the natural paths which cross a public square or courtyard or a piece of common land choose something to stand roughly in the middle: a fountain, a tree, a statue, a clock-tower with seats, a windmill, a bandstand. Make

it something which gives a strong and steady pulse to the square, drawing people in toward the center. Leave it exactly where it falls between the paths; resist the impulse to put it exactly in the middle.

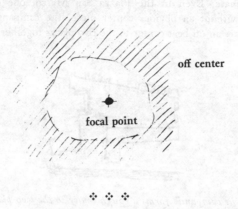

off center

focal point

❖ ❖ ❖

Connect the different "somethings" to one another with the path system—PATHS AND GOALS (120). They may include HIGH PLACES (62), DANCING IN THE STREETS (63), POOLS AND STREAMS (64), PUBLIC OUTDOOR ROOM (69), STILL WATER (71), TREE PLACES (171); make sure that each one has a SITTING WALL (243) around it. . . .

Now, with the paths fixed, we come back to the building: Within the various wings of any one building, work out the fundamental gradients of space, and decide how the movement will connect the spaces in the gradients;

127 INTIMACY GRADIENT**

. . . if you know roughly where you intend to place the building wings—WINGS OF LIGHT (107), and how many stories they will have—NUMBER OF STORIES (96), and where the MAIN ENTRANCE (110) is, it is time to work out the rough disposition of the major areas on every floor. In every building the relationship between the public areas and private areas is most important.

Unless the spaces in a building are arranged in a sequence which corresponds to their degrees of privateness, the visits made by strangers, friends, guests, clients, family, will always be a little awkward.

In any building—house, office, public building, summer cottage—people need a gradient of settings, which have different degrees of intimacy. A bedroom or boudoir is most intimate; a back sitting room or study less so; a common area or kitchen more public still; a front porch or entrance room most public of all. When there is a gradient of this kind, people can give each encounter different shades of meaning, by choosing its position on the gradient very carefully. In a building which has its rooms so interlaced that there is no clearly defined gradient of intimacy, it is not possible to choose the spot for any particular encounter so carefully; and it is therefore impossible to give the encounter this dimension of added meaning by the choice of space. This homogeneity of space, where every room has a similar degree of intimacy, rubs out all possible subtlety of social interaction in the building.

We illustrate this general fact by giving an example from Peru—a case which we have studied in detail. In Peru, friendship is taken very seriously and exists at a number of levels. Casual neighborhood friends will probably never enter the house at all.

Formal friends, such as the priest, the daughter's boyfriend, and friends from work may be invited in, but tend to be limited to a well-furnished and maintained part of the house, the *sala*. This room is sheltered from the clutter and more obvious informality of the rest of the house. Relatives and intimate friends may be made to feel at home in the family room (*comedor-estar*), where the family is likely to spend much of its time. A few relatives and friends, particularly women, will be allowed into the kitchen, other workspaces, and, perhaps, the bedrooms of the house. In this way, the family maintains both privacy and pride.

The phenomenon of the intimacy gradient is particularly evident at the time of a *fiesta*. Even though the house is full of people, some people never get beyond the *sala;* some do not even get beyond the threshold of the front door. Others go all the way into the kitchen, where the cooking is going on, and stay there throughout the evening. Each person has a very accurate sense of his degree of intimacy with the family and knows exactly how far into the house he may penetrate, according to this established level of intimacy.

Even extremely poor people try to have a *sala* if they can: we saw many in the *barriadas*. Yet modern houses and apartments in Peru combine *sala* and family room in order to save space. Almost everyone we talked to complained about this situation. As far as we can tell, a Peruvian house must not, under any circumstances, violate the principle of the intimacy gradient.

The intimacy gradient is unusually crucial in a Peruvian house. But in some form the pattern seems to exist in almost all cultures. We see it in widely different cultures—compare the plan of an African compound, a traditional Japanese house, and early American colonial homes—and it also applies to almost every building type—compare a house, a small shop, a large office building, and even a church. It is almost an archetypal ordering principle for all man's buildings. All buildings, and all parts of buildings which house well-defined human groups, need a definite gradient from "front" to "back," from the most formal spaces at the front to the most intimate spaces at the back.

In an office the sequence might be: entry lobby, coffee and reception areas, offices and workspaces, private lounge.

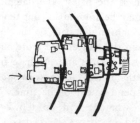

Office intimacy gradient.

In a small shop the sequence might be: shop entrance, customer milling space, browsing area, sales counter, behind the counter, private place for workers.

In a house: gate, outdoor porch, entrance, sitting wall, common space and kitchen, private garden, bed alcoves.

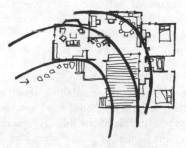

Intimacy gradient in a house.

And in a more formal house, the sequence might begin with something like the Peruvian *sala*—a parlor or sitting room for guests.

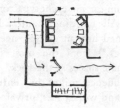

Formal version of the front of the gradient.

Therefore:

Lay out the spaces of a building so that they create a sequence which begins with the entrance and the most public parts of the building, then leads into the slightly more private areas, and finally to the most private domains.

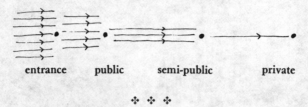

entrance　　public　　semi-public　　private

❖ ❖ ❖

At the same time that common areas are to the front, make sure that they are also at the heart and soul of the activity, and that all paths between more private rooms pass tangent to the common ones—COMMON AREAS AT THE HEART (129). In private houses make the ENTRANCE ROOM (130) the most formal and public place and arrange the most private areas so that each person has a room of his own, where he can retire to be alone—A ROOM OF ONE'S OWN (141). Place bathing rooms and toilets half-way between the common areas and the private ones, so that people can reach them comfortably from both—BATHING ROOM (144); and place sitting areas at all the different degrees of intimacy, and shape them according to their position in the gradient—SEQUENCE OF SITTING SPACES (142). In offices put RECEPTION WELCOMES YOU (149) at the front of the gradient and HALF-PRIVATE OFFICE (152) at the back. . . .

128 INDOOR SUNLIGHT*

. . . according to SOUTH FACING OUTDOORS (105), the building is placed in such a way as to allow the sun to shine directly into it, across its gardens. From INTIMACY GRADIENT (127), you have some idea of the overall distribution of public and private rooms within the building. This pattern marks those rooms and areas along the intimacy gradient which need the sunlight most, and helps to place them so that the indoor sunlight can be made to coincide with the rooms in the INTIMACY GRADIENT which are most used.

❖ ❖ ❖

If the right rooms are facing south, a house is bright and sunny and cheerful; if the wrong rooms are facing south, the house is dark and gloomy.

Everyone knows this. But people may forget about it, and get confused by other considerations. The fact is that very few things have so much effect on the feeling inside a room as the sun shining into it. If you want to be sure that your house, or building, and the rooms in it are wonderful, comfortable places, give this pattern its due. Treat it seriously; cling to it tenaciously; insist upon it. Think of the rooms you know which do have sunshine in them, and compare them with the many rooms you know that don't.

From the pattern SOUTH FACING OUTDOORS (105), the building gets an orientation toward the south. Now the issue is the particular arrangement of rooms along this south edge. Here are some examples: (1) a porch that gets the evening sun late in the day; (2) a breakfast nook that looks directly into a garden which is sunny in the morning; (3) a bathing room arranged to get full morning sun; (4) a workshop that gets full southern exposure during the middle of the day; (5) an edge of a living room where the sun falls on an outside wall and warms a flowering plant.

The key diagram for this pattern summarizes the relations between parts of the house and the morning, the afternoon and

the late afternoon sun. To get the sun right in your design, first decide upon your requirements for sun: make a diagram for yourself, like the key diagram, but with your own special needs. Then arrange spaces along the south, southeast, and southwest of the building to capture the sun. Take special care to detail the south edge properly, so that the sun is working indoors throughout the day. This will most often need a building which is long along the east-west axis.

If we approach the problem of indoor sunlight from the point of view of thermal considerations, we come to a similar conclusion. A long east-west axis sets up a building to keep the heat in during winter, and to keep the heat out during the summer. This makes buildings more pleasant, and cheaper to run. The "optimum shape" of an east-west building is given by the following table, adapted from Victor Olgyay, *Design with Climate* (New Jersey: Princeton University Press, 1963, p. 89). Note that it is always best to orient the long axis east-west.

climate	summer optimum	winter optimum	composite optimum	reasonable efficiency
cool (Minneapolis)	1.4	1.1	1.1	1.3
temperate (New York)	1.63	1.56	1.6	2.4
hot-arid (Phoenix)	1.26	none	1.3	1.6
hot-humid (Miami)	1.7	2.69	1.7	3.0

Rough shape for different climates.

Therefore:

Place the most important rooms along the south edge of the building, and spread the building out along the east-west axis.

Fine tune the arrangement so that the proper rooms are exposed to the south-east and the south-west sun. For example: give the common area a full southern exposure, bedrooms south-east, porch south-west. For most climates, this means the shape of the building is elongated east-west.

south-facing rooms

❖ ❖ ❖

When you can, open up these indoor sunny rooms to the outdoors, and build a sunny place and outdoor rooms directly outside—SUNNY PLACE (161), OUTDOOR ROOM (163), WINDOWS WHICH OPEN WIDE (236). Give the bedrooms eastern exposure—SLEEPING TO THE EAST (138), and put storage and garages to the north—NORTH FACE (162). Where there is a kitchen, try to put its work counter toward the sun—SUNNY COUNTER (199); perhaps do the same for any work bench or desk in a HOME WORKSHOP (157), WORKSPACE ENCLOSURE (183). . . .

129 COMMON AREAS
AT THE HEART**

. . . along the INTIMACY GRADIENT (127), in every building and in every social group within the building, it is necessary to place the common areas. Place them on the sunlit side to reinforce the pattern of INDOOR SUNLIGHT (128); and, when they are large, give them the higher roofs of the CASCADE OF ROOFS (116).

❖ ❖ ❖

No social group—whether a family, a work group, or a school group—can survive without constant informal contact among its members.

Any building which houses a social group supports this kind of contact by providing common areas. The form and location of the common areas is critical. Here is a perfect example—a description of the family room in a Peruvian worker's house:

For a low-income Peruvian family, the family room is the heart of family life. The family eat here, they watch TV here, and everyone who comes into the house comes into this room to say hello to the others, kiss them, shake hands with them, exchange news. The same happens when people leave the house.

The family room functions as the heart of the family life by helping to support these processes. The room is so placed in the house, that people naturally pass through it on their way into and out of the house. The end where they pass through it allows them to linger for a few moments, without having to pull out a chair to sit down. The TV set is at the opposite end of the room from this throughway, and a glance at the screen is often the excuse for a moment's further lingering. The part of the room for the TV set is often darkened; the family room and the TV function just as much during midday as they do at night.

Let us now generalize from this example. If a common area is

located at the end of a corridor and people have to make a special, deliberate effort to go there, they are not likely to use it informally and spontaneously.

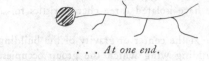

. . . At one end.

Alternatively, if the circulation path cuts too deeply through the common area, the space will be too exposed, it will not be comfortable to linger there and settle down.

. . . Through the middle.

The only balanced situation is the one where a common path, which people use every day, runs *tangent* to the common areas and is open to them in passing. Then people will be constantly passing the space; but because the path is to one side, they are not forced to stop. If they want to, they can keep going. If they want to, they can stop for a moment, and see what's happening; if they want to, they can come right in and settle down.

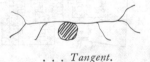

. . . Tangent.

It is worth mentioning, that this pattern has occurred, in some form, in every single project we have worked on. In the multi-service center, we had a pattern called *Staff lounge* based on the same geometry (*A pattern language which generates multi-service centers*, C.E.S., 1968, p. 241); in our work on mental health centers, we had *Patient's choice of being involved*, the same pattern again, as an essential element in therapy; in our work on Peruvian housing, we had *Family room circulation*—this is the example we have given for a family (*Houses generated by patterns*, C.E.S., 1969, p. 140); and in our work on universities, *The*

Oregon Experiment, we had a pattern called *Department hearth,* again the same, for each department. It is perhaps the most basic pattern there is in forming group cohesion.

In detail, we have isolated three characteristics for a successful common area:

1. It must be at the center of gravity of the building complex, building, or building wing which the group occupies. In other words, it must be at the physical heart of the organization, so that it is equally accessible to everyone and can be felt as the center of the group.

2. Most important of all, it must be "on the way" from the entrance to private rooms, so people always go by it on the way in and out of the building. It is crucial that it not be a dead-end room which one would have to go out of one's way to get to. For this reason, the paths which pass it must lie tangent to it.

The common area of a clinic we have built in Modesto, California, where we managed to put tangent paths on all four sides.

3. It must have the right components in it—usually a kitchen and eating space, since eating is one of the most communal of activities, and a sitting space—at least some comfortable chairs, so people will feel like staying. It should also include an outdoor area—on nice days there is always the longing to be outside— to step out for a smoke, to sit down on the grass, to carry on a discussion.

Therefore:

Create a single common area for every social group. Locate it at the center of gravity of all the spaces the group occupies, and in such a way that the paths which go in and out of the building lie tangent to it.

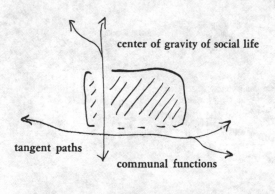

center of gravity of social life

tangent paths

communal functions

❖ ❖ ❖

Most basic of all to common areas are food and fire. Include FARMHOUSE KITCHEN (139), COMMUNAL EATING (147), and THE FIRE (181). For the shape of the common area in fine detail, see LIGHT ON TWO SIDES OF EVERY ROOM (159) and THE SHAPE OF INDOOR SPACE (191). Make sure that there are plenty of different sitting places, different in character for different kinds of moments—SEQUENCE OF SITTING SPACES (142). Include an OUTDOOR ROOM (163). And make the paths properly tangent to the common areas—ARCADES (119), THE FLOW THROUGH ROOMS (131), SHORT PASSAGES (132). . . .

130 ENTRANCE ROOM**

. . . the position and overall shape of entrances is given by FAMILY OF ENTRANCES (102), MAIN ENTRANCE (110) and ENTRANCE TRANSITION (112). This pattern gives the entrances their detailed shape, their shape and body and three dimensions, and helps complete the form begun by CAR CONNECTION (113), and the PRIVATE TERRACE ON THE STREET (140).

✣ ✣ ✣

Arriving in a building, or leaving it, you need a room to pass through, both inside the building and outside it. This is the entrance room.

The most impressionistic and intuitive way to describe the need for the entrance room is to say that the time of arriving, or leaving, seems to swell with respect to the minutes which precede and follow it, and that in order to be congruent with the importance of the moment, the space too must follow suit and swell with respect to the immediate inside and the immediate outside of the building.

We shall see now that there are a tremendous number of miniscule forces which all come together to support this general intuition. All these forces, tendencies, and solutions were originally describe by Alexander and Poyner, in the Atoms of Environmental Structure, Ministry of Public Works, Research and Development, SFB Ba4, London, 1966. At that time it seemed important to emphasize the separate and individual patterns defined by these forces. However, at the present writing it seems clear that these original patterns are, in fact, all faces of the one larger and more comprehensive entity, which we call the ENTRANCE ROOM (130).

1. The relationship of windows to the entrance

(a) A person answering the door often tries to see who is at the door before they open it.

(b) People do not want to go out of their way to peer at people on the doorstep.

623

(c) If the people meeting are old friends, they seek a chance to shout out and wave in anticipation.

The entrance room therefore needs a window—or windows— on the path from the family room or kitchen to the door, facing the area outside the door from the side.

2. The need for shelter outside the door

(a) People try to get shelter from the rain, wind, and cold while they are waiting.

(b) People stand near the door while they are waiting for it to open.

On the outside, therefore, give the entrance room walls enclosing three sides of a covered space.

3. The subtleties of saying goodbye

When hosts and guests are saying goodbye, the lack of a clearly marked "goodbye" point can easily lead to endless "Well, we really must be going now," and then further conversations lingering on, over and over again.

(a) Once they have finally decided to go, people try to leave without hesitation.

(b) People try to make their goodbye as nonabrupt as possible and seek a comfortable break.

Give the entrance room, therefore, a clearly defined area, at least 20 square feet, outside the front door, raised with a natural threshold—perhaps a railing, or a low wall, or a step—between it and the visitors' cars.

4. Shelf near the entrance

When a person is going into the house with a package:

(a) He tries to hold onto the package; he tries to keep it upright, and off the ground.

(b) At the same time he tries to get both hands free to hunt through pockets or handbag for a key.

And leaving the house with a package:

(c) At the moment of leaving people tend to be preoccupied with other things, and this makes them forget the package which they meant to take.

You can avoid these conflicts if there are shelves both inside and outside the door, at about waist height; a place to leave packages in readiness; a place to put them down while opening the door.

5. Interior of the entrance room

(a) Politeness demands that when someone comes to the door, the door is opened wide.

(b) People seek privacy for the inside of their houses.

(c) The family, sitting, talking, or at table, do not want to feel disturbed or intruded upon when someone comes to the door.

Make the inside of the entrance room zigzag, or obstructed, so that a person standing on the doorstep of the open door can see no rooms inside, except the entrance room itself, nor through the doors of any rooms.

6. Coats, shoes, children's bikes . . .

(a) Muddy boots have got to come off.

(b) People need a five foot diameter of clear space to take off their coats.

(c) People take prams, bicycles, and so on indoors to protect them from theft and weather; and children will tend to leave all kinds of clutter—bikes, wagons, roller skates, trikes, shovels, balls—around the door they use most often.

Therefore, give the entrance room a dead corner for storage, put coat pegs in a position which can be seen from the front door, and make an area five feet in diameter next to the pegs.

Therefore:

At the main entrance to a building, make a light-filled room which marks the entrance and straddles the boundary between indoors and outdoors, covering some space outdoors and some space indoors. The outside part may be like an old-fashioned porch; the inside like a hall or sitting room.

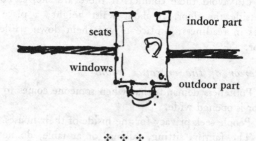

❖ ❖ ❖

Give that part of the entrance which sticks out into the street or garden a physical character which, as far as possible, make it one of the family of entrances along the street—FAMILY OF ENTRANCES (102); where it is appropriate, make it a porch—GALLERY SURROUND (166); and include a bench or seat, where people can watch the world go by or wait for someone—FRONT DOOR BENCH (242). As for the indoor part of the entrance room, above all, make sure that it is filled with light from two or even three sides, so that the first impression of the building is of light—TAPESTRY OF LIGHT AND DARK (135), LIGHT ON TWO SIDES OF EVERY ROOM (159). Put windows in the door itself—SOLID DOORS WITH GLASS (237). Put in BUILT-IN SEATS (202) and make the room part of the SEQUENCE OF SITTING SPACES (142); provide a WAIST-HIGH SHELF (201) for packages. And finally, for the overall shape of the entrance room and its construction, begin with THE SHAPE OF INDOOR SPACE (191). . . .

131 THE FLOW THROUGH ROOMS

. . . next to the gradient of spaces created by INTIMACY GRA-DIENT (127) and COMMON AREAS AT THE HEART (129), the way that rooms connect to one another will play the largest role in governing the character of indoor space. This pattern describes the most fundamental way of linking rooms to one another.

❖ ❖ ❖

The movement between rooms is as important as the rooms themselves; and its arrangement has as much effect on social interaction in the rooms, as the interiors of the rooms.

The movement between rooms, the circulation space, may be generous or mean. In a building where the movement is mean, the passages are dark and narrow—rooms open off them as dead ends; you spend your time entering the building, or moving between rooms, like a crab scuttling in the dark.

Compare this with a building where the movement is generous. The passages are broad, sunlit, with seats in them, views into gardens, and they are more or less continuous with the rooms themselves, so that the smell of woodsmoke and cigars, the sound of glasses, whispers, laughter, all that which enlivens a room, also enlivens the places where you move.

These two approaches to movement have entirely different psychological effects.

In a complex social fabric, human relations are inevitably subtle. It is essential that each person feels free to make connections or not, to move or not, to talk or not, to change the situation or not, according to his judgment. If the physical environment inhibits him and reduces his freedom of action, it will prevent him from doing the best he can to keep healing and improving the social situations he is in as he sees fit.

The building with generous circulation allows each person's instincts and intuitions full play. The building with ungenerous circulation inhibits them. It not only separates rooms from one another to such an extent that it is an ordeal to move from room

to room, but kills the joy of time spent between rooms and may discourage movement altogether.

The following incident shows how important freedom of movement is to the life of a building. An industrial company in Lausanne had the following experience. They installed TV-phone intercoms between all offices to improve communication. A few months later, the firm was going down the drain—and they called in a management consultant. He finally traced their problems back to the TV-phones. People were calling each other on the TV-phone to ask specific questions—but as a result, people never talked in the halls and passages any more—no more "Hey, how are you, say, by the way, what do you think of this idea. . ." The organization was falling apart, because the informal talk—the glue which held the organization together—had been destroyed. The consultant advised them to junk the TV-phones—and they lived happily ever after.

This incident happened in a large organization. But the principle is just the same in a small work group or a family. The possibility of small momentary conversations, gestures, kindnesses, explanations which clear up misunderstandings, jokes and stories is the lifeblood of a human group. If it gets prevented, the group will fall apart as people's individual relationships go gradually downhill.

It is almost certain that the building with ungenerous circulation makes it harder for people to maintain their social fabric. In the long run, there is a good chance that social order in the building with ungenerous circulation will break down altogether.

The generosity of movement depends on the overall arrangement of the movement in the building, not on the detailed design of individual passages. In fact, it is at its most generous, when there are no passages at all and movement is created by a string of interconnecting rooms with doors between them.

A sequence of rooms without a passage.

Even better, is the case where there is a loop. A loop, which passes through all the major rooms, public and common, establishes an enormous feeling of generosity. With a loop it is always possible to come and go in two different directions. It is possible to walk around and around, and it ties the rooms together. And, when such a loop passes through rooms (at one end so as not to disturb them), it connects rooms far more than a simple passage does.

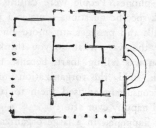

A generous circulation loop.

A building where there is a chain of rooms in sequence also works like this, if there is a passage in parallel with the chain of rooms.

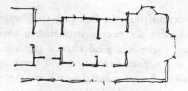

Passage in parallel forms the loop.

Therefore:

As far as possible, avoid the use of corridors and passages. Instead, use public rooms and common rooms as rooms for movement and for gathering. To do this, place the common rooms to form a chain, or loop, so that it becomes possible to walk from room to room—and so that private rooms open directly off these public rooms. In every

case, give this indoor circulation from room to room a feeling of great generosity, passing in a wide and ample loop around the house, with views of fires and great windows.

loops through rooms

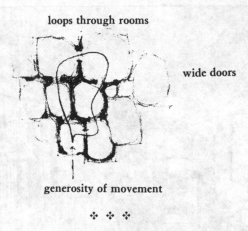

wide doors

generosity of movement

❖ ❖ ❖

Whenever passages or corridors are unavoidable, make them wide and generous too; and try to place them on one side of the building, so that they can be filled with light—SHORT PASSAGES (132). Furnish them like rooms, with carpets, bookshelves, easy chairs and tables, filtered light, and do the same for ENTRANCE ROOM (130) and STAIRCASE AS A STAGE (133). Always make sure that these rooms for movement have plenty of light in them and perhaps a view—ZEN VIEW (134), TAPESTRY OF LIGHT AND DARK (135), and LIGHT ON TWO SIDES OF EVERY ROOM (159). Keep doors which open into rooms, or doors between rooms which create the flow through rooms, in the corners of the rooms—CORNER DOORS (196). . . .

132 SHORT PASSAGES*

. . . THE FLOW THROUGH ROOMS (131) describes the generosity of light and movement in the way that rooms connect to one another and recommends against the use of passages. But when there has to be a passage in an office or a house and when it is too small to be a BUILDING THOROUGHFARE (101), it must be treated very specially, as if it were itself a room. This pattern gives the character of these smallest passages, and so completes the circulation system laid down by CIRCULATION REALMS (98) and BUILDING THOROUGHFARE (101) and THE FLOW THROUGH ROOMS (131).

❖ ❖ ❖

". . . long, sterile corridors set the scene for everything bad about modern architecture."

In fact, the ugly long repetitive corridors of the machine age have so far infected the word "corridor" that it is hard to imagine that a corridor could ever be a place of beauty, a moment in your passage from room to room, which means as much as all the moments you spend in the rooms themselves.

Long corridors.

We shall now try to pinpoint the difference between the corridors which live, which give pleasure, and make people feel

633

alive, and those which do not. There are four main issues. The most profound issue, to our minds, is natural light. A hall or passage that is generously lit by the sun is almost always pleasant. The archetype is the one-sided hall, lined with windows and doors on its open side. (Notice that this is one of the few places where it is a good idea to light a space from one side). The second issue is the relation of the passage to the rooms which open off it. Interior windows, opening from these rooms into the hall, help animate the hall. They establish a flow between the rooms and the passage; they support a more informal style of communication; they give the person moving through the hall a taste of life inside the rooms. Even in an office, this contact is fine so long as it is not extreme; so long as the workplaces are protected individually by distance or by a partial wall—see HALF-PRIVATE OFFICE (152), WORKSPACE ENCLOSURE (183).

The third issue which makes the difference between a lively passage and a dead one is the presence of furnishings. If the passage is made in a way which invites people to furnish it with book cases, small tables, places to lean, even seats, then it becomes very much a part of the living space of the building, not something entirely separate.

And finally, there is the critical issue of length. We know intuitively that corridors in office buildings, hospitals, hotels, apartment buildings—even sometimes in houses—are far too long. People dislike them: they represent bureaucracy and monotony. And there is even evidence to show that they do actual damage.

Consider a study by Mayer Spivack on the unconscious effects of long hospital corridors on perception, communication, and behavior:

> Four examples of long mental hospital corridors are examined . . . it is concluded that such spaces interfere with normal verbal communication due to their characteristic acoustical properties. Optical phenomena common to these passageways obscure the perception of the human figure and face, and distort distance perception. Paradoxical visual cues produced by one tunnel created interrelated, cross-sensory illusions involving room size, distance, walking speed and time. Observations of patient behavior suggest the effect of narrow corridors upon anxiety is via the penetration of the personal

space envelope. (M. Spivack, "Sensory Distortion in Tunnels and Corridors," *Hospital and Community Psychiatry*, 18, No. 1, January 1967.)

When does a corridor become too long? In an earlier version of this pattern (*Short corridors* in *A Pattern Language Which Generates Multi-Service Centers*, CES, 1967, pp. 179–82), we have presented evidence which suggests that there is a definite cognitive breakpoint between long corridors and short halls: the evidence points to a figure of some 50 feet as a critical threshold. Beyond that, passages begin to feel dead and monotonous.

Of course it is possible to make even very long corridors in a human way; but if they have to be longer than 50 feet, it is essential to break down their scale in some fashion. For example, a long hall that is lit in patches from one side at short intervals can be very pleasant indeed: the sequence of light and dark and the chance to pause and glance out, breaks down the feeling of the endless dead corridor; or a hall which opens out into wider rooms, every now and then, has the same effect. However, do everything you can to keep the passages really short.

Therefore:

Keep passages short. Make them as much like rooms as possible, with carpets or wood on the floor, furniture, bookshelves, beautiful windows. Make them generous in shape, and always give them plenty of light; the best corridors and passages of all are those which have windows along an entire wall.

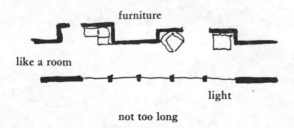

furniture

like a room

light

not too long

635

Put in windows, bookshelves, and furnishings to make them as much like actual rooms as possible, with alcoves, seats along the edge—LIGHT ON TWO SIDES OF EVERY ROOM (159), ALCOVES (179), WINDOW PLACE (180), THICK WALLS (197), CLOSETS BETWEEN ROOMS (198); open up the long side into the garden or out onto balconies—OUTDOOR ROOM (163), GALLERY SURROUND (166), LOW SILL (222). Make interior windows between the passage and the rooms which open off it—INTERIOR WINDOWS (194), SOLID DOORS WITH GLASS (237). And finally, for the shape of the passages, in detail, start with THE SHAPE OF INDOOR SPACE (191). . . .

I 33 STAIRCASE AS A STAGE

. . . if the entrances are in position—MAIN ENTRANCE (110); and the pattern of movement through the building is established —THE FLOW THROUGH ROOMS (131), SHORT PASSAGES (132), the main stairs must be put in and given an appropriate social character.

A staircase is not just a way of getting from one floor to another. The stair is itself a space, a volume, a part of the building; and unless this space is made to live, it will be a dead spot, and work to disconnect the building and to tear its processes apart.

Our feelings for the general shape of the stair are based on this conjecture: changes of level play a crucial role at many moments during social gatherings; they provide special places to sit, a place where someone can make a graceful or dramatic entrance, a place from which to speak, a place from which to look at other people while also being seen, a place which increases face to face contact when many people are together.

If this is so, then the stair is one of the few places in a building which is capable of providing for this requirement, since it is almost the only place in a building where a transition between levels occurs naturally.

This suggests that the stair always be made rather open to the room below it, embracing the room, coming down around the outer perimeter of the room, so that the stairs together with the room form a socially connected space. Stairs that are enclosed in stairwells ·or stairs that are free standing and chop up the space

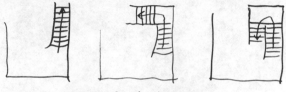

Examples of stair rooms.

638

below, do not have this character at all. But straight stairs, stairs that follow the contour of the walls below, or stairs that double back can all be made to work this way.

Furthermore, the first four or five steps are the places where people are most likely to sit if the stair is working well. To support this fact, make the bottom of the staircase flare out, widen the steps, and make them comfortable to sit on.

Stair seats.

Finally, we must decide where to place the stair. On the one hand, of course, the stair is the key to movement in a building. It must therefore be visible from the front door; and, in a building with many different rooms upstairs, it must be in a position which commands as many of these rooms as possible, so that it forms a kind of axis people can keep clearly in their minds.

However, if the stair is too near the door, it will be so public that its position will undermine the vital social character we have described. Instead, we suggest that the stair be clear, and central, yes—but in the common area of the building, a little further back from the front door than usual. Not usually in the ENTRANCE ROOM (130), but in the COMMON AREA AT THE HEART (129). Then it will be clear and visible, and also keep its necessary social character.

Therefore:

Place the main stair in a key position, central and

ible. Treat the whole staircase as a room (or if it is out-side, as a courtyard). Arrange it so that the stair and the room are one, with the stair coming down around one or two walls of the room. Flare out the bottom of the stair with open windows or balustrades and with wide steps so that the people coming down the stair become part of the action in the room while they are on the stair, and so that people below will naturally use the stair for seats.

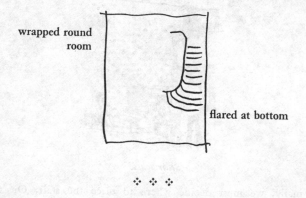

wrapped round room

flared at bottom

❖ ❖ ❖

Treat the bottom steps as STAIR SEATS (125); provide a win-dow or a view half-way up the stair, both to light the stair and to create a natural focus of attention—ZEN VIEW (134), TAPESTRY OF LIGHT AND DARK (135); remember to calculate the length and shape of the stair while you are working out its position—STAIRCASE VOLUME (195). Get the final shape of the staircase room and the beginnings of its construction from THE SHAPE OF INDOOR SPACE (191). . . .

I 34 ZEN VIEW*

. . . how should we make the most of a view? It turns out that the pattern which answers this question helps to govern not the rooms and windows in a building, but the places of transition. It helps to place and detail ENTRANCE TRANSITION (112), ENTRANCE ROOM (130), SHORT PASSAGES (132), THE STAIRCASE AS A STAGE (133)—and outside, PATHS AND GOALS (120).

❖ ❖ ❖

The archetypal zen view occurs in a famous Japanese house, which gives this pattern its name.

A Buddhist monk lived high in the mountains, in a small stone house. Far, far in the distance was the ocean, visible and beautiful from the mountains. But it was not visible from the monk's house itself, nor from the approach road to the house. However, in front of the house there stood a courtyard surrounded by a thick stone wall. As one came to the house, one passed through a gate into this court, and then diagonally across the court to the front door of the house. On the far side of the courtyard there was a slit in the wall, narrow and diagonal, cut through the thickness of the wall. As a person walked across the court, at one spot, where his position lined up with the slit in the wall, for an instant, he could see the ocean. And then he was past it once again, and went into the house.

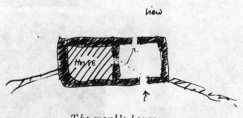

The monk's house.

What is it that happens in this courtyard? The view of the distant sea is so restrained that it stays alive forever. Who, that

642

natural target. The reason is simple. If there are places which have more light than the entrances and circulation nodes, people will tend to walk toward *them* (because of their phototropic tendency) and will therefore end up in the wrong place—with frustration and confusion as the only possible result.

If the places where the light falls are not the places you are meant to go toward, or if the light is uniform, the environment is giving information which contradicts its own meaning. The environment is only functioning in a single-hearted manner, as information, when the lightest spots coincide with the points of maximum importance.

Therefore:

Create alternating areas of light and dark throughout the building, in such a way that people naturally walk toward the light, whenever they are going to important places: seats, entrances, stairs, passages, places of special beauty, and make other areas darker, to increase the contrast.

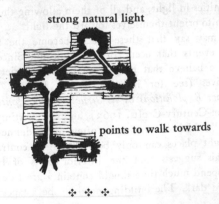

strong natural light

points to walk towards

❖ ❖ ❖

Where the light to walk toward is natural light, build seats and alcoves in those windows which attract the movement—WINDOW PLACE (180). If you use skylights, then make the surfaces around the skylight warm in color—WARM COLORS (250); otherwise the direct light from the sky is almost always cold. At night make pools of incandescent light which guide the movement—POOLS OF LIGHT (252). . . .

has ever seen that view, can ever forget it? Its power will never fade. Even for the man who lives there, coming past that view day after day for fifty years, it will still be alive.

This is the essence of the problem with any view. It is a beautiful thing. One wants to enjoy it and drink it in every day. But the more open it is, the more obvious, the more it shouts, the sooner it will fade. Gradually it will become part of the building, like the wallpaper; and the intensity of its beauty will no longer be accessible to the people who live there.

Therefore:

If there is a beautiful view, don't spoil it by building huge windows that gape incessantly at it. Instead, put the windows which look onto the view at places of transition—along paths, in hallways, in entry ways, on stairs, between rooms.

If the view window is correctly placed, people will see a glimpse of the distant view as they come up to the window or pass it: but the view is never visible from the places where people stay.

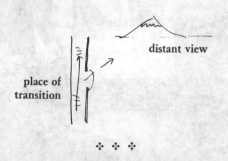

distant view

place of transition

❖ ❖ ❖

Put in the windows to complete the indirectness of the view —NATURAL DOORS AND WINDOWS (221); place them to help the TAPESTRY OF LIGHT AND DARK (135); and build a seat from which a person can enjoy the view—WINDOW PLACE (180). If the view must be visible from inside a room, make a special corner of the room which looks onto the view, so that the enjoyment of the view becomes a definite act in its own right. . . .

135 TAPESTRY OF LIGHT
AND DARK *

. . . passages, entrances, stairs are given their rough position by THE FLOW THROUGH ROOMS (131), SHORT PASSAGES (132), STAIRCASE AS A STAGE (133), ZEN VIEW (134). This pattern helps you fine tune their positions by placing light correctly.

❖ ❖ ❖

In a building with uniform light level, there are few "places" which function as effective settings for human events. This happens because, to a large extent, the places which make effective settings are defined by light.

People are by nature phototropic—they move toward light, and, when stationary, they orient themselves toward the light. As a result the much loved and much used places in buildings, where the most things happen, are places like window seats, verandas, fireside corners, trellised arbors; all of them defined by non-uniformities in light, and all of them allowing the people who are in them to orient themselves toward the light.

We may say that these places become the settings for the human events that occur in the building. Since there is good reason to believe that people need a rich variety of settings in their lives (see for instance, Roger Barker, *The Stream of Behavior: Explorations of its Structure and Content*, New York: Appleton-Century-Crofts, 1963), and since settings are defined by "places," which in turn seem often to be defined by light, and since light places can only be defined by contrast with darker ones, this suggests that the interior parts of buildings where people spend much time should contain a great deal of alternating light and dark. The building needs to be a tapestry of light and dark.

This tapestry of light and dark must then fit together with the flow of movement, too. As we have said, people naturally tend to walk toward the light. It is therefore obvious that any entrance, or any key point in a circulation system, must be systematically lighter than its surroundings—with light (daylight and artificial light) flooded there, so that its intensity becomes a

within the framework of the wings and their internal gradients of space and movement, define the most important areas and rooms. First, for a house;

136 COUPLE'S REALM*

. . . this pattern helps to complete THE FAMILY (75), HOUSE FOR A SMALL FAMILY (76) and HOUSE FOR A COUPLE (77). It also ties in to a particular position on the INTIMACY GRADIENT (127), and can be used to help generate that gradient, if it doesn't exist already.

The presence of children in a family often destroys the closeness and the special privacy which a man and wife need together.

Every couple start out sharing each other's adult lives. When children come, concern for parenthood often overwhelms the private sharing, and everything becomes exclusively oriented toward the children.

In most houses this is aggravated by the physical design of the environment. Specifically:

1. Children are able to run everywhere in the house, and therefore tend to dominate all of it. No rooms are private.

2. The bathroom is often placed so that adults must walk past children's bedrooms to reach it.

3. The walls of the master bedroom are usually too thin to afford much acoustical privacy.

The result is that the private life of the couple is continually interrupted by the awareness that the children are nearby. Their role as parents rather than as a couple permeates all aspects of their private relations.

On the other hand, of course, they do not want to be completely separated from the children's rooms. They also want to be close to them, especially while the children are young. A mother wants to run quickly to the bed of an infant in an emergency.

These problems can only be solved if there is a part of the house, which we call the couple's realm; that is, a world in which the intimacy of the man and woman, their joys and sorrows, can be shared and lived through. It is a place not only insulated from the children's world, but also complete in itself, a

world, a domain. In many respects it is a version of the pattern
HOUSE FOR A COUPLE (77), embedded in the larger house with
children.

The couple's realm needs to be the kind of place that one
might sit in and talk privately, perhaps with its own entrance to
the outdoors, to a balcony. It is a sitting room, a place for privacy,
a place for projects; the bed is part of it, but tucked away into an
alcove with its own window; a fireplace is wonderful; and it
needs some kind of a double door, an ante-room, to protect its
privacy.

Therefore:

Make a special part of the house distinct from the common areas and all the children's rooms, where the man and woman of the house can be together in private. Give this place a quick path to the children's rooms, but, at all costs, make it a distinctly separate realm.

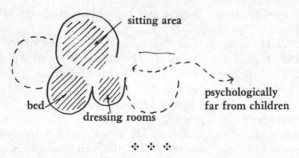

sitting area

bed

dressing rooms

psychologically far from children

❖ ❖ ❖

Even if it's very tiny, give it a sitting area, a place to relax,
read, make love, play music—SITTING CIRCLE (185). Give it
LIGHT ON TWO SIDES (159). At the heart of the couple's realm,
place the bed—MARRIAGE BED (187) so it has morning light—
SLEEPING TO THE EAST (138), and, beside it, the DRESSING ROOM
(189); if possible, try to place the bathing room to open off the
couple's realm—BATHING ROOM (144). For the shape of this
room in fine detail and its construction, see THE SHAPE OF INDOOR
SPACE (191). And keep the area private with a LOW DOORWAY
(224) or two doors—CLOSETS BETWEEN ROOMS (198). . . .

137 CHILDREN'S REALM*

. . . in a HOUSE FOR A SMALL FAMILY (76), there are three main areas: a COMMON AREA AT THE HEART (129), a COUPLE'S REALM (136), and a CHILDREN'S REALM which overlaps the common area. If the common area and couple's realm are in position, it is now possible to weave in this partly separate, partly overlapping place for children, which we call a realm, although we recognize that it is not a separate realm but more an aspect of the house, reserved for children, a mode of functioning which is physically separate only in certain parts. It is that component of CONNECTED PLAY (68) which acts within the individual houses.

❖ ❖ ❖

If children do not have space to release a tremendous amount of energy when they need to, they will drive themselves and everybody else in the family up the wall.

A frenzy in the dining room.

For a graphic example, visualize what happens when children bring in friends after school and have a whole number of ideas in their heads of what to do or play. They are loud and boisterous after being pent up in school all day and they need a lot of indoor and outdoor space to expend all this energy. Obviously, the mood calls for space which contains long distances because they suggest the possibility of physical freedom much more.

And, in general, the child's world is not some single space or room—it is a continuum of spaces. The sidewalk where he sells lemonade and talks with friends, the outdoor play area of his house into which he can invite his friends, the indoor play-space, his private space in the house where he can be alone with a friend, the bathroom, the kitchen where his mother is, the family room where the rest of the family is—for the child, all of these together form his world. If any other kind of space interrupts this continuum, it will be swallowed up into the child's world as part of his circulation path.

If the private rooms, the couple's realm, the quiet sitting areas are scattered randomly among the places that form the children's world, then they will certainly be violated. But if the children's world is one continuous swath, then these quiet, private, adult places will be protected by the mere fact that they are not part of the continuum. We therefore conclude that all the places which children need and use should form one continuous geometrical swath, which does not include the couple's realm, the adult private rooms, or any formal, quiet sitting spaces. This continuous playspace needs certain additional properties.

1. Children are apt to be very demanding of everyone's attention when they are in this specially energetic state. The mother is particularly susceptible to being totally swallowed up by them. They will want to show her things, ask her questions, ask her to do things . . . "Look what I found. Look what I made. Where shall I put this? Where's the clay? Make some paint." The mother must be available for all this, but not forced to be in the thick of it. Her workroom and the kitchen need to be protected, yet tangential to the playspace.

2. The family room is also part of the continuum since it is where children and the rest of the family have contact with each other. The playspace, therefore, should enter the common area— preferably to one side—see COMMON AREA AT THE HEART (129).

3. The children's private spaces (whether they are alcoves or bedrooms) can be off the playspace, but it must be possible to close them off. Children naturally want to be exclusive at times— they often invite their closest friends into such a space for a private chat or to show off some prized possession.

4. It is usually too expensive to create a special playspace; but it is always possible to make a hallway function as the indoor part of the playspace. It needs to be a bit wider than a normal hall (perhaps seven feet) with nooks and stages along the edge. Children take up the suggestive qualities of spaces—on sight of a little cave-like space, they will decide to play house; on sight of a raised platform, they will decide to put on a play. Thus, both indoor and outdoor parts of the playspace need different levels, little nooks, counters, or tables, and so on. A lot of open storage for toys, costumes, and so forth should also be provided in these spaces. When toys are visible, they are more likely to be used.

5. The outdoor space just adjacent to the indoor space should be partially roofed, to provide transition between the two and to reinforce the continuity.

Remember that this kind of playspace is as much in the interest of the adults in the family, as in the interest of the children. If the house is organized so that the children's world gradually spreads throughout the home, it will disrupt and dominate the world of tranquility, preciousness, and freedom that adults need, to live their own lives. If there is an adequate children's world, in the manner described in this pattern, then both the adults and children can co-exist, each without dominating the other.

Therefore:

Start by placing the small area which will belong entirely to the children—the cluster of their beds. Place it in a separate position toward the back of the house, and in such a way that a continuous playspace can be made from this cluster to the street, almost like a wide swath inside the house, muddy, toys strewn along the way, touching those family rooms which children need—the bathroom and the kitchen most of all—passing the common area along one side (but leaving quiet sitting areas and the couple's realm entirely separate and inviolate), reaching out to the street, either through its own door or through the entrance room, and ending in an outdoor room, connected

to the street, and sheltered, and large enough so that the children can play in it when it rains, yet still be outdoors.

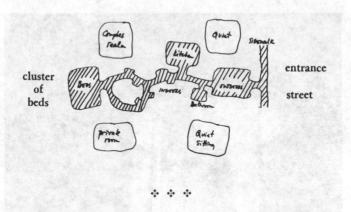

❖ ❖ ❖

As you place this swath between the children's beds and the street, place the FARMHOUSE KITCHEN (139) and the HOME WORKSHOP (157) to one side of the path, touching it, yet not violated by it. Do the same for BATHING ROOM (144), and give it some connection to the children's beds. Develop the cluster of children's beds according to BED CLUSTERS (143); make the long passages which form the realm as light and warm as possible —SHORT PASSAGES (132); make the OUTDOOR ROOM (163) large enough for boisterous activity. . . .

138 SLEEPING TO THE EAST*

. . . at the back of the INTIMACY GRADIENT (127), the position of the COUPLE'S REALM (136) and CHILDREN'S REALM (137), give some idea of where bedrooms will be. This pattern settles the position of the bedrooms by placing them to face the east, and thereby complements the effect of INDOOR SUNLIGHT (128), which places the more public rooms toward the south.

❖ ❖ ❖

This is one of the patterns people most often disagree with. However, we believe they are mistaken.

People's attitude to this pattern often runs along the following lines: "The pattern suggests that I should sleep somewhere where the sun can wake me up; but I don't want the sun to wake me up; I want to be able to sleep late, whenever I can. I guess I have a different style of life; so the pattern doesn't apply to me."

We believe there may be fundamental biological matters at stake here and that no one who once understands them will want to ignore them, even if his present style of life does seem to contradict them.

The facts, as far as we can tell, are these. Our human organism contains a number of very sensitive biological clocks. We are creatures of rhythms and cycles. Whenever we behave in a way which is not in tune with our natural rhythms and cycles, we run a very good chance of disturbing our natural physiological and emotional functioning.

Specifically, these cycles have a great deal to do with sleep. And the cycle of the sun governs our physiology to such an extent, that we cannot afford to sleep out of touch with this cycle. Consider the fact that the body reaches its lowest metabolic activity in the middle of the sun's night, at about 2 A.M. It seems very likely, then, that the most nourishing kind of sleep is a sleep whose curve more or less coincides with the curve of metabolic activity—which is in turn dependent on the sun.

It has recently been shown by Dr. London at the San Francisco Medical School, that our whole day depends critically on the

conditions under which we waken. If we wake up immediately after a period of dreaming (REM sleep), we will feel ebullient, energetic, and refreshed for the whole day, because certain critical hormones are injected into the bloodstream immediately after REM sleep. If, however, we wake up during delta sleep (another type of sleep, which happens in between periods of dreaming), we will feel irritable, drowsy, flat, and lethargic all day long: the relevant hormones are not in the bloodstream at the critical moment of awakening.

Now, obviously, anyone who is woken by an alarm clock, will sometimes be woken in the middle of delta sleep and will, on those days, have a lethargic day; and will sometimes wake up just after REM sleep and will, on those days, have an energetic day. Of course this is tremendously oversimplified—many other matters intervene. But if these facts about sleep are correct, they cannot help but have *some* impact on your waking hours.

Now, the only way to make sure that you wake up at the right time, with the closure of REM sleep, is to wake up naturally. But you can only wake up naturally, and in accordance with the other, larger cycle of metabolic activity, if you wake up with the sun. The sun warms you, increases the light, gently nudges you to wake up—but in a way that is so gentle, that you will still actually wake up at the moment which serves you best— that is, just *after* a dream.

We believe, in short, that this pattern is fundamental to the process of having a healthy, active, energetic day—and that anyone who rejects this pattern on the grounds that he does not want to be woken by the sun, is making a serious mistake about the functioning of his or her own body.

What about details? You want to see the sunlight, but you don't want the sun to shine on the bed itself or you'll wake up hot and uncomfortable. The right kind of place is one which provides morning light—consequently a window in the room that lets in the eastern light—and a bed that provides a view of the light without being directly in the light shaft.

And finally, the matter of the view from the bed is worth mentioning. People look out in the morning to see what kind of day its going to be. Some views give this information very well; others not at all. A good morning window looks out on some kind

of constant object or growing thing, which reflects the changes of season and the weather, and allows a person to establish the mood of the day as soon as he wakes up.

Therefore,

Give those parts of the house where people sleep, an eastern orientation, so that they wake up with the sun and light. This means, typically, that the sleeping area needs to be on the eastern side of the house; but it can also be on the western side provided there is a courtyard or a terrace to the east of it.

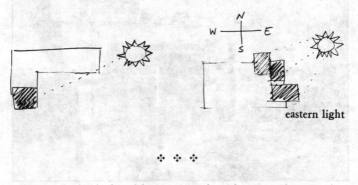

eastern light

❖ ❖ ❖

Place all the beds with care, so that they get the morning light, not only as a group—COUPLE'S REALM (136), BED CLUS-TER (143), but individually, so that each gets eastern light from some specific window—MARRIAGE BED (187), BED ALCOVE (188). Use FILTERED LIGHT (238) to prevent the sun from shining too directly on the bed. If there is room, make this window function as a WINDOW PLACE (180). Place the window nearest the bed carefully so that it frames a view which tells a person waking what the weather is like—NATURAL DOORS AND WINDOWS (221). . . .

139 FARMHOUSE KITCHEN**

clude the "family room" space, and place it near the center
of the commons, not so far back in the house as an ordinary kitchen. Make it large enough to hold a good big
table and chairs, some soft and some hard, with counters
and stove and sink around the edge of the room; and make
it a bright and comfortable room.

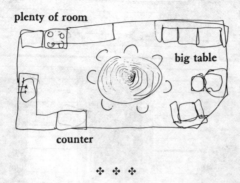

plenty of room

big table

counter

❖ ❖ ❖

Give the kitchen LIGHT ON TWO SIDES (159). When you place
the kitchen counters later, make them really long and generous
and toward the south to get the light—COOKING LAYOUT (184),
SUNNY COUNTER (199); leave room for an alcove or two around
the kitchen—ALCOVES (179); make the table in the middle big,
and hang a nice big warm single light right in the middle to
draw the family around it—EATING ATMOSPHERE (182); surround the walls, when you detail them, with plenty of open
shelves for pots, and mugs, and bottles, and jars of jam—OPEN
SHELVES (200), WAIST-HIGH SHELF (201). Put in a comfortable
chair somewhere—SEQUENCE OF SITTING SPACES (142). And for
the room shape and construction, start with THE SHAPE OF INDOOR
SPACE (191). . . .

140 PRIVATE TERRACE
ON THE STREET**

. . . among the common areas and sitting spaces—COMMON AREAS AT THE HEART (129), SEQUENCE OF SITTING SPACES (142) —there is a need for one, at least, which puts the people in the house in touch with the world of the street outside the house. This pattern helps to create the HALF-HIDDEN GARDEN (111) and gives life to the street—GREEN STREET (51) or PEDESTRIAN STREET (100).

❖ ❖ ❖

The relationship of a house to a street is often confused: either the house opens entirely to the street and there is no privacy; or the house turns its back on the street, and communion with street life is lost.

We have within our natures tendencies toward both communality and individuality. A good house supports *both* kinds of experience: the intimacy of a private haven *and* our participation with a public world.

But most homes fail to support these complementary needs. Most often they emphasize one, to the exclusion of the other: we have, for instance, the fishbowl scheme, where living areas face the street with picture windows and the "retreat," where living areas turn away from the street into private gardens.

The old front porch, in traditional American society, solved this problem perfectly. Where the street is quiet enough, and the house near enough to the street, we cannot imagine a much better solution. But if the street is different, a slightly different solution will be necessary.

Early in his career, Frank Wright experimented with one possible solution. When he built beside lively streets he built a wide terrace between the living room and the street.

To our knowledge, Grant Hildebrand first pointed out this pattern in Wright's work, in his paper, "Privacy and Participation: Frank Lloyd Wright and the City Street," School of

Section of private terrace and street.

Architecture, University of Washington, Seattle, Washington: 1970. Hildebrand gives an interesting account of the way this pattern works in the Cheney house:

> As the pedestrian looks toward the house from the sidewalk, the masonry terrace wall is located so that his line of sight over its top falls at the lower edge of the elaborately leaded upper glass zone of the terrace doors. Vision into the living room from the sidewalk thus is carefully controlled. If the occupant within the house is standing near the doors only his head and shoulders are dimly visible through a diffusing surface. If the occupant is sitting he is, of course, completely hidden from the pedestrian's view.
>
> But whereas the pedestrian cannot effectively intrude on the privacy of the house, the inhabitant on the other hand has a number of options available at will. As he stands or sits on the terrace itself, well above the sidewalk, the effect is of easy participation in the full panorama of the street. From the elevated platform vision is unobstructed. Neighbors and friends can be waved at, greeted, invited in for a chat. Thus the terrace, projecting toward the street, linked— and still links—the Cheney house and its inhabitants to the community life of Oak Park. The configuration is so successful that, as in the Robie house, there has never been much need for curtains. The parapets and the leaded glass, carefully placed, do it all. Thus out of the decision to face the living room toward the street has come not a sacrifice of privacy, but a much richer range of alternative experiences for the occupant.

We believe that Wright's use of this pattern was based on accurate intuitions about a fundamental human need. Indeed, there are empirical grounds for believing that the need for a house to be in touch with the street outside is a fundamental psychological necessity: and that its opposite—the tendency some people have to keep their houses away from the street, locked up, barred, and disconnected from the street—is a symptom of a serious emotional disorder—the autonomy-withdrawal syndrome. See Alexander, "The City as a Mechanism for Sustaining Human Contact," W. Ewald, ed., *Environment for Man*, Indiana University Press, 1967, pp. 60–102.

Here is an example of this pattern from Greece. It is clear that

the pattern can be expressed in many ways, so long as the relationship, the balance of privacy and street contact, is maintained.

Private terrace on the street.

Therefore:

Let the common rooms open onto a wide terrace or a porch which looks into the street. Raise the terrace slightly above street level and protect it with a low wall, which you can see over if you sit near it, but which prevents people on the street from looking into the common rooms.

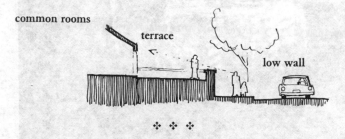

❖ ❖ ❖

If possible, place the terrace in a position which is also congruent with natural contours—TERRACED SLOPE (169). The wall, if low enough, can be a SITTING WALL (243); in other cases, where you want more privacy, you can build a full garden wall, with openings in it, almost like windows, which make the connection with the street—GARDEN WALL (173), HALF-OPEN WALL (193). In any case, surround the terrace with enough things to give it at least the partial feeling of a room—OUTDOOR ROOM (163). . . .

141 A ROOM OF ONE'S OWN**

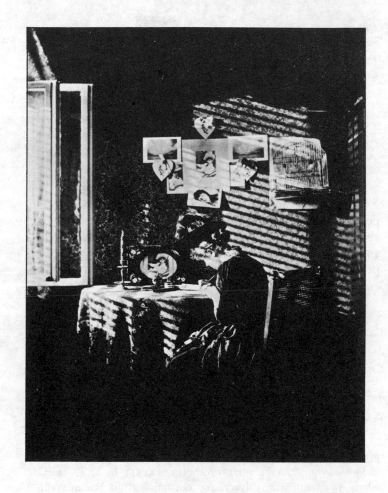

. . . the INTIMACY GRADIENT (127) makes it clear that every house needs rooms where individuals can be alone. In any household which has more than one person, this need is fundamental and essential—THE FAMILY (75), HOUSE FOR A SMALL FAMILY (76), HOUSE FOR A COUPLE (77). This pattern, which defines the rooms that people can have to themselves, is the natural counterpart and complement to the social activity provided for in COMMON AREAS AT THE HEART (129).

❖ ❖ ❖

No one can be close to others, without also having frequent opportunities to be alone.

A person in a household without a room of his own will always be confronted with a problem: he wants to participate in family life and to be recognized as an important member of that group; but he cannot individualize himself because no part of the house is totally in his control. It is rather like expecting one drowning man to save another. Only a person who has a well-developed strong personal self, can venture out to participate in communal life.

This notion has been explored by two American sociologists, Foote and Cottrell:

There is a critical point beyond which closer contact with another person will no longer lead to an increase in empathy. (A) Up to a certain point, intimate interaction with others increases the capacity to empathize with them. But when others are too constantly present, the organism appears to develop a protective resistance to responding to them. . . . This limit to the capacity to empathize should be taken into account in planning the optimal size and concentration of urban populations, as well as in planning the schools and the housing of individual families. (B) Families who provide time and space for privacy, and who teach children the utility and satisfaction of withdrawing for private reveries, will show higher average empathic capacity than those who do not. (Foote, N. and L. Cottrell, *Identity and Interpersonal Competence*, Chicago, 1955, pp. 72–73, 79.)

Alexander Leighton has made a similar point, emphasizing the mental damage that results from a *systematic lack of privacy*

["Psychiatric Disorder and Social Environment," *Psychiatry*, 18 (3), p. 374, 1955].

In terms of space, what is required to solve the problem? Simply, a room of one's own. A place to go and close the door; a retreat. Visual and acoustic privacy. And to make certain that the rooms are truly private, they must be located at the extremities of the house: at the ends of building wings; at the ends of the INTIMACY GRADIENT (127); far from the common areas.

We shall now look at the individual members of the family one at a time, in slightly more detail.

Wife. We put the wife first, because, classically, it is she who has the greatest difficulty with this problem. She belongs everywhere, and every place inside the house is in a vague sense hers— yet it is only very rarely that the woman of the house has a small room which is specifically and exclusively her own. Virginia Woolf's famous essay "A room of one's own" is the strongest and most important statement on this issue—and has given this pattern its name.

Husband. In older houses, the man of the house usually had a study or a workshop of his own. However, in modern houses and apartments, this has become as rare as the woman's own room. And it is certainly just as essential. Many a man associates his house with the mad scene of young children and the enormous demands put on him there. If he has no room of his own, he has to stay at his office, away from home, to get peace and quiet.

Teenagers. For teenage children, we have devoted an entire pattern to this problem: TEENAGER'S COTTAGE (154). We have argued there that it is the teenagers who are faced with the problem of building a firm and strong identity; yet among the adults, it is the young who are most often prevented from having a place in the home that is clearly marked as their own.

Children. Very young children experience the need for privacy less—but they still experience it. They need some place to keep their possessions, to be alone at times, to have a private visit with a playmate. See BED CLUSTER (143) and BED ALCOVE (188). John Madge has written a good survey of a family's need for private space ("Privacy and Social Interaction," Transactions of the Bartlett Society, Vol. 3, 1964–65), and concerning the children he says:

The bedroom is often the repository of most of these items of personal property around which the individual builds his own satisfactions and which help to differentiate him from the other members of the inner circle of his life—indeed he will often reveal them more freely to a peer in age and sex than to a member of his own family.

In summary then, we propose that a room of one's own—an alcove or bed nook for younger children—is essential for each member of the family. It helps develop one's own sense of identity; it strengthens one's relationship to the rest of the family; and it creates personal territory, thereby building ties with the house itself.

Therefore:

Give each member of the family a room of his own, especially adults. A minimum room of one's own is an alcove with desk, shelves, and curtain. The maximum is a cottage—like a TEENAGER'S COTTAGE (154), or an OLD AGE COTTAGE (155). In all cases, especially the adult ones, place these rooms at the far ends of the intimacy gradient— far from the common rooms.

private rooms

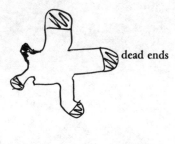

dead ends

❖ ❖ ❖

Use this pattern as an antidote to the extremes of "togetherness" created by COMMON AREAS AT THE HEART (129). Even for

small children, give them at least an alcove in the communal sleeping area—BED ALCOVE (188); and for the man and woman, give each of them a separate room, beyond the couples realm they share; it may be an expanded dressing room—DRESSING ROOM (189), a home workshop—HOME WORKSHOP (157), or once again, an alcove off some other room—ALCOVES (179), WORKSPACE ENCLOSURE (183). If there is money for it, it may even be possible to give a person a cottage, attached to the main structure—TEENAGER'S COTTAGE (154), OLD AGE COTTAGE (155). In every case there must at least be room for a desk, a chair, and THINGS FROM YOUR LIFE (253). And for the detailed shape of the room, see LIGHT ON TWO SIDES OF EVERY ROOM (159) and THE SHAPE OF INDOOR SPACE (191). . . . .

142 SEQUENCE OF SITTING SPACES*

. . . at various points along the INTIMACY GRADIENT (127) of a house, or office, or a public building, there is a need for sitting space. Some of this space may take the form of rooms devoted entirely to sitting, like the formal sitting rooms of old; others may be simply areas or corners of other rooms. This pattern states the range and distribution of these sitting spaces, and helps create the intimacy gradient by doing so.

Every corner of a building is a potential sitting space. But each sitting space has different needs for comfort and enclosure according to its position in the intimacy gradient.

We know from INTIMACY GRADIENT (127) that a building has a natural sequence of spaces in it, ranging from the most public areas, outside the entrance, to the most private, in individual rooms and couples realms. Here is a sequence of sitting spaces that would correspond roughly to the INTIMACY GRADIENT (127):

1. Outside the entrance—ENTRANCE ROOM (130), FRONT DOOR BENCH (242)
2. Inside the entrance—ENTRANCE ROOM (130), RECEPTION WELCOMES YOU (149)
3. Common rooms—COMMON AREAS AT THE HEART (129), SHORT PASSAGES (132), FARMHOUSE KITCHEN (139), SMALL MEETING ROOMS (151)
4. Half-private rooms—CHILDREN'S REALM (137), PRIVATE TERRACE ON THE STREET (140), HALF-PRIVATE OFFICE (152), ALCOVES (179)
5. Private rooms—COUPLE'S REALM (136), A ROOM OF ONE'S OWN (141), GARDEN SEAT (176).

Now, what is the problem? Simply, it is the following. People have a tendency to think about *the* sitting room, as though a building, and especially a house, has just one room made for sitting. Within this frame of reference, this one sitting room gets a great deal of care and attention. But the fact that human activity naturally occurs all through the house, at a variety of degrees of intensity and intimacy, is forgotten—and the sitting spaces throughout the building fail to support the real rhythms of sitting and hanging around.

To solve the problem, recognize that your building should contain a sequence of sitting spaces of varying degrees of intimacy, and that each space in this sequence needs the degree of enclosure and comfort appropriate to its position. Pay attention to the full sequence, not just to one room. Ask yourself if the building you are making or repairing has the full sequence of sitting spaces, and what needs to be done to create this sequence, in its full richness and variety.

Of course, you may want to build a special sitting room—a *sala* or a parlor or a library or a living room—as one of the sitting spaces in your house. But remember that each office and workroom needs a sitting space too; so does a kitchen, so does a couple's realm, so does a garden, so does an entrance room, so does a corridor even, so does a roof, so does a window place. Pick the sequence of sitting spaces quite deliberately, mark it, and pay equal attention to the various spaces in the sequence as you go further into the details of the design.

Therefore:

Put in a sequence of graded sitting spaces throughout the building, varying according to their degree of enclosure. Enclose the most formal ones entirely, in rooms by themselves; put the least formal ones in corners of other rooms, without any kind of screen around them; and place the intermediate one with a partial enclosure round them to keep them connected to some larger space, but also partly separate.

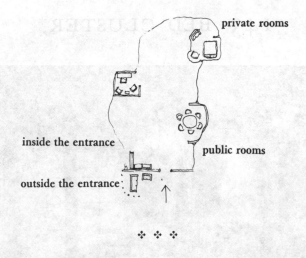

❖ ❖ ❖

Put the most formal sitting spaces in the COMMON AREAS AT THE HEART (129) and in the ENTRANCE ROOM (130); put the intermediate spaces also in the COMMON AREAS AT THE HEART (129), in FLEXIBLE OFFICE SPACE (146), in a PLACE TO WAIT (150), and on the PRIVATE TERRACE ON THE STREET (140); and put the most intimate and most informal sitting spaces in the COUPLE'S REALM (136), the FARMHOUSE KITCHEN (139), the ROOMS OF ONE'S OWN (141), and the HALF-PRIVATE OFFICES (152). Build the enclosure round each space, according to its position in the scale of sitting spaces—THE SHAPE OF INDOOR SPACE (191); and make each one, wherever it is, comfortable and lazy by placing chairs correctly with respect to fires and windows —ZEN VIEW (134), WINDOW PLACE (180), THE FIRE (181), SITTING CIRCLE (185), SEAT SPOTS (241). . . .

143 BED CLUSTER*

. . . the sleeping areas have been defined to be inside the COUPLE'S REALM (136) and CHILDREN'S REALM (137). Beyond that, they are in places facing east to get the morning light—SLEEPING TO THE EAST (138). This pattern defines the grouping of the beds within the sleeping areas, and also helps to generate the general sleeping areas themselves.

Every child in the family needs a private place, generally centered around the bed. But in many cultures, perhaps all cultures, young children feel isolated if they sleep alone, if their sleeping area is too private.

Let us consider the various possible configurations of the children's beds. At one extreme, they can all be in one room—one shared bedroom. At the other extreme, we can imagine an arrangement in which each child has a private room. And then, in between these two extremes, there is a kind of configuration in which children have their own, small, private spaces, not as large as rooms, clustered around a common playspace. We shall try to show that both extremes are bad; and that some version of the cluster of alcoves is needed to solve the conflict between forces in a young child's life.

Three configurations: the shared bedroom, isolated rooms, a cluster of alcoves.

We first discuss the one room version. The problems in this case are obvious. Children are jealous of one another's toys; they fight over the light, the radio, the game being played, the door open or closed. In short, for young children, especially in that

age when feelings of possession and control are developing, the one room with many beds is just too difficult.

In the effort to avoid these difficulties, it is not surprising that many parents go to the other extreme—if they can afford it —an arrangement in which each child has his own room. But this creates new difficulties, of an entirely different sort: Young children feel isolated when they are forced to be alone.

The need for contact in the sleeping area is particularly true in strongly traditional cultures like Peru and India, where even adults sleep in groups. In these countries, people simply do not like to feel isolated and draw a great deal of comfort and security from the fact that they are constantly surrounded by people. But even in "privacy-oriented" cultures like the United States, where isolation is common and taken for granted, children, at least, feel the same way. They prefer to sleep in the company of others. For instance, we know that little children like to leave their door ajar at night, and to sleep with some light on; they like to go off to sleep hearing the voices of the adults around the house.

This instinct is so strongly developed in children of all cultures, that we believe it may be unhealthy for little children to have whole rooms of their own, regardless of cultural habit. It is very easy for a cultural relativist to argue that it depends on the cultural setting, and that a culture which puts high value on privacy, self-sufficiency, and aloneness, might very well choose to put each child in his own room in order to foster these attitudes. However, in spite of this potentially reasonable cultural relativism, it seems to us that although adults do need their own rooms, the isolation of a private room for a small child may perhaps be fundamentally incompatible with healthy psycho-social development; and might even do organic damage. It is significant that there is no culture in the world except the United States, and the offshoots of the United States, where this one-child-one-room pattern is widely practiced. And our observations do certainly suggest that this pattern is correlated with emotional withdrawal, and exaggerated conceptions of the individual's self-sufficiency, which, in the end, bring a person into inner conflicts between the need for contact and the need for withdrawal.

We thus face two conflicting forces. Children need some

privacy, some way of retreating from endless squabbles about territory, some way of having a miniature version of the adult's "room of his own." Yet at the same time, they also need extensive, almost animal, contact with others—their talk, their care, their touch, their sound, their smell.

We believe that this conflict can only be resolved in an arrangement which gives them the opportunity for both; an arrangement of individual spaces which they "own," clustered around a common playspace so that they are all in sight and sound of one another, never too alone. In a culture with relatively little need for privacy, the clustered beds can get enough privacy by being set into simple, curtained bed-alcoves, see BED ALCOVE (188). In a culture where people have a strong need for privacy, the clustered beds may be in tiny rooms, surrounding a communal space.

Finally, two examples: One shows the way one lay-designer, working with this pattern language, interpreted this pattern. The other shows a cluster of beds in a Breton farmhouse.

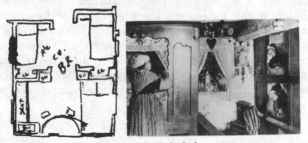

Two homemade bed clusters.

Therefore:

Place the children's beds in alcoves or small alcove-like rooms, around a common playspace. Make each alcove large enough to contain a table, or chair, or shelves—at least some floor area, where each child has his own things. Give the alcoves curtains looking into the common space, but not walls or doors, which will tend once more to isolate the beds too greatly.

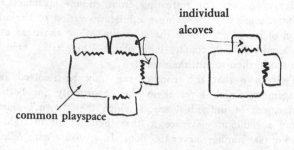

individual
alcoves

common playspace

❖ ❖ ❖

Another version of this pattern, more suitable for adults, is given by COMMUNAL SLEEPING (186). In both cases, build the individual alcoves according to BED ALCOVE (188); if the cluster is for children, shape the playspace in the middle according to the specifications of CHILDREN'S REALM (137), and make the path which leads from the beds, past the kitchen, to the outdoors, according to that pattern too. Use the location of dressing areas and closets to help shape the bed cluster and the individual alcoves—DRESSING ROOM (189), CLOSETS BETWEEN ROOMS (198); include some tiny nooks and crannies—CHILD CAVES (203). Give the entire space LIGHT ON TWO SIDES (159). And for the shape of this space in more detail and its construction, start with THE SHAPE OF INDOOR SPACE (191). . . .

144 BATHING ROOM*

. . . this pattern defines and places the main bathroom of a building. It does it by changing the present character of bathing rooms completely: And its position is so clear, and so essential, that it will probably help to form the sleeping areas and public areas given by larger patterns: INTIMACY GRADIENT (127), COMMON AREAS AT THE HEART (129), COUPLE'S REALM (136), CHILDREN'S REALM (137), SLEEPING TO THE EAST (138), BED CLUSTER (143).

❖ ❖ ❖

"The motions we call bathing are mere ablutions which formerly preceded the bath. The place where they are performed, though adequate for the routine, does not deserve to be called a bathroom."

Bernard Rudofsky

Rudofsky points out that cleaning up is only a small part of bathing; that bathing as a whole is a far more basic activity, with therapeutic and pleasurable aspects. In bathing we tend to ourselves, our bodies. It is one of the precious times when we are awake and absolutely naked. The relaxation of the bath puts us into sensual contact with water. It is one of the most direct and simple ways of unwinding. And, most astonishing, there is even evidence that we become less warlike when we tend to ourselves and our children in this way.

Cross culturally there is a correlation between the degree to which a society places restrictions on bodily pleasure—particularly in childhood—and the degree to which the society engages in the glorification of warfare and sadistic practices. (Philip Slater, *Pursuit of Loneliness*, Boston: Beacon Press, 1970, pp. 89–90.)

We ought to remember . . . that the thermae of old, with their routine of daily regeneration, were as much a matter of course to their users as our restaurants are to us. Only more so; they were considered indispensable. In the fourth century, the city of Rome alone counted 856 bathing establishments; six hundred years later, Cordoba boasted an even larger number of public baths—and who ever hears as much as its name? (Rudofsky, *Behind the Picture Window*, New York: Oxford University Press, 1955, p. 118.)

A Finnish sauna.

But bathing for pleasure has had a hard history. It went underground with the Reformation of the Church, the Elizabethan Era, and Puritanism. It became a "scapegoat" for the evils of society—immorality, ungodliness, and disease. It is strange that we have not yet recovered from such nonsense. Contrast our approach to the bath, tub, and shower with these words, written in 1935 by Nikos Kazantzakis, the Greek novelist and poet, after his first Japanese bath:

> I feel unsurpassed happiness. I put on the kimono, wear the wooden sandals, return to my room, drink more tea, and, from the open wall, watch the pilgrims as they go up the road beating drums. . . . I have overcome impatience, nervousness, haste. I enjoy every single second of these simple moments I spend. Happiness, I think, is a simple everyday miracle, like water, and we are not aware of it.

We start, then, with the assumption that there are strong and profound reasons for making something pleasant out of bathing, and that there is something quite wrong with our present way of building several small and separate bathrooms, one for the master bedroom, one for children, perhaps one near the living room— each one of them a compact efficient box. These separate, efficiency bathrooms never give a family the chance to share the intimacies and pleasures of bathing, of being naked and half-naked together. And yet, of course, this sharing has its limits. House guests and casual visitors must be able to use the bathroom too; and one bathroom will not work for a whole family, if any one person can lock the door and keep it to himself. Yet if we imagine a large bathing room, large enough to make bathing a

683

pleasure, we see that we can certainly not afford more than one of them per family.

How can all these problems be resolved? In order to resolve them, we shall list the various forces which seem to be acting. Then we can untangle them.

1. First, the newly re-emerging force, which we have named already—the growing desire that people have to make their bathing into a positive re-generating pleasure.

2. Second, an increasing relaxation about nakedness, which makes it possible to imagine members of a family, and their friends, and even strangers, sharing a bath.

3. Third, the fact that this increasing relaxation has its limits; and that the limits are different for every person. Some people still want to be able to keep their nakedness private: they must be able to have a shower, or use the toilet, unseen, when they want to.

4. The fact that the habit of putting toilets in bathrooms (not next to them as they used to be), springs from the convenience of passing to and fro between the toilet and the bath—or shower— without dressing and undressing to go out into a passage. People want to be comfortably naked while they are in the bathroom— going into the bathroom, going from the toilet to the bath, shaving, and so on. It is a nuisance to have to dress simply to negotiate any one of these connections.

5. And yet, the members of the family must be able to pass between bedrooms and bathroom, in various stages of undress, without passing through public areas. This is especially true of the adults.

6. And visitors must be able to use the bathing room, and must therefore be able to reach it without passing through the private rooms or bedrooms.

The fundamental conflict in these forces seems to be between openness and privacy. There are reasons to draw the functions of the bathroom together, and reasons to keep them separate. This suggests that all the functions of the bathroom be drawn together to form a suite, that this suite or bathing room be conceived of as the only bathroom in the house, but that private realms be created within this suite, where people can shut a door or pull a curtain and be private.

We imagine the entire bathing room tiled and protected from other parts of the house, and the public outdoors. Within this space it is possible to achieve the right connections between the bath itself and the other parts of the bathing room, and yet keep the bathing room proper open to people who want to use only the sink, the shower, or the toilet. We suggest that the room be placed next to the couple's realm—they will use it most—but also *between* the public part of the house and the private part of the house, so that the path from the family commons to the bathing room does not pass through the bedrooms or private workspace. And make sure paths from bedrooms to bathroom do not pass through any area which is visible from the common rooms.

A simple way to cope with the subtleties of nakedness and gowns is to give the bathing room prominent towel racks in several places, each with a few giant towels, towels that people can wrap up in. Under these circumstances a person can simply throw a towel around himself and twist it together when he is uneasy about his nakedness, and otherwise let it drop. This is far better than the formal robes, which are always in the wrong place, and are too much like dressing.

The bath itself should be large enough so that two or three people can get themselves comfortably in the water—so that you feel like staying, not rushing in and out. Light helps a lot. If privacy is an issue, natural light can filter through translucent glass; or a window with clear glass can overlook a private garden.

Finally, a word about the doors: It is important to place them correctly, as they do the most to establish the subtle balance between openness and privacy. We imagine solid unlockable doors to the bathing room as a whole; perhaps swinging doors to establish the fluidity of the area; and then opaque glass doors or curtains on the shower stall; a simple door for the toilet stalls—this is the most private spot; and an open doorway to the alcove which contains the bath. The sinks and the towels, the shelves, and all the other odds and ends are in the tiled outer zone.

Therefore:

Concentrate the bathing room, toilets, showers, and basins of the house in a single tiled area. Locate this bathing

room beside the couple's realm—with private access—in a position half-way between the private secluded parts of the house and the common areas; if possible, give it access to the outdoors; perhaps a tiny balcony or walled garden.

Put in a large bath—large enough for at least two people to get completely immersed in water; an efficiency shower and basins for the actual business of cleaning; and two or three racks for huge towels—one by the door, one by the shower, one by the sink.

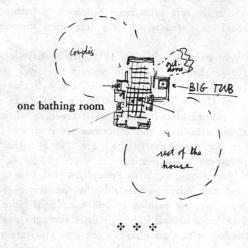

❖ ❖ ❖

Above all, make sure that there is light, plenty of light—LIGHT ON TWO SIDES OF EVERY ROOM (159) and FILTERED LIGHT (238); try to place the bathing room so that it opens out into a private part of the garden—GARDEN WALL (173), and perhaps even gives direct access to some local swimming pool—STILL WATER (71). Line up the toilet with the compost chamber—COMPOST (178); and for the detailed shape of the room and its construction, start with THE SHAPE OF INDOOR SPACE (191). . . .

145 BULK STORAGE

. . . . this pattern helps to complete any HOUSE FOR A SMALL FAMILY (76), SELF-GOVERNING WORKSHOPS AND OFFICES (80), and INDIVIDUALLY OWNED SHOPS (87). More generally, it is needed to fill out every BUILDING COMPLEX (95).

In houses and workplaces there is always some need for bulk storage space; a place for things like suitcases, old furniture, old files, boxes—all those things which you are not ready to throw away, and yet not using everyday.

Some old buildings provide for this kind of storage automatically, with their attics, cellars, and sheds. But very often this kind of storage space is overlooked. We find it neglected, for example, in carefully designed buildings, where the designer is watching the square foot costs closely and cannot justify an extra room that is not "living space."

In our experience, however, bulk storage space is terribly important; and when it is not provided, it usually means that some other space becomes the receptacle for all the bulky, marginal things that people need to store.

How much bulk storage should be provided? Certainly there should not be too much of it. That only invites us to keep old things that we have long since finished with. But some bulk storage is essential. Any household or workshop or cluster will have old furniture to store until it can be fixed, old tires, books, chests, tools that are only occasionally used; and the more self-sufficient the household is, the more space it needs. In the extreme case, it is even necessary to have space for storing building materials! The amount needed is never less than 10 per cent of the built area—sometimes as high as 50 per cent—and normally 15 to 20 per cent.

Therefore:

Do not leave bulk storage till last or forget it. Include a volume for bulk storage in the building—its floor area at least 15 to 20 per cent of the whole building area—not less. Place this storage somewhere in the building where it costs less than other rooms—because, of course, it doesn't need a finish.

20 per cent of building area

❖ ❖ ❖

Put the storage in the apex of the roof if the roof has a steep pitch—SHELTERING ROOF (117); if there is a sloping site, put it in a basement—TERRACED SLOPE (169), GROUND FLOOR SLAB (215); otherwise, put it in a shed which can perhaps be made into a cottage later—ROOMS TO RENT (153). No matter whether it is an attic, cellar, or shed, it is usually good advice to follow NORTH FACE (162) and situate bulk storage to the north of the building, leaving the sunny spaces for rooms and gardens. . . .

then the same for offices, workshops, and public buildings.

689

146 FLEXIBLE OFFICE SPACE

. . . imagine that you have laid out the basic areas of a workshop or office—SELF GOVERNING WORKSHOPS AND OFFICES (80), OFFICE CONNECTIONS (82). Once again, as in a house, the most basic layout of all is given by INTIMACY GRADIENT (127) and COMMON AREAS AT THE HEART (129). Within their general framework, this pattern helps to define the working space in more detail, and so completes these larger patterns.

❖ ❖ ❖

Is it possible to create a kind of space which is specifically tuned to the needs of people working, and yet capable of an infinite number of various arrangements and combinations within it?

Every human organization goes through a series of changes. In offices, the clusters of work groups, their size and functions, are all subject to change—often unpredictably. How must office space be designed to cope with this situation?

The standard approaches to the problem of flexibility in office spaces are: (1) uninterrupted modular space with modular partitions (full height or half-height) and (2) entire floors of uninterrupted space with low ceilings and no partitions (known as "office landscape").

But neither of these solutions really work. They are not genuinely flexible. Let us analyze them in turn.

We discuss the partition solution first. In a naïve sense, it seems obvious that the problem can be solved by movable partitions. However, in practice there are a number of serious difficulties.

1. If partitions are made easy to move, they become lightweight and provide inadequate acoustic insulation.

2. If the partitions are both easy to move and acoustically insulated, they are usually very expensive.

3. The actual cost of moving a partition is usually so high that even in highly "flexible" and "modular" systems, the partitions are in fact very rarely moved.

4. Most serious of all: it is usually not possible to make minor changes in a partition system. At the moment when one working group expands and needs more space, it is only by rare accident that the working group next door happens at this same moment to be contracting. In order to make room for the expanding group, a large part of the office must be reshuffled, but this causes so much disruption that many office managements adopt the simpler solutions—they leave the partitions as they are and move the people.

5. Finally, it is in the nature of office space that certain informal, semi-permanent arrangements *grow more permanent over time* (for example, furnishing, filing systems, "ownership" of special spaces or windows). This makes the occupants resistant to change. Though they may be willing to move when the growth of their own working group is at stake, they will resist moving strongly, as part of any general office reshuffle, caused by the expansion or contraction of some other working group.

The modular partition system fails because the partitions become, in effect, ordinary walls; yet they are less useful than real walls for defining territory and for sound insulation; and what is more, the partitions do not necessarily satisfy the need for a semi-enclosed workspace, discussed in WORKSPACE ENCLOSURE (183). It is clear, then, that systems of movable partitions do not really solve the problem.

The office landscape solution, since it has no partitions, is more genuinely flexible. However, this system is only suitable for types of work which require neither a high degree of privacy nor much internal cohesion within individual working groups. Moreover, studies by Brian Wells have made it clear that office workers strongly prefer small work spaces to larger ones—see SMALL WORK GROUPS (148). Wells shows that, when given a choice among different sized offices, people choose desks in small offices rather than large ones. And he shows that working groups in small offices are much more cohesive (defined by a larger percentage of internal sociometric choices), than the working groups in large offices. (Pilkington Research Unit, *Office Design: A*

Study of Environment, Department of Building Science, University of Liverpool, 1965, pp. 113–21.)

It seems then, that neither flexible partitions nor office landscape, really works. Neither creates space that is both well-adapted to specific work arrangements *and* truly flexible. A clue to an altogether different approach to flexibility comes from the fact that organizations which use converted houses as office space have no difficulty with this problem at all. Indeed, it appears that these old buildings actually provide more real flexibility than the apparent flexibility of modular partitioned offices. The reason is simple. In these old houses, there are many small rooms, a few large rooms, and many partially defined spaces, usually interconnected in a variety of ways.

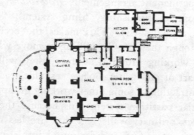

Mixture of room sizes.

Though these spaces were designed to support family life, they turn out also to support the natural structure of work groups: there are small spaces for private and half-private offices, slightly larger spaces for work groups of two to six, usually one space where up to 12 people can gather, and a commons centered around the kitchen and dining room. Furthermore, within each space there are usually a variety of walls, half-walls, window seats, which allow for changes within the rooms.

Although the walls cannot be moved at a moment's notice—the house is genuinely adaptable. Changes in work groups can be made in a few minutes, at no cost, just by opening and closing doors. And the acoustic characteristics are excellent—since most of the walls are solid, often load-bearing walls.

It is occasionally possible to build an office or a workspace like

a house—when you know enough about the working group ahead of time to base the mix of rooms and larger spaces on their specific nature. But, *far more often*, the work groups which will occupy the space are unknown at the time the space is built. In this case, no specific "house-like" design is possible. Instead, it is necessary to design and build a type of space which can gradually, and systematically, be turned into this needed house-like kind of space once it is occupied.

The kind of space which will create this possibility is not "warehouse" space or "office landscape" space but instead, a kind of space which contains the possibility that people need, in the form of columns and ceiling height variety, to encourage them to modify it as they use it. If there are columns, so placed, that a few partitions nailed to the columns will begin to form differentiations and rooms within rooms, then we can be sure that people will actually transform it to meet their needs once they begin to work there.

As far as the geometrical layout of the columns is concerned, we have found that it works best when there is essentially a central space—with aisles down the sides—and the possibility of forming the bays of the aisles into workspaces. The illustration below shows the general idea, together with the ways this pattern may be transformed after a few years.

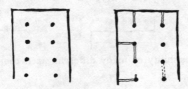

Adding partitions.

Of course, you can add rooms of different sizes and combine spaces to follow this general outline in an almost endless variety of ways. In one case they may be rather simple, with bays laid out in rows. In another case, the bays may twist and turn, with odd sized rooms and spaces in between. The details are irrelevant. What matters is the general position of the columns and, *of course*, the guarantee that they are placed in such a way that

there is plenty of natural light inside—LIGHT ON TWO SIDES OF EVERY ROOM (159).

Therefore:

Lay out the office space as wings of open space, with free standing columns around their edges, so they define half-private and common spaces opening into one another. Set down enough columns so that people can fill them in over the years, in many different ways—but always in a semi-permanent fashion.

If you happen to know the working group before you build the space, then make it more like a house, more closely tailored to their needs. In either case, create a variety of space throughout the office—comparable in variety to the different sizes and kinds of space in a large old house.

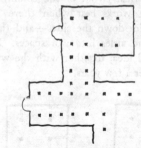

possibility of many different sized rooms

Light is critical. The bays of this kind of workspace must either be free-standing (so that there is light behind the alcoves), or the entire bay must be short enough to bring enough light in from the two ends—LIGHT ON TWO SIDES OF EVERY ROOM (159). Use CEILING HEIGHT VARIETY (190) and COLUMN PLACES (226) to define the proper mix of possible spaces. Above all, lay the

694

workspace out in such a way to make it possible for people to work in twos and threes, always with partial contact and partial privacy—SMALL WORK GROUPS (148) and HALF-PRIVATE OFFICE (152). Place a welcoming reception area at the front—RECEPTION WELCOMES YOU (149); and in the common areas at the heart arrange a place where people can eat together, everyday—COMMUNAL EATING (147). . . .

147 COMMUNAL EATING*

. . . . this pattern helps complete all those human groups and institutions which have COMMON AREAS AT THE HEART (129) in them, and most of all it helps to complete workshops and offices and extended families—THE FAMILY (75), SELF-GOVERNING WORKSHOPS AND OFFICES (80). In all of them, the common area will draw its strength from the sharing of food and drink. This pattern defines it in detail, and shows also how it helps to generate a larger social order.

❖ ❖ ❖

Without communal eating, no human group can hold together.

The importance of communal eating is clear in all human societies. Holy communion, wedding feasts, birthday parties, Christmas dinner, an Irish wake, the family evening meal are Western and Christian examples, but every society has its equivalents. There are almost no important human events or institutions which are not given their power to bind, their sacral character, by food and drink. The anthropological literature is full of references. For example: "Food and Its Vicissitudes: A Cross-Cultural Study of Sharing and Nonsharing," in Yehudi A. Cohen, *Social Structure and Personality: A Casebook*, New York: Holt, 1961. Audrey I. Richards, *Hunger and Work in a Savage Tribe: A Functional Study of Nutrition Among the Southern Bantu*. Glencoe, Ill.: Free Press, 1932.

Thomas Merton summarizes the meaning of communal eating beautifully:

A feast is of such a nature that it draws people to itself, and makes them leave everything else in order to participate in its joys. To feast together is to bear witness to the joy one has at being with his friends. The mere act of eating together, quite apart from a banquet or some other festival occasion, is by its very nature a sign of friendship and of "communion."

In modern times we have lost sight of the fact that even the most ordinary actions of our everyday life are invested, by their very nature, with a deep spiritual meaning. The table is in a

certain sense the center of family life, the expression of family life. Here the children gather with their parents to eat the food which the love of their parents has provided. . . .

So, too, with a banquet. The Latin word *convivium* contains more of this mystery than our words "banquet" or "feast." To call a feast a "convivium" is to call it a "mystery of the sharing of life"—a mystery in which guests partake of the good things prepared and given to them by the love of their host, and in which the atmosphere of friendship and gratitude expands into a sharing of thoughts and sentiments, and ends in common rejoicing. (Thomas Merton, *The Living Bread*, New York, 1956, pp. 126–27.)

It is clear, then, that communal eating plays a vital role in almost all human societies as a way of binding people together and increasing the extent to which they feel like "members" of a group.

But beyond this intrinsic importance of communal eating, as a way of binding the members of a group together, there is another important reason for maintaining the pattern, which applies especially to modern metropolitan society.

Metropolitan society creates the possibility of meeting a wonderful variety of people, a possibility almost entirely new in human history. In a traditional society, one learns to live with the people he knows, but the people he knows form a relatively closed group; there is little possibility of expanding it greatly. In a modern metropolitan society, each person has the possibility of finding those few other people in the city he really wants to be with. In theory, a man in a city of five million people has the possibility of meeting just those half dozen people who are the people he most wants to be with, in all of these five million.

But this is only theory. In practice it is very hard. Few people can feel confident that they have met their closest possible companions or found the informal groups they want to belong to in the cities they inhabit. In fact, on the contrary, people complain constantly that they cannot meet enough people, that there are too few opportunities for meeting people. Far from being free to explore the natures of all the people in society, and free to be together with those others who have the greatest natural and mutual affinities, instead people feel constrained to be with the few people they happen to have run into.

How can the great potential of metropolitan society be realized? How can a person find the other people for whom he has the greatest possible affinity?

To answer this question, we must define the workings of the process by which people meet new people in society. The answer to this question hinges on the following three critical hypotheses:

1. The process hinges entirely on the *overlap* of the human groups in society, and the way a person can pass through these human groups, expanding his associations.

2. The process can only take place if the various human groups in society possess "group territories" where meeting can take place.

3. The process of meeting seems to depend especially on communal eating and drinking and therefore takes place especially well in those groups which have at least partly institutionalized common food and drink.

If these three hypotheses are correct, as we believe, then it is plain that the process by which people meet one another depends very largely on the extent to which people are able to pass from group to group, as visitors and guests, at communal meals. And this of course can happen only if each institution and each social group has its own common meals, regularly, and if its members are free to invite guests to their meals and in turn are free to be invited by the guests they meeet to other meals at other gatherings.

Therefore:

Give every institution and social group a place where people can eat together. Make the common meal a regular event. In particular, start a common lunch in every work place, so that a genuine meal around a common table (not out of boxes, machines, or bags) becomes an important, comfortable, and daily event with room for invited guests. In our own work group at the Center, we found this worked most beautifully when we took it in turns to cook the lunch. The lunch became an event: a gathering: something that each of us put our love and energy into, on our day to cook.

a table

regular meal

people cook it themselves, in turn

❖ ❖ ❖

If the institution is large, find some way of breaking it down into smaller groups which eat together, so that no one group which eats together has more than about a dozen people in it— SMALL WORK GROUPS (148), SMALL MEETING ROOMS (151). Build the kitchen all around the eating place like a FARMHOUSE KITCHEN (139); make the table itself a focus of great importance —EATING ATMOSPHERE (182). . . .

148 SMALL WORK GROUPS**

. . . within the workspace of an institution—SELF-GOVERNING
WORKSHOPS AND OFFICES (80), FLEXIBLE OFFICE SPACE (146),
there need to be still further subdivisions. Above all, as this
pattern shows, it is essential that the smallest human working
groups each have their own physical space.

**When more than half a dozen people work in the same
place, it is essential that they not be forced to work in one
huge undifferentiated space, but that instead, they can
divide their workspace up, and so form smaller groups.**

In fact, people will feel oppressed, both when they are either
working in an undifferentiated mass of workers and when they
are forced to work in isolation. The small group achieves a
nice balance between the one extreme in which there are so
many people, that there is no opportunity for an intimate social
structure to develop, and the other extreme in which there are
so few, that the possibility of social groups does not occur at all.

This attitude toward the size of work groups is supported by
the findings of the Pilkington Research Unit, in their investigations of office life (*Office Design: A Study of Environment*, ed.
Peter Manning, Department of Building Science, University of
Liverpool, 1965, pp. 104–28). In a very large study indeed,
office workers were asked their opinions of large offices and small
offices. The statements they chose most often to describe their
opinions were: "The larger offices make one feel relatively unim-
portant" and "There is an uncomfortable feeling of being watched
all the time in a large office." And when asked to compare five
different possible layouts for offices, workers consistently chose
those layouts in which workgroups were smallest.

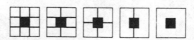

The five layouts in order of preference.

702

Analysis of the results also showed that "the people who work in small office areas are more opposed to large office areas than those who actually work in them." Apparently, once people have had the experience of working in small groups, they find it very uncomfortable to imagine going back to the larger office settings.

In our own survey of attitudes toward workspace—taken among workers at the Berkeley City Hall—we found that people prefer to be part of a group that ranges from two to eight. When there are more than eight, people lose touch with the group as a human gathering; and almost no one likes working alone.

A similar finding is reported by the Japanese architect, T. Takano, in his study of work groups in Japan. In the offices he studied, he found that five persons formed the most useful functional group. (Building Section, Building and Repairs Bureau, Ministry of Construction: The Design of Akita prefectural government office, Public Buildings, 1961.)

How should these small groups be related to each other? Brian Wells points out that while small offices support an intimate atmosphere, they do not support communications between groups. "The Psycho-Social Influence of Building Environment" (*Building Science*, Vol. 1, Pergamon Press, 1965, p. 153). It would seem that this problem can be solved by arranging the small work groups so that several of them share common facilities: drinking fountains, toilets, office equipment, perhaps a common anteroom and garden.

Therefore:

Break institutions into small, spatially identifiable work groups, with less than half a dozen people in each. Arrange these work groups so that each person is in at least partial view of the other members of his own group; and arrange several groups in such a way that they share a common entrance, food, office equipment, drinking fountains, bathrooms.

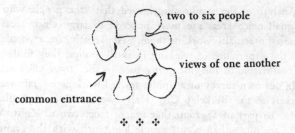

two to six people

views of one another

common entrance

❖ ❖ ❖

Lay the workgroups out with respect to each other so that the distances between groups is within the constraints of OFFICE CONNECTIONS (82), and give each group office space which leaves room to expand and to contract—FLEXIBLE OFFICE SPACE (146); provide a common area, either for the group itself or for several groups together or both—COMMON AREA AT THE HEART (129). Treat each small work group, in every kind of industry and office, as a place of learning—MASTER AND APPRENTICES (83). Give it its own stair, directly to the street—OPEN STAIRS (158). Arrange the individual workspaces within the small work group according to HALF-PRIVATE OFFICE (152) and WORKSPACE ENCLOSURE (183). . . .

149 RECEPTION
WELCOMES YOU

. . . in a public building, or an office where there are many people coming in, SELF-GOVERNING WORKSHOPS AND OFFICES (80), SMALL SERVICES WITHOUT RED TAPE (81), TRAVELER'S INN (91), FLEXIBLE OFFICE SPACE (146)—the place inside the ENTRANCE ROOM (130) plays an essential role; it must be built from the very start with the right atmosphere. This pattern was originally proposed by Clyde Dorsett of the National Institute of Mental Health, in a program for community mental health clinics.

Have you ever walked into a public building and been processed by the receptionist as if you were a package?

To make a person feel at ease, you must do the same for him as you would do to welcome him to your home; go toward him, greet him, offer him a chair, offer him some food and drink, and take his coat.

In most institutions the person arriving has to go toward the receptionist; the receptionist remains passive and offers nothing. To be welcoming the receptionist must initiate the action—come forward and greet the person, offer a chair, food, a seat by the fire, coffee. Since it is first impressions which count, this whole atmosphere should be the first thing a person encounters.

A beautiful example we know is the reception desk at Browns Hotel in London. You pass into the hotel through a small, unassuming entrance, not unlike the entrance to a house. You pass through two or three rooms; then come to the central room in which there are two old writing desks. The receptionist comes forward from an inner office, invites you to sit down in a comfortable chair at one of these writing desks, and sits down with you while you fill out the hotel register.

The reasons most reception areas fail completely to have this quality, is that the receptionist's desk forms a barrier, so that the desk and equipment together help to create an institutional atmosphere, quite at odds with the feeling of welcome.

Therefore:

Arrange a series of welcoming things immediately inside the entrance—soft chairs, a fireplace, food, coffee. Place the reception desk so that it is not between the receptionist and the welcoming area, but to one side at an angle—so that she, or he, can get up and walk toward the people who come in, greet them, and then invite them to sit down.

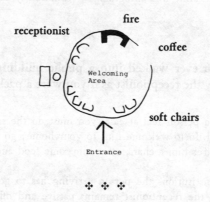

❖ ❖ ❖

Place the fireplace most carefully, to be a focus—THE FIRE (181) give the receptionist a workspace where she can be comfortable in her own work, and still make visitors feel welcome— WORKSPACE ENCLOSURE (183); give the space LIGHT ON TWO SIDES (159); perhaps put in an alcove or a window seat for people who are waiting—A PLACE TO WAIT (150), ALCOVES (179), WINDOW PLACE (180). Make sure that the reception point itself is lighter than surrounding areas—TAPESTRY OF LIGHT AND DARK (135). And for the shape of the reception space start with THE SHAPE OF INDOOR SPACE (191). . . .

150 A PLACE TO WAIT*

. . . in any office, or workshop, or public service, or station, or clinic, where people have to wait—INTERCHANGE (34), HEALTH CENTER (47), SMALL SERVICES WITHOUT RED TAPE (81), OFFICE CONNECTIONS (82), it is essential to provide a special place for waiting, and doubly essential that this place not have the sordid, enclosed, time-slowed character of ordinary waiting rooms.

The process of waiting has inherent conflicts in it.

On the one hand, whatever people are waiting for—the doctor, an airplane, a business appointment—has built in uncertainties, which make it inevitable that they must spend a long time hanging around, waiting, doing nothing.

On the other hand, they cannot usually afford to enjoy this time. Because it is unpredictable, they must hang at the very door. Since they never know exactly when their turn will come, they cannot even take a stroll or sit outside. They must stay in the narrow confine of the waiting room, waiting their turn. But this, of course, is an extremely demoralizing situation: nobody wants to wait at somebody else's beck and call. Kafka's greatest works, *The Castle* and *The Trial*, both deal almost entirely with the way this kind of atmosphere destroys a man.

The classic "waiting room" does nothing to resolve this problem. A tight dreary little room, with people staring at each other, fidgeting, a magazine or two to flip—this is the very situation which creates the conflict. Evidence for the deadening effect of this situation comes from Scott Briar ("Welfare From Below: Recipients' Views of the Public Welfare System," in Jacobus Tenbroek, ed., *The Law and the Poor*, San Francisco: Chandler Publishing Company, 1966, p. 52). We all know that time seems to pass more slowly when we are bored or anxious or restless. Briar found that people waiting in welfare agencies consistently thought they had been waiting for longer than they really had. Some thought they had been wating four times as long.

The fundamental problem then, is this. How can the people

who are waiting, spend their time wholeheartedly—live the hours or minutes while they wait, as fully as the other hours of their day—and yet still be on hand, whenever the event or the person they are waiting for is ready?

It can be done best when the waiting is fused with some other activity: an activity that draws in other people who are not there essentially to wait—a cafe, pool tables, tables, a reading room, where the activities and the seats around them are within earshot of the signal that the interviewer (or the plane, or whatever) is ready. For example, the Pediatrics Clinic at San Francisco General Hospital built a small playground beside the entrance, to serve as a waiting area for children and a play area for the neighborhood.

Waiting room at the pediatrics clinic.

In another example we know, a horseshoe pit was built along-side a terrace where people came to wait for appointments. The people waiting inevitably started pitching horseshoes, others joined in, people left as their appointments came up—there was an easy flow between the horseshoe pit, the terrace, and the offices.

Waiting can also be a situation where the person waiting finds himself with free time, and, with the support of the surroundings, is able to draw into himself, become still, meditative—quite the opposite of the activity described above.

The right atmosphere will come naturally if the waiting area provides some places that are quiet, protected, and do not draw out the anxiety of the wait. Some examples: a seat near a bus

stop, under a tree, protected from the street; a window seat that looks down upon a street scene below; a protected seat in a garden, a swing or a hammock; a dark place and a glass of beer, far enough away from passages so that a person is not always looking up when someone comes or goes; a private seat by a fish tank.

In summary, then, people who are waiting must be free to do what they want. If they want to sit outside the interviewer's door, they can. If they want to get up and take a stroll, or play a game of pool, or have a cup of coffee, or watch other people, they can. If they want to sit privately and fall into a daydream, they can. And all this without having to fear that they are losing their place in line.

Quiet waiting.

Therefore:

In places where people end up waiting (for a bus, for an appointment, for a plane), create a situation which makes the waiting positive. Fuse the waiting with some other activity—newspaper, coffee, pool tables, horseshoes; something which draws people in who are not simply waiting. And also the opposite: make a place which can draw a person waiting into a reverie; quiet; a positive silence.

activities where people meet

within earshot
if some signal

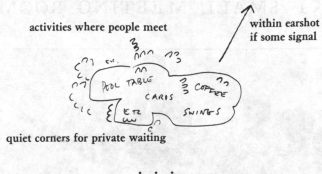

quiet corners for private waiting

❖ ❖ ❖

The active part might have a window on the street—STREET
WINDOWS (164), WINDOW PLACE (180), a cafe—STREET CAFE
(88), games, positive engagements with the people passing by—
OPENING TO THE STREET (165). The quiet part might have a
quiet garden seat—GARDEN SEAT (176), a place for people to
doze—SLEEPING IN PUBLIC (94), perhaps a pond with fish in
it—STILL WATER (71). To the extent that this waiting space
is a room, or a group of rooms, it gets its detailed shape from
LIGHT ON TWO SIDES OF EVERY ROOM (159) and THE SHAPE OF
INDOOR SPACE (191). . . .

151 SMALL MEETING ROOMS*

. . . within organizations and workplaces—UNIVERSITY AS A MARKETPLACE (43), LOCAL TOWN HALL (44), MASTER AND APPRENTICES (83), FLEXIBLE OFFICE SPACE (146), SMALL WORK GROUPS (148), there will, inevitably, be meeting rooms, group rooms, classrooms, of one kind or another. Investigation of meeting rooms shows that the best distribution—both by size and by position—is rather unexpected.

❖ ❖ ❖

The larger meetings are, the less people get out of them. But institutions often put their money and attention into large meeting rooms and lecture halls.

We first discuss the sheer size of meetings. It has been shown that the number of people in a group influences both the number who never talk, and the number who feel they have ideas which they have not been able to express. For example, Bernard Bass (*Organizational Psychology*, Boston: Allyn, 1965, p. 200) has conducted an experiment relating group size to participation. The results of this experiment are shown in the following graph.

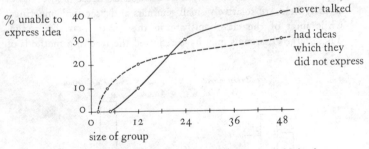

As size of group grows, more and more people hold back.

There is no particularly natural threshold for group size; but it is clear that the number who never talk climbs very rapidly. In a group of 12, one person never talks. In a group of 24, there are six people who never talk.

We get similar thresholds when we consider comfortable distances for talking. Edward Hall has established the upper

range for full casual voice at about 8 feet; a person with 20/20 vision can see details of facial expression up to 12 feet; two people whose heads are 8 to 9 feet apart, can pass an object if they both stretch; clear vision (that is, macular vision) includes 12 degrees horizontally and 3 degrees vertically—which includes one face but not two, at distances up to about 10 feet. (See Edward Hall, *The Silent Language*, New York: Doubleday, 1966, pp. 118–19.)

Thus a small group discussion will function best if the members of the group are arranged in a rough circle, with a maximum diameter of about 8 feet. At this diameter, the circumference of the circle will be 25 feet. Since people require about 27 inches each for their seats, there can be no more than about 12 people round the circle.

Next we shall present evidence to show that in institutions and workgroups, the natural history of meetings tends also to converge on this size.

The following histograms show the relative numbers of different sized classes held at the University of Oregon in the Fall of 1970 and the relative numbers of available classrooms in the different size ranges. We believe these figures are typical for many universities. But it is obvious at a glance that there are too many large classrooms and too few small classrooms. Most of the classes actually held are relatively small seminars and "section" meetings, while most of the classrooms are in the 30 to 150 size range. These large classrooms may have reflected the teaching methods of

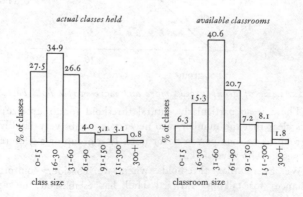

Histogram: Classes don't fit the classrooms.

an earlier period, but apparently they do not conform to the actual practice of teaching in the 1970's.

We found that the meetings of official committees, boards, and commissions in the City of Berkeley have a similar distribution. Among the various city boards, commissions, and committees, 73 per cent have an average attendance of 15 or less. Yet of course, most of these meetings are held in rooms designed for far more than 15 people. Here again, most of the meetings are held in rooms that are too large; the rooms are half-empty; people tend to sit at the back; speakers face rows of empty seats. The intimate and intense atmosphere typical of a good small meeting cannot be achieved under these circumstances.

Finally, the *spatial* distribution of meeting rooms is often as poorly adapted to the actual meetings as the size distribution. The following histograms compare the distribution of classrooms in different sectors of the University of Oregon with the distribution of faculty and student offices.

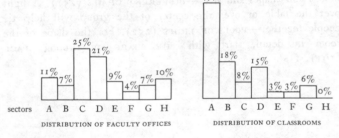

DISTRIBUTION OF FACULTY OFFICES   DISTRIBUTION OF CLASSROOMS

The meeting rooms are not located where people work.

Once again, this discrepancy has a bad effect on the social life of small meetings. The meetings work best when the meeting rooms are fairly near the participants' offices. Then discussions which begin in the meeting rooms are able to continue in the office or the laboratory. When the meeting rooms are a long walk from offices, the chances of this kind of informal business are drastically reduced.

Therefore:

Make at least 70 per cent of all meeting rooms really small—for 12 people or less. Locate them in the most publi parts of the building, evenly scattered among the workpla

70 per cent small meeting rooms

evenly distributed through working areas

❖ ❖ ❖

Shape meeting rooms like any other rooms, perhaps with special emphasis on the fact that there must be no glare—LIGHT ON TWO SIDES OF EVERY ROOM (159)—and on the fact that the rooms should be roughly round or square, and not too long or narrow—SITTING CIRCLE (185). People will feel best if many of the chairs are different, to suit different temperaments and moods and shapes and sizes—DIFFERENT CHAIRS (251). A light over the table or over the center of the group will help tie people together—POOLS OF LIGHT (252). For the shape of the room in detail, start with THE SHAPE OF INDOOR SPACE (191). . . .

152 HALF-PRIVATE OFFICE

. . . within the overall arrangement of group space and individual working space provided by INTIMACY GRADIENT (127), FLEXIBLE OFFICE SPACE (146), and SMALL WORK GROUPS (148), this pattern shapes the individual rooms and offices. The pattern also helps to generate the organization of these larger patterns.

What is the right balance between privacy and connection in office work?

The totally private office has a devastating effect on the flow of human relationships within a work group, and entrenches the ugly quality of office hierarchies. At the same time, there are moments when privacy is essential; and to some extent nearly every job of work needs to be free from random interruption.

Everyone who has experienced office work reports some version of this problem. In our own experience—as members of a working team of architects—we have faced the problem in hundreds of ways. The best evidence we have to report is our own experience as a work group.

Over the last seven years we moved our offices on several occasions. At one point we moved to a large old house: large enough for some of us to have private rooms and others to share rooms. In a matter of months our social coherence as a group was on the point of breakdown. The workings of the group became formalized; easy-going communication vanished; the entire atmosphere changed from a setting which sustained our growth as a group to an office bureaucracy, where people made appointments with each other, left notes in special boxes, and nervously knocked on each other's doors.

For a while we were virtually unable to produce any interesting work.

It gradually dawned on us that the environment of the house was playing a powerful role in the breakdown. As we started to pay attention to it, we noticed that those rooms which were still functioning—the places where we would all gather to talk

over the work—had a special characteristic: they were only *half*-private, even though the workspaces within them were strongly marked.

As we thought it out, it seemed that almost every place where we had found ourselves working well together had these characteristics: no office was entirely private; most offices were for more than one person; but even when an office was only for one, it had a kind of simple common area at its front and everyone felt free to drop in and stay for a moment. And the desks themselves were always built up as private domains within and toward the edges of these offices, so that doors could always be left wide open. Eventually we rearranged ourselves until each person had some version of this pattern.

The pattern works so well, that we recommend it to everyone in similar circumstances.

Therefore:

Avoid closed off, separate, or private offices. Make every workroom, whether it is for a group of two or three people or for one person, half-open to the other workgroups and the world immediately beyond it. At the front, just inside the door, make comfortable sitting space, with the actual workspace(s) away from the door, and further back.

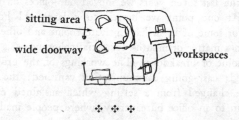

❖ ❖ ❖

Shape each office in detail, according to THE SHAPE OF INDOOR SPACE (191); give it windows on at least two sides—LIGHT ON TWO SIDES OF EVERY ROOM (159); make individual workspaces in the corners—WORKSPACE ENCLOSURE (183), looking out of windows—WINDOWS OVERLOOKING LIFE (192); make the sitting area toward the door as comfortable as possible—SITTING CIRCLE (185). . . .

*add those small outbuildings which must be
slightly independent from the main structure, and
put in the access from the upper stories to the street
and gardens;*

153 ROOMS TO RENT

. . . this pattern is the first which sets the framework for the outbuildings. Used properly, it can help to create NECKLACE OF COMMUNITY PROJECTS (45), THE FAMILY (75), SELF-GOVERNING WORKSHOPS AND OFFICES (80), SMALL SERVICES WITHOUT RED TAPE (81), FLEXIBLE OFFICE SPACE (146), TEENAGER'S COTTAGE (154), OLD AGE COTTAGE (155), HOME WORKSHOP (157): in general it makes any building flexible, useful in a greater variety of circumstances.

As the life in a building changes, the need for space shrinks and swells cyclically. The building must be able to adapt to this irregular increase and decrease in the need for space.

Very simply, when a family or a workgroup shrinks because one or two people leave, the space which becomes empty should be able to find a use. Otherwise, the people who stay behind will rattle around in a hollow shell which is too big for them. They may even be forced to sell their property and move because they cannot afford the upkeep of so big a place.

And by the same token, since swelling and shrinking is almost always unpredictable, this splitting off of space should be reversible. The rooms which are given to outside use or let out when they are not used, may one day be needed again when circumstances change and the workgroup or family swells in size again.

To give buildings this flexibility, it is essential that parts of them be relatively independent. In effect, some rooms should be conceived in advance as potential rooms to let if the size of the group should change. These rooms need a kind of connection to the rest of the house, which allows them to be closed off and separated, and then, just as easily, joined up again. Generally,

this means a private entrance from the outside, either a private bath or direct access to a bathroom, and perhaps access to the kitchen.

In Denmark, Ole Dybbroe has developed a scheme for housing that takes this pattern as a crucial generator of the form of the house. The houses he shows in *Enfamiliehuset 1970* (Landsbankernes Reallanefond, stiftedes den 9. maj 1959) grow slowly, and each part of them can either be united with the larger household or inhabited as an independent unit. Here is his plan for a "four part" house.

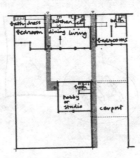

Dybbroe's four-part house.

Though renting in general has a devastating impact on the environment—see YOUR OWN HOME (79) our experience has been that face-to-face rental, with the owners occupying the main structure, is the one kind of rental relationship that is reasonably healthy. The landlord is actually there, so he is directly concerned with the well-being of the life around him and with the environment, unlike the absentee landlords, who own property only for the money which it makes. And the tenants are usually short-term tenants, who prefer to rent a room rather than take on burdens of ownership. Even here a more ideal situation would be for the owner to share out ownership over some part of the building, with certain options for taking back the space. However, in the absence of such subtle forms of legal ownership, face to face renting is, we believe, the only form of renting that is not socially and physically destructive.

Therefore:

Make at least some part of the building rentable: give it a private entrance over and above its regular connection to the rest of the house. Make sure that the regular entrance can be easily closed off without destroying the circulation in the house, and make sure that a bathroom can be directly reached from this room without having to go through the main house.

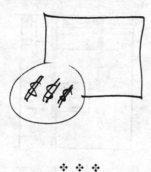

❖ ❖ ❖

Place the rooms to rent in such a way that they can double as a TEENAGER'S COTTAGE (154), or an OLD AGE COTTAGE (155), or a HOME WORKSHOP (157); give the private entrance an ENTRANCE TRANSITION (112), and if the space is on an upper floor, give it direct access to the street by means of OPEN STAIRS (158). And give the rooms themselves LIGHT ON TWO SIDES (159) and THE SHAPE OF INDOOR SPACE (191). . . .

154 TEENAGER'S COTTAGE*

. . . in any house which has teenagers in it—THE FAMILY (75), HOUSE FOR A SMALL FAMILY (76)—it is necessary to give special consideration to their rooms—A ROOM OF ONE'S OWN (141). If possible, these rooms should be attached but separate, and made to help create the possibility of later being ROOMS TO RENT (153).

❖ ❖ ❖

If a teenager's place in the home does not reflect his need for a measure of independence, he will be locked in conflict with his family.

In most family homes the rooms for children and adolescents are essentially the same. But when children become adolescents, their relationship to the family changes considerably. They become less and less dependent on the family; they take on greater responsibilities; their life outside the home becomes richer, more absorbing. Most of the time they want more independence; occasionally they really need the family to fall back on; sometimes they are terrified by the confusion within and around them. All of this places new demands on the organization of the family and, accordingly, on the organization of the house.

To really help a young person go through this time, home life must strike a subtle balance. It must offer tremendous opportunities for initiative and independence, as well as a constant sense of support, no matter what happens. But American family life never seems to strike this balance. The studies of adolescent family life depict a time of endless petty conflict, tyranny, delinquency, and acquiescence. As a social process, adolescence, it seems, is geared more to breaking the spirit of young boys and girls, than to helping them find themselves in the world. (See, for example, Jules Henry, *Culture Against Man*, New York: Random House, 1963.)

In physical terms these problems boil down to this. A teenager needs a place in the house that has more autonomy and character and is more a base for independent action than a child's bedroom or bed alcove. He needs a place from which he can come

and go as he pleases, a place within which his privacy is respected. At the same time he needs the chance to establish a closeness with his family that is more mutual and less strictly dependent than ever before. What seems to be required is a cottage which, in its organization and location, strikes the balance between a new independence and new ties to the family.

The teenager's cottage might be made from the child's old bedroom, the boy and his father knocking a door through the wall and enlarging the room. It might be built from scratch, with the intention that it later serve as a workshop, or a place for grandfather to live out his life, or a room to rent. The cottage might even be an entirely detached structure in the garden, but in this case, a very strong connection to the main house is essential: perhaps a short covered path from the cottage into the main kitchen. Even in row housing, or apartments, it is possible to give teenagers rooms with private entry.

Is the idea of the teenage cottage acceptable to parents? Silverstein interviewed 12 mothers living in Foster City, a suburb of San Francisco, and asked them whether they would like a teenage cottage in their family. Their resistance to the idea revolved around three objections:

1. The cottage would be useful for only a few years, and would then stand empty.

2. The cottage would break up the family; it isolates the teenager.

3. It gives the teenager too much freedom in his comings and goings.

Silverstein then suggested three modifications, to meet these objections:

To meet the first objection, make the space double as a workshop, guest room, studio, place for grandmother; and build it with wood, so it can be modified easily with hand tools.

To meet the second objection, attach the cottage to the house, but with its own entrance; attach the cottage to the house via a short hall or vestibule or keep the cottage to the back of the lot, behind the house.

To meet the third objection, place the cottage so that the path from the room to the street passes through an important communal part of the house—the kitchen, a courtyard.

He discussed these modifications with the same twelve mothers. Eleven of the twelve now felt that the modified version had some merit, and was worth trying. This material is reported by Murray Silverstein, in "The Boy's Room: Twelve Mothers Respond to an Architectural Pattern," University of California, Department of Architecture, December 1967.

Here are some possible variants containing these modifications.

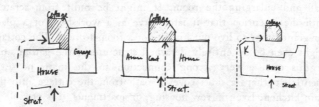

Variations of teenager's cottage.

Among the Comanches, ". . . the boy after puberty was given a separate tepee in which he slept, entertained his friends, and spent most of his time." (Abram Kardiner, *Psychological Frontiers of Society*, New York: Columbia University Press, 1945, p. 75.)

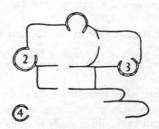

Plan of a Yungur Compound, Africa; 2 is the master bedroom; 3 is the daughter's hut; 4 is the son's hut.

And finally, from Simone De Beauvoir:

When I was twelve I had suffered through not having a private retreat of my own at home. Leafing through *Mon Journal* I had found a story about an English schoolgirl, and gazed enviously at

the colored illustration portraying her room. There was a desk, and a divan, and shelves filled with books. Here, within these gaily painted walls, she read and worked and drank tea, with no one watching her—how envious I felt! For the first time ever I had glimpsed a more fortunate way of life than my own. And now, at long last, I too had a room to myself. My grandmother had stripped her drawing room of all its armchairs, occasional tables, and knick-knacks. I had bought some unpainted furniture, and my sister had helped me to give it a coat of brown varnish. I had a table, two chairs, a large chest which served both as a seat and as a hold-all, shelves for my books. I papered the walls orange, and got a divan to match. From my fifth-floor balcony I looked out over the Lion of Belfort and the plane trees on the Rue Denfert-Rochereau. I kept myself warm with an evil-smelling kerosene stove. Somehow its stink seemed to protect my solitude, and I loved it. It was wonderful to be able to shut my door and keep my daily life free of other people's inquisitiveness. For a long time I remained indifferent to the decor of my surroundings. Possibly because of that picture in *Mon Journal* I preferred rooms that offered me a divan and bookshelves, but I was prepared to put up with any sort of retreat in a pinch. To have a door that I could shut was still the height of bliss for me . . . I was free to come and go as I pleased. I could get home with the milk, read in bed all night, sleep till midday, shut myself up for forty-eight hours at a stretch, or go out on the spur of the moment . . . my chief delight was in doing as I pleased. (Simone De Beauvoir, *The Prime of Life*, New York: Lancer Books, 1966, pp. 9–10.)

Therefore:

To mark a child's coming of age, transform his place in the home into a kind of cottage that expresses in a physical way the beginnings of independence. Keep the cottage attached to the home, but make it a distinctly visible bulge, far away from the master bedroom, with its own private entrance, perhaps its own roof.

cottage

path through
commons

separate entrance

727

❖ ❖ ❖

Arrange the cottage to contain a SITTING CIRCLE (185) and a BED ALCOVE (188) but not a private bath and kitchen—sharing these is essential: it allows the boy or girl to keep enough connection with the family. Make it a place that can eventually become a guest room, room to rent, workshop, and so on—ROOMS TO RENT (153), HOME WORKSHOP (157). If it is on an upper story, give it a separate private OPEN STAIR (158). And for the shape of the cottage and its construction, start with THE SHAPE OF INDOOR SPACE (191) and STRUCTURE FOLLOWS SOCIAL SPACES (205). . . .

155 OLD AGE COTTAGE**

. . . we have explained, in OLD PEOPLE EVERYWHERE (40), that it is essential to have a balanced number of old people in every neighborhood, partly centered around a communal place, but largely strung out among the other houses of the neighborhood. This pattern now defines the nature of the houses for old people in more detail: both those which are a part of clusters and those which are tucked, autonomously, between the larger houses. As we shall see, it seems desirable that every family should have a cottage like this, attached to it—THE FAMILY (75). Like ROOMS TO RENT (153) and TEENAGER'S COTTAGE (154), this cottage can be rented out or used for other purposes in time of trouble.

❖ ❖ ❖

Old people, especially when they are alone, face a terrible dilemma. On the one hand, there are inescapable forces pushing them toward independence: their children move away; the neighborhood changes; their friends and wives and husbands die. On the other hand, by the very nature of aging, old people become dependent on simple conveniences, simple connections to the society about them.

This conflict is reflected often in their children's conflict. On the one hand, children feel responsible for their parents, because, of course, they sense their growing need for care and comfort. On the other hand, as families are whittled down, parent-child conflicts become more acute, and few people can imagine actually being able or willing to take care of their parents in their dotage.

The conflict can be partly resolved, if each house which houses a nuclear family has, somewhere near it, a small cottage where a grandparent can live, far enough away to be independent, and yet close enough to feel some tie and to be cared for in a time of trouble or approaching death.

But the conflict is more general. Even if we ignore, altogether, the complexities of parent-child relationships, the fact is that most old people face enormous difficulties as they grow older. The wel-

fare state tries to replace the comfort of the extended family with payments—social security or pensions. This income is always tiny; and inflation makes it worse. In the United States, one-quarter of the population over 65 lives on less than $4000 a year. Many of the old people in our society are forced to live in miserable tiny rooms, way in the back of some run-down old folks hotel. They cannnot have a decent house, because there are no decent tiny houses compatible with a small income and reduced activity.

This second conflict, between the need for someplace really small and modest and the need for social contact, a view of passing people, someone to nod to, a place in the sun, can also be resolved, like the first conflict, by cottages. It can be resolved, if there are many tiny cottages, dotted among the houses of communities and always strung along pedestrian paths—tiny enough to be really cheap.

Therefore:

Build small cottages specifically for old people. Build some of them on the land of larger houses, for a grandparent; build others on individual lots, much smaller than ordinary lots. In all cases, place these cottages at ground level, right on the street, where people are walking by, and close to neighborhood services and common land.

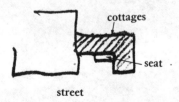

cottages

seat

street

Perhaps the most important part of an old age cottage is the front porch and front door bench outside the door, right on the street—PRIVATE TERRACE ON THE STREET (140), FRONT DOOR BENCH (242); for the rest, arrange the cottage pretty much according to the layout of any HOUSE FOR ONE PERSON (78); make provisions for SETTLED WORK (156); and give the cottage a STREET WINDOW (164). And for the shape of the cottage start with THE SHAPE OF INDOOR SPACE (191) and STRUCTURE FOLLOWS SOCIAL SPACES (205). . . .

156 SETTLED WORK*

. . . as people grow older, simple satisfying work which nourishes, becomes more and more important. This pattern specifies the need for this development to be a part of every family. It helps to form THE FAMILY (75), it helps form OLD AGE COTTAGE (155), and it is a natural embellishment of A ROOM OF ONE'S OWN (141).

❖ ❖ ❖

The experience of settled work is a prerequisite for peace of mind in old age. Yet our society undermines this experience by making a rift between working life and retirement, and between workplace and home.

First of all, what do we mean by "settled work"? It is the work which unites all the threads of a person's life into one activity: the activity becomes a complete and wholehearted extension of the person behind it. It is a kind of work that one cannot come to overnight; but only by gradual development. And it is a kind of work that is so thoroughly a part of one's way of life that it most naturally occurs within or very near the home: when it is free to develop, the workplace and the home gradually fuse and become one thing.

It may be the same kind of work that a man has been doing all his life—but as settled work it becomes more profound, more concrete, and more unique. For example, there is the bureaucrat who finally breaks through all the paper work and finds the underlying organic function in his work. Then he begins to let this function into the world. This is the theme of Kurosawa's most beautiful film, *Ikiru: To Live*. Or it may be work that a person begins in his spare time, away from his occupation, and it gradually expands and becomes more involving, until it replaces his old occupation altogether.

The problem is that very many people never achieve the experience of settled work. This is essentially because a person,

during his working life, has neither the time nor the space to develop it. In today's marketplace most people are forced to adapt their work to the rules of the office, the factory, or the institution. And generally this work is all-consuming—when the weekends come people do not have the energy to start a new, demanding kind of work. Even in the self-governing workshops and offices, where working procedures are created ad hoc by the workers as they go, the work itself is generally geared to the demands of the marketplace. It does not allow time for the slow growth of "settled work"—which comes from within and may not always carry its weight in the marketplace.

To solve the problem, we must first of all create a working environment, where a person, from say middle age, has the opportunity of slowly developing a kind of settled work that is right for him. For instance, if people were able to take off one day a week, with half-time pay, beginning at the age of 40, they could gradually set up for themselves a workshop in their home or in their neighborhood. If the time is increased gradually over the years, a person can explore various kinds of work; and, then, gradually let the settled work replace his working life.

We make special mention of settled work as the work of old age, because, even though it must begin early on in a person's life, it is in old age that having such work becomes a necessity. The crisis of old age, life integrity versus despair and cynicism, can only be solved by a person engaged in some form of settled work —occ LIFE CYCLE (26). People who have the opportunity to develop such work and to relate it in some appropriate way to the world about them, will find their way to a successful resolution of this crisis as they grow old; others will sink into despair.

Therefore:

Give each person, especially as he grows old, the chance to set up a workplace of his own, within or very near his home. Make it a place that can grow slowly, perhaps in the beginning sustaining a weekend hobby and gradually becoming a complete, productive, and comfortable workshop.

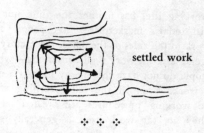

settled work

❖ ❖ ❖

Arrange the workshop, physically, along the lines defined by
HOME WORKSHOP (157), and make the workshop open to the
street, a part of local street life—PRIVATE TERRACE ON THE
STREET (140), OPENING TO THE STREET (165). . . .

157 HOME WORKSHOP

. . . at the center of each HOUSE CLUSER (37) and in YOUR
OWN HOME (79) there needs to be one room or outbuilding, which
is freely attached and accessible from the outside. This is the
workshop. The following pattern tells us how important workshops are, how widely they ought to be scattered, how omni-
present, and when they are built, how easy to reach, and how
public they should always be. It helps to reinforce the patterns of
SCATTERED WORK (9), NETWORK OF LEARNING (18), and MEN
AND WOMEN (27).

❖ ❖ ❖

**As the decentralization of work becomes more and more
effective, the workshop in the home grows and grows in
importance.**

We have explained in SCATTERED WORK (9), NETWORK OF
LEARNING (18), MEN AND WOMEN (27), SELF-GOVERNING
WORKSHOPS AND OFFICES (80), and other patterns that we
imagine a society in which work and family are far more intermingled than today; a society in which people—businessmen,
artists, craftsmen, shopkeepers, professionals—work for themselves,
alone and in small groups, with much more relation to their immediate surroundings than they have today.

In such a society, the home workshop becomes far more than a
basement or a garage hobby shop. It becomes an integral part of
every house; as central to the house's function as the kitchen or
the bedrooms. And we believe its most important characteristic
is its relationship to the public street. For most of us, work life
is relatively public. Certainly, compared to the privacy of the
hearth, it is a public affair. Even where the public relationship is
slight, there is something to be gained, both for the worker and
the community, by enlarging the connection between the two.

In the case of the home workshop, the public nature of the
work is especially valuable. It brings the workshop out of the
realm of backyard hobbies and into the public domain. The
people working there have a view of the street; they are exposed

to the people passing by. And the people passing learn something about the nature of the community. The children especially are enlivened by this contact. And according to the nature of the work, the public connection takes the form of a shopfront, a driveway for loading and unloading materials, a work bench in the open, a small meeting room . . .

We therefore advocate provision for a substantial workshop with all the character of a real workplace and some degree of connection to the public street: at least a glancing connection so that people can see in and out; and perhaps a full connection, like an open shop front.

Therefore:

Make a place in the home, where substantial work can be done; not just a hobby, but a job. Change the zoning laws to encourage modest, quiet work operations to locate in neighborhoods. Give the workshop perhaps a few hundred square feet; and locate it so it can be seen from the street and the owner can hang out a shingle.

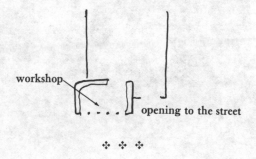

workshop   opening to the street

❖ ❖ ❖

Give the workshop a corner where it is especially nice to work —LIGHT ON TWO SIDES (159), WORKSPACE ENCLOSURE (183); a strong connection to the street—OPENING TO THE STREET (165), WINDOWS OVERLOOKING LIFE (192); perhaps a place to work in the sun on warm days—SUNNY PLACE (161). For the shape of the workshop and its construction, start with THE SHAPE OF INDOOR SPACE (191). . . .

158 OPEN STAIRS*

. . . most of the last patterns—ROOMS TO RENT (153), TEEN-AGER'S COTTAGE (154), SETTLED WORK (156), HOME WORKSHOP (157)—can be upstairs, provided that they have direct connections to the street. Far more generally, it is true that many of the households, public services, and workgroups given by earlier patterns can be successful when they lie upstairs, only if they are given direct connections to the street. For instance, in a work community SELF-GOVERNING WORKSHOPS AND OFFICES (80), SMALL SERVICES WITHOUT RED TAPE (81), SMALL WORK GROUPS (148) all require direct access to the public street when they are on the upper storys of a building. And in the individual households—HOUSE FOR A SMALL FAMILY (76), HOUSE FOR A COUPLE (77), HOUSE FOR ONE PERSON (78) also need direct connections to the street, so people do not need to go through lower floors to get to them. This pattern describes the open stairs which may be used to form these many individual connections to the street. They play a major role in helping to create PEDESTRIAN STREETS (100).

Internal staircases reduce the connection between upper stories and the life of the street to such an extent that they can do enormous social damage.

The simple fact of the matter is that an apartment on the second floor of a building is wonderful when it has a direct stair to the street, and much less wonderful when it is merely one of several apartments served by an internal stair. The following, perhaps rather laborious discussion, is our effort to explain this vital and commonplace intuition.

In a traditional culture where buildings are built incrementally, outdoor stairs leading to upper stories are common. And half "outdoor" stairs—protected by walls and roofs, but nonetheless open to the street—are also common.

The beauty of open stairs.

By contrast, in industrialized, authoritarian societies most stairs are indoor stairs. The access to these stairs is from internal lobbies and corridors; the upper stories are cut off from direct access to the life of the street.

This is not an open stair—don't be fooled.

This difference is not an incidental by-product of fire laws or construction techniques. It is fundamental to the difference between a free anarchical society, in which there is a voluntary exchange of ideas between equals, and a highly centralized authoritarian society, in which most individuals are subservient to large government and business organizations.

In effect we are saying that a centralized entrance, which funnels everyone in a building through it, has in its nature the trappings of control; while the pattern of many open stairs, leading off the public streets, direct to private doors, has in its nature the fact of independence, free comings and goings.

We can see this most easily in the cases where the centralized door is, without question, a source of social control. In workplaces with a central entrance and a time-clock, workers punch in and out, and they have to make excuses when they are leaving at a time that is not normal. In some kinds of student housing, people are asked to sign in and out; and if they are not back by "lock-out" time, they are in trouble.

Then there are cases where the control is more subtle. In an apartment house or a workplace where everyone is free to come or go as he pleases it is not uncommon for the main door to be kept locked. Of course the residents have a key to the building; but their friends do not. When the front door is locked—after normal hours, say—they are effectively cut off from the spontaneous "dropping in" that can occur freely only where all paths are public right up to the thresholds of private territory.

Then there is the still more subtle fact that, even where the centralized entrance carries with it no explicit policy of social control—let us say that it is a door that is always open—it still has an uneasy feeling about it for people who cherish basic liberties. The single, centralized entrance is the precise pattern that a tyrant *would* propose who wanted to control people's comings and goings. It makes one uneasy to live with such a form, even where the social policy is relatively free.

This may very easily sound paranoid. But the point is this: socially, a libertarian society tries to build for itself structures which cannot easily be controlled by one person or one group "at the helm." It tries to decentralize social structures so that there are *many* centers, and no one group can come to have excessive control.

A physical environment which supports the same libertarian ideal will certainly put a premium on structures that allow people freedom to come and go as they please. And it will try to protect this right by building it into the very ground plan of buildings and cities. When we feel uneasy in a building that is spatially over-centralized and authoritarian, it is because we feel unprotected in this way; we feel that one of our basic rights is potentially vulnerable and is not being fully affirmed by the physical structure of the environment.

Open stairs which act as extensions of the public world and which reach up to the very threshold of each household's and each

workgroup's own space solve this problem. These spaces are then connected directly to the world at large. People on the street recognize each entry as the domain of real people—not the domain of corporations and institutions, which have the actual or potential power to tyrannize.

Therefore:

Do away, as far as possible, with internal staircases in institutions. Connect all autonomous households, public services, and workgroups on the upper floors of buildings directly to the ground. Do this by creating open stairs which are approached directly from the street. Keep the stair roofed or unroofed, according to climate, but at all events leave the stair open at ground level, without a door, so that the stair is functionally a continuation of the street. And build no upstairs corridors. Instead, make open landings or an open arcade where upstairs units share a single stair.

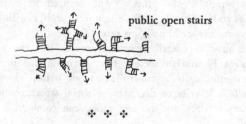

public open stairs

✧ ✧ ✧

Where the stair comes down to the ground, make an entrance which helps to repair the family of entrances that exist already on the street—FAMILY OF ENTRANCES (102); make the landings and the top of the stair, where it reaches the roof, into gardens where things can grow and where people can sit in the sun—ROOF GARDEN (118), SUNNY PLACE (161). Remember STAIR SEATS (125), and build the stair according to STAIRCASE VOLUME (195). . . .

prepare to knit the inside of the building to the outside, by treating the edge between the two as a place in its own right, and making human details there;

159 LIGHT ON TWO SIDES OF EVERY ROOM**

. . . once the building's major rooms are in position, we have to fix its actual shape: and this we do essentially with the position of the edge. The edge has got its rough position already from the overall form of the building—WINGS OF LIGHT (107), POSITIVE OUTDOOR SPACE (106), LONG THIN HOUSE (109), CASCADE OF ROOFS (116). This pattern now completes the work of WINGS OF LIGHT (107), by placing each individual room exactly where it needs to be to get the light. It forms the exact line of the building edge, according to the position of these individual rooms. The next pattern starts to shape the edge.

❖ ❖ ❖

When they have a choice, people will always gravitate to those rooms which have light on two sides, and leave the rooms which are lit only from one side unused and empty.

This pattern, perhaps more than any other single pattern, determines the success or failure of a room. The arrangement of daylight in a room, and the presence of windows on two sides, is fundamental. If you build a room with light on one side only, you can be almost certain that you are wasting your money. People will stay out of that room if they can possibly avoid it. Of course, if all the rooms are lit from one side only, people will have to use them. But we can be fairly sure that they are subtly uncomfortable there, always wishing they weren't there, wanting to leave—just because we are so sure of what people do when they do have the choice.

Our experiments on this matter have been rather informal and drawn out over several years. We have been aware of the idea for some time—as have many builders. (We have even heard that "light on two sides" was a tenet of the old Beaux Arts design tradition.) In any case, our experiments were simple: over and over again, in one building after another, wherever we happened to find ourselves, we would check to see if the pattern held. Were people in fact avoiding rooms lit only on one side, preferring the two-sided rooms—what did they think about it?

We have gone through this with our friends, in offices, in many homes—and overwhelmingly the two-sided pattern seems significant. People are aware, or half-aware of the pattern—they understand exactly what we mean.

With light on two sides . . . . and without

If this evidence seems too haphazard, please try these observations yourself. Bear the pattern in mind, and examine all the buildings you come across in your daily life. We believe that you will find, as we have done, that those rooms you intuitively recognize as pleasant, friendly rooms have the pattern; and those you intuitively reject as unfriendly, unpleasant, are the ones which do not have the pattern. In short, this one pattern alone, is able to distinguish good rooms from unpleasant ones.

The importance of this pattern lies partly in the social atmosphere it creates in the room. Rooms lit on two sides, with natural light, create less glare around people and objects; this lets us see things more intricately; and most important, it allows us to read in detail the minute expressions that flash across people's faces, the motion of their hands . . . and thereby understand, more clearly, the meaning they are after. *The light on two sides allows people to understand each other.*

In a room lit on only one side, the light gradient on the walls and floors inside the room is very steep, so that the part furthest from the window is uncomfortably dark, compared with the part near the window. Even worse, since there is little reflected light on the room's inner surfaces, the interior wall immediately next to the window is usually dark, creating discomfort and glare against this light. *In rooms lit on one side, the glare which sur-*

748

rounds people's faces prevents people from understanding one another.

Although this glare may be somewhat reduced by supplementary artificial lighting, and by well-designed window reveals, the most simple and most basic way of overcoming glare, is to give every room two windows. The light from each window illuminates the wall surfaces just inside the other window, thus reducing the contrast between those walls and the sky outside. For details and illustrations, see R. G. Hopkinson, *Architectural Physics: Lighting*, London: Building Research Station, 1963, pp. 29, 103.

A supreme example of the complete neglect of this pattern is Le Corbusier's Marseilles Block apartments. Each apartment unit is very long and relatively narrow, and gets all its light from one end, the narrow end. The rooms are very bright just at the windows and dark everywhere else. And, as a result, the glare created by the light-dark contrast around the windows is very disturbing.

In a small building, it is easy to give every room light on two sides: one room in each of the four corners of a house does it automatically.

In a slightly larger building, it is necessary to wrinkle the edge, turn corners, to get the same effect. Juxtaposition of large rooms and small, helps also.

Wrinkle the edge.

In an even larger building, it may be necessary to build in some sort of systematic widening in the plan or to convolute the edge still further, to get light on two sides for every room.

But of course, no matter how clever we are with the plan, no matter how carefully we convolute the building edge, sometimes it is just impossible. In these cases, the rooms can get the effect of light on two sides under two conditions. They can get it, if the room is very shallow—not more than about eight feet deep —with at least two windows side by side. The light bounces off the back wall, and bounces sideways between the two windows, so that the light still has the glare-free character of light on two sides.

And finally, if a room simply has to be more than eight feet deep, but cannot have light from two sides—then the problem can be solved by making the ceiling very high, by painting the walls very white, and by putting great high windows in the wall, set into very deep reveals, deep enough to offset the glare. Elizabethan dining halls and living rooms in Georgian mansions were often built like this. Remember, though, that it is very hard to make it work.

Therefore:

Locate each room so that it has outdoor space outside it on at least two sides, and then place windows in these outdoor walls so that natural light falls into every room from more than one direction.

each room has light on two sides

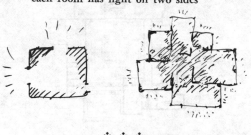

❖ ❖ ❖

Don't let this pattern make your plans too wild—otherwise you will destroy the simplicity of POSITIVE OUTDOOR SPACE (106), and you will have a terrible time roofing the building—ROOF

LAYOUT (209). Remember that it is possible to keep the essence of the pattern with windows on one side, if the room is unusually high, if it is shallow compared with the length of the window wall, the windows large, the walls of the room white, and massive deep reveals on the windows to make quite certain that the big windows, bright against the sky, do not create glare.

Place the individual windows to look onto something beautiful—WINDOWS OVERLOOKING LIFE (192), NATURAL DOORS AND WINDOWS (221); and make one of the windows in the room a special one, so that a place gathers itself around it—WINDOW PLACE (180). Use DEEP REVEALS (223) and FILTERED LIGHT (238). . . .

160 BUILDING EDGE**

. . . assume that the position of the building edge is fixed—most recently by LIGHT ON TWO SIDES OF EVERY ROOM (159)—and before that by the position of the building wings and their interior spaces and by the courts and gardens and streets between the buildings—WINGS OF LIGHT (107), POSITIVE OUTDOOR SPACE (106). This pattern now sets the stage for the development of the zone between the indoors and the outdoors. Often this "zone" is thought of as an edge, a line on paper without thickness, a wall. But this is altogether wrong . . .

A building is most often thought of as something which turns inward—toward its rooms. People do not often think of a building as something which must also be oriented toward the outside.

But unless the building is oriented toward the outside, which surrounds it, as carefully and positively as toward its inside, the space around the building will be useless and blank—with the direct effect, in the long run, that the building will be socially isolated, because you have to cross a no-man's land to get to it.

Look, for example, at this machine age slab of steel and glass. You cannot approach it anywhere except at its entrance—because the space around it is not made for people.

The edge cannot support any life.

And compare it with this older, warmer building, which has a continuous surrounding of benches, galleries, balconies, flowers, corners to sit, places to stop. This building edge is alive. It is connected to the world around it by the simple fact that it is made into a positive place where people can enjoy themselves.

An edge that can be used . . .

Think of the effect of this small difference. The machine-like building is cut off from its surroundings, isolated, an island. The building with a lively building edge, is connected, part of the social fabric, part of the town, part of the lives of all the people who live and move around it.

We get empirical support for this contrast from the following: apparently people prefer being at the edges of open spaces—and when these edges are made human, people cling to them tenaciously. In observing people's behavior in outdoor spaces, for example, Jan Gehl discovered that "there is a marked tendency for both standing and sitting persons to place themselves near something—a facade, pillar, furniture, etc." ["Mennesker til Fods (Pedestrians)," *Arkitekten*, No. 20, 1968.] This tendency for people to stay at the edges of spaces, is also discussed in the pattern ACTIVITY POCKETS (124).

If this propensity were taken as seriously outdoors as it is indoors, then the exterior walls of buildings would look very different indeed from the way they look today. They would be

more like places—walls would weave in and out, and the roof would extend over them to create little places for benches, posters, and notices for people to look at. For the niches to have the right depth, they would have to be occasionally as much as 6 feet deep—see the arguments for SIX-FOOT BALCONY (167).

When it is properly made, such an edge is a realm between realms: it increases the connection between inside and outside, encourages the formation of groups which cross the boundary, encourages movement which starts on one side and ends on the other, and allows activity to be either on, or in the boundary itself. A very fundamental notion.

Therefore:

Make sure that you treat the edge of the building as a "thing," a "place," a zone with volume to it, not a line or interface which has no thickness. Crenelate the edge of buildings with places that invite people to stop. Make places that have depth and a covering, places to sit, lean, and walk, especially at those points along the perimeter which look onto interesting outdoor life.

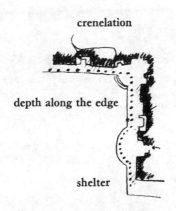

crenelation

depth along the edge

shelter

BUILDINGS

Do it with arcades, galleries, porches, and terraces—ARCADES (119), OUTDOOR ROOM (163), GALLERY SURROUND (166), SIX-FOOT BALCONY (167), CONNECTION TO THE EARTH (168); take special account of the sun—SUNNY PLACE (161), NORTH FACE (162); and put in seats and windows which complete the feeling of connection—STAIR SEATS (125), STREET WINDOWS (164), SEAT SPOTS (241), FRONT DOOR BENCH (242). . . .

161 SUNNY PLACE**

. . . this pattern helps to embellish and give life to any SOUTH FACING OUTDOORS (105); and, in a situation where the outdoors is not to the south, but east or west, it can help to modify the building so that the effective part of the outdoors moves towards the south. It also helps to complete BUILDING EDGE (160), and to place OUTDOOR ROOM (163).

The area immediately outside the building, to the south —that angle between its walls and the earth where the sun falls—must be developed and made into a place which lets people bask in it.

We have already made the point that important outdoor areas should be to the south of buildings which they serve, and we presented the empirical evidence for this idea in SOUTH FACING OUTDOORS (105). But even if the outdoor areas around a building are toward the south, this still won't guarantee that people actually will use them.

In this pattern, we shall now discuss the subtler fact that a south-facing court or garden will still not work, unless there is a functionally important sunny place within it, intently and specifically placed for sun, at a central juncture between indoors and outdoors and immediately next to the indoor rooms which it serves.

We have some evidence—presented in SOUTH-FACING OUTDOORS (105)—that a deep band of shade between a building and a sunny area can act as a barrier and keep the area from being well used. It is this evidence which makes us believe that the most important sunny places occur up against the exterior walls of buildings, where people can see into them from inside and step directly out into the light, leaning in the doorway of the building. Furthermore, we have observed that these places are more inviting if they are placed in the crook of a building or wall, where there is just enough enclosure from a hedge, a low wall, a column, to provide a backdrop, a place to sit up against and take in the sun.

And finally, of course, if the place is really to work, there
must be a good reason for going there: something special which
draws a person there—a swing, a potting table for plants, a special
view, a brick step to sit upon and look into a pool—whatever, so
long as it has the power to bring a person there almost without
thinking about it.

Here is an example—a sunny place at the edge of a building,
directly related to the inside, and set in a nook of the building.
Someone comes there every day to sit for a moment, water the
hanging plants, see how they are doing, and take in some sun.

Sunny place . . .

A particularly beautiful version of this pattern can be made
when several sunny places are placed together—perhaps for a
HOUSE CLUSTER (37) or a WORK COMMUNITY (41). If the places
can be set down so that they form a south-facing half-necklace of
sunny spots, each within hailing distance of all the others, it
makes the act of coming out into the sun a communal affair.

Therefore:

**Inside a south-facing court, or garden, or yard, find the
spot between the building and the outdoors which gets
the best sun. Develop this spot as a special sunny place—
make it the important outdoor room, a place to work in
the sun, or a place for a swing and some special plants, a
place to sunbathe. Be very careful indeed to place the**

sunny place in a position where it is sheltered from the wind. A steady wind will prevent you from using the most beautiful place.

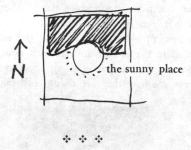

❖ ❖ ❖

Make the place itself as much as possible like a room—PRIVATE TERRACE ON THE STREET (140), OUTDOOR ROOM (163); always at least six feet deep, no less—SIX-FOOT BALCONY (167); perhaps with foliage or a canvas to filter the light on hot days—FILTERED LIGHT (238), TRELLISED WALK (174), CANVAS ROOF (244). Put in seats according to SEAT SPOTS (241). . . .

162 NORTH FACE

. . . even if the building has been placed correctly according to
SOUTH-FACING OUTDOORS (105) and there is little outdoor space
toward the north, there is usually still some kind of area or
volume on the north face of the building. It is necessary to take
care of this north-facing place to supplement the work of INDOOR
SUNLIGHT (128) and SUNNY PLACE (161).

❖ ❖ ❖

**Look at the north sides of the buildings which you know.
Almost everywhere you will find that these are the spots
which are dead and dank, gloomy and useless. Yet there are
hundreds of acres in a town on the north sides of buildings;
and it is inevitable that there must always be land in this
position, wherever there are buildings.**

If a building has a sheer north face, during many months of
the year it will cast a long shadow out behind it.

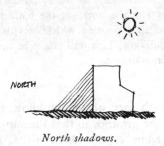

North shadows.

These dead and gloomy north sides not only waste enormous
areas of land; they also help to kill the larger environment, by

cutting it up with shadow areas which no one wants to cross, and which therefore break up the various areas of the environment from one another. It is essential to find a way of making these north-facing areas alive, at least in their own terms, so that they help the land around them instead of breaking it apart.

The shadow cast by the north face is essentially triangular. To keep this triangle of shade from becoming a forlorn place, it is necessary to fill it up with things and places which do not need the sun. For example, the area to the north may form a gentle cascade which contains the car shelter, perhaps a bath suite, storage, garbage cans, a studio. If this cascade is properly made, then for most of the year the outdoors beyond it to the north will have enough sun for a garden, a greenhouse, a private garden seat, a workshop, paths.

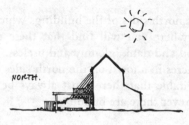

North cascade.

Furthermore, if there are north rooms that are inevitably gloomy, it helps enormously to make a reflecting wall: a wall standing some ways to the north of the building, painted white or yellow, and set in a position which gets the sun and reflects it back into the building. This wall might be the wall of a nearby building, a garden wall, etc.

Therefore:

Make the north face of the building a cascade which slopes down to the ground, so that the sun which normally casts a long shadow to the north strikes the ground immediately beside the building.

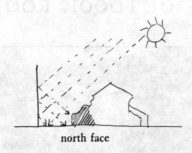

north face

❖ ❖ ❖

Use the triangle inside this north cascade for car, garbage, storage, shed, a studio which requires north light, closets—those parts of the building which can do very well without interior sunlight—CAR CONNECTION (113), BULK STORAGE (145), COMPOST (178), CLOSETS BETWEEN ROOMS (198). If it is at all practical, use a white or yellow wall to the north of the building to reflect sunlight into the north-facing rooms—INDOOR SUNLIGHT (128), LIGHT ON TWO SIDES OF EVERY ROOM (159), GARDEN WALL (173). . . .

163 OUTDOOR ROOM**

. . . every building has rooms where people stay and live and talk together—COMMON AREAS AT THE HEART (129), FARMHOUSE KITCHEN (139), SEQUENCE OF SITTING SPACES (142). Whenever possible, these rooms need to be embellished by a further "room" outdoors. This kind of outdoor room also helps to form a part of any PUBLIC OUTDOOR ROOM (69), HALF-HIDDEN GARDEN (111), PRIVATE TERRACE ON THE STEET (140), or SUNNY PLACE (161).

❖ ❖ ❖

A garden is the place for lying in the grass, swinging, croquet, growing flowers, throwing a ball for the dog. But there is another way of being outdoors: and its needs are not met by the garden at all.

For some moods, some times of day, some kinds of friendship, people need a place to eat, to sit in formal clothes, to drink, to talk together, to be still, and yet outdoors.

They need an outdoor room, a literal outdoor room—a partly enclosed space, outdoors, but enough like a room so that people behave there as they do in rooms, but with the added beauties of the sun, and wind, and smells, and rustling leaves, and crickets.

This need occurs everywhere. It is hardly too much to say that every building needs an outdoor room attached to it, between it and the garden; and more, that many of the special places in a garden—sunny places, terraces, gazebos—need to be made as outdoor rooms, as well.

The inspiration for this pattern comes from Bernard Rudofsky's chapter, "The Conditioned Outdoor Room," in *Behind the Picture Window* (New York: Oxford Press, 1955).

In a superbly layed out house-garden, one ought to be able to work and sleep, cook and eat, play and loaf. No doubt, this sounds specious to the confirmed indoor dweller and needs elaboration.

As a rule, the inhabitant of our climate makes no sallies into his immediate surroundings. His farthest outpost is the screened porch. The garden—if there is one—remains unoccupied between garden

BUILDINGS

parties. Indeed, when he talks about the outdoors, he seldom means
his garden. He does not think of gardens as potential living space.
. . . Like the parlor of our grandmothers, the garden is an object
of excessive care. Like the parlor, it is not meant to be lived in. In
an age that puts a premium on usefulness this is most irregular. Para-
doxical though it may sound, the use of glass walls in recent years
alienated the garden. Even the "picture window," as the domestic
version of the show-window is called, has contributed to the estrange-
ment between indoors and outdoors; the garden has become a
spectator garden.

The historical concept of the house-garden is entirely different.
Domestic gardens as we have known them through the centuries were
valued mostly for their habitableness and privacy, two qualities that
are conspicuously absent in contemporary gardens. Privacy, so little
in demand these days, was indispensable to people with a taste for
dignified living. The house-gardens of antiquity furnish us, even
in their fragmentary and dilapidated state, perfect examples of how
a diminutive and apparently negligible quantity of land can, with
some ingenuity, be transformed into an oasis of delight. Miniature
gardens though they were, they had all the ingredients of a happy
environment.

These gardens were an essential part of the house; they were,
mind you, contained *within* the house. One can best describe them as
rooms without ceilings. They were true outdoor living rooms,
and invariably regarded as such by their inhabitants. The wall- and
floor-materials of Roman gardens, for example, were no less
lavish than those used in the interior part of the house. The combined
use of stone mosaic, marble slabs, stucco reliefs, mural decorations
from the simplest geometric patterns to the most elaborate murals
established a mood particularly favorable to spiritual composure. As
for the ceiling, there was always the sky in its hundred moods.
(pp. 157–59)

An outdoor space becomes a special outdoor room when it is
well enclosed with walls of the building, walls of foliage, columns, trellis, and sky; and when the outdoor room, together
with an indoor space, forms a virtually continuous living area.

Here are several examples of outdoor rooms. Each one uses a
different combination of elements to establish its enclosure; each
one is related to its building in a slightly different way. Rudofsky gives many other examples in the book we have cited. For
instance, he describes how a front lawn can be rebuilt to become
an outdoor room.

766

Two outdoor rooms.

Finally, a note. Since there is another pattern with a rather similar name—PUBLIC OUTDOOR ROOM (69)—we want to remind you of the following distinction: in a certain sense, the two are opposites. An OUTDOOR ROOM has walls around it and is only partially roofed; while a PUBLIC OUTDOOR ROOM has a roof, but essentially no walls.

Therefore:

Build a place outdoors which has so much enclosure round it, that it takes on the feeling of a room, even though it is open to the sky. To do this, define it at the corners with columns, perhaps roof it partially with a trellis or a sliding canvas roof, and create "walls" around it, with fences, sitting walls, screens, hedges, or the exterior walls of the building itself.

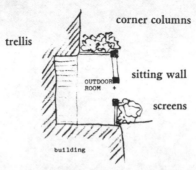

767

This outdoor room is formed, most often, by free standing columns—COLUMN PLACE (226), walls—GARDEN WALL (173), low SITTING WALLS (243), perhaps a trellis overhead—TRELLISED WALK (174), or a translucent canvas awning—CANVAS ROOFS (244), and a ground surface which helps to provide CONNECTION TO THE EARTH (168). Like any other room, for its construction start with THE SHAPE OF INDOOR SPACE (191) and STRUCTURE FOLLOW SOCIAL SPACES (205). . . .

164 STREET WINDOWS*

. . . wherever there are GREEN STREETS (51), SMALL PUBLIC SQUARES (61), PEDESTRIAN STREETS (100), BUILDING THOROUGH-FARES (101)—in short, any streets with people in them, these streets will only come to life if they are helped to do so by the people looking out on them, hanging out of windows, laughing, shouting, whistling.

❖ ❖ ❖

A street without windows is blind and frightening. And it is equally uncomfortable to be in a house which bounds a public street with no window at all on the street.

The street window provides a unique kind of connection between the life inside buildings and the street. Franz Kafka wrote a short commentary entitled "The Street Window," which expresses beautifully the power of this relationship.

Whoever leads a solitary life and yet now and then wants to attach himself somewhere, whoever, according to changes in the time of day, the weather, the state of his business, and the like, suddenly wishes to see any arm at all to which he might cling—he will not be able to manage for long without a window looking onto the street. And if he is in the mood of not desiring anything and only goes to his window sill a tired man, with eyes turning from his public to heaven and back again, not wanting to look out and having thrown his head up a little, even then the horses below will draw him down into their train of wagons and tumult, and so at last into the human harmony. (Franz Kafka, *The Complete Stories*, ed. Nahum N. Glatzer, New York: Schocken Books, 1972, p. 384).

The process of watching the street from upper story windows is strongly embedded in traditional Peruvian culture in the form of the *mirador*, the beautiful ornamented gallery which sticks out over the street from many of the colonial buildings in Lima. Peruvian girls especially love to watch the street, but only if they are not too visible. They can watch the street from the mirador without any impropriety, something they cannot do so easily from the front door. If anyone looks at them too hard, they can pull back into the window.

The mirador—the lookout.

Street windows are most successful on the second and third floors. Anything higher, and the street becomes a "view"—the vitality of the connection is destroyed. From the second and third floors people can shout down to the street, throw down a jacket or a ball; people in the street can whistle for a person to come to the window, and even glimpse the expressions on a person's face inside.

At ground level, street windows are less likely to work. If they are too far back from the street, they don't really give a view onto the street—though of course they still give light. If they are too close to the street, they don't work at all, because they get boarded up or curtained to protect the privacy of the rooms inside —see the empirical findings presented in *Houses Generated by Patterns,* Center for Environmental Structure, 1969, pp. 179–80.

One possible way of making a street window at ground level might be to build an alcove, two or three steps up, with a window on the street, its window-sill five feet above the street. People in the alcove, can lean on the window sill, and watch the street; people in the street can see them, without being able to see into the room behind them. It is even easier, of course, if the

An alcove street window at ground level.

771

ground floor of the house is two or three feet above the street, as many ground floors are.

Finally, on whatever floor it is, a street window must be placed in a position which the people inside pass often, a place where they are likely to pause and stand beside the window: the head of a stair, the bay window of a favorite room, a kitchen, bedroom, or window in a passage.

Therefore:

Where buildings run alongside busy streets, build windows with window seats, looking out onto the street. Place them in bedrooms or at some point on a passage or stair, where people keep passing by. On the first floor, keep these windows high enough to be private.

❖ ❖ ❖

On the inside, give each of these windows a substantial place, so that a person feels encouraged to sit there or stand and watch the street—WINDOW PLACE (180); make the windows open outward—WINDOWS WHICH OPEN WIDE (236); enrich the outside of the window with flower boxes and climbing plants—then people, in the course of caring for the flowers, will have the opportunity for hanging out—FILTERED LIGHT (238), CLIMBING PLANTS (246). . . .

connection. When the wall is open it is possible to hear what is going on inside, to smell the inside, to exchange words, and even to step in all along the opening. Street cafes, open food stalls, workshops with garage door openings are examples.

We passed the workshop every day on our way home from school. It was a furniture shop, and we would stand at the opening and watch men building chairs and tables, sawdust flying, forming legs on the lathe. There was a low wall, and the foreman told us to stay outside it; but he let us sit there, and we did, sometimes for hours.

3. The most involving case of all: activity is not only open to sight and sound on one side of the path, but some part of the activity actually crosses the path, so that people who walk down the sidewalk find themselves walking *through* the activity. The extreme version is the one where a shop is set up to straddle the path, with goods displayed on either side. A more modest version is the one where the roof of the space covers the path, the wall is entirely open, and the paving of the path is continuous with the "interior" of the space.

No matter how the opening is formed, it is essential that it expose the ordinary activity inside in a way that invites people passing to take it in and have some relationship, however modest, to it. The doctors of the Pioneer Health Center in Peckham believed this principle to be so essential that they deliberately built the center's gymnasium, swimming pool, dance floor, cafeteria, and theater in such a way that people passing could not help but see others, often people they knew, inside:

. . . dancing goes on there and moving figures can be seen on the floor of the main building at night when the whole building is lit up attracting the attention of the passers by. . . .

. . . it must be remembered that it is not the action of the skilled alone that is to be seen in the Centre, but *every degree* of proficiency in all that is going on. This point is crucial to an understanding of how vision can work as a stimulus engendering action in the company gathering there. In ordinary life the spectator of any activity is apt to be presented *only* with the exhibition of the specialist; and this trend has been gathering impetus year by year with alarming progression. Audiences swell in their thousands to watch the expert game, but as the "stars" grow in brilliance, the conviction of an in-

eptitude that makes trying not worth while, increasingly confirms the inactivity of the crowd. It is not then all forms of action that invite the attempt to action: it is the sight of action that is within the possible scope of the spectator that affords a temptation eventually irresistible to him. Short though the time of our experiment has been, this fact has been amply substantiated, as the growth of activities in the Centre demonstrates. (*The Peckham Experiment*, I. Pearse and L. Crocker, New Haven: Yale University Press, 1947, pp. 67–72.)

Therefore:

In any public space which depends for its success on its exposure to the street, open it up, with a fully opening wall which can be thrown wide open, and if it is possible, include some part of the activity on the far side of the pedestrian path, so that it actually straddles the path, and people walk through it as they walk along the path.

There are dozens of ways to build such an opening. For example, a wall can be made very cheaply with a simple plywood hanging shutter sliding on an overhead rail, which can be removed to open up completely, and locked in place at night.

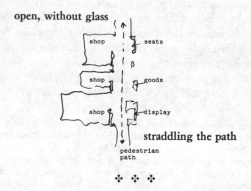

open, without glass

shop   seats

shop   goods

shop   display

straddling the path

pedestrian path

❖ ❖ ❖

Give the opening a boundary, when it is entirely open, with a low solid wall which people can sit on—SITTING WALL (243); and make an outdoor room out of the part of the path which runs past it—PATH SHAPE (121), OUTDOOR ROOM (163). . . .

166 GALLERY SURROUND*

. . . we continue to fill out the BUILDING EDGE (160). Assume that arcades have been built wherever they make sense—ARCADES (119); there are still large areas within the building edge where BUILDING EDGE tells you to make something positive—but so far no patterns have explained how this can be done physically. This pattern shows you how you can complete the edge. It complements ROOF GARDEN (118) and ARCADES (119) and helps to enliven the PEDESTRIAN STREET (100).

❖ ❖ ❖

If people cannot walk out from the building onto balconies and terraces which look toward the outdoor space around the building, then neither they themselves nor the people outside have any medium which helps them feel the building and the larger public world are intertwined.

We have discussed the importance of the building edge in two other patterns: BUILDING EDGE (160) itself, and ARCADES (119). In both cases, we explained how the arcades and the edge help to create space which people who are *outside* the building can use to help them feel more intimately connected with the building. These patterns, in short, look at the problem of connection from the point of view of the people *outside* the building.

In this pattern we discuss the same problem—but from the point of view of the people *inside* the building. We believe, simply, that every building needs at least one place, and preferably a whole range of places, where people can be still within the building, but in touch with the people and the scene outside. This problem has also been discussed in PRIVATE TERRACE ON THE STREET (140). But that pattern deals only with one very important and highly specific occurrence of this need. The present pattern suggests that the need is completely general: very plainly, it is fundamental, an all-embracing necessity which applies to all buildings over and again.

The need has been documented extensively. (See, for example, Anthony Wallace, *Housing and Social Structure*, Philadelphia Housing Authority, 1952; Federal Housing Authority, *The Livability Problem of 1,000 Families*, Washington, D. C., 1945.)

Windows on the street, while they have their own virtues, are simply not enough to satisfy this need. They usually occupy a very small part of the wall, and can only be used if a person stands at the edge of the room. The kinds of situations that are needed are far more rich and engrossing. We need places along the upper stories of the building's edge where we can live comfortably, for hours, in touch with the street—playing cards, bringing work out on the terrace on a hot day, eating, scrambling with children or setting up an electric train, drying and folding the wash, sculpting with clay, paying the bills.

In short, almost all the basic human situations can be enriched by the qualities of the gallery surround. This is why we specify that each building should have as many versions of it as possible along its edge—porches, arcades, balconies, awnings, terraces, and galleries.

Four examples of this pattern.

Therefore:

Whenever possible, and at every story, build porches, galleries, arcades, balconies, niches, outdoor seats, awnings, trellised rooms, and the like at the edges of buildings— especially where they open off public spaces and streets, and connect them by doors, directly to the rooms inside.

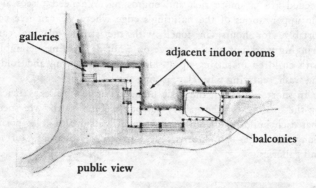

galleries

adjacent indoor rooms

balconies

public view

❖ ❖ ❖

A warning: take care that such places are not stuck artificially onto the building. Keep them real; find the places along the building edge that offer a direct and useful connection with the life indoors—the space outside the stair landing, the space to one side of the bedroom alcove, and so on.

These places should be an integral part of the building territory, and contain seats, tables, furniture, places to stand and talk, places to work outside—all in the public view—PRIVATE TERRACE ON THE STREET (140), OUTDOOR ROOM (163); make the spaces deep enough to be really useful—SIX-FOOT BALCONY (167)—with columns heavy enough to provide at least partial enclosure—HALF-OPEN WALL (193), COLUMN PLACES (226). . . .

167 SIX-FOOT BALCONY**

. . . in various places ARCADES (119) and GALLERY SURROUND (166) have helped you to imagine some kind of a balcony, veranda, terrace, porch, arcade along the building edge or half-way into it. This pattern simply specifies the depth of this arcade or porch or balcony, to make sure that it really works.

❖ ❖ ❖

Balconies and porches which are less than six feet deep are hardly ever used.

Balconies and porches are often made very small to save money; but when they are too small, they might just as well not be there.

A balcony is first used properly when there is enough room for two or three people to sit in a small group with room to stretch their legs, and room for a small table where they can set down glasses, cups, and the newspaper. No balcony works if it is so narrow that people have to sit in a row facing outward. The critical size is hard to determine, but it is at least six feet. The following drawing and photograph show roughly why:

Six feet
minimum

Six feet deep.

Our observations make it clear that the difference between deep balconies and those which are not deep enough is simply astonishing. In our experience, almost no balconies at all which are 3 or 4 feet deep manage to gather life to them or to get used. And almost no balconies which are more than six feet deep are *not* used.

Narrow balconies are useless.

Two other features of the balcony make a difference in the degree to which people will use it: its enclosure and its recession into the building.

As far as enclosure goes, we have noticed that among the deeper balconies, it is those with half-open enclosures around them—columns, wooden slats, rose-covered trellises—which are used most. Apparently, the partial privacy given by a half-open screen makes people more comfortable—see HALF-OPEN WALL (193).

And recesses seem to have a similar effect. On a cantilevered balcony people must sit outside the mass of the building; the balcony lacks privacy and tends to feel unsafe. In an English study ("Private Balconies in Flats and Maisonettes," *Architect's Journal*, March 1957, pp. 372–76), two-thirds of the people that never used their balconies gave lack of privacy as their reason,

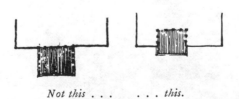

Not this . . .   . . . this.

and said that they preferred recessed balconies, because, in contrast to cantilevered balconies, the recesses seemed more secure.

Therefore:

**Whenever you build a balcony, a porch, a gallery, or a
terrace always make it at least six feet deep. If possible,
recess at least a part of it into the building so that it is not
cantilevered out and separated from the building by a
simple line, and enclose it partially.**

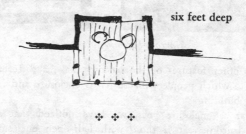

six feet deep

❖ ❖ ❖

Enclose the balcony with a low wall—SITTING WALL (243),
heavy columns—COLUMN PLACES (226), and half-open walls or
screens—HALF-OPEN WALL (193). Keep it open toward the
south—SUNNY PLACE (161). Treat it as an OUTDOOR ROOM
(163), and get the details of its shape and its construction from
THE SHAPE OF INDOOR SPACE (191). . . .

168 CONNECTION TO THE EARTH**

. . . this pattern helps to create the BUILDING EDGE (160) and its ARCADES (119), PRIVATE TERRACE ON THE STREET (140), the GALLERY SURROUND (166), and SIX-FOOT BALCONY (167), by specifying the way the floor of the building reaches out into the land and gardens round about it.

A house feels isolated from the nature around it, unless its floors are interleaved directly with the earth that is around the house.

We shall understand this best by contrasting those houses which are sharply separated from the earth with those in which there is a continuity between the two.

Look first at this house where there is no continuity.

An average house—but look at it closely.
It lacks this pattern utterly.

The inside and the outside are abruptly separate. There is no way of being partly inside, yet still connected to the outside; there is no way in which the inside of the house allows you, in your bare feet, to step out and feel the dew collecting or pick blossoms off a climbing plant because there is no surface near the house on which you can go out and yet still be the person that you are inside.

Compare it with the house in our main picture, where there *is*

786

continuity. Here, there is an intermediate area, whose surface is connected to the inside of the house—and yet it is in plain outdoors. This surface is part of the earth—and yet a little smoother, a little more beaten, more swept—stepping out on it is not like stepping out into a field in your bare feet—it is as if the earth itself becomes in that small area a part of your indoor terrain.

When we compare the examples, there seems little doubt that some deep feeling is involved, and we are confident in presenting this pattern as a fundamental one. But we can only speculate about its origins or why it is important.

Perhaps the likeliest of all the explanations we are able to imagine is one which connects the earth boundness and rootedness of a man or a woman to their physical connection to the earth. It is very plain, and we all discover for ourselves, that our lives become satisfactory to the extent that we are rooted, "down to earth," in touch with common sense about everyday things—not flying high in the sky of concepts and fantasies. The path toward this rootedness is personal and slow—but it may just be true that it is helped or hindered by the extent to which our physical world is itself rooted and connected to the earth.

In physical terms, the rootedness occurs in buildings when the building is surrounded, along at least a part of its perimeter, by terraces, paths, steps, gravel, and earthen surfaces, which bring the floors outside, into the land. These surfaces are made of intermediate materials more natural than the floors inside the house—and more man-made than earth and clay and grass. Brick terraces, tiles, and beaten earth tied into the foundations of the house all help make this connection; and, if possible, each house should have a reasonable amount of them, pushing out into the land around the house and opening up the outdoors to the inside.

Therefore:

Connect the building to the earth around it by building a series of paths and terraces and steps around the edge. Place them deliberately to make the boundary ambiguous— so that it is impossible to say exactly where the building stops and earth begins.

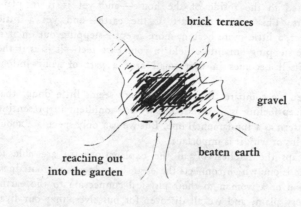

brick terraces

gravel

reaching out
into the garden

beaten earth

❖ ❖ ❖

Use the connection to the earth to form the ground for outdoor rooms, and entrances, and terraces—ENTRANCE ROOM (130),
PRIVATE TERRACE ON THE STREET (140), OUTDOOR ROOM (163),
TERRACED SLOPE (169); prepare to tie the terraces continuously
into the wall which forms the edge of the ground floor slab, to
make the very structure of the building feel connected to the
earth—GROUND FLOOR SLAB (215); and where you come to form
the terrace surfaces, use things like hand-made bricks and soft-
baked crumbling biscuit-fired tile—SOFT TILE AND BRICK (248);
and further out, along the paths a little distance from the house,
leave cracks between the tiles to let the grass and flowers grow
between them—PAVING WITH CRACKS BETWEEN THE STONES
(247). . . .

decide on the arrangement of the gardens, and the places in the gardens;

169 TERRACED SLOPE*

. . . this pattern helps to complete SITE REPAIR (104). Where there are buildings, it ties into the BUILDING EDGE (160) and can help form it; and it helps create the CONNECTION TO THE EARTH (168). If the ground is sloping at all, this pattern tells you how to handle the slope of the ground in a way that makes sense for the people in the building, and for the plants and grasses on the ground.

❖ ❖ ❖

On sloping land, erosion caused by run off can kill the soil. It also creates uneven distribution of rainwater over the land, which naturally does less for plant life than it could if it were evenly distributed.

Terraces and bunds, built along contour lines, have been used for thousands of years to solve this problem. Erosion starts when the water runs down certain lines, erodes the earth along these lines, makes it hard for plants to grow there, then forms rills in the mud and dust, which are then still more vulnerable to more runoff, and get progressively worse and worse. The terraces control erosion by slowing down the water, and preventing the formation of these rills in the first place.

Even more important, the terraces spread the water evenly over the entire landscape. In a given area, each square meter of earth gets the same amount of water since the water stays where it falls. Under these conditions, plants can grow everywhere—on the steepest parts of hillsides as easily as in the most luscious valleys.

The pattern of terracing makes as much sense on a small house lot as it does on the hills around a valley. Proper terracing on a small lot creates a stable micro-system of drainage, and protects the top soil for the local gardens. Our main photograph shows a small building that is built on a terraced site. Once the terracing has been accomplished, the building can fit to it, and stretch across the lines of the terrace.

At both scales—the house lot and the hills—this method of

conserving the land and making it healthy is ancient. "Only very lately has modern anti-erosion practice, for example, through contour ploughing, managed to match the effectiveness of traditional methods of terracing long practiced in countries as far apart as Japan and Peru." (M. Nicholson, *The Environmental Revolution*, New York: McGraw Hill, 1970, p. 192.)

At the scale of hillsides and valleys, China is making an impressive attempt to reclaim her eroded land in this way. For instance, Joseph Alsop, "Terraced Fields in China":

> In the Chinese countryside, no effort has ever been spared to get a maximum crop with the resources available. Even so, I was hardly prepared for the "terrace fields" that they took me to see in the farming communes around Chungking.
>
> The countryside hereabouts is both rocky and largely composed of such steep hills that even Chinese would not think of trying to grow rice on them. The old way, ruinously eroding, was to grow as much rice as possible in the valleys: and then plant the hillsides, too, where soil remained.
>
> The new way is to make "terrace fields." The rocks are dynamited to get the needed building materials. Heavy dry-stone walls are then built to heights of six or seven feet, following the contours of the land. And earth is finally brought to fill in behind the stone walls, thereby producing a terrace field.

Therefore:

On all land which slopes—in fields, in parks, in public gardens, even in the private gardens around a house—make a system of terraces and bunds which follow the contour lines. Make them by building low walls along the contour lines, and then backfilling them with earth to form the terraces.

There is no reason why the building itself should fit into the terraces—it can comfortably cross terrace lines.

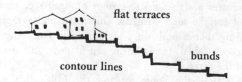

flat terraces

contour lines

bunds

Plant vegetables and orchards on the terraces—VEGETABLE
GARDEN (177), FRUIT TREES (170); along the walls which form
the terraces, plant flowers high enough to touch and smell—
RAISED FLOWERS (245). And it is also very natural to make the
walls so people can sit on them—SITTING WALL (243). . . .

170 FRUIT TREES*

. . . both the COMMON LAND (67) outside the workshops, offices and houses, and the private gardens which belong to individual buildings—HALF-HIDDEN GARDEN (111), can be helped by planting fruit trees. After all, a garden, whether it is public or private, is a thing of use. Yet it is not a farm. That half way kind of garden which is useful, but also beautiful in spring and autumn, and a marvelous place to walk because it smells so wonderful, is the orchard.

❖ ❖ ❖

In the climates where fruit trees grow, the orchards give the land an almost magical identity: think of the orange groves of Southern California, the cherry trees of Japan, the olive trees of Greece. But the growth of cities seems always to destroy these trees and the quality they possess.

The fact that the trees are seasonal and bear fruit has special consequences. The presence of orchards adds an experience that has all but vanished from cities—the experience of growth, harvest, local sources of fresh food; walking down a city street, pulling an apple out of a tree, and biting into it.

Fruit trees on common land add much more to the neighborhood and the community than the same trees in private backyards: privately grown, the trees tend to produce more fruit than one household can consume. On public land, the trees concentrate the feeling of mutual benefit and responsibility. And because they require yearly care, pruning, and harvesting, the fruit trees naturally involve people in their common land. It is an obvious place where people can take responsibility for their local common land, have pride in the results, employ themselves and their children part time.

Imagine a community gradually being able to produce a portion of its own need for fruit, or cider, or preserves. In the beginning it would be a small portion indeed, but it would serve as a beginning. There is not much work involved if it is tackled communally, and the satisfaction is great.

795

Therefore:

Plant small orchards of fruit trees in gardens and on common land along paths and streets, in parks, in neighborhoods: wherever there are well-established groups that can themselves care for the trees and harvest the fruit.

fruit trees

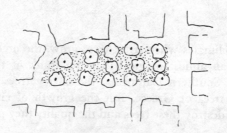

❖ ❖ ❖

If you have an especially nice fruit tree, make a TREE PLACE (171) under it, with a GARDEN SEAT (176), or arrange a path so the tree can provide a natural goal along the path—PATHS AND GOALS (120). . . .

171 TREE PLACES**

. . . trees are precious. Keep them. Leave them intact. If you have followed SITE REPAIR (104), you have already taken care to leave the trees intact and undisturbed by new construction; you may have planted FRUIT TREES (170); and you may perhaps also have other additional trees in mind. This pattern re-emphasizes the importance of leaving trees intact, and shows you how to plant them, and care for them, and use them, in such a way that the spaces which they form are useful as extensions of the building.

❖ ❖ ❖

When trees are planted or pruned without regard for the special places they can create, they are as good as dead for the people who need them.

Trees have a very deep and crucial meaning to human beings. The significance of old trees is archetypal; in our dreams very often they stand for the wholeness of personality: "Since . . . psychic growth cannot be brought about by a conscious effort of will power, but happens involuntarily and naturally, it is in dreams frequently symbolized by the tree, whose slow, powerful involuntary growth fulfills a definite pattern." (M. L. von Franz, "The process of individuation," in C. G. Jung, *Man and his Symbols*, New York: Doubleday, 1964, pp. 161, 163–64.)

There is even indication that trees, along with houses and other people, constitute one of the three most basic parts of the human environment. The House-Tree-Person Technique, developed by Psychologist John Buck, takes the drawings a person makes of each of these three "wholes" as a basis for projective tests. The mere fact that trees are considered as full of meaning, as houses and people, is, alone, a very powerful indication of their importance (V. J. Bieliauskas, *The H-T-P Research Review*, 1965 Edition, Western Psychological Services, Los Angeles, California, 1965; and Isaac Jolles, *Catalog for the Qualitative Interpretation of the House-Tree-Person*, Los Angeles, California: Western Psychological Services, 1964, pp. 75–97).

But for the most part, the trees that are being planted and transplanted in cities and suburbs today do not satisfy people's craving for trees. They will never come to provide a sense of beauty and peace, because they are being set down and built around *without regard for the places they create.*

The trees that people love create special social places: places to be in, and pass through, places you can dream about, and places you can draw. Trees have the potential to create various kinds of social places: an *umbrella*—where a single, low-sprawling tree like an oak defines an outdoor room; a *pair*—where two trees form a gateway; a *grove*—where several trees cluster together; a *square*—where they enclose an open space; and an *avenue*— where a double row of trees, their crowns touching, line a path or street. It is only when a tree's potential to form places is realized that the real presence and meaning of the tree is felt.

The trees that are being set down nowadays have nothing of this character—they are in tubs on parking lots and along streets, in specially "landscaped areas" that you can see but cannot get to. They do not form places in any sense of the word—and so they mean nothing to people.

Now, there is a great danger that a person who has read this argument so far, may misinterpret it to mean that trees should be "used" instrumentally for the good of people. And there is, unfortunately, a strong tendency in cities today to do just that —to treat trees instrumentally, as means to our own pleasure.

But our argument says just the opposite. Trees in a city, round a building, in a park, or in a garden are not in the forest. They need attention. As soon as we decide to have trees in a city, we must recognize that the tree becomes a different sort of ecological being. For instance, in a forest, trees grow in positions favorable to them: their density, sunlight, wind, moisture are all chosen by the process of selection. But in a city, a tree grows where it is planted, and it will not survive unless it is most carefully tended —pruned, watched, cared for when its bark gets pierced . . .

But now we come to a very subtle interaction. The trees will not get tended unless the places where they grow are liked and used by people. If they are randomly planted in some garden or in the shrubbery of some park, they are not near enough to

people to make people aware of them; and this in turn makes it unlikely that they will get the care they need.

So, finally, we see the nature of the complex interactive symbiosis between trees and people.

1. First, people need trees—for the reasons given.

2. But when people plant trees, the trees need care (unlike the forest trees).

3. The trees won't get the care they need unless they are in places people like.

4. And this in turn requires that the trees form social spaces.

5. Once the trees form social spaces, they are able to grow naturally.

So we see, by a curious twist of circumstances, trees in cities can only grow well, and in a fashion true to their own nature, when they cooperate with people and help to form spaces which the people need.

Therefore:

If you are planting trees, plant them according to their nature, to form enclosures, avenues, squares, groves, and single spreading trees toward the middle of open spaces. And shape the nearby buildings in response to trees, so that the trees themselves, and the trees and buildings together, form places which people can use.

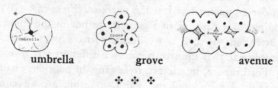

umbrella   grove   avenue

❖ ❖ ❖

Make the trees form "rooms" and spaces, avenues, and squares, and groves, by placing trellises between the trees, and walks, and seats under the trees themselves—OUTDOOR ROOM (163), TRELLISED WALK (174), GARDEN SEAT (176), SEAT SPOTS (241). One of the nicest ways to make a place beside a tree is to build a low wall, which protects the roots and makes a seat—SITTING WALL (243). . . .

. . . with terracing in place and trees taken care of—TERRACED SLOPE (169), FRUIT TREES (170), TREE PLACES (171), we come to the garden itself—to the ground and plants. In short, we must decide what kind of garden to have, what kind of plants to grow, what style of gardening is compatible with both artifice and nature.

❖ ❖ ❖

A garden which grows true to its own laws is not a wilderness, yet not entirely artificial either.

Many gardens are formal and artificial. The flower beds are trimmed like table cloths or painted designs. The lawns are clipped like perfect plastic fur. The paths are clean, like new polished asphalt. The furniture is new and clean, fresh from the department store.

These gardens have none of the quality which brings a garden to life—the quality of a wilderness, tamed, still wild, but cultivated enough to be in harmony with the buildings which surround it and the people who move in it. This balance of wilderness and cultivation reached a high point in the oldest English gardens.

In these gardens things are arranged so that the natural processes which come into being will maintain the condition of the garden and not degrade it. For example, mosses and grasses will grow between paving stones. In a sensible and natural garden, the garden is arranged so that this process enhances the garden and does not threaten it. In an unnatural garden these kinds of small events have constantly to be "looked after"—the gardener must constantly try to control and eradicate the processes of seeding, weeds, the spread of roots, the growth of grass.

In the garden growing wild the plants are chosen, and the boundaries placed, in such a way that the growth of things regulates itself. It does not need to be regulated by control. But it does not grow fiercely and undermine the ways in which it is planted. Natural wild plants, for example, are planted among

flowers and grass, so that there is no room for so-called weeds to fill the empty spaces and then need weeding. Natural stone edges form the boundaries of grass so that there is no need to chop the turf and clip the edge every few weeks. Rocks and stones are placed where there are changes of level. And there are small rock plants placed between the stones, so that once again there is no room for weeds to grow.

A garden growing wild is healthier, more capable of stable growth, than the more clipped and artificial garden. The garden can be left alone, it will not go to ruin in one or two seasons.

And for the people too, the garden growing wild creates a more profound experience. The gardener is in the position of a good doctor, watching nature take its course, occasionally taking action, pruning, pulling out some species, only to give the garden more room to grow and become itself. By contrast, the gardens that have to be tended obsessively, enslave a person to them; you cannot learn from them in quite the same way.

Therefore:

Grow grasses, mosses, bushes, flowers, and trees in a way which comes close to the way that they occur in nature: intermingled, without barriers between them, without bare earth, without formal flower beds, and with all the boundaries and edges made in rough stone and brick and wood which become a part of the natural growth.

cultivated plants growing wild

rough
natural edges

Include no formal elements, except where something is specifically called for by function—like a greenhouse—GREEN-HOUSE (175), a quiet seat—GARDEN SEAT (176), some water—STILL WATER (71), or flowers placed just where people can touch them and smell them—RAISED FLOWERS (245). . . .

173 GARDEN WALL*

. . . in private houses, both the HALF-HIDDEN GARDEN (111) and the PRIVATE TERRACE ON THE STREET (140) require walls. More generally, not only private gardens, but public gardens too, and even small parks and greens—QUIET BACKS (59), ACCESSIBLE GREEN (60), need some kind of enclosure round them, to make them as beautiful and quiet as possible.

❖ ❖ ❖

Gardens and small public parks don't give enough relief from noise unless they are well protected.

People need contact with trees and plants and water. In some way, which is hard to express, people are able to be more whole in the presence of nature, are able to go deeper into themselves, and are somehow able to draw sustaining energy from the life of plants and trees and water.

In a city, gardens and small parks try to solve this problem; but they are usually so close to traffic, noise, and buildings that the impact of nature is entirely lost. To be truly useful, in the deepest psychological sense, they must allow the people in them to be in touch with nature—and must be shielded from the sight and sound of passing traffic, city noises, and buildings. This requires walls, substantial high walls, and dense planting all around the garden.

In those few cases where there are small walled gardens in a city, open to the public—Alhambra, Copenhagen Royal Library Garden—these gardens almost always become famous. People understand and value the peace which they create.

. . . your garden or park wall of brick . . . has indeed often an unkind look on the outside, but there is more modesty in it than unkindness. It generally means, not that the builder of it wants to shut you out from the view of his garden, but from the view of himself: it is a frank statement that as he needs a certain portion of time to himself, so he needs a certain portion of ground to himself, and must not be stared at when he digs there in his shirt-

806

Walled gardens—Mughal.

sleeves, or plays at leapfrog with his boys from school, or talks over old times with his wife, walking up and down in the evening sunshine. Besides, the brick wall has good practical service in it, and shelters you from the east wind, and ripens your peaches and nectarines, and glows in autumn like a sunny bank. And, moreover, your brick wall, if you build it properly, so that it shall stand long enough, is a beautiful thing when it is old, and has assumed its grave purple red, touched with mossy green. . . . (John Ruskin, *The Two Paths,* New York: Dutton, 1907, pp. 202–205.)

This pattern applies to all private gardens and to small parks in cities. We are not convinced that it applies to *all* small parks—but it is hard to differentiate precisely between the places where a walled garden is desirable and the places where it is not. There are definitely situations where a small park, and perhaps even a small garden that is *open* to the rush of life around it, is just right. However, there are far more parks and gardens left open, that need to be walled, than vice versa, so we emphasize the walled condition.

Therefore:

Form some kind of enclosure to protect the interior of a quiet garden from the sights and sounds of passing traffic. If it is a large garden or a park, the enclosure can

be soft, can include bushes, trees, slopes, and so on. The smaller the garden, however, the harder and more definite the enclosure must become. In a very small garden, form the enclosure with buildings or walls; even hedges and fences will not be enough to keep out sound.

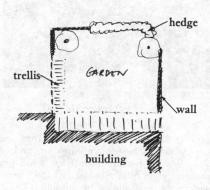

❖ ❖ ❖

Use the garden wall to help form positive outdoor space— POSITIVE OUTDOOR SPACE (106); but pierce it with balustrades and windows to make connections between garden and street, or garden and garden—PRIVATE TERRACE ON THE STREET (140), TRELLISED WALK (174), HALF-OPEN WALL (193), and above all, give it openings to make views into other larger and more distant spaces—HIERARCHY OF OPEN SPACE (114), ZEN VIEW (134). . . .

174 TRELLISED WALK**

. . . suppose the main spots of the garden have been defined—
OUTDOOR ROOM (163), TREE PLACES (171), GREENHOUSE (175),
FRUIT TREES (170). Now, where there is a special need to emphasize a path—PATHS AND GOALS (120)—or, even more important, where the edges between two parts of a garden need to be
marked without making a wall, an open trellised walk which can
enclose space, is required. Above all, these trellised walks help to
form the POSITIVE OUTDOOR SPACES (106) in a garden or a park;
and may perhaps help to form an ENTRANCE TRANSITION (112).

**Trellised walks have their own special beauty. They are
so unique, so different from other ways of shaping a path,
that they are almost archetypal.**

In PATH SHAPE (121), we have described the need for outdoor
paths to have a shape, like rooms. In POSITIVE OUTDOOR SPACE
(106), we have explained the need for larger outdoor areas to
have positive shape. A trellised walk does both. It makes it possible to implement both these patterns at the same time—simply
and elegantly. But it does it in such a fundamental way that we
have decided to treat it as a separate pattern; and we shall try
to define the places where a trellised structure over a path is
appropriate.

1. Use it to emphasize the path it covers, and to set off one
part of the path as a special section of a longer path in order to
make it an especially nice and inviting place to walk.

A trellis gives shape to an outdoor area.

2. Since the trellised path creates enclosure around the spaces which it bounds, use it to create a virtual wall to define an outdoor space. For example, a trellised walk can form an enormous outdoor room by surrounding, or partially surrounding, a garden. Therefore:

Where paths need special protection or where they need some intimacy, build a trellis over the path and plant it with climbing flowers. Use the trellis to help shape the outdoor spaces on either side of it.

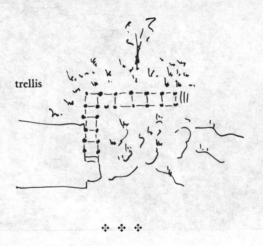

trellis

❖ ❖ ❖

Think about the columns that support the trellis as themselves capable of creating places—seats, bird feeders—COLUMN PLACES (226). Pave the path with loosely set stones—PAVING WITH CRACKS BETWEEN THE STONES (247). Use climbing plants and a fine trellis work to create the special quality of soft, filtered light underneath the trellis—FILTERED LIGHT (238), CLIMBING PLANTS (246). . . .

175 GREENHOUSE

. . . to keep a garden alive, it is almost essential that there be a "workshop"—a kind of halfway house between the garden and the house itself, where seedlings grow, and where, in temperate climates, plants can grow in spite of cold. In a HOUSE CLUSTER (37) or a WORK COMMUNITY (41), this workshop makes an essential contribution to the COMMON LAND (67).

❖ ❖ ❖

Many efforts are being made to harness solar energy by converting it into hot water or electric power. And yet the easiest way to harness solar energy is the most obvious and the oldest: namely, to trap the heat inside a greenhouse and use it for growing flowers and vegetables.

Imagine a simple greenhouse, attached to a living room, turned to the winter sun, and filled with shelves for flowers and vegetables. It has an entrance from the house—so you can go into it and use it in the winter without going outdoors. And it has an entrance from the garden—so you can use it as a workshop while you are out in the garden and not have to walk through the house.

This greenhouse then becomes a wonderful place: a source of life, a place where flowers can be grown as part of the life of the house. The classic conservatory was a natural part of countless houses in the temperate climates.

For someone who has not experienced a greenhouse as an extension of the house, it may be hard to recognize how fundamental it becomes. It is a world unto itself, as definite and wonderful as fire or water, and it provides an experience which can hardly be matched by any other pattern. Hewitt Ryan, the psychiatrist for whom we built the clinic in Modesto with the help of this pattern language, thought greenhouses so essential that he included one as a basic part of the clinic: a place beside the common area, where people could reintegrate themselves by growing seedlings that would be gradually transplanted to form gardens for the clinic.

Several recent "energy-systems" inspired by the ecology movement have sought to make greenhouses a fundamental part of human settlements. For example, Grahame Gaines' self-contained eco-house includes a large greenhouse as a source of heat and food. (See *London Observer*, October 1972.) And Chahroudi's Grow Hole—a glazed sunken pit for growing vegetables in winter—is another kind of greenhouse (*Progressive Architecture*, July 1970, p. 85).

Therefore:

In temperate climates, build a greenhouse as part of your house or office, so that it is both a "room" of the house which can be reached directly without going outdoors and a part of the garden which can be reached directly from the garden.

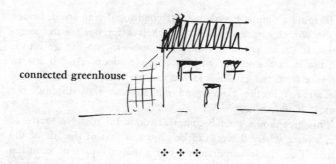

connected greenhouse

✧ ✧ ✧

Place the greenhouse so that it has easy access to the VEGETABLE GARDEN (177) and the COMPOST (178). Arrange its interior so that it is surrounded with WAIST-HIGH SHELVES (201) and plenty of storage space—BULK STORAGE (145); perhaps give it a special seat, where it is possible to sit comfortably—GARDEN SEAT (176), WINDOW PLACE (180). . . .

. . . with the character of the garden fixed—GARDEN GROWING
WILD (172), we consider the special corners which make the
garden valuable and somewhat secret. Of these, the most important is the SUNNY PLACE (161), which has already been described, because it is so fundamental to the building. Now we
add to this another seat, more private, where a person can go to
sit and think and dream.

❖ ❖ ❖

**Somewhere in every garden, there must be at least one
spot, a quiet garden seat, in which a person—or two
people—can reach into themselves and be in touch with
nothing else but nature.**

Throughout the patterns in this pattern language we have said,
over and again, how very essential it is to give ourselves environments in which we can be in touch with the nature we have
sprung from—see especially CITY COUNTRY FINGERS (3) and
QUIET BACKS (59). But among all the various statements of this
fact there is not one so far which puts this need right in our own
houses, as close to us as fire and food.

Wordsworth built his entire politics, as a poet, around the
fact that tranquility in nature was a basic right to which everyone was entitled. He wanted to integrate the need for solitude-
in-nature with city living. He imagined people literally stepping
off busy streets and renewing themselves in private gardens—
every day. And now many of us have come to learn that without
such a place life in a city is impossible. There is so much activity,
days are so easily filled with jobs, family, friends, things to do—
that time alone is rare. And the more we live without the habit of
stillness, the more we tie ourselves to this active life, the stranger
and more disquieting the experience of stillness and solitude
becomes: city people are notoriously busy-busy, and cannot be
alone, without "input," for a moment.

It is in this context that we propose the isolated garden seat:
a place hidden in the garden where one or two people can sit
alone, undisturbed, near growing things. It may be on a roof

top, on the ground, perhaps even half-sunken in an embankment.

There are literally hundreds of old books about gardens which testify to this pattern. One is Hildegarde Hawthorne's *The Lure of the Garden*, New York: The Century Co., 1911. We quote from a passage describing the special kind of small talk that is drawn out of people by quiet garden seats:

> Perhaps, of all the various forms of gossip overheard by the garden, the loveliest is that between a young and an old person who are friends. Real friendship between the generations is rare, but when it exists it is of the finest. That youth is fortunate who can pour his perplexities into the ear of an older man or woman, and who knows a comradeship and an understanding exceeding in beauty the facile friendships created by like interests and common pursuits; and fortunate too the girl who is able to impart the emotions and ideas aroused in her by her early meetings with the world and life to some one old in experience but comprehendingly young in heart. Both of them will remember those hours long after the garden gate has closed behind their friend forever; as long, indeed, as they remember anything that went to the making of the best in them.

Therefore:

Make a quiet place in the garden—a private enclosure with a comfortable seat, thick planting, sun. Pick the place for the seat carefully; pick the place that will give you the most intense kind of solitude.

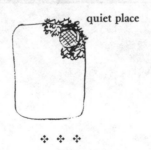

quiet place

❖ ❖ ❖

Place the garden seat, like other outdoor seats, where it commands a view, is in the sun, is sheltered from the wind—SEAT SPOTS (241); perhaps under bushes and trees where light is soft and dappled—FILTERED LIGHT (238). . . .

817

177 VEGETABLE GARDEN*

. . . we have one pattern, already, which brings out the useful character of gardens—both public and private ones—FRUIT TREES (170); we supplement this with a smaller, but as important aspect of the garden—one which every public and private garden should contain: enhance common land—COMMON LAND (67) and private gardens—HALF-HIDDEN GARDEN (111) with a patch where people can grow vegetables.

❖ ❖ ❖

In a healthy town every family can grow vegetables for itself. The time is past to think of this as a hobby for enthusiasts; it is a fundamental part of human life.

Vegetables are the most basic foods. If we compare dairy products, vegetables and fruits, meats, and synthetic foods, the vegetables play the most essential role. As a class, they are the only ones which are by themselves wholly able to support human life. And, in an ecologically balanced world, it seems almost certain that man will have to work out some balanced relationship with vegetables for his daily food. (See, for example, F. Lappe, *Diet for a Small Planet*, New York: Ballantine, 1971.)

Since the industrial revolution, there has been a growing tendency for people to rely on impersonal producers for their vegetables; however, in a world where vegetables are central and where self-sufficiency increases, it becomes as natural for families to have their own vegetables as their own air.

The amount of land it takes to grow the vegetables for a household is surprisingly small. It takes about one-tenth of an acre to grow an adequate year round supply of vegetables for a family of four. And apparently vegetables give a higher "nutrient return" for fixed quantities of energy—sun, labor—than any other food. This means that every house or house cluster can create its own supply of vegetables, and that every household which does not have its own private land attached to it should have a portion of a *common vegetable garden* close at hand.

Beside this fundamental need for vegetable gardens in cities,

there is a subtler need. Parks, street trees, and manicured lawns do very little to establish the connection between us and the land. They teach us nothing of its productivity, nothing of its capacities. Many people who are born, raised, and live out their lives in cities simply do not know where the food they eat comes from or what a living garden is like. Their only connection with the productivity of the land comes from packaged tomatoes on the supermarket shelf. But contact with the land and its growing process is not simply a quaint nicety from the past that we can let go of casually. More likely, it is a basic part of the process of organic security. Deep down, there must be some sense of insecurity in city dwellers who depend entirely upon the supermarkets for their produce.

Community gardens needn't be expensive propositions either. When Santa Barbara residents decided to start a downtown garden back in May, 1970, they used their ingenuity. A vacant downtown lot was acquired (at a cost of one dollar for 6 months), and the city provided free water and a tractor with operator for two days. Compost was no problem. The group got leaves from the park department, hard sludge from the local sanitation district, and horse manure from a nearby riding club. Tools and seeds were donated. ("Community Gardens," Bob Rodale, *San Francisco Chronicle*, May 31, 1972, p. 16.)

School garden in Amsterdam, worked by the children.

Therefore:

Set aside one piece of land either in the private garden or on common land as a vegetable garden. About one-tenth of

an acre is needed for each family of four. Make sure the vegetable garden is in a sunny place and central to all the households it serves. Fence it in and build a small storage shed for gardening tools beside it.

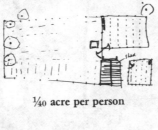

¼₀ acre per person

❖ ❖ ❖

To fertilize the vegetables, use the natural compost which is generated by the house and the neighborhood—COMPOST (178); and if possible, try to use water from the sinks and drains to irrigate the soil—BATHING ROOM (144). . . .

178 COMPOST*

In Chekiang Province, as in many other parts of China, roadside toilets abound. They are built by farmers to entice passersby into favoring them with a gift of valued fertilizer.

. . . the garden is a valuable part of the house, because it can help you grow fruit and vegetables—FRUIT TREES (170), VEGETABLE GARDEN (177). But it can only flourish if it gets nourishment; and this nourishment, in the form of compost, can only be created when the garbage and the wastes from the individual houses and HOUSE CLUSTERS (37) and from the ANIMALS (74) are properly organized.

❖ ❖ ❖

Our current ways of getting rid of sewage poison the great bodies of natural water, and rob the land around our buildings of the nutrients they need.

To the average individual in the city, it probably appears that the sewage system works beautifully—no muss, no fuss. Just pull the toilet chain, and everything is fine. In fact, city dwellers who have had the experience of using a smelly outhouse would probably argue that our modern system of sewage disposal is a tremendous advance over earlier practices. Unfortunately, this is simply not the case. Almost every step in modern sewage disposal is either wasteful, expensive, or dangerous.

We can start by remembering that every single time a toilet is flushed, seven gallons of drinking water go down the drain. In fact, around half of our domestic water consumption goes to flushing out the toilet.

Beyond the cost of the water, there is an enormous cost in the hardware of the sewer system. The average new homeowner today, living on a 50 x 150 foot lot in the city, has paid $1500 as his share of the collection system which takes sewage from his house to the sewage treatment plant. In lower density residential areas, this cost may be $2000 or even $6000. Each house pays an additional $500 toward the cost of the sewage treatment plant. We see then that the initial cost of today's sewage system is at least $2000 per house, often more. And these prices do not include monthly service charges for water and sewer facilities: around $50 per year for a single family household.

In addition we must add those costs which are less easily measurable in dollars and cents, but which may, in the long run, prove even higher than those already discussed. These include: (1) the value of lost nutrients which are allowed to flow away into the rivers and oceans—nutrients which could have been used to build up the soil they came from; and (2) the cost of the pollution: effluents cause "eutrophication"—the sewage depletes the oxygen in water and causes it to become clogged with algae.

What can be done? Some of this effluent might be recycled back to the land in the form of sludge. But residential sewage is usually mixed with industrial waste which often contains extremely noxious elements. And even if industrial wastes were not allowed into the sewage system, an additional distribution system would be needed to get the sludge back to the land. We see, therefore, that additional costs required to make the existing system ecologically sound are prohibitive.

What is needed is not a larger, more centralized and complex system, but a smaller, more decentralized and simpler one. We need a system that is less expensive; and we need a system that is an ecological benefit rather than an ecological drain.

We propose that individual small-scale composting plants begin to replace our present disposal system. Small buildings would be equipped with their own miniature sewage plants, located directly under the toilets. All bulky garbage produced on-site would be added to the plants. The resultant humus would be used to replenish the soil surrounding the building and throughout the neighborhood, as would the waste water from bathing and washing.

Such miniature sewage plants are commercially available and are currently in use in Sweden, Norway, and Finland. They are sold under the trade names Multrum or Clivus, and they can even be imported to the United States for a total price of $1500: much lower than the lowest figure of $2000, currently being charged for the conventional system. For a worked example, see Van der Ryn, Anderson and Sawyer, "Composting Privy", Technical Bulletin #1, Natural Energy Design Center, University of California, Berkeley, Dept. of Architecture, January 1974.

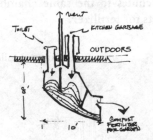

Clivus compost chamber.

These composting plants are so simple that they can be built by amateurs for much less money. An extremely simple home-made composting system is described below:

The privy is built adjoining a larger outbuilding which is built over a root cellar. From overhead joists to floor, the cellar is about 7′ deep. And so it was simplest to make the composting chamber beneath the privy 7′ deep. . . .

In the composting chamber underneath our privy, we have been using peat-moss—both because it is highly absorbent, and because it comes compactly baled and is convenient to store. We also use some garden dirt and a little lime.

We keep a garbage can full of peat moss in the privy, and dump in about a quart of the moss after each use. The privy is fairly odorless. Whenever there gets to be a smell I add lime, dirt and an extra layer of peat moss. That takes care of it. I figure that we will use three or four bales of peat moss a year—for a family of four plus a large number of guests.

My privy is of the kind familiarly known as a two-holer, which seems necessary for my composting system.

We use only one hole at a time. We use A until there is an accumulation 18 inches deep. We then shift to B and use it until the accumulation there is as great as that of A. Then the heap at A is shoveled to C, and so on. When all four positions are filled, C and D are shoveled into a heap on the ground outside, where I mean to let it stay for at least several weeks before use. (*Organic Gardening and Farming,* Emmaus, Pennsylvania: Rodale Press, February 1972.)

Therefore:

Arrange all toilets over a dry composting chamber. Lead

organic garbage chutes to the same chamber, and use the combined products for fertilizer.

grouped toilets

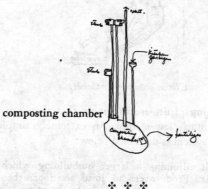

composting chamber

❖ ❖ ❖

Add to the effect of dry composting by re-using waste water; run all water drains into the garden to irrigate the soil; use organic soap—BATHING ROOM (144). . . .

go back to the inside of the building and attach the necessary minor rooms and alcoves to complete the main rooms;

179 ALCOVES**

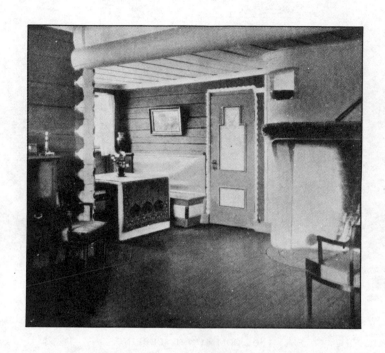

. . . many large rooms are not complete unless they have smaller rooms and alcoves opening off them. This pattern, and several which follow it, define the form of minor rooms and alcoves which help to complete COMMON AREAS AT THE HEART (129), FARMHOUSE KICHEN (139), SEQUENCE OF SITTING SPACES (142), FLEXIBLE OFFICE SPACE (146), A PLACE TO WAIT (150), SMALL MEETING ROOMS (151), and many others.

❖ ❖ ❖

No homogeneous room, of homogeneous height, can serve a group of people well. To give a group a chance to be together, as a group, a room must also give them the chance to be alone, in one's and two's in the same space.

This problem is felt most acutely in the common rooms of a house—the kitchen, the family room, the living room. In fact, it is so critical there, that the house can drive the family apart when it remains unsolved. Therefore, while we believe that the pattern applies equally to workplaces and shops and schools—in fact, to all common rooms wherever they are—we shall focus our discussion on the house, and the use of alcoves around the family common rooms.

In modern life, the main function of the family is emotional; it is a source of security and love. But these qualities will only come into existence if the members of the house are *physically able to be together as a family*.

This is often difficult. The various members of the family come and go at different times of day; even when they are in the house, each has his own private interests: sewing, reading, homework, carpentry, model-building, games. In many houses, these interests force people to go off to their own rooms, away from the family. This happens for two reasons. First, in a normal family room, one person can easily be disturbed by what the others are doing: the person who wants to read, is disturbed by the fact that the others are watching TV. Second, the family room does not usually have any space where people can leave

things and not have them disturbed. Books left on the dining table get cleared away at meal times; a half-finished game cannot be left standing. Naturally, people get into the habit of doing these things somewhere else—away from the family.

To solve the problem, there must be some way in which the members of the family can be together, even when they are doing different things. This means that the family room needs a number of small spaces where people can do different things. The spaces need to be far enough away from the main room, so that any clutter that develops in them does not encroach on the communal uses of the main room. The spaces need to be connected, so that people are still "together" when they are in them: this means they need to be open to each other. At the same time they need to be secluded, so a person in one of them is not disturbed by the others. In short, the family room must be surrounded by small alcoves. The alcoves should be large enough for one or two people at a time: about six feet wide, and between three and six feet deep. To make it clear that they are separate from the main room, so they do not clutter it up, and so that people in them are secluded, they should be narrower than the family room walls, and have lower ceilings than the main room.

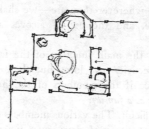

Family room alcoves.

Since this pattern is so fundamental, we now present several quotes from various writers to underscore the fact that many people have made roughly similar observations:

From *Psychosocial Interior of the Family*, Gerald Handel, ed., Chicago, Ill.: Aldine Publishing Company, 1967, p. 13.

This fundamental duality of family life is of considerable significance, for the individual's efforts to take his own kind of interest

in the world, to become his own kind of person, proceed apace with his efforts to find gratifying connection to the other members. At the same time, the other members are engaged in taking their kinds of interest in him, and in themselves. This is the matrix of interaction in which a family develops its life. The family tries to cast itself in a form that satisfies the ways in which its members want to be together and apart. . . .

From *Children in the Family* by Florence Powdermaker and Louise Grimes, New York: Farrar & Reinhart, Inc., 1940, p. 108: "Even if a child has a room of his own, he doesn't like being kept there all day long but wants to spend much of his time in other parts of the house. . . ." And p. 112: ". . . he enjoys and craves attention. He likes to show things to adults and have them share in the pleasure of his discoveries. Besides, he is entranced by their activities and would like to have a finger in every pie."

And from Svend Riemer, "Sociological Theory of Home Adjustment," *American Soc. Rev.*, Vol. 8, No. 3, June 1943, p. 277:

In adjustment to the activities of other members of the family, it will be necessary to "migrate" . . . between the different rooms of the family home. Even the same activity may have to be moved from one room to the other at different times of the day,

Home studies for example may have to be carried out in the living room during the afternoon, while food is being prepared in the kitchen; they may have to be continued in the kitchen during the evening hours, when the living room is occupied by leisure time activities of other members of the family. This "migration" between different rooms is apt to impair intellectual concentration. It may convey a sense of insecurity. Its possible disadvantages have to be seriously considered whenever children are reared in the family home.

It is clear then, that the opposing needs for some seclusion and some community at the same time in the same space, occur in almost every family. It is not hard to see that only slightly different versions of the very same forces exist in all communal rooms. People want to be together; but at the same time they want the opportunity for some small amount of privacy, without giving up community.

If ten people, or five, are together in a room, and two of them want to pull away to one side to have a quiet talk together, they need a place to do it. Only the alcove, or some version of the

alcove, can give them the privacy they need, without forcing them to give the group up altogether.

Therefore:

Make small places at the edge of any common room, usually no more than 6 feet wide and 3 to 6 feet deep and possibly much smaller. These alcoves should be large enough for two people to sit, chat, or play and sometimes large enough to contain a desk or a table.

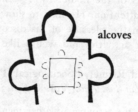

alcoves

Give the alcove a ceiling which is markedly lower than the ceiling height in the main room—CEILING HEIGHT VARIETY (190); make a partial boundary between the alcove and the common room by using low walls and thick columns—HALF-OPEN WALL (193), COLUMN PLACE (226); when the alcove is on an outside wall, make it into a window place, with a nice window, low sill, and a built-in seat—WINDOW PLACE (180), BUILT-IN SEATS (202); and treat it as THICKENING THE OUTER WALLS (211). For details on the shape of the alcove, see THE SHAPE OF INDOOR SPACE (191). . . .

. . . this pattern helps complete the arrangement of the windows given by ENTRANCE ROOM (130), ZEN VIEW (134), LIGHT ON TWO SIDES OF EVERY ROOM (159), STREET WINDOWS (164). According to the pattern, at least one of the windows in each room needs to be shaped in such a way as to increase its usefulness as a space.

❖ ❖ ❖

Everybody loves window seats, bay windows, and big windows with low sills and comfortable chairs drawn up to them.

It is easy to think of these kinds of places as luxuries, which can no longer be built, and which we are no longer lucky enough to be able to afford.

In fact, the matter is more urgent. These kinds of windows which create "places" next to them are not simply luxuries; they are *necessary*. A room which does not have a place like this seldom allows you to feel fully comfortable or perfectly at ease. Indeed, a room without a window place may keep you in a state of perpetual unresolved conflict and tension—slight, perhaps, but definite.

This conflict takes the following form. If the room contains no window which is a "place," a person in the room will be torn between two forces:

1. He wants to sit down and be comfortable.
2. He is drawn toward the light.

Obviously, if the comfortable places—those places in the room where you most want to sit—are away from the windows, there is no way of overcoming this conflict. You see, then, that our love for window "places" is not a luxury but an organic intuition, based on the natural desire a person has to let the forces he experiences run free. A room where you feel truly comfortable will always contain some kind of window place.

Now, of course, it is hard to give an exact definition of a

834

"place." Essentially a "place" is a partly enclosed, distinctly identifiable spot within a room. All of the following can function as "places" in this sense: bay windows, window seats, a low window sill where there is an obvious position for a comfortable armchair, and deep alcoves with windows all around them. To make the concept of a window place more precise, here are some examples of each of these types, together with discussion of the critical features which make each one of them work.

A bay window. A shallow bulge at one end of a room, with windows wrapped around it. It works as a window place because of the greater intensity of light, the views through the side windows, and the fact that you can pull chairs or a sofa up into the bay.

A bay window.

A window seat. More modest. A niche, just deep enough for the seat. It works best for one person, sitting parallel to the window, back to the window frame, or for two people facing each other in this position.

A window seat.

A low sill. The most modest of all. The right sill height for a window place, with a comfortable chair, is very low: 12 to 14 inches. The feeling of enclosure comes from the armchair—best of all, one with a high back and sides.

A low sill.

A glazed alcove. The most elaborate kind of window place: almost like a gazebo or a conservatory, windows all around it, a small room, almost part of the garden.

A glazed alcove.

And, of course, there are other possible versions too. In principle, any window with a reasonably pleasant view can be a window place, provided that it is taken seriously as a space, a volume, not merely treated as a hole in the wall. Any room that people use often should have a window place. And window places should even be considered for waiting rooms or as special places along the length of hallways.

Therefore:

In every room where you spend any length of time during the day, make at least one window into a "window place."

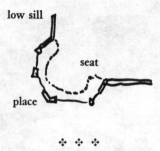

❖ ❖ ❖

Make it low and self-contained if there is room for that—ALCOVES (179); keep the sill low—LOW SILL (222); put in the exact positions of frames, and mullions, and seats after the window place is framed, according to the view outside—BUILT-IN SEATS (202), NATURAL DOORS AND WINDOWS (221). And set the window deep into the wall to soften light around the edges—DEEP REVEALS (223). Under a sloping roof, use DORMER WINDOWS (231) to make this pattern. . . .

181 THE FIRE*

. . . this pattern helps to create the spirit of the COMMON AREAS AT THE HEART (129), and even helps to give its layout and position, because it influences the way that paths and rooms relate to one another.

❖ ❖ ❖

There is no substitute for fire.

Television often gives a focus to a room, but it is nothing but a feeble substitute for something which is actually alive and flickering within the room. The need for fire is almost as fundamental as the need for water. Fire is an emotional touchstone, comparable to trees, other people, a house, the sky. But the traditional fireplace is nearly obsolete, and new ones are often added to homes as "luxury items." Perhaps this explains why these showpiece fireplaces are always so badly located. Stripped of the logic of necessity, they seem an afterthought, not truly integrated.

The most convincing statement of the need for fire that we have found is in Gaston Bachelard's book, *The Psychoanalysis of Fire*. Here is a long quote from Bachelard to give you some idea of the power of his argument.

The fire confined to the fireplace was no doubt for man the first object of reverie, the symbol of repose, the invitation to repose. One can hardly conceive of a philosophy of repose that would not include a reverie before a flaming log fire. Thus, in our opinion, to be deprived of a reverie before a burning fire is to lose the first use and the truly human use of fire. To be sure, a fire warms us and gives us comfort. But one only becomes fully aware of this comforting sensation after quite a long period of contemplation of the flames; one only receives comfort from the fire when one leans his elbows on his knees and holds his head in his hands. This attitude comes from the distant past. The child by the fire assumes it naturally. Not for nothing is it the attitude of the Thinker. It leads to a very special kind of attention which has nothing in common with the attention involved in watching or observing. Very rarely is it utilized for any other kind of contemplation. When near the fire, one must be seated; one must rest without sleeping; one must engage in reverie on a specific object. . . .

BUILDINGS

Of course the supporters of the theory of the utilitarian formation of the mind will not accept a theory so facile in its idealism, and they will point out to us the multiple uses of fire in order to ascertain the exact interest that we have in it: not only does fire give heat, but it also cooks meats. As if the complex hearth, the peasant's hearth, precluded reverie! . . .

. . . From the notched teeth of the chimney hook there hung the black cauldron. The three-legged cooking pot projected over the hot embers. Puffing up her cheeks to blow into the steel tube, my grandmother would rekindle the sleeping flames. Everything would be cooking at the same time: the potatoes for the pigs, the choice potatoes for the family. For me there would be a fresh egg cooking under the ashes . . . on days when I was on my good behavior, they would bring out the waffle iron. Rectangular in form, it would crush down the fire of thorns burning red as the spikes of sword lilies. And soon the *gaufre* or waffle would be pressed against my pinafore, warmer to the fingers than to the lips. Yes, then indeed I was eating fire, eating its gold, its odor and even its crackling while the burning gaufre was crunching under my teeth. . . .

And it is always like that, through a kind of extra pleasure—like dessert—that fire shows itself a friend of man. It does not confine itself to cooking; it makes things crisp and crunchy. It puts the golden crust on the griddle cake; it gives a material form to man's festivities. As far back in time as we can go, the gastronomic value has always been more highly prized than the nutritive value, and it is in joy and not in sorrow that man discovered his intellect. The conquest of the superfluous gives us a greater spiritual excitement than the conquest of the necessary. Man is a creation of desire, not a creation of need.

But the reverie by the fireside has axes that are more philosophical. Fire is for the man who is contemplating it an example of a sudden change or development and an example of a circumstantial development. Less monotonous and less abstract than flowing water, even more quick to grow and to change than the young bird, we watch every day in its nest in the bushes, fire suggests the desire to change, to speed up the passage of time, to bring all of life to its conclusion, to its hereafter. In these circumstances the reverie becomes truly fascinating and dramatic; it magnifies human destiny; it links the small to the great, the hearth to the volcano, the life of a log to the life of a world. The fascinated individual hears the call of the funeral pyre. For him destruction is more than a change, it is a renewal. . . .

Love, death and fire are untied at the same moment. Through its sacrifice in the heart of the flames, the mayfly gives us a lesson in eternity. This total death which leaves no trace is the guarantee that our whole person has departed for the beyond. To lose everything in order to gain everything. The lesson taught by the fire is clear: "After having gained all through skill, through love or

through violence you must give up all, you *must* annihilate your-
self." (Gaston Bachelard, *The Psychoanalysis of Fire*, Boston · Beacon
Press, 1964, pp. 14–16. Originally published as *La Psychanalyse du
Feu*, Librarie Gallimard, 1938. Reprinted by permission of Beacon
Press.)

Another, more down-to-earth, view of the need for fire comes
from Mrs. Field, quoted in Robert Woods Kennedy, *The House
and the Art of Its Design*, New York: Reinhold, 1953, pp. 192–
93:

> During the winter months, when the children are often confined
> indoors for their play, it often happens that around four o-clock
> or a little after they become cross and grumpy in their playroom,
> or wild and almost hysterical with boredom. Then I light a fire in
> the living-room fireplace, and send the children in there to watch it;
> if the fire were not lighted they would continue their quarreling and
> perhaps try to turn the quiet room into another bedlam, but with
> the burning flames on the hearth, they relax into easy interest.
> They see things in the fire, someone tells a story that interests the
> whole group, they quiet down, leaving me free to prepare the
> supper and serve it. It has a definitely hypnotic quality that can be
> turned to good account.

Of course, we must face the fact that in many parts of the world
wood and coal fires are ecologically unsound. They pollute the
air; they are inefficient for heating; they are a drain on wood
reserves. If we wish to maintain the habit of burning fires in the
home, we shall have to find a way of supplementing wood fuel.
For example, we can cultivate the habit of burning the in-
flammable materials that become waste around the house and
throughout the community—paper, cloth, non-chlorinated plastics,
wood scraps and sawdust. In short, if we want the emotional
comfort that can be drawn from a fireplace, we shall have to
learn to use the fireplace in a concentrated way, producing our
own fuel from materials that would otherwise go to waste in our
neighborhoods. It is easy to imagine, a simple hand press which
people can use in their homes to press this waste into dense "logs"
to make the fire more substantial.

Assume then that we are to have some kind of fireplace—
perhaps something entirely simple, but an open fire nonetheless.
Where shall we put it? There are four points to consider:

1. Certainly, the main fireplace should be located in the com-

mon area of the house. it will help to draw people together in this area, and when it is burning, it provides a kind of counterpoint to conversation.

2. However, the fireplace should be in view for people passing through the room and people in adjoining rooms, especially the kitchen. The fire will tend to pull people ·in and make it more likely for the family to gather. And also it is good to view the fire in passing. A welcome time for a fire is in the evening when the family is gathering for the evening meal; and the activity tends to balance between the kitchen and the fire.

3. Make certain, too, that there is a space where people can sit in front of the fire; and that this space is not cut by paths between doors or adjacent rooms.

4. And be sure that the fire is not a dead place when the fire is *not* burning. A fireplace without a fire, full of ashes and dark, will turn the chairs away, unless the chairs which face the fire when it is lit face something else—a window, or activity, or a view—when it is not lit. Only then will the circle of chairs which forms around the fire be stable and keep the place alive, both when the fire is burning and when it isn't.

A daytime focus.

Therefore:

Build the fire in a common space—perhaps in the kitchen —where it provides a natural focus for talk and dreams and thought. Adjust the location until it knits together the social spaces and rooms around it, giving them each a glimpse of the fire; and make a window or some other focus to sustain the place during the times when the fire is out.

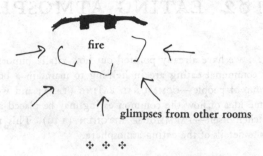

fire

glimpses from other rooms

❖ ❖ ❖

Even where the traditional open fireplace is obsolete for heating
or where fuel is scarce, find some way of converting refuse, paper,
scraps of wood and cardboard into logs which can be burned, and
which smell good—perhaps with some kind of natural resin in a
home-made press. Burn all the dry organic materials that do not
go to the COMPOST (178), so that the leftovers from the materials
which come into the house all serve a useful function, either as
fertilizer or as fuel; indeed, the ashes from the fire may go into
the compost. Make a circle of chairs around the fire—SITTING
CIRCLE (185); perhaps these chairs include a WINDOW PLACE
(180).

182 EATING ATMOSPHERE

. . . we have already pointed out how vitally important all kinds of communal eating are in helping to maintain a bond among a group of people—COMMUNAL EATING (147); and we have given some idea of how the common eating may be placed as part of the kitchen itself—FARMHOUSE KITCHEN (139). This pattern gives some details of the eating atmosphere.

❖ ❖ ❖

When people eat together, they may actually be together in spirit—or they may be far apart. Some rooms invite people to eat leisurely and comfortably and feel together, while others force people to eat as quickly as possible so they can go somewhere else to relax.

Above all, when the table has the same light all over it, and has the same light level on the walls around it, the light does nothing to hold people together; the intensity of feeling is quite likely to dissolve; there is little sense that there is any special kind of gathering. But when there is a soft light, hung low over the table, with dark walls around so that this one point of light lights up people's faces and is a focal point for the whole group, then a meal can become a special thing indeed, a bond, communion.

Therefore:

Put a heavy table in the center of the eating space—large enough for the whole family or the group of people using it. Put a light over the table to create a pool of light over the group, and enclose the space with walls or with contrasting darkness. Make the space large enough so the chairs can be pulled back comfortably, and provide shelves and counters close at hand for things related to the meal.

light in the middle

❖ ❖ ❖

Get the details of the light from POOLS OF LIGHT (252); and choose the colors to make the place warm and dark and comfortable at night—WARM COLORS (250); put a few soft chairs nearby—DIFFERENT CHAIRS (251); or put BUILT-IN SEATS (202) with big cushions against one wall; and for the storage space—OPEN SHELVES (200) and WAIST-HIGH SHELF (201). . . .

183 WORKSPACE ENCLOSURE **

. . . this pattern plays a vital role in helping to create an atmosphere in which people can work effectively. You can use it piecemeal to generate the larger patterns for workspace like FLEXIBLE OFFICE SPACE (146), HALF-PRIVATE OFFICE (152), and HOME WORKSHOP (157). Or, of course, it can be used to help complete these larger patterns, if you have already built them into your design. Even in an alcove off the family commons—ALCOVES (179), you can make the workspace more suitable for work, by placing and shaping the enclosure immediately around it according to this pattern.

People cannot work effectively if their workspace is too enclosed or too exposed. A good workspace strikes the balance.

In many offices, people are either completely enclosed and feel too isolated, or they are in a completely open area as in the office landscape and feel too exposed. It is hard for a person to work well at either of these two extremes—the problem is to find the right balance between the two.

To find the proper balance, we conducted a simple experiment. We first defined 13 variables, which we thought might influence a person's sense of enclosure in his workspace.

These 13 variables are:

1. Presence or absence of a wall immediately behind you.
2. Presence or absence of a wall immediately beside you.
3. Amount of open space in front of you.
4. Area of the workspace.
5. Total amount of enclosure around the immediate workspace.
6. View to the outside.
7. Distance to nearest person.
8. Number of people you are aware of from your workplace.
9. Noise: level and type.
10. Presence or absence of a person facing you directly.
11. Number of different positions you can sit in.

847

12. Number of people you can see from your workspace.

13. The number of people you can talk to without raising your voice.

We then formulated thirteen hypotheses which connect these variables with the comfort of the work space. The hypotheses are listed below. We interviewed 17 men and women who had all worked in several different offices. In the interview, we first asked each person to think of the very best workspace he (or she) had ever worked in and the very worst; and then asked him (or her) to make a sketch plan of both spaces. Then we asked questions to identify the value of each of these 13 variables in the "best" and "worst" workspaces. Thus, for instance, we might point to one of the sketches a person had drawn, and say "How far away was that wall" to establish the value of the third variable. The values of the variables for the 17 best and worst workspaces are given in the following table.

On the basis of this table, we then calculated the probable significance of our hypotheses, according to the chi-squared test. Nine of the hypotheses appear to be significant according to the chi-squared test, and four are not. We now list the nine "significant" hypotheses, and with each one, in parentheses, we venture an explanation for its success.

1. You feel more comfortable in a workspace if there is a wall behind you. (If your back is exposed you feel vulnerable—you can never tell if someone is looking at you, or if someone is coming toward you from behind.) The data support this hypothesis at the 1 per cent level of significance.

2. You feel more comfortable in a workspace if there is a wall to one side. (If your workspace is open in front and on both sides, you feel too exposed. This is probably due to the fact that though it is possible to be vaguely aware of everything that goes on 180 degrees around you, you cannot feel in real control of such a wide angle without moving your head all the time. If you have a wall on one side, you only have to manage an angle of 90 degrees, which is much easier, so you feel more secure.) The data support this hypothesis at the 5 per cent level of significance.

3. There should be no blank wall closer than 8 feet in front of you. (As you work you want to occasionally look up and rest your

	Wall Behind in Workspace?		Wall to Side in Workspace?		Wall in Front Within 8'?		Area of Workspace?		Enclosure		View to Outside?		Aural Privacy?		No. of People in Awareness		Bother by Noise of a Different Kind?		Catch Somebody's Eye?		No. of Different Views While Working		No. of People in Sight		No. of People Available for Chat	
Question Number	1		2		3		4		5		6		7		8		9		10		11		12		13	
*	B	W	B	W	B	W	B	W	B	W	B	W	B	W	B	W	B	W	B	W	B	W	B	W	B	W
Tony	Y	N	Y	N	N	Y	35	20	50	37	Y	N	–	–	2	1	Y	Y	Y	N	1	1	2	1	2	1
Irene	Y	N	Y	N	Y	N	135	35	60	0	Y	N	Y	N	3	4	N	Y	N	N	3	2	2	2	0	1
Effie	Y	N	Y	N	Y	Y	150	35	86	25	Y	Y	Y	N	4	5	N	Y	N	N	2	2	0	5	0	3
Peggy	Y	N	Y	N	N	N	90	36	50	2	Y	N	Y	N	8	16	N	Y	Y	N	4	2	8	16	0	1
Ron	Y	N	Y	Y	Y	Y	63	22	57	44	Y	N	Y	N	8	1	N	Y	N	N	2	1	4	1	3	1
Joan	Y	N	Y	N	N	N	120	20	50	0	Y	N	Y	N	3	9	N	N	N	Y	2	1	3	9	3	2
Leslie	Y	N	N	N	N	N	50	20	25	0	Y	Y	Y	Y	10	0	N	Y	N	N	3	1	9	0	7	0
Virginia	Y	N	Y	Y	N	N	80	20	50	25	Y	N	Y	N	3	50	N	Y	N	N	2	1	3	8	1	4
Fran	N	N	Y	N	N	Y	100	50	55	50	Y	N	N	N	2	2	N	Y	N	N	1	4	1	2	1	1
Dendal	N	N	N	Y	Y	Y	20	20	25	50	Y	N	N	N	4	150	N	N	N	N	1	1	4	2	4	1
Phyllis	Y	Y	Y	Y	N	N	70	150	50	0	Y	Y	Y	Y	3	1	Y	Y	N	N	3	3	0	15	0	1
Ina	Y	Y	Y	Y	N	N	20	20	37	25	Y	N	Y	Y	3	1	Y	Y	N	N	2	2	2	0	2	0
Mary	Y	N	Y	Y	N	N	400	20	75	25	Y	N	Y	N	21	2	Y	N	N	Y	2	2	1	1	0	1
Fred	N	Y	Y	Y	N	N	200	100	37	43	Y	Y	Y	N	1	5	N	Y	N	N	1	1	1	15	1	3
Jerry	N	N	Y	N	N	Y	20	40	25	31	N	Y	N	Y	3	3	N	Y	N	N	2	1	3	2	2	2
Gerry	N	N	Y	Y	Y	N	50	64	50	25	Y	N	N	Y	2	60	N	N	N	N	2	1	2	60	2	1
Lyle	Y	Y	Y	Y	N	Y	100	112	75	95	Y	Y	Y	N	20	16	Y	Y	N	N	1	1	20	2	0	0

* Best & Worst

Values of the variables for each hypothesis.

eyes by focusing them on something farther away than the desk. If there is a blank wall closer than 8 feet your eyes will not change focus, and they get no relief. In this case you feel too enclosed.) The data support this hypothesis at the 5 per cent level of significance.

4. Workspaces where you spend most of the day should be at least 60 square feet in area. (If your workspace is any smaller than 60 square feet you feel cramped and claustrophobic.) The data support this hypothesis at the 5 per cent level of significance.

5. Each workspace should be 50 to 75 per cent enclosed by walls or windows. (We guess that enclosure by windows creates about half the feeling of enclosure that solid walls have, so that a workspace which is surrounded half by wall and half by

849

window is considered to have 75 per cent enclosure, while a workspace completely surrounded by a half-height wall and otherwise open, is considered to have 50 per cent enclosure.) The data support this hypothesis at the 1 per cent level of significance.

6. Every workspace should have a view to the outside. (If you do not have a view to the outside, you feel too enclosed and oppressed by the building, even if you are working in a large open office. See WINDOWS OVERLOOKING LIFE (192).) The data support this hypothesis at the 0.1 per cent level of significance.

7. No other person should work closer than 8 feet to your workspace. (You should be able to hold conversations either on the phone or in person with someone, without feeling as though someone else can hear every word you are saying. The noise level in an average office is 45 db. At 45 db people closer than 8 feet to you are virtually forced to overhear your conversations. From the *Handbook of Noise Measurement* by Peterson and Gross, Sixth Edition, West Concord, Mass.: General Radio Company, 1967.) The data support this hypothesis at the 5 per cent level of significance.

8. It is uncomfortable if you are not aware of at least two other persons while you work. On the other hand, you do not want to be aware of more than eight people. (If you are aware of more than eight people, you lose a sense of where you are in the whole organization. You feel like a cog in a huge machine. You are exposed to too many people. On the other hand, if you are not aware of anyone else around you, you feel isolated and as though no one cares about you or your work. In this case, you are too enclosed.) The data support this hypothesis at the 5 per cent level of significance.

9. You should not be able to hear noises very different from the kind of noise you make, from your workplace. (Your workplace should be sufficiently enclosed to cut out noises which are of a different kind from the ones you make. There is some evidence that one can concentrate on a task better if people around him are doing the same thing, not something else.) The data support this hypothesis at the 5 per cent level of significance.

Four of the hypotheses we tested were not supported to a statistically significant extent by the data. They are the following:

10. No one should be sitting directly opposite you and facing you.

11. Workspaces should allow you to face in different directions.

12. From your workspace, you should be able to see at least two other persons; but no more than four.

13. There should be at least one other person close enough to talk to.

Therefore:

Give each workspace an area of at least 60 square feet. Build walls and windows round each workspace to such an extent that their total area (counting windows at one-half) is 50 to 75 per cent of the full enclosure that would be there if all four walls around the 60 square feet were solid. Let the front of the workspace be open for at least 8 feet in front, always into a larger space. Place the desk so that the person working at it has a view out, either to the front or to the side. If there are other people working nearby, arrange the enclosure so that the person has a sense of connection to two or three others; but never put more than eight workspaces within view or earshot of one another.

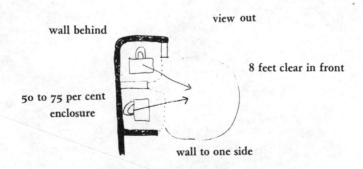

wall behind

view out

8 feet clear in front

50 to 75 per cent
enclosure

wall to one side

For the view, give each workspace a window to the outside—
WINDOWS OVERLOOKING LIFE (192); surround the space with
thick walls which contain shelves and storage space—HALF-OPEN
WALL (193), THICK WALLS (197), OPEN SHELVES (200), WAIST-
HIGH SHELF (201); arrange a pool of incandescent light over the
work table to set it off—POOLS OF LIGHT (252); and try to make a
sitting place, next to the workspace, so that the pulse of work, and
talk can happen easily throughout the day—SITTING CIRCLE
(185). For details on the shape of the workspace, see THE SHAPE
OF INDOOR SPACE (191). . . .

184 COOKING LAYOUT*

. . . within the FARMHOUSE KITCHEN (139), or any other kind of kitchen, it is essential that the cooking area be fashioned as a workshop for the preparation of food, and not as some kind of magazine kitchen with built-in counters and decorator colors. This down-to-earth and working character of a good kitchen comes in large part from the arrangement of the stove and food and counter.

Cooking is uncomfortable if the kitchen counter is too short and also if it is too long.

Efficiency kitchens never live up to their name. They are based on the notion that the best arrangement is one that saves the most steps; and this has led to tiny, compact kitchens. These compact layouts do save steps, but they usually don't have enough counter space. Preparing dinner for a family is a complex operation; several things must go on at once, and this calls for the simultaneous use of counter space for different projects. If there isn't enough counter space, then the ingredients and utensils for one thing must be moved, washed, or put away before the next thing can be prepared; or else things become so jumbled that extra time and effort must be taken to find what's needed at the proper moment. On the other hand, if the counter is too long or too spread out, the various points along its length are too far apart—and cooking is again uncomfortable, because your movements as you cook are so inefficient and slow.

Empirical support for the notion that there is insufficient counter space in many kitchens comes from a recent work by the Small Homes Council, University of Illinois. The Council found that in over a hundred housing developments, 67 per cent had too little counter space. No one complained that their kitchens were too large.

In *The Owner Built Home* (Yellow Springs, Ohio, 1961, Volume IV, p. 30), Ken Kern notes that a principal concept in cooking design is to provide for storage and workspace at each of

the major cooking centers in the kitchen. Drawing on a Cornell University study he identifies the major cooking centers as the sink, the stove, the refrigerator, the mixing, and the serving areas. To provide storage for each center requires 12 to 15 feet of free counter space, excluding the sink, drainboards, and stove. (*The Cornell Kitchen*, Glenn Beyer, Cornell University, 1952.)

As far as the limits on the distance between these major cooking centers are concerned, there is less empirical evidence. Estimates vary. The rule of thumb we postulate is that no two of them should be more than three or four steps, or about 10 feet, apart.

A kitchen that really works: huge, but great.

Therefore:

To strike the balance between the kitchen which is too small, and the kitchen which is too spread out, place the stove, sink, and food storage and counter in such a way that:

1. **No two of the four are more than 10 feet apart.**
2. **The total length of counter—excluding sink, stove, and refrigerator—is at least 12 feet.**
3. **No one section of the counter is less than 4 feet long.**

There is no need for the counter to be continuous or entirely "built-in" as it is in many modern kitchens—it can even consist of free-standing tables or counter tops. Only the three functional relationships described above are critical.

855

12 feet of counter

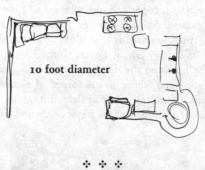

10 foot diameter

❖ ❖ ❖

Place the most important part of the working surface in the sunlight—SUNNY COUNTER (199); put all the kitchen tools and plates and saucepans and nonperishable food around the walls, one deep, so all of it is visible, and all of it directly open to reach—THICK WALLS (197), OPEN SHELVES (200). . . .

185 SITTING CIRCLE*

. . . according to the SEQUENCE OF SITTING SPACES (142), there will be a variety of different kinds of sitting space throughout an office building or a house or workshop—some formal, some informal, some large, some small, laid out in part according to the INTIMACY GRADIENT (127). This pattern deals with the actual physical layout of any one of these sitting spaces. And of course, it can be used to help create the sequence of sitting spaces, piecemeal, one space at a time.

❖ ❖ ❖

A group of chairs, a sofa and a chair, a pile of cushions —these are the most obvious things in everybody's life— and yet to make them work, so people become animated and alive in them, is a very subtle business. Most seating arrangements are sterile, people avoid them, nothing ever happens there. Others seem somehow to gather life around them, to concentrate and liberate energy. What is the difference between the two?

Most important of all, perhaps, is their position. A sitting circle needs essentially the same position as a COMMON AREA AT THE HEART (129), but in miniature: a well defined area, with paths running past it, not cutting through it, and placed so that people naturally pass by it, stop and talk, lean on the backs of chairs, gradually sit down, move position, get up again. These characteristics are vital. The reasons are exactly the same as those given in COMMON AREAS AT THE HEART (129); only the scale is different.

Second, the rough shape of a circle. When people sit down to talk together they try to arrange themselves roughly in a circle. Empirical evidence for this has been presented by Margaret Mead ("Conference Behavior," *Columbia University Forum*, Summer, 1967, pp. 20–25). Perhaps one reason for the circle, as opposed to other forms, is the fact that people like to sit at an angle to one another, not side by side (Robert Sommer, "Studies in Personal Space," *Sociometry*, 22 September 1959, pp. 247–60.)

In a circle, even neighbors are at a slight angle to one another. This, together with the first point, suggests that a rough circle is best.

But it is not enough for the chairs to be in a circle. The chairs themselves will only hold this position if the actual architecture—the columns, walls, fire, windows—subtly suggest a partly contained, defined area, which is roughly a circle. The fire especially helps to anchor a sitting circle. Other things can do it almost as well.

Third, we have observed that the seating arrangement needs to be slightly loose—not too formal. Relatively loose arrangements, where there are many different sofas, cushions, and chairs, all free to move, work to bring a sitting circle to life. The chairs can be adjusted slightly, they can be turned at slight angles; and if there are one or two too many, all the better: this seems to animate the group. People get up and walk around, then sometimes sit back down in a new chair.

Therefore:

Place each sitting space in a position which is protected, not cut by paths or movement, roughly circular, made so that the room itself helps to suggest the circle –not too strongly—with paths and activities around it, so that people naturally gravitate toward the chairs when they get into the mood to sit. Place the chairs and cushions loosely in the circle, and have a few too many.

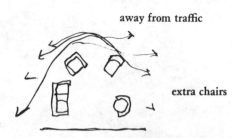

away from traffic

extra chairs

rough circle

loose overcrowded arrangement

Use a fire, and columns, and half-open walls to form the shape of the circle—THE FIRE (181), THE SHAPE OF INDOOR SPACE (191), HALF-OPEN WALL (193); but do not make it too formal or too enclosed—COMMON AREAS AT THE HEART (129), SEQUENCE OF SITTING SPACES (142). Use DIFFERENT CHAIRS (251), big ones, small ones, cushions, and a few too many, so that they are never too perfectly arranged, but always in a bit of a jumble. Make a POOL OF LIGHT (252) to mark the sitting circle, and perhaps a WINDOW PLACE (180). . . .

186 COMMUNAL SLEEPING

. . . by this time the sleeping areas have been defined—COUPLE's REALM (136), CHILDREN's REALM (137), SLEEPING TO THE EAST (138), BED CLUSTER (143). It remains only to build in the actual detailed space which forms the beds themselves—MARRIAGE BED (187), BED ALCOVE (188). However, before we consider these patterns, we wish to draw attention to a slightly more general pattern which may affect their detailed positions.

In many traditional and primitive cultures, sleep is a communal activity without the sexual overtones it has in the West today. We believe that it may be a vital social function, which plays a role as fundamental and as necessary to people as communal eating.

For instance, in Indian villages during the dry season the men pull their beds into the compound at sundown and talk and smoke together, then drift off to sleep. It is a vital part of the social life of the community. The experience of the campfire is the closest western equivalent: people's love of camping suggests that the urge is still a common one.

It is possible that sleep as a communal activity may be a vital part of healthy social life, not only for children, but for all adults. How might we harmonize this need with the obvious facts of privacy and sexuality that are linked with sleeping?

Of course, it is a beautifully intimate thing—the moment in the morning and at night when a couple are together, in private, falling asleep or waking up together. But we believe that it is also possible to create a situation where, occasionally, people can sleep together in big, family-size groups.

In particular, we can imagine a special version of this activity for metropolitan culture, where so often friends live many miles

away from each other. How many times have you experienced this situation: You have been out for the night with your friends and end up back at their house for drinks, to talk, to build a fire. Finally, late into the night, it is time to leave. Often they will say, "Please, spend the night"—but this rarely happens. You decline, and make the weary, half-drunken drive home to "your own bed."

It seems to us that under these conditions especially, communal sleeping makes sense. It would help to intensify the social occasions when we do see our friends who live far away.

But the environment must invite it, or we shall never overcome our reluctance. People are uneasy about spending the night because it usually means having to make up a guest bed, or sleeping on the rug, or cramped on the sofa. Think how much more inviting it would be if, at the end of the night, people simply dozed off, in ones and twos, in alcoves, and on mats with quilts, around the main sleeping area of the house, or around the commons.

From a practical point of view, there are two alternative positions for the alcoves:

1. There might be a place in the commons—not in any one person's private space—a place where late at night after people have been together for the evening and the fire is dying out, it is simple to draw together and sleep—a place where children and parents can sleep together on special nights. It could be very simple: one large mat and some blankets.

2. The other solution is a more deliberate version of the pattern: the couple's realm in a family house could be slightly larger than normal, with one or two alcoves or window seats that could double as beds. A built-in seat, for example, that is wide enough and long enough to lay down on, with a thin mat spread across it, becomes a bed. A few places like this, and, at a moment's notice the couple's bedroom becomes a setting for communal sleeping.

In either case, the solution must be simple and must involve nothing more than reaching for a blanket and a mat. If special beds must be made and the room rearranged, it will never happen. And, of course, the space for guest's beds must be made so that it is not dead when it is not used for sleeping. It needs a com-

patible double function—a place to put a crib, a seat, a place to lay out clothes—ALCOVE (179), WINDOW PLACE (180), DRESSING ROOM (189).

This pattern may seem strange at first, but when our typist, read it, she was fascinated and decided to try it one Saturday night with her family. They spread a big mat across the living room. They all got up together and helped the youngest son on his paper route; then they had some breakfast. Ed: Are they still doing it? ? Au: No, after 2 weeks they were arrested.

Seriously though:

Arrange the sleeping area so that there is the possibility for children and adults to sleep in the same space, in sight and sound of one another, at least as an occasional alternative to their more usual sleeping habits.

This can be done in the common area near the fireplace, where the entire household and guests can sleep together— one large mat and some blankets in an alcove. It is also possible to build bed alcoves for overnight guests, in an extended couple's realm.

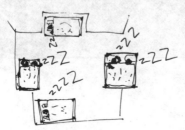

beds within sight and sound of other beds

❖ ❖ ❖

Place the ALCOVES (179) and MARRIAGE BED (187) and the BED ALCOVES (188) and DRESSING ROOMS (189) accordingly. The children have this pattern for themselves already—if bed alcoves are placed in a cluster—BED CLUSTER (143). . . .

187 MARRIAGE BED

. . . the pattern COUPLE'S REALM (136) gives emphasis to the importance of the couple's private life together within a household. Within that couple's realm, the placing and nature of the bed is naturally the most important thing.

The bed is the center of a couple's life together: the place where they lie together, talk, make love, sleep, sleep late, take care of each other during illness. But beds and bedrooms are not often made in ways which intensify their meaning, and these experiences cannot take hold.

It is true that there are extra wide beds, special bedspreads and frames, water beds, soft lighting, and all kinds of accessories on the night table. But these are all essentially gadgets. They still don't make a bed which nourishes intimacy and love.

There are three far more basic points which go to establish the marriage bed.

1. The space around the bed is *shaped* around the bed. There is a low ceiling, or a partial ceiling, over the bed. The walls and windows are made to contain the bed. See BED ALCOVE (188).

2. It is crucial that the couple choose the right time to build the bed, and not buy one at the drop of the hat. It is unlikely that the bed can come to have the right feeling until a couple has weathered some hard times together and there is some depth to their experience.

3. Find a way of adding to the bed and the space around it, so that it will become more personal and unique over the years; for example, a headboard that can be carved, painted, repainted, or a cloth ceiling that can be changed, embroidered.

The importance of the bed as an anchor point in a couple's life is brought home in this passage from Homer. Odysseus is home after 20 years of wandering and misadventure. His wife, Penelope, does not recognize him—there have been so many imposters, and he has been away so long. He pleads with her to believe it is him, but she is unsure. Frustrated, Odysseus turns away from her. Penelope speaks:

"Strange man, I am not proud, or contemptuous, or offended, but I know what manner of man you were when you sailed away from Ithaca. Come Eurycleia, make the bed outside the room which he built himself; put the fine bedstead outside, and lay out the rugs and blankets and fleeces."

This was a little trap for her husband. He burst into a rage:

"Wife, that has cut me to the heart! Who has moved my bed? That would be a difficult job for the best workman, unless God himself should come down and move it. It would be easy for God, but no man could easily prize it up, not the strongest man living! There is a great secret in that bed. I made it myself, and no one else touched it. There was a strong young olive tree in full leaf growing in an enclosure, the trunk as thick as a pillar. Round this I built our bridal chamber; I did the whole thing myself, laid the stones and built a good roof over it, jointed the doors and fitted them in their places. After that I cut off the branches and trimmed the trunk from the root up, smoothed it carefully with the adze and made it straight to the line. This tree I made the bedpost. That was the beginning of my bed; I bored holes through it, and fitted the other posts about it, and inlaid the framework with gold and silver and ivory, and I ran through it leather straps coloured purple. Now I have told you my secret. And I don't know if it is still there, wife, or if some one has cut the olive at the root and moved my bed!"

She was conquered, she could hold out no longer when Odysseus told the secret she knew so well. She burst into tears and ran straight to him, throwing her arms about his neck. She kissed his head, and cried:

"Don't be cross with me, my husband, you were always a most understanding man! The gods brought affliction upon us because they grudged us the joy of being young and growing old together! Don't be angry, don't be hurt because I did not take you in my arms as soon as I saw you! My heart has been frozen all this time with a fear that some one would come and deceive me with a false tale; there were so many imposters! But now you have told me the secret of our bed, that settles it." (From *The Odyssey*, translated by W. H. D. Rouse. Reprinted by arrangement with The New American Library, Inc., New York, New York.)

The translator footnotes this incident as follows: "This is the first time in all the eventful tale when Odysseus speaks on impulse; he has been prepared for everything, but this unexpected trifle unlocks his heart."

Quite honestly, we are not certain whether or not this pattern makes sense. On the one hand, it does: it is a beautiful idea; idyllic almost. Yet, face to face with cold hard fact and with the

dissolution and struggles in the marriages around us, it seems hard to hope that it could ever be quite real. We have decided to leave it in, just because it is a beautiful idea. But we ask you to treat it like Oblomov's dream, a picture more real than reality, an impossible dream of perfect and idyllic circumstances, which may help perhaps, to make a little more sense of our muddled everyday reality—but only if we take it with a pinch of salt.

Therefore:

At the right moment in a couple's life, it is important that they make for themselves a special bed—an intimate anchor point for their lives; slightly enclosed, with a low ceiling or a canopy, with the room shaped to it; perhaps a tiny room built around the bed with many windows. Give the bed some shape of its own, perhaps as a four-poster with head board that can be hand carved or painted over the years.

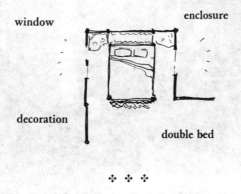

window   enclosure

decoration

double bed

❖ ❖ ❖

Make two separate dressing rooms or alcoves near the bed—DRESSING ROOMS (189); for more details on the space around the bed, see BED ALCOVE (188); lower the ceiling over the bed—CEILING HEIGHT VARIETY (190), and provide some way of creating special ornament all around it—ORNAMENT (249). For the detailed shape of the space around the bed, see THE SHAPE OF INDOOR SPACE (191). . . .

188 BED ALCOVE**

. . . bed alcoves help to generate the form of BED CLUSTERS (143), COMMUNAL SLEEPING (186) and MARRIAGE BED (187). For children, each alcove also functions as A ROOM OF ONE'S OWN (141), so that even in the smallest house, not only the adults, but every child can have at least a small place to call his own.

❖ ❖ ❖

Bedrooms make no sense.

The valuable space around the bed is good for nothing except access to the bed. And all the other functions—dressing, working, and storage of personal belongings which people stuff uncomfortably into the corners of their bedrooms—in fact, need their own space, and are not at all well met by the left over areas around a bed.

In BED CLUSTERS (143), we have already argued that each child in a family should have a bed alcove of his own, opening off a common play-space. This is based purely on the balance between community and privacy. We shall now try to establish the fact that, for everyone in the house, isolated beds, not only those in clusters, are better off in alcoves than in bedrooms. There are two reasons.

First, the bed in a bedroom creates awkward spaces around it: dressing, working, watching television, sitting, are all rather foreign to the side spaces left over around a bed. We have found that people have a hard time adapting the space around the bed to their needs for bedroom space.

Second, the bed itself seems more comfortable in a space that is adjusted to it. In our design experiments, where lay people have used these patterns to design their own houses, we have noticed a rather strong urge to give the bed a nook of its own, some kind of enclosure. Apparently this particular pattern strikes a chord in people.

Once the bed has been built into a space that is right for it, then the rest of the bedrom space is free to shape itself around the needs for sitting space, play areas, dressing, and storage.

What are the issues at stake in making a good bed alcove?

Spaciousness. Don't make it too tight. It must be comfortable to get in and out and to make the bed. If the alcove is going to function as A ROOM OF ONE'S OWN (141) for a child, then it needs to be almost a tiny room, with one wall missing.

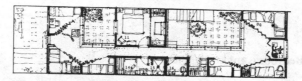

Six bed alcoves in one of our houses in Peru.

Ventilation. Bed alcoves need fresh air; at least a vent of some kind that is adjustable, and better still a window.

Privacy. People will want to draw into the alcove and be private. The opening of the alcove needs a curtain or some other kind of enclosure.

Ceiling. According to the arguments developed with the pattern CEILING HEIGHT VARIETY (190), the bed, as an intimate social space for one or two, needs a ceiling height somewhat lower than the room beside it.

Bed alcoves off a family room.

Therefore:

Don't put single beds in empty rooms called bedrooms, but instead put individual bed alcoves off rooms with other nonsleeping functions, so the bed itself becomes a tiny private haven.

If you are building a very small house no more than 300 or 400 square feet—perhaps with the idea of adding to it gradually—this pattern plays an essential role. It will probably be best then to put the alcoves off the family room.

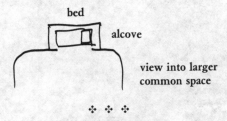

❖ ❖ ❖

Build the ceiling low—CEILING HEIGHT VARIETY (190); add some storage in the walls around the alcove—THICK WALLS (197), OPEN SHELVES (200), and a window, in a natural position—NATURAL DOORS AND WINDOWS (221). Perhaps HALF-OPEN WALL (193) will help to give the alcove the right enclosure. Where space is very tight, combine the bed alcove with DRESSING ROOM (189). And finally, give each alcove, no matter how small, the characteristics of any indoor space—THE SHAPE OF INDOOR SPACE (191). . . .

189 DRESSING ROOMS*

. . . if the beds are in position—MARRIAGE BED (187), BED ALCOVES (188)—we can give detailed attention to the dressing spaces—both to the closets where people keep their clothes and to the space they use for dressing. These dressing spaces may also help to form the BATHING ROOM (144).

Dressing and undressing, storing clothes, having clothes lying around, have no reason to be part of any larger complex of activities. Indeed they disturb other activities: they are so self-contained that they themselves need concentrated space which has no other function.

We have argued, in BED ALCOVES (188), that the concept of the bedroom leads to wasted space around the bed. This pattern lends further support to the idea that "bedrooms" in their present form are not valuable entities to have in a house.

The arguments are:

1. Clothes lying around are messy; they can take over a great deal of space; they need some kind of individual space. A dressing space can be for one person or shared by a couple. The important thing is that it be organized as a small space where it is comfortable to store clothes and to dress. When such a space is not provided, *the whole bedroom* is potentially the dressing room; and this can destroy its integrity as a room. It becomes more a big closet to "keep neat," than a room to stay in and relax.

2. People tend to take up a private position while they dress, even where they are relatively intimate with the people they live with. Even in a locker room, people will make a half-turn away from others as they dress. This suggests that the space for dressing be relatively private. The old fashioned standing screens in a green room or a boudoir worked this way; they created a half-private dressing space.

3. The time of dressing, the activity, is a natural moment of transition in the day. It is a time when people think about the day ahead, or unwind at the end of the day and get ready for bed. If you dwell, for a moment, on this transitional quality of

873

dressing, it seems clear that the dressing space can be made to help support it. For example, a good place to dress will have beautiful natural light; this requires as much thought in your design as any room—see, for example, LIGHT ON TWO SIDES OF EVERY ROOM (159).

4. The dressing space should be large enough, with room to stretch your arms and turn around. This means six or seven feet of open area. It must also have about six feet of clothes hanging space, another six feet of open shelves, and a few drawers for each person. These figures are rough. Check your own closet and shelves, think about what you really need, and make an estimate.

Therefore:

Give everyone a dressing room—either private or shared —between their bed and the bathing room. Make this dressing room big enough so there is an open area in it at least six feet in diameter; about six linear feet of clothes hanging space; and another six feet of open shelves; two or three drawers; and a mirror.

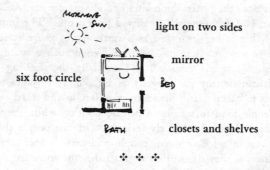

❖ ❖ ❖

Place each dressing room so that it gets plenty of natural LIGHT ON TWO SIDES (159). Use THICK WALLS (197), CLOSETS BETWEEN ROOMS (198), and OPEN SHELVES (200) to form its walls; include a wide shelf around the edge—WAIST-HIGH SHELF (201); and for the detailed shape of the room, see THE SHAPE OF INDOOR SPACE (191). . . .

fine tune the shape and size of rooms and alcoves to make them precise and buildable;

190 CEILING HEIGHT
VARIETY**

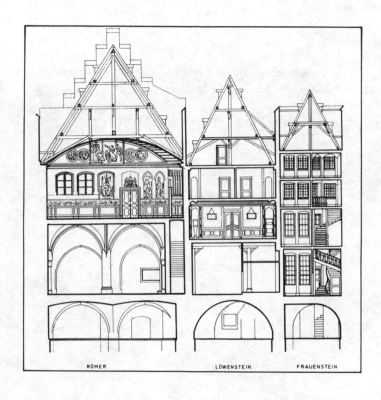

RÖMER   LÖWENSTEIN   FRAUENSTEIN

. . . this pattern helps to form the rooms. It therefore helps to complete all the patterns which define rooms, or arcades, or balconies, or outdoor rooms or minor rooms: in short, just about all of the last 100 patterns. If you have been imagining these spaces while you walk about on the actual site, then all these spaces will already be three-dimensional in your mind: they will be volumes of space, not merely areas on plan. Now, with this pattern, which determines ceiling heights, the next pattern which determines the exact shape of each room, and the remaining patterns in the language, we fill out this three dimensional conception of the building.

❖ ❖ ❖

A building in which the ceiling heights are all the same is virtually incapable of making people comfortable.

In some fashion, low ceilings make for intimacy, high ceilings for formality. In older buildings which allowed the ceiling heights to vary, this was almost taken for granted. However, in buildings which are governed by standard components, it is very hard to make the ceiling height vary from room to room, so it tends to be forgotten. And people are willing to let it go, because they have forgotten what an important psychological reason there is for making the heights vary.

We have presented three different theories over the years in our attempts to explain the significance of ceiling height variety, and we shall present the evolution of all three theories here, because it puts the matter in perspective and will perhaps allow you to formulate the pattern most coherently for yourself.

Theory one. The ceiling height should be related to the length and breadth of the room, because the problem is one of proportion, and people feel comfortable or uncomfortable according to the room's proportions.

Many efforts have been made to establish rules which will make sure that rooms are "well proportioned." Thus, for instance, Palladio laid down three rules of proportion: all of them shared

the feature that the height of a room should be intermediate between its length and its breadth.

In traditional Japanese architecture, this idea is captured by a simple rule of thumb. The ceiling height of a room is 6 feet 3 inches + (3.7 × the number of tatami in the room) inches. This creates a direct relationship between floor area and ceiling height. A very small room (3 mats) has a ceiling height of 7 feet 2 inches. A large room (12 mats) has a ceiling height of 9 feet 11 inches. (See Heinrich Engle, *The Japanese House*, Rutland Vermont: Charles E. Tuttle Company, 1964, pp. 68–71.)

However sound this approach may seem in certain cases, it is clearly not a completely valid geometric principle. There are many rooms with extremely low ceilings, especially in cottages and informal houses, which are extremely pleasant—even though they violate Palladio's principle and the Japanese rule of thumb utterly.

Theory two. The ceiling height is related to the *social distance* between people in the room, and is therefore directly related to their relative intimacy or nonintimacy.

This theory makes it clear what is wrong with badly proportioned rooms, and gives the beginning of a functional basis for establishing the right height for different spaces. The problem hinges on the question of appropriate social distance. It is known that in various kinds of social situations there are appropriate and inappropriate distances between people. (See Edward Hall, *The Silent Language*, New York: Doubleday, 1959, pp. 163–64; and Robert Sommer, "The Distance for Comfortable Conversation," *Sociometry*, 25, 1962, pp. 111–16.) Now, the ceiling height in a room has a bearing on social distance in two ways:

A. The height of a ceiling appears to affect the *apparent distance* of sound sources from a hearer. Thus, under a low ceiling sound sources seem nearer than they really are; under a high ceiling they seem further than they really are.

Since the sound is an important cue in the perception of distance between people (voice, footstep, rustle, and so on), this means that the ceiling height will alter the apparent distance between people. Under a high ceiling people seem further apart than they actually are.

On the basis of this effect, it is clear that intimate situations require very low ceilings, less intimate situations require higher ceilings, formal places require high ceilings, and the most public situations require the highest ceilings: for example, the canopy over the double bed, a fireside nook, high-ceilinged formal reception room, Grand Central Station.

B. Through the medium of three-dimensional "bubbles". We know that each social situation has a certain horizontal dimension or diameter. We may think of this as a kind of membrane or bubble which encloses the situation. It is likely that this bubble needs a vertical component—equal in height to its diameter. If so, the height of the ceiling should, for comfort, be equal to the dominant social distance in the room. Since people in Grand Central are strangers, and have an effective social distance of as much as 100 feet, this would explain why the ceiling has to be very high; similarly, in an intimate nook, or over a double bed, where the social distance is no more than five or six feet, the ceiling has to be very low.

Theory three. Although both of the previous theories contain valuable insights, they must be at least slightly wrong because they assume that the absolute ceiling height in any one room has a critical functional effect. In fact, the *absolute* ceiling height does not matter as much as one would expect from theories one and two.

For example, the most intimate room in an igloo may be no more than five feet high; yet in a very hot climate even the most intimate rooms may be nine feet high. This makes it clear that the absolute height of rooms is governed by other factors too—climate and culture. Obviously, then, no theory which prescribes an absolute height for any given social situation, or room size, can be correct. What then, is going on? Why do ceiling heights vary? What functional effect does their variation have?

We have been led, finally, to the conclusion that it is the *variation itself* which matters, not merely the absolute height in any given room. For if a building contains rooms with several different ceiling heights in it and the height has an effect on social relationships (for the reasons given), then the mere fact that the ceiling heights vary, allows people to move from high

rooms to low rooms, and vice versa, according to the degree of intimacy they seek—because they know that everyone correlates intimacy with ceiling height.

According to this theory, the effect of the ceiling height is not direct; there is instead a complex interaction between people and space, in which people read the different ceiling heights in a building as messages, and take up positions according to these messages. They are comfortable or uncomfortable according to whether they can take part in this process, and can then feel secure in the knowledge that they have chosen a place of appropriate intimacy.

Finally, some special notes are required on the implementation of this pattern. In a one story structure there is no problem; the ceiling heights may vary freely. In buildings with several stories however, it is not so clear cut. The floors of the upper stories must be more or less flat; and this obviously creates problems as you try to vary the ceiling heights underneath. Here are some notes which may help you to solve this problem:

1. Build storage between floors and ceilings—at least two feet deep—where you want to lower ceiling heights.

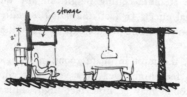

Storage over a low ceiling.

2. Put two alcoves over each other. If each is 6 feet 3 inches, this gives a main ceiling of 13 feet, which is good for very public spaces.

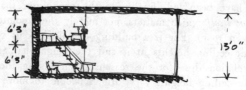

Stacked alcoves.

3. Raise the floor level with steps, instead of lowering the ceiling.

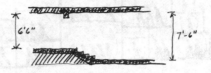

The floor does it.

4. It is very important to have some rooms with ceilings as low as 7 feet or 7 feet 6 inches—these are very beautiful.

5. Except in one-story buildings, the low ceilinged rooms will make most sense on upper stories; indeed, the average ceiling height will probably get lower and lower with successive stories —the most public rooms, for the largest gatherings, are typically on the ground, and rooms get progressively more intimate the further they are from the ground.

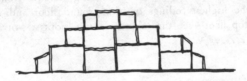

Lower ceilings upstairs.

Therefore:

Vary the ceiling heights continuously throughout the building, especially between rooms which open into each other, so that the relative intimacy of different spaces can be felt. In particular, make ceilings high in rooms which are public or meant for large gatherings (10 to 12 feet), lower in rooms for smaller gatherings (7 to 9 feet), and very low in rooms or alcoves for one or two people (6 to 7 feet).

complete range of ceiling heights

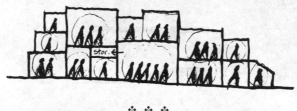

❖ ❖ ❖

The construction of floor vaults will create variations in ceiling height almost automatically since the vault starts about 6 feet 6 inches high and rises a further distance which is one-fifth of the room diameter—FLOOR-CEILING VAULTS (219). Where ceiling height varies within one story, put storage in the spaces between the different heights—BULK STORAGE (145). Get the shape of individual rooms under any given ceiling height from THE SHAPE OF INDOOR SPACE (191) and STRUCTURE FOLLOWS SOCIAL SPACES (205); and vary ceiling heights from story to story—the highest ceilings on the ground floor and the lowest on the top floor—see the table in FINAL COLUMN DISTRIBUTION (213). . . .

191 THE SHAPE OF
INDOOR SPACE**

. . . from CEILING HEIGHT VARIETY (190) you have an overall
conception of each floor in the building as a cascade of heights,
typically highest in the middle where the largest rooms are,
lower toward the edge where the small rooms are, and varying
with floor also, so that the lower floors will tend to have a
higher average ceiling height than upper floors. This pattern
takes each individual space, within this overall cascade, and gives
it a more definite shape.

❖ ❖ ❖

**The perfectly crystalline squares and rectangles of ultra-
modern architecture make no special sense in human or
in structural terms. They only express the rigid desires and
fantasies which people have when they get too preoccupied
with systems and the means of their production.**

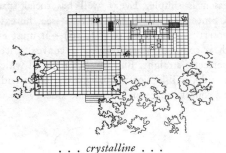

. . . crystalline . . .

To get away from this madness a new wave of thought has
thrown the right angle away completely. Many of the new
organic technologies create buildings and rooms shaped more or
less like wombs and holes and caves.

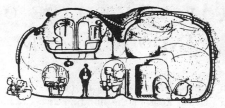

. . . pseudo biological . . .

But these biological rooms are as irrational, as much based on images and fantasies as the rigid crystals they are trying to replace. When we think about the human forces acting on rooms, we see that they need a shape which lies between the two. There are reasons why their sides should be more or less straight; and there are reasons why their angles, or many of them anyway, should be rough right angles. Yet their sides have no good reason to be perfectly equal, their angles have no good reason to be perfectly right angles. They only need to be irregular, rough, imperfect rectangles.

The core of our argument is this. We postulate that every space, which is recognizable and walled enough to be distinct, must have walls which are roughly straight, except when the walls are thick enough to be concave in both directions.

The reason is simple. Every wall has social spaces on both sides of it. Since a social space is convex—see the extensive argument in POSITIVE OUTDOOR SPACE (106)—it must either have a wall which is concave (thus forming a convex space) or a wall which is perfectly straight. But any "thin" wall which is concave toward one side, will be convex toward the other and will, therefore, leave a concave space on at least one side.

Two convex spaces pressed up against each other,
form a straight wall between them.

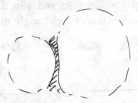

A wall thick enough to be concave on both sides.

*A thin wall, makes a convex space on one side,
and destroys the other side.*

Essentially then, every wall with social spaces on both sides
of it, must have straight walls, except where it is thick enough
to be concave on both sides. And, of course, a wall may be
curved whenever there is no significant social space on the outside of it. This happens sometimes in a position where an entrance butts out into a street, or where a bay window stands in a
part of a garden which is unharmed by it.

*A place where a wall can be curved,
because it works with the outside.*

So much for the walls. They must most often be roughly
straight. Now for the angles between walls. Acute angles are
hardly ever appropriate, for reasons of social integrity again. It is
an uphill struggle to make an acute angle in a room, which works.
Since the argument for convexity rules out angles of more than
180 degrees, this means that the corners of spaces must almost

always be obtuse angles between 80 and 180 degrees. (We say 80, because a few degrees less than a right angle makes no difference.)

The range of possible corners.

And one further word about the angles. Most often rooms will pack in such a way that angles somewhere near right angles (say between 80 and 100 degrees) make most sense. The reason, simply, is that other obtuse angles do not pack well at corners where several rooms meet. Here are the most likely typical kinds of corners:

Only angles that are nearly right angles pack successfully.

This means that the majority of spaces in a building must be polygons, in plan, with roughly straight walls and obtuse-angled corners. Most often they will probably be irregular, squashed, rough rectangles. Indeed, respect for the site and the subtleties of the plan will inevitably lead to slightly irregular shapes. And occasionally they may have curved walls—either if the wall is thick enough to be concave on both sides or, on an exterior wall, where there is no important social space outside.

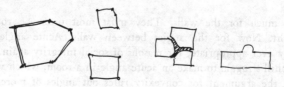

Polygon, rough rectangle, thick curved wall,
exterior curved wall.

A final point. Our experience has led us to an even stronger version of this pattern—which constrains the shape of ceilings too. Specifically, we believe that people feel uncomfortable in spaces like these:

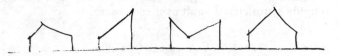

Rooms whose ceilings can make you uncomfortable.

We can only speculate on the possible reasons for these feelings. It seems just possible that they originate from some kind of desire for a person to be surrounded by a spherical bubble roughly related to the human axis. Room shapes which are more or less versions of this bubble are comfortable; while those which depart from it strongly are uncomfortable. *Perhaps when the space around us is too sharply different from the imaginary social bubble around us, we do not feel quite like persons.*

The shape of the space bubble.

A ceiling that is flat, vaulted in one direction or vaulted in two directions, has the necessary character. A ceiling sloping to one side does not. We must emphasize that this conjecture is not intended as an argument in favor of rigidly simple or symmetric spaces. It only speaks against those rather abnormal spaces with one-sided sloping ceilings, high apexed ceilings, weird bulges into the room, and re-entrant angles in the wall.

Therefore:

With occasional exceptions, make each indoor space or each position of a space, a rough rectangle, with roughly straight walls, near right angles in the corners, and a roughly symmetrical vault over each room.

rough rectangles

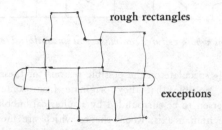

exceptions

rough vertical symmetry

❖ ❖ ❖

You can define the room with columns, one at each corner— COLUMNS AT THE CORNERS (212); and the shape of the ceiling can be given exactly by the ceiling vault—FLOOR AND CEILING LAYOUT (210), FLOOR-CEILING VAULT (219). Avoid curved walls except where they are strictly necessary—WALL MEMBRANES (218). Where occasional curved walls like bay windows do jut out into the outside, place them to help create POSITIVE OUTDOOR SPACES (106). Make the walls of each room generous and deep —THICK WALLS (197), CLOSETS BETWEEN ROOMS (198); and where it is appropriate, make them HALF-OPEN WALLS (193). For the patterns on the load-bearing structure, engineering, and construction, begin with STRUCTURE FOLLOWS SOCIAL SPACES (205). . . .

. . . this pattern helps to complete the earlier patterns which give each room its shape: LIGHT ON TWO SIDES OF EVERY ROOM (159), CEILING HEIGHT VARIETY (190), and THE SHAPE OF INDOOR SPACE (191). Once these patterns are clear, this pattern helps to place the windows rather more precisely in the walls. It defines just how many windows there should be, how far apart, and what their total area should be.

Rooms without a view are prisons for the people who have to stay in them.

When people are in a place for any length of time they need to be able to refresh themselves by looking at a world different from the one they are in, and with enough of its own variety and life to provide refreshment.

Amos Rapoport gives written descriptions of three windowless seminar rooms at the University of California. The descriptions —by teachers and students of English who were asked to write descriptions of the rooms as part of a writing exercise—are heavily negative, even though they were not asked to be, and in many cases refer directly to the windowless, boxed-in, or isolated-from-the-world character of the rooms.

Here are two examples:

Room 5646 is an unpleasant room in which to attend class because in it one feels detached and isolated from the rest of the world under the buzzing fluorescent lights and the high sound-proofed ceilings, amid the sinks, cabinets, and pipes, surrounded by empty space.

The large and almost empty, windowless room with its sturdy, enclosing, and barren grey walls inspired neither disgust nor liking; one might easily have forgotten how trapped one was. (Amos Rapoport, "Some Consumer Comments on a Designed Environment," *Arena—The Architectural Association Journal*, January 1967, pp. 176–78.)

Brian Wells, studying office workers' choice of working positions, found that 81 per cent of all subjects chose positions next to

a window. (*Office Design: A Study of Environment,* Peter Manning, ed., Pilkington Research Unit, Department of Building Science, University of Liverpool, 1965, pp. 118–21.) Many of the subjects gave "daylight" rather than "view" as a reason for their choice. But it is shown elsewhere in the same report that subjects who are far from windows grossly overestimate the amount of daylight they receive as compared with artificial light (*Office Design* p. 58). This suggests that people want to be near windows for other reasons over and above the daylight. Our conjecture that it is the view which is critical is given more weight by the fact that people are less interested in sitting near windows which open onto light wells, which admit daylight, but present no view.

And Thomas Markus presents evidence which shows clearly that office workers prefer windows with meaningful views—views of city life, nature—as against views which also take in large areas, but contain uninteresting and less meaningful elements. (Thomas A. Markus, "The Function of Windows: A Reappraisal," *Building Science,* 2, 1967, pp. 97–121; see especially p. 109.)

Assume then that people do need to be able to look out of windows, at some world different from their immediate surroundings. We now give very rough figures for the total area of the windows in a room. The area of window needed will depend to a large extent on climate, latitude, and the amount of reflecting surfaces around the outside of the building. However, it is fairly reasonable to believe that the floor/window ratio, though different in different regions, may be more or less constant within any given region.

We suggest, therefore, that you go round the town where you live, and choose half a dozen rooms in which you really like the light. In each case, measure the window area as a percentage of the floor area; then take the average of the different percentages.

In our part of the world—Berkeley, California—we find that rooms are most pleasant when they have about 25 per cent window—sometimes as much as 50 per cent—(that is, 25–50 square feet of window for every 100 square feet of floor). But we repeat, obviously this figure will vary enormously from one part of the world to another. Imagine: Rabat, Timbuctoo, Antarctica, Northern Norway, Italy, Brazilian jungle. . . .

Therefore:

In each room, place the windows in such a way that their total area conforms roughly to the appropriate figures for your region (25 per cent or more of floor area, in the San Francisco Bay Area), and place them in positions which give the best possible views out over life: activities in streets, quiet gardens, anything different from the indoor scene.

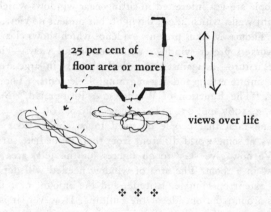

25 per cent of floor area or more

views over life

❖ ❖ ❖

Fine tune the exact positions of the windows at the time that you build them—NATURAL DOORS AND WINDOWS (221); break the area of each window into SMALL PANES (239); give each window a very LOW SILL (222) to improve the view and DEEP REVEALS (223) to make the light as soft as possible inside. . . .

193 HALF-OPEN WALL*

. . . THE SHAPE OF INDOOR SPACE (191) defines the shapes of rooms and minor rooms. This pattern gives more detail to the walls between these rooms. Wherever there are HALF-PRIVATE OFFICES (152), SIX-FOOT BALCONIES (167), ALCOVES (179), SITTING CIRCLES (185), BED ALCOVES (188), BUILDING THOROUGHFARES (101), ARCADES (119), or THE FLOW THROUGH ROOMS (131), the spaces must be given a subtle balance of enclosure and openness by partly opening up the walls or keeping them half-open.

Rooms which are too closed prevent the natural flow of social occasions, and the natural process of transition from one social moment to another. And rooms which are too open will not support the differentiation of events which social life requires.

A solid room, for instance, with four walls around it can obviously sustain activities which are quite different from the activities in the next room. In this sense it is excellent. But it is very hard for people to join in these activities or leave them naturally. This is only possible if the door is glazed, or if there is a window in the wall, or if there is an opening, so that people can gradually come forward, just when there is a lull in the conversation, and naturally become a part of what is happening.

On the other hand, an open space with no walls around it, just a place marked by a carpet on the floor and a chair arrangement, but entirely open to the spaces all around it, is so exposed that people never feel entirely comfortable there. No one activity can establish itself because it is too vulnerable; and so the things that happen there tend to be rather bland—a drink, reading the paper, watching television, staring at the view, "sitting around": you will not find animated conversations, arguments, excitement,

people making things, painting, card games, charades, or someone practicing the violin. People let themselves go into these more highly differentiated activities, when there is some degree of enclosure around them—at least a half-wall, a railing, columns, some separation from the other nearby spaces.

In short, the subtle conflict between exposure and enclosure naturally requires a balance. But for some reason the modern images of rooms and indoor space lead people to the two extremes, and hardly ever to the balance which is needed.

The kind of space which most easily supports both differentiation of activities and the transition between different activities has less enclosure than a solid room, and more enclosure—far more —than a space inside an open plan.

A wall which is half-open, half-enclosed—an arch, a trellised wall, a wall that is counter height with ornamented columns, a wall suggested by the reduction of the opening or the enlargement of the columns at the corners, a colonnade of columns in the wall—all these help get the balance of enclosure and openness right; and in these places people feel comfortable as a result.

Examples.

From WORKSPACE ENCLOSURE (183) we have some evidence for the amount of enclosure required. We found there that a person is comfortable when he is about "half" enclosed—when he has material around him on about two sides, or the four sides around him are about half solid and half-open.

We therefore guess that the enclosure of any half-open wall should itself consist of about 50 per cent void and 50 per cent solid. This does not mean that it has to be a screen. For example,

a combination of thick columns, deep beams, arched openings, also creates this balance of openings and enclosures. A railing is too open. But a balustrade with thick supports will often be just right.

This applies very strongly to outdoor rooms and balconies; and equally to all those indoor spaces which are connected to larger rooms but partly separate from them—an alcove, workspace, kitchen, bed. In all these cases the wall which forms the enclosure and separates the smaller space from the larger one, needs to be partially open and partially closed.

Among ourselves and many of our friends, we have found that the urge to remodel a house is virtually one and the same with the urge to create half-open walls between various parts of the house. It seems that without ever naming this pattern, people have the instinct to "open up" a room; or to give "more enclosure" to some other space.

Therefore:

Adjust the walls, openings, and windows in each indoor space until you reach the right balance between open, flowing space and closed cell-like space. Do not take it for granted that each space is a room; nor, on the other hand, that all spaces must flow into each other. The right balance will always lie between these extremes: no one room entirely enclosed; and no space totally connected to another. Use combinations of columns, half-open walls, porches, indoor windows, sliding doors, low sills, french doors, sitting walls, and so on, to hit the right balance.

50 per cent opening

50 per cent solid

Wherever a small space is in a larger space, yet slightly separate from it, make the wall between the two about half-open and half-solid—ALCOVES (179), WORKSPACE ENCLOSURE (183). Concentrate the solids and the openings, so that there are essentially a large number of smallish openings, each framed by thick columns, waist high shelves, deep soffits, and arches or braces in the corners, with ornament where solids and openings meet—INTERIOR WINDOWS (194), COLUMNS AT THE CORNERS (212), COLUMN PLACE (226), COLUMN CONNECTIONS (227), SMALL PANES (239), ORNAMENT (249). . . .

. . . at various places in the building, there are walls between rooms where windows would help the rooms to be more alive by creating more views of people and by letting extra light into the darkest corners. For instance, between passages and rooms or between adjacent living rooms, or between adjacent work rooms —BUILDING THOROUGHFARE (101), ENTRANCE ROOM (130), THE FLOW THROUGH ROOMS (131), SHORT PASSAGES (132), TAPESTRY OF LIGHT AND DARK (135), SEQUENCE OF SITTING SPACES (142), HALF-OPEN WALL (193).

Windows are most often used to create connections between the indoor and the outdoors. But there are many cases when an indoor space needs a connecting window to another indoor space.

This is most often true for corridors and passages. These places can easily seem deserted. People feel more connected to one another by interior windows, and the passages in the building become less deserted.

The same may hold for certain rooms, especially small rooms. Three bare walls and a window can seem like a prison. Windows placed between rooms, or between a passage and a room, will help to solve these problems and will make both the passages and the rooms more lively.

Furthermore, when rooms and passages are visibly connected to one another, it is possible to grasp the overall arrangement of a building far more clearly than in a building with blank walls between all the rooms.

It is enough if these windows allow people to see through them; they do not need to be open nor the kind which can be opened. Ordinary, cheap, fixed glazing will do all that is required.

Therefore:

Put in fully glazed fixed windows between rooms which

tend to be dead because they have too little action in them or where inside rooms are unusually dark.

ordinary fixed window

❖ ❖ ❖

Make the windows the same as any other windows, with small panes of glass—SMALL PANES (239). In some case it may be right to build interior windows in the doors—SOLID DOORS WITH GLASS (237). . . .

195 STAIRCASE VOLUME*

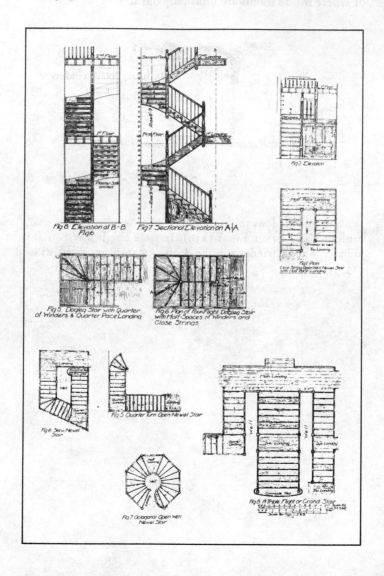

Fig 8 Elevation at B-B Fig 6

Fig 7 Sectional Elevation on A-A

Fig 2 Elevation

Fig 1 Plan
Close String Open Well Newel Stair
with Half Pace Landing

Fig 5 Dogleg Stair with Quarter
of Winders & Quarter Pace Landing

Fig 6 Plan of Four Flight Dogleg Stair
with Half-Spaces of Winders and
Close Strings

Fig 6 Skew Newel Stair

Fig 5 Quarter Turn Open Newel Stair

Fig 7 Octagonal Open Well Newel Stair

Fig 8 A Triple Flight or Grand Stair

. . . STAIRCASE AS A STAGE (133) and OPEN STAIRS (158) will tell you roughly where to place the various stairs, both indoors and outdoors. This pattern gives each stair exact dimensions and treats it like a room so that it becomes realistic in the plan.

We are putting this pattern in the language because our experiments have shown us that lay people often make mistakes about the volume which a staircase needs and therefore make their plans unbuildable.

Here are some examples of the stairs which people who are not used to building, draw, or think of, when they try to lay out houses for themselves.

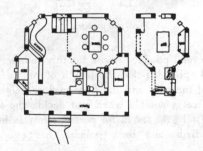

Staircase problems—too short

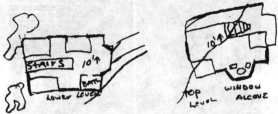

. . . no upstairs volume.

Obviously, these stairs will not work; and the misunderstandings of the nature of the stair are so basic, that it is hard to correct

these plans without destroying them. In order to put in a realistic stair, it would be necessary to rethink the plan entirely. To avoid this kind of mental backtracking, it is essential that stairs be more or less realistic *from the very start*.

The simplest way to understand a stair is this. *Every staircase occupies a volume, two stories high.* If this volume is the right shape, and large enough to give the stair its rise, then it will be possible to fill it later, with a stair which works.

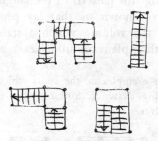

Two-story space.

There are several possible layouts for this volume: any one of them will work, provided that the length of run is long enough for the slope of the stair, and the floor to floor height. We urge you to be as free as possible when you decide the slope of the stair. Unfortunately, the search for perfect safety in housing laws, insurance standards, and bank policies, has exaggerated the

Different slopes.

standardisation of slopes. For example, Federal Housing Authority regulations specify that stairs should be between 30 and 35 degrees in slope. But in some cases—a very small house, a stair to the roof—such a shallow stair is a waste of space; a steep stair is far more appropriate. And in other cases—a main stair in a public building, or an outdoor stair—a much shallower stair is more generous, and more appropriate.

Therefore:

Make a two story volume to contain the stairs. It may be straight, L-shaped, U-shaped, or C-shaped. The stair may be 2 feet wide (for a very steep stair) or 5 feet wide for a generous shallow stair. But, in all cases, the entire stairwell must form one complete structural bay, two stories high.

Do not assume that all stairs have to have the "standard" angle of 30 degrees. The steepest stair may almost be a ladder. The most generous stair can be as shallow as a ramp and quite wide. As you work out the exact slope of your stair, bear in mind the relationship: riser + tread = 17½ inches.

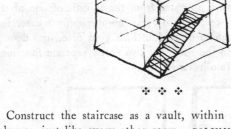

❖ ❖ ❖

Construct the staircase as a vault, within a space defined by columns, just like every other room—COLUMNS AT THE CORNERS (212), STAIR VAULT (228). And make the most of the staircase; underneath it is a place where the children can play and hide—CHILD CAVES (203); and it is a place to sit and talk—STAIR SEATS (125). . . .

196 CORNER DOORS*

. . . this pattern helps you place doors exactly. Use it to help create the larger FLOW THROUGH ROOMS (131). You can use it too, to generate a SEQUENCE OF SITTING SPACES (142), by leaving small corners for sitting, uninterrupted by the doors; and you can use it to create TAPESTRY OF LIGHT AND DARK (135), since every door, if glazed and near a window, will create a natural pool of light which people gravitate toward.

The success of a room depends to a great extent on the position of the doors. If the doors create a pattern of movement which destroys the places in the room, the room will never allow people to be comfortable.

First there is the case of a room with a single door. In general, it is best if this door is in a corner. When it is in the middle of a wall, it almost always creates a pattern of movement which breaks the room in two, destroys the center, and leaves no single area which is large enough to use. The one common exception to this rule is the case of a room which is rather long and narrow. In this case it makes good sense to enter from the middle of one of the long sides, since this creates two areas, both roughly square, and therefore large enough to be useful. This kind of central door is especially useful when the room has two partly separate functions, which fall naturally into its two halves.

Rooms with one door.

Now, the case of a room with two or more doors: the individual doors should still be in the corners for the reasons given above. But we must now consider not only the position of the

individual doors, but the relation between the doors. If possible, they should be placed more or less along the same side, so as to leave the rest of the room untouched by movement.

More generally, if we draw lines which connect the doors, then the spaces which are left uncut by these lines, should be large enough to be useful, and should have a strong positive shape—a triangular space left between paths of circulation will hardly ever be used.

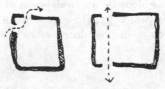

Rooms with more than one door.

Finally, note that this pattern does not apply to very large rooms. In a very large room, or in a room with a big table in the middle, the doors can be in the middle, and still create a special formal, spacious feeling. In fact, in this case, it may even be better to put them in the middle, just to create this feeling. But this only works when the room is large enough to benefit from it.

Therefore:

Except in very large rooms, a door only rarely makes sense in the middle of a wall. It does in an entrance room, for instance, because this room gets its character essentially from the door. But in most rooms, especially small ones, put the doors as near the corners of the room as possible. If the room has two doors, and people move through it, keep both doors at one end of the room.

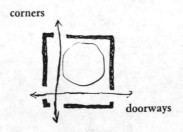

❖ ❖ ❖

When a door marks a transition, as it does into a bedroom or a private place, for instance, make it as low as you dare—LOW DOORWAY (224); and thicken the entry way with closet space where it needs to be especially private—CLOSETS BETWEEN ROOMS (198). Later, when you make the door frame, make it integral with the wall, and decorate it freely—FRAMES AS THICKENED EDGES (225), ORNAMENT (249); except when rooms are very private, put windows in the door—SOLID DOORS WITH GLASS (237). . . .

*give all the walls some depth, wherever there are to
be alcoves, windows, shelves, closets or seats.*

197 THICK WALLS**

. . . once the plan is accurate to the nearest 5 or 6 feet, there is a final process in which the smallest spaces—niches, built-in seats, counters, closets and shelves—get built to form the walls. Or of course, you can build this pattern into an existing house. In either case, use the pattern so that it helps to create the proper shapes for rooms—THE SHAPE OF INDOOR SPACE (191), the ceiling heights—ALCOVES (179), WINDOW PLACES (180), and CEILING HEIGHT VARIETY (190), and, on the outside of the rooms, the nooks and crannies of the BUILDING EDGE (160).

❖ ❖ ❖

Houses with smooth hard walls made of prefabricated panels, concrete, gypsum, steel, aluminum, or glass always stay impersonal and dead.

In the world we live in today, newly built houses and apartments are more and more standardized. People no longer have a chance to make them personal and individual. A personal house tells us about the people who live there. A child's swing hanging in a doorway reflects the attitude of parents to their children. A window seat overlooking a favorite bush supports a contemplative, dreamy nature. Open counters between kitchen and living space are specific to informal family life; small closable hatches between the two are specific to more formal styles. An open shelf around a room should be seen at one height to display a collector's porcelain, best seen from above; at another height and depth if it is to be used to support a photographer's latest pictures; at another height again for setting down drinks in the house of a perennial party-giver. A large enough fireplace nook, with enough built-in seats, invites a family of six to sit together.

Each of these things gives us a sense about the people living in the house because each expresses some special personal need. And everyone needs the opportunity to adapt his surroundings to his own way of life.

In traditional societies this personal adaptation came about very easily. People lived in the same place for very long periods,

often for whole lifetimes. And houses were made of hand-processed materials like wood, brick, mud, straw, plaster, which are easily modified by hand by the inhabitants themselves. Under these conditions, the personal character of the houses came about almost automatically from the fact of occupancy.

However, in a modern technological society, neither of these two conditions holds good. People move frequently, and houses are increasingly built of factory-made, factory-finished materials, like 4 x 8 foot sheets of finished plaster board, aluminum windows, prefabricated baked enamel steel kitchens, glass, concrete, steel—these materials do not lend themselves at all to the gradual modification which personal adaptation requires. Indeed, the processes of mass production are almost directly incompatible with the possibility of personal adaptation.

The crux of the matter lies in the walls. Smooth hard flat industrialized walls make it impossible for people to express their own identity, because most of the identity of a dwelling lies in or near its surfaces—in the 3 or 4 feet near the walls. This is where people keep most of their belongings; this is where special lighting fixtures are; this is where special built-in furniture is placed; this is where the special cosy nooks and corners are that individual family members make their own; this is where the identifiable small-scale variation is; this is the place where people

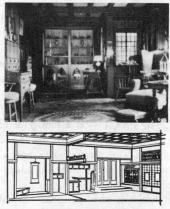

The identity of a house comes from its walls.

can most easily make changes and see the product of their own craftsmanship.

The house will become personal only if the walls are so constructed that each new family can leave its mark on them—they must, in other words, invite incremental fine adjustments, so that the variety of the inhabitants who live in it rubs off on them. And the walls must be so constructed that these fine adjustments are permanent—so that they do accumulate over time and so that the stock of available dwellings becomes progressively more and more differentiated.

All this means that the walls must be extremely deep. To contain shelves, cabinets, displays, special lights, special surfaces, deep window reveals, individual niches, built in seats and nooks, the walls must be at least a foot deep; perhaps even three or four feet deep.

And the walls must be made of some material which is inherently structural—so that however much of it gets carved out, the whole remains rigid and the surface remains continuous almost no matter how much is removed or added.

Then, as time goes on, each family will be able to work the wall surfaces in a very gradual, piecemeal, incremental manner. After a year or two of occupancy, each dwelling will begin to show its own characteristic pattern of niches, bay windows, breakfast nooks, seats built into the walls, shelves, closets, lighting arrangements, sunken parts of the floor, raised parts of the ceiling.

Each house will have a memory; the characteristics and personalities of different human individuals can be written in the thickness of the walls; the houses will become progressively more and more differentiated as they grow older, and the process of personal adaptation—both by choice and by piecemeal modification—has room to breathe. The full version of this pattern was originally published by Christopher Alexander: "Thick Walls," *Architectural Design*, July 1968, pp. 324–26.

Therefore:

Open your mind to the possibility that the walls of your building can be thick, can occupy a substantial volume— even actual usable space—and need not be merely thin

membranes which have no depth. Decide where these thick walls ought to be.

1 to 4 feet thick

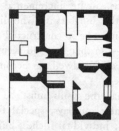

hand-carveable

❖ ❖ ❖

Where the thickness is 3 or 4 feet, build the thickness and the volume of the walls according to the process described in THICKENING THE OUTER WALLS (211); where it is less, a foot or 18 inches, build it from open shelves stretched between deep vertical columns—OPEN SHELVES (200), COLUMNS AT THE CORNERS (212). Get the detailed position of the various things within the wall from the patterns which define them: WINDOW PLACE (180), CLOSETS BETWEEN ROOMS (198), SUNNY COUNTER (199), WAIST HIGH SHELF (201), BUILT-IN SEATS (202), CHILD CAVES (203), SECRET PLACE (204). . . .

. . . given the layout of rooms, it is now necessary to decide exactly where to put the built-in cupboards and closets. Use them, especially, to help form the enclosure around a workspace—WORK-SPACE ENCLOSURE (183), around a dressing space—DRESSING ROOM (189), and around the doors of rather private rooms so that the doorway itself gets some depth—CORNER DOOR (196).

The provision of storage and closets usually comes as an afterthought.

But when they are correctly placed, they can contribute greatly to the layout of the building.

Perhaps the most important secondary feature of storage space is its sound insulating quality. The extra wall sections, and the doors enclosing the closet, as well as the clothes, boxes, and so on, that are being stored, all work to create substantial acoustical barriers. You can take advantage of this feature of closet space by locating all required storage areas within the walls separating rooms rather than in exterior walls, where they cut off natural light.

In addition, when storage is placed in the interior walls of a room, around the doorway, the resulting thickness will make the transitions between rooms and corridors more distinct. For the person entering such a room, the thickness of the wall creates a subtle "entry" space, which makes the room more private. This way of making the closet "thickness" around an entrance is therefore appropriate for spaces like the COUPLE'S REALM (136) and the various private rooms—A ROOM OF ONE'S OWN (141).

Closets form the entrance to the room.

Therefore:

Mark all the rooms where you want closets. Then place the closets themselves on those interior walls which lie between two rooms and between rooms and passages where you need acoustic insulation. Place them so as to create transition spaces for the doors into the rooms. On no account put closets on exterior walls. It wastes the opportunity for good acoustic insulation and cuts off precious light.

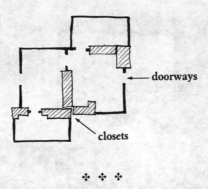

doorways

closets

❖ ❖ ❖

Later, include the closets as part of the overall building structure—THICK WALLS (197). . . .

199 SUNNY COUNTER*

. . . FARMHOUSE KICHEN (139) and COOKING LAYOUT (184) give the overall design of the kitchen, and its workspace. INDOOR SUNLIGHT (128) makes sure of sunshine in the kitchen. But to help create these larger patterns, and to make the kitchen as warm and beautiful as possible, it is worth taking a great deal of care placing the counter and its windows.

Dark gloomy kitchens are depressing. The kitchen needs the sun more than the other rooms, not less.

Look how beautiful the workspace in our main picture is. Nearly the whole counter is lined with windows. The work surface is bathed in light, and there is a sense of spaciousness all around. There is a view out, an air of calm.

A gloomy kitchen.

Compare it with this gloomy kitchen. There is no natural light on the work counter, the cabinets are a clutter; it is a shabby experience to work there—to work below a cabinet, facing a wall with artificial light in the middle of the day.

This gloomy kitchen is typical of many thousands of kitchens in modern houses. It happens for two reasons. First, people often place kitchens to the north, because they reserve the south for living rooms and then put the kitchen in the left over areas. And it happens, secondly, when the kitchen is thought of as

917

an "efficient" place, only meant for the mechanical cooking operations. In many apartments, efficiency kitchens are even in positions where they get no natural light at all. But, of course, the arguments we have presented in FARMHOUSE KITCHEN (139) for making the kitchen a living room, not merely a machine-shop, change all this.

Therefore:

Place the main part of the kitchen counter on the south and southeast side of the kitchen, with big windows around it, so that sun can flood in and fill the kitchen with yellow light both morning and afternoon.

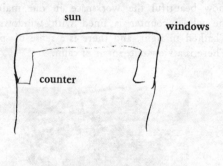

❖ ❖ ❖

Give the windows a view toward a garden or the area where children play—WINDOWS OVERLOOKING LIFE (192). If storage space is tight, you can build open shelves for bowls and plates and plants right across the windows and still let in the sun— OPEN SHELVES (200). Build the counter as a special part of the room, integral with the building structure, able to take many modifications later—THICKENING THE OUTER WALLS (211). Use WARM COLORS (250) around the window to soften and warm the sunlight. . . .

200 OPEN SHELVES*

. . . within the THICK WALLS (197), especially around the FARMHOUSE KITCHEN (139) and WORKSPACE ENCLOSURE (183), but possibly throughout the building, there is a need for shelves. This pattern helps you decide exactly where you want them and how they shall be organized. Mary Louise Rogers first made the pattern explicit for us.

❖ ❖ ❖

Cupboards that are too deep waste valuable space, and it always seems that what you want is behind something else.

It is easy to think that you have good storage in a room or in a building just because you have enough closets, cupboards, and shelves. But the value of storage depends as much on the ease of access as on the amount. An enormous amount of cupboard space in a place where no one can get to it is not very useful. It is useful when you can find the things which you have put away at a glance.

This means, essentially, that except for BULK STORAGE (145), things should be stored on open shelves, "one deep." Then you can see them all. It means, in effect, that you are flattening out the total storage all over the walls—instead of having it in solid lumps, hidden, and hard to reach.

The need for open storage is most obvious in kitchens. In badly planned kitchens, the shelves are filled with things three or four items deep, sometimes stacked on top of each other, and something is always in the way of what you need. But in well-planned kitchens, all storage is one item deep. Shelves are one can deep, glasses are stored one row deep, pots and pans are hung one deep on the wall; for small jars and spices there are special spice shelves that hold the items just one deep.

We think this property is common to all convenient storage. A family's most prized possessions, gifts, whether for the kitchen or any place else in the house, are hidden away when they are stored in cupboards and the back shelves of closets. Openly stored, one deep, these things are beautiful around the house.

Many forms of storage can be one-deep: swinging cabinets that have shelves inside the doors; pegboards for pots and pans; tool racks. It is even possible to create narrow open shelves in front of windows. When things are just one deep, there is still enough light coming in to make the window useful.

Open shelves across a window.

Therefore:

Cover the walls with narrow shelves of varying depth but always shallow enough so that things can be placed on them one deep—nothing hiding behind anything else.

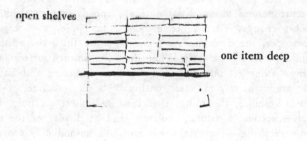

❖ ❖ ❖

At waist height put in an extra deep shelf for plates, phonograph, TV, boxes, displays, treasures—WAIST-HIGH SHELF (201). Mark the open shelves along with all the other deep spaces in the walls—THICKENING THE OUTER WALL (211). . . .

201 WAIST-HIGH SHELF

. . . anywhere where there are open shelves, and around any
room which tends to accumulate potted plants, books, plates, bits
of paper, boxes, beautiful vases, and little things you have picked
up along your travels, there is a need for space where these
things can lie undisturbed, without making the room a mess—
THICK WALLS (197), OPEN SHELVES (200).

**In every house and every workplace there is a daily
"traffic" of the objects which are handled most. Unless
such things are immediately at hand, the flow of life is
awkward, full of mistakes; things are forgotten, misplaced.**

The essence of this problem lies in the phrase "at hand." This
is literally true and needs to be interpreted as such. When a
person reaches for something, his hands are roughly at waist
height. When there are surfaces here and there, around the
rooms and passages and doors, which are at waist height, they
become natural places to leave things and later pick them up.
Pocket change, pictures, open books, an apple, a package, a
newspaper, the day's mail, a reminder note: these things are at
hand on a waist high shelf. When there are no such surfaces, then
things either get put away and are then forgotten and lost, or
they are in the way and must continually be cleared aside.

Furthermore, the things that tend to collect on waist high
shelves become a natural, evolving kind of display of the most
ordinary things—the things that are most immediately a part of
one's life. And since for each person these things will vary, the
waist high shelf helps a room become unique and personal, effort-
lessly.

Therefore:

Build waist-high shelves around at least a part of the

main rooms where people live and work. Make them long, 9 to 15 inches deep, with shelves or cupboard underneath. Interrupt the shelf for seats, windows, and doors.

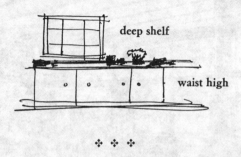

❖ ❖ ❖

Build the shelf right into the structure of the building— THICKENING THE OUTER WALL (211). It is a good place to put your personal treasures—THINGS FROM YOUR LIFE (253). . . .

202 BUILT-IN SEATS*

. . . throughout the building—SEQUENCE OF SITTING SPACES (142)—there are alcoves, entrances, corners, and windows where it is natural to make built-in seats—ENTRANCE ROOM (130), ALCOVES (179), WINDOW PLACE (180). This pattern helps complete them.

❖ ❖ ❖

Built-in seats are great. Everybody loves them. They make a building feel comfortable and luxurious. But most often they do not actually work. They are placed wrong, or too narrow, or the back does not slope, or the view is wrong, or the seat is too hard. This pattern tells you what to do to make a built-in seat that really works.

Why do built-in seats so often not work properly? The reasons are simple and fairly easy to correct. But the problems are critical. If the seats are wrongly made, they just will not be used, and they will be a waste of space, a waste of money, and a wasted golden opportunity. What are the critical considerations?

Position: It is natural to put the built-in seat into an unobtrusive corner—that is where it melts most easily into the structure and the wall. But, as a result, it is often out of the way. If you want to build a seat, ask yourself where you would place a sofa or a comfortable armchair—and build the seat *there*, not tucked into some hopeless corner.

Width and comfort: Built-in seats are often too hard, too narrow, and too stiff-backed. No one wants to sit on a shelf, especially not for any length of time. Make the seat as wide as a really comfortable chair (at least 18 inches), with a back that slopes gently (not upright), and put a warm soft cushion on it and on the back, so that it is really comfortable.

View: Most people want to look at something when they sit—either at other people or a view. Built-in seats often place you so that you are facing away from the view or *away* from the other people in the room. Place the seat so that a person sitting down is looking at something interesting.

Therefore:

Before you build the seat, get hold of an old arm chair or a sofa, and put it into the position where you intend to build a seat. Move it until you really like it. Leave it there for a few days. See if you enjoy sitting in it. Move it if you don't. When you have got it into a position which you like, and where you often find yourself sitting, you know it is a good position. Now build a seat that is just as wide, and just as well padded—and your built-in seat will work.

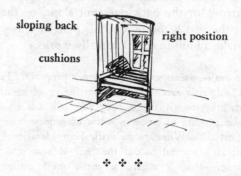

sloping back

right position

cushions

❖ ❖ ❖

Once you decide where to put the seat, make it part of the THICK WALLS (197), so that it is a part of the structure, not just an addition—THICKENING THE OUTER WALL (211). . . .

. . . the places specially devoted to children's play—ADVENTURE PLAYGROUND (73), CHILDREN'S HOME (86), CHILDREN'S REALM (137)—and THICK WALLS (197)—can be embellished with a special detail.

Children love to be in tiny, cave-like places.

In the course of their play, young children seek out cave-like spaces to get into and under—old crates, under tables, in tents, etc. (For evidence see L. E. White, "The Outdoor Play of Children Living in Flats," *Living in Towns*, Leo Kuper, ed., London, 1953, pp. 235–64.)

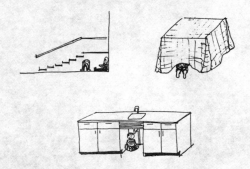

They try to make special places for themselves and for their friends—most of the world about them is "adult space" and they are trying to carve out a place that is kid size.

When children are playing in such a "cave"—each child takes up about 5 square feet; furthermore, children like to do this in groups, so the caves should be large enough to accommodate this: these sorts of groups range in size from three to five—so 15 to 25 square feet, plus about 15 square feet for games and circulation, gives a rough maximum size for caves.

Therefore:

Wherever children play, around the house, in the neighborhood, in schools, make small "caves" for them. Tuck these caves away in natural left over spaces, under stairs, under kitchen counters. Keep the ceiling heights low—2 feet 6 inches to 4 feet—and the entrance tiny.

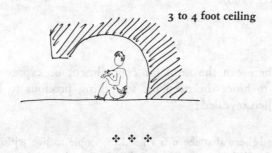

3 to 4 foot ceiling

❖ ❖ ❖

Build the caves right into the fabric of the walls—THICKENING THE OUTER WALLS (211). Make the doors very tiny to match the caves—an extreme version of LOW DOORWAY (224). . . .

204 SECRET PLACE

. . . and here is a finishing touch to the thick walls, perhaps even to the low ceilings—THICK WALLS (197), CEILING HEIGHT VARIETY (190).

❖ ❖ ❖

Where can the need for concealment be expressed; the need to hide; the need for something precious to be lost, and then revealed?

We believe that there is a need in people to live with a secret place in their homes: a place that is used in special ways, and revealed only at very special moments.

To live in a home where there is such a place alters your experience. It invites you to put something precious there, to conceal, to let only some in on the secret and not others. It allows you to keep something that is precious in an entirely personal way, so that no one may ever find it, until the moment you say to your friend, "Now I am going to show you something special"—and tell the story behind it.

There is strong support for the reality of this need in Gaston Bachelard's *The Poetics of Space* (New York: The Omen Press, 1964). We quote from Chapter 3:

> With the theme of drawers, chests, locks and wardrobes, we shall resume contact with the unfathomable store of daydreams of intimacy.
>
> Wardrobes with their shelves, desks with their drawers, and chests with their false bottoms are veritable organs of the secret psychological life. Indeed, without these "objects" and a few others in equally high favor, our intimate life would lack a model of intimacy. They are hybrid objects, subject objects. Like us, through us and for us, they have a quality of intimacy. . . .
>
> If we give objects the friendship they should have, we do not open a wardrobe without a slight start. Beneath its russet wood, a wardrobe is a very white almond. To open it, is to experience an event of whiteness.

An anthology devoted to small boxes, such as chests and caskets, would constitute an important chapter in psychology. These complex pieces that a craftsman creates are very evident witnesses of the need for secrecy, of an intuitive sense of hiding places. It is not merely a matter of keeping a possession well guarded. The lock doesn't exist that could resist absolute violence, and all locks are an invitation to thieves. A lock is a psychological threshold. . . .

Therefore:

Make a place in the house, perhaps only a few feet square, which is kept locked and secret; a place which is virtually impossible to discover—until you have been shown where it is; a place where the archives of the house, or other more potent secrets, might be kept.

secret place

life history of family

precious objects

history of the house

❖ ❖ ❖

Classic types of secret places are the panel that slides back, revealing the cavity in the wall, the loose board beneath the rug, the trap door—CLOSETS BETWEEN ROOMS (198), THICKENING THE OUTER WALLS (211), FLOOR-CEILING VAULTS (219). . . .

CONSTRUCTION

*At this stage, you have a complete design for an indi-
vidual building. If you have followed the patterns given,
you have a scheme of spaces, either marked on the
ground, with stakes, or on a piece of paper, accurate to
the nearest foot or so. You know the height of rooms,
the rough size and position of windows and doors, and
you know roughly how the roofs of the building, and
the gardens are laid out.*

*The next, and last part of the language, tells you how
to make a buildable building directly from this rough
scheme of spaces, and tells you how to build it, in detail.*

❖ ❖ ❖

The patterns in this last section present a physical attitude to construction that works together with the kinds of
buildings which the second part of the pattern language
generates. These construction patterns are intended for
builders—whether professional builders, or amateur
owner builders.

Each pattern states a principle about structure and
materials. These principles can be implemented in any
number of ways when it comes time for actual building.
We have tried to state various ways in which the principles can be built. But, partly because these patterns are
the least developed, and partly because of the nature of
building patterns, the reader will very likely have much
to add to these patterns. For example, the actual materials used to implement them will vary greatly from
region to region . . .

Perhaps the main thing to bear in mind, as you look
over this material, is this: Our intention in this section

has been to provide an alternative to the technocratic and rigid ways of building that have become the legacy of the machine age and modern architecture.

The way of building described here leads to buildings that are unique and tailored to their sites. It depends on builders taking responsibility for their work; and working out the details of the building as they go—mocking up entrances and windows and the dimensions of spaces, making experiments, and building directly according to the results.

The patterns in this section are unique in several ways.

First, the sequence of the patterns is more concrete than in any of the earlier portions of the language. It not only corresponds to the order in which a design matures *conceptually*, in the user's mind, but also corresponds to the actual physical order of construction. That is, except for the first four patterns, which deal with structural philosophy, the remaining patterns can actually be used, in the sequence given, to build a building. The sequence of the language corresponds almost exactly, to the actual sequence of operations on the building site. In addition, the patterns themselves in this section are both more concrete, and more abstract, than any other patterns in the language.

They are more concrete because, with each pattern, we have always given at least one interpretation which can be built directly. For instance, with the pattern ROOT FOUNDATION, we have given one particular interpretation, to show that it can be done, and also to give the reader an immediate, and practical, buildable approach to construction.

Yet at the same time, they are also more abstract. The particular concrete formulation which we have given for each pattern, can also be interpreted, and remade in a thousand ways. Thus, it is also possible to take the general idea of the pattern, the idea that the foundation functions like a tree root, in the way that it anchors the building in the ground—and invent a dozen entirely different physical systems, which all work in this fundamental way. In this sense, these patterns are more abstract than any others in the book, since they have a wider range of possible interpretations.

To illustrate the fact that a great variety of actual building systems can be developed, based on these patterns, we present three versions that we have developed, in response to different contexts.

In Mexico: Concrete block foundations with re-bar connectors; hollow self-aligning molded earth blocks reinforced with bamboo for walls and columns; burlap formed concrete beams; steep barrel vaults with earth and asphalt covering—everything whitewashed.

In Peru: Slab floors poured integrally with wall foundations; finished with soft baked tiles; hard wood (diablo fuerte) columns and beams; plaster on bamboo lath acting as shear walls between columns; diagonal wood plank ceiling/floors; bamboo lattice partitions.

In Berkeley: Concrete slab finished with colored wax; walls of exterior skin of 1 x boards and interior skin of gypboard filled with light weight concrete; box columns made of 1 x boards, filled with lightweight concrete; 2-inch concrete ceiling/floor vaults formed with wood lattice and burlap forms.

As you can see from these examples, we have formulated these patterns with very careful attention to cost. We have tried to give examples of these patterns which use the cheapest, and most easily available, materials; we have designed them in such a way that such buildings can be built by lay people (who can therefore avoid the cost of labor altogether); and we have designed it so that the cost of labor, if done professionally, is also low.

Of the three parts of the language, this third part is the least developed. Both the part on *Towns* and the part on *Buildings* have been tested, one partially, the other very thoroughly, in practice. This third part has so far only been tested in a small number of relatively minor buildings. That means, obviously, that this material needs a good deal of improvement.

However, we intend, as soon as possible, to test all these patterns thoroughly in various different buildings —houses, public buildings, details, and additions. Once again, as soon as we have enough examples to make it worth reporting on them, we shall publish another volume which describes them, and our findings.

In many ways, rough though it is, this is the most exciting part of the language, because it is here, in these few patterns, that we can most vividly see a building literally grow before our eyes, under the impact of the patterns.

The actual process of construction, in which the sequence of their patterns creates a building, is described in chapter 23 of *The Timeless Way*.

Before you lay out construction details, establish a philosophy of structure which will let the structure grow directly from your plans and your conception of the buildings.

939

205 STRUCTURE FOLLOWS
SOCIAL SPACES**

. . . if you have used the earlier patterns in the language, your plans are based on subtle arrangements of social spaces. But the beauty and subtlety of all these social spaces will be destroyed, when you start building, unless you find a way of building which is able to follow the social spaces without distorting or rearranging them for engineering reasons.

This pattern gives you the beginning of such a way of building. It is the first of the 49 patterns which deal specifically with structure and construction; it is the bottleneck through which all languages pass from the larger patterns for rooms and building layout to the smaller ones which specify the process of construction. It not only has its own intrinsic arguments about the relation between social spaces and load-bearing structure—it also contains, at the end, a list of all the connections which you need for patterns on structure, columns, walls, floors, roofs, and all the details of construction.

❖ ❖ ❖

No building ever feels right to the people in it unless the physical spaces (defined by columns, walls, and ceilings) are congruent with the social spaces (defined by activities and human groups).

And yet this congruence is hardly ever present in modern construction. Most often the physical and social spaces are incongruent. Modern construction—that is, the form of construction most commonly practiced in the mid-twentieth century—usually forces social spaces into the framework of a building whose shape is given by engineering considerations.

There are two different versions of this incongruence.

On the one hand, there are those buildings whose structural form is very demanding indeed and actually forces the social space to follow the shape of the construction—Buckminster Fuller domes, hyperbolic paraboloids, tension structures are examples.

On the other hand, there are those buildings in which there are very few structural elements—a few giant columns and no

941

Geodesic dome.   *Steel and glass.*

more. In these buildings the social spaces are defined by light-weight nonstructural partitions floating free within the "neutral" physical structure given by the engineering. The buildings of Mies van der Rohe and Skidmore Owings and Merrill are examples.

We shall now argue that both these kinds of incongruence do fundamental damage—for entirely different reasons.

In the first case the structure does damage simply because it constrains the social space and makes it different from what it naturally wants to be. To be specific: we know from our experiments that people are able to use this pattern language to design buildings for themselves; and that the plans they create, unhampered by other considerations, have an astonishing range of free arrangements, always finely tuned to the details of their lives and habits.

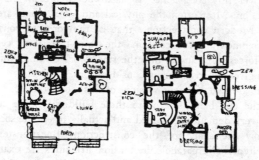

User's house plan.

Any form of construction which makes it impossible to implement these plans and forces them into the strait jacket of an alien geometry, simply for structural reasons, is doing social damage.

Of course, it could be argued that the structural needs of a building are as much a part of its nature as the social and psychological needs of its inhabitants. This argument might perhaps, perhaps, hold water if there were indeed no way of building buildings which conform more exactly to the loose plans based on activities alone.

But the next few patterns in this book make it very clear that there do exist ways of building which are structurally sound and yet perfectly congruent with social space, without any compromise whatever. It is therefore clear that we may legitimately reject any form of construction which cannot adapt itself perfectly to the forms of space required by social action.

What of the second kind of incongruence between social space and building form—the kind where the structure creates huge areas of almost uninterrupted "flexible" space, punctuated by occasional columns, and the social spaces are created inside this framework by nonstructural partitions.

Once again, many important patterns cannot be incorporated into the design—LIGHT ON TWO SIDES OF EVERY ROOM (159), for example simply cannot be included in a giant rectangle. But in this type of building, there is an additional kind of incongruence between social space and engineering structure which comes from the fact that the two are virtually independent of each other. The engineering follows its own laws, the social space follows its laws—and they do not match.

This mismatch is perceived and felt not merely as a mismatch, but as a fundamental and disturbing incoherence in the fabric of the building, which makes people feel uneasy and unsure of themselves and their relation to the world. We offer four possible explanations.

First: the spaces called for by the patterns dealing with social and psychological needs are critical. If the spaces are not right, the needs are not met and problems are not solved. Since these spaces are so critical, it stands to reason that they must be felt as real spaces, not flimsily or haphazardly partitioned spaces, which

only pay lip-service to the needs people experience. For instance, if an entrance room is created with flimsy partitions, it will not take hold; people won't take it seriously. Only when the most solid elements of the building form the spaces will the spaces be fully felt and the needs which call for the space then fully be satisfied.

Second: a building will also seem alien unless it gives to its users a direct and intuitive sense of its structure—how it is put together. Buildings where the structure is hidden leave yet another gap in people's understanding of the environment around them. We know this is important to children and suspect it must be important to adults too.

Third: when the social space has, as its own surrounding, the fabric of the load-bearing structure which supports that space, then the forces of gravity are integrated with the social forces, and one feels the resolution of *all* the forces which are acting in this one space. The experience of being in a place where the forces are resolved together at once is completely restful and whole. It is like sitting under an oak tree: things in nature resolve all the forces acting on them together: they are, in this sense, whole and balanced.

Fourth: it is a psychological fact that a space is defined by its corners. Just as four dots define a rectangle to your eye, so four posts (or more) define an imaginary space between them.

Four points make a rectangle.

This is the most fundamental way in which solids define space. Unless the actual solids which make up the building lie at the corners of its social spaces, they must, instead, be creating *other* virtual spaces at odds with the intended ones. The building will only be at rest psychologically if the corners of its rooms are clearly marked and coincide, at least in the majority of cases, with its most solid elements.

Therefore:

A first principle of construction: on no account allow the engineering to dictate the building's form. Place the load bearing elements—the columns and the walls and floors—according to the social spaces of the building; never modify the social spaces to conform to the engineering structure of the building.

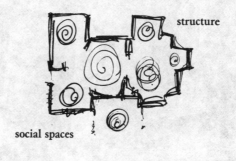

structure

social spaces

❖ ❖ ❖

You will be able to guarantee that structure follows social spaces by placing columns at the corner of every social space—COLUMNS AT THE CORNERS (212); and by building a distinct and separate vault over each room and social space—FLOOR-CEILING VAULTS (219).

For the principles of structure which will make it possible to build your building according to this pattern, begin with EFFICIENT STRUCTURE (206); for the class of compatible materials, see GOOD MATERIALS (207); for the fundamentals of the process of construction, see GRADUAL STIFFENING (208). . . .

. . . this pattern complements the pattern STRUCTURE FOLLOWS SOCIAL SPACES (205). Where that pattern defines the relationship between the social spaces and the structure, this pattern lays down the kind of structure which is dictated by pure engineering. As you will see, it is compatible with STRUCTURE FOLLOWS SOCIAL SPACES, and will help to create it.

❖ ❖ ❖

Some buildings have column and beam structures; others have load-bearing walls with slab floors; others are vaulted structures, or domes, or tents. But which of these, or what mixture of them, is actually the most efficient? What is the best way to distribute materials throughout a building, so as to enclose the space, strongly and well, with the least amount of material?

Engineers usually say that there is no answer to this question. According to current engineering practice it is first necessary to make an arbitrary choice among the basic possible systems—and only then possible to use theory and calculation to fix the size of members within the chosen system. But, the basic choice itself—at least according to prevailing dogma—cannot be made by theory.

To anyone with an enquiring mind, this seems quite unlikely. That such a fundamental choice, as the choice between column and beams systems and load-bearing wall systems and vaulted systems, should lie purely in the realm of whim—and that the possible myriad of mixed systems, which lie between these archetypes, cannot even be considered—all this has more to do with the status of available theory than with any fundamental insight.

Indeed, as we shall now try to show, the archetypal, best solution to the problem of efficient structure in a building is one which does lie in between the three most famous archetypes. It is a system of load-bearing walls, supported at frequent intervals by thickened stiffeners like columns, and floored and roofed by a system of vaults.

We shall derive the character of the most efficient structure in

three steps. First, we shall define the three-dimensional character of a typical system of rooms and spaces in a building. We shall then define an efficient structure as the smallest cheapest amount of stable material, placed only in the interstices between the rooms, which can support itself and the loads which the rooms generate. Finally, we shall obtain the details of an efficient structure. For a similar discussion, see Christopher Alexander, "An attempt to derive the nature of a human building system from first principles," in Edward Allen, *The Responsive House*, M.I.T. Press, 1974.

I. The three-dimensional character of a typical building based purely on the social spaces and the character of rooms.

In order to obtain this from fundamental considerations, let us first review the typical shape of rooms—see THE SHAPE OF INDOOR SPACE (191)—and then go on to derive the most efficient structure for a building made up of these kinds of rooms:

1. The boundary of any space, seen in plan, is formed by segments which are essentially straight lines—though they need not be perfectly straight.

2. The ceiling heights of spaces vary according to their social functions. Roughly speaking, the ceiling heights vary with floor areas—large spaces have higher ceilings, small ones lower—CEILING HEIGHT VARIETY (190).

3. The edges of the space are essentially vertical up to head height—that is, about 6 feet. Above head height, the boundaries of the space may come in toward the space. The upper corners between wall and ceiling of a normal room serve no function, and it is therefore not useful to consider them as an essential part of the space.

4. Each space has a horizontal floor.

5. A building then is a packing of polygonal spaces in which each polygon has a beehive cross section, and a height which varies according to its size.

If we follow the principle of STRUCTURE FOLLOWS SOCIAL SPACES (205), we may assume that this three-dimensional array of spaces must remain intact, and not be interrupted by structural

A packing of polygonal beehive spaces.

elements. This means that an efficient structure must be one of the arrangements of material which occupies only the interstices between the spaces.

We may visualize the crudest of these possible structures by means of a simple imaginary process. Make a lump of wax for each of the spaces which appears in the building, and construct a three-dimensional array of these lumps of wax, leaving gaps between all adjacent lumps. Now, take a generalized "structure fluid," and pour it all over this arrangements of lumps, so that it completely covers the whole thing, and fills all the gaps. Let this fluid harden. Now dissolve out the wax lumps that represent spaces. The stuff which remains is the most generalized building structure.

II. *The most efficient structure for a given system of spaces.*

Obviously, the imaginary structure made from the structure fluid is not real. And besides, it is rather inefficient: it would, if actually carried out, use a great deal of material. We must now ask how to make a structure, similar to this imaginary one, but one which uses the smallest amount of material. As we shall see, this most efficient structure will be *a compression structure*, in which bending and tension are reduced to a minimum and *a continuous structure*, in which all members are rigidly connected in such a way that each member carries at least some part of the stresses caused by any pattern of loading.

1. *A compression structure.* In an efficient structure, we want every ounce of material to be working to its capacity. In more precise terms, we want the stress distributed throughout the materials in such a way that every cubic inch is stressed to the same degree. This is not happening, for example, in a simple wooden beam. The material is most stressed at the top and bottom

of the beam; the middle of the beam has only very low stresses, because there is too much material there relative to the stress distribution.

As a general rule, we may say that members which are in bending always have uneven stress distributions and that we can therefore only distribute stresses evenly throughout the materials if the structure is entirely free of bending. In short, then, a perfectly efficient structure must be free of bending.

There are two possible structures which avoid bending altogether: pure tension structures and pure compression structures. Although pure tension structures are theoretically interesting and suitable for occasional special purposes, the considerations described in GOOD MATERIALS (207) rule them out overwhelmingly on the grounds that tension materials are hard to obtain, and expensive, while almost all materials can resist compression. Note especially that wood and steel, the two principle tension materials in buildings, are both scarce, and can—on ecological grounds—no longer be used in bulk—again, see GOOD MATERIALS (207).

2. *A continuous structure.* In an efficient structure, it is not only true that individual elements have even stress distributions in them when they are loaded. It is also true that the structure acts as a whole.

Consider, for example, the case of a basket. The individual strands of the basket are weak. By itself no one strand can resist much load. But the basket is so cunningly made, that all the strands work together to resist even the smallest load. If you press on one part of the basket with your finger, all the strands in the basket—even those in the part furthest from your finger—work together to resist the load. And of course, since the whole structure works as one, to resist the load, no one part has, individually, to be very strong.

This principle is particularly important in a structure like a building, which faces a vast range of different loading conditions. At one minute, the wind is blowing very strong in one direction; at another moment an earthquake shakes the building; in later years, uneven settlement redistributes dead loads because some foundations sink lower than others; and, of course, throughout its life the people and furniture in the building are moving

all the time. If each element is to be strong enough, by itself, to resist the maximum load it can be subjected to, it will have to be enormous.

But when the building is continuous, like a basket, so that each part of the building helps to carry the smallest load, then, of course, the unpredictable nature of the loads creates no difficulties at all. Members can be quite small, because no matter what the loads are, the continuity of the building will distribute them among the members as a whole, and the building will act as a whole against them.

The continuity of a building depends on its connections: actual continuity of material and shape. It is very hard, almost impossible, to make continuous connections between different materials, which transfer load as efficiently as a continuous material; and it is therefore essential that the building be made of one material, which is actually continuous from member to member. And the shape of the connections between elements is vital too. Right angles tend to create discontinuities: forces can be distributed throughout the building only if there are diagonal fillets wherever walls meet ceilings, walls meet walls, and columns meet beams.

III. The details of an efficient structure.

If we assume now that an efficient building will be both compressive and continuous, we can obtain the main morphological features of its structure by direct inference.

1. Its ceilings, floors, and rooms must all be vaulted. This follows directly. The dome or vault shape is the only shape which works in pure compression. Floors and roofs can only be continuous with walls, if they curve downward at their edges. And the shape of social spaces also invites it directly—since the triangle of space between the wall and ceiling serves no useful purpose, it is a natural place for structural material.

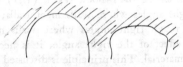

Vaults.

951

3. Walls must all be load-bearing. Any non load-bearing partition evidently contradicts the principle of continuity which says that every particle of the building is helping to resist loads. Furthermore, columns with non load-bearing partitions between them need shear support. The wall provides it naturally; and the continuity of the walls, floor, and ceiling can only be created by the action of a wall that ties them together.

Load-bearing walls.

3. Walls must be stiffened at intervals along their length by columnar ribs. If a wall is to contain a given amount of material, then the wall acts most efficiently when its material is redistributed, nonhomogeneously, to form vertical ribs. This wall is most efficient in resisting buckling—indeed, at most thicknesses this kind of stiffening is actually *required* to let the wall act at its full compressive capacity—see FINAL COLUMN DISTRIBUTION (213). And it helps to resist horizontal loads, because the stiffeners act as beams against the horizontal forces.

Vertical stiffeners.

4. Connections between walls and floors, and between walls and walls, must all be thickened by extra material that forms a fillet along the seam. Connections are the weakest points for continuity, and right-angled connections are the worst. However, we know from THE SHAPE OF INDOOR SPACE (191) that we cannot avoid rough right angles where walls meet walls; and of course, there must be rough right angles where walls meet floors. To counteract the effect of the right angle, it is necessary to "fill" the angle with material. This principle is discussed under COLUMN CONNECTIONS (227).

Thickened connections.

5. *Openings in walls must have thickened frames, and rounding in the upper corners.* This follows directly from the principle of continuity and is fully discussed in FRAMES AS THICKENED EDGES (225).

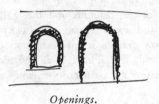

Openings.

Therefore:

Conceive the building as a building made from one continuous body of compressive material. In its geometry, conceive it as a three-dimensional system of individually vaulted spaces, most of them roughly rectangular, with thin load-bearing walls, each stiffened by columns at intervals along its length, thickened where walls meet walls and where walls meet vaults and stiffened around the openings.

continuity of material

compressive material

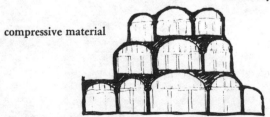

CONSTRUCTION

The layout of the inner vaults is given in FLOOR AND CEILING LAYOUT (210) and FLOOR-CEILING VAULTS (219); the layout of the outer vaults which form the roof is given in ROOF LAYOUT (209) and ROOF VAULTS (220). The layout of the stiffeners which make the walls is given in FINAL COLUMN DISTRIBUTION (213); the layout of the thickening where walls meet walls is given by COLUMNS AT THE CORNERS (212); the thickening where walls meet vaults is given by PERIMETER BEAMS (217); the construction of the columns and the walls is given by BOX COLUMNS (216) and WALL MEMBRANES (218); the thickening of doors and window frames is given by FRAMES AS THICKENED EDGES (225); and the non-right-angled connection between columns and beams by COLUMN CONNECTION (227). . . .

207 GOOD MATERIALS**

. . . the principles of structure allow you to imagine a building in which materials are distributed in the most efficient way, congruent with the social spaces given by the plan—STRUCTURE FOLLOWS SOCIAL SPACES (205), EFFICIENT STRUCTURE (206). But of course the structural conception is still only schematic. It can only become firm and cogent in your mind when you know what materials the building will be made of. This pattern helps you settle on materials.

❖ ❖ ❖

There is a fundamental conflict in the nature of materials for building in industrial society.

On the one hand, an organic building requires materials which consist of hundreds of small pieces, put together, each one of them hand cut, each one shaped to be unique according to its position. On the other hand, the high cost of labor, and the ease of mass production, tend to create materials which are large, identical, not cuttable or modifiable, and not adaptable to idiosyncracies of plan. These "modern" materials tend to destroy the organic quality of natural buildings and, indeed, to make it impossible. In addition, modern materials tend to be flimsy and hard to maintain—so that buildings deteriorate more rapidly than in a pre-industrial society where a building can be maintained and improved for hundreds of years by patient attention.

The central problem of materials, then, is to find a collection of materials which are small in scale, easy to cut on site, easy to work on site without the aid of huge and expensive machinery, easy to vary and adapt, heavy enough to be solid, longlasting or easy to maintain, and yet easy to build, not needing specialized labor, not expensive in labor, and universally obtainable and cheap.

Furthermore, this class of good materials must be ecologically sound: biodegradable, low in energy consumption, and not based on depletable resources.

When we take all these requirements together, they suggest a

rather startling class of "good materials"—quite different from the materials in common use today. The following discussion is our attempt to begin to define this class of materials. It is certainly incomplete; but perhaps it can help you to think through the problem of materials more carefully.

We start with what we call "bulk materials"—the materials that occur in the greatest volume in a given building. They may account for as much as 80 per cent of the total volume of materials used in a building. Traditionally, bulk materials have been earth, concrete, wood, brick, stone, snow. . . . Today the bulk materials are essentially wood and concrete and, in the very large buildings, steel.

When we analyze these materials strictly, according to our criteria, we find that stone and brick meet most of the requirements, but are often out of the question where labor is expensive, because they are labor intensive.

Wood is excellent in many ways. Where it is available people use it in great quantities, and where it is not available people are trying to get hold of it. Unfortunately the forests have been terribly managed; many have been devastated; and the price of heavy lumber has skyrocketed. From today's paper: "Since the end of federal economic controls the price of lumber has been jumping about 15 percent a month and is now about 55 percent above what it was a year ago." *San Francisco Chronicle*, February 11, 1973. We shall therefore look upon wood as a precious material, which should not be used as a bulk material or for structural purposes.

Steel as a bulk material seems out of the question. We do not need it for high buildings since they do not make social sense— FOUR-STORY LIMIT (21). And for smaller buildings it is expensive, impossible to modify, high energy in production.

Earth is an interesting bulk material. But it is hard to stabilize, and it makes incredibly heavy walls because it has to be so thick. Where this is appropriate, and where the earth is available, however, it is certainly one of the "good materials."

Regular concrete is too dense. It is heavy and hard to work. After it sets one cannot cut into it, or nail into it. And its surface is ugly, cold, and hard in feeling, unless covered by expensive finishes not integral to the structure.

And yet concrete, in some form, is a fascinating material. It is fluid, strong, and relatively cheap. It is available in almost every part of the world. A University of California professor of engineering sciences, P. Kumar Mehta, has even just recently found a way of converting abandoned rice husks into Portland cement.

Is there any way of combining all these good qualities of concrete and also having a material which is light in weight, easy to work, with a pleasant finish? *There is. It is possible to use a whole range of ultra-lightweight concretes which have a density and compressive strength very similar to that of wood. They are easy to work with, can be nailed with ordinary nails, cut with a saw, drilled with wood-working tools, easily repaired.*

We believe that ultra-lightweight concrete is one of the most fundamental bulk materials of the future.

To make this as clear as possible, we shall now discuss the range of lightweight concretes. Our experiments lead us to believe that the best lightweight concretes, the ones most useful for building, are those whose densities lie in the range of 40 to 60 pounds per cubic foot and which develop some 600 to 1000 psi in compression.

Oddly enough, this particular specification lies in the least developed part of the presently available range of concretes. As we can see from the following diagram, the so-called "structural" concretes are usually more dense (at least 90 pounds per cubic foot) and much stronger. The most common "lightweight" concretes use vermiculite as an aggregate, are used for underflooring and insulation, and are very light, but they do not usually develop enough strength to be structurally useful—most

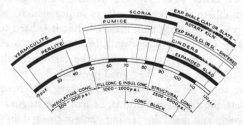

Currently available concrete mixes.

often about 300 psi in compression. However, a range of mixed lightweight aggregates, containing vermiculite, perlite, pumice, and expanded shale in different proportions, can easily generate 40–60 pound, 600 psi concretes anywhere in the world. We have had very good luck with a mix of 1-2-3: cement-kylite-vermiculite.

Beyond the bulk materials, there are the materials used in relatively smaller quantities for framework, surfaces, and finishes. These are the "secondary" materials.

When buildings are built with manageable secondary materials, they can be repaired with the same materials: repair becomes continuous with the original building. And the buildings are more apt to be repaired if it is easy to do so and if the user can do it himself bit by bit without having to rely on skilled workers or special equipment. With prefabricated materials this is impossible, the materials are inherently unrepairable. When prefabricated finish materials are damaged they must be replaced with an entirely new component.

Take the case of a garden patio. It can be made as a continuous concrete slab. When the ground shifts slightly underneath this slab, the slab cracks and buckles. This is quite unrepairable for the user. It requires that the entire slab be broken out (which requires relatively heavy-duty equipment) and replaced—by professional skilled labor. On the other hand, it would have been possible to build the patio initially out of many small bricks, tiles, or stones. When the ground shifts, the user is then able to lift up the broken tiles, add some more earth, and replace the tile—all without the aid of expensive machinery or professional help. And if one of the tiles or bricks becomes damaged, it can be easily replaced.

What are the good secondary materials? Wood, which we want to avoid as a bulk material, is excellent as a secondary material for doors, finishes, windows, furniture. Plywood, particle board, and gypsum board can all be cut, nailed, trimmed, and are relatively cheap. Bamboo, thatch, plaster, paper, corrugated metals, chicken wire, canvas, cloth, vinyl, rope, slate, fiberglass, nonchlorinated plastics are all examples of secondary materials which do rather well against our criteria. Some are dubious ecologically —that is, the fiberglass and the corrugated metals—but again,

these sheet materials need only be used in moderation, to form and finish and trim the bulk materials.

Finally, there are some materials which our criteria exclude entirely—either as bulk or secondary materials. They are expensive, hard to adapt to idiosyncratic plans, they require high energy production techniques, they are in limited reserves. . . . for example: steel panels and rolled steel sections; aluminum; hard and prestressed concrete; chlorinated foams; structural lumber; cement plaster; immense sections of plate glass. . . .

And, for any optimist who thinks he can go on using steel reinforcing bars forever—consider the following fact. Even iron, abundant as it is all over the earth's surface, is a depletable resource. If consumption keeps growing at its present rate of increase (as it very well may, given the vast parts of the world not yet using resources at American and western consumption levels), the resources of iron will run out in 2050.

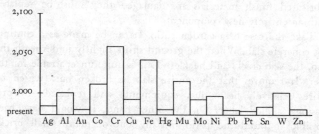

Years at which various metals will be depleted assuming current usage rate continues to increase as it did between 1960 and 1968.

Therefore:

Use only biodegradable, low energy consuming materials, which are easy to cut and modify on site. For bulk materials we suggest ultra-lightweight 40–60 lbs. concrete and earth-based materials like tamped earth, brick, and tile. For secondary materials, use wood planks, gypsum, plywood, cloth, chickenwire, paper, cardboard, particle board, corrugated iron, lime plasters, bamboo, rope, and tile.

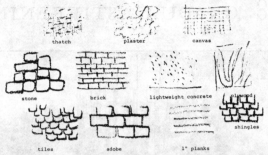

ultra-light weight concrete or organic or earth-based materials

❖ ❖ ❖

In GRADUAL STIFFENING (208), we shall work out the way of using these materials that goes with STRUCTURE FOLLOWS SOCIAL SPACES (205) and EFFICIENT STRUCTURE (206). Try to use the materials in such a way as to allow their own texture to show themselves—LAPPED OUTSIDE WALLS (234), SOFT INSIDE WALLS (235). . . .

. . . in STRUCTURE FOLLOWS SOCIAL SPACES (205) and EFFI-CIENT STRUCTURE (206) we have set down the beginnings of a philosophy, an approach, to construction. GOOD MATERIALS (207) tells us something about the materials we ought to use in order to meet human and ecological demands. Now, before we start the practical task of making a structural layout for a building, it is necessary to consider one more philosophical pattern: one which defines the process of construction that will make it possible to use the right materials and get the overall conception of the structure right.

The fundamental philosophy behind the use of pattern languages is that buildings should be uniquely adapted to individual needs and sites; and that the plans of buildings should be rather loose and fluid, in order to accommodate these subtleties.

This requires an entirely new attitude toward the process of construction. We may define this attitude by saying that it is desirable to build a building in such a way that it starts out loose and flimsy while final adaptations in plan are made, and then gets stiffened gradually during the process of construction, so that each additional act of construction makes the structure sounder.

To understand this philosophy properly, it is helpful to imagine a building being made like a basket. A few strands are put in place. They are very flimsy. Other strands are woven in. Gradually the basket gets stiffer and stiffer. Its final structural strength is only reached from the cooperation of all the members, and is not reached until the building is completely finished. In this sense, such a process produces a building in which all parts of it are working structurally—see EFFICIENT STRUCTURE (206).

Why does the principle of gradual stiffening seem so sensible as a *process* of building?

To begin with, such a structure allows the actual building process to be a creative act. It allows the building to be built up

gradually. Members can be moved around before they are firmly in place. All those detailed design decisions which can never be worked out in advance on paper, can be made during the building process. And it allows you to see the space in three dimensions as a whole, each step of the way, as more material is added.

This means that since each new material that is added in the process must adapt perfectly to the framework that is there, each new material must be more adaptable, more flexible, more capable of coping with variation, than the last. Thus, though the building as a whole goes from flimsy to strong, the actual materials that are added go from the strongest and stiffest, to the gradually less stiff, until finally fluid materials are added.

The essence of this process is very fundamental indeed. We may understand it best by comparing the work of a fifty-year-old carpenter with the work of a novice. The experienced carpenter keeps going. He doesn't have to keep stopping, because every action he performs, is calculated in such a way that some later action can put it right to the extent that it is imperfect now. What is critical here, is the sequence of events. The carpenter never takes a step which he cannot correct later; so he can keep working, confidently, steadily.

The novice, by comparison, spends a great deal of his time trying to figure out what to do. He does this essentially because he knows that an action he takes now may cause unretractable problems a little further down the line; and if he is not careful, he will find himself with a joint that requires the shortening of some crucial member—at a stage when it is too late to shorten that member. The fear of these kinds of mistakes forces him to spend hours trying to figure ahead: and it forces him to work as far as possible to exact drawings because they will guarantee that he avoids these kinds of mistakes.

The difference between the novice and the master is simply that the novice has not learnt, yet, how to do things in such a way that he can afford to make small mistakes. The master knows that the sequence of his actions will always allow him to cover his mistakes a little further down the line. It is this simple but essential knowledge which gives the work of a master carpenter its wonderful, smooth, relaxed, and almost unconcerned simplicity.

In a building we have exactly the same problem, only greatly magnified. Essentially, most modern construction has the character of the novice's work, not of the master's. The builders do not know how to be relaxed, how to deal with earlier mistakes by later detailing; they do not know the proper sequence of events; and they do not, usually, have a building system, or a construction process, which allows them to develop this kind of relaxed and casual wisdom. Instead, like the novice, they work exactly to finely detailed drawings; the building is extremely uptight as it gets made; any departure from the exact drawings is liable to cause severe problems, may perhaps make it necessary to pull out whole sections of the work.

This novice-like and panic-stricken attention to detail has two very serious results. First, like the novice, the architects spend a great deal of time trying to work things out ahead of time, not smoothly building. Obviously, this costs money; and helps create these machine-like "perfect" buildings. Second, a vastly more serious consequence: the details control the whole. The beauty and subtlety of the plan in which patterns have held free sway over the design suddenly becomes tightened and destroyed because, in fear that details won't work out, the details of connections, and components, are allowed to control the plan. As a result, rooms get to be slightly the wrong shape, windows go out of position, spaces between doors and walls get altered just enough to make them useless. In a word, the whole character of modern architecture, namely the control of larger space by piddling details of construction, takes over.

What is needed is the opposite—a process in which details are fitted to the whole. This is the secret of the master carpenter; it is described in detail in *The Timeless Way of Building* as the foundation of all organic form and all successful building. The process of gradual stiffening, which we describe here, is the physical and procedural embodiment of this essential principle. We now ask how, in practice, it is possible to create a gradually stiffened structure within the context defined by the pattern GOOD MATERIALS (207).

Facts about materials give us the starting point we need.

1. Sheet materials are easy to produce and make the best connections.

In traditional society there are few sheet materials. However, factory production tends to make sheets more easily than other forms of material. As we move into an age of mass production, sheet materials become plentiful and are naturally strong, light, and cheap. Gypsum board, plywood, cloth, vinyl, canvas, fiberglass, particle board, wood planks, corrugated metals, chicken wire, are all examples.

And sheet materials are the strongest for connections. Connections are the weak points in a structure. Sheet materials are easy to connect, because connections can join surfaces to one another. Anything made out of sheets is inherently stronger than something made of lumps or sticks.

2. Ultra-lightweight concrete is an excellent fill material— it has the density of wood, is strong, light, easy to cut, easy to repair, easy to nail into—and is available everywhere. This is discussed fully in GOOD MATERIALS (207).

3. However, any kind of concrete needs formwork: and the cost of formwork is enormous.

This makes it very expensive indeed to build any complex form; and within conventional building systems, it more or less rules out the kind of "organic" structure which we have described. Furthermore, in regular concrete work, the formwork is eventually wasted, thrown away.

We believe that the finishes in any sensible building system should be integral with the process of construction and the structure itself (as they are in almost all traditional buildings)— and that any building system in which finishes have to be "added" to the building are wasteful, and unnatural.

4. We therefore propose that ultra-lightweight concrete be poured into forms which are made of the easily available sheet materials: and that these materials are then left in place to form the finish.

The sheet materials can be any combination of cloth, canvas, wood planks, gypsum boards, fiberboards, plywood, paper, plastered chickenwire, corrugated metals, and where it is possible, tile, brick, or stone—see GOOD MATERIALS (207). For the ultra-lightweight concrete we recommend a perlite, expanded shale, or pumice aggregate. Tamped earth, adobe, nonchlorinated foams, may also do instead of the concrete, if loads allow it.

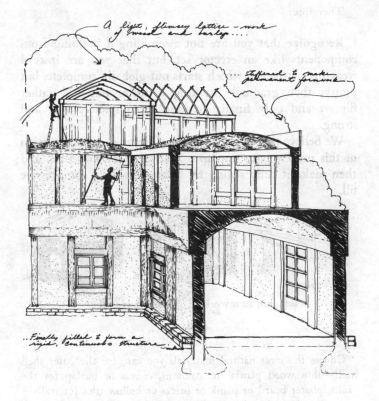

A light, flimsy lattice - work of wood and burlap ....

.... Stiffened to make permanent formwork

...Finally filled to form a rigid, continuous structure....

One version of gradual stiffening, using one inch planks, gypsum board and burlap as sheets, with ultra-lightweight concrete as fill.

The drawing above, shows one particular realisation of this kind of gradual stiffening. But the principle is far more general than this particular use of it. Indeed, it occurs, in one way or another, in almost all traditional forms of building. Eskimo igloo construction and African basket structures are both gradually stiffened structures, where each next step copes with the existing framework, adds to it, and stiffens it. The stone buildings of Alberobello in southern Italy are examples. So is Elizabethan half-timber construction.

Therefore:

Recognize that you are not assembling a building from components like an erector set, but that you are instead weaving a structure which starts out globally complete, but flimsy; then gradually making it stiffer but still rather flimsy; and only finally making it completely stiff and strong.

We believe that in our own time, the most natural version of this process is to put up a shell of sheet materials, and then make it fully strong by filling it with a compressive fill.

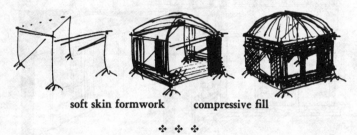

soft skin formwork   compressive fill

❖ ❖ ❖

Choose the most natural materials you can, for the outer shell itself—thin wood planks for columns, canvas or burlap for the vaults, plaster board or plank or bricks or hollow tiles for walls— GOOD MATERIALS (207).

Use ultra-lightweight 40 to 60 pounds perlite concrete for the compressive fill—it has the same density as wood and can be cut and nailed like wood, both during the construction and in later years when repairs become necessary—GOOD MATERIALS (207).

Build up the columns first, then fill them with the ultra-lightweight concrete; then build up the beams and fill them; then the vaults, and cover them with a thin coat of concrete which hardens to form a shell; then fill that shell with even lighter weight materials to form the floors; then make the walls and window frames, and fill them; and finally, the roof, again a thin cloth vault covered with a coat of concrete to form a shell— BOX COLUMNS (216), PERIMETER BEAM (217), WALL MEMBRANE (218), FLOOR-CEILING VAULTS (219), ROOF VAULTS (220). . . .

*within this philosophy of structure, on the basis of
the plans which you have made, work out the
complete structural layout; this is the last thing you
do on paper, before you actually start to build;*

209 ROOF LAYOUT*

. . . assume now that you have a rough plan, to scale, for each floor of the building. In this case you already know roughly how the roofs will go, from CASCADE OF ROOFS (116) and SHELTERING ROOF (117); and you know exactly where the roof is flat to form roof gardens next to rooms at different floors—ROOF GARDEN (118). This pattern shows you how to get a detailed roof plan for the building, which helps those patterns come to life, for any plan which you have drawn.

What kind of roof plan is organically related to the nature of your building?

We know, from arguments presented in THE SHAPE OF INDOOR SPACE (191), that the majority of spaces in an organic building will have roughly—not necessarily perfectly—straight walls because it is only then that the space on *both* sides of the walls can be positive, or convex in shape.

And we know, from similar arguments, that the majority of the angles in the building will be roughly—again, not exactly— right angles, that is, in the general range of 80 to 100 degrees.

We know, therefore, that the class of natural plans may contain a variety of shapes like half circles, octagons, and so on—but that for the most part, it will be made of very rough, sloppy rectangles.

We also know, from SHELTERING ROOF (117), that entire wings should be under one roof whenever possible and that the building is to be roofed with a mixture of flat roofs and sloping or domical roofs, with the accent on those which are *not* flat.

We may therefore state the problem of defining a roof layout as follows: *Given an arbitrary plan of the type described above, how can we fit to it an arrangement of roofs which conforms to the* CASCADE OF ROOFS (116) *and* SHELTERING ROOF (117) *and* ROOF GARDENS (118)?

Before explaining the procedure for laying out roofs in detail, we underline five assumptions which provide the basis for the procedure.

1. The "pitched" roofs may actually be pitched, or they may be vaults with a curved pitch, or barrel vaults—as described in ROOF VAULTS (220). The general procedure, in all three cases, is the same. (For curved vaults, define slope as height-to-width ratio.)

The "pitch" of a vaulted roof.

2. Assume that all roofs in the building, which are not flat, have roughly the same slope. For a given climate and roof construction, one slope is usually best; and this greatly simplifies construction.

The same slope throughout.

3. Since all roofs have the same slope, the roofs which cover the widest wings and/or rooms will have the highest peaks; those covering smaller wings and rooms will be relatively lower. This is consistent with MAIN BUILDING (99), CASCADE OF ROOFS (116), and CEILING HEIGHT VARIETY (190).

Wide roofs are highest.

4. Any place where the building helps to enclose an outdoor room or courtyard needs an even eave line so that it has the space of a "room." An irregular roof line, with gable ends, will usually destroy the space of a small courtyard. It is necessary, therefore, that roofs be hipped in these positions to make the roof edge horizontal.

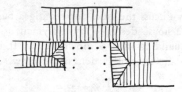

Low roof edge round a courtyard.

5. In all other positions, leave the ends of buildings and wings as gable ends.

One version of a roof layout, using ultra-lightweight concrete vaults as roofs.

We shall now discuss the rules for roofing a building by using an example of a house designed by a layman using the pattern language. This building plan is shown below. It is a single-story house and it contains no roof gardens or balconies.

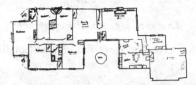

We first identify the largest rectangular cluster of rooms and roof it with a peaked roof, the ridge line of which runs the long direction:

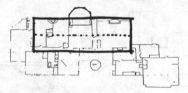

Then we do the same with smaller clusters, until all the major spaces are roofed.

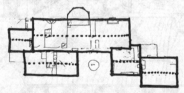

Then we roof remaining small rooms, alcoves, and thick walls with shed roofs sloping outward. These roofs should spring from the base of the main roofs to help relieve them of outward thrusts; their outside walls should be as low as possible.

Finally, we identify the outdoor spaces (shown as A, B, and C), and hip the roofs around them to preserve a more continuous eave line around the spaces.

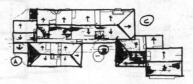

We shall now discuss a slightly more complicated example, a two story building.

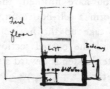

We begin with the top story, roofing the entire master bedroom and bath under one peaked roof with the ridge running lengthwise:

Next we move to the lower story, roofing the children's wing under a flat roof to form a ROOF GARDEN (118) for the master bedroom, and the larger living room under a pitched roof, again with the ridge running lengthwise.

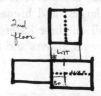

Then we bring the roof over the master bedroom down over the interior loft.

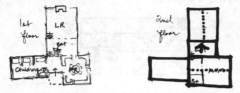

Finally, we smooth the living room roof ridge line into the side of the roof over the loft. This completes the roof layout.

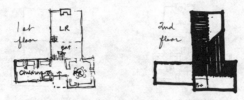

It is very helpful, when you are laying out roofs, to remember the structural principle outlined in CASCADE OF ROOFS (116). When you have finished, the overall arrangement of the roofs should form a self-buttressing cascade in which each lower roof helps to take up the horizonal thrust generated by the higher roofs—and the overall section of the roofs, taken in very very general terms, tends toward a rough upside down catenary.

Therefore:

Arrange the roofs so that each distinct roof corresponds to an identifiable social entity in the building or building complex. Place the largest roofs—those which are highest and have the largest span—over the largest and most important and most communal spaces; build the lesser roofs off these largest and highest roofs; and build the smallest roofs of all off these lesser roofs, in the form of half-vaults and sheds over alcoves and thick walls.

major roofs

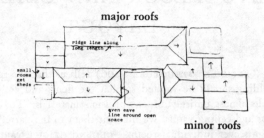

minor roofs

❖ ❖ ❖

You can build all these roofs, and the connections between them, by following the instructions for roof vaults—ROOF VAULTS (220). When a wing ends in the open, leave the gable end at full height; when a wing ends in a courtyard, hip the gable, so that the horizontal roof edge makes the courtyard like a room— COURTYARDS WHICH LIVE (115).

Treat the smallest shed roofs, which cover thick walls and alcoves, as buttresses, and build them to help take the horizontal thrust from floor vaults and higher roof vaults—THICKENING THE OUTER WALLS (211). . . .

2 1 0 FLOOR AND CEILING LAYOUT

. . . EFFICIENT STRUCTURE (206) tells us that the spaces in the building should be vaulted so that the floors and ceilings can be made almost entirely of compression materials. To lay out the floor and ceiling vaults, we must fit them to the variety of ceiling heights over individual rooms—CEILING HEIGHT VARIETY (190) and, on the top story, to the layout of the roof vaults—ROOF LAYOUT (209).

❖ ❖ ❖

Again, the basic problem is to maintain the integrity of the social spaces in the plan.

We know, from STRUCTURE FOLLOWS SOCIAL SPACES (205), that floor and ceiling vaults must correspond to the important social spaces in the plan. But there are a great number of social spaces, and they range in size from spaces like WINDOW PLACE (180), perhaps five feet across, to spaces like FARMHOUSE KITCHEN (139), perhaps 15 feet across, to collections of spaces, like COMMON AREAS AT THE HEART (129), perhaps 35 feet across.

Where vaults of different width are near each other, you must remember to pay attention to the level of the floor above. Either you can level out the floor by making the smaller vaults have proportionately higher arches, or you can put extra material in between to keep the small vaults low—see CEILING HEIGHT VARIETY (190), or you can make steps in the floor above to correspond to changes in the vault sizes below.

Vaults on different floors do not have to line up perfectly with one another. In this sense they are far more flexible than column-beam structures, and for this reason also better adapted to STRUCTURE FOLLOWS SOCIAL SPACES (205). However, there are limits. If one vault is placed so that its loads come down over

978

the arch of the vault below, this will put undue stress on the lower vault. Instead, we make use of the fact that vertical forces, passing through a continuous compressive medium, spread out downward in a 45 degree angle cone. If the lower columns are always within this cone, the upper vault will do no structural damage to the vault below it.

The angle at which a vertical force spreads downward.

To maintain reasonable structural integrity in the system of vaults as a whole, we therefore suggest that every vault be placed so that its loads come down in a position from which the forces can go to the columns which support the next vault down, by following a 45 degree diagonal.

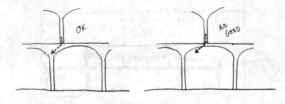

Good . . .   . . . no good.

With all this in mind then, work out a vault plan for your building. We suggest that you try to keep the vaults aligned with the rooms, with occasional adjustments to suit a very big room, or a very small nook or alcove. The drawing on the next page shows a floor and ceiling layout for a simple building.

Each space that you single out for a vault may have either a two-way vault (a domical ceiling on a rectangular base) or a one-way vault (a barrel vault). The two-way vaults are the most efficient structurally; but when a space is long and narrow, the domical shape begins to act like a barrel vault. We therefore

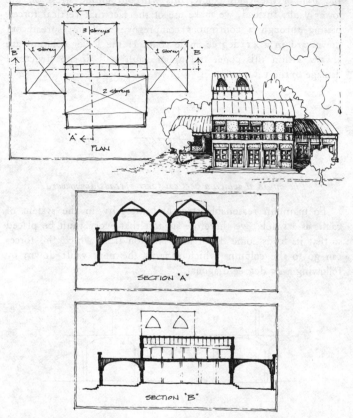

*A version of floor-ceiling layout, shown in plan and
section, for a simple ultra-lightweight concrete building.*

suggest domical vaults for spaces where the long side is not more
than twice the short side and barrel vaults for the spaces which
are narrower.

We also suggest that you use barrel vaults for the rooms immediately under the roof. The roof itself is generally a barrel vault—
see ROOF VAULT (220)—so it is most natural to give the ceiling
of the space just under the roof a barrel vault as well.

The vaults described in FLOOR-CEILING VAULTS (219) may

span from 5 to 30 feet. And they require a rise of at least 13 per cent of the short span.

Therefore:

Draw a vault plan, for every floor. Use two-way vaults most often; and one-way barrel vaults for any spaces which are more than twice as long as they are wide. Draw sections through the building as you plan the vaults, and bear the following facts in mind:

1. Generally speaking, the vaults should correspond to rooms.

2. There will have to be a support under the sides of each vault: this will usually be the top of a wall. Under exceptional circumstances, it can be a beam or arch.

3. A vault may span as little as 5 feet and as much as 30 feet. However, it must have a rise equal to at least 13 per cent of its shorter span.

4. If the edge of one vault is more than a couple of feet (in plan) from the edge of the vault below it—then the lower vault will have to contain an arch to support the load from the upper vault.

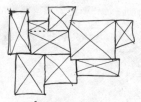

vaults over rooms

upper vaults/lower vaults reconciled

Put a PERIMETER BEAM (217) on all four sides of every vault, along the top of the bearing wall, or spanning openings. Get the shape of the vaults from FLOOR-CEILING VAULTS (219) and as you lay out the sections through the vaults, bear in mind that the perimeter beams get lower and lower on higher floors, because the

columns on upper stories must be shorter (top floor columns about
4 feet, one below top 6 feet, two below top 6 to 7 feet, three below top 8 feet)—FINAL COLUMN DISTRIBUTION (213). Make sure
that variations in floor level coincide with the distinctions between quiet and more public areas—FLOOR SURFACE (233).
Complete the definition of the individual spaces which the vaults
create with COLUMNS AT THE CORNERS (212). Include the
smallest vaults of all, around the building edge, in THICKENING
THE OUTER WALLS (211). . . .

211 THICKENING THE
OUTER WALLS*

. . . the arrangement of roof and floor vaults will generate horizontal outward thrust, which needs to be buttressed—CASCADE OF ROOFS (116). It also happens, that in a sensibly made building every floor is surrounded, at various places, by small alcoves, window seats, niches, and counters which form "thick walls" around the outside edge of rooms—WINDOW PLACE (180), THICK WALLS (197), SUNNY COUNTER (199), BUILT-IN SEATS (202), CHILD CAVES (203), SECRET PLACE (204). The beauty of a natural building is that these thick walls—since they need lower ceilings, always, than the rooms they come from—can work as buttresses.

Once the ROOF LAYOUT (209), and the FLOOR AND CEILING LAYOUT (210) are clear these thick walls can be laid out in such a way as to form the most effective butresses, against the horizontal thrust developed by the vaults.

We have established in THICK WALLS (197), how important it is for the walls of a building to have "depth" and "volume," so that character accumulates in them, with time. But when it comes to laying out a building and constructing it, this turns out to be quite hard to do.

The walls will not usually be thick in the literal sense, except in certain special cases where mud construction, for example, lends itself to the making of walls. More often, the thickness of the wall has to be built up from foam, plaster, columns, struts, and membranes. In this case columns, above all, play the major role, because they do the most to encourage people to develop the walls. For instance, if the framework of a wall is made of columns standing away from the back face of the wall, then the wall invites modification—it becomes natural and easy to nail planks to the columns, and so make seats, and shelves, and changes there. But a pure, flat, blank wall does not give this kind of encouragement. Even though, theoretically, a person can always add things which stick out from the wall, the very smoothness of the

wall makes it much less likely to happen. Let us assume then, that a thick wall becomes effective when it is a volume defined by columns.

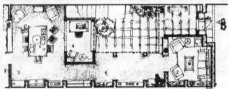

Thick walls made effective by columns.

How is it possible for a wall of this kind to justify its expense by helping the structure of the building? The fact that the building is conceived as a compressive structure, whose floors and roofs are vaults—EFFICIENT STRUCTURE (206), means that there are horizontal thrusts developed on the outside of the building, where the vaults do not counterbalance one another.

To some extent this horizontal thrust can be avoided by arranging the overall shape of the building as an upside down catenary—see CASCADE OF ROOFS (116). If it were a perfect catenary, there would be no outward thrust at all. Obviously, though, most buildings are narrower and steeper than the ideal structural catenary, so there are horizontal thrusts remaining. Although these thrusts can be resolved by tensile reinforcing in the perimeter beams—see PERIMETER BEAMS (217)—it is simplest, and most natural, and stable to use the building itself to buttress the horizontal thrusts.

This possibility occurs naturally wherever there are "thick walls"—alcoves, window seats, or any other small spaces at the outside edge of rooms, which can have lower ceilings than the main room and can therefore have their roofs shaped as continuations of the ceiling vault inside. This requires that thick walls be outside the structure of the main room, so that their roofs and walls come close to forming a catenary with the main vault.

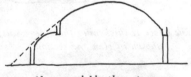

Alcoves within the catenary.

It is of course rare to be able to have the alcove or thick walls approach a true catenary section—we hardly ever want them that deep or that low. But even when the thick walls and alcoves are inside the line of the catenary, they are still helping to counter outward thrusts. And their buttressing effect can be improved still more by making their roofs heavy. The extra weight will tend to redirect the forces coming from the main vault slightly more toward the ground.

The drawing below shows the way this pattern works, and the kind of effect it has on a building.

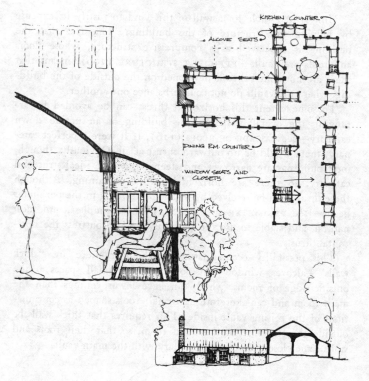

*The effect of thickening the outer walls,
shown in plan and section.*

986

Therefore:

Mark all those places in the plan where seats and closets are to be. These places are given individually by ALCOVES (179), WINDOW PLACES (180), THICK WALLS (197), SUNNY COUNTER (199), WAIST-HIGH SHELF (201), BUILT-IN SEATS (202), and so on. Lay out a wide swath on the plan to correspond to these positions. Make it two or three feet deep; recognize that it will be outside the main space of the room; your seats, niches, shelves, will feel attached to the main space of rooms but not inside them. Then, when you lay out columns and minor columns, place the columns in such a way that they surround and define these thick volumes of wall, as if they were rooms or alcoves.

For shelves and counters less than 2 feet deep, there is no need to go to these lengths. The thickening can be built simply by deepening columns and placing shelves between them.

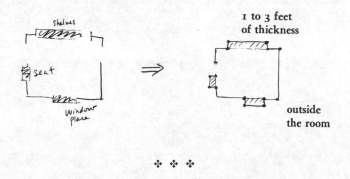

❖ ❖ ❖

In order to make an alcove or thick wall work as a buttress, build its roof as near as possible to a continuation of the curve of the floor vault immediately inside. Load the roof of the buttress with extra mass to help change the direction of the forces—ROOF VAULTS (220). Recognize that these thick walls must be *outside*

the main space of the room, below the main vault of the room—FLOOR-CEILING VAULTS (219), so that they help to buttress the horizontal forces generated by the main vault of the ceiling. When you lay out columns and minor colunms, put a column at the corner of every thick wall, so that the wall space, like other social spaces, becomes a recognizable part of the building structure—COLUMNS AT THE CORNERS (212). . . .

212 COLUMNS AT THE
CORNERS**

. . . assume that you have worked out the roof plan, and laid out ceiling vaults for every room on every floor—ROOF LAYOUT (209), FLOOR AND CEILING LAYOUT (210). These vaults are not only the basis of the structure, but also define the social spaces underneath them. Now it is time to put columns at the corners of the vaults. This will both complete them as clearly defined social spaces—STRUCTURE FOLLOWS SOCIAL SPACES (205)—and also be the first constructive step in the erection of the building —GRADUAL STIFFENING (208).

❖ ❖ ❖

We have already established the idea that the structural components of a building should be congruent with its social spaces.

In STRUCTURE FOLLOWS SOCIAL SPACES (205) we have established that the columns need to be at corners of social spaces for psychological reasons. In EFFICIENT STRUCTURE (206) we have established that there needs to be a thickening of material at the corners of a space for purely structural reasons.

Now we give yet a third still different derivation of the same pattern—not based on psychological arguments or structural arguments, but on the process by which a person can communicate a complex design to the builder, and ensure that it can be built in an organic manner.

We begin with the problem of measurement and working drawings. For the last few decades it has been common practice to specify a building plan by means of working drawings. These measured drawings are then taken to the site; the builder transfers the measurements to the site, and every detail of the drawings is built in the flesh, on site.

This process cripples buildings. It is not possible to make such a drawing without a T-square. The necessities of the drawing itself change the plan, make it more rigid, turn it into the kind of plan which can be drawn and can be measured.

But the kind of plans which you can make by using the pattern

language are much freer than that—and not so easy to draw and measure. Whether you conceive these plans out on the site—and mark them on the site with sticks and stones and chalk marks—or draw them roughly on the back of envelopes or scraps of tracing paper—in all events, the richness which you want to build into the plan can only be preserved if the builder is able to generate a living building, with all its slightly uneven lines and imperfect angles.

Chalk marks on the ground.

In order to achieve this aim, the building must be generated in an entirely different manner. It cannot be made by following a working drawing slavishly. What must be done, essentially, is to fix those points which generate the spaces—*as few of them as possible*—and then let these points generate the walls, right out on the building site, during the very process of construction.

You may proceed like this: first fix the corner of every major space by putting a stake in the ground. There are no more than a few dozen of these corners in a building, so this is possible, even if the measurements are intricate and irregular. Place these corner markers where they seem right, without regard for the

exact distances between them. There is no reason whatever to try and make modular distances between them. If angles are slightly off, as they often will be, the modular dimensions are impossible anyway.

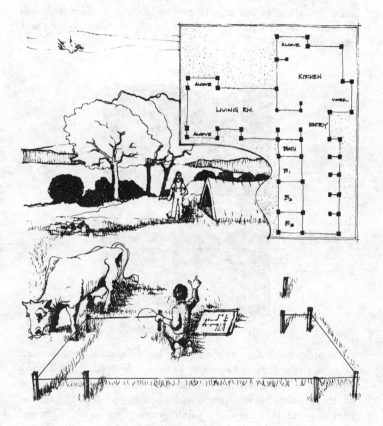

"Staking out"

These simple marks are all you need to build the building. Once construction starts, you can start very simply, by building a column, over each of these marks. These columns will then generate the rest of the building, by their mere presence, without

any further need for detailed measurements or drawings, because the walls will simply be built along the lines which connect adjacent columns: and everything else follows.

For the upper storys, you can make drawings of the column positions and once again transfer them to the actual building while it is being built. As you will see from FINAL COLUMN DISTRIBUTION (213), upper story columns do not need to line up perfectly with downstairs columns.

With this procedure, it becomes possible to transfer a rather complex building from your mind, or from a scrap of paper, to the site—and regenerate it in a way which makes it live out there.

The method hinges on the fact that you can fix the corners of the spaces first—and that these corners may then play a significant role in the construction of the building. It is interesting that although it is based on entirely different arguments from STRUCTURE FOLLOWS SOCIAL SPACES (205), it leads to almost exactly the same conclusion.

Therefore:

On your rough building plan, draw a dot to represent a column at the corner of every room and in the corners formed by lesser spaces like thick walls and alcoves. Then transfer these dots onto the ground out on the site with stakes.

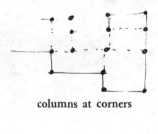

columns at corners

❖ ❖ ❖

Once you have the columns for each floor on your vault plan, reconcile them from floor to floor and put in intermediate col-

umns—FINAL COLUMN DISTRIBUTION (213). Note, especially, that it is not necessary for the corner columns to fall on a grid. The floor vaults and roof vaults can be made to fit any arrangement of columns, and still make a coherent structure—thus allowing the social spaces to determine the building shape without undue constraint from purely structural considerations—FLOOR-CEILING VAULTS (219), ROOF VAULTS (220).

These columns will not only guide your mental image of the building, they will also guide construction: first put the columns and the column foundations in place; then, to make the frame complete, tie the columns together around each room with the perimeter beam—ROOT FOUNDATIONS (214), BOX COLUMNS (216), PERIMETER BEAMS (217). Give special emphasis to all free-standing columns with the idea that when you build them, you will make them very thick—COLUMN PLACE (226). . . .

213 FINAL COLUMN DISTRIBUTION**

. . . assume that you have placed the corner columns which define the spaces—COLUMNS AT THE CORNERS (212). It is now necessary to fill in the gaps between the columns with intermediate stiffener columns as required by EFFICIENT STRUCTURE (206). This pattern gives the spacing of these intermediate stiffener columns, and helps to generate the kind of walls which EFFI-CIENT STRUCTURE (206) requires. It also helps to generate CEILING HEIGHT VARIETY (190).

How should the spacing of the secondary columns which stiffen the walls, vary with ceiling height, number of stories and the size of rooms?

In some very gross intuitive way we know the answer to this question. Roughly, if we imagine a building with the walls stiffened at intervals along their length, we can see that the texture of these stiffeners needs to be largest near the ground, where social spaces are largest and where loads are largest, and smallest near the roof, where rooms are smallest and where loads are least. In its gross intuitive form this is the same as the intuition which tells us to expect the finest texture in the ribbing at the fine end of a leaf where everything is smallest, and to expect the grosser, cruder structure to be near the large part of the leaf.

Leaf.

These intuitions are borne out by many traditional building forms where columns, or frames, or stiffeners are larger and further apart near the ground, and finer and closer together higher up. Our key picture shows examples. But what is the structural basis for these intuitions?

Elastic plate theory gives us a formal explanation.

Consider an unstiffened thin wall carrying an axial load. This wall will usually fail in buckling before it fails in pure compression because it is thin. And this means that the material in the wall is not being used efficiently. It is not able to carry the compressive loads which its compressive strength makes possible because it is too thin.

It is therefore natural to design a wall which is either thick enough or stiffened enough so that it can carry loads up to its full compressive capacity without buckling. Such a wall, which uses its material to the limits of its compressive capacity, will then also satisfy the demands of EFFICIENT STRUCTURE (206).

The critical factor is the slenderness of the wall: the ratio of its height to its thickness. For the simple case of an unstiffened concrete wall, the ACI code tells us that the wall will be able to work at 93 per cent efficiency (that is, carry 93 per cent of its potential compressive load without buckling), if it has a slenderness ratio of 10 or less. A wall 10 feet high and 1 foot thick is therefore efficient in this sense.

Suppose now, that we extrapolate to the case of a stiffened wall using elastic plate theory. By using the equation which relates allowable stress to the spacing of stiffeners, we can obtain similar figures for various walls with stiffeners. These figures are presented in the curve below. For example, a wall with a slenderness of 20 needs stiffeners at 0.5H apart (where H is the height) thus creating panels half as wide as they are high. In general, obviously, the thinner the wall is, in relation to its height, the more often it needs to be stiffened along its length.

In every case, the curve gives the spacing of stiffeners which is needed to make the wall work at 93 per cent of its compressive strength. In short, we may say that a wall built according to the principle of EFFICIENT STRUCTURE (206) ought to be stiffened in accordance with this curve.

The gradient of column spacing over different floors follows

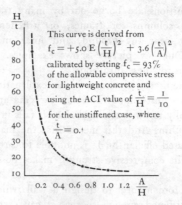

The curve which relates wall slenderness
to the spacing of stiffeners.

directly from this curve. We may see this in the following manner. The walls in a four story building carry loads which are very roughly in the ratio 4:3:2:1 (only very roughly). In any case, the loads the walls carry get less and less the higher we go in the building. If all the walls are reaching their full compressive capacity, this means that they must be getting steadily thinner too, the higher one goes in the building. If we assume that the walls all have the same height, then the four walls will therefore have progressively greater and greater slenderness ratios, and *will therefore fall further and further to the left on the curve, and will therefore need to be stiffened at closer and closer intervals.*

For example, suppose a four story building has 8 foot high walls on all floors and has wall thicknesses of 12 inches, 9 inches, 6 inches, and 3 inches on its four floors. The slenderness ratios are 8, 11, 17, and 33. In this case, reading off the curve, we find the ground floor has no stiffeners at all (they are infinitely far apart), the second floor has stiffeners at about 8 feet apart, the third floor has them about 5 feet apart, and the top floor has them about 2 feet apart.

In another case, where the walls are thinner (because materials are lighter and loads smaller), the spacing will be closer. Suppose, for example, that the necessary wall thicknesses are 8, 6, 4, and

998

2 inches. Then the slenderness ratios are 12, 16, 24, and 48, and the stiffeners need to be spaced closer together than before: nine feet apart on the ground story, 5 feet apart on the second story, 3 feet apart on the third, and 15 inches apart on the top.

As you can see from these examples, the variation in column spacing is surprisingly great; greater, in fact, than intuition would allow. But the variation is so extreme because we have assumed that ceiling heights are the same on every floor. In fact, in a correctly designed building, the ceiling height will vary from floor to floor; and under these circumstances, as we shall see, the variation in column spacing becomes more reasonable. There are two reasons why the ceiling height needs to vary from floor to floor, one social and one structural.

In most buildings, the spaces and rooms on the first floor will tend to be larger—since communal rooms, meeting rooms, and so on, are generally better located near the entrance to buildings, while private and smaller rooms will be on upper stories, deeper into the building. Since the ceiling heights vary with the size of social spaces—see CEILING HEIGHT VARIETY (190)—this means that the ceiling heights are higher on the ground floor, getting lower as one goes up. And the roof floor has either very short walls or no wall at all—see SHELTERING ROOF (117).

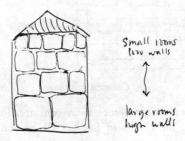

Variation of room sizes.

And there is a second, purely structural explanation of the fact that ceilings need to be lower on upper stories. It is embodied in the drawing of the granary shown below. Suppose that a system of columns is calculated for pure structure. The columns on upper stories will be thinner, because they carry less load than

those on lower stories. But because they are thinner, they have
less capacity to resist buckling, and must therefore be shorter if
we are to avoid wasting material. As a result, even in a granary,
where there are no social reasons for variation in ceiling height,
purely structural considerations create the necessity for thick columns and high ceilings on the lower stories and for thinner and
thinner columns and lower and lower ceilings the higher one gets
in the building.

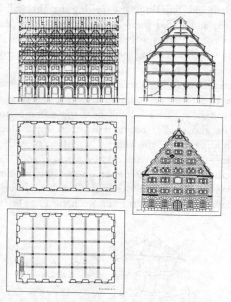

German granary.

The same conclusion comes from consideration of our curve.
We have used the curve, so far, to tell us that stiffeners need
to be closer together on upper stories, because the walls are more
slender. We may also use the curve to tell us that, for a given
load, we should try to keep the slenderness ratio as low as possible.
On the upper stories, where walls are most apt to be thin, we
should therefore make the walls as low as possible, in order to
keep the slenderness ratios low.

Let us assume now, that the wall heights do vary in a building, in a manner consistent with these arguments. A four story building, with an attic story on top, might then have these wall heights (remember that the vault height, in a vaulted room, is higher than the wall height): 9 feet on the ground floor, 7 feet on the second, 6 feet on the third, and 4 feet on the fourth, where the pitched roof comes down low over the eaves. And let us assume that the wall thicknesses are 12 inches, 6 inches, 5 inches, and 3 inches, respectively. In this case, the slenderness ratios will be 9, 14, 14, 15. The ground floor needs no stiffeners at all; the second has them 6 feet apart; the third has them 5 feet apart; and the fourth has them 3 feet apart. We show a similar distribution in the drawing opposite.

When you try to apply this pattern to floor plan, you will find a certain type of difficulty. Since the corners of rooms may already be fixed by COLUMNS AT THE CORNERS (212), it is not always possible to space the stiffeners correctly within the wall of any given room. Naturally this does not matter a great deal; the stiffeners only need to be *about* right; the spacing can comfortably vary from room to room to fit the dimensions of the walls. However, on the whole, you must try and put the stiffeners closer together where the rooms are small and further apart where rooms are large. If you do not, the building will seem odd, because it defies one's structural intuitions.

Consider two rooms on the same floor, one twice as large as the other. The larger room has twice the perimeter, but its ceiling generates four times the load; it therefore carries a greater load per unit length of wall. In an ideal efficient structure, this means that the wall must be thicker; and therefore, by the arguments already given, it will need stiffeners spaced further apart than the smaller room which carries less load and has thinner walls.

We recognize that few builders will take the trouble to make wall thicknesses vary from room to room on one floor of the building. However, even if the wall is uniformly thick, we believe that the stiffeners must at least not contradict this rule. If, for reasons of layout, it is necessary that the spacing of stiffeners varies from room to room, then it is essential that the larger spacings of the stiffeners fall on those walls which enclose the

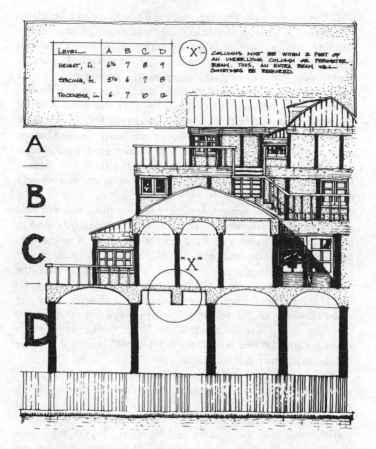

LEVEL	A	B	C	D
HEIGHT, ft.	6½	7	8	9
SPACING, ft.	5½	6	7	8
THICKNESS, in	6	7	10	12

"X" COLUMNS MUST BE WITHIN 2 FEET OF AN UNDERLYING COLUMN OR PERIMETER BEAM. THUS, AN EXTRA BEAM WILL SOMETIMES BE REQUIRED.

*The final column distribution in a four story building,
built according to our patterns for columns,
walls and vaults.*

larger rooms. If the greater spacing of stiffeners were to coincide with smaller rooms, the eye would be so deceived that people might misunderstand the building.

One important note. All of the preceding analysis is based on the assumption that walls and stiffeners are behaving as elastic plates. This is roughly true, and helps to explain the general

phenomenon we are trying to describe. However, no wall behaves perfectly as an elastic plate—least of all the kind of lightweight concrete walls we are advocating in the rest of the construction patterns. We have therefore used a modified form of the elastic plate theory, calibrated according to the ACI code, so that the numbers in our analysis are based on the elastic behavior of concrete (and fall within the limits of its tension and compression). However, when the plate goes out of the elastic range and cracks, as it almost certainly will in a concrete design, other factors will enter in. We therefore caution the reader most strongly not to take the actual numbers presented in our analysis as more than illustrations. The numbers reflect the general mathematical behavior of such a system, but they are not reliable enough to use in structural computations.

Therefore:

Make column stiffeners furthest apart on the ground floor and closer and closer together as you go higher in the building. The exact column spacings for a particular building will depend on heights and loads and wall thicknesses. The numbers in the following table are for illustration only, but they show roughly what is needed.

building height in stories	ground floor	2nd floor	3rd floor	4th floor
1	2'-5'			
2	3'-6'	1'-3'		
3	4'-8'	3'-6'	1'-3'	
4	5'-∞'	4'-8'	3'-6'	1'-3'

Mark in these extra stiffening columns as dots between the corner columns on the drawings you have made for different floors. Adjust them so they are evenly spaced between each pair of corner columns; but on any one floor, make sure that they are closer together along the walls of small rooms and further apart along the walls of large rooms.

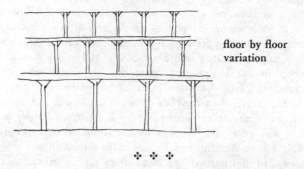

floor by floor
variation

❖ ❖ ❖

To the extent consistent with CEILING HEIGHT VARIETY (190),
make walls and columns progressively shorter the higher you go
in the building to keep slenderness ratios low.

And make wall thicknesses and column thicknesses vary with
the height—see WALL MEMBRANE (218). Our calculations, for a
typical lightweight concrete building of the kind we have been
discussing, suggest the following orders of magnitude for wall
thicknesses: Top story—2 inches thick; one below top story—3
inches; two below top story—4 inches; three storys below top
(ground floor on a four story building)—5 inches. Of course
these numbers will change for different loads, or for different
materials, but they show the type of variation you can expect.

Column thicknesses must be proportional to wall thicknesses,
so that the thinnest walls have the thinnest columns. If they are
very thin, it will be possible to make them simply by placing
boards, or one thickness of material, outside the outer skins which
form the wall membrane—see WALL MEMBRANE (218). If the
walls are thick, they will need to be full columns, twice as
thick as the walls, and roughly square in section, built before the
walls, but made in such a way that they can be poured integrally
with the walls—BOX COLUMNS (216). . . .

put stakes in the ground to mark the columns on the
site, and start erecting the main frame according to
the layout of these stakes;

214 ROOT FOUNDATIONS

. . . once you have a rough column plan for the building—COLUMNS AT THE CORNERS (212), FINAL COLUMN DISTRIBUTION (213)—you are ready to start the site work itself. First, stake out the positions of the ground floor columns, before you do any other earthwork, so that you can move the columns whenever necessary to leave rocks or plants intact—SITE REPAIR (104), CONNECTION TO THE EARTH (168). Then dig the foundation pits and prepare to make the foundations.

The best foundations of all are the kinds of foundations which a tree has—where the entire structure of the tree simply continues below ground level, and creates a system entirely integral with the ground, in tension and compression.

When the column and the foundations are separate elements which have to be connected, the connection becomes a difficult and critical joint. Both bending and shear stresses are extremely high just at the joint. If a connector is introduced as a third element, there are even more joints to worry about, and each member works less effectively to resist these stresses.

We suspect that it would be better to build the foundations and the columns in such a way that the columns get rooted in the foundation and become integral and continuous with the ground.

In the realization of this pattern which we illustrate, the root foundation takes a very simple form. Since columns start out hollow, BOX COLUMNS (216), we can form a root foundation by setting the hollow column into the foundation pit, and then pouring the lower part of the column and the foundation, integrally, in a single pour.

As far as the wood version is concerned, the problem of placing

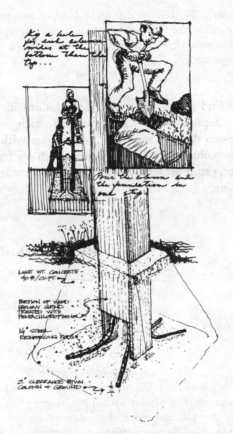

*One version of a root foundation for a hollow wooden box
column which we have built.*

wood in contact with wet underground concrete is very serious.
The wood of the column can be protected from dry rot and ter-
mites by pressure dipping in pentachlorophenol. We also believe
that painting with thick asphalt or dampproof mastic might work;
but the problem isn't really solved. Of course, masonry versions
in which columns are made of terracotta pipe or concrete pipe
and filled with dense concrete, ought to work alright. But even
in these cases, we are doubtful about the exact structural validity

of the pattern. We believe that some kind of structure which is continuous with the ground is needed: but we quite haven't been able to work it out. Meanwhile, we state this pattern as a kind of challenge.

Namely:

Try to find a way of making foundations in which the columns themselves go right into the earth, and spread out there—so that the footing is continuous with the material of the column, and the column, with its footing, like a tree root, can resist tension and horizontal shear as well as compression.

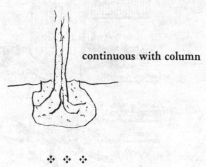

continuous with column

❖ ❖ ❖

To make foundations like this for hollow concrete, filled box columns, start with a pit for each foundation, place the hollow column in the pit, and pour the column and the foundation integrally, in one continuous pour—BOX COLUMNS (216). Later, when you build the ground floor slab, tie the concrete into the foundations—GROUND FLOOR SLAB (215).

215 GROUND FLOOR SLAB

. . . this pattern helps to complete CONNECTION TO THE EARTH (168), EFFICIENT STRUCTURE (206), COLUMNS AT THE CORNERS (212), and ROOT FOUNDATIONS (214). It is a simple slab, which forms the ground floor of the building, ties the root foundations to one another, and also allows you to form simple strip foundations as part of the slab, to support the walls.

❖ ❖ ❖

The slab is the easiest, cheapest, and most natural way to lay a ground floor.

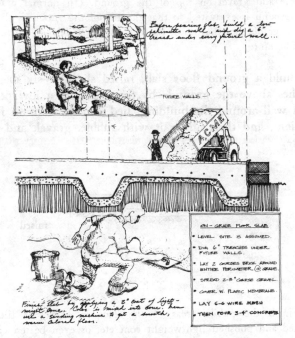

A raised ground floor slab built inside a brick perimeter wall.

When the ground is relatively level, a concrete slab which sits directly on the ground is the most natural and cheapest way of building a ground floor. Wood floors are expensive, need air space underneath them, and need to be built up on continuous foundation walls or beams. Prefabricated floor panels also need a structure of some sort to support them. A slab floor, on the other hand, uses the earth for support, and can supply the foundations which are needed to support walls, by simple thickening.

The one trouble with slabs is that they can easily feel cold and damp. We believe that this feeling is at least as much a psychological one as a physical one (given a well-made and insulated slab), and that the feeling is most pronounced with slabs that are on grade. We therefore propose that the slab be raised from the ground. This can be done by not excavating the ground at all, instead only leveling it, and placing the usual bed of rubble and gravel on top of the ground. (In normal practice, the ground is excavated so that the top of the rubble is slightly below grade, and the top of the slab only *just* above the ground.)

Therefore:

Build a ground floor slab, raised slightly—six or nine inches above the ground—by first building a low perimeter wall around the building, tied into the column foundations, and then filling it with rubble, gravel, and concrete.

❖ ❖ ❖

Finish the public areas of the floor in brick, or tile, or waxed and polished lightweight concrete, or even beaten earth; as for those areas which will be more private, build them one

step up or one step down, with a lightweight concrete finish that can be felted and carpeted—FLOOR SURFACE (233).

Build the low wall which forms the edge of the ground floor slab out of brick, and tie it directly into all the terraces and paths around the building—CONNECTION TO THE EARTH (168), SOFT TILE AND BRICK (248). If you are building on a steep sloped site, build part of the ground floor as a vaulted floor instead of excavating to form a slab—FLOOR-CEILING VAULTS (219). . . .

216 BOX COLUMNS**

. . . if you use ROOT FOUNDATIONS (214), the columns must be made at the same time as the foundations, since the foundation and the column are integral. The height, spacing, and thickness of the various columns in the building are given by FINAL COLUMN DISTRIBUTION (213). This pattern describes the details of construction for the individual columns.

❖ ❖ ❖

In all the world's traditional and historic buildings, the columns are expressive, beautiful, and treasured elements. Only in modern buildings have they become ugly and meaningless.

The fact is that no one any longer knows how to make a column which is at the same time beautiful and structurally efficient. We discuss the problem under seven separate headings:

1. Columns feel uncomfortable unless they are reasonably thick and solid. This feeling is rooted in structural reality. A long thin column, carrying a heavy load, is likely to fail by buckling: and our feelings, apparently, are particularly tuned in to this possibility.

We do not wish to exaggerate the need for thickness. Taken too far, it could easily become a mannerism of a rather ridiculous sort. But columns do need to be comfortable and solid, and only thin when they are short enough to be in no danger of buckling. When the column is a free-standing one, then the need for thickness becomes essential. This is fully discussed under COLUMN PLACE (226).

2. Structural arguments lead to exactly the same conclusion. Thin, high strength materials, like steel tubes and prestressed concrete, are ruled out by GOOD MATERIALS (207). Lower strength materials which are ecologically sound have to be relatively fat to cope with the loads.

3. The column must be cheap. An 8 by 8 solid wood column is too expensive; thick brick or stone columns are almost out of the question in today's market.

4. It must be warm to the touch. Concrete columns and painted steel columns have an unpleasant surface and are not very easy to face.

5. If the column takes bending, the highest strength materials should be concentrated toward the outside. Buckling and bending strength both depend on the moment of inertia, which is highest when the material is as far as possible from the neutral axis. A stalk of grass is the archetypal example.

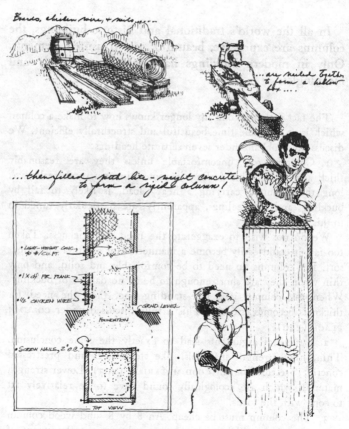

A version of box columns made of 1 inch wood planks, nailed together with spiral groove nails, and filled with chicken wire and ultra-lightweight concrete.

6. The column must be easy to connect to foundations, beams, and walls. Precast concrete columns are very hard to connect. So are metal columns. Brick columns are easy to connect to brick walls—not to the lighter weight skin structures required by WALL MEMBRANE (218).

7. The column must be hand nailable, and hand cuttable to make on-site modification and later repair as easy as possible. Again, current materials do not easily meet this requirement.

A column which has all these features is a box column, where the hollow tube can be made as thick as is required, and then filled with a strong compressive material. Such a column can be made cheaper than comparable wood and steel columns; the outer skin can be made with a material that is beautiful, easy to repair, and soft to the touch; the column can be stiffened for bending, either by the skin itself, or by extra reinforcing; and, for structural integrity, the fill material can be made continuous with the column's footings and beams.

An example of a box column which we have built and tested is a wooden box column, made with 1 inch wooden planks and filled with lightweight concrete the same density as wood, so that it has the overall volume and mass of a heavy 8 inch solid column. The drawing opposite shows these wooden box columns being made.

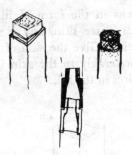

Possible box columns

Box columns can be made in many other ways. One kind is made by stacking 8 by 8 inch lightweight concrete blocks, and filling the cavity with a concrete of the same density. Some wire reinforcing inside the column is required to give the column tensile strength. A hollow brick column, filled with earth is

another possibility. Concrete, vinyl, and terracotta sewer pipe filled with lightweight concrete and reinforced with mesh; a resin-impregnated cardboard tube filled with earth; or two concentric cardboard tubes with the outer ring filled with concrete and the inner ring filled with earth; still another is made from a tube of chicken wire wesh, filled with rubble, plastered and whitewashed on the outside. And still another can be made with self-aligning hollow tiles for the skin. The tiles can be molded by hand with a hand press—in concrete or tile; the soft tile will make beautiful rose red, soft warm columns.

Box columns made from concrete sewer pipe,
filled with concrete.

Therefore:

Make the columns in the form of filled hollow tubes, with a stiff tubular outer skin, and a solid core that is strong in compression. Give the skin of the column some tensile strength—preferably in the skin itself, but perhaps with reinforcing wires in the fill.

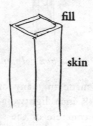

As you already know, it is best to build the columns integral with ROOT FOUNDATIONS (214) on the ground floor, or integral with the FLOOR-CEILING VAULTS (219) on upper floors, and to fill them in one continuous pour. Once the columns are in position, put in the PERIMETER BEAMS (217), and fill the beams at the same time that you fill the upper part of the column. If the column is free standing, put in column braces or column capitals—COLUMN CONNECTION (227)—to brace the connection between the two. And make the columns especially thick, or build them in pairs, where they are free-standing, so that they form a COLUMN PLACE (226). . . .

217 PERIMETER BEAMS*

. . . this pattern helps to complete BOX COLUMNS (216), by tying the tops of the columns together once they are in position. It also helps to form the bearing surface for the edge of the FLOOR-CEILING VAULTS (219). For this reason, the positions of the perimeter beams must correspond exactly to the edges of the vaults laid out in FLOOR AND CEILING LAYOUT (210).

❖ ❖ ❖

If you conceive and build a room by first placing columns at the corners, and then gradually weaving the walls and ceiling round them, the room needs a perimeter beam around its upper edge.

It is the beam, connecting the columns which creates a volume you can visualize, before it is complete; and when the columns are standing in the ground, you need the actual physical perimeter beam, to generate this volume before your eyes, to let you see the room as you are building it, and to tie the tops of the columns together, physically.

These reasons are conceptual. But of course, the conceptual simplicity and rightness of the beam around the room comes, in the end, from the more basic fact that this beam has a number of related structural functions, which make it an essential part of any room built as a natural structure. The perimeter beam has four structural functions:

1. It forms the natural thickening between the wall membrane and vault membrane, described in EFFICIENT STRUCTURE (206).

2. It resists the horizontal thrust of the ceiling vault, wherever there are no outside external buttresses to do it, and no other vaults to lean against.

3. It functions as a lintel, wherever doors and windows pierce the wall membrane.

4. It transfers loads from columns in upper storys to the columns and the wall membrane below it, and spreads these loads out to distribute them evenly between the columns and the membrane.

These functions of the perimeter beam show that the beam must be as continuous as possible with walls and columns above, the walls and columns below, and with the floor. If we follow GOOD MATERIALS (207), the beam must also be easy to make, and easy to cut to different lengths.

Available beams do not meet these requirements. Steel beams and precast or prestressed beams cannot easily be tied into the wall and floor to become continuous with these membranes. Far more important, they cannot easily be cut on site to conform to the exact dimensions of the different rooms which will occur in an organic plan.

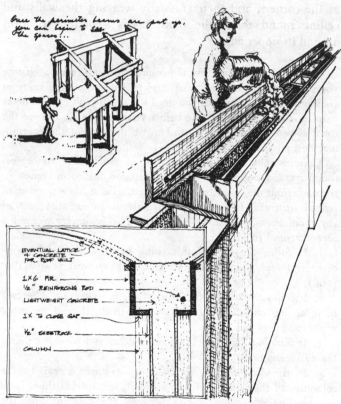

Once the perimeter beams are put up, you can begin to see the spaces...

EVENTUAL LATTICE
& CONCRETE
FOR ROOF VAULT

1×6 FIR

1/2" REINFORCING ROD

LIGHTWEIGHT CONCRETE

1× TO CLOSE GAP

1/2" SHEETROCK

COLUMN

A version of the perimeter beam consistent with the box column shown before.

Of course, wood beams meet both requirements: they are easy to cut and can be tied along their lengths to wall and floor membranes. However, as we have said in GOOD MATERIALS (207), wood is unavailable in many places, and even where it is available, it is becoming scarce and terribly expensive, especially in the large sizes needed for beams.

To avoid the use of wood, we have designed a perimeter beam—shown opposite—which is consistent with our box column, and designed to be used together with it. It is a beam made by first nailing up a channel made of wooden planks to the columns, before the wall membranes are made; then putting in reinforcing, and filling up with ultra-lightweight 60 pounds per cubic foot concrete, after the walls are made and filled. This beam is excellent for continuity. The wooden channel can first be made continuous with other skin elements by nailing, and the fill can then be made continuous by filling columns and beams and walls and vault in one continuous pour—see WALL MEMBRANES (218) and FLOOR-CEILING VAULTS (219).

Of course, there are many other ways of making a perimeter beam. First of all, there are several variants of our design: the U-shaped channel can be made of fiberboard, plywood, precast lightweight concrete, and, in every case, filled with lightweight concrete. Then there are various traditional perimeter beams— the Japanese version or the early American versions come to mind. And then there are a variety of structures which are not exactly even beams—but still act to spread vertical loads and counteract horizontal thrusts. A row of brick arches might function in this way, in a far fetched case so might a tension ring of jungle creeper.

Therefore:

Build a continuous perimeter beam around the room, strong enough to resist the horizontal thrust of the vault above, to spread the loads from upper stories onto columns, to tie the columns together, and to function as a lintel over openings in the wall. Make this beam continuous with columns, walls and floor above, and columns and walls below.

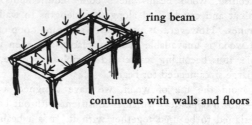

ring beam

continuous with walls and floors

❖ ❖ ❖

Remember to place reinforcing in such a way that the perimeter beam acts in a *horizontal* direction as well as vertical. When it forms the base for a FLOOR-CEILING VAULT (219) it must be able to act as a ring beam to resist all those residual horizontal outward thrusts not contained by the vault. Strengthen the connection between the columns and the perimeter beam with diagonal braces where the columns are free standing—COLUMN CONNECTION (227). . . .

218 WALL MEMBRANE*

. . . according to EFFICIENT STRUCTURE (206) and FINAL COLUMN DISTRIBUTION (213), the wall is a compressive load-bearing membrane, "stretched" between adjacent columns and continuous with them, the columns themselves placed at frequent intervals to act as stiffeners. The intervals vary from floor to floor, according to column height; and the wall thickness (membrane thickness) varies in a similar fashion. If the column stiffeners are already in place according to BOX COLUMN (216), this pattern describes the way to stretch the membrane from column to column to form the walls.

In organic construction the walls must take their share of the loads. They must work continuously with the structure on all four of their sides; and act to resist shear and bending, and take loads in compression.

When walls are working like this, they are essentially structural membranes: they are continuous in two dimensions; together with stiffeners and columns they resist loads in compression; and they create a continuous rigid connection between columns, beams, and floors, both above and below, to help resist shear and bending.

By contrast, curtain walls and walls which are essentially "in-fill," do not act as membranes. They may function as walls in other respects—they insulate, enclose, they define space—but they do not contribute to the overall structural solidity of the building. They let the frame do all the work; structurally they are wasted. [For the details of the argument that every part of the structure must cooperate to take loads, see EFFICIENT STRUC-TURE (206).]

A membrane, on the other hand, makes the wall an integral thing, working with the structure around it. How should we build such a wall membrane?

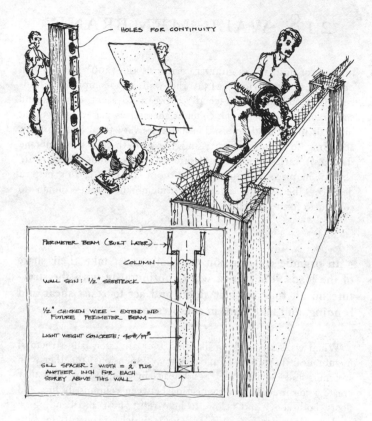

A version of an interior wall membrane which uses gypsum board as skin, and ultra-lightweight concrete for the fill.

GOOD MATERIALS (207) tells us that we should use hand cuttable, nailable, ecologically sound materials, which one can work with home tools, with the emphasis on earthen fill materials and sheet materials.

GRADUAL STIFFENING (208) tells us that the process of building should be such that one can start with a flimsy structure and stiffen it during the course of construction, as materials are put in place, so that the process can be smooth and continuous.

An example of such a wall that we have built and tested uses gypboard for the inner skin, ship-lapped wooden boards for the outer skin and ultra-lightweight concrete for the fill. The wall is built by fixing nailing blocks to the sides of columns. We nail the skin to the nailing blocks, put chickenwire into the cavity to reinforce the concrete against shrinkage, and then pour the lightweight concrete into the cavity. The wall needs to be braced during pouring, and you can't pour more than two or three feet at a time: the pressure gets too great. The last pour fills the perimeter beam and the top of the wall, and so makes them integral. The drawing opposite shows one way that we have made this particular kind of wall membrane.

This wall is solid (about the density of wood), has good acoustic and thermal properties, can easily be built to conform to free and irregular plans, and can be nailed into. And because of its stiffeners, the wall is very strong for its thickness.

Other versions of this pattern: (1) The skin can be formed from hollow structural tiles or concrete blocks, with a concrete or earthen fill. (2) The exterior skin might be brick, the interior skin plywood or gypboard. In either case the columns would have to be hollow tile, or concrete pipe, or other masonry box columns. (3) The skin might be formed with wire mesh, gradually filled with concrete and rubble, and stuccoed on the outside, with plaster on the inside. The columns in this case can be built in the same way—out of a wire mesh tube filled with rubble and concrete. (4) It may also be possible to use gypboard for both skins, inside and out. The gypboard on the outer side could then be covered with building paper, lath, and stucco.

Therefore:

Build the wall as a membrane which connects the columns and door frames and windows frames and is, at least in part, continuous with them. To build the wall, first put up an inner and an outer membrane, which can function as a finished surface; then pour the fill into the wall.

inner and outer membrane

fill

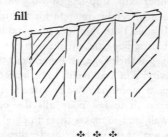

❖ ❖ ❖

Remember that in a stiffened wall, the membranes can be much thinner than you might expect, because the stiffeners prevent buckling. In some cases they can be as thin as two inches in a one story building, three inches at the bottom of a two-story building and so on—see FINAL COLUMN DISTRIBUTION (213).

Membranes can be made from hollow tile, lightweight concrete block, plywood, gypboard, wood planks, or any other sheet type material which would make a nice surface, which is easy to nail into, comfortable to touch, and so on. If the inner sheet is gypsum board, it can be finished with a skim coat of plaster—SOFT INSIDE WALLS (235). The outer sheet can be made of 1 inch boards, tongue and grooved; or exterior grade plywood; or exterior board hung with tile, shingles, or plastered—LAPPED OUTSIDE WALLS (234). It is also possible to build the outer skin of brick or tile: in this case, columns must be of the same material—SOFT TILE AND BRICK (248). . . .

219 FLOOR-CEILING
VAULTS**

. . . we have already discussed the fact that ordinary joist floors and slab floors are inefficient and wasteful because the tension materials they use to resist bending are less common than pure compression materials—EFFICIENT STRUCTURE (206), GOOD MATERIALS (207), and that it is therefore desirable to use vaults wherever possible. This pattern gives the shape and construction of the vaults. The vaults will help to complete FLOOR AND CEILING LAYOUT (210), and PERIMETER BEAMS (217); and, most important of all, they will help to create the CEILING HEIGHT VARIETY (190) in different rooms.

❖ ❖ ❖

We seek a ceiling vault shape which will support a live load on the floor above, form the ceiling of the room below, and generate as little bending and tension as possible so that compressive materials can be relied on.

The vault shape is governed by two constraints: the ceiling cannot be lower than about 6 feet at the edge of the room, except in occasional attic rooms; and the ceiling in the middle of the room should vary with the room size (8 to 12 feet for large rooms, 7 to 9 feet for middle sized rooms, and 6 to 7 feet for the very smallest alcoves and corners—see CEILING HEIGHT VARIETY (190)).

We know, from structural considerations, that a circular shell dome will generate virtually no bending moments when its rise is at least 13 to 20 per cent of its diameter. (This is established in studies and tests of shell structures, and is corroborated by our own computer studies.) For a room 8 feet across, this requires a rise of about 18 inches, making a total height of 7 to 8 feet in the middle; for a room 15 feet across, it requires a rise of 2–3 feet, making a height of 8 to 10 feet in the middle.

Luckily, these vault heights are just congruent with the needed ceiling heights. We may say, therefore, that the ideal vault for an inhabited space is one which springs from 6 to 7 feet at the edge, and rises 13 to 20 per cent of the smaller diameter.

There are various possible ways of making a circular or elliptical vault spring from a square or rectangular room.

1. One type of vault is made by arching diagonal ribs from corner to corner; and then spacing straight line elements across the ribs.

2. Another type is a pure dome supported on squinches.

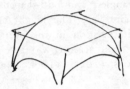

3. Another is based on a rectangular grid of arched ribs. The edge ribs are entirely flat, and the center ribs have the greatest curvature. In the end, each part of the vault is curved in three dimensions, and the corners are slightly flattened.

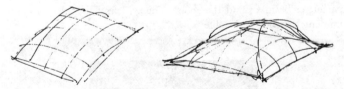

Each of these three vaults makes sense in slightly different circumstances. The first is the easiest to conceive, but it has a slight structural disadvantage: its surface panels are curved in one direction only—because they are made of straight line elements —and cannot therefore achieve the strength of a doubly curved vault. The second is the hardest to conceive; however, it comes naturally from the intersection of a spherical shape and a rectangular one. If one were to make a vault by using a balloon as a form, pushed up within the perimeter beams, the second type would be the easiest to use. In the particular building technique we have been using, the third type is easiest to use, because it is particularly

simple to lay out the arched ribs which provide the formwork. It flattens out at the corners, which could create bending moments and require tension materials. However, in lightweight concrete we have found that it does not require any more than the shrinkage reinforcement, which is needed anyway.

We shall now describe a very simple way of making a vault. Bear in mind that we considered it essential that the vault be built up gradually, and that it could be fitted to any room shape, without difficulty. This technique is not only cheap and simple. It is also one of the only ways we have found of fitting a vault to an arbitrary room shape. It works for rectangular rooms, rooms that are just off-rectangles, and odd-shaped rooms. It can be applied to rooms of any size. The height of the vault can be varied according to its position in the overall array of ceiling heights and floors—CEILING HEIGHT VARIETY (190), STRUCTURE FOLLOWS SOCIAL SPACES (205), FLOOR AND CEILING LAYOUT (210).

First, place lattice strips at one foot centers, spanning in one direction, from one perimeter beam to the opposite perimeter beam, bending each strip to make a sensible vault shape. Now weave strips in the other direction, also at almost one foot centers, to form a basket. The strips can be nailed onto the form of the perimeter beam around the room. You will find that the basket is immensely strong and stable.

Lattice strips in position.

Now stretch burlap over the lattice strips, tacking it on the strips so it fits tightly. Paint the burlap with a heavy coat of polyester resin to stiffen it.

Burlap over the lattice work.

The burlap-resin skin is strong enough to support 1 to 2 inches of lightweight concrete. In preparation for this, put a layer of chickenwire, as shrinkage reinforcement, over the stiffened burlap. Then trowel on a 1- to 2-inch layer of lightweight concrete. Once again, use the ultra-lightweight 40–60 pound concrete described in GOOD MATERIALS (207).

Resin over burlap.

The shell which forms is strong enough to support the rest of the vault, and the floor above.

Lightweight concrete on.

The rest of the vault should not be poured until all edges are in, columns for the next floor are in position, and ducts are in—see BOX COLUMNS (216), DUCT SPACE (229). In order to keep the weight of the vault down, it is important that even the ultralightweight concrete be further lightened, by mixing it with 50 per cent voids and ducts. Any kind of voids can be used—empty

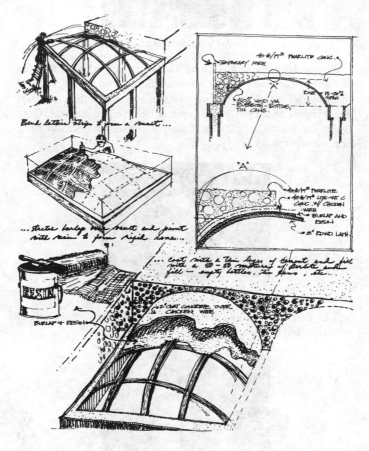

One version of a floor-ceiling vault, made of thin wooden lattice strips woven like a basket, burlap, resin, chicken-wire and ultra lightweight concrete.

beer cans, wine jugs, sono tubes, ducts, chunks of polyurethane. Or voids can be made very much like the vaults themselves by making arches with latticing between columns and then stretching burlap from these arches to the dome. The drawing opposite shows the sequence of construction.

A 16 by 20 foot vault similar to the one shown in our photographs has been analyzed by a computerized finite element analysis. The concrete was assumed to be 40 pounds perlite, with a

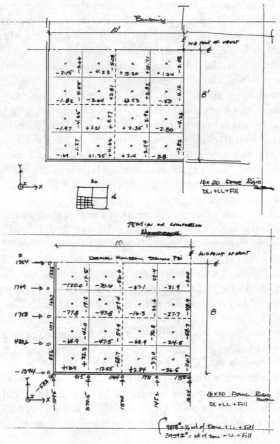

Results of computer analysis.

test compressive strength of 600 psi. Tensile strength is taken as 34 psi, and bending as 25.5 inch pounds per inch. These figures are based on the assumption that the concrete is unreinforced. Dead loads were figured at 60 pounds per square foot assuming 50 per cent voids in the spandrels of the vault. Live loads were taken to be 50 pounds per square foot.

According to the analysis, under such loading the largest compressive stress in this dome occurs near the base at mid points of all four sides and is 120 psi. Outward thrust is the greatest at quarter points along all four walls, and is 1769 pounds. The maximum tension of 32 psi occurs at the corners. Maximum bending is 10 inch pounds per inch. All of these are well within the capacity of the vault, and besides, shrinkage reinforcement in the vault will make it even stronger.

The analysis shows, then, that even though the vault is an impure form (it contains square panels which are actually sagging within the overall configuration of the vault shape), its structural behavior is still close enough to that of a pure vault to work essentially as a compression structure. There are small amounts of local bending; and the corner positions of the dome suffer small amounts of tension, but the chickenwire needed for shrinkage will take care of both these stresses.

Here are some other possible ways of building such a vault:

To begin with, instead of wood for the lattice work, many other materials can be used: plastic strips, thin metal tubes, bamboos. Other resins besides polyester resins can be used to stiffen the burlap. If resins are unavailable, then the form for the vault can be made by placing lattice strips as described, and then stretching chickenwire over it, then burlap soaked in mortar which is allowed to harden before concrete is placed. It might also be possible to use matting stiffened with glue, perhaps even papier mache.

It is possible that similar vaults could be formed by altogether different means: perhaps with pneumatic membranes or balloons. And it is of course possible to form vaults by using very traditional methods: bricks or stones, on centering, like the beautiful vaults used in renaissance churches, gothic cathedrals, and so on.

Therefore:

Build floors and ceilings in the form of elliptical vaults which rise between 13 and 20 per cent of the shorter span. Use a type of construction which makes it possible to fit the vault to any shaped room after the walls and columns are in position: on no account use a prefabricated vault.

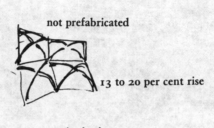

not prefabricated

13 to 20 per cent rise

❖ ❖ ❖

When the main vault is finished, mark the positions of all those columns which will be placed on the floor above it—FINAL COLUMN DISTRIBUTION (213). Whenever there are columns which are more than 2 feet away from the perimeter beam, strengthen the vault with ribs and extra reinforcing to withstand the vertical forces.

Put all the upper columns in position before you pour the floor of the vault, so that when you pour it, the concrete will pour around the column feet, and anchor them firmly in the same way that they are anchored in the foundations—ROOT FOUNDATIONS (214).

To finish the under surface of the vault paint it or plaster it—SOFT INSIDE WALLS (235). As for the floor surface above, either wax it and polish it or cover it with soft materials—FLOOR SURFACE (233). . . .

220 ROOF VAULTS*

. . . if the roof is a flat ROOF GARDEN (118), it can be built just like any FLOOR-CEILING VAULT (219). But when it is a sloping roof, according to the character of SHELTERING ROOF (117), it needs a new construction, specifically adapted to the shape which can enclose a volume.

❖ ❖ ❖

What is the best shape for a roof?

For some reason, this is the most loaded, the most emotional question, that can be asked about building construction. In all our investigations of patterns, we have not found any other pattern which generates so much discussion, so much disagreement, and so much emotion. Early childhood images play a vital role; so does cultural prejudice. It is hard to imagine an Arab building with a pitched roof; hard to imagine a New England farmhouse with a Russian onion roof over a tower; hard to imagine a person who has grown up among pitched steep wooden roofs, happy under the stone cones of the trulli.

All over the world.

For this reason, in this pattern we make our discussion as fundamental as we can. We shall do everything we can to obtain the necessary features which we can treat as invariant for all roofs, regardless of people or culture—yet deep enough to allow a rich assortment of cultural variations.

We approach the problem with the assumption that there are no constraints created by techniques or availability of materials. We are merely concerned with the optimum shape and distribution of materials. Given a roughly rectangular plan, or plan composed of rectangular pieces connected, what is the best shape for the shell of the roof which covers them?

The requirements influencing the shape are these:

1. The feeling of shelter—SHELTERING ROOF (117). This requires that the roof cover a whole wing (that is, not merely room by room). It requires that some of the roof be highly visible—hence, that it have a fairly steep slope—and that some of the roof be flat and usable for gardens or terraces.

2. The roof must definitely contain lived-in space—that is, not just sit on top of the rooms which are all below—see SHELTERING ROOF (117). This means it needs rather a steep slope at the edge—because otherwise there is no headroom. This requires an elliptical section dome, or a barrel vault (which starts going up vertically at the edge), or a very steep slope.

3. In plan, each individual roof is a very rough rectangle, with occasional variations. This follows from the way the roofs of a building must, together, follow the social layout of the plan—ROOF LAYOUT (209).

4. The roof shape must be relaxed—that is, it can be used in any plan layout—and can be generated very simply from a few generating lines which follow automatically from the plan—that is, it must not be a tricky or contrived shape which needs a lot of fiddling around to define it—STRUCTURE FOLLOWS SOCIAL SPACES (205).

5. Structural considerations require a curved shell, dome or vault to eliminate as much bending as possible—see EFFICIENT STRUCTURE (206) and GOOD MATERIALS (207). Of course, to the extent that wood or steel or other tension materials are available, this requirement can be relaxed.

6. The roof is steep enough to shed rain and snow in climates

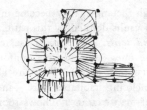

. . . relaxed.

where they occur. Obviously, this aspect of the roof will vary from climate to climate.

These requirements eliminate the following kinds of roofs:

1. *Flat roofs.* Flat roofs, except ROOF GARDENS (118), are already eliminated by the psychological arguments of SHELTERING ROOFS (117) and, of course, by structural considerations. A flat roof is necessary where people are going to walk on it; but it is a very inefficient structural shape since it creates bending.

2. *Pitched Roofs.* Pitched roofs still require materials that can withstand bending moment. The most common material for pitched roofs—wood—is becoming scarce and expensive. As we have said in GOOD MATERIALS (207), we believe it is most sensible to keep wood for surfaces and not to use it as a structural material, except in wood rich areas. Pitched roofs also need to be very steep, indeed, to enclose habitable space as required by SHELTER-ING ROOF (117)—and hence rather inefficient.

3. *Dutch barn and mansard roofs.* These roofs enclose habitable space more efficiently than pitched roofs; but they have the same structural drawbacks.

4. *Geodesic domes.* These domes cover essentially circular areas, and are not therefore useful in their ordinary form—CASCADE OF ROOFS (116), STRUCTURE FOLLOWS SOCIAL SPACES (205). In the modified form, which comes when you stretch

the base into a rough rectangle, they become more or less congruent with the class of vaults defined by this pattern.

5. *Cable nets and tents.* These roofs use tensile materials instead of compressive ones—they do not conform to the requirements of GOOD MATERIALS (207). They are also very inefficient when it comes to enclosing habitable space—and thus fail to meet the requirements of STRUCTURE FOLLOWS SOCIAL SPACES (205).

The roofs which satisfy the requirements are all types of rectangular barrel vaults or shells, with or without a peak, gabled or hipped, and with a variety of possible cross sections. Almost any one of these shells will be further strengthened by additional undulations in the direction of the vault. Examples of possible cross sections are given below. (Remember that this does not include those flat ROOF GARDENS (118) built over FLOOR-CEILING VAULTS (219).)

Possible roof vaults.

We have developed a range of roof vaults which are rather similar to a pitched roof—but with a convex curve great enough to eliminate bending, in some cases actually approaching barrel vaults. One is shown in the drawing opposite; another is shown below.

Another version of a roof vault, built by Bob Harris in Oregon.

We build the roof vault very much like the floor vaults:

1. First span the wing to be roofed with pairs of lattice strips which are securely nailed at their ends to the perimeter beam, and weighted at their apex so that the two pieces become slightly curved.

2. Make the frame for the ceiling under the roof frame at the same time according to FLOOR-CEILING VAULTS (219).

3. Repeat this frame every 18 inches, until the entire wing is

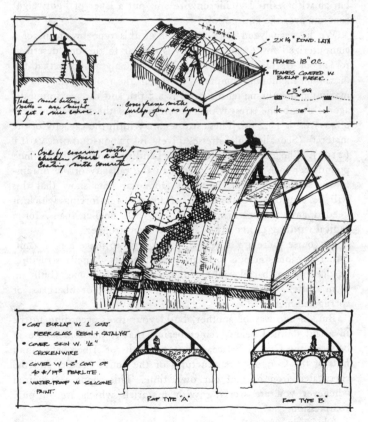

A type of roof vault, similar to the floor-ceiling vault, made from lattice strips, burlap, chicken-wire and ultra-lightweight concrete, but with an apex, and a pitch, and undulations for strength.

framed. The outer one will be the same, while the inner frame for the ceiling may change according to the rooms under it.

4. Now lay burlap over the ceiling frame, then resin, then 1½ inches of ultra-lightweight concrete—as for FLOOR-CEILING VAULTS (219).

5. Now lay burlap over the roof frame, tacking it onto the lattice strips so that there is a 3-inch scallop in between the ribs— to form structural undulations in the skin. Again, paint the burlap with resin; lay chickenwire and put a layer of lightweight concrete over the entire roof.

We have analyzed a 48-foot roof of this type by means of a computerized finite element analysis similar to the one described for FLOOR-CEILING VAULTS (219). The analysis shows that the maximum membrane compressive stress in the roof is 39.6 psi; the maximum membrane tensile stress is 2.5 psi, and the maximum diagonal membrane stress which develops from the maximum shear of 41.7 psi is 15.2 psi. These stresses are within the capacity of the material (See allowable stresses given in FLOOR-CEILING VAULT (219)). The maximum membrane bending moment is 46 inch pounds per inch which is higher than the capacity of the unreinforced section, but extrapolations from our data show that this will be comfortably taken care of by the reinforcing which is needed anyway for shrinkage. Roofs with smaller spans, for a typical WING OF LIGHT (106), will be even stronger.

Of course there are dozens of other ways to make a roof vault. Other versions include ordinary barrel vaults, lamella structures in the form of barrel vaults, elongated geodesic domes (built up from struts), vaults built up from plastic sheets, or fiberglass, or corrugated metal.

But, in one way or another, build your roofs according to the invariant defined below, remembering that it lies somewhere in between the Crystal Palace, the stone vaults of Alberobello, mud huts of the Congo, grass structures of the South Pacific, and the corrugated iron huts of our own time. This shape is required whenever you are working with materials which are in pure compression.

Obviously, if you have access to wood or steel and want to use it, you can modify this shape by adding tension members. However, we believe that these tension materials will become more

Experimental roof vaults.

and more rare as time goes on and that the pure compression shape will gradually become a universal.

Therefore:

Build the roof vault either as a cylindrical barrel vault, or like a pitched roof with a slight convex curve in each of the two sloping sides. Put in undulations along the vault, to make the shell more effective. The curvature of the main shell, and of the undulations, can vary with the span; the bigger the span, the deeper the curvature and undulations need to be.

barrel vault

undulations

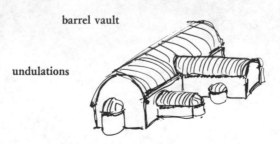

Leave space for dormers at intervals along the vault—DORMER WINDOWS (231), and build them integral with it. Finish the roof with ROOF CAPS (232). And once the vault is complete, it needs a waterproof paint or skin applied to its outer surface—LAPPED OUTSIDE WALLS (234). It can be painted white to protect it against the sun; the undulations will carry the rainwater. . . .

within the main frame of the building, fix the exact positions for openings—the doors and the windows —and frame these openings.

221 NATURAL DOORS
AND WINDOWS**

. . . imagine that you are now standing in the built-up frame of a partly constructed building, with the columns and beams in place—BOX COLUMNS (216), PERIMETER BEAMS (217). You know roughly where you want doors and windows from ZEN VIEW (134), STREET WINDOWS (164), WINDOW PLACE (180), WINDOWS OVERLOOKING LIFE (192), CORNER DOORS (196). Now you can settle on the exact positions of the frames.

Finding the right position for a window or a door is a subtle matter. But there are very few ways of building which take this into consideration.

In our current ways of building, the delicacy of placing a window or a door has nearly vanished. But it is just this refinement, down to the last foot, even to the last inch or two, which makes an immense difference. Windows and doors which are just right are always like this. Find a beautiful window. Study it. See how different it would be if its dimensions varied a few inches in either direction.

Now look at the windows and doors in most buildings made during the last 20 years. Assume that these openings are in roughly the right place, but notice how they could be improved if they were free to shift around, a few inches here and there, each one taking advantage of its own special circumstances—the space immediately inside and the view outside.

It is almost always a rigid construction system, combined with a formal aesthetic, which holds these windows in such a death grip. There is nothing else to this regularity, for it is possible to relax the regularity without losing structural integrity.

It is also important to realize that this final placing of windows and doors can only be done on site, with the rough frame of the building in position. It is impossible to do it on paper. But on the site it is quite straightforward and natural: mock up the openings with scraps of lumber or string and move them around until they feel right; pay careful attention to the organization of the view and the kind of space that is created inside.

Getting it just right.

As we shall see in a later pattern—SMALL PANES (239), it is not necessary to make the windows any special dimensions, or to try and make them multiples of any standard pane size. Whatever dimensions this pattern gives each window, it will then be possible to divide it up, to form small panes, which will be different in their exact shape and size, according to the window they are in.

However, although there is no constraint on the exact dimension of the windows, there is a general rule of thumb, which will make window sizes vary: Windows, as a rule, should become smaller as you get higher up in the building.

1. The area of windows needed for light and ventilation depends on the size of rooms, and rooms are generally smaller on upper stories of the building—the communal rooms are generally on the ground floor and more private rooms upstairs.

2. The amount of daylight coming through a window depends on the area of open sky visible through the window. The higher the window, the more open sky is visible (because nearby trees and buildings obscure less)—so less window area is needed to get sufficient daylight in.

3. To feel safe on the upper stories of a building, one wants more enclosure, smaller windows, higher sills—and the higher off the ground one is, the more one needs these psychological protections.

Therefore:

On no account use standard doors or windows. Make each window a different size, according to its place.

Do not fix the exact position or size of the door and win-

dow frames until the rough framing of the room has actually been built, and you can really stand inside the room and judge, by eye, exactly where you want to put them, and how big you want them. When you decide, mark the openings with strings.

Make the windows smaller and smaller, as you go higher in the building.

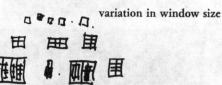

variation in window size

the position of the doors and windows "felt"

❖ ❖ ❖

Fine tune the exact position of each edge, and mullion, and sill, according to your comfort in the room, and the view that the window looks onto—LOW SILL (222), DEEP REVEALS (223). As a result, each window will have a different size and shape, according to its position in the building. This means that it is obviously impossible to use standard windows and even impossible to make each window a simple multiple of standard panes. But it will still be possible to glaze each window, since the procedure for building the panes makes them divisions of the whole, instead of making up the whole as a multiple of standard panes—SMALL PANES (239). . . .

222 LOW SILL

. . . this pattern helps to complete NATURAL DOORS AND WINDOWS (221), and the special love for the view, and for the earth outside, which ZEN VIEW (134), WINDOW PLACE (180) and WINDOWS OVERLOOKING LIFE (192) all need.

❖ ❖ ❖

One of a window's most important functions is to put you in touch with the outdoors. If the sill is too high, it cuts you off.

The "right" height for a ground floor window sill is astonishingly low. Our experiments show that sills which are 13 or 14 inches from the floor are perfect. This is much lower than the window sills which people most often build: a standard window sill is about 24 to 36 inches from the ground. And it is higher than French doors and windows which usually have a bottom rail of 8 to 10 inches. The best height, then, happens to be a rather uncommon one.

We first give the detailed explanation for this phenomenon, and we then explain the modifications which are necessary on upper floors.

People are drawn to windows because of the light and the view outside—they are natural places to sit by when reading, talking, sewing, and so on, yet most windows have sill heights of 30 inches or so, so that when you sit down by them you cannot see the ground right near the window. This is unusually frustrating—you almost have to stand up to get a complete view.

In "The Function of Windows: A Reappraisal" (*Building Science*, Vol. 2, Pergamon Press, 1967, pp. 97–121), Thomas Markus shows that the primary function of windows is not to provide light but to provide a link to the outside and, furthermore, that this link is most meaningful when it contains a view of the ground and the horizon. Windows with high sills cut out the view of the ground.

On the other hand, glass all the way down to the floor is undesirable. It is disturbing because it seems contradictory and

even dangerous. It feels more like a door than a window; you have the feeling that you ought to be able to walk through it. If the sill is 12 to 14 inches high, you can comfortably see the ground, even if you are a foot or two away from the window, and it still feels like a window rather than a door.

On upper stories the sill height needs to be slightly higher. The sill still needs to be low to see the ground, but it is unsafe if it is too low. A sill height of about 20 inches allows you to see most of the ground, from a chair nearby, and still feel safe.

Therefore:

When determining exact location of windows also decide which windows should have low sills. On the first floor, make the sills of windows which you plan to sit by between 12 and 14 inches high. On the upper stories, make them higher, around 20 inches.

12 to 14 inches high

❖ ❖ ❖

Make the sill part of the frame, and make it wide enough to put things on—WAIST-HIGH SHELF (201), FRAMES AS THICKENED EDGES (225), WINDOWS WHICH OPEN WIDE (236). Make the window open outward, so that you can use the sill as a shelf, and so that you can lean out and tend the flowers. If you can, put flowers right outside the window, on the ground or raised a little, too, so that you can always see the flowers from inside the room—RAISED FLOWERS (245). . . .

. . . this pattern helps to complete the work of LIGHT ON TWO SIDES OF EVERY ROOM (159), by going even further to reduce glare; and it helps to shape the FRAMES AS THICKENED EDGES (225).

Windows with a sharp edge where the frame meets the wall create harsh, blinding glare, and make the rooms they serve uncomfortable.

They have the same effect as the bright headlights of an on-coming car: the glare prevents you from seeing anything else on the road because your eye cannot simultaneously adapt to the bright headlights and to the darkness of the roadway. Just so, a window is always much brighter than an interior wall; and the walls tend to be darkest next to the window's edge. The difference in brightness between the bright window and the dark wall around it also causes glare.

Glare . . . and no glare.

To solve this problem, the edge of the window must be splayed, by making a reveal between the window and the wall. The splayed reveal then creates a transition area—a zone of intermediate brightness—between the brightness of the window and the darkness of the wall. If the reveal is deep enough and the angle just right, the glare will vanish altogether.

But the reveal must be quite deep, and the angle of the splay quite marked. In empirical studies of glare, Hopkinson and

Petherbridge have found: (1) that the larger the reveal is, the less glare there is; (2) the reveal functions best, when its brightness is just halfway between the brightness of the window and the brightness of the wall. ("Discomfort Glare and the Lighting of Buildings," *Transactions of the Illuminating Engineering Society,* Vol. XV, No. 2, 1950, pp. 58–59.)

Our own experiments show that this happens most nearly, when the reveal lies at between 50 and 60 degrees to the plane of the window; though, of course, the angle will vary with local conditions. And, to satisfy the need for a "large" reveal, we have found that the reveal itself must be a good 10 to 12 inches wide.

Therefore:

Make the window frame a deep, splayed edge: about a foot wide and splayed at about 50 to 60 degrees to the plane of the window, so that the gentle gradient of daylight gives a smooth transition between the light of the window and the dark of the inner wall.

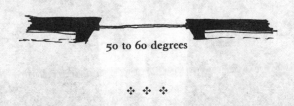

50 to 60 degrees

❖ ❖ ❖

Build the depth of the frame so that it is continuous with the structure of the walls—FRAMES AS THICKENED EDGES (225); if the wall is thin, make up the necessary depth for the reveal on the inside face of the wall, with bookshelves, closets or other THICK WALLS (197); embellish the edge of the window even further, to make light even softer, with lace work, tracery, and climbing plants—FILTERED LIGHT (238), HALF-INCH TRIM (240), CLIMBING PLANTS (246). . . .

224 LOW DOORWAY

. . . some of the doors in a building play a special role in creating transitions and maintaining privacy: it may be any of the doors governed by FAMILY OF ENTRANCES (102), or MAIN ENTRANCE (110), or THE FLOW THROUGH ROOMS (131) or CORNER DOORS (196), or NATURAL DOORS AND WINDOWS (221). This pattern helps to complete these doors by giving them a special height and shape.

❖ ❖ ❖

High doorways are simple and convenient. But a lower door is often more profound.

The 6′ 8″ rectangular door is such a standard pattern, and is so taken for granted, that it is hard to imagine how strongly it dominates the experience of transition. There have been times, however, when people were more sensitive to the moment of passage, and made the shape of their doors convey the feeling of transition.

An extreme case is the Japanese tea house, where a person entering must literally kneel down and crawl in through a low hole in the wall. Once inside, shoes off, the guest is entirely a guest, in the world of his host.

Among architects, Frank Lloyd Wright used the pattern many times. There is a beautifully low trellised walk behind Taliesin West, marking the transition out of the main house, along the path to the studios.

If you are going to try this pattern, test it first by pinning cardboard up to effectively lower the frame. Make the doorway low enough so that it appears "lower than usual"—then people will immediately adapt to it, and tall people will not hit their heads.

Therefore:

Instead of taking it for granted that your doors are simply 6′ 8″ rectangular openings to pass through, make at least some of your doorways low enough so that the act of going through the door is a deliberate thoughtful passage

from one place to another. Especially at the entrance to a house, at the entrance to a private room, or a fire corner— make the doorway lower than usual, perhaps even as low as 5′ 8″.

❖ ❖ ❖

Test the height before you build it, in place—NATURAL DOORS AND WINDOWS (221). Build the door frame as part of the structure—FRAMES AS THICKENED EDGES (225), and make it beautiful with ORNAMENT (249) around the frame. If there is a door, glaze it, at least partially—SOLID DOORS WITH GLASS (237). . . .

225 FRAMES AS THICKENED EDGES **

. . . assume that columns and beams are in and that you have marked the exact positions of the doors and windows with string or pencil marks—NATURAL DOORS AND WINDOWS (221). You are ready to build the frames. Remember that a well made frame needs to be continuous with the surrounding wall, so that it helps the building structurally—EFFICIENT STRUCTURE (206), GRADUAL STIFFENING (208).

Any homogeneous membrane which has holes in it will tend to rupture at the holes, unless the edges of the holes are reinforced by thickening.

The most familiar example of this principle at work is in the human face itself. Both eyes and mouth are surrounded by extra bone and flesh. It is this thickening, around the eyes and mouth, which gives them their character and helps to make them such important parts of human physiognomy.

A building also has its eyes and mouth: the windows and the doors. And following the principle which we observe in nature, almost every building has its windows and doors elaborated, made more special, by just the kind of thickening we see in eyes and mouths.

The fact that openings in naturally occurring membranes are invariably thickened can be easily explained by considering how the lines of force in the membrane must flow around the hole.

The density of the lines represent increasing stress concentrations.

The increasing density of lines of force around the perimeter of the hole requires that additional material be generated there to prevent tearing.

Consider a soap film. When you prick the film, the tension pulls the film apart, and it disintegrates. But if you insert a ring of string into the film, the hole will hold, because the tensile forces which accumulate around the opening can be held by the thicker ring. This is in tension. The same is true for buckling and compression. When a thin plate is functioning in compression and a hole is made in it, the hole needs stiffening. It is important to recognize that this stiffening is not only supporting the opening itself against collapse, but it is taking care of the stresses in the membrane which would normally be distributed in that part of the membrane which is removed. Familiar examples of such stiffening in plates are the lips of steel around the portholes in a ship or in a locomotive cab.

A door frame as a thickening.

The same is true for doors and windows in a building. Where the walls are made of wood planks and lightweight concrete fill—see WALL MEMBRANES (218)—the thickened frames can be made from the same wood planks, placed to form a bulge, and then filled to be continuous with the wall. If other types of skin are used in the wall membranes, there will be other kinds of thickening: edges formed with chicken wire, burlap, and resin, filled with concrete; edges formed with chicken wire filled with rubble, and then mortar, plaster; edges formed with brick, filled, then plastered.

More general examples of frames as thickened edges exist all over the world. They include the thickening of the mud around the windows of a mud hut, the use of stone edges to the opening in a brick wall because the stone is stronger, the use of double studs around an opening in stud construction, the extra stone around the windows in a gothic church, the extra weaving round the hole in any basket hut.

Therefore:

Do not consider door and window frames as separate rigid structures which are inserted into holes in walls. Think of them instead as thickenings of the very fabric of the wall itself, made to protect the wall against the concentrations of stress which develop around openings.

In line with this conception, build the frames as thickenings of the wall material, continuous with the wall itself, made of the same materials, and poured, or built up, in a manner which is continuous with the structure of the wall.

wall thickening

✦ ✦ ✦

In windows, splay the thickening, to create DEEP REVEALS (223); the form of doors and windows which will fill the frame, is given by the later patterns—WINDOWS WHICH OPEN WIDE (236), SOLID DOORS WITH GLASS (237), SMALL PANES (239). . . .

as you build the main frame and its openings, put in the following subsidiary patterns where they are appropriate;

226. COLUMN PLACE

227. COLUMN CONNECTION

228. STAIR VAULT

229. DUCT SPACE

230. RADIANT HEAT

231. DORMER WINDOWS

232. ROOF CAPS

226 COLUMN PLACE*

. . . certain columns, especially those which are free standing, play an important social role, beyond their structural role as COLUMNS AT THE CORNERS (212). These are, especially, the columns which help to form arcades, galleries, porches, walkways, and outdoor rooms—PUBLIC OUTDOOR ROOM (69), ARCADES (119), OUTDOOR ROOM (163), GALLERY SURROUND (166), SIX-FOOT BALCONY (167), TRELLISED WALK (174). This pattern defines the character these columns need to make them function socially.

Thin columns, spindly columns, columns which take their shape from structural arguments alone, will never make a comfortable environment.

The fact is, that a free-standing column plays a role in shaping human space. It marks a point. Two or more together define a wall or an enclosure. The main function of the columns, from a human point of view, is to create a space for human activity.

In ancient times, the structural arguments for columns coincided in their implications with the social arguments. Columns made of brick, or stone, or timber were always large and thick. It was easy to make useful space around them.

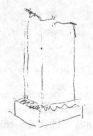

A big thick column.

But with steel and reinforced concrete, it is possible to make a very slender column; so slender that its social properties disap-

pear altogether. Four inch steel pipes or 6 inch reinforced concrete columns break up space, but they destroy it as a place for human action, because they do not create "spots" where people can be comfortable.

Thin columns of the plastic world.

In these times, it is therefore necessary to reintroduce, consciously, the social purposes which columns have, alongside their structural functions. Let us try to define these social purposes exactly.

A column affects a volume of space around it, according to the situation. The space has an area that is roughly circular, perhaps 5 feet in radius.

The space around the column.

When the column is too thin, or lacks a top or bottom, this entire volume—an area of perhaps 75 square feet—is lost. It cannot be a satisfactory place in its own right: the column is too thin to lean against, there is no way to build a seat up against it, there is no natural way to place a table or a chair against the column. On the other hand, the column still breaks up the space. It subtly prevents people from walking directly through that area: we notice

that people tend to give these thin columns a wide berth; and it prevents people from forming groups.

In short, if the column has to be there, it will destroy a considerable area unless it is made to be a place where people feel comfortable to stay, a natural focus, a place to sit down, a place to lean.

Therefore:

When a column is free standing, make it as thick as a man—at least 12 inches, preferably 16 inches: and form places around it where people can sit and lean comfortably: a step, a small seat built up against the column, or a space formed by a pair of columns.

thick columns

✣ ✣ ✣

You can get the extra thickness quite cheaply if you build the column as a BOX COLUMN (216); complete the "place" the column forms, by giving it a "roof" in the form of a column capital, or vault which springs from the column, or by bracing the column against the beams—COLUMN CONNECTION (227). And when it makes sense, make the column base a SITTING WALL (243), a place for flowers—RAISED FLOWERS (245), or a place for a chair or table—DIFFERENT CHAIRS (251). . . .

. . . the columns are in position, and have been tied together by a perimeter beam—BOX COLUMNS (216), PERIMETER BEAMS (217). According to the principles of continuity which govern the basic structure—EFFICIENT STRUCTURE (206), the connections need stiffening to lead the forces smoothly from the beams into the columns, especially when the columns are free standing as they are in an arcade or balcony—ARCADE (119), GALLERY SURROUND (166), SIX-FOOT BALCONY (167), COLUMN PLACE (226). You may also do the same in the upper corners of your door and window frames—FRAMES AS THICKENED EDGES (225)—making arched openings.

The strength of a structure depends on the strength of its connections; and these connections are most critical of all at corners, especially at the corners where the columns meet the beams.

There are two entirely different ways of looking at a connection:

1. As a source of rigidity, which can be strengthened by triangulation, to prevent racking of the frame. This is a moment connection: a brace. See the upper picture.

2. As a source of continuity, which helps the forces to flow easily around the corner in the process of transferring loads by changing the direction of the force. This is a continuity connection: a capital. See the lower picture.

1. A column connection as a brace.

As a building is erected, and throughout its life, it settles, creating tiny stresses within the structure. When the settling is uneven, as it most always is, the stresses are out of balance; there is strain in every part of the building, whether or not that part of the building was designed to accept strain and transmit the forces on down to the ground. The parts of the building that are not designed to carry these forces become the weak points of the building subject to fracture and rupture.

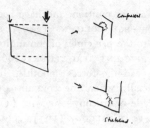

Effects of uneven stresses on a frame.

Rectangular frames, especially, have these cracks at the corners because the transmission of the load is discontinuous there. To solve this problem the frame must be braced—made into a rigid frame that transmits the forces around it as a whole without distorting. The bracing is required at any right-angled corner between columns and beams or in the corners of door and window frames.

2. *A column connection as a capital.*

This happens most effectively in an arch. The arch creates a continuous body of compressive material, which transfers vertical forces from one vertical axis to another. It works effectively because the line of action of a vertical force in a continuous compressive medium spreads out downward at about 45 degrees.

And a column capital is, in this sense, acting as a small, underdeveloped arch. It reduces the length of the beam—and so reduces bending stress. And it begins to provide the path for the forces as they move from one vertical axis to another, through the medium of the beam. The larger the capital, the better.

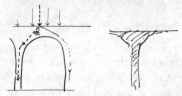

A capital that acts the same way as an arch.

A column connection will work best when it acts both as a column capital and as a column brace. This means that it needs to

be thick and solid, like a capital, so that there is a lot of material for the forces to travel through, and stiff and strong and completely continuous with the column and perimeter beam, like the brace, so that it can work against shear and bending.

The bone structure, shown below uses both principles, to transfer compressive stress from one strut to another, continuously, throughout a three-dimensional space frame of struts. The structure is most massive at the connections, where the forces change direction.

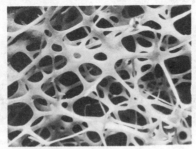

Connections inside a bone.

A similar column connection can be made integral with poured hollow columns and beams. The forms for the connection are gussets made of skin material: then fill the column and the gussets and the beam in a continuous concrete pour.

Of all the patterns in the book, this is one of the most widespread and has taken the greatest variety of outward forms throughout the course of history. A solid wood capital on a wood column, or a continuously poured column top, and arches of stone, brick, or poured concrete are all examples. And, of course, typical column capitals—a larger stone on a stone column or typical gusset plate or brace—even if weak in some ways, also help a great deal. But only relatively few of the historical column connections succeed fully in acting both as braces and as capitals.

Therefore:

Build connections where the columns meet the beams. Any distribution of material which fills the corner up will do: fillets, gussets, column capitals, mushroom column, and

most general of all, the arch, which connects column and
beam in a continuous curve.

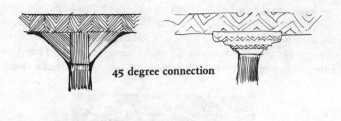

45 degree connection

❖ ❖ ❖

The connection is one of the most natural places for ORNAMENT
(249): there is a wide variety of possible connections, carvings,
fretwork, painting, for this critical position. In certain cases, the
connection may act as an umbrella for a COLUMN PLACE
(226). . . .

228 STAIR VAULT*

. . . this pattern helps complete the rough shape and location of stairs given by STAIRCASE AS A STAGE (133) and by STAIRCASE VOLUME (195). If you want to build a conventional stair, you can find what you need in any handbook. But how to build a stair in a way which is consistent with the compressive structure of EFFICIENT STRUCTURE (206), without using wood or steel or concrete—GOOD MATERIALS (207)?

❖ ❖ ❖

Within a building technology which uses compressive materials as much as possible, and excludes the use of wood, it is natural to build stairs over a vaulted void, simply to save weight and materials.

A concrete stair is usually made from precast pieces supported by steel stringers; or it is formed in place, and then stripped of its forms. But for the reasons already given in GOOD MATERIALS (207), precast concrete and steel are undesirable materials to use—they call for modular planning; they are unpleasant materials to touch, look at, and walk on; they are hard to work with and modify in any relaxed way, since they call for special tools.

Given the principles of EFFICIENT STRUCTURE (206), GOOD MATERIALS (207), and GRADUAL STIFFENING (208), we suggest that stairs be made like FLOOR-CEILING VAULTS (219)—by making a half-vault (to the slope of the stair), with lattice strips, burlap, resin, chickenwire, and lightweight concrete. The steps themselves can then be formed by using wood planks, or tiles, as risers, and filling in the steps with trowelled concrete.

When we first wrote this pattern, we thought it was very doubtful—and put it in mainly to be consistent with floor and roof vaults. Since then we have built a vaulted stair. It is a great success —beautiful—and we recommend it heartily.

Therefore:

Build a curved diagonal vault in the same way that you

build your FLOOR-CEILING VAULTS (219). Once the vault hardens, cover it with steps of lightweight concrete, trowel-formed into position.

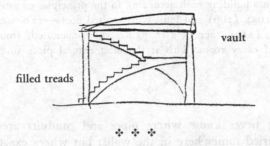

❖ ❖ ❖

A lightweight concrete tread, colored, waxed, and polished can be quite beautiful and soft enough to be comfortable—see FLOOR SURFACE (233)—and will eventually take on the patina of wear called for in SOFT TILE AND BRICK (248).

The vaulted space under the stair can be used as an ALCOVE (179) a CHILD CAVE (203), or CLOSETS BETWEEN ROOMS (198). If it is plastered, like a regular ceiling—see FLOOR-CEILING VAULTS (219), it makes a much more pleasant and useful space than the space under an ordinary stair.

229 DUCT SPACE

. . . in a building built according to the principles of EFFICIENT STRUCTURE (206) and built with vaulted floors—FLOOR-CEILING VAULTS (219), there is a triangular volume, unused, around the edge of every room. This is the most natural place to put the ducts.

❖ ❖ ❖

You never know where pipes and conduits are; they are buried somewhere in the walls; but where exactly are they?

In most buildings electric conduits, plumbing, drains, gas pipes, telephone wires, and so on, are buried in the walls, in a completely uncoordinated and disorganized way. This makes the initial construction of the building complicated since it is difficult to coordinate the installation of the various services with the building of various parts of the building. It makes it difficult to think about making any changes or additions to the building once it is built since you don't know where the service lines are. And it leaves a gap in our understanding of our surroundings: the organization of utilities and services in the buildings we live in are a mystery to us.

We propose that all the services be located together and run around the ceiling of each room in the spandrel between the vaulted ceiling and the floor above—FLOOR-CEILING VAULTS (219).

Heating and electrical conduits will be universal throughout the building and should thus be run around every room. Plumbing and gas lines will be around some rooms only. All lines will also be concentrated vertically at the corners of rooms. Thus the lines form vertical trunks from which horizontal loops spring. This configuration of pipes and conduits is easy to understand and plug into.

All in one place.

Therefore:

Make ducts to carry hot air conduit, plumbing, gas, and other services in the triangular space, within the vault, around the upper edge of every room. Connect the ducts for different rooms by vertical ducts, in special chases, in the corners of rooms. Build outlets and panels at intervals along the duct for access to the conduits.

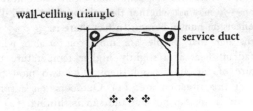

❖ ❖ ❖

Once the duct is in, you can fill up the triangle with light-weight concrete—FLOOR-CEILING VAULTS (219). Place heating panels along the surface of the triangle—RADIANT HEAT (230); and place outlets for lights at frequent intervals below the duct, with leads and conduits running down in rebates along the window frames—POOLS OF LIGHT (252). . . .

230 RADIANT HEAT*

. . . to complete WALL MEMBRANES (218), FLOOR-CEILING VAULTS (219) and DUCT SPACE (229), use a biologically sensible heating system.

❖ ❖ ❖

This pattern is a biologically precise formulation of the intuition that sunlight and a hot blazing fire are the best kinds of heat.

Heat can be transmitted by radiation (heat waves across empty space), convection (flow in air or liquids by mixing of molecules and hot air rising), and conduction (flow through a solid).

In most places, we get heat in all three ways from our environment: conducted heat from the solids we touch, convected heat in the air around us, and radiated heat from those sources of radiation in our line of sight.

Of the three, conducted heat is trivial, since any surface hot enough to conduct heat to us directly is too hot for comfort. As far as the other two are concerned—convected heat and radiant heat—we may ask whether there is any biological difference in their effects on human beings. In fact there is.

It turns out that people are most comfortable when they receive radiant heat at a slightly higher temperature than the temperature of the air around them. The two most primitive examples of this situation are: (1) Outdoors, on a spring day when the air is not too hot but the sun is shining. (2) Around an open fire, on a cool evening.

Most people will recognize intuitively that these are two unusually comfortable situations. And in view of the fact that we evolved as organisms in the open air, with plenty of sun, it is not surprising that this condition happens to be so comfortable for us. It is built into our systems, biologically.

Unfortunately, it happens that many of the most widely used heating systems ignore this basic fact.

Hot air systems, and buried pipes, and the so-called hot water "radiators" do transmit some of their heat to us by means of radiation, but most of the heat we get from them comes from convection. The air gets heated and warms us as it swirls around us. But, as it does so it creates that very uncomfortable stuffy, over-heated, dry sensation. When convection heaters are warm enough to heat us we feel stifled. If we turn the heat down, it gets too cold.

The conditions in which people feel most comfortable require a subtle balance of convected heat and radiant heat. Experiments have established that the most comfortable balance between the two, occurs when the average radiant temperature is about two degrees higher than the ambient temperature. To get the average radiant temperature in a room, we measure the temperature of all the visible surfaces in a room, multiply the area of each surface by its temperature, add these up, and divide by the total area. For comfort, this average radiant temperature needs to be about two degrees higher than the air temperature.

Since some of the surfaces in a room (windows and outside walls), will usually be cooler than the indoor air temperature, this means that at least some surfaces must be considerably warmer to get the average up.

An open fire, which has a small area of very high temperature, creates this condition in a cool room. The beautiful Austrian and Swedish tiled stoves also do it very well. They are massive stoves, made of clay bricks or tiles, with a tiny furnace

Austrian tiled stove.

in the middle. A handful of twigs in the furnace give all their heat to the clay of the stove itself, and this clay, like the earth, keeps this heat and radiates it slowly over a period of many hours.

Radiant panels, with individual room control, and infrared heaters hung from walls and ceilings, are possible high technology sources of radiant heat. It is possible that sources of low-grade radiant heat—like a hot water tank—might also work to very much the same effect. Instead of insulating the tank, it might be an excellent source of radiant heat, right in the center of the house.

Therefore:

Choose a way of heating your space—especially those rooms where people are going to gather when it is cold—that is essentially a radiative process, where the heat comes more from radiation than convection.

radiant sources

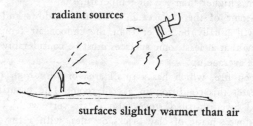

surfaces slightly warmer than air

If you have followed earlier patterns, you may have rooms which have a vaulted ceiling, with a steeply sloping surface close to the wall, and with the major ducts behind that surface—FLOOR-CEILING VAULTS (219), DUCT SPACE (229). In this case, it is natural to put the radiant heating panels on that sloping surface.

But it is also very wonderful to make at least some part of the radiant surfaces low enough so that seats can be built round them and against them; on a cold day there is nothing better than a seat against a warm stove—BUILT-IN SEATS (202). . . .

. . . this pattern helps to complete SHELTERING ROOF (117). If you have followed sheltering roof, your roof has living space within it: and it must therefore have windows in it, to bring light into the roof. This pattern is a special kind of WINDOW PLACE (180), which completes the ROOF VAULTS (220), in these situations.

❖ ❖ ❖

We know from our discussion of SHELTERING ROOF (117) that the top story of the building should be right inside the roof, surrounded by it.

Obviously, if there is habitable space inside the roof, it must have some kind of windows; skylights are not satisfactory as windows—except in studios or workshops—because they do not create a connection between the inside and the outside world—WINDOWS OVERLOOKING LIFE (192).

It is therefore natural to pierce the roof with windows; in short, to build dormer windows. This simple, fundamental fact would hardly need mentioning if it were not for the fact that dormer windows have come to seem archaic and romantic. It is important to emphasize how sensible and ordinary they are—simply because people may not build them if they believe that they are old fashioned and out of date.

Dormers make the roof livable. Aside from bringing in light and air and the connection to the outside, they relieve the low ceilings along the edge of the roofs and create alcoves and window places.

How should the dormers be constructed? Within the roof vault we have described, the basket which forms the vault can simply be continued to form the roof of the dormer, over a frame of columns and perimeter beams which form the opening.

The other ways of building dormer windows depend on the construction system you are using. Whatever you are using for lintels, columns, and walls, can simply be modified and used in combination to build the dormer.

Therefore:

Wherever you have windows in the roof, make dormer windows which are high enough to stand in, and frame them like any other alcoves in the building.

dormer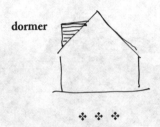

❖ ❖ ❖

Frame them like ALCOVES (179) and WINDOW PLACE (180) with GRADUAL STIFFENING (208), COLUMNS AT THE CORNERS (212), BOX COLUMNS (216), PERIMETER BEAMS (217), WALL MEMBRANES (218), FLOOR-CEILING VAULTS (219), ROOF VAULTS (220) and FRAMES AS THICKENED EDGES (225).

Put WINDOWS WHICH OPEN WIDE (236) in them, and make SMALL PANES (239). . . .

. . . and this pattern finishes the ROOF GARDENS (118) or the ROOF VAULTS (220). Assume that you have built the roof vaults —or at least that you have started to build up the splines which will support the cloth which forms the vault. Or assume that you have begun to build a roof garden, and have begun to fence it or surround it. In either case—how shall the roof be finished?

❖ ❖ ❖

There are few cases in traditional architecture where builders have not used some roof detail to cap the building with an ornament.

The pediments on Greek buildings; the caps on the trulli of Alberobello; the top of Japanese shrines; the venting caps on barns. In each of these examples there seems to be some issue of the building system that needs resolution, and the builder takes the opportunity to make a "cap."

We suspect there is a reason for this which should be taken seriously. The roof cap helps to finish the building; it tops the building with a human touch. Yet, the power of the cap, its overall effect on the feeling of the building, is of much greater proportions than one would expect. Look at these sketches of a building, with and without a roof cap. They look like different buildings. The difference is enormous.

With and without a roof cap.

Why is it that these caps are so important and have such a powerful effect on the building as a whole?

Here are some possible reasons.

1. They crown the roof. They give the roof the status that it deserves. The roof is important, and the caps emphasize this fact.

2. They add detail. They make the roof less homogeneous, and

they relieve the roof from being a single uninterrupted thing. The walls get this relief from windows, doors, balconies, which add scale and character; when a roof has many dormers, it seems to need the caps less.

3. The caps provide a connection to the sky, in a way that might have had religious overtones at one time. Just as the building needs a sense of connection to the earth—see CONNECTION TO THE EARTH (168)—perhaps the roof needs a connection to the sky.

In the building system we propose, the roof caps are weights we use at the ridge of the roof to make the slight curve in the pitched sides of the roof. They happen at regular intervals, at the ridges of the scallops. They need not be large—a small bag of sand or a stone will do, plastered with concrete and shaped so the bulge is obvious. It may be nice to paint them a different color from the roof.

Of course, there are hundreds of other possible kinds of roof caps. They can be brick chimneys, statues, vents, structural details, the pinnacles on a gothic buttress, weather vanes, or even windmills.

Therefore:

Choose a natural way to cap the roof—some way which is in keeping with the kind of construction, and the meaning of the building. The caps may be structural; but their main function is decorative—they mark the top—they mark the place where the roof penetrates the sky.

connection to the sky

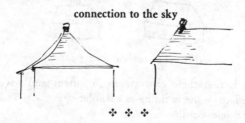

❖ ❖ ❖

Finish the roof caps any way you want, but don't forget them—ORNAMENT (249). . . .

put in the surfaces and the indoor details;

233 FLOOR SURFACE**

. . . this pattern tells you how to put the surface on the floors, to finish the GROUND FLOOR SLAB (215) and FLOOR-CEILING VAULTS (219). When properly made, the floor surfaces will also help intensify the gradient of intimacy in the building— INTIMACY GRADIENT (127).

We want the floor to be comfortable, warm to the touch, inviting. But we also want it to be hard enough to resist wear, and easy to clean.

When we think of floors, we think of wood floors. We hope, if we can afford it, to have a wooden floor. Even in hot countries, where tiles are beautiful, many people want hardwood floors whenever they can afford them. But the wood floor, though it seems so beautiful, does little to solve the fundamental problem of floors. The fact is that a room in which there is a bare wood floor, seems rather barren, forbidding, makes the room sound hollow and unfurnished. To make the wooden floor nice, we put down carpets. But then it is not really a wood floor at all. This confusion makes it clear that the fundamental problem of "the floor" has not been properly stated.

When we look at the problem honestly, we realize that the wooden floor, *and* the wooden floor with a carpet on it, are both rather uneven compromises. The bare wooden floor is too bare, too hard to be comfortable; but not in fact hard enough to resist wear particularly well if it is left uncovered—it scratches and dents and splinters. And when the floor is covered with a carpet, the whole point of the beauty of the wood is lost. You cannot see it any more, except round the edges of the carpet; and the carpet on the floor is certainly not hard enough to resist any substantial wear. Furthermore, the most beautiful carpets, handmade rugs and tapestries, are so delicate that they cannot take very rough wear. The practice of walking on a Persian rug with outdoor shoes on is a barbarian habit, never practiced by the people who make those rugs, and know how to treat them—they always take their shoes off. But the modern nylon and acrylic rugs, machine-made for hard wear, lose all the sumptuousness and

pleasure of the carpet: they are, as it were, soft kinds of concrete.

The problem cannot be solved. The conflict is fundamental. The problem can only be *avoided* by making a clear distinction in the house between those areas which have heavy traffic and so need hard wearing surfaces which are easy to clean, and those other areas which have only very light traffic, where people can take off their shoes, and where lush, soft, beautiful rugs, pillows, and tapestries can easily be spread.

Traditional Japanese houses and Russian houses solve the problem in exactly this way: they divide the floor into two zones— serviceable and comfortable. They use very clean, and often precious materials in the comfortable zone, and often make the serviceable zone an extension of the street—that is, dirt, paving, and so on. People take their shoes off, or put them on, when they pass from one zone to the other.

The threshold between hard and soft.

We are not sure whether taking shoes off and on could become a natural habit in our culture. But it still makes sense to zone the house so that the floor material changes as one gets deeper into the house. The pattern INTIMACY GRADIENT (127) calls for a gradient of public, semi-public, and private rooms. It follows that one wants the floor to get softer as one goes deeper into the house—that is, the entrance and the kitchen are better floored with a hard, serviceable surface, while the dining, family room, and children's playrooms need a serviceable floor but with comfortable spots, and the bedrooms, studies, rooms of one's own need soft comfortable floors, on which people can sit, lie, and walk barefoot.

What should the materials be? Of the hard and soft materials, the hard is more of a problem. Since children are close to these floors, as well as the soft ones, they must be warm to the touch, —and at the same time they must be easy to clean. For these hard floors, a "soft" concrete might work. It can be made serviceable and pleasant at the same time if it is finished off with a light-weight textured floor finish, which is relatively porous. It can be made to wear and repel water by making the color integral with the mix and by waxing and polishing after it is set. It is fairly cheap and makes sense if the floor is a concrete floor anyway. Other materials which would work as hard floors are earth, rubber or cork tile, soft unbaked tile known as pastelleros in Peru—see SOFT TILE AND BRICK (248)—and wood planks, but these materials are more expensive.

For soft materials, carpet is the most satisfactory—for sitting, lying, and being close to the ground. We doubt that an improvement can be made on it—in fact we guess that if a substitute is used instead, it will eventually get carpeted over, anyway. This means that the areas which are going to be carpeted might as well have a cheap subfloor with matting laid wall to wall.

To emphasize the two zones, and to promote the taking off and on of shoes from one zone to the next, we suggest that there be a step up or a step down between the zones. This will help tremendously in keeping each zone "pure," and it is sure to help the activities in each zone.

Therefore:

Zone the house, or building, into two kinds of zones: public zones, and private or more intimate zones. Use hard materials like waxed, red polished concrete, tiles, or hardwood in the public zones. In the more intimate zone, use an underfloor of soft materials, like felt, cheap nylon carpet, or straw matting, and cover it with cloths, and pillows, and carpets, and tapestries. Make a clearly marked edge between the two—perhaps even a step—so that people can take their shoes off when they pass from the public to the intimate.

CONSTRUCTION

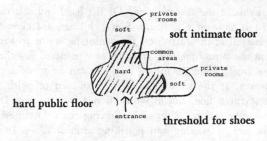

On the hard floor, you can use the same floor as you use on outdoor paths and terraces—hand fired brick and tile—soft tile and brick (248). On the soft intimate floors, use materials and cloths that are rich in ornament and color—ornament (249), warm colors (250). . . .

. . . this pattern finishes the WALL MEMBRANES (218), and ROOF VAULTS (220). It defines the character of their outside surfaces.

❖ ❖ ❖

The main function of a building's outside wall is to keep weather out. It can only do this if the materials are joined in such a way that they cooperate to make impervious joints.

At the same time, the wall must be easy to maintain; and give the people outside some chance of relating to it.

None of these functions can be very well managed by great sheets of impervious material. These sheets, always in the same plane, have tremendous problems at the joints. They require highly complex, sophisticated gaskets and seals, and, in the end, it is these seals and joints which fail.

Consider a variety of natural organisms: trees, fish, animals. Broadly speaking, their outside coats are rough, and made of large numbers of similar but not identical elements. And these elements are placed so that they often overlap: the scales of a fish, the fur of an animal, the crinkling of natural skin, the bark of a tree. All these coats are made to be impervious and easy to repair.

In simple technologies, buildings follow suit. Lapped boards, shingles, hung tiles, thatch, are all examples. Even stone and brick though in one plane, are still in a sense lapped internally to prevent cracks which run all the way through. And all of these walls are made of many small elements, so that individual pieces can be replaced as they are damaged or wear out.

Bear in mind then, as you choose an exterior wall finish, that it should be a material which can be easily lapped against the weather, which is made of elements that are easy to repair locally, and which therefore can be maintained piecemeal, indefinitely. And of course, whatever you choose, make it a surface which invites you to touch it and lean up against it.

In making our filled lightweight concrete structures, we have

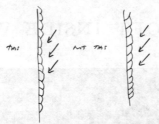

The internal structure of an imaginary lapped material.

used lapped boards as the exterior formwork for the lightweight concrete fill. And it is, of course, possible to use many other kinds of external cladding if they are available and if one can afford them. Slate, corrugated iron, ceramic tiles will produce excellent shingled wall claddings, and can all be placed in such a way as to provide exterior formwork for the pouring of a wall. It is also conceivable (though we have no evidence for it), that scientists might be able to create an oriented material whose internal crystal or fiber structure is in effect "lapped," because all the split lines run diagonally outward and downward.

Therefore:

Build up the exterior wall surface with materials that are lapped against the weather: either "internally lapped," like exterior plaster, or more literally lapped, like shingles and boards and tiles. In either case, choose a material that is easy to repair in little patches, inexpensively, so that little by little, the wall can be maintained in good condition indefinitely.

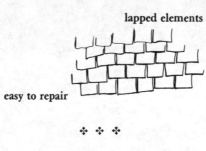

❖ ❖ ❖

235 SOFT INSIDE WALLS*

. . . and this pattern finishes the inner surface of the WALL
MEMBRANES (218), and the under surface of FLOOR-CEILING
VAULTS (219). If it is possible to use a soft material for the inner
sheet of the wall membrane, then the wall will have the right
character built in from the beginning.

❖ ❖ ❖

**A wall which is too hard or too cold or too solid is un-
pleasant to touch; it makes decoration impossible, and
creates hollow echoes.**

A very good material is soft white gypsum plaster. It is warm
in color (even though white), warm to the touch, soft enough to
take tacks and nails and hooks, easy to repair, and makes a
mellow sound, because its sound absorption capacity is reasonably
high.

However, cement plaster, though only slightly different—and
even confused with gypsum plaster—is opposite in all of these
respects. It is too hard to nail into comfortably; it is cold and
hard and rough to the touch; it has very low absorption acoustically—that is, very high reflectance—which creates a harsh, hollow sound; and it is relatively hard to repair, because once a
crack forms in it, it is hard to make a repair that is homogeneous
with the original.

In general, we have found that modern construction has gone
more and more toward materials for inside walls that are hard
and smooth. This is partly an effort to make buildings clean and
impervious to human wear. But it is also because the kinds of materials used today are machine made—each piece perfect and
exactly the same.

Buildings made of these flawless, hard and smooth surfaces
leave us totally unrelated to them. We tend to stay away from
them not only because they are psychologically strange, but because in fact they are physically uncomfortable to lean against;
they have no give; they don't respond to us.

The solution to the problem lies in the following:

1. Gypsum plaster as opposed to cement plaster. Soft baked tiles as opposed to hard fired ones. When materials are porous and low in density they are generally softer and warmer to the touch.

2. Use materials which are granular and have natural texture, and which can be used in small pieces, or in such a way that there is repetition of the same small element. Walls finished in wood have the quality—the wood itself has texture; boards repeat it at a larger scale. Plaster has this character when it is hand finished. First there is the granular quality of the plaster and then the larger texture created by the motion of the human hand.

One of the most beautiful versions of this pattern is the one used in Indian village houses. The walls are plastered, by hand, with a mixture of cow dung and mud, which dries to a beautiful soft finish and shows the five fingers of the plasterer's hand all over the walls.

Cow dung plaster in an Indian village house.

Therefore:

Make every inside surface warm to the touch, soft enough to take small nails and tacks, and with a certain slight "give" to the touch. Soft plaster is very good; textile hangings, canework, weavings, also have this character. And wood is fine, where you can afford it.

soft to the touch

enough "give" for nails

In our own building system, we find it is worth putting on a light skim coat of plaster over the inner surfaces of the WALL MEMBRANE (218) and FLOOR-CEILING VAULTS (219). Wherever finish plaster meets columns, and beams, and doors and window frames, cover the joint with half-inch wooden trim—HALF-INCH TRIM (240). . . .

236 WINDOWS WHICH OPEN WIDE*

. . . this pattern helps to complete WINDOW PLACE (180), WINDOWS OVERLOOKING LIFE (192), and NATURAL DOORS AND WINDOWS (221).

❖ ❖ ❖

Many buildings nowadays have no opening windows at all; and many of the opening windows that people do build, don't do the job that opening windows ought to do.

It is becoming the rule in modern design to seal up windows and create "perfect" indoor climates with mechanical air conditioning systems. This is crazy.

A window is your connection to the outside. It is a source of fresh air; a simple way of changing the temperature, quickly, when the room gets too hot or too cold; a place to hang out and smell the air and trees and flowers and the weather; and a hole through which people can talk to each other.

What is the best kind of window?

Double-hung windows cannot be fully opened—only half of the total window area can ever be opened at once. And they often get stuck—sometimes because they have been painted, sometimes because their concealed operating system of cords, counter-weights, and pulleys gets broken, it becomes such an effort to open them that no one bothers.

Sliding windows have much of the same problem—only part of the window area can be open, since one panel goes behind another; and they often get stuck too.

The side hung casement is easy to open and close. It gives the greatest range of openings, and so creates the greatest degree of control over air and temperature; and it makes an opening which is large enough to put your head and shoulders through. It is the easiest window to climb in and out of too.

The old time French windows are a stunning example of this pattern. They are narrow, full length upstairs windows, which swing out onto a tiny balcony, large enough only to contain the open windows. When you open them you fill the frame, and can stand drinking in the air: they put you intensely close to the out-

side—yet in a perfectly urban sense, as much in Paris or Madrid as in the open countryside.

Therefore:

Decide which of the windows will be opening windows. Pick those which are easy to get to, and choose the ones which open onto flowers you want to smell, paths where you might want to talk, and natural breezes. Then put in side-hung casements that open outward. Here and there, go all the way and build full French windows.

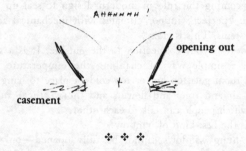

❖ ❖ ❖

Complete the subframe of the casement with SMALL PANES (239). . . .

237 SOLID DOORS
WITH GLASS

. . . this pattern finishes the doors defined by CORNER DOORS
(196) and LOW DOORWAY (224). It also helps to finish TAPESTRY
OF LIGHT AND DARK (135) and INTERIOR WINDOWS (194), since it
requires glazing in the doors, and can help to create daylight in
the darker parts of indoor places.

❖ ❖ ❖

**An opaque door makes sense in a vast house or palace,
where every room is large enough to be a world unto itself;
but in a small building, with small rooms, the opaque door
is only very rarely useful.**

What is needed is a kind of door which gives some sense of
visual connection together with the possibility of acoustic isolation: a door which you can see through but can't hear through.
Glazed doors have been traditional in certain periods—they are
beautiful, and enlarge the sense of connection and make the life
in the house one, but still leave people the possibility of privacy
they need. A glazed door allows for a more graceful entrance into
a room and for a more graceful reception by people in the room,
because it allows both parties to get ready for each other. It also
allows for different degrees of privacy: You can leave the door
open, or you can shut it for acoustical privacy but maintain the
visual connection; or you can curtain the window for visual and
acoustic privacy. And, most important, it gives the feeling that
everyone in the building is connected—not isolated in private
rooms.
Therefore:

**As often as possible build doors with glazing in them,
so that the upper half at least, allows you to see through
them. At the same time, build the doors solid enough, so**

that they give acoustic isolation and make a comfortable "thunk" when they are closed.

solid and with glass

"thunk"

❖ ❖ ❖

Glaze the door with small panes of glass—SMALL PANES (239); and make the doors more solid, by building them like WALL MEMBRANES (218). . . .

. . . even if the windows are beautifully placed, glare can still be a problem—NATURAL DOORS AND WINDOWS (221). The softness of the light, in and around the window, makes an enormous difference to the room inside. The shape of the frames can do a part of it—DEEP REVEALS (223)—but it still needs additional help.

❖ ❖ ❖

Light filtered through leaves, or tracery, is wonderful. But why?

We know that light filtering through a leafy tree is very pleasant—it lends excitement, cheerfulness, gaiety; and we know that areas of uniform lighting create dull, uninteresting spaces. But why?

1. The most obvious reason: direct light coming from a point source casts strong shadows, resulting in harsh images with strong contrasts. And people have an optical habit which makes this contrast worse: our eye automatically reinforces boundaries so that they read sharper than they are. For example, a color chart with strips of different colors set next to each other will appear as though there are dark lines between the strips. These contrasts and hard boundaries are unpleasant—objects appear to have a hard character, and our eyes, unable to adjust to the contrast, cannot pick up the details.

For all these reasons, we have a natural desire to diffuse light with lamp shades or indirect lighting, so that the images created by the light will be "softer," that is, that the boundaries perceived are not sharp, there is less contrast, fewer shadows, and the details are easier to see. This is also why photographers use reflected light instead of direct light when photographing objects; they pick up details which otherwise would be lost in shadow.

2. The second reason: to reduce the glare around the window. When there is bright light coming in through the window, it creates glare against the darkness of the wall around the window —see DEEP REVEALS (223). Filtering the light especially at the

1106

edges of the window cuts down the glare by letting in less light.

3. A third reason which is pure conjecture: it may simply be that an object which has small scale patterns of light dancing on it is sensually pleasing, and stimulates us biologically. Some film-makers claim the play of light upon the retina is naturally sensuous, all by itself.

To create filtered light, partially cover those windows which get direct sunlight, with vines and lattices. Leaves are special because they move. And the edge of the window can have fine tracery—that is, the edge of the glass itself, not the frame, so that the light coming in is gradually stronger from the edge to the center of the window; the tracery is best toward the top of the window where the light is strongest. Many old windows combine these ideas.

Therefore:

Where the edge of a window or the overhanging eave of a roof is silhouetted against the sky, make a rich, detailed taspestry of light and dark, to break up the light and soften it.

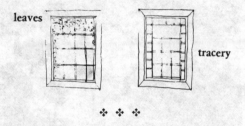

leaves   tracery

❖ ❖ ❖

You can do this, most easily, with climbing plants trained to climb around the outside of the window—CLIMBING PLANTS (246). If there are no plants, you can also do it beautifully with simple canvas awnings—CANVAS ROOFS (244), perhaps colored—WARM COLORS (250). You can also help to filter light by making the panes smaller, more delicate, and more elaborate high in the window where the light is strong—SMALL PANES (239). . . .

239 SMALL PANES**

. . . this pattern gives the glazing for the windows in INTERIOR WINDOWS (194), NATURAL DOORS AND WINDOWS (221), WINDOWS WHICH OPEN WIDE (236), and SOLID DOORS WITH GLASS (237). In most cases, the glazing can be built as a continuation of the FRAMES AS THICKENED EDGES (225).

❖ ❖ ❖

When plate glass windows became possible, people thought that they would put us more directly in touch with nature. In fact, they do the opposite.

They alienate us from the view. The smaller the windows are, and the smaller the panes are, the more intensely windows help connect us with what is on the other side.

This is an important paradox. The clear plate window seems as though it ought to bring nature closer to us, just because it seems to be more like an opening, more like the air. But, in fact, our contact with the view, our contact with the things we see through windows is affected by the way the window frames them. When we consider a window as an eye through which to see a view, we must recognize that it is the extent to which the window frames the view, that increases the view, increases its intensity, increases its variety, even increases the number of views we seem to see—and it is because of this that windows which are broken into smaller windows, and windows which are filled with tiny panes, put us so intimately in touch with what is on the other side. It is because they create far more frames: and it is the multitude of frames which makes the view.

Thomas Markus, who has studied windows extensively, has arrived at the same conclusion: windows which are broken up make for more interesting views. ("The Function of Windows— A Reappraisal," *Building Science*, Vol. 2, 1967, pp. 101–4). He points out that small and narrow windows afford different views from different positions in the room, while the view tends to be the same through large windows or horizontal ones.

We believe that the same thing, almost exactly, happens

within the window frame itself. The following picture shows
a simple landscape, broken up as it might be by six panes. Instead of one view, we see six views. The view becomes alive
because the small panes make it so.

Six views.

Another argument for small panes: Modern architecture and
building have deliberately tried to make windows less like
windows and more as though there was nothing between you and
the outdoors. Yet this entirely contradicts the nature of windows.
It is the function of windows to offer a view and provide a relationship to the outside, true. But this does not mean that they
should not at the same time, like the walls and roof, give you a
sense of protection and shelter from the outside. It is uncomfortable to feel that there is nothing between you and the outside,
when in fact you are *inside* a building. It is the nature of windows to give you a relationship to the outside *and* at the same
time give a sense of enclosure.

Small panes in Mendocino.

Not only that. Big areas of clear glass are sometimes even dangerous. People walk into plate glass windows, because they look like air. By comparison, windows with small panes give a clear functional message—the frames of the panes definitely tell you that something is there separating you from the outside. And they help to create FILTERED LIGHT (238).

Therefore:

Divide each window into small panes. These panes can be very small indeed, and should hardly ever be more than a foot square. To get the exact size of the panes, divide the width and height of the window by the number of panes. Then each window will have different sized panes according to its height and width.

small panes

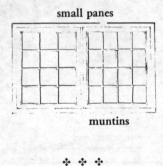

muntins

❖ ❖ ❖

In certain cases you may want to make the small panes even finer near the window edge, to filter the light around the upper edge of windows which stand out against the sky—FILTERED LIGHT (238). As for the muntins, they can be made from the same materials as trim—HALF-INCH TRIM (240). . . .

240 HALF-INCH TRIM**

. . . and this pattern finishes the joints between SOFT INSIDE WALLS (235), or LAPPED OUTSIDE WALLS (234) and the various floors and vaults and frames and stiffeners and ornaments which are set into the walls: BOX COLUMNS (216), PERIMETER BEAMS (217), FLOOR-CEILING VAULTS (219), FRAMES AS THICKENED EDGES (225), and ORNAMENT (249).

Totalitarian, machine buildings do not require trim because they are precise enough to do without. But they buy their precision at a dreadful price: by killing the possibility of freedom in the building plan.

A free and natural building cannot be conceived without the possibility of finishing it with trim, to cover up the minor variations which have arisen in the plan, and during its construction.

For example, when nailing a piece of gypsum board to a column—if the board is cut on site—it is essential that the cut can be inaccurate within a half-inch or so. If it has to be more accurate, there will be a great waste of material, and on-site cutting time and labor will increase, and, finally, the very possibility of adapting each part of the building to the exact subtleties of the plan and site will be in jeopardy.

It is in response to difficulties of this sort that modern system building has arisen. Here tolerances are very low indeed—$\frac{1}{8}$ inch and even lower—and there is no need for trim to cover up inaccuracies. However, the precision of the components can only be obtained by the most tyrannical control over the plan. This one aspect of construction has by itself destroyed the builder's capacity to make a building which is natural, organic, and adapted to the site.

If, as we suggest, the building procedure is looser and allows much larger tolerance—even mistakes on the order of half an inch or more—then the use of trim to cover the connection between materials becomes essential. Indeed, within this attitude to building, the trim is not a trivial decoration added as a finishing touch, but an essential phase of the construction. We see, then,

that trim, so often associated with older buildings, and treated as an emblem of nostalgia, is in fact a vital part of the process of making buildings natural.

Finally, it is worth adding a note about the actual size of the trim pieces. Buildings built in the last 25 years often make a virtue out of boldness, and there is a tendency to use very large oversized pieces of trim instead of small pieces. Within the framework of this philosophy, it might seem right to use pieces of trim 2 or 3 inches thick for their effect and heaviness. We believe that this is wrong: Trim which is too large, or too thick, doesn't do its job. This is not a matter of style. There is a psychological reason for making sure that every component in the building has at least some pieces of trim which are of the order of half an inch or an inch thick, *and no more.*

Compare the following two examples of trim. For some reason the right-hand one, in which the trim is finer, is closer and better adapted to our feelings than the left-hand one.

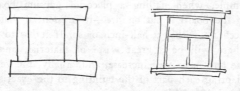

Chunky trim . . . . . fine scale trim.

The reason for this seems to be the following. Our own bodies and the natural surroundings in which we evolved contain a continuous hierarchy of details, ranging all the way from the molecular fine structure to gross features like arms and legs (in our own bodies) and trunks and branches (in our natural surroundings).

We know from results in cognitive psychology that any one step in this hierarchy can be no more than 1:5, 1:7, or 1:10 if we are to perceive it as a natural hierarchy. We cannot understand a hierarchy in which there is a jump in scale of 1:20 or more. It is this fact which makes it necessary for our surroundings, even when man-made, to display a similar continuum of detail.

Most materials have some kind of natural fibrous or crystalline

structure at the scale of about $\frac{1}{20}$ inch. But if the smallest building detail dimensions are of the order of 2 or 3 inches, this leaves a jump of 1:40 or 1:60 between these details and the fine structure of the material.

In order to allow us to perceive a connection between the fine building construction and the fine structure of the materials, it is essential that the smallest building details be of the order of a half inch or so, so that it is no more than about 10 times the size of the granular and fibrous texture of the materials.

Therefore:

Wherever two materials meet, place a piece of trim over the edge of the connection. Choose the pieces of trim so that the smallest piece, in each component, is always of the order of ½ inch wide. The trim can be wood, plaster, terracotta. . . .

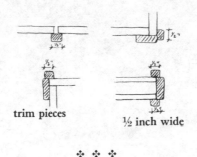

trim pieces   ½ inch wide

❖ ❖ ❖

In many cases, you may be able to use the trim to form the ornaments—ORNAMENT (249); and trims may occasionally be colored: even tiny amounts can help to make the light in a room warm—WARM COLORS (250). . . .

build outdoor details to finish the outdoors as fully as the indoor spaces;

241 SEAT SPOTS**

. . . assume that the main structure of the building is complete. To make it perfectly complete you need to build in the details of the gardens and the terraces around the building. In some cases, you will probably have laid out the walls and flowers and seats, at least in rough outline; but it is usually best to make the final decisions about them after the building is really there—so that you can make them fit the building and help to tie it into its surroundings—PATH SHAPE (121), ACTIVITY POCKETS (124), PRIVATE TERRACE ON THE STREET (140), BUILDING EDGE (160), SUNNY PLACE (161), OUTDOOR ROOM (163), CONNECTION TO THE EARTH (168), TRELLISED WALK (174), GARDEN SEAT (176), etc. First, the outdoor seats, public and private.

Where outdoor seats are set down without regard for view and climate, they will almost certainly be useless.

We made random spot checks on selected benches in Berkeley, California, and recorded these facts about each bench: Was it occupied or empty? Did it give a view of current activity or not? Was it in the sun or not? What was the current wind velocity? Three of the eleven benches were occupied; eight were empty.

At the moment of observation, all three occupied benches looked onto activity, were in the sun, and had a wind velocity of less than 1.5 feet per second. At the moment of observation, none of the eight empty benches had all three of these characteristics. Three of them had shelter and activity but no sun; three of them had activity but no sun, and wind greater than 3 feet per second; two of them had sun and shelter but no activity.

A second series of observations compared the numbers of old people sitting in Union Square at 3:00 P.M. on a sunny day with the number at 3:00 P.M. on a cloudy day: 65 people on the sunny day and 21 on the cloudy day, even though the air temperature was the same on both days.

It's obvious, of course—but the point is this—when you are going to mark in spots in your project for the location of outdoor

seats, sitting walls, stair seats, garden seats, look for places with these characteristics:

1. Benches facing directly onto pedestrian activity.

2. Benches open to the south for sun exposure during winter months.

3. A wall on those sides where the winter wind comes down.

4. In hot climates—cover to give sun protection during the midday hours of summer months, and the bench open to the direction of the summer breeze.

New England benches.

Therefore:

Choosing good spots for outdoor seats is far more important than building fancy benches. Indeed, if the spot is right, the most simple kind of seat is perfect.

In cool climates, choose them to face the sun, and to be protected from the wind; in hot climates, put them in shade and open to summer breezes. In both cases, place them to face activities.

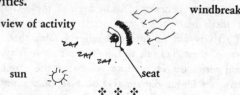

If these seats can be made continuous with stairs or building entrances or low walls or ballustrades, so much the better— STAIR SEATS (125), FRONT DOOR BENCH (242), SITTING WALL (243). . . .

242 FRONT DOOR BENCH*

. . . SEAT SPOTS (241), acting within several larger patterns, creates an atmosphere around the edge of the building which invites lingering—ARCADES (119), BUILDING EDGE (160), SUNNY PLACE (161), CONNECTION TO THE EARTH (168); it is most marked and most important near the entrance—ENTRANCE ROOM (130). This pattern defines a special SEAT SPOT (241): a bench which helps to form the entrance room and the building edge around the entrance. It is always important; but perhaps most important of all, at the door of an OLD AGE COTTAGE (155).

People like to watch the street.

But they do not always want a great deal of involvement with the street. The process of hanging out requires a continuum of degrees of involvement with the street, ranging all the way from the most private kind to the most public kind. A young girl watching the street may want to be able to withdraw the moment anyone looks at her too intently. At other times people may want to be watching the street, near enough to it to talk to someone who comes past, yet still protected enough so that they can withdraw into their own domain at a moment's notice.

The most public kind of involvement with the street is sitting out. Many people, especially older people, pull chairs out to the front door or lean against the front of their houses, either while

Front door benches in Peru.

1122

they are working at something or just for the pleasure of watching street life. But since there is some reluctance to be too public, this activity requires a bench or seat which is clearly private, even though in the public world. It is best of all when the bench is placed so that people are sitting on the edge of *their* world on private land—yet so placed that the personal space it creates overlaps with land that is legally public.

Therefore:

Build a special bench outside the front door where people from inside can sit comfortably for hours on end and watch the world go by. Place the bench to define a half-private domain in front of the house. A low wall, planting, a tree, can help to create the same domain.

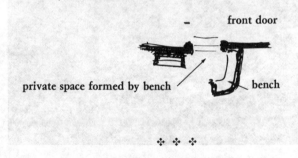

front door

private space formed by bench   bench

❖ ❖ ❖

The bench may help to make the entrance visible—MAIN EN-TRANCE (110); it can be part of a wall—SITTING WALL (243), with flowers in the sunshine next to it—RAISED FLOWERS (245). Place it with care, according to the rules given in SEAT SPOTS (241). . . .

243 SITTING WALL**

. . . if all is well, the outdoor areas are largely made up of positive spaces—POSITIVE OUTDOOR SPACES (106); in some fashion you have marked boundaries between gardens and streets, between terraces and gardens, between outdoor rooms and terraces, between play areas and gardens—GREEN STREETS (51), PEDESTRIAN STREET (100), HALF-HIDDEN GARDEN (111), HIERARCHY OF OPEN SPACE (114), PATH SHAPE (121), ACTIVITY POCKETS (124), PRIVATE TERRACE ON THE STREET (140), OUTDOOR ROOM (163), OPENING TO THE STREET (165), GALLERY SURROUND (166), GARDEN GROWING WILD (172). With this pattern, you can help these natural boundaries take on their proper character, by building walls, just low enough to sit on, and high enough to mark the boundaries.

If you have also marked the places where it makes sense to build seats—SEAT SPOTS (241), FRONT DOOR BENCH (242)—you can kill two birds with one stone by using the walls as seats which help enclose the outdoor space wherever its positive character is weakest.

In many places walls and fences between outdoor spaces are too high; but no boundary at all does injustice to the subtlety of the divisions between the spaces.

Consider, for example, a garden on a quiet street. At least somewhere along the edge between the two there is a need for a seam, a place which unites the two, but does so without breaking down the fact that they are separate places. If there is a high wall or a hedge, then the people in the garden have no way of being connected to the street; the people in the street have no way of being connected to the garden. But if there is no barrier at all—then the division between the two is hard to maintain. Stray dogs can wander in and out at will; it is even uncomfortable to sit in the garden, because it is essentially like sitting in the street.

The problem can only be solved by a kind of barrier which functions as a barrier which separates, and as a seam which joins, at the same time.

A low wall or balustrade, just at the right height for sitting, is perfect. It creates a barrier which separates. But because it invites people to sit on it—invites them to sit first with their legs on one side, then with their legs on top, then to swivel round still further to the other side, or to sit astride it—it also functions as a seam, which makes a positive connection between the two places.

Examples: A low wall with the children's sandbox on one side, circulation path on the other; low wall at the front of the garden, connecting the house to the public path; a sitting wall that is a retaining wall, with plants on one side, where people can sit close to the flowers and eat their lunch.

Ruskin describes a sitting wall he experienced:

Last summer I was lodging for a little while in a cottage in the country, and in front of my low window there were, first, some beds of daisies, then a row of gooseberry and currant bushes, and then a low wall about three feet above the ground, covered with stonecress. Outside, a corn-field, with its green ears glistening in the sun, and a field path through it, just past the garden gate. From my window I could see every peasant of the village who passed that way, with basket on arm for market, or spade on shoulder for field. When I was inclined for society, I could lean over my wall, and talk to anybody; when I was inclined for science, I could botanize all along the top of my wall—there were four species of stone-cress alone growing on it; and when I was inclined for exercise, I could jump over my wall, backwards and forwards. That's the sort of fence to have in a Christian country; not a thing which you can't walk inside of without making yourself look like a wild beast, nor look at out of your window in the morning without expecting to see somebody impaled upon it in the night. (John Ruskin, *The Two Paths*, New York: Everyman's Library, 1907, p. 203.)

Therefore:

Surround any natural outdoor area, and make minor boundaries between outdoor areas with low walls, about 16 inches high, and wide enough to sit on, at least 12 inches wide.

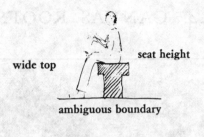

wide top   seat height

ambiguous boundary

Place the walls to coincide with natural seat spots, so that extra benches are not necessary—SEAT SPOTS (241); make them of brick or tile, if possible—SOFT TILE AND BRICK (248); if they separate two areas of slightly different height, pierce them with holes to make them balustrades—ORNAMENT (249). Where they are in the sun, and can be large enough, plant flowers in them or against them—RAISED FLOWERS (245). . . .

244 CANVAS ROOFS*

. . . around every building there are ROOF GARDENS (118), ARCADES (119), PRIVATE TERRACES ON THE STREET (140), OUTDOOR ROOMS (163), GALLERY SURROUNDS (166), TRELLISED WALKS (174), and WINDOW PLACES (180), even SMALL PARKING LOTS (103), which all become more subtle and more beautiful with canvas roofs and awnings. And the awnings always help to create FILTERED LIGHT (238).

❖ ❖ ❖

There is a very special beauty about tents and canvas awnings. The canvas has a softness, a suppleness, which is in harmony with wind and light and sun. A house or any building built with some canvas will touch all the elements more nearly than it can when it is made only with hard conventional materials.

In conventional building, it is easy to think that walls and roofs must either be solid, or missing altogether. But cloth and canvas lie just exactly halfway in between. They are translucent, let a little breeze pass through, and they are very cheap, and easy to roll up and easy to pull down.

We can identify three kinds of places that need these properties:

1. Awnings—sunshades over windows, retractable, and used to filter very bright hot sunlight.

2. Curtains—moveable, half-open walls on outdoor rooms, balconies, and galleries—places that are occupied mainly during the day, but might benefit from extra wind protection.

3. Tent-like roofs on outdoor rooms—a tent which can hold off a drizzle and make outdoor rooms, or trellises, or courtyards habitable in the spring and autumn and at night.

Here is Frank Lloyd Wright describing his use of the canvas roof in the very early structures at Taliesin West:

. . . the Taliesin Fellowship (is a) desert camp on a great Arizona mesa which the boys, together with myself, are now building to work and live in during the winter-time. Many of the building units have canvas tops carried by red-wood framing resting on massive

stone walls made by placing the flat desert stones into wood boxes and throwing in stones and concrete behind them. Most of the canvas frames may be opened or kept closed. . . . The canvas overhead being translucent, there is a very beautiful light to live and work in; I have experienced nothing like it elsewhere except in Japan somewhat, in their houses with sliding paper walls or "shoji." (*The Future of Architecture*, London: The Architectural Press, 1955, pp. 255–56.)

Another example: In Italy, the canvas awning is used quite commonly as a simple awning over south and west windows. The canvas is often a bright and beautiful orange, giving color to the street and a warm glow to the interior rooms.

As a final example, we report on our own use of this pattern in the housing project in Lima. We roofed interior patios with movable canvas material. In hot weather the covers are rolled back, and a breeze blows through the house. In cold weather, the canvas is rolled out, sealing the house, and the patio is still useful. In Lima, there is a winter dew which normally makes patio floors damp and cold for eight months in the year. The cover on the patios keeps them dry and warm and triples their useful life. They eliminate the need for glass windows almost entirely. The windows which look into patios give light to rooms and may be curtained for visual control—but since the cold and damp are kept out by the patio canvas there need be no glass in the windows and no expensive moving parts.

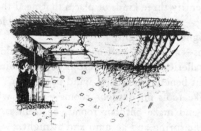

Our patio covers in Peru.

Therefore:

Build canvas roofs and walls and awnings wherever there are spaces which need softer light or partial shade in sum-

mer, or partial protection from mist and dew in autumn
and winter. Build them to fold away, with ropes or wires
to pull them, so that they can easily be opened.

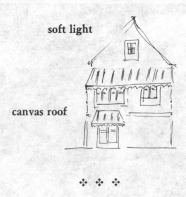

❖ ❖ ❖

Use the canvas awnings, especially, to filter light over those
windows which face west and south and glare because they face
the sky—FILTERED LIGHT (238). Colored canvas will add
special life—ORNAMENT (249), WARM COLORS (250). . . .

245 RAISED FLOWERS*

. . . outdoors there are various low walls at sitting height—
SITTING WALL (243); terraced gardens, if the garden has a natural slope in it—TERRACED SLOPE (169); and paths and steps
and crinkled building edges—PATHS AND GOALS (120), STAIR
SEATS (125), BUILDING EDGE (160), GARDEN WALL (173).
These are the best spots for flowers, and flowers help to make
them beautiful.

❖ ❖ ❖

**Flowers are beautiful along the edges of paths, buildings,
outdoor rooms—but it is just in these places that they
need the most protection from traffic. Without some protection they cannot easily survive.**

Look at the positions that wildflowers take in nature. They
are as a rule in protected places when they occur in massive quantities: places away from traffic—often on grassy banks, on corners
of fields, against a wall. It is not natural for flowers to grow in
bundles like flower beds; they need a place to nestle.

What are the issues?

1. The sun—they need plenty of sun.
2. A position where people can smell and touch them.
3. Protection from stray animals.
4. A position where people see them, either from inside a
house or along the paths which they naturally pass coming and
going.

Typical flower borders are often too deep and too exposed.
And they are so low the flowers are out of reach. Concrete
planter boxes made to protect flowers often go to the other extreme. They are so protected that people have no contact with
them, except from a distance. This is next to useless. The flowers
need to be close, where you can touch them, smell them.

Therefore, instead of putting the flowers in low borders, on
the ground, where people walk, or in massive concrete tubs, build
them up in low beds, with sitting walls beside them, along the
sides of paths, around entrances and edges. Make quite certain

that the flowers are placed in positions where people really can enjoy them—and not simply as ornament: outside favorite windows, along traveled paths, near entrances and round doorways, by outdoor seats.

Raised flowers.

Therefore:

Soften the edges of buildings, paths, and outdoor areas with flowers. Raise the flower beds so that people can touch the flowers, bend to smell them, and sit by them. And build the flower beds with solid edges, so that people can sit on them, among the flowers too.

raised flowers   1–3 feet high

❖ ❖ ❖

. . . two earlier patterns can be helped by climbing plants around the building: TRELLISED WALK (174) and FILTERED LIGHT (238).

❖ ❖ ❖

A building finally becomes a part of its surroundings when the plants grow over parts of it as freely as they grow along the ground.

There is no doubt that buildings with roses or vines or honeysuckle growing on them mean much more to us than buildings whose walls are blank and bare. That is reason enough to plant wild clematis around the outside of a building, to make boxes to encourage plants to grow at higher storys, and to make frames and trellises for them to climb on.

We can think of four ways to ground this intuition in function.

1. One argument, consistent with others in the book, is that climbing plants effect a smooth transition between the built and the natural. A sort of blurring of the edges.

2. The quality of light. When the plants grow around the openings of buildings, they create a special kind of filtered light inside. This light is soft, reduces glare, and stark shadows—FILTERED LIGHT (238).

3. The sense of touch. Climbing and hanging plants also give the outside walls a close and subtle texture. The same kind of texture can be achieved in the building materials, but it is uniquely beautiful when it comes from a vine growing across a wall or winding around the eaves of an arcade. Then, the texture invites you to touch and smell it, to pick off a leaf. Perhaps most important, the texture of climbing plants is ever different; it is subtly different from day to day, as the wind and sun play upon it; and it is greatly different from season to season.

4. Tending the plants. When they are well-tended, healthy plants and flowers growing around the windows and out of flower boxes in the upper storys, make the street feel more

comfortable. They bespeak a social order of some repose within the buildings, and therefore it is comfortable to be on the streets —one feels at home. It is as if the plants were a gift from the people inside to people on the street.

The contribution to the street.

Therefore:

On sunny walls, train climbing plants to grow up round the openings in the wall—the windows, doors, porches, arcades, and trellises.

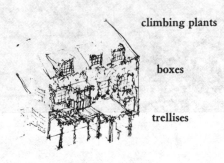

climbing plants

boxes

trellises

❖ ❖ ❖

247 PAVING WITH CRACKS BETWEEN THE STONES**

. . . many patterns call for paths and terraces and places where the outdoor areas around a building feel connected to the earth—GREEN STREETS (51), PATH SHAPE (121), PRIVATE TERRACE ON THE STREET (140), OUTDOOR ROOM (163), CONNECTION TO THE EARTH (168), TERRACED SLOPE (169). This pattern provides a way of building the ground surface that makes these larger patterns come to life.

❖ ❖ ❖

Asphalt and concrete surfaces outdoors are easy to wash down, but they do nothing for us, nothing for the paths, and nothing for the rainwater and plants.

Look at a simple path, made by laying bricks or paving stones directly in the earth, with ample cracks between the stones. It is good to walk on, good for the plants, good for the passage of time, good for the rain. You walk from stone to stone, and feel the earth directly under foot. It does not crack, because as the earth settles, the stones move with the earth and gradually take on a rich uneven character. As time goes by, the very age and history of all the moments on that path are almost recorded in its slight unevenness. Plants and mosses and small flowers grow between the cracks. The cracks also help preserve the delicate ecology of worms and insects and beetles and the variety of plant species. And when it rains, the water goes directly to the ground; there is no concentrated run-off, no danger of erosion, no loss of water in the ground around the path.

All these are good reasons to set paving stones loosely. As for the flat, smooth, hard concrete and asphalt surfaces, they have almost nothing to recommend them. They are built when people forget these small advantages that come about when paving is made out of individual stones with cracks between the stones.

Therefore:

On paths and terraces, lay paving stones with a 1 inch crack between the stones, so that grass and mosses and

small flowers can grow between the stones. Lay the stones directly into earth, not into mortar, and, of course, use no cement or mortar in between the stones.

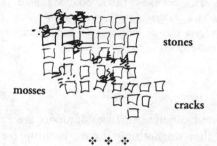

stones

mosses

cracks

❖ ❖ ❖

Use paving with cracks, to help make paths and terraces which change and show the passage of time and so help people feel the earth beneath their feet—CONNECTION TO THE EARTH (168); the stones themselves are best if they are simple soft baked tiles—SOFT TILE AND BRICK (248). . . .

248 SOFT TILE AND BRICK

. . . several patterns call for the use of tiles and bricks—
CONNECTION TO THE EARTH (168), GOOD MATERIALS (207),
FLOOR SURFACE (233), SITTING WALL (243), PAVING WITH
CRACKS BETWEEN THE STONES (247).

❖ ❖ ❖

**How can a person feel the earth, or time, or any connec-
tion with his surroundings, when he is walking on the
hard mechanical wash-easy surfaces of concrete, asphalt,
hard-fired architectural paving bricks, or artificially con-
cocted mixes like terrazo.**

It is essential, above all, that the ground level surfaces we
walk on—both around our buildings and indoors in those places
like passages and kitchens where the floor has to be hard—be soft
enough, at least, to show the passage of time, in gradual undulations and unevenness, that tell the story of a thousand passing
feet, and make it clear that buildings are like people—not
impervious and alien, but alive, changing with time, remembering
the paths which people tread.

Nothing shows the passage of time so well as very soft, baked
or lightly fired, bricks and tiles. They are among the cheapest
tiles that can be made; they use ordinary clay, are biodegradable, and always develop a beautiful sense of wear and time in
the undulations made by people walking over them.

In addition, those paved areas around a building required by
CONNECTION TO THE EARTH (168) play a special role. They are
the places which are halfway between the building—with its
artificial materials—and the earth—which is entirely natural.
To make this connection felt, the materials themselves must also
be halfway, in character, between the building and the earth.
Again, soft, lightly fixed tiles are most appropriate.

We consider this so important, that we advocate, specifically, that the people who are making the building, make the quantity of bricks and tiles they need for ground floor and outdoor surfaces—and that these be made in local clay and soft fired, in stacks, right on the site.

It is easy to do. We shall now give detailed instructions for making the tiles themselves and for making a rudimentary outdoor firing pit.

We start with the clay: it would be best to make one's own clay from scratch.

Clay is decomposed feldspathic rock. There is an abundance of it all over the earth. One may be fortunate enough to find it in one's back yard.

To test whether it is clay, pick up a bit of it and wet it. If it is plastic and sticky enough to form a smooth ball, it is clay. . . .

Process the clay as follows:

1. First, remove impurities such as twigs, leaves, roots and stones.
2. Then, let the chunks dry in the sun.
3. Break up these chunks and grind them up as finely as possible.
4. Put this ground-up clay in water so that there is a mound above water.
5. Let this mixture soak for one day, then stir it, and sieve it through a screen.
6. Let stand again for another day, and remove excess water.
7. Then put the clay in a plaster container; plaster absorbs water, thus stiffening the mixture into workable clay.
8. Work the clay a little to test it. If cracks appear, it is "short"; when that happens, add to the mixture, up to 7% bentonite. If clay is too plastic, add "grog." . . .

Shrinkage may be decreased by adding flint or grog to the clay. Grog is clay that has been biscuit-fired and then crushed. Some people prepare their own grog from broken biscuit-fired pieces. It can be bought at very little cost at any supply company in varying degrees of fineness. The coarser the particles of grog added to the clay, the coarser the texture of the fired object will be.

Grog makes clay porous and is used for objects which are not intended to hold water. Grog also prevents warpage and is, therefore, very useful for tile making and for sculpture. 20% is a good proportion of grog in a clay mixture.

(Muriel Pargh Turoff, *How to Make Pottery and Other Ceramic Ware*, New York: Crown Publishers, 1949, p. 13.)

Once you have the clay, you can make the tiles.

In this method of tile making, a wooden form is used that has the dimensions desired for the finished tiles. It is put together by

nailing four strips of wood to a smooth piece of board. The strips should be 1 inch wide and their height may vary from ⅜ inch to ¾ inch, depending on how thick you wish the finished tiles to be. It is a good plan to put a piece of oilcloth on the base board before nailing down the strips. This will keep the board from warping. . . .

Roll out a slab of clay. . . . Then cut from the slab a piece that will fit comfortably into the form and roll it down with a rolling pin. Do not roll the pin all the way across the surface of the clay, but work from the center outwards to all four sides. . . . Let the tile dry until it is leather-hard; then separate it from the form by running a knife around its edges. . . .

Clay tiles should be allowed to dry very slowly, and for this reason should be put in a cool place. If they dry too quickly under heat, they are apt to crack or warp. The edges have a tendency to dry more rapidly than the center and usually should be dampened from time to time to prevent this. (Joseph Leeming, *Fun With Clay*, Philadelphia and New York: J. B. Lippincott Company.)

To fire soft tiles and bricks, it is not necessary to build real kilns. They can be fired in open pits much like those which primitive potters used to fire their pottery. This type of open pit firing is described in detail by Daniel Rhodes, in *Kilns: Design, Construction and Operation*, Philadelphia: Chilton Book Company. Briefly:

Dig a shallow pit about 14 to 20 inches deep, and several square feet in area. Line this pit (bottom and sides) with branches, reeds, twigs, etc. Place the tiles and bricks to be fired on the lining, so that they are compactly piled with just a tiny bit of airspace between them—(they can be criss crossed). . . . If you use old tiles to line the pit, it will keep the heat in even better; and air holes low down at one end will help combustion. . . . Put some fuel in between stacks and over them. Then light the fuel in the pit, and allow it to burn slowly—which it will to begin with because not much air can get to it. Pile more fuel on as the fire burns up to a level above the pit. After the entire pit and its contents reach red heat, allow the fire to die down, and cover the top of the fire with wet leaves, dung or ashes to retain the heat. After the fire has died down, and the embers cooled, the tiles can be removed.

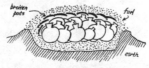

A simple kiln.

Therefore:

Use bricks and tiles which are soft baked, low fired—so that they will wear with time, and show the marks of use. You can make them in a simple mold from local clay, right on the site; surround the stack with twigs and firewood; and fire them, to a soft pink color which will leave them soft enough to wear with time.

low fired clay

❖ ❖ ❖

The soft pink color helps to create WARM COLORS (250). Before firing, you may want to give the tiles some ORNAMENT (249). . . .

complete the building with ornament and light and color and your own things.

249 ORNAMENT**

. . . once buildings and gardens are finished; walls, columns, windows, doors, and surfaces are in place; boundaries and edges and transitions are defined—MAIN ENTRANCE (110), BUILDING EDGE (160), CONNECTION TO THE EARTH (168), GARDEN WALL (173), WINDOW PLACE (180), CORNER DOORS (196), FRAMES AS THICKENED EDGES (225), COLUMN PLACE (226), COLUMN CONNECTION (227), ROOF CAPS (232), SOFT INSIDE WALLS (235), SITTING WALL (243), and so on—it is time to put in the finishing touches, to fill the gaps, to mark the boundaries, by making ornament.

❖ ❖ ❖

All people have the instinct to decorate their surroundings.

But decorations and ornaments will only work when they are properly made: for ornaments and decorations are not only born from the natural exuberance and love for something happy in a building; they also have a function, which is as clear, and definite as any other function in a building. The joy and exuberance of carvings and color will only work, if they are made in harmony with this function. And, further, the function is a necessary one —the ornaments are not just optional additions which may, or may not be added to a building, according as the spirit moves you—a building needs them, just as much as it needs doors and windows.

In order to understand the function of ornament, we must begin by understanding the nature of space in general. Space, when properly formed, is whole. Every part of it, every part of a town, a neighborhood, a building, a garden, or a room, is whole, in the sense that it is both an integral entity, in itself, and at the same time, joined to some other entities to form a larger whole. This process hinges largely on the boundaries. It is no accident that so many of the patterns in this pattern language concern the importance of the boundaries between things, as places that are as important as the things themselves—for ex-

ample, SUBCULTURE BOUNDARY (13), NEIGHBORHOOD BOUNDARY (15), ARCADES (119), BUILDING EDGE (160), GALLERY SURROUND (166), CONNECTION TO THE EARTH (168), HALF-OPEN WALLS (193), THICK WALLS (197), FRAMES AS THICKENED EDGES (225), HALF-INCH TRIM (240), SITTING WALL (243).

A thing is whole only when it is itself entire and also joined to its outside to form a larger entity. But this can only happen when the boundary between the two is so thick, so fleshy, so ambiguous, that the two are not sharply separated, but can function either as separate entities or as one larger whole which has no inner cleavage in it.

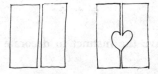

Split . . . and whole.

In the left-hand diagram where there is a cleavage that is sharp, the thing and its outside are distinct entities—they function individually as wholes—but they do not function together as a larger whole. In this case the world is split. In the right-hand diagram where there is ambiguous space between them, the two entities are individually entire, as before, but they are also entire together as a larger whole. In this case the world is whole.

This principle extends throughout the material universe, from the largest organic structures in our surroundings, to the very atoms and molecules.

Extreme examples of this principle at work in manmade objects are in the endless surfaces of objects from the so-called "dark ages" and in the carpets and tilework of Turkey and Persia. Leaving aside the profound meaning of these "ornaments," it is a fact that they function mainly by creating surfaces in which each part is simultaneously figure and boundary and in which the design acts as boundary and figure at several different levels simultaneously.

*A decoration which is whole, because it cannot
be broken into parts.*

Since none of the parts can be separated from their surroundings, because each part acts as figure and as boundary, at several
levels, this ancient carpet is whole, to an extraordinary degree.

*The main purpose of ornament in the environment—in build-
ings, rooms, and public spaces—is to make the world more whole
by knitting it together in precisely the same way this carpet
does it.*

If the patterns in this language are used correctly, then these
unifying boundaries will already come into existence without
ornament at almost all the scales where they are necessary in
spaces and materials. It will happen in the large spaces, like the
entrance transition or the building edge. And, of course, it happens of its own accord, in those smaller structures which occur
within the materials themselves—in the fibers of wood, in the
grain of brick and stone. But there is an intermediate range of
scales, a twilight zone, where it will not happen of its own accord.
It is in this range of scales that ornament fills the gap.

As far as specific ways of doing it are concerned, there are
hundreds, of course. In this balustrade the ornament is made
entirely of the boundary, of the space between the boards. The
boards are cut in such a way, that when they are joined together in the fence, they make something of the space between
them.

. . . A balustrade.

Here is a more complicated case—the entrance to a Romanesque church.

A doorway.

The ornament is built up around the edge of the entrance. It creates a unifying seam between the entrance *space* and the stone. Without the ornament, there would be a gap between the arch of the entry and the passage itself: the ornament works on the seam, between the two, and holds them together. It is especially lavish and developed in this place, because just this seam—the boundary of the entrance to the church—is so important, symbolically, to the people who worship there.

In fact, doors and windows are always important for ornament, because they are places of connection between the elements of buildings and the life in and around them. It is very likely that we shall find a concentration of ornament at the edges of doors and windows, as people try to tie together these edges with the space around them.

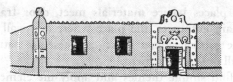

Nubian door.

And exactly the same happens at hundreds of other places in the environment; in rooms, around our houses, in the kitchen, on a wall, along the surface of a path, on tops of roofs, around a column—in fact, anywhere at all where there are edges between things which are imperfectly knit together, where materials or objects meet, and where they change.

Early American stencilling.

Most generally of all, the thing that makes the difference in the use of ornament is the eye for the significant gap in the continuum: the place where the continuous fabric of interlock and connectivity is broken. When ornament is applied badly it is always put into some place where these connections are not really missing, so it is superfluous, frivolous. When it is well used, it is always applied in a place where there is a genuine gap, a need for a little more structure, a need for what we may call metaphorically "some extra binding energy," to knit the stuff together where it is too much apart.

Therefore:

Search around the building, and find those edges and transitions which need emphasis or extra binding energy.

Corners, places where materials meet, door frames, windows, main entrances, the place where one wall meets another, the garden gate, a fence—all these are natural places which call out for ornament.

Now find simple themes and apply the elements of the theme over and again to the edges and boundaries which you decide to mark. Make the ornaments work as seams along the boundaries and edges so that they knit the two sides together and make them one.

repetition   boundaries   themes

❖ ❖ ❖

Whenever it is possible, make the ornament while you are building—not after—from the planks and boards and tiles and surfaces of which the building is actually made—WALL MEMBRANE (218), FRAMES AS THICKENED EDGES (225), LAPPED OUTSIDE WALLS (234), SOFT INSIDE WALLS (235), SOFT TILE AND BRICK (248). Use color for ornament—WARM COLORS (250); use the smaller trims which cover joints as ornament—HALF-INCH TRIM (240); and embellish the rooms themselves with parts of your life which become the natural ornaments around you—THINGS FROM YOUR LIFE (253). . . .

250 WARM COLORS**

. . . this pattern helps to create and generate the right kind of GOOD MATERIALS (207), FLOOR SURFACE (233), SOFT INSIDE WALLS (235). Where possible leave the materials in their natural state. Just add enough color for decoration, and to make the light inside alive and warm.

❖ ❖ ❖

The greens and greys of hospitals and office corridors are depressing and cold. Natural wood, sunlight, bright colors are warm. In some way, the warmth of the colors in a room makes a great deal of difference between comfort and discomfort.

But just what are warm colors and cold colors? In a very simple minded sense, red and yellow and orange and brown are warm; blue and green and grey are cold. But, obviously, it is not true that rooms with red and yellow feel good; while rooms with blue and grey feel cold. There is some superficial truth to this simple statement: it is true that reds and browns and yellows *help* to make rooms comfortable; but it is also true that white and blue and green can all make people comfortable too. After all, the sky is blue, and grass is green. Obviously, we feel comfortable out in the green grass of a meadow, under the blue sky.

The explanation is simple and fascinating. It is not the color of the things, the surfaces, which make a place warm or cold, *but the color of the light*. What exactly does this mean? We can estimate the color of the light at a particular point in space by holding a perfectly white surface there. If the light is warm, this surface will be slightly tinted toward the yellow-red. If the light is cold, this surface will be slightly tinted toward the blue-green. This tinting will be very slight: indeed, on a small white surface it may be so hard to see that you need a spectrometer to do it.

But when you realize that everything in that space is lightly tinted—people's faces, hands, shirts, dresses, food, paper, everything—it is not so hard to see that this can have a huge effect on the emotional quality that people experience there.

Now, the color of the light in a space does not depend in any simple way on the color of the surface. It depends on a complex interaction between the color of the light sources and the way this light then bounces on and off the many surfaces. In a meadow, on a spring day, the sunlight bouncing off the green grass is still warm light—that is, in the yellowish reddish range. The light in a hospital corridor, lit by fluorescent tubes, bouncing off green walls is cold light—in the green-blue range. In a room with lots of natural light, the overall light is warm. In a room whose windows face onto a grey building across the street, the light may be cold, unless there is a very strong concentration of yellow and red fabrics.

If you are in any doubt about the objective character of the light in the room and you don't have a spectrometer, all you need to do is to try to use color film. If the light is warm and the film is properly exposed, white walls will come out slightly pink. If the light is cold, white walls will come out slightly blue.

So, in order to make a room comfortable, you must use a collection of colors which together with the sources of light and the reflecting surfaces outside the room, combine to make the reflected light which exists in the middle of the room warm, that is, toward the yellow-red. Yellow and red colors will always do it. Blues and greens and whites will only do it in the proper places, balanced with other colors, and when the light sources are helping.

To complete the discussion we now make the concept of warm light precise in terms of chromaticity. Consider the light falling on any given surface in the middle of the room. This light contains a variety of different wavelengths. Its character is specified, exactly, by some distribution of spectral energies $p(\lambda)$, which gives the relative proportions of different wavelengths present in this light.

We know that any light whatsoever—in short, any $p(\lambda)$—can be plotted as a single point on the color triangle—more formally known as the two-dimensional chromaticity diagram—by means of the standard color matching functions given in Gunter Wyszecki

and W. S. Stiles, *Color Science*, New York, 1967, pp. 228–317. The coordinates of a plot in this color triangle define the *chromaticity* of any given energy distribution.

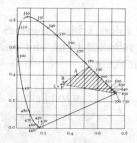

Chromaticity diagram.

We may now identify a region on the chromaticity diagram which we shall call the *warm region*. It is shown hatched on the drawing.

This hatched area is based on a number of empirical results. For example, we know that people have a clear subjective impression of the relative warmth, or coldness, of different spaces. See, for instance, Committee on Colorimetry of the Optical Society of America, *The Science of Color*, New York, 1953, p. 168. One study which attempts to identify the objective correlates of perceived "warmth" is S. M. Newhall, "Warmth and Coolness of Colors," *Psychological Record*, 4, 1941, pp. 198–212. This study revealed a maximum for "warmest" judgments at dominant wave-length 610 millimicrons, which is in the middle of the orange range. And individual observer stability in such judgments is high. Thus, one study gives reliability coefficients of 0.95 for warmth and 0.82 for coolness—N. Collins, "The Appropriateness of Certain Color Combinations in Advertising," M. A. thesis, Columbia University, New York, 1924.

Finally, it is vital to remember that this pattern requires only that the *light*—the total light in the middle of a room, coming from sunlight, artificial lights, reflections from walls, reflections from outside, from carpets—the total *light*, lies in that part of the color triangle we call "warm." It does not require that any individual color surfaces in the room should be red or orange or

yellow—only that the combined effect of all the surfaces and lights together, creates light in the middle of the room which lies in the warm part of the color triangle.

Therefore:

Choose surface colors which, together with the color of the natural light, reflected light, and artificial lights, create a warm light in the rooms.

warm light

oranges   yellows   reds   and browns

❖ ❖ ❖

This means that yellows, reds, and oranges will often be needed to pick out trim and lampshades and occasional details— HALF-INCH TRIM (240), ORNAMENT (249), POOLS OF LIGHT (252). Colored CANVAS ROOFS (244) and SOFT TILE AND BRICK (248) also help to make warm colored light. Blues and greens and greys are much harder to use; especially on the north side where the light is cold and grey, but they can always be used for ornament, where they help to set off the warmer colors—ORNAMENT (249). . . .

251 DIFFERENT CHAIRS

. . . when you are ready to furnish rooms, choose the variety of furniture as carefully as you have made the building, so that each piece of furniture, loose or built in, has the same unique and organic individuality as the rooms and alcoves have—each different, according to the place it occupies—SEQUENCE OF SITTING SPACES (142), SITTING CIRCLE (185), BUILT-IN SEATS (202).

⟡ ⟡ ⟡

People are different sizes; they sit in different ways. And yet there is a tendency in modern times to make all chairs alike.

Of course, this tendency to make all chairs alike is fueled by the demands of prefabrication and the supposed economies of scale. Designers have for years been creating "perfect chairs"— chairs that can be manufactured cheaply in mass. These chairs are made to be comfortable for the average person. And the institutions that buy chairs have been persuaded that buying these chairs in bulk meets all their needs.

But what it means is that some people are chronically uncomfortable; and the variety of moods among people sitting gets entirely stifled.

Obviously, the "average chair" is good for some, but not for everyone. Short and tall people are likely to be uncomfortable. And although situations are roughly uniform—in a restaurant everyone is eating, in an office everyone is working at a table— even so, there are important distinctions: people sitting for different lengths of time; people sitting back and musing; people sitting aggressively forward in a hot discussion; people sitting formally, waiting for a few minutes. If the chairs are all the same, these differences are repressed, and some people are uncomfortable.

What is less obvious, and yet perhaps most important of all, is this: we project our moods and personalities into the chairs we sit in. In one mood a big fat chair is just right; in another

mood, a rocking chair; for another, a stiff upright; and yet again, a stool or sofa. And, of course, it isn't only that we like to switch according to our mood; one of them is our favorite chair, the one that makes us most secure and comfortable; and that again is different for each person. A setting that is full of chairs, all slightly different, immediately creates an amosphere which supports rich experience; a setting which contains chairs that are all alike puts a subtle straight jacket on experience.

Therefore:

Never furnish any place with chairs that are identically the same. Choose a variety of different chairs, some big, some small, some softer than others, some rockers, some very old, some new, with arms, without arms, some wicker, some wood, some cloth.

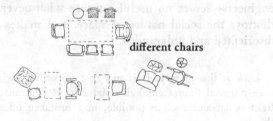

different chairs

❖ ❖ ❖

Where chairs are placed alone and where chairs are gathered, reinforce the character of the places which the chairs create with POOLS OF LIGHT (252), each local to the group of chairs it marks. . . .

252 POOLS OF LIGHT**

. . . this pattern helps to finish small social spaces like ALCOVES (179) and WORKSPACE ENCLOSURE (183), larger places like COMMON AREAS AT THE HEART (129), ENTRANCE ROOM (130), and FLEXIBLE OFFICE SPACE (146), and the furnishing of rooms like EATING ATMOSPHERE (182), SITTING CIRCLE (185), and DIFFERENT CHAIRS (251). It even helps to generate WARM COLORS (250).

Uniform illumination—the sweetheart of the lighting engineers—serves no useful purpose whatsoever. In fact, it destroys the social nature of space, and makes people feel disoriented and unbounded.

Look at this picture. It is an egg-crate ceiling, with dozens of evenly spaced fluorescent lights above it. It is meant to make the light as flat and even as possible, in a mistaken effort to imitate the sky.

Flat, even light.

But it is based on two mistakes. First of all, the light outdoors is almost never even. Most natural places, and especially the

conditions under which the human organism evolved, have dappled light which varies continuously from minute to minute, and from place to place.

More serious, it is a fact of human nature that the space we use as social space is in part defined by light. When the light is perfectly even, the social function of the space gets utterly destroyed: it even becomes difficult for people to form natural human groups. If a group is in an area of uniform illumination, there are no light gradients corresponding to the boundary of the group, so the definition, cohesiveness, and "existence" of the group will be weakened. If the group is within a "pool" of light, whose size and boundaries correspond to those of the group, this enchances the definition, cohesiveness, and even the phenomenological existence of the group.

One possible explanation is suggested by the experiments of Hopkinson and Longmore, who showed that small bright light sources distract the attention less than large areas which are less bright. These authors conclude that local lighting over a work table allows the worker to pay more attention to his work than uniform background lighting does. It seems reasonable to infer that the high degree of person to person attention required to maintain the cohesiveness of a social group is more likely to be sustained if the group has local lighting, than if it has uniform background lighting. (See R. G. Hopkinson and J. Longmore, "Attention and Distraction in the Lighting of Workplaces," *Ergonomics*, 2, 1959, p. 321 ff. Also reprinted in R. G. Hopkinson, *Lighting*, London: HMSO, 1963, pp. 261–68.)

On-the-spot observation supports this conjecture. At the International House, University of California, Berkeley, there is a large room which is a general waiting and sitting lounge for guests and residents. There are 42 seats in the room, 12 of them are next to lamps. At the two times of observation we counted a total of 21 people sitting in the room; 13 of them chose to sit next to lamps. These figures show that people prefer sitting near lights ($X^2 = 11.4$, significant at the 0.1% level). Yet the overall light level in the room was high enough for reading. We conclude that people do seek "pools of light."

Everyday experience bears out the same observation in hundreds of cases. Every good restaurant keeps each table as a

separate pool of light, knowing that this contributes to its privai
and intimate ambience. In a house a truly comfortable old chaii
"yours," has its own light in dimmer surroundings—so tha
you retreat from the bustle of the family to read the paper in
peace. Again, house dining tables often have a single lamp sus-
pended over the table—the light seems almost to act like glue for
all the people sitting round the table. In larger situations the
same thing seems to be true. Think of the park bench, under a
solitary light, and the privacy of the world which it creates for
a pair of lovers. Or, in a trucking depot, the solidarity of the
group of men sipping coffee around a brightly lit coffee stand.

One word of caution. This pattern is easy to understand; and
perhaps it is easy to agree with. But it is quite a subtle matter to
actually create functioning pools of light in the environment. We
know of many failures: for example, places where small lights do
break down even illumination, but do not correspond in any real
way with the places where people tend to gather in the space.

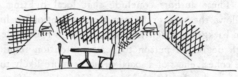

Light pools at odds with social space.

Therefore:

**Place the lights low, and apart, to form individual pools
of light which encompass chairs and tables like bubbles to
reinforce the social character of the spaces which they form.
Remember that you can't have pools of light without the
darker places in between.**

pools of light

❖ ❖ ❖

Color the lampshades and the hangings near the lights to make the light which bounces off them warm in color—WARM COLORS (250). . . .

253 THINGS FROM
YOUR LIFE*

. . . lastly, when you have taken care of everything, and you start living in the places you have made, you may wonder what kinds of things to pin up on the walls.

❖ ❖ ❖

"Decor" and the conception of "interior design" have spread so widely, that very often people forget their instinct for the things they really want to keep around them.

There are two ways of looking at this simple fact. We may look at it from the point of view of the person who owns the space, and from the point of view of the people who come to it. From the owner's point of view, it is obvious that the things around you should be the things which mean most to you, which have the power to play a part in the continuous process of self-transformation, which is your life. That much is clear.

But this function has been eroded, gradually, in modern times because people have begun to look outward, to others, and over their shoulders, at the people who are coming to visit them, and have replaced their natural instinctive decorations with the things which they believe will please and impress their visitors. This is the motive behind all the interior design and decor in the women's magazines. And designers play on these anxieties by making total designs, telling people they have no right to move anything, paint the walls, or add a plant, because they are not party to the mysteries of Good Design.

But the irony is, that the visitors who come into a room don't want this nonsense any more than the people who live there. It is far more fascinating to come into a room which is the living expression of a person, or a group of people, so that you can see their lives, their histories, their inclinations, displayed in manifest form around the walls, in the furniture, on the shelves. Beside such experience—and it is as ordinary as the grass—the artificial scene-making of "modern decor" is totally bankrupt.

Jung describes the room that was his study, how he filled the stone walls with paintings that he made each day directly on

the stones—mandalas, dream images, preoccupations—and he tells us that the room came gradually to be a living thing to him—the outward counterpart to his unconscious.

Examples we know: A motel run by a Frenchman, mementos of the Resistance all around the lounge, the letter from Charles de Gaulle. An outdoor market on the highway, where the proprietor has mounted his collection of old bottles all over the walls; hundreds of bottles, all shapes and colors; some of them are down for cleaning; there is an especially beautiful one up at the counter by the cash register. An anarchist runs the hot dog stand, he plasters the walls with literature, proclamations, manifestoes against the State.

A hunting glove, a blind man's cane, the collar of a favorite dog, a panel of pressed flowers from the time when we were children, oval pictures of grandma, a candlestick, the dust from a volcano carefully kept in a bottle, a picture from the news of prison convicts at Attica in charge of the prison, not knowing that they were about to die, an old photo, the wind blowing in the grass and a church steeple in the distance, spiked sea shells with the hum of the sea still in them.

Therefore:

Do not be tricked into believing that modern decor must be slick or psychedelic, or "natural" or "modern art," or "plants" or anything else that current taste-makers claim. It is most beautiful when it comes straight from your life —the things you care for, the things that tell your story.

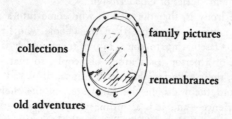

collections

family pictures

remembrances

old adventures

❖ ❖ ❖

ACKNOWLEDGMENTS

We have had a great deal of help and support over the eight years it has taken us to conceive and create this work. And we should here like to express our feelings of gratitude to everyone who helped us.

The Center has always been a small workgroup, fluctuating in size from 3 to 8, according to the demands of the work. Since the Center was incorporated in 1967, a number of people have worked with us, for different lengths of time, and helped in many ways. Denny Abrams was financial manager of the Center for three years. He played a critical role in the early days of the Center, helping to shape our nature as a work group. He also helped with layout and photographic experiments in the early drafts of the book and worked with us on the Oregon experiment. Ron Walkey spent two years at the Center, and helped especially to develop the patterns and the overall conception of the city portrayed in the first section of the book. The two of them were very close to the development of the pattern language, from the beginning; and above all, their music, after lunch, made unforgettable times together for all of us.

In more general terms, both Sim Van der Ryn and Roslyn Lindheim gave us help and encouragement when we first began the project, years ago. Christie Coffin, Jim Jones, and Barbara Schreiner all helped us develop the contents of the earliest versions of the language.

Jim Axley helped more than anyone on the very difficult development of the structural patterns, in the last part of the language. And earlier, Sandy Hirshen, collaborating with us during the Peru project, had begun to develop our attitude to construction techniques.

Harlean Richardson has worked tremendously hard on the detailed design of the book itself. And we have had wonderful secretarial help over the years from Helen Green, who typed many many versions of the patterns, and from Mary Louise Rogers who helped in many ways coordinating the work and providing support.

Another invaluable kind of help we have had was that given by people who believed in what we were trying to do, gave us an opportunity to work on it, and to do projects for them which incorporated these ideas. Ken Simmons, who allowed us to develop our very first pattern language in a professional job, Johannes Olivegren, John Eberhard, Bob Harris, Don Conway, Fried Wittman, Hewitt Ryan, and Edgar Kaufmann all helped us in this way. What they gave us in confidence, and emotional support, and friendship, and, often, in money that supported the work, cannot be counted.

Even more specifically, we want to thank Dick Wakefield, Coryl Jones, and Clyde Dorsett at the National Institute for Mental Health. The evolution of the pattern language was supported for the four most important years by a sequence of grants from the Center for the Study of Metropolitan Problems of the National Institute for Mental Health—and it would have been quite impossible for us to do the work if it had not been for those grants.

Finally, we owe a great deal to Oxford University Press, especially to James Raimes, our editor, who first

agreed to try and publish all three books, in a series, and also to James Huws-Davies and Byron Hollinshead. All three of them supported the publication of this book, and the other books, before they had even seen them: and once again, gave us enormous energy to do the work, by putting their confidence in us at a time when we badly needed it. During the production of the book, we have often created severe difficulties for Oxford; but they have stood by us throughout.

It is only because all of our friends have helped us as they did that it has actually been possible.

PHOTO ACKNOWLEDGMENTS

Many of the pictures we have selected for this book come from secondary and tertiary sources. In every case we have tried to locate the original photographer and make the appropriate acknowledgment. In some cases, however, the sources are too obscure, and we have simply been unable to track them down. In these cases, we regret that our acknowledgments are incomplete and hope that we have not offended anyone.

376	Ken Heyman	737	Orhan Ozguner
385	Robert Doisneau	740	Marian O. Hooker
389	Edwin Smith	746	Erik Lundberg
412	Alfred Eisenstaedt	769	Henri Cartier-Bresson
436	André Kertesz	794	Berthe Morisot
444	Ralph Crane	805	A. F. Sieveking
451	Eugene Atget	822	R. Rodale
454	V. S. Pritchett	857	C. H. Baer
457	André Kertesz	872	Pierre Bonnard
473	Charles E. Rotkin	876	G. Nagel
492	Bernard Rudofsky	889	Henri Matisse
508	Wu Pin	897	Dorothy and
524	Tonk Schneiders		Richard Pratt
531	Eugene Atget	962	Alan Fletcher
540	Erik Lundberg	970	Erik Lundberg
569	Martin Hurlimann	989	Clifford Yeich
580	Bernard Rudofsky	1027	Erik Lundberg
585	François Enaud	1046	Carl Anthony
589	Bernard Rudofsky	1050	Winslow Homer
596	Herbert Hagemann	1053	Edwin Smith
599	Lazzardo Donati	1056	Avraham Wachman
641	Pierre Bonnard	1064	Ivy De Wolfe
651	Russell Lee	1088	Bruno Taut
656	Joanne Leonard	1105	Izis Bidermanas
664	Joanne Leonard	1118	André Kertesz
696	Ken Heyman	1121	Pfister
707	Dorien Leigh	1128	Roderick Cameron
729	Ernest Rathnau	1135	Marc Foucault
733	Aniela Jaffé	1164	J. Szarhouski

PA

JUN 18